# The Cambridge Handbook of Translation

Translation plays a vital role in society – it allows us to share knowledge and enrich our lives through access to other cultures. Translation studies is a rapidly evolving academic discipline, directly impacted by advances in technological aids, and with close connections between theory and practice. Bringing together contributions from internationally renowned scholars, this handbook offers an authoritative, up-to-date account of the many facets of this buoyant discipline. It covers different themes, areas of practice and developing trends, and provides an overview of the major sub-fields and the connections among them. It is organized into six parts covering the nature of translation, its roles in society, its relationships with other disciplines, a selection of its factual genres, a selection of its art-related genres and, finally, its role in history. Comprehensive yet accessible, it is essential reading for students, teachers and scholars of translation studies, modern languages, linguistics, social studies and literary studies.

KIRSTEN MALMKJÆR is Professor Emeritus of Translation Studies at the University of Leicester. Recent publications include *The Routledge Handbook of Translation Studies and Linguistics* (2018), *Key Cultural Texts in Translation* (co-edited with Serban and Louwagie, 2018) and *Translation and Creativity* (2020). She co-edits the Cambridge Elements of Translation and Interpreting series.

Genuinely broad in scope, each handbook in this series provides a complete state-of-the-field overview of a major sub-discipline within language study and research. Grouped into broad thematic areas, the chapters in each volume encompass the most important issues and topics within each subject, offering a coherent picture of the latest theories and findings. Together, the volumes will build into an integrated overview of the discipline in its entirety.

## Published titles

*The Cambridge Handbook of Phonology*, edited by Paul de Lacy

*The Cambridge Handbook of Linguistic Code-switching*, edited by Barbara E. Bullock and Almeida Jacqueline Toribio

*The Cambridge Handbook of Child Language, Second Edition*, edited by Edith L. Bavin and Letitia Naigles

*The Cambridge Handbook of Endangered Languages*, edited by Peter K. Austin and Julia Sallabank

*The Cambridge Handbook of Sociolinguistics*, edited by Rajend Mesthrie

*The Cambridge Handbook of Pragmatics*, edited by Keith Allan and Kasia M. Jaszczolt

*The Cambridge Handbook of Language Policy*, edited by Bernard Spolsky

*The Cambridge Handbook of Second Language Acquisition*, edited by Julia Herschensohn and Martha Young-Scholten

*The Cambridge Handbook of Biolinguistics*, edited by Cedric Boeckx and Kleanthes K. Grohmann

*The Cambridge Handbook of Generative Syntax*, edited by Marcel den Dikken

*The Cambridge Handbook of Communication Disorders*, edited by Louise Cummings

*The Cambridge Handbook of Stylistics*, edited by Peter Stockwell and Sara Whiteley

*The Cambridge Handbook of Linguistic Anthropology*, edited by N.J. Enfield, Paul Kockelman and Jack Sidnell

*The Cambridge Handbook of English Corpus Linguistics*, edited by Douglas Biber and Randi Reppen

*The Cambridge Handbook of Bilingual Processing*, edited by John W. Schwieter

*The Cambridge Handbook of Learner Corpus Research*, edited by Sylviane Granger, Gaëtanelle Gilquin and Fanny Meunier

*The Cambridge Handbook of Linguistic Multicompetence*, edited by Li Wei and Vivian Cook

*The Cambridge Handbook of English Historical Linguistics*, edited by Merja Kytö and Päivi Pahta

*The Cambridge Handbook of Formal Semantics*, edited by Maria Aloni and Paul Dekker

*The Cambridge Handbook of Morphology*, edited by Andrew Hippisley and Greg Stump

*The Cambridge Handbook of Historical Syntax*, edited by Adam Ledgeway and Ian Roberts

*The Cambridge Handbook of Linguistic Typology*, edited by Alexandra Y. Aikhenvald and R. M. W. Dixon

*The Cambridge Handbook of Areal Linguistics*, edited by Raymond Hickey

*The Cambridge Handbook of Cognitive Linguistics*, edited by Barbara Dancygier

*The Cambridge Handbook of Japanese Linguistics*, edited by Yoko Hasegawa

*The Cambridge Handbook of Spanish Linguistics*, edited by Kimberly L. Geeslin

# The Cambridge Handbook of Translation

Edited by

**Kirsten Malmkjær**
*University of Leicester*

CAMBRIDGE
UNIVERSITY PRESS

CAMBRIDGE
UNIVERSITY PRESS

Shaftesbury Road, Cambridge CB2 8EA, United Kingdom

One Liberty Plaza, 20th Floor, New York, NY 10006, USA

477 Williamstown Road, Port Melbourne, VIC 3207, Australia

314–321, 3rd Floor, Plot 3, Splendor Forum, Jasola District Centre, New Delhi – 110025, India

103 Penang Road, #05–06/07, Visioncrest Commercial, Singapore 238467

Cambridge University Press is part of Cambridge University Press & Assessment,
a department of the University of Cambridge.

We share the University's mission to contribute to society through the pursuit of
education, learning and research at the highest international levels of excellence.

www.cambridge.org
Information on this title: www.cambridge.org/9781108727358

DOI: 10.1017/9781108616119

First published 2022
First paperback edition 2024

*A catalogue record for this publication is available from the British Library*

ISBN    978-1-108-48040-6    Hardback
ISBN    978-1-108-72735-8    Paperback

For David

# Contents

# Figures

# Tables

# Contributors

**Fabio Alves**, Professor of Translation Studies, Universidade Federal de Minas Gerais; Research Fellow of the National Research Council (CNPq), Brazil

**Brian James Baer**, Professor of Russian and Translation Studies, Kent State University, United States; Leading Research Fellow at the Higher School of Economics, Moscow, Russia

**Bergljot Behrens**, Professor Emeritus, University of Oslo, Norway

**Łucja Biel**, Associate Professor of Translation Studies, Institute of Applied Linguistics, University of Warsaw, Poland

**Albert Branchadell**, Associate Professor, Universitat Autònoma de Barcelona, Spain

**Geraldine Brodie**, Associate Professor in Translation Theory and Theatre Translation, Centre for Translation Studies, University College London, UK

**Anthony Cordingley**, Associate Professor, Université Paris 8, France; Robinson Fellow, Department of English, University of Sydney, Australia

**Lucile Davier**, Research and Teaching Fellow, University of Geneva, Switzerland

**Julie McDonough Dolmaya**, Associate Professor, School of Translation, York University, Canada

**Arnt Lykke Jakobsen**, Professor Emeritus, Copenhagen Business School, Denmark

**Krisztina Károly**, Full Professor of Linguistics, Eötvös Loránd University, Budapest, Hungary

**Duncan Large**, Academic Director of the British Centre for Literary Translation and Professor of European Literature and Translation, University of East Anglia, UK

**Sara Laviosa**, Associate Professor in English Language and Translation, Department of Letters, Language, Arts, Italian Studies and Comparative Cultures, University of Bari 'Aldo Moro', Italy

**Tong King Lee**, Associate Professor of Translation, University of Hong Kong, HKSAR, China

**Xiaofan Amy Li**, Lecturer in Comparative Cultural Studies, University College London, UK

**Peter Low**, Adjunct Senior Fellow, University of Canterbury, New Zealand

**Kirsten Malmkjær**, Professor Emeritus of Translation Studies, University of Leicester, UK

**Denise Merkle**, Professor and Head of the Department of Translation and Languages, Université de Moncton, Canada

**Vicent Montalt**, Department of Translation and Communication Studies, Universitat Jaume I, Castelló, Spain

**Jeremy Munday**, Professor of Translation Studies, University of Leeds, UK

**Paschalis Nikolaou**, Assistant Professor in Literary Translation, Ionian University, Greece

**Gabriel González Núñez**, Associate Professor, Translation and Interpreting Programs, University of Texas Rio Grande Valley, United States

**Maeve Olohan**, Professor of Translation Studies, Centre for Translation and Intercultural Studies, University of Manchester, UK

**Hanting Pan**, Associate Professor of Translation Studies, College of Education for the Future, Beijing Normal University at Zhuhai, China

**Cecilia Rossi**, Senior Lecturer in Literature and Translation, University of East Anglia, UK

**Akiko Sakamoto**, Senior Lecturer in Translation Studies and Japanese Language, University of Portsmouth, UK

**Moritz Schaeffer**, Senior Research Associate, Johannes Gutenberg-Universität, Mainz, Germany

**Karen Seago**, Independent Scholar, London, UK

**Rakefet Sela-Sheffy**, Associate Professor, Semiotics and Culture Research, Unit of Culture Research, Tel Aviv University, Israel

**Roberto A. Valdeón**, Full Professor in English Studies, Universidad de Oviedo, Spain; Honorary Professor, South China Business College (SCBC), Guangzhou, China; Research Associate, University of the Free State, South Africa

**Serenella Zanotti**, Associate Professor in English Language and Translation, Università degli Studi Roma Tre, Italy

**Karen Korning Zethsen**, Professor of Translation Studies, University of Aarhus, Denmark

**Meifang Zhang**, Professor of Translation Studies, University of Macau, China

# Acknowledgements

I thank the reviewers of the handbook proposal for their insightful and constructive criticism, which helped me greatly in finalizing the planning of the volume. I am immensely indebted to the contributors who gave up time and effort to comply with deadlines and style sheets and most of all with my relentless editing! I owe very particular thanks to Rebecca Taylor, Laura Simmons and Isabel Collins at Cambridge University Press for their patience and guidance throughout, to Lori Heaford for her vigilant copy-editing, to Vidya Ashwin for expert project management and most especially to Work Till Late Ltd for generously applying their expertise to enhancing the quality of the figures in the handbook. Mange tak [thank you very much]!

# Introduction

Kirsten Malmkjær

The translation phenomenon has intrigued me for as long as I have known more than one language. When my interest turned academic in the late 1970s, the discipline of translation studies had only recently acquired its name, on James Holmes's suggestion (see Chapter 1). Now, as that name nears its fiftieth year, the discipline has expanded so extensively that the term 'translation' can seem too narrow to reflect all that it encompasses. Relevant arguments for and against the continued use of the term can be found in Chapter 20. For me, 'translation' still conjures up a world of variety of play and work with and within languages, and aptly names a set of practices and processes crucial to communication within and between cultures. I chose the title, *The Cambridge Handbook of Translation*, for this volume with breadth and comprehensiveness in mind, and I hope that the *Handbook* reflects this intention.

The *Handbook* is divided into six parts of five chapters each, except for the final part which consists of four chapters only, leaving room and scope to grow into further centuries!

Part I addresses the nature of the phenomenon – its theories in Chapter 1, its processes in Chapter 2, its relationship with technology in Chapter 3, translations made by the author of the initial text themselves in Chapter 4 and the nature of translated text in Chapter 5.

Chapter 1, 'Theories of Translation', by Jeremy Munday, discusses the nature of theory, how theory can be applied and the interaction between theories. The last issue is especially important for a discipline like translation studies, which interacts in a variety of ways with other disciplines, as Part III highlights. The chapter takes us from St Jerome in his study at the end of the fourth decade of the Christian Era, when he was commissioned by Pope Damasus to revise the existing Latin translation of the Old Testament, through early and towards contemporary theories of the translation endeavour, and towards the terminology that has been developed along the way, to pinpoint the discipline's important concepts, considerations and approaches.

Chapter 2, 'The Translation Process', by Fabio Alves and Arnt Lykke Jakobsen, tackles aspects of cognitive processing that can be observed in the course of a translation task, from the moment a translator begins to read a text-to-be-translated until the translation has been finalized. It begins by recording the historical development of research into the translation process and how the task of translation has been modelled. It moves on to examining how advances in methodological approaches have contributed to the development of early models, providing empirical evidence from verbal reports, keylogging and eye tracking. Contemporary translation process research focuses on text reading, segmentation and production; and advances in computational linguistics have enhanced descriptions and identification of translation units, attention, production and alignment.

Chapter 3, 'Translation and Technology', by Akiko Sakamoto, describes major advances in translation technologies and explains how these have influenced our understanding of translation, particularly the concept of translation quality and the translation production process. Sakamoto argues that these changes have created a rift between translation studies theories and a new notion of translation circulating in the industry. The chapter identifies new trends in translation studies research which seek to develop new knowledge to address this rift.

Chapter 4, 'Self-Translation', by Anthony Cordingley, argues that self-translators are not bound by the same professional code that typically constrains translators. The chapter examines how self-translators balance the need to represent their source accurately and the freedom to recreate it. It describes the differences between self-translation and other forms of bilingual writing and explains how self-translation has been categorized with respect to a range of literary, geopolitical and commercial influences and motivations. Finally, it considers how the metaphor of self-translation is used within literary and translation studies.

The last in Part I, Chapter 5, 'Translated Text', by Bergljot Behrens, discusses claims that different norms govern translation and the nature of translated text in different temporal and geographical contexts, and that translated texts differ from first-written texts. It considers the troubled relationship between the notions of norms and translation universals, and addresses the question of what constitutes a translation 'proper', and what characterizes the task a translator takes on when translating a piece of literature. It gives an account of the variety of approaches and attitudes taken to this task since ancient Roman times, through to the work of Gideon Toury on translation laws and later developments that this has inspired, including work on norms, the nature of translated text, and translation universals. Translations and re-translations into English of Henrik Ibsen's plays are used for purposes of illustration.

Part II moves from the nature of translation as such to considering the role of translation in society. In Chapter 6, 'Translation and Translanguaging in (Post)multilingual Societies', Tong King Lee addresses the complex, multi-faceted relationship between translation and society in general, before discussing translation in the context of multilingual societies. He examines translation in connection with translanguaging in the contexts of superdiversity and metrolingualism, drawing on findings of the AHRC-funded project, 'Translation and Translanguaging: Investigating Linguistic and Cultural Transformations in Superdiverse Wards in Four UK Cities', arguing that translation should be seen as part of assemblages that constitute the discursive and semiotic character of multilingual societies.

In Chapter 7, 'Less Translated Languages', Albert Branchadell considers languages that are less translated from and into than other languages. Focusing on institutional translation, he examines the translation regimes of the United Nations, the European Union, selected multilingual states and selected multilingual regions within or without multilingual states, focusing, in the first case, on Spanish with respect to English and French in the UN system; in the second case, on translation in several EU institutions; in the third case, on the asymmetric interpreting regime of the Spanish Senate, in which Spain's minority languages may be translated from but not into, and there is no translation at all *between* minority languages; and, in the fourth case, on multilingual regions like Catalonia and South Tyrol.

In Chapter 8, 'The Translation Professions', Rakefet Sela-Sheffy addresses the question of how and to what extent translation practices have become professions. In sociology, a profession is understood as an occupation that has been formally established, with boundaries determined by a canonized body of knowledge and formulated ethics, methods and technologies and recognition and authority given by the state. In contrast, translation occupations mostly form a heteronomous field that lacks formalized standards and controls. She argues that this reflects a tension between professionalization as defined in sociology and 'the rules of art' or 'the intellectual field' as described by Bourdieu. In the latter, norms and value-scales depend on practitioners' ethos and images rather than on institutional parameters.

Nevertheless, relationships do exist between translation and public policy. These are addressed in Chapter 9, 'Translation Studies and Public Policy', by Gabriel González Núñez. When challenges of organizing public spaces involve the use of more than one language, translation is often employed, and, in such circumstances, translation may serve a variety of functions, including the deployment of language policies alongside other policy aims such as the promotion of human rights or multiculturalism. The chapter explores this link between public policy and translation, presenting a survey of insights that have been provided by scholars, and suggesting areas where scholarship can provide further understandings. These insights are important, given the continuing multi-lingualism and diversity of societies.

The last in Part II, Chapter 10, 'Translator Associations and Networks', by Julie McDonough Dolmaya, begins by addressing the differences between the two groupings, associations and networks. It divides these into four categories, profession-oriented, practice-oriented, education-oriented and research-oriented, and presents examples of each type of grouping. It examines the activities that translator associations and networks typically engage in, focusing in particular on advocacy efforts, training and certifi-cation, and social and professional networking. The chapter also intro-duces the codes of ethics and codes of practice that guide translation professionals.

In Part III, relationships that obtain between translation and other dis-ciplines are in focus. In Chapter 11, 'Translation and Comparative Literature', Xiaofan Amy Li offers historical reflections on the role that translation has played in comparative literature as a discipline in Europe and in East Asia. She examines current scholarship to cast light on the relationship between translation and comparative literature and the polemics that this relationship has sparked. She argues for a diversified view of translation and comparative literature that acknowledges not one but many conceptualizations of their interrelations.

In Chapter 12, 'Translation and Linguistics', Hanting Pan and Meifang Zhang trace the role of linguistics within translation studies back to Roman Jakobson's 'On Linguistic Aspects of Translation' of 1959. To illus-trate how linguistic theories and concepts have developed and contributed to translation studies, they present a map drawn up on the basis of a bibliometric survey, focusing on three major stages, pure linguistics, discourse analysis and multimodality. In light of the way in which the relationship has developed between translation studies and aspects of linguistics that have been applied to translation research, in particular multimodal discourse analysis, they suggest how the relationship might continue to develop in the future.

In Chapter 13, 'Translation and Philosophy', Duncan Large argues for the central importance of translation to philosophy, which is 'born trans-lated' and constantly renews itself through translation. He considers lead-ing philosophical accounts of translation, focusing on the question of untranslatability, before addressing complementary ways in which trans-lation studies as a discipline has been exercised by philosophical ques-tions, especially concerning translation equivalence and the ethical duty of the translator. Finally, he examines some of the purposes met by trans-lations of philosophical texts, and some of the practical issues involved in translating philosophical texts by canonical German philosophers into English.

Moving from translation's relationships with the intellectual pursuits of linguistics and philosophy, the discipline's relationship with the less ethereal (though, of course, no less theorized) notions of gender and sexuality, and education, respectively, is addressed in the last two chapters in Part III, Chapters 14 and 15.

Chapter 14, 'Translation, Gender and Sexuality', by Brian James Baer, addresses the relationships between translation and gender and sexuality which began to be discussed in translation studies in the 1980s by scholars often informed by feminist theory and by the minority rights and independence movements of the time. The chapter deals with translation and gender and with sexuality and translation in separate sections, to reflect the fact that gender identity and sexual orientation are not mutually determining. It surveys current research within those discrete but intersecting categories, before discussing emerging themes and future directions.

Chapter 15, 'Translation and Education', by Sara Laviosa, highlights the shared concerns of translation scholars and teachers that derive from the recognition that communities and people are increasingly multilingual. Scholars increasingly favour a model of education that privileges mutual exchange and co-construction of knowledge between teacher and students and which fosters translanguaging as a pedagogical model in bilingual education and in a variety of educational contexts where the school language and the learners' languages do not coincide. The chapter examines the principles embraced by the multilingual turn in educational linguistics and explains how these tenets underpin novel translation teaching approaches and methods in higher education.

The chapter by Laviosa completes Part III of the volume and is an apt transitional chapter between the volume's generally theory-focused first half and the application and practice-focused Parts IV and V.

Part IV begins with Maeve Olohan's Chapter 16, 'Translating Technical Texts'. Given the problematic concept of 'text' in the context of technical content, and of what is 'technical', for that matter, Olohan focuses on practices in which technical content figures. Technical translation is closely connected to technical authoring, and the two activities share some of the materials that are used, the competences that are required, the motivations that drive them, and their ultimate purposes of producing technical content that will enable users to achieve their goals. Drawing on work in genre analysis, she suggests that it would be useful for translation studies to research professional contexts in which translated technical content is focal in, for example, software development and industrial manufacturing, in laboratories and research centres, and in diverse installation and operation settings.

In Chapter 17, 'Translating Academic Texts', Krisztina Károly highlights how translation studies' interaction with genre analysis, register studies, critical language study, contrastive rhetoric and the study of languages for special purposes relates to the translation of academic texts. Most investigations contrast English with languages such as French, Spanish,

Portuguese, German, Russian, Chinese, Arabic, Slovene, Hungarian, Finnish and Danish, and the foci of analyses relate to a wide range of topics, such as translation strategies, style and register, terminology, and culture-specific discourse conventions. Károly identifies the challenges that the field faces and the areas where further research is needed.

In the case of medical and legal text translation, the expert–lay divide often presents particular challenges for translators, as the authors of Chapters 18 and 19 show.

In Chapter 18 on 'Translating Medical Texts', Karen Korning Zethsen and Vicent Montalt chart the history of medical translation, and developments in the field. They introduce the main genres and target groups and discuss important challenges that medical translators face. A shift from the biomedical paradigm to patient-centredness and patient empowerment means that people want to understand information involving their own health, so that intralingual translation is often required for expert–lay medical translation. The chapter discusses the challenges that such intralingual translation presents, especially when coupled with interlingual translation. The importance of medical ethics in medical translation is also highlighted.

The second genre in which the lay–expert divide can be challenging is the translation of legal texts, which Łucja Biel discusses in Chapter 19, 'Translating Legal Texts'. The chapter maps the field of legal translation practice, research and training, beginning with an overview of the history of legal translation and its reorientation from literalness towards functional, receiver-oriented approaches which ensure equivalent effects, and which perceive legal translation as an act of legal communication. The chapter identifies the key characteristics of legal translation, both inter-systemic and institutional, and discusses attempts to standardize legal translation by way of an ISO standard. The chapter also reviews key research trends and methods in legal translation studies, and outlines the competencies that legal translators need to acquire, suggesting how these can be developed.

In contrast to the two genres that are the foci of Chapters 18 and 19, 'Translating News', the focus of Chapter 20 by Lucile Davier, is generally meant for a broad, mainly lay audience. The challenge here is less a divide between lay and expert text user, and more the fact that news translation tends to be undertaken by non-professional translators, namely journalists themselves. This particularity makes news translation an integral part of non-professional translation. The organizations that translate news are discussed, and the chapter outlines the stages of text production at which translation occurs. Finally, it offers a glimpse into the past to the beginning of news translation with the birth of newswires, and suggests a view of the future of news translation.

The chapter on news translation completes the first of the two parts of the volume that focus on practices of translation, in this case factual genres.

The practical focus continues in Part V, although the genres under scrutiny here are largely art texts, beginning, in Chapter 21, by Geraldine Brodie, with 'Translating for the Theatre'. Theatre translation has connections with literary and poetry translation but is always focused on a performed text and its users. Readers of translated theatrical texts include theatre practitioners engaged in the design and development of performance, and actors who reproduce the text as dialogue and movement. The chapter contrasts direct translation by a specialist translator with the frequent practice of commissioning an expert linguist to make a literal translation to be used by a theatre practitioner to create a text for performance. It considers the role of the translator in the theatrical environment, and concludes with a discussion of the implications for theatre translation of relevant theories from the wider translation arena.

In Chapter 22 on 'Audiovisual Translation', Serenella Zanotti offers an overview of the field focusing on both established and emerging modalities, from traditional transfer modes such as dubbing, subtitling and voice-over, to modes that provide accessibility for people with sensory impairment, such as subtitling for the deaf and hard-of-hearing, audio description, live-subtitling and sign language. Non-professional translation practices such as fansubbing, fandubbing and film remakes are also discussed. For each mode, the chapter illustrates the associated medium-specific constraints and creative possibilities, highlighting the power of audiovisuals to contribute to meaning in ways that lend themselves to manipulation during the translation process.

Chapter 23, 'Translating Literary Prose', by Karen Seago, focuses on a broad genre that ranges among children's literature, genre fiction, and literary and lyrical fiction. Each subgenre presents different primary foci, from style to plot, but each tends towards a narrative core of characters, setting and process. Translators of literary prose face textual and contextual practical challenges in catching the cadence, rhythm and music of a text, since stylistic variation can be crucial in characterization and plot development. Figurative language, selectional restrictions, humour, allusions and quotations tend to be culturally specific and to add to the challenges presented by indeterminacy, ambiguity, inference and implicatures, all of which rely on contextual understanding and may need to be explicitated in a translation.

In Chapter 24, 'Translating Poetry', Paschalis Nikolaou and Cecilia Rossi provide a history of thought on poetry translation ranging from the Roman poets translating Greek, to the experiments of Louis and Celia Zukovsky. They explore how poetic forms, for example the haiku and the sonnet, have been introduced to literary systems beyond their origins through translation, and how the poetry of the classical world has been reanimated through modernism's shifts in practices and views of translation. They discuss the 'translation' of texts in a literary context by poets and versioners who may or may not read the source languages concerned.

Throughout, the emphasis is on exemplification and on the connection between theoretical perspectives and paratextual reflection.

The final chapter in Part V on the translation of art texts is Chapter 25, 'Translating the Texts of Songs and Other Vocal Music', by Peter Low. Translations of songs may be required for various purposes – for singers to sing, for announcers to speak, for CD listeners to read, for singing students to study, and for display as surtitles at a performance. Since no translation is ideal for every purpose, translators need to choose strategies and options that best suit the end-users. Particularly complex is the 'singable translation' (singable in the target language) which is intended to fit a pre-existing melody – here translators are subject to unusual constraints, such as the need to achieve the right number of syllables and a workable rhythm. Often, a singable translation may include so many changes that the term 'adaptation' is more accurate than the term 'translation'.

In Part VI, the *Handbook* turns its attention to translation in history – not the history of translation so much as the roles of translation in different temporal periods, from the pre-Christian era until our own millennium.

In Chapter 26, 'Translation before the Christian Era', Roberto A. Valdeón discusses the role of translation in the years before the birth of Christ in Ancient Egypt, the Near and Middle East, Ancient Greece and Rome, and China. Despite the difficulties of finding texts in translated form stemming from a time when writing was generally limited to stone inscriptions and papyri, many of which have been lost, discoveries made since the 1900s in areas such as Egypt or the Iranian plateau have demonstrated that the practice of translation was not unknown. These discoveries show that the aims of translating into foreign languages were the same as those of modern times: conquest, trade, dissemination of religious beliefs, and literary appropriation or adaptation.

Documentation concerning translation activity in the first millennium is less hard to come by, and Chapter 27, 'Translation in the First Millennium', by Denise Merkle, covers the period from the beginning of the Christian Era to the advent of the Renaissance. The Eastern Roman and Byzantine, (Holy) Roman, Umayyad and Abbasid as well as Chinese empires, in addition to the Indian subcontinent, documented translation and interpreting activity during the millennium when expansionist empires and kingdoms rose and fell, and Silk Road trade flourished. Classical Greek, Latin, Persian, Sanskrit and Arabic texts were revered and much translated, as were the texts of two religions founded during the period, Christianity and Islam. The Chinese invention of paper early in the second century reduced the cost of producing translations.

The second chapter authored by Denise Merkle, Chapter 28, 'Translation in the Second Millennium', presents an overview of translation and interpreting activity through the second millennium in Africa, the Americas (the 'New World'), Asia (China, India, Japan, Turkey) and the Old World. The chapter concludes with a section on the twentieth century that links the professionalization of translation, terminology and interpretation with the development of transnational organizations like UNESCO and supranational unions like the European Union in the aftermath of World War II, along with continued globalization and technological progress.

The final chapter in the volume, Chapter 29, by Moritz Schaeffer, entitled 'Translation in the Third Millennium', completes the account of translation in history as well as the volume itself. As Schaeffer points out, to predict what will happen over the course of a millennium is reckless; but observing the current state of affairs of technological development relating to translation studies and assuming that future developments will follow a linear path, he argues that the impact of technology on translation is likely to play a significant role in how translators and consumers of translations will experience translation itself in this millennium. He predicts that we will achieve a better understanding of the brain, and that technology will become more integrated with humans; this will have a revolutionary influence on how translation is conceptualized, practised and used. The concept of the original would be turned on its head, so to speak, and global connectivity would acquire a new meaning if brains were to be connected the way we are currently connected via machines external to our bodies. In these circumstances, translation would be central in the endeavour to build an interface between individuals.

And so, the volume comes to its conclusion. It has charted a complex, multifaceted field of study, practice and theorization which – my own prediction here – will continue to fascinate for the foreseeable future.

# Part I

## The Nature of Translation

# 1

# Theories of Translation

Jeremy Munday

## 1.1 Introduction

Along with other performance-based disciplines, translation has both a theoretical and a practical core. There is an unresolved friction between theoreticians and practitioners. Translation is taught as an academic or professional competence at undergraduate and postgraduate level, while translation studies encompasses the research and theoretical investigation of the subject. The theory of translation, or translation theory, previously the denomination of the whole field, is now usually a subset of the discipline. Multiple theories have evolved, and there is no formal consensus. Each theory reflects a different approach to the practice and study of translation.

Questions of theory delve into the fundamentals of a field: what a theory of it is, how theory can be applied and how different theories interact. Translation of some sort must have been in existence since the invention of language, yet until the middle of the twentieth century relatively few translators had received formal training. In such circumstances, what 'formal' theory existed was generally limited to impressionistic, philosophical or religious commentary located in some paratext of the translation, in a preface or other foreword or afterword. Even attempts at more systematic writings, such as Dryden's (1680) or Tytler's (1797), did not go much further than identifying certain translation strategies and selecting various translation solutions. The nineteenth-century German Romantics such as Goethe, Schlegel and Schleiermacher trod a different path through the hermeneutic world, Schleiermacher ([1813] 1992) devoting a public lecture in 1813 to discussing different methods of translation.

## 1.2  Classic Depiction of the Translator

Let us start with the classic depiction of the translator in Western civilization, Domenico Ghirlandaio's fresco *St Jerome in His Study* (see Figure 1.1), painted for the All Saints Church in Florence in 1480.

The church retains both this and its companion piece of another translator, St Augustine, painted by Botticelli.

Jerome was commissioned in CE 390 by Pope Damasus to revise the existing Latin translation of the Old Testament using the Hebrew Bible and the Greek Septuagint as a basis. The justification for the revision was concern in the Church about discrepancies among the existing translations; it was felt that the time had come to publish a 'standard' translation to ensure that, literally, everyone was reading from or listening to the same hymn sheet. Ghirlandaio's painting reinforces a stereotype that persisted until the end of the twentieth century: translation as a solitary occupation in which the translator works like an artist or artisan, surrounded by the tools of the trade, books and papers, manipulating a quill/

**Figure 1.1** Domenico Ghirlandaio, *St Jerome in His Study* (1480)

pen and, more recently, a computer/computer-assisted translation (CAT) tool.

St Jerome is the Catholic saint of translators, celebrated on 30 September, International Translation Day. Jerome's contribution to theory rests on brief comments in a letter, where he defends himself from attacks from those who were unhappy with his translation of the Bible. Jerome emphasized his opinion that the better translation is normally 'sense-for-sense' rather than 'word-for-word': 'Now I not only admit but freely announce that in translating from the Greek – except of course in the case of the Holy Scripture, where even the syntax contains a mystery – **I render not word-for-word but sense-for-sense**' (St Jerome, Letter to Pammachius, 395 CE). The brief clause, highlighted in bold in the example, earns Jerome a place in the translation theory books. Preceding this point in the text, Jerome makes a useful comment on a facet of translation that may depend on contextual features of the situation. Thus, he says that his preference is for sense translation *except* in the case of the Bible, where 'even the syntax contains a mystery'. In such cases literal translation is to be preferred because of the peculiar character of the source text and the special properties of sacred language. The underlying theory of translation expressed by Jerome may be explicitly articulated as follows: there are two translation strategies available, one focused on the (form of the) word and the other on recreating the sense. For most translation, the sense-focused strategy is the default, but the word-focused strategy is more appropriate for sensitive, high-status religious texts.

## 1.3 Early Theories

In a major edited volume published in 1997, Douglas Robinson brought together a collection of the best-known historical writing on translation theory from a Western perspective. The subtitle of the book shows the breadth of the writers and the collection: from Herodotus in the fifth century BCE to Nietzsche in the nineteenth century CE. This was a remarkable endeavour, but Robinson notes some important limitations in his editor's preface. The first is that much of the material was relatively inaccessible and dependent upon the quasi-archaeological excavation of previous anthologies or was enhanced by new translations for those texts written in French, German and Greek principally. Secondly, Robinson points out that anthologies of the time were rapidly becoming outdated because they often ended up regurgitating the same texts and ideas. It was a time when elsewhere Robinson was writing on the then novel theory of translation as empire, the poetics of imperialism and post-colonialism and the growing field of gender studies in translation. A schism in the field was pitching linguistics-oriented writing, such as the anthology *Readings in*

*Translation Theory* (Chesterman, 1989), against the rapidly expanding studies coming from a cultural angle.

The scope of the so-called 'linguistic theories' of translation covered in Chesterman's (1989) volume was greater than previously contemplated. It ranges from Dryden and Walter Benjamin to then cutting-edge research in machine translation and Skopos theory. This gives the lie to the description by Robinson (1997, p. xviii) of linguistic theories as being 'concerned ... specifically with a fairly narrow range of sense-for-sense, word-for-word, and "free" translation – the field as it has long been defined'. Robinson's dismissal of linguistics because it is concerned with translation in its most practical sense shows the theoretical battleground defining this study.

## 1.4  Definition of the Term 'Translation Theory'

Following Christensen (2002, p. 2), the word *theory* in English has a visual origin and is said to come from the Greek *theoria* ('seeing' or 'observing') and *theoros* ('spectator'). According to the *Oxford English Dictionary* (OED, n. d.), the term was first used in English in the late sixteenth century as 'a mental scheme of something to be done'. It is given with six modern senses, of which the following are of most relevance to us:

1.a The conceptual basis of a subject or area of study. Contrasted with *practice*.
2.   [Without article.] Abstract knowledge or principles, as opposed to practical experience or activity: theorising, theoretical speculation.

. . .

6.a An explanation of a phenomenon arrived at through examination and contemplation of the relevant facts; a statement of one or more laws or principles which are generally held as describing an essential property of something.

The visual nature of the process (the spectator who observes) joins with the reasoning element (examination/speculation) as the essence of the term. Senses 1.a and 2 both stress the contrast of theory with 'practice'; it is a classic distinction for translation and will be discussed in Section 1.5. Sense 6.a centres on the visual observation leading to the identification of laws or principles of behaviour. This will be crucial in the later discussion of descriptive translation studies (DTS).

Theories may be abstract, but they do not exist in a vacuum. First published in 1962, Thomas Kuhn's *The Structure of Scientific Revolutions* remains a seminal philosophical text to understand the history and flow of ideas. In Kuhn's account, a scientific status quo or 'paradigm' is maintained until a situation arises that cannot be resolved or explained using the normal methods. New approaches are tested, and when one is successful, it becomes a new paradigm for future studies or practice. In the introduction to his book *Exploring Translation Theories*, Anthony Pym ([2010] 2014, p. 1) points out that there is terminological overlap among 'theory', 'model' and 'paradigm'. He follows Kuhn in defining paradigms as configurations of principles that support different groups of theories. The translation paradigms proposed by Pym are: equivalence, purpose, description, uncertainty, localization and cultural translation. We shall discuss several of these, but it should be acknowledged that there is no general agreement among translation theorists about the number and content of such paradigms.

Then comes the question concerning how theory is used. Pym claims reasonably that translators are theorizing all the time: they identify translation problems, generate possible solutions and then choose between the candidate equivalents. In similar fashion, discussing the relation of theory and practice in translation, Boase-Beier (2010, p. 26) contends that 'everyone needs theory, because any act which is not a reflex or purely the result of intuition (and perhaps even then) must be based on a theory, which is simply a way of looking at the world'. However, that word *simply* underplays the complexity of language. It is as a guide through that complexity that theory may assist a translator to translate better. It also allows translators conceptual tools to defend their choices, underpinned by argumentation that is more solid than simply saying 'it sounds better'.

## 1.5 Metalanguage

As translation theory has developed, so research has become more systematic. Or vice versa. The area of metalanguage is one where innovation and the weight of theory are most evident. Since the 1950s, there have been numerous attempts to classify the small changes or 'shifts' that occur in the move from source to target text. Considered from the standpoint of the translator, these are variously known as translation techniques / procedures / methods / solutions / tactics. Perhaps the earliest taxonomy of this type was constructed in Canada by Vinay and Darbelnet in 1958, a comparative stylistics of French and English designed to function as a manual of translation. The taxonomy they produced included seven 'procedures' (borrowing, calque, literal translation, transposition, modulation, equivalence and adaptation) at three levels (lexicon, syntax, message) and with an overall orientation that was either 'direct' or 'oblique' translation. The advantage of such a systematic approach is that it is evidence-based and the precision of the terminology allows for easy reference and comprehension: hopefully, everyone knows what they are referring to and hopefully it is to the same thing. The disadvantage is that the metalanguage used may clash with the metalanguage coined by another scholar and this may cause confusion. For instance, the term 'equivalence' in the above list of procedures denotes an idiomatic rendering of a source text element (e.g., a proverb, onomatopoeia); this is different from the concept called 'equivalence of meaning' that is central to the work of Nida and others.

An added complexity, inherent to their function, is that these taxonomies were published based on different language pairs. They would circulate with inconsistent renderings of newly coined terms years before an official translation was made. Thus, Vinay and Darbelnet's categorization of methods existed in French for nearly four decades before it was translated into English, during which time the specific method of *emprunt* had been variously translated as *borrowing* or *loan*. Similarly, Reiss and Vermeer's 1984 monograph existed in German and its Spanish translation for three decades before appearing in English, the language which, for better or worse, has become the lingua franca of academia, including contemporary translation theory.

## 1.6  Theory and Practice

More than half a century has passed since Eugene Nida and Charles Taber published their classic *The Theory and Practice of Translation* (Nida and Taber, 1969). This was one of a series of publications based on Eugene Nida's experience of training Bible translators working into a myriad languages, some of which had no previously written form. Nida and Taber discuss the effect of the translation on the receptor and the necessity of seeking 'equivalent effect'. This is linked to the choice of overall translation strategy. For Nida and Taber it is achieved through what they call 'dynamic equivalence' (later 'functional equivalence'), defined as the 'quality of a translation in which the message of the original text has been so transported into the receptor language that the response of the receptor is essentially like that of the original receptors' (Nida and Taber, 1969, p. 200). This frequently requires adaptation of the form of the source text in order to preserve the message.

Dynamic equivalence should be considered in opposition to the strategy of formal correspondence, which, in its severest form, 'mechanically reproduces the form of the source text leading to a distortion of the message' (Nida and Taber, 1969, p. 201). The binary distinction of two types of translation strategy was a theoretically more advanced extension of the old 'literal versus free' distinction. It brought in new concepts from generative grammar to underpin a more systematic analysis. Over the following thirty years a number of other translation theorists proposed their own binary. In many cases the binary hides a cline, because translation is rarely completely systematic. Some of the more prominent classifications can be seen in Table 1.1.

Table 1.1 *Binary terminology of translation strategies (adapted from Munday, 2016, p. 311)*

| Theorist | Orientation Strategy | |
| --- | --- | --- |
| Friedrich Schleiermacher | Naturalizing translation | Alienating translation |
| Eugene Nida | Dynamic equivalence (later called 'functional equivalence') | Formal equivalence (later called 'formal correspondence') |
| Peter Newmark | Communicative translation | Semantic translation |
| Jean-Paul Vinay and Jean Darbelnet | Oblique translation | Direct translation |
| Christiane Nord | Instrumental translation | Documentary translation |
| Juliane House | Covert translation | Overt translation |
| Gideon Toury | Acceptability | Adequacy |
| Theo Hermans | Target-oriented | Source-oriented |
| Lawrence Venuti | Domestication | Foreignization |

The list in Table 1.1 is far from being fully comprehensive. One of the difficulties is the inconsistency in terminology. Each of the theorists in the left-hand column has approached the question from a slightly different angle (see Munday, 2016 for a summary of these differences). In essence, each pair of terms in columns 2 and 3 may be distilled into a distinction between a translation that is oriented linguistically and one that is oriented culturally towards, in column 2, the values of the source culture or, in column 3, the values of the lingua-culture.

Then there is the thorny question of whether theory is actually needed at all. It is a question that needs to be confronted. First, we must note that it is sometimes possible to translate well without studying translation. Translation and interpreting have been carried out for centuries during which time there was little or no training available. Today, although the number of translator training institutes has grown widely and it is no longer possible to land a secure translator/interpreter's post at an international organization such as the European Union or the United Nations without an advanced qualification, which normally requires the study of translation theory, the argument about theory and practice continues.

One of the pithiest examples of the differentiation between theory and practice and their mutual commensurability is found in the essay by the linguist Michael Halliday (2001) in a collection that draws on his contribution to the 25th Systemic Functional Linguistics conference in Cardiff in 1998 in which Halliday made a distinction between the purpose of translation theory for practitioners (the translators) and that for linguists (for whom we can read 'translation studies scholars'):

**For a linguist, translation theory is the study of how things are:** what is the nature of the translation process and the relation between texts in translation. **For a translator, translation theory is the study of how things ought to be:** what constitutes good or effective translation and what can help to achieve a better or more effective product . . ..                                (Halliday, 2001, p. 13, bold highlight added)

Here Halliday makes clear academics' interest in understanding how the translation comes into being (the process) as well as what changes occur in the move from source to target text (the product in comparison with the starting text). By contrast, the professional translator will more often than not be focused on identifying specific equivalents that will function appropriately in the specific context of the time-sensitive translation task at hand.

Theory provides valuable concepts that allow translators to use their wide linguistic store and repertoire of responses in order to find solutions consistently rather than relying on intuition or luck of the draw. There are comparable situations in other disciplines, for example music or art. It is possible to play an instrument without knowledge of theory much in the way that an untrained translator may work. The translator draws on linguistic competence acquired or learned of both source and target languages and a finely tuned instinct (if untrained, or from theory if trained) about what makes a good translation; the untrained musician may have an innate ability to create or reproduce music, an ability that can be expanded by exposure to theory. It should be stressed that an individual without a theoretical background may still be capable of intuitively arriving at a solution endorsed by theory.

Music theory has a much longer formal history than translation theory but faces a similar hierarchical divide between theory and practice. For music, this hierarchy has shifted over time and expanded to encompass music analysis, as described in the survey of the field that begins the *Cambridge History of Western Music Theory* (Christensen, 2002).

## 1.7  The Study of Translation Theory

Until late into the twentieth century, the concept of the theory of translation was still firmly attached to literary texts and to an eclectic series of readings from mostly well-known and mostly male authors who happened to have written something about translation. For example, in 1992 the University of Chicago Press published a volume edited by Rainer Schulte and John Biguenet of the prestigious Center for Translation Studies at the University of Texas at Dallas. Entitled *Theories of Translation* (Schulte and Biguenet, 1992), the volume brought together in English a collection of twenty Western language texts by almost exclusively male writers from the nineteenth and twentieth centuries. The aim of the volume was expressed in a very clear statement: 'A study of the various theoretical concepts that are drawn from or brought to the **practice** of translation can provide entrance into the mechanisms that, through the **art** of translation, make cross-cultural communication and understanding possible' (Schulte and Biguenet, 1992, p. 1, bold highlight added). The field is here construed very much in terms of literary translation and creative writing, and with a philosophical underpinning that explores the transfer of the foreign content to the target text. Translation is also seen to be an energizing force for the target language (Schulte and Biguenet, 1992, p. 9). But how this actually works is left to interpretation and is not best served by being described as an art or craft, as in the quote earlier in this section. However, the volume affords some space to more systematic analysis. For example, one of the readings is Roman Jakobson's (1959) still seminal 'On Linguistic Aspects of Translation', in which he puts forward the definition of three types of translation: intralingual, interlingual and intersemiotic. In their introduction, Schulte and Biguenet (1992) also discuss the links between research and practice and assert that research into translation theory is about reconstructing the process by analysing the product alongside the source text. It is about analysing choices open to the translator and deducing reasons for the selections made. This concentration on process as well as product chimes with the approach proposed by James S. Holmes (1988) in a paper that was to revolutionize research in translation studies.

## 1.8 Holmes and Translation Theory

Holmes (1924–86) was a Dutch-American poet, translator and lecturer in the Netherlands. His seminal article 'The Name and Nature of Translation Studies' (Holmes, 1988) coined the English name for this discipline. Subsequently, Gideon Toury ([1995] 2012) made use of Holmes's structure when he put together a visual representation of the field.

The famous map can be seen in Figure 1.2. Translation studies (that is, the field as a whole) is subdivided into a 'pure' (theoretical) and an 'applied' (practical) side. The 'applied translation' branch was, at that time, very much the junior partner. Our interest in the theoretical side of translation studies will centre on the triangle formed by **'pure'** and its subordinates, **'theoretical'** (**general** or **partial**) and **'descriptive'** (later differentiated, according to **'product'**, **'process'** and **'function'**). Let us consider each of these overarching terms and how each subdivision serves to construct that part of the field of translation theory.

'Pure' [2] is an epithet designed to put translation studies [1] on a par with systematic scientific investigation. For Holmes, the theoretical side encompasses both [4] and [5]. Further, [4] is subdivided between 'general

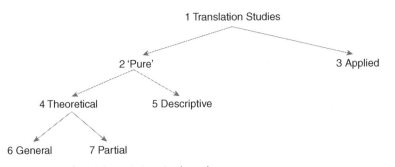

**Figure 1.2** Holmes's/Toury's 'map', adapted
Source: Toury [1995] 2012, p. 10.

theory' [6] and 'partial theory' [7]; in line with this, [6] should be reserved for theory that is applicable across the board, while [7] may be limited to a specific language pair, a certain domain of knowledge or a particular translation problem. However, although some texts, including introductory textbooks, lay claim to being applicable *generally*, it behoves us to question to what extent a feature is really 'general', that is, relevant for all contexts and situations.

The concept of observing or viewing inherent in the definition of 'theory' is very much in tune with the approach adopted by DTS, number [5] in Figure 1.2. The positioning and interaction of theory with the other forms of translation research is important. Toury ([1995] 2012, p. 15) emphasizes that 'one of the aims of translation studies should definitely be to bring the results of descriptive-explanatory studies executed within DTS to bear on the theoretical branch'. This advancement of DTS as a necessary counter to the often-prescriptive nature of more practical volumes is reinforced by following an approach that privileges description, explanation and prediction.

Holmes (1988) discusses six relevant factors that prevent a general theoretical statement being made for translation. These subdivisions, or 'restrictions', mark important distinctions in translation theory research that are still valid. The six are:

1. **Medium-restricted.** Written translation may still be the norm, but the range of forms encompassed by the general term 'translation' is far greater and more sophisticated than in Holmes's time: interpreting, audio-visual translation including video-game localization, machine translation (full or human-assisted) and CAT, among others.
2. **Area-restricted**. This includes phenomena such as language-specific pairs, and different language or cultural groups within the same geographical area. It is important to recognize that there is an overlap between language-specific pairs and contrastive linguistics; however, while translation theory is centred on identifying solutions to translation problems in the two languages, contrastive linguistics has the primary goal of assisting language learning.

3. **Rank-restricted**. When Holmes wrote, the linguistic category of rank was most often applied to the individual word, phrase or sentence. It was an important element in Catford's prominent book on linguistic approaches to translation (Catford, 1965). Subsequently, rank has been superseded by whole text analysis and by discourse analysis using systemic functional linguistics, which sees function in choice.
4. **Text-type restricted**. This relates to questions of translating specific text types and genres, which may have different formal or pragmatic conventions in the two lingua-cultures. An example would be formal business correspondence in French, which has strict conventions about the language used for opening and closing a letter.
5. **Time-restricted**. Translation is dependent on its historical context. It changes over time and descriptive studies are necessarily located in a particular time frame; hence, for example, studies devoted to translations of Latin American fiction into English in the 1960s and 1970s.
6. **Problem-restricted**. The focus is placed on one feature. Holmes gives the examples of the translation of metaphor and of proper names.

All these restrictions constrain the scope of the findings. Furthermore, Holmes accepts that theories can be restricted in more than one way. The translation of metaphor and of proper names necessarily depends on narrowing down the categories of text type (would a name be translated the same whether it appears in a novel or a newspaper report?) and time (names of places can be subject to change for political reasons, such as Salisbury, Rhodesia, which on independence became Harare, Zimbabwe). Current translation studies, priding itself on its interdisciplinarity and its openness, has moved towards the collaborative investigation of such questions.

## 1.9  Descriptive Laws, Probabilities and Universals

The advance of the descriptive translation paradigm by Gideon Toury and others represented a landmark in the theorization of the field. Before Toury ([1995] 2012), much descriptive research was constituted by one-off, isolated studies of a particular source and target text pair. Without the systematic and rigorous assemblage of DTS, there would be no formal way in which to properly evaluate the significance of each new study. What the DTS structure permitted was the comparison and discussion of the new findings within a replicable research framework that overtly builds on prior research.

What Toury was leading to in his more scientific methods was a more solid means of seeing the bigger picture. Individual studies, however brilliant, will always remain one tree in the dense wood and, on their own, will not be able to answer some larger questions, for instance about the consistency of a translation method at a given time or by a given translator (or group of translators) in given genres or languages. It is only by comparing the findings to similar studies of similar/different genres or the same/different translators, etc. that the single study may be contextualized. Only thus may descriptive research escape isolation and succeed in contributing to the greater understanding as well as theorization of the case.

For Toury ([1995] 2012, p. 267ff.), the 'bigger picture' meant the identification of probabilistic 'laws' of translation: 1) the **law of growing standardization** and 2) the **law of interference**. That is to say, translations would tend in 1) to be less diverse than the source texts (they would be more standard in the choice of lexis and syntax and so on) and in 2) to show the effect of the source text on the target text composition. Thus, we can interpret Toury's words as meaning both that

1) the vocabulary and structures in translations will be less varied compared with the source (for example, a 'grubby railway station' may be translated as 'dirty ...') and that
2) the translation is constrained by the features of the source (in effect, 'dirty' in the source text would be more likely to be translated as 'dirty' in the target text even if that were an unnatural or infrequent collocation in the target language).

These two points seem to be contradictory and have been challenged. Pym (2008) suggested that the coexistence of the two laws depends on a range of 'conditioning factors' (the need to deal with an ambiguous source text, for example) that allow the translator to manage risk (by choosing the standard term or borrowing a source text term). In addition, the more popular choices in target texts may reflect the specific cultural, sociological and historical circumstances in which the translation took place. Therefore, the patterns that we see may better be considered as 'tendencies' or 'trends' rather than 'laws' or 'universals'. 'Universals' would suggest a feature that occurs in every translation, and Toury ([1995] 2012, p. 80) acknowledged that this would be something so general (such as 'translation shifts occur') that it would be unable to say anything very useful.

## 1.10  Functional Theories of Translation

Of course, there have been other attempts to formulate a general theory of translation. Early work in the Soviet Union by Andrey Fedorov (1953/2021) produced a monograph in Russian entitled *An Introduction to the Theory of Translation*. As Vasserman (forthcoming) describes, it was first published in 1953 with subsequent editions up to the posthumous fifth in 2002. Targeted mainly at literary translation, it nevertheless reveals a network of academics working on translation theory across the Eastern and Western blocs. This included Roman Jakobson and Jiří Levý (2011) in the then Czechoslovakia and Edmond Carey and Georges Mounin in Switzerland and France. We should remember that, ironically for a discipline of translation studies, one of the impediments to knowledge transfer was the range of languages in which academics were writing at the time: Fedorov's use of Russian was a significant indicator of power in the Soviet sphere, but it did mean that the audience for his work was restricted among academics in the West. Finally, in 2021, Fedorov's major book appeared in English translation, supported by funding from the European Society for Translation Studies.

Fedorov's work on functional equivalence was a forerunner for theoretical advances in the 1970s and 1980s in Germany (West and East), major centres for translation-based research. The work of Katharina Reiss and Hans Vermeer was geared towards providing what they explicitly termed 'Foundation of a general theory of Translation': *Grundlegung einer allgemeinen Translationstheorie*. This was based on Reiss's work on text type and genre together with the later Skopos theory developed by her student Vermeer. Text type describes the text according to its rhetorical function (arguing, informing, persuading ...); as the textual manifestation of a social process, genre would be considered at the level of, for example, 'health-care information leaflet' rather than a superordinate such as 'health communication'. Admittedly, it is possible to provide a more delicate description of the genre; thus, the health-care information leaflet could be restricted to specific areas of health, such as cancer, which itself can be subdivided into the varieties of the illness (skin, bowel, etc.). One crucial claim of Reiss and Vermeer's theory is that the text type and genre determine to a great extent the form of the translation. So, an informing text type (such as the health-care information leaflet) would require a translation that privileges the transfer of information through 'straight-forward', unambiguous language, while a denser text translated for health-care experts would tolerate (and even demand) that the subject-specific terminology be retained.

Just as importantly, however, Skopos, or purpose, indicates the success of the operation. Fulfilling the translation 'commission', or 'brief', is central to achieving a satisfactory result. The question then arises as to the status of the source text. If, for example, the purpose of the dense information leaflet was to alert a young public to the measures to be taken in the event of a future pandemic, would it be satisfactory, in seeking to achieve its Skopos, to produce a heavily adapted text based on pictures? Indeed, what theoretical limits are there to the manipulation of the text to meet translation instructions? Vermeer (1989) himself spoke of the 'dethroning' of the source text since it was no longer the gold standard against which deviation was to be measured. In view of the consequences of this theoretical question, another German functionalist, Christiane

Nord (2003), proposed a solution of 'functionality plus loyalty': that is, fulfilling the functional instructions given to the translator and at the same time remaining 'loyal' to the source text author's intention. However, such theoretical terms themselves are problematic. The whole area of loyalty/fidelity/faithfulness harks back to the times of what were known in France as *les belles infidèles*, a sexist trope that described translations as beautiful or faithful but never both. The author's intention is another problematic concept: if we see each new reading as different, how can we be sure to know the author's intention, and what should the translator do if there are multiple interpretations possible? Linguistic expressions of loyalty to the author, unless conveyed in very clear terms, are subject to just the same reservations as Nida and Taber's (1969) notion of equivalent effect. That is, how do we measure it reliably? This is the main reason why functionalism initially placed most emphasis on the nature of the target text: if the target text fulfilled the purpose for which it was commissioned, then the translation brief was deemed to have been achieved. In the case of a specialized technical text such as the manufacturer's details or the global warranty of a product, the success of the translation may be measured by whether or not the target text users were able to understand how to contact the manufacturer or how to claim under the guarantee. The measure of success is whether it functions in the real world. Functionalism, therefore, has a socio-cultural perspective; translation succeeds if the target text works in the target culture, which may be more important than a close relation to the source text. This was central to subsequent developments in translation theory.

One direction, which began in the 1990s and continues today, is the move from text analysis to discourse analysis. Whereas work on the functionalist paradigms mainly involved the application of a model of text analysis that examined a detailed list of both intra-textual and extra-textual factors when planning a translation or when judging its efficacy, new moves subsequently came in the direction of discourse analysis. Two models of analysis have been especially popular within translation studies: systemic functional linguistics (SFL), following the tradition of Halliday (1985) and Halliday and Matthiessen (2014), and a specialist off-shoot version designed for the analysis of political texts, namely critical discourse analysis (Fairclough, 1989; Fairclough and Fairclough, 2012).

The development of 'linguistic' translation theory is highly intricate and revealing of the interdisciplinary nature of translation studies. Thus, the pedagogical origins of Halliday's research in the 1960s underpinned the work of Juliane House in the 1970s in her model of Translation Quality Assessment (most recently, House, 2015), perhaps the first comprehensive use of register analysis for the study of translation. Halliday's later work was incorporated into the discourse analytic models of Hatim and Mason (1990, 1997) and Steiner (2004). It has continued to prosper in more recent volumes devoted to the application of specific discourse elements for the analysis of translation (e.g., Munday, 2012; Munday and Zhang, 2015; Kim et al., 2021).

There are two key theoretical points here: one is that it is not easy to establish the specific cause and effect links between lexico-grammatical choices and the wider context of culture. The second point is the feasibility and desirability of importing a theoretical model from another discipline (here, linguistics) with the expectation that it will work for the analysis of a source text–target text pair. Sometimes there is a certain disconnect between imported theory and translated data. This may manifest itself by a mismatch made vivid by the attempted classification of phenomena into categories originally devised for the study of monolingual material. For example, the application of the appraisal framework to the study of political discourse in translation (Munday, 2012) leads to the identification of a series of translation shifts in intensification and explicitation. Yet a full classification of the two texts based on monolingual text features may not be the most effective methodology when, in reality, many of the phenomena display translation shifts only when there is a clash in the value system between the source and the target lingua-cultures.

This is indeed the question that should be asked of translation theories in general: why is translation studies so dependent on the importation of basic ideas from other disciplines? While the trend may be explained by chronology, since theories of linguistics have preceded those of translation studies, some (e.g., Gutt, 2000) have argued that relevance theory already covers communication, including translation, and therefore no separate theory of translation is required to supplement it. The response would be that theoretical concepts from linguistics may be imported initially, but that translation theory soon develops through its own pathways. This can be seen in translation-specific theoretical notions such as 'loss', 'gain', 'compensation', 'explicitation', 'shifts' and so on.

## 1.11 Current Translation Theory Expands the Definition of Translation

The 'one small step for a translator but one giant leap for translation theory' moment was the 'cultural turn' ushered in by the members of the so-called Manipulation School (Hermans, 1985), prominent being Gideon Toury, Susan Bassnett and André Lefevere. For Bassnett and Lefevere (1990), the aim was to move the discipline away from its reliance on sometimes superficial linguistic analysis towards a consideration of the socio-cultural, historical and other contexts in which communication takes place. Although this turn may disregard linguistic theories, as soon as it is accepted that linguistics alone cannot account for all observations in translation, the field opens up to the cultural and other paradigms.

The cultural and other 'turns' in translation studies have been reflected in the abundance of new theories, imported from other disciplines (cultural theory, deconstruction, post-colonial theory, feminist theory, gender theory, film theory and so on). This has been particularly evident in the desire to shift the focus of translational research onto new ground, such as narrative theory (Baker, 2006), the sociological approach (using the work of Bourdieu (1991) and others), the historical approach and the translatorial approach. The last investigates the figure of the translator/interpreter, ironically almost completely overlooked by Holmes and Toury.

Another key element since the new millennium is the rise of China as a player in translation studies. The resulting research has promoted a greater understanding of the Chinese tradition in translation, which goes back beyond the translation projects of the Buddhist sutras; it encompasses the meeting or clash of cultures in locations where treaties and commercial papers were drafted in two or more languages for the regulation of activities between China and a foreign power. There has also been greater understanding and critical appreciation of the work of Yán Fù (1854–1921), whose predominant pronouncements on translation are to be found in the foreword he wrote to his translation of Thomas Henry Huxley's *Evolution and Ethics* (see Hsu, 1973). His three principles of translation – *xìn*, *dá* and *yǎ*, which broadly equate to faithfulness, accessibility and elegance – became central to Chinese translation theory throughout the twentieth century.

The dissemination of these principles is illustrative of the obstacles encountered by non-Western and especially non-anglophone concepts. Yán Fù's three terms are by no means translated consistently when they are discussed in Western translation theory (Hermans, 2003). Yán Fù was a leading figure in cultural and intellectual circles, which may explain why he maintained his status as the major Chinese translation theorist into the twenty-first century (Chan, 2004). It was only then that younger Chinese scholars, who had studied modern linguistic theories, emerged onto the national stage, and adopted a more systematic and rigorous methodology especially for the study of the translation process.

The emergence of China as a major player in research has been accompanied by a concerted effort to develop theories of translation originating in China. This can be seen in the interest in Chinese discourse in translation, richly displayed by Martha Cheung's (2006) publications; this pioneering project was left unfinished at her death in 2013 but was continued by her colleagues at Hong Kong Baptist University. Another, very different example is Gengshen Hu's development of 'eco-translatology', a fusion of translation theory (going by the 'scientific' name of 'translatology') and ecology; the key concept is that translation is an organic system, ever-shifting in nature through evolution, adaptation, natural selection and extinction. It was first promoted at a conference in China in 2006 and consolidated by the publication of a monograph *Eco-Translatology: Towards an Eco-paradigm of Translation Studies* (Hu, 2020). The success that this paradigm has received can be gauged by the fact that the 7th IATIS conference in Barcelona in 2021 had at its main theme *The Cultural Ecology of Translation.* Likewise, it is testament to the many years of research into translation and ecology, as well as translation and globalization, by Michael Cronin (2016).

Another point to bear in mind is the link being forged by translation theorists working on broader, interdisciplinary research into cultural and social aspects of the field. One excellent example, from South Africa, is the work of Kobus Marais on translation and development and on biosemiotics (Marais, 2014, 2018).

## 1.12 The Technological and Digital Revolution

Among theoretical developments since Holmes are those which affect what he would have called the 'medium', and what now is more commonly known as 'mode'. This is, above all, audio-visual translation: the subtitling, dubbing or voice-over of films, documentaries, video games and similar. This field has developed into the major player in research in the twenty-first century. New technological developments go hand-in-hand with new theories of communication, notably theories of multimodality (Kress and van Leeuwen, 2021; Bateman, 2008). Underlying this development is the absolute conviction that visual and other multimodal products be viewed as an integral part of a semiotic code and not as a mere appendage to the communication. Where once film and TV were relegated to a remote outpost on the boundaries of academia, in current translation studies research they are central to the evolution of new theories of meaning and translation (see Thomas, 2020; Adami and Ramos-Pinto, forthcoming).

There are several consequences. One is the relationship between medium/mode and theory. Is it possible to devise a theory of translation that encompasses both conventional written translation and audio-visual translation, or are these best retained as separate beasts? Not to mention the other elephant in the room, which is interpreting. The distinction between (written) translation and (spoken) interpreting is now justifiably considered to be unreliable since the two may coexist in many situations. Instances might include a politician who reads aloud a written speech for simultaneous interpreting and for later written translation, and the combination in a film or documentary of spoken dialogue and on-screen writing (a series of SMS or WhatsApp messages, for example) translated intersemiotically into written subtitles or spoken voice-over/dubbing. These increasingly blurred distinctions between modes accompany more sophisticated information technology in the translation workplace. Audio-visual translators also now have at their disposal freely available subtitling software which allows subtitles to be entered and recorded by fansubbers working from the comfort of the home.

The equivalence paradigm (Pym, [2010] 2014) has also been extended and challenged with the development of the digital apparatus of localization. The rapid deployment of CAT tools and project management software has revolutionized not only the work station and working processes but also the very form of research and the theory underpinning it. For example, the automatic segmentation of the source text into word, phrase, clause and sentence often determines the rank at which equivalence is to be sought. And the largest segment is never more than the sentence. At the same time, the use of translation memories aims to ensure consistency of terminology both within a text and intertextually throughout the database.

Much effort has also been invested in developing empirical research methods to investigate the translation process, using brain scans, eye tracking, keystroke logging, think-aloud protocols and so on (Saldanha and O'Brien, 2014). In the same vein, the improved production of fully automatic machine translation and human-assisted machine translation, along with research which makes use of corpus linguistic methods, fits into a more objective and measurable research methodology compared to earlier more subjective and intuitive work. For the present, the reality is that translation cannot be an exact science. There is too much variation, and too many extenuating circumstances and extratextual factors affect the process and the product. For translation theory in the future, it may be that technological and digital change will prove to be the harbingers of consistency that will wage war with translation's many contextual constraints and variables over the fate of 'true' universals, as well as transforming (and perhaps disrupting) the working practice of translators themselves.

# Bibliography

Adami, E., and Ramos Pinto, S. (forthcoming). *Translation and Multimodality.* Abingdon: Routledge.

Baker, M. (2006). *Translation and Conflict: A Narrative Account.* Abingdon: Routledge.

Bassnett, S., and Lefevere, A., eds. (1990). *Translation, History and Culture.* London: Pinter.

Bateman, J. (2008). *Multimodality and Genre.* Basingstoke: Palgrave Macmillan.

Boase-Beier, J. (2010). Who needs theory? In A. Fawcett, K. Guadarrama García and R. Hyde Parker, eds., *Translation: Theory and Practice in Dialogue.* London/New York: Continuum, pp. 25–38.

Bourdieu, P. (1991). *Language and Symbolic Power,* trans. G. Raymond and M. Adamson. Cambridge: Polity Press.

Catford, I. (1965). *A Linguistic Theory of Translation*. Oxford: Oxford University Press.

Chan, L. T.-h., ed. (2004). *Twentieth Century Chinese Translation Theory: Modes, Issues and Debates*. Amsterdam: John Benjamins.

Chesterman, A., ed. (1989). *Readings in Translation Theory*. Helsinki: Finn Lectura.

Cheung, M., ed. (2006). *An Anthology of Chinese Discourse on Translation: From Earliest Times to the Buddhist Project* (vol. 1). Manchester: St Jerome.

Christensen, T., ed. (2002). *The Cambridge History of Western Music Theory*. Cambridge: Cambridge University Press.

Cronin, M. (2016). *Eco-translation: Translation and Ecology in the Age of the Anthropocene*. London/New York: Routledge.

Dryden, J. ([1680] 1992). Metaphrase, paraphrase and imitation: Extracts of preface to Ovid's Epistles (1680). In R. Schulte and J. Biguenet, eds., *Theories of Translation*. Chicago: University of Chicago Press, pp. 17–31.

Fairclough, N. (1989). *Language and Power*. London: Longman.

Fairclough, I., and Fairclough, N. (2012). *Political Discourse Analysis: A Method for Advanced Students*. London: Routledge.

Fedorov, A. V. (1953/2021). *Vvedenie v teoriiu perevoda*. Trans. and ed. B. J. Baer as *Introduction to Translation Theory*. London: Routledge.

Gutt, E. A. (2000). *Translation and Relevance: Cognition and Context*. 2nd ed. Manchester: St Jerome.

Halliday M. A. K. (1985). *An Introduction to Functional Grammar*. London: Arnold.

Halliday M. A. K. (2001). Towards a theory of good translation. In E. Steiner and C. Yallop, eds., *Exploring Translation and Multilingual Text Production: Beyond Content*. Berlin: Mouton de Gruyter, pp. 13–18.

Halliday M. A. K., and Matthiessen, C. (2014). *An Introduction to Functional Grammar*. 4th ed. London: Routledge.

Hatim, B., and Mason, I. (1990). *Discourse and the Translator*. London: Longman.

Hatim, B., and Mason, I. (1997). *The Translator as Communicator*. London/New York: Routledge.

Hermans, T., ed. ([1985] 2014). *The Manipulation of Literature: Studies in Literary Translation*. Abingdon: Routledge.

Hermans, T. (2003). Cross-cultural translation studies as thick translation. *Bulletin of the School of Oriental and African Studies*, **66**(3), 380–9.

Holmes, J. S. (1988). *Translated! Papers on Literary Translation and Translation Studies*. Amsterdam: Rodopi.

House, J. (2015). *Translation Quality Assessment: Past and Present*. London: Routledge.

Hsu, C. Y., trans. (Autumn 1973). General remarks on translation by Yen Fu (1854–1921). *Renditions*, **1**, 4–6. Available at www.cuhk.edu.hk/rct/pdf/e_outputs/b01/v01p004.pdf.

Hu, G. (2020). *Eco-Translatology: Towards an Eco-paradigm of Translation Studies*. Abingdon: Routledge.

Jakobson, R. (1959). On linguistic aspects of translation. In R. Brower, ed., *On Translation*. Cambridge, MA: Harvard University Press, pp. 232–9.

Jerome, E. H. (St Jerome) (395 CE). De optime genere interpretandi (Letter 101, to Pammachius), trans. P. Carroll as On the best kind of translator. In D. Robinson, ed. (1997). *Western Translation Theory: From Herodotus to Nietzsche*. Manchester: St Jerome, pp. 22–30.

Kim, M., Munday, J., Wang Z., and Wang P., eds. (2021). *Systemic Functional Linguistics and Translation Studies*. London/New York: Bloomsbury.

Kress, G., and van Leeuwen, T. (2021). *Reading Images: The Grammar of Visual Design*. 3rd ed. Abingdon: Routledge.

Kuhn, T. (1962). *The Structure of Scientific Revolutions*. Chicago: University of Chicago Press.

Levý, J. (2011). *The Art of Translation*, trans. P. Corness, ed. Z. Jettmarová. Amsterdam:John Benjamins.

Marais, K. (2014). *Translation Theory and Development Studies: A Complexity Theory Approach*. Abingdon/New York: Routledge.

Marais, K. (2018). *A (Bio)Semiotic Theory of Translation: The Emergence of Socio-cultural Reality*. Abingdon: Routledge.

Munday, J. (2012). *Evaluation in Translation: Critical Points of Translator Decision-Making*. London/New York: Routledge.

Munday, J. (2016). *Introducing Translation Studies*. 4th ed. London/New York: Routledge.

Munday, J., and Zhang, M., eds. (2015). *Discourse Analysis in Translation Studies*. Special issue of *Target*, **27**(3).

Nida, E., and Taber, C. R. (1969). *The Theory and Practice of Translation*. Leiden: E. J. Brill.

Nord, C. (2003). Function and loyalty in Bible translation. In M. Calzada-Pérez, ed., *Apropos of Ideology*. Manchester: St Jerome, pp. 89–112.

OED. (n.d.). Entry: 'theory'. Available at www.oed.com/view/Entry/200431.

Pym, A. (2007). Natural and directional equivalence in theories of translation. *Target*, 19(2), 271–94.

Pym, A. ([2010] 2014). *Exploring Translation Theories*. London: Routledge.

Reiss, K., and Vermeer, H. ([1984] 2013). *Towards a General Theory of Translational Action: Skopos Theory Explained*, trans. C. Nord, English reviewed by M. Dudenhöfer. Manchester: St Jerome.

Robinson, D., ed. (1997). *Western Translation Theory: From Herodotus to Nietzsche*. Manchester: St Jerome.

Saldanha G., and O'Brien, S. (2014). *Research Methodologies in Translation Studies*. Abingdon: Routledge.

Schleiermacher, F. ([1813] 1992). On the different methods of translating. In R. Schulte and J. Biguenet, eds., *Theories of Translation*. Chicago/London: University of Chicago Press, pp. 36–54.

Schulte, R., and Biguenet, J., eds. (1992). *Theories of Translation*. Chicago/London: University of Chicago Press.

Steiner, E. (2004). *Translated Text: Properties, Variants, Evaluations* (Sabest Saarbrucker Beitrage Zur Sprach- Und Translationswissenschaft 4). Bern: Peter Lang.

Thomas, M. (2020). Multimodality and media archaeology: Complementary optics for looking at digital stuff? *Digital Scholarship in the Humanities*, 36(2), 482–500.

Toury, G. ([1995] 2012). *Descriptive Translation Studies–And Beyond*. Amsterdam/Philadelphia: John Benjamins.

Tytler, A. F. (Lord Woodhouselee). (1797). *Essay on the Principles of Translation*. Extracted in D. Robinson, ed. (1997). *Western Translation Theory: From Herodotus to Nietzsche*. Manchester: St Jerome, pp. 208–12.

Vasserman, E. (forthcoming). The theory of translation by Russian scholar Andrei Fedorov. Unpublished PhD thesis. University of Leeds.

Vermeer, H. (1989). Skopos and commission in translation action. In A. Chesterman, ed., *Readings in Translation Theory*. Helsinki: Finn Lectura, pp. 173–200.

# 2

# The Translation Process

Fabio Alves and Arnt Lykke Jakobsen

## 2.1   Introduction

Within translation studies (TS), the term *translation process* usually refers to the process by which a translator produces a translation of a text. This process is physical, behavioural and mental. There is a material text representation, there is body movement involved in reading and writing text, and there is thinking. Translation process research (TPR) has not been much concerned with the material aspects; rather, it has mostly focused on how inferences about cognitive processes could be reliably made from observations of translators' behaviour as they translate. Particular attention has been given to translators' finger movements on a keyboard and their eye movements across a computer screen on which are displayed both the text-to-be-translated and the emerging translation. Inferences about cognition can also be made from other measurable activity in the body such as changes in heart rate, blood pressure and other symptoms of affect and cognitive strain or relaxation. Finally, a translator's brain activity can be measured with electroencephalography (EEG), brain imaging technology like positron emission tomography (PET) or functional magnetic resonance imaging (fMRI) scanning. Such technologies provide information about what areas of the brain are particularly active during translation. Information about neuronal activity is hypothesized to provide particularly important evidence of the nature of cognitive processes.

When reading a translation, we can sometimes guess why a certain phrase was translated in a particular way, especially if it has been translated awkwardly, but in most cases we cannot know how the translator arrived at a certain solution or what earlier versions existed. Recording and studying how a translation comes into being, in addition to studying the end product, gives us insight into the thought processes that underlie the final version of a translation. This insight is important from a pedagogical perspective as well as for understanding how the human mind handles meaning when it has to cross a language border.

The translation process is typically studied from the moment a translator begins to read a text-to-be-translated, a source text, until the translation has been finalized as a target text. Regarded in this manner, the translation process is really three interrelated processes: (1) reading the source text, (2) meaning translation and (3) writing the target text. The means by which the translation process is studied include direct observation, recordings of verbalizations either during concurrent think aloud or in retrospective interviews, questionnaires and other experimental procedures like video/audio recording, keylogging, eye tracking and various neuroscientific methods (EEG, fMRI and others). Different combinations of these methods, yielding both subjective qualitative and technology-recorded quantitative data, are often used in so-called multi-method approaches. Empirical data elicited by these means are analysed statistically to identify significant findings, often in a process of data triangulation.

The translation process thus described is strongly focused on what has been called the translation *act* following Holmes's map of TS which fore-saw a special branch of TS dealing with 'the process or act of translation itself' (Holmes, 1972, p. 177). Toury (2012) and Chesterman (2013) distin-guished between the cognitive act and the observable *event*, the event being everything that happens in the situation, including what happens in the translator's body. By this distinction, translation process research may be said to be aimed at inferring knowledge about the translation act from evidence in the translation event.

In some research, the translation process is construed as the entire social and economic sequence of transactional processes, including the cognitive processes and ergonomic conditions involved, from when a client orders a translation from a translation agency to when the agency delivers the translation to the client. Here, the focus may be on the social status of translators, their interaction in the workplace with colleagues, translation tools and other 'agents', and how all of this affects their cogni-tion. An even wider perspective includes study of the socio-cultural pro-cesses by which texts are selected for translation (e.g., in majority or minority cultures), how translations are disseminated, and their impact in recipient cultures. In research of this kind, the methods used are socio-logical, cultural or anthropological.

Our main focus in the present account is on what happens behaviourally and cognitively in the bodies and minds of translators when they translate.

## 2.2 Modelling the Translation Process

As far as models of the translation process are concerned, Seleskovitch (1968) can be considered a point of departure. This work is based on theoretical considerations and intuitive experience that drew attention to the specificities of the translation process. Seleskovitch (1968) and later Seleskovitch and Lederer (1984) built on the phases of understanding and re-expression but also explored the idea of an intermediate phase of de-verbalization between understanding and re-expression.

Their innovative research paved the way for attempts to model the translation process from an empirical perspective. In the beginning, empirically oriented approaches to investigating the translation process drew heavily on think-aloud protocols (TAPs) (Gerloff, 1988; Séguinot, 1989; Jääskeläinen, 1990; Tirkkonen-Condit, 1991). As research evolved, several models of the translation process were developed from the mid-1980s to the mid-1990s, particularly at German universities. Arising as an alternative to the German functional tradition in TS (Reiß and Vermeer, 1984), German scholars used TAPs (Ericsson and Simon, 1980) to try to investigate the translation process in real time. In Section 2.3, we present a chronological overview of some of the most important models of the translations process from the mid-1980s to the present and offer brief descriptions of their main features.

## 2.3    A Chronological Overview of Models of the Translation Process

The models of the translation process developed at German universities from 1986 to 1995 used think-aloud data to analyse cognitive processing and flow charts to display traits of the translation process. All of these models drew on the information-processing paradigm, included top-down and bottom-up features, and examined the use of strategies and instances of problem solving and decision making.

Krings (1986) used TAPs to look at translations performed by students of French. He designed a model of the translation process in the form of a flow chart with several intermediate steps which require yes/no answers. The point of departure is the source text and the end point the target text. The first question asked is whether there is a translation problem. If not, a solution is transferred into the target text. If there is a problem, the next step is problem identification, which leads to another question on the nature of that identification. Krings proposes a series of strategic steps to help with problem solving and decision making. When the problem is solved in terms of understanding it, the process moves into a phase of strategic decisions which lead to equivalent renderings being established for the target text. Several alternative procedures are suggested to achieve equivalence between source text problems and target text items. Finally, there is a phase of strategic assessment before the original translation problem is solved and the solution transferred into the target text.

Königs (1987) also used TAPs to examine translations rendered from Spanish into German by novice translators. He proposed a three-step model involving automatic and reflexive processes. It is displayed in the form of a simple flow chart with few intermediate steps but a detailed description of what these steps entail. On the one hand are automatic processes which are part of the *Adhoc Block* containing previously established correspondences between source and target text items. On the other hand are reflexive processes which occur in the *Rest Block*; these require you to search for adequate strategies to solve a given translation problem. *Adhoc Block* processes constitute a default procedure in the search for 1:1 equivalences between source and target text segments. Such equivalences often arise from internalized decisions based on previous experience. They are processed automatically by translators and are resistant to revision even when they fail to provide adequate renderings. Whenever the default procedure fails to be implemented, translators resort to *Rest Block* procedures where strategies of internal and external support are used to implement problem-solving and decision-making mechanisms. Finally, a third block leads to revision of interim decisions, and translators are given a chance to improve their work.

Hönig (1988) used verbal reports by students working from German into English. He presented a model which builds on assumptions formulated by functional approaches to translation to assess the performance of translation students during the translation of several informative texts, describing a series of behavioural patterns. For Hönig, the translation process is a monitored process in which translators employ macro- and micro-strategies to broadly understand the source text and produce a target text which fits the purpose of the translation task, to the expectations of the target text readership and to other external factors.

Lörscher (1991) also used verbal reports from students working from German into English to design a model of the translation process in the form of a flow chart of translational problem-solving. He analyses verbalizations by novice translators with a focus on reconstructing the translation strategies which underlie their translation performance, assuming that such underlying strategies steer the unfolding of the translation process but are not accessible to direct inspection. Lörscher's model consists of two hierarchical levels, namely a lower level containing elements of translation strategies (i.e., discrete problem-solving steps) and a higher level that captures the manifestations of translation strategies. For Lörscher, interim versions captured during translation task execution can comprise several strategies and are intra- or inter-strategic phenomena.

Kiraly (1995) used think-aloud data from novice and professional translators between English and German to model the translation process as a communicative and social activity as well as a cognitive activity. The model is graphically displayed as dual: a social model and a cognitive model. From a communicative and social perspective, Kiraly's model looks at the social implications of the communicative act of translation and the contextual features related to the source and target texts as well as the translator. From a cognitive perspective, the model portrays the translator's mind as part of an information processing system which interacts with relatively uncontrolled and relatively controlled processes. Kiraly distinguished between a subconscious workspace and a controlled processing centre and suggested the existence of an intuitive workspace (which is relatively uncontrolled). When automatic processing does not yield provisional solutions, translation problems move into the intuitive workspace and are processed in the controlled processing centre until a strategy is selected and applied. For Kiraly, strategies alone do not solve translation problems but they do contribute in the attempt to solve them.

Alves (1995) used TAPs to assess the performance of bilinguals, professional and novice translators and translation students working from German into Portuguese. He presented a psycholinguistically oriented model of the translation process that draws on the relevance-theoretic approach to translation proposed by Gutt (1991). Alves (1995) built on Königs's (1987) model and designed a graphic display in the form of a flow chart with both top-down and bottom-up processes interacting recursively. The entry point of Alves's model was the translation unit which, for him, is dependent on the translator's focus of attention on the source text. A given translation unit is first processed automatically in the *Adhoc Block* as a default procedure; it moves into the *Rest Block* only when a solution cannot be found. As in other models at the time, yes/no questions indicate several steps in the process. In the *Rest Block*, mechanisms of external and internal support interact recursively. Alves's model also focuses on the principle of relevance (Sperber and Wilson, 1986) as a mediating factor between processing effort and cognitive effects, suggesting that additional cognitive processing is unnecessary when there is nothing to gain from the generation of new cognitive effects. Throughout the process, the principle of relevance guides translators in their problem-solving and decision-making processes. The search for interpretive resemblance is considered to be the driving force behind the translation process and its ultimate goal.

For several years after the 1990s, there were no novel attempts at modelling the translation process. When new attempts emerged in the early 2000s, the focus on graphic modelling had changed towards more robust theoretical and methodological considerations. In the following paragraphs, we will focus on three models of the translation process which try to provide some theoretical grounding for their formulation and aim at creating the necessary conditions for empirical validation. Instead of only describing the models, we will also examine their impact on future work.

Halverson (2003) investigates a possible cognitive basis for the patterns and processes that have been referred to in TS as simplification/generalization, normalization, standardization, sanitization and exaggeration of target language features. She uses cognitive grammar to suggest that these patterns mostly arise from the existence of asymmetries in the cognitive organization of semantic information. Halverson uses the term 'gravitational pull' to offer an explanation for some general features of translated language and for the fact that frequent patterns in the source language tend to lead translators to choose literal renderings in the target language.

Halverson (2017) revisits her original assumptions related to cognitive asymmetries to suggest that highly salient linguistic items are more prone to be chosen in a 'gravitational pull' model. Therefore, they end up being over-represented in translational corpus data. If put to empirical test, she argues, the 'gravitational pull' hypothesis could develop into a cognitive-linguistic model of the translation process, incorporating salience phenomena in source and target texts as well as the effects of entrenched links between translated segments.

Halverson (2019) elaborates on the concept of 'default' translation as a specific phase of translation production, characterized by rapid, relatively uninterrupted production involving primarily bilingual linguistic knowledge, including communication norms. It also comprises metalinguistic knowledge and a specific understanding of the translation task. Her modelling of 'default translation' places the concept relative to the idea of 'literal translation'. Although her work is theoretical in nature, Halverson also suggests a means of identifying the phase of 'default translation' in translation process data.

Tirkkonen-Condit's (2005) monitor model is primarily theoretical, but it is supported by empirical evidence provided by keylogged data. She draws on Ivir (1981) to elaborate on the translator's search for equivalence and endorses Toury's (1995, pp. 191–2) statement that 'only when the identical-meaning formal correspondent is either not available or not able to ensure equivalence' do translators 'resort to formal correspondents with not-quite-identical meanings or to structural and semantic shifts which destroy formal correspondence altogether'. Building on the notion of a monitor model to inquire into translators' monitoring skills and self-awareness, Tirkkonen-Condit (2005) claims that translators resort to literal translation as a sort of default translation procedure. She argues that there is a tendency to translate literally, word by word, until the translator is interrupted by a monitor that points to a problem in rendering a particular text segment. The monitor interrupts the automatic unfolding of the translation process and triggers conscious strategies of problem solving and decision making to handle the problem.

Tirkkonen-Condit's (2005) monitor model was put to an empirical test by Carl and Dragsted (2012). They proposed an extended version of the monitor model in which comprehension and production are processed in parallel by the default procedure. Carl and Dragsted (2012, p. 127) hypothesize that 'the monitor supervises text production processes, and triggers disintegration of the translation activity into chunks of sequential reading and writing behavior'. To corroborate their hypothesis, they compare copying tasks with translation tasks, assuming that copying represents a typical literal default rendering procedure. Both tasks entail decoding, retrieval and encoding of text segments. However, translation tasks require an additional transfer phase into another language. Using key-logged and eye-tracking data, Carl and Dragsted (2012) observed many similarities in the two tasks pointing to similarities in the underlying cognitive processes. The need for effortful text understanding forces both copyists and translators to deviate from automatized procedures and to engage in monitoring the processes for the sake of understanding what they are copying or translating. Both copyists and translators also engage in sequential reading and writing patterns until target text produc-tion problems trigger the monitor and lead them into monitoring activ-ities for the sake of solving problems and making decisions.

Schaeffer and Carl (2015) also revisit the monitor model to investigate automated processing during translation. The analysis of translation-process data provides evidence that translation involves strong activation of lexico-semantic and syntactical representations which share cognitive representations of both source and target language items. Schaeffer and Carl (2015) argue that activation of shared representations leads to auto-mated processing which is interrupted when a monitor is triggered. This leads to a recursive model of translation.

Altogether, Carl and Dragsted (2012) and Schaeffer and Carl (2015) man-aged to provide robust empirical evidence to consubstantiate Tirkkonen-Condit's (2005) claims and validate the monitor model empirically.

Subsequently, Carl and Schaeffer (2017a) built on Shannon and Weaver's (1949) model of communication to propose a noisy channel model of the translation process. The noisy channel model conceptualizes communication as a problem of decoding a message sent through a noisy communication channel by a receiver who receives a noisy signal encod-ing a version of the original message. It is a probabilistic model which indicates the probability of the original message and the conditional probability of the message received. Carl and Schaeffer (2017a) consider the translation processes a temporal sequence of translational events, which may be segmented into coherent chunks or behavioural units, including pauses in the process. They assume that translation processes and behavioural observations are probabilistic in nature and suggest a probabilistic framework to assess and integrate empirical findings. Similar to connectionist networks, the translation process is modelled as a network of hidden states which implement the actual translation processes.

It is interesting that the notion of monitoring has been present in all models of the translation process presented over the decades. In addition, the notions of translation units, segmentation, inferencing mechanisms, problem solving and decision making have always been included when modelling the translation process. The tools and techniques to achieve that end have changed over the years, and we describe them in more detail in Section 2.4.

## 2.4  Methodological Development of TPR

The translation process has been investigated methodologically in ways that have strongly marked the development of the field. Starting in the mid-1980s with only one technique, think-aloud protocols, TPR has seen developments arising from the combined use of keylogging, eye tracking and, more recently, biometric and neuroimaging techniques. In this section, we look at the development of each technique and comment on the main implications concerning their use.

### 2.4.1  Think Aloud

The interest in cognitive science that has developed at US universities since 1956 (Miller, 2003, p. 142) brought with it an interest in cognitive processes like learning and decision making. Flower and Hayes (1981) wrote about the act of putting organized ideas into writing as a cognitive process of translation. Ericsson and Simon (1980) went on to publish their *Protocol Analysis: Verbal Reports as Data* (1984), which offered a detailed, new methodology for gaining access to information in the 'black box' of the human mind. Their TAP method was enthusiastically received by the first generation of researchers interested in studying the translation process in addition to studying translation products. From the mid-1980s and for almost twenty years, think aloud was the preferred method in process-oriented TS. After training a translator in the think-aloud technique, the researcher would ask the translator to translate while concurrently speaking her/his mind, thereby producing the 'verbal data' the researcher would record and subsequently transcribe in a protocol. Here the data was annotated with codes and analysed as evidence of cognitive processes in the translator's mind. Among the early users of the method for studying translation were Dechert and Sandrock, Gerloff, Königs, Krings, and Lörscher, all in 1986. A wave of further studies followed, including Tirkkonen-Condit (1987, 1989), Jääskeläinen (1987, 1989), Gerloff (1987, 1988), Königs (1987), Krings (1987), Séguinot (1989, 1991) and Lörscher (1991), resulting in some of the models described above in Section 2.1. (See further Jääskeläinen (2002).)

The focus of attention of this research was process-oriented and cognitive as reflected in the titles of some of the key publications: *The Translation Process* (Séguinot, 1989), *Was beim Übersetzen passiert* (What happens in translation) (Königs, 1987), *Was in den Köpfen von Übersetzern vorgeht* (What goes on in the heads of translators) (Krings, 1986). As apparent from the various models of the translation process, including those described in Section 2.1, the translation process was generally understood as a three-phase (reading, translating, writing) problem-solving and decision-making strategic process with multiple sub-processes. With the emerging interest in computing, the presumptive processes inferred from the verbal data were often represented in flow charts with binary choice options and recursive loops.

Language is our main instrument for sharing personal thoughts and emotions, and the idea of accessing the mind through verbal utterances is fundamentally attractive. Think aloud is an effective method for collecting and categorizing verbal data and also for identifying problem triggers, but analysing the data beyond categorization is fraught with problems. In particular, problems concerning completeness, consistency, reliability and attitude have been identified. It is often difficult to determine if a translator is indeed verbalizing thoughts or is constructing a report. The degree to which the entire method of concurrent think aloud might itself distort the process under investigation (the 'reactivity' issue) has also been much debated (Bowles, 2010), but, despite much criticism, it is fair to say that TAP methodology and the studies inspired by it laid the foundation for the development of TPR.

According to think-aloud theory, only information available in verbal form in short-term memory can be verbalized. This means that translators can report only on instances of non-automatic translation requiring conscious decision making, not on unconscious or routinized processes. As it is generally assumed that translation can be quite extensively automatized (Jääskeläinen and Tirkkonen-Condit, 1991, p. 89; cf. also Ericsson and Simon, 1993 [1984], pp. 15, 90), this is a serious problem, which the keylogging program Translog, invented in 1995 (Jakobsen and Schou, 1999; Jakobsen, 2006), was an attempt to address.

### 2.4.2 Keylogging

The most characteristic activity a translator performs when translating is moving the eyes to read and moving the hand and fingers to write. These are actions which can be video recorded for study but are now mostly recorded with specialist technologies: keylogging and eye tracking. Video is used in research where it is important to have access to information about facial expressions, gestures and other body movements, as well as information about events in the situational context that might have had an impact on other recorded data.

A keylogging program records ('logs') a translator's every keystroke on a keyboard and thereby provides evidence of all the editing the target text undergoes during production and the temporal rhythm by which this happens. It shows the entire textual transformation of the source text into a target text. Such a program makes no distinction between automatic and non-automatic text production or between problematic and non-problematic production. It therefore offered a new opportunity to obtain behavioural information about a translator's typing process, regardless of what kind of processing was involved and who the translator or the researcher was. Everything the program recorded, including words typed and deleted, typos, corrections made, as well as the dynamic timing of it all was interpreted as evidence of the translator's cognitive process. Pauses, in particular, stood out as important indicators of cognitive ease or difficulty, depending on their duration (Goldman-Eisler, 1972; Schilperoord, 1996).

Keylogging changed the course of TPR in more ways than by offering a new technology for recording a translator's typing activity. It opened up the possibility of triangulating observations and findings based on quali-tative data from interviews, questionnaires and TAPs with observations and findings based on quantitative keystroke data (Alves, 2003). Altogether, TPR developed a stronger computational orientation, and with it came increased awareness of the importance of methodological and experimental rigour and greater awareness of the importance of statistical analysis.

Keylogging made it possible to compare translation tasks performed with concurrent think aloud with identical or similar tasks performed without think aloud (Jakobsen, 2003). As it appeared that concurrent think aloud affected the translation process negatively by forcing transla-tors to work in smaller segments, the preferred methodology for combin-ing qualitative and quantitative data elicitation now became to collect qualitative data from post-translation-task sessions where the translator observed a replay of her/his typing process while saying what s/he recol-lected thinking about at the time ('cued retrospection'). Cued retrospec-tion avoided some of the issues with think aloud, and yielded very rich data that often helped in interpreting the keystroke behaviour, but pro-blems remained. Translation students were often very vociferous about what thinking had guided their production, while expert translators either had poor recollection or were less willing to speak their thoughts. Obviously, there was no straightforward relationship between processes in the mind and what was verbalized.

The production rhythm of bursts alternating with pauses of a second or more (for discussions of segment boundary criteria, see Alves and Vale, 2009; Dragsted, 2004; O'Brien, 2006) was visually obvious from the dynamic replay of the keystrokes, indicating the size of production units, which in turn indicated what segments of source text words and associated units of meaning had previously been processed to enable a burst. Pauses of diminishing duration could be seen to occur at sentence, clause, phrase and word boundaries, indicating overall correlation between grammatical and cognitive syntax. Systematic pause distribution was also found at morpheme and syllable levels and even between keystrokes (Immonen, 2006; Immonen and Mäkisalo, 2010). This overall, predictable rhythm was observed to be often randomly broken by very long pauses triggered by local comprehension, meaning construction or formulation problems requiring extra cognitive effort or external help. The so-called linear representation of keystrokes showed a clear distinction between typing/pausing behaviour during the three main phases of the translation process, thus supporting this construal.

Keystroke-based studies also investigated differences caused by different external conditions: different levels of time constraint (Jensen, 2000), availability or not of external resources (Livbjerg and Mees, 1999, 2003) and effects on segmentation of different types of source text (Dragsted, 2005). There were also studies of differences caused by directionality (Lorenzo, 1999; Pavlović, 2007; Pokorn, 2005) and of revision behaviour (Breedveld, 2002). Although most studies of keystrokes were targeted at exploring the topics just mentioned, often without explicit theoretical grounding, attempts were also made to situate TPR in the context of relevance theory (Alves, 2007; Alves and Gonçalves, 2003, 2015).

Keylogging has one serious drawback in that it records only activity coming at the end of the translation process when the source-text reading and probably most of the thinking about how to render the construed meaning in the target language have been done. As is clear from frequent 'online' revisions in the drafting phase, a lot of thinking still takes place as the translation is being typed and also after, but earlier processing is at best only very indirectly reflected in a keylog. A log file shows that the typing process is not nicely sequential from reading and comprehension via translation to representation in the target text. The overall direction of the process is linear from beginning to end, but along the way many wrong garden paths are often taken and better solutions are suddenly thought of, indicating both that the process is far from straightforwardly linear and that meaning processing does not stop once a translation has been typed. Depending on the translator's typing skill, more or less 'technical effort' (Krings, 2001) may be required, but technical effort, measured as time delay, is generally slight in comparison with the delay caused by the efforts required to 'interpret' the source text and to find a good way of representing the interpreted meaning in the target language.

Thus, with keystroke data alone, much can be known, for example about overall phases of translation, units of segmentation, distribution of pauses in the typing process, occurrences of problem triggers, and revision behaviour, but knowing in specific instances if a typing pause was occasioned by a source text comprehension problem, a formulation problem, a planning activity or by evaluation of an earlier portion of translation is not really possible. By adding eye tracking to keylogging, a much stronger basis for hypothesizing about such things could be obtained.

### 2.4.3 Eye Tracking

An eye tracker provides detailed evidence of what words, in a text displayed on a computer monitor, a translator looks at, and for how long, while producing the translation. Unlike the translator's fingers, the eyes rarely pause. They mostly provide uninterrupted data about gaze activity all through the production process. Eye-movement data therefore importantly complement keylogging data in which there are frequent pauses showing no activity (no data).

The amount of visual attention given to the source text and the emerging target text varies considerably. Most translators spend more time looking at their translation than at the source text (Hvelplund, 2011). This is particularly noticeable in translators who visually track the result of their typing on-screen as they type or immediately after. The behavioural gaze pattern that appears again supports the division of the process into three phases: (1) initial orientation, (2) reading of the source text and production of the translation and (3) final checking and revision. The combination of gaze and keystroke data further sharpens the definition of the (mostly phrase-level) units from which a translator works.

Most reading research has targeted adult reading of text in the reader's first language. Rayner and Pollatsek (1989) and others have described how such reading progresses in an overall linear succession of fixations and saccades (short movements of the eyes between fixations), but with frequent regressions when meaning construction fails or attention lapses. However, reading differs according to its purpose. This was pointed out by Buswell (1935) and documented experimentally by Yarbus (1967). Jakobsen and Jensen (2008) illustrated how fixation count and average duration differed depending on whether readers expected to be asked to translate a text or not. The different gaze behaviour indicated that if readers expected to be asked to translate the text they were reading, they engaged in mental acts of pre-translation in addition to reading for comprehension.

What mainly distinguishes translational reading from other kinds of reading is that when translating, most translators are reading two texts in parallel, with visual and cognitive attention constantly shifting between them. This slows down the process considerably, for, with every shift, time is spent retrieving the earlier reading point. Translators who dictate their translation or translators who touch-type do not need to attend visually to their emerging text or to the keyboard, so they can devote unbroken visual attention to the source text, but even they read it differently. Experiments with sight translation show considerably increased visual attention to the source text compared to reading for comprehension. This is probably caused by the need to co-ordinate fast eye movements with relatively slow vocal production (or typing). In a post-editing situation, the strain on a translator's cognitive capacity may be increased, and the process slowed down, by the need to refer to three texts: the source text, the machine-translated version of it and the translator's own.

Various technical measures of the distance in time between the moment when the eyes look at a word and when the matching word is typed are in use, on the model of the ear-voice span (EVS) in simultaneous interpreting. The eye-key span (EKS) (Dragsted, 2010) is measured from the time of the first fixation on a word (from the beginning or the end of the fixation) to the time of the typing of the first (or last) letter of the matching word. As with *décalage* in simultaneous interpreting (the time lapse between the start of a stretch of speech and the beginning of its interpretation), this EKS measure is an indicator of the amount of meaning handled by a translator in a single chunk. If a word is fixated several times, as is frequently the case in written translation, EKS can also be measured from the moment of the last fixation on a word before the matching word is typed. This measure indicates how close to production the translator needs information in memory to be refreshed and how closely meaning construal, reformulation and production are connected.

Just and Carpenter's (1980) eye-mind and immediacy assumptions still have general validity. The eye-mind assumption is that there is a general correlation between what the eyes are looking at and what is being processed by the mind. The relationship between what is looked at and what is processed is not as direct as Just and Carpenter assumed: sometimes the eyes run ahead of the mind, sometimes the mind anticipates meaning before the eyes have seen its verbal representation, and sometimes our eyes wander across a whole page without our mind attending, but in general a translator will attend to what the eyes are looking at. Similarly, we can also generally assume that the longer a translator looks at a word (phrase, clause), the more cognitively difficult it is either to construe optimal meaning or to reformulate it.

The combination of gaze and keystroke data provides a detailed image of how a translator co-ordinates comprehension, translation and text production in a process somewhat reminiscent of purling and knitting. In the first move to make a stitch, the eyes look at a segment of new text to which the mind begins to attribute meaning (with 'no appreciable lag') and to work on reformulating it. Once that has been done, attention shifts to producing a representation of the reformulated meaning. As the eyes are not engaged in supplying new text-to-be-translated at this point, they can be employed to visually oversee that production is executed as planned. Before production is completed and in order to enable fluent production by ensuring constant, in-time availability of new text to the processing mind, the eyes are already on their way to reading the next source text segment, and a new stitch in the knitting process has begun to be made.

Referring to the combination of keystroke and gaze data in time as 'user activity data' (UAD) and building the Center for Research and Innovation in Translation and Translation Technology (CRITT) TPR database (CRITT, n. d.), Carl (2012) developed methods of building computational models of translation processing. Progression graphs created from alignment of translators' fixation points and keystrokes with source text words (Carl, 2009) illustrated different translator profiles graphically and showed that some translators spend considerable time getting to know the source text before embarking on translating it. Others start translating after a very quick orientation. Progression graphs also made it possible to identify translators' characteristic processing style. Some translators are locally oriented short-term planners; others are globally oriented long-term planners (Dragsted and Carl, 2013). Computation of UAD was also the technique used to develop the monitor and noisy channel models of translation mentioned in Section 2.1.

### 2.4.4 Biometric and Neuroimaging Techniques

While translating, translators also breathe, their hearts beat, and all kinds of metabolic and hormonal processes are active. Such body processes are *sine qua non* for a translator to be able to translate, but they do not specifically contribute to translation. Nevertheless, many such processes are measurably affected by the translation situation. Changing levels of breathing, blood pressure, heart rate and electrodermal activity, for example, may therefore constitute evidence of such emotional-cognitive phenomena as uncertainty, nervousness and mental strain. Biometrical evidence of this kind may in turn be used to support assumptions about cognitive issues like meaning construal problems or difficulties with cross-linguistic meaning representation.

Neuroimaging methods (fNIRS (functional near-infrared spectroscopy), fMRI, PET) for studying what areas in a translator's brain are particularly active during translation provide further evidence for inferences about the highly complex cognitive processes underlying translation. Brain imaging methods are often used in combination with EEG (electroencephalography) because measures from EEG complement neuroimaging data well. The strength of neuroimaging methods lies in their excellent spatial resolution. They identify active areas very accurately, but since they work from relatively slow (metabolic) processes in the body, they are less accurate with respect to temporal resolution. EEG, by contrast, has very accurate temporal resolution, but as data are measured on the outside of the scalp, it is difficult to know very precisely what area of the brain the activity measured comes from. From the point of view of studying cognitive translation processes, these methods, excellently described in García (2019), open up fascinating new prospects for TPR.

## 2.5 Concluding Remarks

Hurtado Albir (2001/2011, p. 375) defines translating as a complex cognitive activity 'which has an interactive and non-linear nature, encompassing controlled and uncontrolled processes, and requiring problem solving, decision making and the use of translation strategies and tactics' (see Alves and Hurtado Albir, 2010, p. 28). Most of the models of the translation process we described in the previous sections and most of the empirical results obtained in TPR support that definition. Alves and Hurtado Albir (2017, pp. 538–9) have summarized the main traits of the translation process, highlighting the importance of basic processes of comprehension and re-expression, the role of documentation sources in supporting problem-solving and decision-making and the dynamic nature of the translation process. Carl and Schaeffer (2017b) have also looked at models of the translation process. They stress the need to formalize, operationalize and test many relevant aspects that have been identified in TPR because (Carl and Schaeffer, 2017b, p. 66), 'once predictions can be made and validated or rejected, existing models can be modified and/or extended'. We agree with Carl and Schaeffer (2017b) and with Alves and Hurtado Albir (2017) in their plea for more robust studies in order to strengthen future empirical research on models and traits of the translation process.

Finally, in our discussion, we have deliberately excluded topics such as translation competence and translation competence acquisition. Although they have also been modelled empirically, we believe that they fall outside the scope of the present context. We have also refrained from discussing models of the translation process that place a strong focus on embodied, embedded, enacted, extended and affective (4EA) factors (see Muñoz Martín, 2010, for a discussion of the interface between cognitive translatology and 4EA cognition). There is still much research to be done and many questions still need to be answered.

## References

Alves, F. (1995). *Zwischen Schweigen und Sprechen: Wie bildet sich eine transkulturelle Brücke? Eine psycholinguistisch orientierte Untersuchung von Übersetzungsvorgängen zwischen portugiesischen und brasilianischen Übersetzern.* Hamburg: Dr. Kovac.

Alves, F., ed. (2003). *Triangulating Translation: Perspectives in Process Oriented Research.* Amsterdam: John Benjamins.

Alves, F. (2007). Cognitive effort and contextual effect in translation: A relevance theoretic approach. *Journal of Translation Studies*, **10**(1), 18–35.

Alves, F., and Gonçalves, J. L. (2003). A relevance theory approach to the investigation of inferential processes in translation. In F. Alves, ed.,

*Triangulating Translation: Perspectives in Process Oriented Research.* Amsterdam: John Benjamins, pp. 3–24.

Alves, F., and Gonçalves, J. L. (2015). Investigating the conceptual-procedural distinction in the translation process: A relevance-theoretic analysis of micro and macro translation units. In M. Ehrensberger-Dow, S. Göpferich and S. O'Brien, eds., *Interdisciplinarity in Translation and Interpreting Process Research.* Amsterdam: John Benjamins, pp. 109–26.

Alves, F., and Hurtado Albir, A. (2010). Cognitive approaches. In Y. Gambier and L. van Doorslaer, eds., *The Handbook of Translation Studies*, Vol. 1. Amsterdam: John Benjamins, pp. 28–35.

Alves, F., and Hurtado Albir, A. (2017). Evolution, challenges and perspectives for research on cognitive aspects of translation. In J. W. Schwieter and A. Ferreira, eds., *The Handbook of Translation and Cognition.* Hoboken, NJ: Wiley-Blackwell, pp. 537–54.

Alves, F., and Vale, D. C. (2009). Probing the unit of translation in time: Aspects of the design and development of a web application for storing, annotating, and querying translation process data. *Across Languages and Cultures*, **10**(2), 251–73.

Bowles, M. (2010). *The Think-Aloud Controversy in Second-Language Research.* London: Routledge.

Breedveld, H. (2002). Writing and revising processes in professional translation. *Across Languages and Cultures*, **3**(1), 91–100.

Buswell, G. (1935). *How People Look at Pictures: A Study of the Psychology of Perception in Art.* Chicago, IL: University of Chicago Press.

Carl, M. (2009). Triangulating product and process data: Quantifying alignment units with keystroke data. In I. M. Mees, F. Alves and S. Göpferich, eds., *Methodology, Technology and Innovation in Translation Process Research.* Copenhagen: Samfundslitteratur, pp. 225–47.

Carl, M. (2012). Translog-II: A program for recording user activity data for empirical translation process research. Paper presented at the 8th International Conference on Language Resources and Evaluation. Istanbul, Turkey.

Carl, M., and Dragsted, B. (2012). Inside the monitor model: Processes of default and challenged translation production. *Translation: Corpora, Computation, Cognition*, **2**(1), 127–45.

Carl, M., and Schaeffer, M. (2017a). Sketch of a noisy channel model for the translation process. In S. Hansen-Schirra, O. Czulo and S. Hofmann, eds., *Empirical Modelling of Translation and Interpreting.* Berlin: Language Science Press, pp. 71–116.

Carl, M., and Schaeffer, M. (2017b). Models of the translation process. In J. W. Schwieter and A. Ferreira, eds., *The Handbook of Translation and Cognition.* Hoboken, NJ: Wiley-Blackwell, pp. 50–70.

Chesterman, A. (2013). Models of what processes? *Translation and Interpreting Studies*, **8**(2), 155–68. Reprinted in M. Ehrensberger-Dow,

B. Englund Dimitrova, S. Hubscher-Davidson and U. Norberg, eds., *Describing Cognitive Processes in Translation: Acts and Events*. Amsterdam: John Benjamins, pp. 7–20.

CRITT (n.d.) TPR database: https://sites.google.com/site/centretranslationin novation/tpr-db.

Dechert, H.-W., and Sandrock, U. (1986). Thinking-aloud protocols: The decomposition of language processing. In V. Cook, ed., *Experimental Approaches to Second Language Learning*. Oxford: Pergamon, pp. 111–26.

Dragsted, B. (2004). *Segmentation in Translation and Translation Memory Systems: An Empirical Investigation of Cognitive Segmentation and Effects of Integrating a TM System into the Translation Process*. Copenhagen: Samfundslitteratur.

Dragsted, B. (2005). Segmentation in translation: Differences across levels of expertise and difficulty. *Target*, **17**(1), 49–70.

Dragsted, B. (2010). Coordination of reading and writing processes in translation: An eye on uncharted territory. In G. Shreve and E. Angelone, eds., *Translation and Cognition*. Amsterdam: John Benjamins, pp. 41–62.

Dragsted, B., and Carl, M. (2013). Towards a classification of translation styles based on eye-tracking and key-logging data. *Journal of Writing Research*, **5**(1), 133–58.

Ericsson, K., and Simon, H. (1980). Verbal reports as data. *Psychological Review*, **87**, 215–51.

Ericsson, K., and Simon, H. (1993 [1984]). *Protocol Analysis: Verbal Reports as Data*. Cambridge, MA: MIT Press.

Flower, L., and Hayes, J. R. (1981). A cognitive process theory of writing. *College Composition and Communication*, **32**(4), 365–87.

García, A. M. (2019). *The Neurocognition of Translation and Interpreting*. Amsterdam: John Benjamins.

Gerloff, P. A. (1986). Second language learners' reports on the interpretive process: Talk-aloud protocols of translation. In J. House and S. Blum-Kulka, eds., *Interlingual and Intercultural Communication, Discourse and Cognition in Translation and Second Language Acquisition Studies*. Tübingen: Gunter Narr, pp. 243–62.

Gerloff, P. A. (1987). Identifying the unit of analysis in translation: Some uses of think-aloud protocol data. In C. Færch and G. Kasper, eds., *Introspection in Second Language Research*. Clevedon, UK: Multilingual Matters, pp. 135–58.

Gerloff, P. A. (1988). From French to English: A look at the translation process in students, bilinguals and professional translators. Unpublished DEd thesis, Harvard University.

Goldman-Eisler, F. (1972). Pauses, clauses, sentences. *Language and Speech*, **15**, 103–13.

Gutt, E.-A. (1991). *Translation and Relevance: Cognition and Context*. Oxford: Blackwell. (2nd ed. published by Routledge, 2000.)

Halverson, S. (2003). The cognitive basis of translation universals. *Target*, **15**(2), 197–241.

Halverson, S. (2017). Gravitational pull in translation: Testing a revised model. In G. de Sutter, M.-A. Lefer and I. Delaere, eds., *Empirical Translation Studies: New Methodological and Theoretical Traditions*. Berlin: De Gruyter, pp. 9–46.

Halverson, S. (2019). 'Default' translation: A construct for cognitive translation and interpreting studies. *Translation, Cognition & Behavior*, **2**(2), 187–210.

Holmes, J. S. (1972). The name and nature of translation studies. In J. Holmes, ed., *Translated! Papers on Literary Translation and Translation Studies*. Amsterdam: Rodopi, pp. 67–80. Reprinted in L. Venuti, ed. (2000). *The Translation Studies Reader*. London: Routledge, pp. 172–85.

Hönig, H. G. (1988). Wissen Übersetzer eigentlich, was sie tun? *Lebende Sprachen*, **33**(1), 10–14.

Hurtado Albir, A. (2001/2011). *Traducción y Traductología. Introducción a la Traductología*. Madrid: Cátedra.

Hvelplund, K. T. (2011). Allocation of cognitive resources in translation: An eye-tracking and key-logging study. Unpublished PhD dissertation, Copenhagen Business School.

Immonen, S. (2006). Pauses in translation versus monolingual text production. *Target*, **18**(2), 313–36.

Immonen, S., and Mäkisalo, J. (2010). Pauses reflecting the processing of syntactic units in monolingual text production and translation. *Hermes – Journal of Language and Communication Studies*, **44**, 45–61.

Ivir, V. (1981). Formal correspondence vs. translation equivalence revisited. *Poetics Today*, **2**(4), 1–7.

Jääskeläinen, R. (1987). *What Happens in a Translation Process: Think-Aloud Protocols of Translation*. A pro gradu thesis. University of Joensuu, Savonlinna School of Translation Studies.

Jääskeläinen, R. (1989). Translation assignment in professional vs. non-professional translation. In C. Séguinot, ed., *The Translation Process*. Toronto: H. G. Publications, York University, pp. 87–98.

Jääskeläinen, R. (1990). *Features of Successful Translation Processes: A Think-Aloud Protocol Study*. Joensuu: University of Joensuu.

Jääskeläinen, R. (2002). Think-aloud protocol studies into translation: An annotated bibliography. *Target*, **14**(1), 107–36.

Jääskeläinen, R., and Tirkkonen-Condit, S. (1991). Automatised processes in professional vs. non-professional translation: A think-aloud protocol study. In S. Tirkkonen-Condit, ed., *Empirical Research in Translation and Intercultural Studies*. Tübingen: Narr, pp. 89–109.

Jakobsen, A. L. (2003). Effects of think aloud on translation speed, revision, and segmentation. In F. Alves, ed., *Triangulating Translation: Perspectives in Process Oriented Research*. Amsterdam: John Benjamins, pp. 69–95.

Jakobsen, A. L. (2006). Research methods in translation – Translog. In K. P. H. Sullivan and E. Lindgren, eds., *Keystroke Logging and Writing: Methods and Applications*. Oxford: Elsevier, pp. 95–105.

Jakobsen, A. L., and Jensen, K. T. H. (2008). Eye movement behaviour across four different types of reading task. In S. Göpferich, A. L. Jakobsen and I. M. Mees, eds., *Looking at Eyes: Eye-Tracking Studies of Reading and Translation Processing*. Copenhagen: Samfundslitteratur, pp. 103–24.

Jakobsen, A. L., and Schou, L. (1999). Translog documentation. In G. Hansen, ed., *Probing the Process in Translation*. Copenhagen: Samfundslitteratur, pp. 151–86.

Jensen, A. (2000). *The Effect of Time on Cognitive Processes and Strategies in Translation*. PhD thesis. Copenhagen: Copenhagen Business School.

Just, M. A., and Carpenter, P. A. (1980). A theory of reading: From eye fixations to comprehension. *Psychological Review*, **87**, 329–54.

Kiraly, D. (1995). *Pathways to Translation: Pedagogy and Process*. Kent, OH: Kent State University Press.

Königs, F. G. (1987). Was beim Übersetzen passiert. Theoretische Aspekte, empirische Befunde und praktische Konsequenzen. *Die neueren Sprachen*, **86**(2), 162–85.

Krings, H. P. (1986). *Was in den Köpfen von Übersetzern vorgeht: eine Untersuchung zur Struktur des Übersetzungsprozesses an fortgeschrittenen Französischlernern*. Tübingen: Gunter Narr.

Krings, H. P. (1987). The use of introspective data in translation. In C. Færch and G. Kasper, eds., *Introspection in Second Language Research*. Clevedon, UK: Multilingual Matters, pp. 158–76.

Krings, H. P. (2001). *Repairing Texts: Empirical Investigations of Machine Translation Post-Editing Processes*. Kent, OH: Kent State University Press.

Livbjerg, I., and Mees, I. M. (1999). A study of the use of dictionaries in Danish-English translation. In G. Hansen, ed., *Probing the Process in Translation*. Copenhagen: Samfundslitteratur, pp. 135–49.

Livbjerg, I., and Mees, I. M. (2003). Patterns of dictionary use in non-domain-specific translation. In F. Alves, ed., *Triangulating Translation: Perspectives in Process Oriented Research*. Amsterdam: John Benjamins, pp. 123–36.

Lorenzo, M. P. (1999). La seguridad del traductor profesional en la traducción a una lengua extranjera. In G. Hansen, ed. *Probing the Process in Translation*. Copenhagen: Samfundslitteratur, pp. 121–35.

Lörscher, W. (1986). Linguistic aspects of translation processes: Towards an analysis of translation performance. In J. House and S. Blum-Kulka, eds., *Interlingual and Intercultural Communication, Discourse and Cognition in Translation and Second Language Acquisition Studies*. Tübingen: Gunter Narr, pp. 277–92.

Lörscher, W. (1991). *Translation Performance, Translation Process, and Translation Strategies: A Psycholinguistic Investigation*. Tübingen: Narr.

Miller, G. (2003). The cognitive revolution: A historical perspective. *TRENDS in Cognitive Sciences*, **7**(3), 141–4.

Muñoz Martín, R. (2010). Leave no stone unturned: On the development of cognitive translatology. *Translation and Interpreting Studies*, **5**(2), 145–62.

O'Brien, S. (2006). Pauses as indicators of cognitive effort in post-editing machine translation output. *Across Languages and Cultures*, **7** (1), 1–21.

Pavlović, N. (2007). Directionality in translation and interpreting practice: Report on a questionnaire survey in Croatia. *Forum*, **5**(2), 77–99.

Pokorn, N. (2005). *Challenging the Traditional Axioms: Translation into a Non-mother Tongue*. Amsterdam: John Benjamins.

Rayner, K., and Pollatsek, A. (1989). *The Psychology of Reading*. Englewood Cliffs, NJ: Prentice Hall.

Reiß, K., and Vermeer, H. (1984). *Grundlegung einer allgemeinen Translationstheorie*. Tübingen: M. Niemeyer.

Schaeffer, M., and Carl, M. (2015). Shared representations and the translation process: A recursive model. In M. Ehrensberger-Dow, B. Englund Dimitrova, S. Hubscher-Davidson and U. Norberg, eds., *Describing Cognitive Processes in Translation: Acts and Events*. Amsterdam: John Benjamins, pp. 21–42.

Schilperoord, J. (1996). *It's about Time: Temporal Aspects of Cognitive Processes in Text Production*. Amsterdam: Rodopi.

Séguinot, C. (1989). The translation process: An experimental study. In C. Séguinot, ed., *The Translation Process*. York University, School of Translation: H. G. Publications, pp. 21–53.

Séguinot, C. (1991). A study of student translation strategies. In S. Tirkkonen-Condit, ed., *Empirical Research in Translation and Intercultural Studies*. Tübingen: Gunter Narr, pp. 79–88.

Seleskovitch, D. (1968). *L'interprète dans les conférences internationales. Problèmes de langage et de communication*. Paris: Minard.

Seleskovitch, D., and Lederer, M. (1984). *Interpréter pour traduire*. Paris: Didier Érudition.

Shannon, C., and Weaver, W. (1949). *The Mathematical Theory of Communication*. Urbana: University of Illinois Press.

Sperber, D., and Wilson, D. (1986) *Relevance: Communication and Cognition*. Oxford: Blackwell.

Tirkkonen-Condit, S. (1987). Think-aloud protocols in the study of the translation process. In H. Nyyssönen, R. Kataja and V. Komulainen, eds., *CDEF 86. Papers from the Conference of Departments of English in Finland*. Publications of the Department of English 7. Oulu: University of Oulu, pp. 39–49.

Tirkkonen-Condit, S. (1989). Professional vs non-professional translation: A think-aloud protocol study. In C. Séguinot, ed., *The Translation Process*. Toronto: H. G. Publications, York University, pp. 73–85.

Tirkkonen-Condit, S., ed. (1991). *Empirical Research in Translation and Intercultural Studies*. Tübingen: G. Narr.

Tirkkonen-Condit, S. (2005). The monitor model revisited: Evidence from process research. *Meta*, **50**(2), 405–14.

Toury, G. (2012). *Descriptive Translation Studies—and Beyond. Revised Edition*. Amsterdam: John Benjamins.

Yarbus, A. L. (1967). *Eye Movements and Vision*. New York: Plenum Press.

# 3

# Translation and Technology

Akiko Sakamoto

## 3.1  Introduction

This chapter describes major advances in translation technologies (translation memory (TM) and machine translation (MT)) and explains how they have influenced our understanding of translation, particularly the concept of translation quality. The discussion focuses on the notion of translation as 'text', showing that technological changes have created a rift between translation studies theories and a new notion of translation circulating in the industry. The chapter finally identifies trends in research which seek to develop new knowledge to address the aforementioned rift.

## 3.2  Technologies in Translation Practice

A wide range of electronic tools and systems are available to support the production of translation (Austermühl, 2014, pp. 18–67). ISO 17100, published by the International Organization for Standardization (British Standards Institution, 2018, p. 17), defines 'translation technology' as 'a set of tools used by human translators, revisers, reviewers, and others to facilitate their work' and lists the following as examples: a) content management systems (CMSs); b) authoring systems; c) desktop publishing; d) word-processing software; e) translation management systems (TMSs); f) TM tools and computer-aided translation (CAT); g) quality assurance tools; h) revision tools; i) localization tools; j) MT; k) terminology management systems; l) project management software; and m) speech-to-text recognition software. Drugan (2013, ch. 3) provides a comprehensive summary of the nature of most of these technologies, although, inevitably, some parts (particularly those focusing on MT) need updating owing to the innovative nature of the tools (see Sections 3.2.1–3.2.3).

This chapter focuses on two technologies used extensively in the standard translation production processes: TM tools and MT.

### 3.2.1  Translation Memory (TM)

TM and MT are often confused, partly because the acronyms are similar and also because they have been increasingly used together in a CAT tool (see Section 3.2.3). They were, however, originally conceived and developed as distinct technologies with unique histories and philosophies behind them.

TM is a key component of a CAT tool. Simply put, TM is a collection of data in the form of a computer file, which contains sets of source language sentences and their translations in a target language. Those sets are called 'segments'. A segment consists of a pair composed of a source text (ST) sentence and its translation. When translating a new text in a CAT tool with one or more TMs uploaded, the software compares the sentences in the new ST with the ST sentences stored in the TM. It detects sentences that are identical or similar in the two, and shows on the screen the translations of the sentences stored in the TM as 'translation suggestions'. The similarity of the ST sentences is measured by the 'match rate'. A '100 per cent match' means that the two ST sentences (one in the TM and the other in the new text) are identical. Any match rates smaller than 100 per cent are called 'fuzzy matches'. The principle of TM technology is that the more sentences of higher matches the TM contains as against the new text for translation, the better the translation suggestions that will be provided, which facilitates faster translation as the number of corrections the translator has to make is smaller. As a TM *helps* translators to translate (but *does not produce the translation* for translators), translation produced with a TM (and often with other functions in the CAT tools such as a terminology tool) is defined as 'machine-assisted human translation' ('MAHT'). For detailed accounts of TM functions and development, see Bowker (2002) and Bowker and Fisher (2010).

### 3.2.2  Machine Translation (MT)

MT, in contrast, uses a computer system which produces automated translations from one natural language to another. In the mid-twentieth century, MT was originally conceived with the aim of producing translations without any human involvement, known as 'fully automatic high-quality translation' ('FAHQT'), but the developers soon realized that this aim was unachievable. The current practice of MT use is thus defined as 'human-assisted machine translation' ('HAMT'), as some assistance by humans is necessary to achieve high-quality translation.

The methods used in MT systems have changed over time. Broadly speaking, there are two approaches: rule-based and data-driven.

Rule-based machine translation (RBMT) is a system built by programming the grammatical and lexical rules of both languages. Because of limitations in the quality of the target language output of rule-based systems, since the 1990s, MT development has gradually moved towards data-driven approaches. Data-driven MT systems are built by letting the system learn patterns of translations from a large number of parallel corpora consisting of ST sentences and translations of them made by humans. The system produces translations by calculating the statistically most probable translation. The two main methods used are statistical machine translation (SMT) and the more recently developed neural machine translation (NMT). Most major MT systems (including free online ones like Google Translate and Microsoft Translator) now use NMT. SMT and NMT both use data-driven approaches, but NMT uses artificial neural networks as an analysis method and is said to be capable of producing more fluent translations, although it has its own limitations such as a tendency to produce semantically inaccurate passages or non-words.

In this chapter, MT refers to data-driven MT systems because these are the mainstream systems. For detailed accounts of the history of different MT systems, see Kenny (2018). For the basic working principles of NMT, see Forcada (2017).

### 3.2.3   How TMs and MTs Are Used in Practice

Since the mid-1990s, many CAT-tool products have become more affordable for translators, and practising translators are often expected to use TMs in the CAT-tool environment to speed up translation processes. The effectiveness of TM use for translation productivity is affected by several factors, such as the number of suggestions that the TM can offer and their match rates. The effectiveness is also influenced by the nature of the ST: translations of texts that follow a standard format (such as users' manuals, legal texts and IT documents) are more likely to achieve high productivity with TM. TM is also effective when only some parts of the ST need translating (such as an updated version of a user's manual) as the CAT tool can pick up the sentences which need updated translations while it reuses previous translations for 100 per cent matches (source text sentences which have not been changed from the previous version).

Owing to their typically imperfect quality, MT outputs often undergo a process called 'machine translation post-editing' ('MTPE'), in which human operators (often called 'post-editors' or 'linguists') correct mistakes in the MT outputs. Owing to the low quality of MT in the early development period, MTPE was limited to producing gist translations for corporations' internal uses (Garcia, 2011, p. 218). However, since the quality of data-driven MT systems' output has improved, MTPE has become widely used in the commercial translation market. For a description of a typical MTPE process in the industry, see Zaretskaya (2017).

Although TM and MT were originally conceived and developed for different purposes, as explained in Sections 3.2.1 and 3.2.2, the boundary between the two technologies has become blurred because of a function called 'MT assisted TM' (Garcia, 2010), which many CAT tools incorporate. This function offers MT outputs as translation suggestions when TMs cannot offer good enough suggestions. For example, a user can calibrate the CAT tool so that if matches of higher than 70 per cent are not offered by the TMs, the tool will retrieve MT outputs from a specified online MT system via a plugin, a piece of software code which allows the CAT tool to access and use an external MT system. When using this function, the translator's translation process is assisted by TMs and MTs at the same time. The use of two kinds of leverage (TM matches and MT outputs) is believed to improve translation efficiency.

## 3.3 The Influence of Technologies on the Understanding of Translation Quality

### 3.3.1 The Sentential Approach to Translation

TM and MT share as a fundamental working principle the use of the sentence as the unit of translation.

A TM holds its data in the form of a parallel corpus, in which each segment consists of a sentence from the ST and its translation in the target language. 'A sentence' here means a string of words which ends with a full stop. A segment can consist of other text units such as a phrase or even a word (e.g., in a chapter heading in a text), but, for ease of argument, we use the word 'sentence' here.

A CAT tool retrieves translation suggestions from TMs for each sentence. A CAT tool's interface is designed so that the translator translates sentence by sentence: the translator evaluates the suggestions for a current sentence (the sentence in which the cursor is placed and is highlighted on the screen), chooses the suggestion that he or she considers the most useful, and amends the sentence as necessary. If the TMs do not offer any usable suggestion, the translator rejects the suggestions and translates the sentence from scratch. Once the translator 'confirms' (accepts) the translation, the CAT tool highlights the next segment, showing suggestions. This procedure limits the translator's cognitive processing of the text to the sentence level, making cross-sentential operation difficult.

With MT, too, the unit of translation is a sentence. The MT algorithm recognizes one source language (SL) sentence as a unit of translation and produces a translation of that sentence. Text production is thus achieved by accruing translated sentences in a linear mode.

Assessment of the quality of MT outputs is also carried out at a sentence level. There are two types of MT assessment: automatic and human. In automatic assessment, the quality of MT outputs is typically measured using human translation as a benchmark. The implicit assumption in automatic assessment is that quality can be assessed by the similarity to the human reference translation at the word or sentence level. The closer the MT output is to the reference translation in terms of the number of identical words included in the sentence, the higher the score it achieves. In human assessment, human assessors assess each sentence of MT output by using their judgement of quality with regard to different criteria (such as accuracy and fluency). This assessment is also carried out at the sentence level, that is, without a context. For a summary of these assessment methods, see Doherty (2017).

In the context of MTPE, efficiency is related to the amount of effort spent to correct errors in raw MT outputs, so knowing the number and types of errors in MT outputs is important. A body of MT research has identified a number of different error classifications and techniques of error analysis (Popović, 2018), again carried out at a sentence level (or at the level of a segment within a sentence).

### 3.3.2 Catford – the Sentence-Bound Linguistic Approach to Translation

This sentence-focused principle of translation assessment reminds us of Catford's early linguistic approach to translation (1965). According to Catford (1965, p. 1), because translation is 'an operation performed on languages', a theory of translation needs to draw on a linguistic theory, and Catford selects the General Linguistic Theory presented by Halliday (1961). The highest rank of this grammar is (as in most grammars) the sentence, and Catford considers that it is at this grammatical level that translation equivalence can most often be established: 'SL [source language] and TL [target language] texts or items are translation equivalents when they are *interchangeable in a given situation*. This is why translation equivalence can nearly always be established at sentence-rank—the sentence is the grammatical unit most directly related to speech-function within a situation' (Catford, 1965, p. 49, italics in original). That said, his model allowed for shifts, 'departures from formal correspondence' between levels and between categories (Catford, 1965, p. 73). For example, a sentence can be translated into a phrase or a word, and vice versa, which constitutes a level shift. A category shift occurs when structures, classes and units do not correspond formally between an ST and a TT. For example, a clause structure shift takes place when the English clause 'John loves Mary', which has the structure Subject – Predicator – Complement, is translated into Gaelic as 'Tha gradh aig Iain air Mairi', which has the structure Predicator – Subject – Complement – Adjunct (Catford, 1965, pp. 76–7).

### 3.3.3  The Textual Approach to Translation

The notion of translation equivalence at the sentence level and the observation of its manifestation in the target text has limitations. For example, it does not explain what the translator really does when translating (Fawcett, 1997, p. 56). Since the late twentieth century, translation studies scholars have drawn on other branches of linguistics which had developed by then to explain the real-world experiences of producers, readers and translators of texts. These include, among others, text linguistics. 'Text' is understood in different ways by different schools of linguistics, often being interchangeably used with 'discourse'. The concepts were famously imported into translation by Hatim and Mason (1990) from De Beaugrande and Dressler (1981).

De Beaugrande and Dressler (1981, p. 3) maintain that a text is a communicative occurrence which meets seven standards of textuality: cohesion, coherence, intentionality, acceptability, informativity, situationality and intertextuality. These seven standards are all necessary to make the text 'communicative', but the standards that are particularly relevant in the current discussion are cohesion and coherence. Cohesion in text is produced by certain linguistic devices, which are language specific. For instance, English has five such devices: reference, substitution, ellipsis, conjunction and lexical cohesion (Halliday and Hasan, 1976). These devices link different parts of text together, which enables the reader to recognize one part of a text as connected to another part of the text. However, textuality involves another important concept, coherence, because a text must hang together 'both linguistically and conceptually' (Hatim and Mason, 1990, p. 192). For it to hang together conceptually, it needs coherence as well as cohesion. Coherence is not an observable textual feature but, instead, is produced by assumptions held by the reader. To recognize a set of linguistic devices as a vehicle for creating coherence, the reader needs to have world knowledge along with knowledge of coherence relations such as cause–effect, problem–solution and temporal sequence.

Application of these concepts is not straightforward in translation, though. This is because while knowledge of the sequence of coherence relations is (most likely) shared by users of the source and the target languages, cohesive devices in those languages are language specific. The translator's job is to negotiate between the two systems and produce a translation which satisfies both systems and achieves equivalence at the text level (Baker, 2018/1992, pp. 134–234). As Shreve puts it, paying attention to textual properties can lead to a 'quantum leap … in the "textual quality" of the translation' (Shreve, 2017, p. 175); but text production through negotiating between two systems (i.e., translation) requires considerable linguistic knowledge and skills and major cognitive effort. This is because the unit of translation is considered to be a sentence (Huang and

Wu, 2009) and, as a body of cognitive research indicates, the way that translation proceeds (i.e., sequential and step-by-step) brings the translator's focus, necessarily, down to the sentential level (Shreve, 2017, p. 175). This leads us to deduce that producing a cohesive and coherent text on the text level in translation requires additional effort and skills (such as cross-sentential revision) by the translator compared to monolingual text production.

### 3.3.4 The Influence of Technologies on Translation Practice

#### 3.3.4.1 The Influence of TM on Text Production

Considering the cognitive processes involved in translational text production, as well as the mechanism of the TM function in a CAT tool, it is easy to understand that TM-assisted translation exacerbates the difficulty of producing translation with appropriate textuality. The translator is required to minimize the adverse effects caused by the sentential restrictions as well as the influence from the CAT tool interface and the nature of TM. Under these circumstances, the translator must pay sufficient attention to translation suggestions from the TM and apply necessary edits so that the final translation achieves maximum textuality.

Bowker (2006) offers detailed examples of the difficulties involved in this. One obvious example is related to the sequence of coherence relations. A sentence in a text stands in certain logical relations to other parts of the text, but these relationships obtain only in that particular text–context configuration. When a sentence is stored in a TM, the context is stripped away. And when the sentence is suggested as a recyclable segment in a new translation, the suggestion is not only made without regard to context but may conflict with the new context in the target text (TT). Therefore, to make the suggested sentence work in the new translation, the translator needs to 'work outside the artificial boundaries of sentences, so the sentence-by-sentence approach imposed by TMs may not be conducive to effective translation of the text's message as a whole' (Bowker, 2006, p. 180). Another example concerns polysemy. Bowker uses the example of the French translation of the English expression 'empty the pipe', which will have different translations in a text about plumbing (pipe=tuyau) and in a text about smoking (pipe=pipe) (Bowker, 2006, p. 179). Since a suggestion from the TM database is presented out of context, the translator will need to check the context and, if necessary, consult relevant reference materials.

These examples indicate that, although the use of TMs was originally introduced to improve the productivity of translation processes, the resultant translations require a high level of effort by the translator to ensure that the suggested sentences are adjusted so that they sit well in the whole text. In addition, the effort to accomplish this task is influenced by some TM-related factors, typically 'terminological train wreck' and 'sentence salad' (Bowker, 2006, p. 181). 'Terminological train wreck' occurs because translators tend to use inconsistent or inappropriate terminology for the context of a new translation when the TM contains terminology from different translations made for different clients at different times. Terminology can evolve quickly; thus, terms stored in a TM may become out of date quickly. 'Sentence salad' is a similar phenomenon, but at the sentence level. If a TM offers translation suggestions from translations produced by different translators in different styles about different topics, the new translation based on suggestions from the TM may present a 'stylistic hodgepodge'.

Dragsted's (2006) process study investigated how professional and student translators deal with these challenges posed by TM. The study showed that, when translating without a TM, professional translators tended not to recognize the sentence as a translation unit (whereas student translators did tend to translate sentence-by-sentence), but when translating with a TM, their focus was more sentential: they spent more time translating each sentence, reducing the length of time spent on cross-sentential revisions at the end of the whole translation (Dragsted, 2006, pp. 449–53). The professionals also made fewer cross-sentential shifts from the source text to the target text, such as combining or splitting up sentences, when using a TM (Dragsted, 2006, pp. 453–9). Most professionals recognized this cognitive restriction caused by the TM mechanism as a disadvantage, while student translators tended to regard it as an advantage, saying that they could concentrate on translating one sentence at a time. These findings suggest that student translators do not recognize the restrictions caused by a TM because their translation competence is not sufficiently developed to deal with the text-level translation problems when translating without a TM (Dragsted, 2006, p. 457). In contrast, professionals are aware of these restrictions but, in the study, said that solving text-level translation problems at the final cross-sentential revision stage was not always possible in professional situations because it requires time and effort (Dragsted, 2006, p. 458).

These findings provide a convincing explanation for another TM-related phenomenon called 'blind faith' (Bowker, 2005). 'Blind faith' refers to the tendency of translators to accept suggestions from a TM without checking the appropriateness of the segment in the new translation sufficiently owing to the pressure to increase productivity. The pressure for higher productivity in the professional environment is highlighted in translation workplace studies (e.g., LeBlanc, 2017) which show that translators are increasingly deprived of time to spend on translation to meet management's expectations that technologies like TM should reduce the time spent on translation.

### 3.3.4.2 The Influence of MT on Text Production

The rift between the concepts of translation quality at the text level and at the sentence level is evident in text production involving MT, too.

Lumeras and Way (2017), drawing on Kay (2014), illustrate the rift using the dichotomous concepts of 'syntactic translation' and 'pragmatic translation'. Lumeras and Way (2017, p. 30) provide the following example.

(i) 'Est-ce que c'est ta cousine?' 'Non, je n'ai pas de cousine.'

The cousin who is talked about in this conversation is female, which is clearly marked by the female form of the word 'cousine' in French. However, as the English language does not have lexical items to distinguish male and female cousins, an MT engine is most likely to render the French sentences as in (ii).

(ii) 'Is that your cousin?' 'No, I don't have a cousin.'

On the other hand, if the conversation is to be translated by a human translator, the translator will infer the gender of the cousin from the other parts of the text, or from their world knowledge about the text, and may produce a text like (iii).

(iii) 'Is that girl your cousin?' 'No, she's not my cousin.'

A sentence like (ii) is called a 'syntactic translation' and a sentence like (iii) is called a 'pragmatic translation'. On the sentence level, (ii) is correct, but it is not the optimal translation on the text level.

MT translates a text which consists of more than one sentence through a production model that Lumeras and Way (2017, p. 30), following Kay (2014), call the Syntactic Model of Translation. The model bases itself on the idea that 'a long translation is a sequence of short(er) translations, we memorize short translations (lexical items), and these short translations can be reordered' (p. 30). This model is obviously incongruent with the notion of text we saw above.

The adherence to sentence-level text production is evident in MTPE training, too. A piece of training material of one of the major localization companies (SDL, 2017, p. 32) advises:

1. Read the source segment first then the MT output.
2. Determine the usable elements (single words and phrases) and make them the basis for your translation.
3. Build from the MT output and use every part of the MT output that can speed up your work.

The guidelines then suggest that all grammatical and terminological errors be corrected whereas corrections of stylistic errors are optional. After editing MT outputs to the end of the text in this way, the post-editor is instructed to run the automatic quality check function available in the

CAT tool, which detects spelling, grammar and terminological errors. There are, however, no instructions in these guidelines to check text-level errors (cross-sentential checks). This indicates that quality assessment on the text level is not expected in MTPE. In the same vein, the post-editing guidelines published by the Translation Automation User Society (TAUS) (Massardo et al., 2016, p. 17) encourage post-editors, while verifying edits, to '[e]nsure that no information has been accidentally added or omitted [to the source segment]'.

The reason behind these instructions is easy to deduce: trying to assess the quality at text level, which may necessitate additional cross-sentential translation strategies, will make the exercise complex and time-consuming, which defeats the purpose of MTPE, namely, fast turnaround.

This sentence-focused process in MTPE tends to cause text-level problems just like translation using TMs does. Čulo et al. (2014, p. 208) report a case of English-German post-editing.

> Killer nurse receives four life sentences. Hospital nurse C.N. was imprisoned for life today for the killing of four of his patients.    (Source Text)

> Killer-Krankenschwester zu viermal lebenslanger Haft verurteilt. Der Krankenpfleger C.N. wurde heute auf Lebenszeit eingesperrt für die Tötung von vier seiner Patienten.    (Post-Edited Text)

> 'Killer woman-nurse to four times life-long imprisonment sentenced. The man-nurse C.N. was today for lifetime imprisoned for the killing of four of his patients.'    (Back Translation)

The Source Text sentence is a newspaper headline. The word 'nurse' was machine translated as 'Krankenschwester' (female nurse), which the post-editor accepted. In the second sentence, however, the post-editor edited the same word as 'Krankenpfleger' (male nurse) as the gender of the nurse was clarified by the pronoun 'seiner' (=his) in the same sentence. The inconsistency across the two sentences in this example leaves the text incoherent at the text level. Čulo et al. (2014, p. 212) conclude that the post-editing task required the post-editors to use the translation strategy of 'explicitation'.

### 3.3.5   Justification from the Industry

We have seen that the translator's ability to produce high-quality translation text tends to be affected by the use of both TM and MT. These tools turn the process of translation into a mechanical task of producing and assessing translation sentence by sentence, which can be considered to be side effects of the technologies. When the phenomena are considered in sociological frameworks, the side effects of TM and MT can be understood as a burden imposed on translators by tool makers and employers/commissioners of translators who prioritize the operationality of technology over and above the importance of the concept of 'text'. As a result, the translator's pursuit of quality translation as text is subjected to 'the industrialization and globalization forces that demand higher productivity and speed' (Jiménez-Crespo, 2017, p. 161). Despite the importance of the concept of text as the basis of many new translation research and training projects, the concept is undermined in practice by technologies such as TM and MT (Jiménez-Crespo, 2017, pp. 158–9).

However, this does not stop the industry from using these technologies in translation. A common ground for a defence of this practice is the notion of 'good enough translation' or 'fit-for-purpose translation' (Bowker, 2019). When time and budget resources are limited, one of the strategies used in the industry is to target resources according to the purposes of translation. If the text is highly 'perishable', that is, to be used only for a short time, perfect translation may not be necessary. Texts such as forum posts on social media or product support texts (which are updated frequently) are good examples. Another criterion for resource allocation is the risk involved in the translation (Nitzke, Hansen-Schirra and Canfora, 2019). Outward communication from a company to its customers is important for the business and the risk of damaging the business is high with translation of texts of, for example, advertisement. In contrast, texts used for internal information carry a lower risk. Users of translation may decide to have perishable and lower-risk texts translated at a lower quality, that is, 'good enough' translation.

The concept of 'good enough' translation manifests itself clearly in the two-tier quality classification of MTPE, which is commonly used in the industry. The classification consists of two distinct post-editing processes: 'full post-editing' and 'light post-editing'. ISO 18587 (British Standards Institution, 2017), an international industry standard which sets standards of MTPE services, defines 'full-editing' as editing required 'to obtain a product comparable to a product obtained by human translation' and 'light post-editing' as required to 'obtain merely comparable text without any attempt to produce a product comparable to a product obtained by human translation'. The concept of light post-editing embodies the industry's belief that a substandard translation has its own market value, depending on the client's needs and requirements, budgets or time constraints.

The discrepancy in the fundamental attitudes to quality between academic theories and professional beliefs is evident in Drugan's (2013) extensive ethnographic study of translation quality in the industry. Drugan points out that no professionals or practitioners who participated in the study mentioned a single translation studies model to explain their practice of quality assessment: academic theories are ignored in professional environments (Drugan, 2013, p. 41). At the same time, Drugan (2013, p. 47) points out that much of the industry debate on 'fit-for-purpose' translation, for instance, is clearly linked to ideas from Skopos theory, even if this is rarely acknowledged, or perhaps even realized.

Skopos theory (Reiss and Vermeer, 2013/1984) postulates that textual features of translation are governed by the purpose (=*skopos*) of translation. The purpose of translation is decided by the situation, which includes what the recipient of the translation expects from it (Reiss and Vermeer, 2013/1984, p. 89). Consequently, the message in the translation should be '"sufficiently" coherent with the situation in which it is received', which is more important than the massage being 'coherent "in itself"' (Reiss and Vermeer, 2013/1984, p. 98). '"Understanding" means to relate something to one's own situation and the background knowledge it implies' (Reiss and Vermeer, 2013/1984, p. 98). Although the practice of MTPE was not common when Skopos theory was developed, this reasoning, particularly the understanding of 'coherence', agrees with the practice of MTPE. For example, a mechanical engineer will find a light post-edited technical document about a new machine sufficient for their purpose as they can use their own world knowledge about the subject in interpreting the text correctly. Light post-editing of MT will be adequate for the purpose.

So, although the notion of translation commonly observed in the technological industry environment seems to conflict with the academic concept of translation quality as determined by the quality of the translated text in the context of its source text, the notion used in the technological environment shares much common ground with one of the most authoritative translation theories, that is, Skopos theory.

### 3.3.6  Future Outlook for Technologies and Translation Studies

We have seen that technologies such as TM and MT are not capable of addressing the notion of text sufficiently owing to their sentence-focused mechanisms. One may hastily deduce, then, that, as technologies develop further, the gap between the understanding of translation in translation studies and that in the industry will widen. In reality, however, this seems not to be the case. A survey of research and tool development shows increasing engagement with the notion of text by translation technology developers.

With regard to TM, most CAT tools incorporate a function called 'preview'. A separate preview pane on the computer screen shows the target text in the form it will appear on the final printed page. With this function on, the translator can check how the translation looks on the page, that is, on the text level in the intended context. This function facilitates assessment of the level of cohesion and coherence in the translation.

In MT research, an increasing number of investigations are carried out with a view to improving the text-level quality of MT outputs. This includes the development of translation and quality assessment models which can refer to discourse information from outside the current sentences. In the late 2010s, an increasing number of research projects explored methods to materialize this (e.g., Bawden et al., 2018; Li, Nakazawa and Tsuruoka, 2019; Wang, 2019). This shows that language technology research in the computing and engineering disciplines is actively importing the notion of quality from translation studies.

This kind of text-level MT research is still in its infancy and how much of this goal can be achieved remains to be seen. Also, how this new stage of MT development influences the perception held by users of MT, as well as translators, will be an important focus for observation. It may be welcomed by the translation community as a sign of diminishing polarization and opposition between humans and machines, a common trait seen thus far in the translation community (Sakamoto, 2019a). On the other hand, this may exacerbate the feeling of threat experienced by translators if understood as a sign that MTs are catching up with humans to eventually make human translators obsolete. The relation between translation and technology is fluid, and if, or how, our understanding of translation will be changed by technologies in the future remains to be seen.

## 3.4  Future Directions of Research

O'Hagan (2013, p. 508) points out that there is a disconnection between the theory and the practice of translation, claiming that the changes occurring in technologies and their effects on translation practice, and the studies in the applied branches of translation which investigate these phenomena, are not influencing theorizing or modelling in the pure branch of translation studies on Holmes's map of translation studies (Holmes, 1972). The examples offered in this chapter are relevant. As we have seen, methods and evidence used in technology-related research in the applied branch have been restricted to the sentence level owing to technological limitations. Text-level engagement is, however, increasingly becoming possible thanks to technological advancement, which promises increased interaction between the pure and the applied branches.

Diverse approaches in studies of translation, including both cognitive and sociological studies, are needed in the pursuit of such interaction, and to make the outcomes useful for the real world. The influence of technology on translation, both positive and negative, is enormous and consequently affects all parties involved in it (i.e., translators, post-editors, business owners, clients of translation services, etc.). What follows shows some examples of such studies and future directions of research.

### 3.4.1  Cognitive Studies of Translation Technologies

Process studies have been popular in translation studies since the 1980s. Methods such as think-aloud protocols (TAPs), keystroke logging, screen recording and eye tracking are typically used, as well as concurrent and retrospective verbal reports (Göpferich and Jääskeläinen, 2009). The processes of translation with tools such as TM and MT have been an important target of such studies. Christensen and Schjoldager (2010) and Christensen (2011) offer good reviews of studies of TM. More recently, in tandem with the increasing prevalence of MT and its integration in CAT tools, the number of process studies with MT has increased, particularly concerning MTPE processes. For a review of such studies, see Koponen (2016). For collections of studies on MTPE, see O'Brien (2014), O'Brien and Simard (2014) and Vieira, Alonso and Bywood (2019).

One of the main questions in MTPE research is whether MTPE is worth adopting (Garcia, 2011; Koponen, 2016). To answer this question, studies have examined the quality of translations produced by MTPE, their difference from human translation and their efficiency. But such investigations tend to measure quality in terms of the number of errors, and inevitably face the fundamental questions: What is quality in translation? How can it be measured?

An innovative approach to these questions is to investigate 'post-editese', a concept derived from 'translationese'. Daems, De Clercq and Macken (2017) investigated whether post-edited products carried more typical MTPE features and concluded that sufficiently post-edited MT outputs do not carry post-editese features which machines can detect. In contrast, Toral (2019) investigated lexical variety in MT outputs as well as post-edited texts and argues that post-editese is observable in post-edited texts. These studies are good examples of how a traditional translation studies concept (in this case, translation universals) and new practices involving technologies can be linked to explore the question of quality.

Another noticeable development in MT research is the emphasis on 'prediction' of MT quality, dubbed the 'predictive turn' in translation studies (Schaeffer, Nitzke and Hansen-Schirra, 2019). Accurate prediction of MT output quality will allow us to filter out suitable MT outputs for an efficient MTPE process. Furthermore, researchers are interested in estimating the cognitive effort required in post-editing by certain features of texts. Outcomes of such studies will have applied value in professional workflow design and management, including time planning and economic modelling of MTPE services.

### 3.4.2   Sociological Studies on Translation Technologies

The other side of the coin of translation technology studies is the sociology of translation. To understand the influence of technologies on translation practice and on the people involved with it, researchers have imported different sociological frameworks into translation studies. For example, in studying the way users' agency resists tool development, Olohan (2011) adopts Pickering's notion of a 'Mangle of Practice' (Pickering, 1993). In an attempt to answer why many translators resist post-editing work, Sakamoto (2019b) draws on Bourdieu's field theory (Bourdieu, 1984/1979. In examining how stakeholders' legal rights and power relations are affected by the way translation resources (MT's machine learning data) are used, Moorkens and Lewis (2019) use Hess and Ostrom's institutional analysis and development (IAD) framework (Hess and Ostrom, 2007). These and a growing number of related works can be grouped together under an umbrella paradigm of 'science and technology and studies (STS) inspired translation studies research' (Kenny, 2017; Olohan, 2017; Sakamoto, Evans and Torres-Hostench, 2018). This research paradigm examines relations and interactions between technology and translation from critical angles using historical, economic, sociological and anthropological methodologies.

This paradigm covers a wide range of topics in translation. These include technology-induced power relations among different stakeholders (e.g., Garcia, 2007), economics of translation (e.g., Moorkens, 2017; Vieira, 2018), ethical use of data resources (e.g., Drugan and Babych, 2010; Kenny, 2011), and translators' perceptions of technology use (e.g., Guerberof Arenas, 2013; LeBlanc, 2017). There are also fields of research beyond commercial translation environments. For example, the utility of MT has been explored for literary translation (e.g., Moorkens et al., 2018; Toral and Way, 2018).

It is important to remember that the two approaches (the cognitive and the sociological) do not, or should not, position themselves separately from each other if we are to achieve a holistic understanding of translation in the technologized society and benefit from it in the real world. One good example of such holistic enquiry is workplace research. Because it uses controlled, experimental methods, cognitive research has limited ecological validity. To overcome this limitation, some researchers are going out of the labs to examine the interactions between humans and technologies in workplaces. This approach may be described as 'socio-cognitive' (Risku, Rogl and Milosevic, 2017), 'socio-technical' (Ehrensberger-Dow and Massey, 2017) or 'cognitive-ergonomic' (Lavault-Olléon, 2011; Teixeira and O'Brien, 2017), but they all investigate how technologies influence and shape practice in the real world, and vice versa. These interactions among different branches of translation studies have the potential to lead us to yet further enhanced understanding of translation.

# References

Austermühl, F. (2014). *Electronic Tools for Translators*. Abingdon: Routledge. Available at http://capitadiscovery.co.uk/port/items/1133149.

Baker, M. (2018/1992). *In Other Words: A Coursebook on Translation*, 3rd ed. London: Routledge. Available at http://capitadiscovery.co.uk/port/items/1276427.

Bawden, R., Sennrich, R., Birch, A., and Haddow, B. (2018). Evaluating discourse phenomena in neural machine translation. In *Proceedings of NAACL-HLT 2018* (pp. 1304–13). Available at http://arxiv.org/abs/1711.00513.

Bourdieu, P. (1979). *La distinction. Critique sociale du jugement*. Paris: Minuit.

Bourdieu, P. (1984). *Distinction: A Social Critique of the Judgement of Taste*. London: Routledge and Kegan Paul.

Bowker, L. (2002). Translation-memory systems. In L. Bowker, ed. *Computer-Aided Translation Technology: A Practical Introduction*. Ottawa: University of Ottawa Press, pp. 93–128.

Bowker, L. (2005). Productivity vs. quality? A pilot study on the impact of translation memory systems. *Localization Focus*, **4**(1), 13–20. Available at www.localisation.ie/sites/default/files/publications/Vol4_1Bowker.pdf.

Bowker, L. (2006). Translation memory and 'text'. In L. Bowker, ed., *Lexicography, Terminology, and Translation: Text-Based Studies in Honour of Ingrid Meyer*. Ottawa: University of Ottawa Press, pp. 175–87.

Bowker, L. (2019). Fit-for-purpose translation. In M. O'Hagan, ed., *The Routledge Handbook of Translation and Technology* London: Taylor and Francis, pp. 453–68.

Bowker, L., and Fisher, D. (2010). Computer-aided translation. In Y. Gambier and L. van Doorslaer, eds., *Handbook of Translation Studies: Volume 1*. Amsterdam/Philadelphia: John Benjamins, pp. 60–5.

British Standards Institution. (2017). *BS ISO 18587:2017 BSI Standards Publication Translation services – Post-editing of machine translation output – Requirements*. London.

British Standards Institution. (2018). *BS EN 17100:2015+A1:2017 BSI Standards Publication Translation Services – Requirements for translation services*. London.

Catford, J. C. (1965). *A Linguistic Theory of Translation: An Essay in Applied Linguistics*. Oxford: Oxford University Press.

Christensen, T. P. (2011). Studies on the mental processes in translation memory-assisted translation: The state of the art. *Trans-Kom*, **4**, 137–60. Available at www.trans-kom.eu/bd04nr02/trans-kom_04_02_02_Christensen_Translation_Memory.20111205.pdf.

Christensen, T. P., and Schjoldager, A. (2010). Translation-memory (TM) research: What do we know and how do we know it? *Hermes – Journal of Language and Communication Studies*, **44**, 89–102.

Čulo, O., Gutermuth, S., Hansen-Schirra, S., and Nitzke, J. (2014). The influence of post-editing on translation strategies. In S. O'Brien, M. Carl, M. Simard, L. Specia and L. Winther Balling, eds., *Post-Editing of Machine Translation: Processes and Applications*. Newcastle upon Tyne: Cambridge Scholars Publishing, pp. 200–18.

Daems, J., De Clercq, O., and Macken, L. (2017). Translationese and post-editese: How comparable is comparable quality? *Linguistica Antverpiensia, New Series: Themes in Translation Studies*, **16**, 89–103. Available at https://biblio.ugent.be/publication/8516838/file/8554001.pdf.

De Beaugrande, R., and Dressler, W. (1981). *Introduction to Text Linguistics*. London/New York: Longman.

Doherty, S. (2017). Issues in human and automatic translation quality assessment. In D. Kenny, ed., *Human Issues in Translation Technology*. London/New York: Taylor and Francis, pp. 131–49.

Dragsted, B. (2006). Computer-aided translation as a distributed cognitive task. *Pragmatics & Cognition*, **14**(2), 443–64. Available at https://doi.org/10.1075/pc.14.2.17dra.

Drugan, J. (2013). *Quality in Professional Translation: Assessment and Improvement*. London: Bloomsbury Academic.

Drugan, J., and Babych, B. (2010). Shared resources, shared values? Ethical implications of sharing translation resources. In *Proceedings of the Second Joint EM+/CNGL Workshop 'Bringing MT to the User: Research on Integrating MT in the Translation Industry'*, pp. 3–9.

Ehrensberger-Dow, M., and Massey, G. (2017). Socio-technical issues in professional translation practice. *Translation Spaces*, **6**(1), 104–21. Available at https://doi.org/10.1075/ts.6.1.06ehr.

Fawcett, P. (1997). *Translation and Language: Linguistic Theories Explained*. Manchester: St Jerome.

Forcada, M. (2017). Making sense of neural machine translation. *Translation Spaces*, **6**(2), 291–309. Available at https://doi.org/10.1075/ts.2.06for.

Garcia, I. (2007). Power shifts in web-based translation memory. *Machine Translation*, **21**(1), 55–68. Available at https://doi.org/10.1007/s10590-008-9033-6.

Garcia, I. (2010). The proper place of professionals (and non-professionals and machines) in web translation. *Revista Tradumàtica*, **8**, 1–7.

Garcia, I. (2011). Translating by post-editing: Is it the way forward? *Machine Translation*, **25**(3), 217–37. Available at https://doi.org/10.1007/s10590-011-9115-8.

Göpferich, S., and Jääskeläinen, R. (2009). Process research into the development of translation competence: Where are we, and where do we need to go? *Across Languages and Cultures*, **10**(2), 169–91.

Guerberof Arenas, A. (2013). What do professional translators think about post-editing? *Journal of Specialised Translation*, **19**, 75–95.

Halliday, M. (1961). Categories of the theory of grammar. *Word*, **17**(3), 241–92.

Halliday, M., and Hasan, R. (1976). *Cohesion in English*. London: Longman.

Hatim, B., and Mason, I. (1990). *Discourse and the Translator*. London: Longman.

Hess, C., and Ostrom, E. (2007). *Understanding Knowledge as a Commons: From Theory to Practice*. Cambridge, MA: MIT Press.

Holmes, J. (1972). The name and nature of translation studies. In *Translated: Papers on Literary Translation and Translation Studies*. Amsterdam: Rodopi, pp. 66–80. Reprinted in L. Venuti, ed. (2004). *The Translation Studies Reader*. 2nd ed. London: Routledge, pp. 180–92.

Huang, H., and Wu, C. (2009). The unit of translation: Statistics speak. *Meta*, **54**(1), 110–30. Available at https://doi.org/https://doi.org/10.7202/029796ar.

Jiménez-Crespo, M. A. (2017). *Crowdsourcing and Online Collaborative Translations: Expanding the Limits of Translation Studies*. Amsterdam: John Benjamins.

Kay, M. (2014). Does a computational linguist have to be a linguist? Invited Talk, COLING 2014, 25th International Conference on Computational Linguistics, Dublin, Ireland [online]. www.coling-2014.org/martin-kay.php.

Kenny, D. (2011). The ethics of machine translation. In New Zealand Society of Translators and Interpreters Annual Conference *2011*. Auckland, New Zealand. Available at http://doras.dcu.ie/17606/.

Kenny, D. (2017). Introduction. In D. Kenny, ed., *Human Issues in Translation Technology*. London/New York: Taylor and Francis, pp. 131–49.

Kenny, D. (2018). Machine translation. In P. Rawling and P. Wilson, eds., *The Routledge Handbook of Translation and Philosophy*. Abingdon, UK: Routledge, pp. 428–45.

Koponen, M. (2016). Is machine translation post-editing worth the effort? A survey of research into post-editing and effort. *Journal of Specialised Translation*, **25**, 131–48. Available at www.jostrans.org/issue25/art_koponen.pdf.

Lavault-Olléon, É. (2011). L'ergonomie, nouveau paradigme pour la traductologie [Ergonomics as a New Paradigm for Translation Studies]. In *ILCEA* 14. Available at http://ilcea.revues.org/1078.

LeBlanc, M. (2017). 'I can't get no satisfaction!' Should we blame translation technologies or shifting business practices? In D. Kenny, ed., *Human Issues in Translation Technology*. London/New York: Taylor and Francis, pp. 45–62.

Li, L., Nakazawa, T., and Tsuruoka, Y. (2019). Bunmyakujouhou o kouryoshita nichiei nyuuraru kikaihonyaku:文脈情報を考慮した日英ニューラル機械翻訳 [Japanese-English Neural Machine Translation in consideration of discourse information]. In *25th Natural Language Processing NLP2019 Conference Proceedings*, pp. 101–4. Available at www.anlp.jp/proceedings/annual_meeting/2019/pdf_dir/A2-2.pdf.

Lumeras, M. A., and Way, A. (2017). On the complementarity between human translators and machine translation. *Hermes*, **56**, 21–42. Available at https://doi.org/https://tidsskrift.dk/her/article/view/97200.

Massardo, I., van der Meer, J., O'Brien, S., Hollowood, F., Aranberri, N., and Drescher, K. (2016). *MT Post-Editing Guidelines*. Available at www.taus.net/academy/bestpractices/postedit-best-practices/machine-translation-post-editing-guidelines.

Moorkens, J. (2017). Under pressure: Translation in times of austerity. *Perspectives*, **25**(3), 1–14. Available at https://doi.org/10.1080/0907676X.2017.1285331.

Moorkens, J., and Lewis, D. (2019). Research questions and a proposal for the future governance of translation data. *Journal of Specialised Translation*, **32**, 2–25.

Moorkens, J., Toral, A., Castilho, S., and Way, A. (2018). Translators' perceptions of literary post-editing using statistical and neural machine translation. *Translation Spaces*, **7**(2), 240–62. Available at https://doi.org/10.1075/ts.18014.moo.

Nitzke, J., Hansen-Schirra, S., and Canfora, C. (2019). Risk management and post-editing competence. *Journal of Specialised Translation*, **31**, 239–59.

O'Brien, S., ed. (2014). *Post-Editing of Machine Translation: Processes and Applications*. Newcastle upon Tyne: Cambridge Scholars Publishing. Available at http://capitadiscovery.co.uk/port/items/1216444.

O'Brien, S., and Simard, M., eds. (2014). Special issue: Post-Editing. *Machine Translation*, **28**. https://link.springer.com/journal/10590/volumes-and-issues/28-3.

O'Hagan, M. (2013). The impact of new technologies on translation studies: A technological turn? In C. Millán-Varela and F. Bartrina, eds., *The Routledge Handbook of Translation Studies*. London: Routledge, pp. 503–18.

Olohan, M. (2011). Translators and translation technology: The dance of agency. *Translation Studies*, **4**(3), 342–57. Available at https://doi.org/10.1080/14781700.2011.589656.

Olohan, M. (2017). Technology, translation and society. *Target*, **29**(2), 264–83. Available at https://doi.org/10.1075/target.29.2.04olo.

Pickering, A. (1993). The mangle of practice: Agency and emergence in the sociology of science. *American Journal of Sociology*, **99**(3), 559–89.

Popović, M. (2018). Error classification and analysis for machine translation quality assessment. In J. Moorkens, S. Castilho, F. Gaspari and S. Doherty, eds., *Translation Quality Assessment: From Principles to Practice*. Cham, Switzerland: Springer, pp. 129–58.

Reiss, K., and Vermeer, H. J. (2013/1984). *Towards a General Theory of Translational Action: Skopos Theory Explained*. Manchester: St Jerome.

Risku, H., Rogl, R., and Milosevic, J. (2017). Translation practice in the field. *Translation Spaces*, **66**(1), 3–26. Available at https://doi.org/10.1075/ts.6.1.01ris.

Sakamoto, A. (2019a). Unintended consequences of translation technologies: From project managers' perspectives. *Perspectives*, **27**(1), 58–73. Available at https://doi.org/10.1080/0907676X.2018.1473452.

Sakamoto, A. (2019b). Why do many translators resist post-editing? A sociological analysis using Bourdieu' s concepts. *Journal of Specialised Translation*, **31**, 201–16.

Sakamoto, A., Evans, J., and Torres-Hostench, O. (2018). *Introduction to the Special Dossier Section: Translation and Disruption. Revista Tradumàtica*, 16. Available at https://doi.org/https://doi.org/10.5565/rev/tradumatica.223.

Schaeffer, M., Nitzke, J., and Hansen-Schirra, S. (2019). Predictive turn in translation studies: Review and prospects. In S. D. Brunn and R. Kehrein, eds., *Handbook of the Changing World Language Map*. Cham, Switzerland: Springer, pp. 1–23. Available at https://doi.org/10.1007/978-3-319-73400-2_217-1.

SDL. (2017). *SDL Certification: Post-Editing Certification*.

Shreve, G. M. (2017). Text linguistics, translating, and interpreting. In K. Malmkjær, ed., *The Routledge Handbook of Translation Studies and Linguistics*. London: Routledge, pp. 165–78. Available at https://doi.org/10.4324/9781315692845-12.

Teixeira, C. S. C., and O'Brien, S. (2017). Investigating the cognitive ergonomic aspects of translation tools in a workplace setting. *Translation Spaces*, **6**(1), 79–103. Available at https://doi.org/10.1075/ts.6.1.05tei.

Toral, A. (2019). Post-editese: An exacerbated translationese. In *Proceedings of MT Summit XVII*, Vol. 1. Dublin, pp. 272–81.

Toral, A., and Way, A. (2018). What level of quality can neural machine translation attain on literary text? In J. Moorkens, F. Gaspari, S. Castilho and S. Doherty, eds., *Translation Quality Assessment: From Principles to Practice*. Cham, Switzerland: Springer International, pp. 263–87. Available at https://doi.org/10.1007/978-3-319-91241-7_12.

Vieira, L. N. (2018). Automation anxiety and translators. *Translation Studies*, 1–21. Available at https://doi.org/10.1080/14781700.2018.1543613.

Vieira, L. N., Alonso, E., and Bywood, L. (2019). Introduction: Post-editing in practice – Process, product and networks. Special issue of the *Journal of Specialised Translation*, **31**, 2–13.

Wang, L. (2019). *Discourse-Aware Neural Machine Translation*. PhD thesis, Dublin City University.

Zaretskaya, A. (2017). Machine translation post-editing at TransPerfect: The 'human' side of the process. *Revista Tradumàtica*, **15**, 116–23. Available at https://doi.org/https://doi.org/10.5565/rev/tradumatica.201.

# 4

# Self-Translation

Anthony Cordingley

## 4.1 Introduction

Self-translation occurs when an author composes a text in one language and translates it into another. Necessarily, the author decides how much liberty to allow themselves in rewriting and to what extent the text should be adapted to a new readership. This produces a form of writing once studied as literary authorship but more recently theorized as translation (López López-Gay, 2006, pp. 218, 222). Yet others believe that all writing reformulates existing words and narratives, so there is no such thing as an 'original' and self-translation only renders this fact more visible (Bassnett, 2013). More commonly, however, self-translation is understood as a hybrid activity, uniquely and 'eminently *at once* translation and writing' (Oustinoff, 2001, p. 57, author's emphasis).

Perhaps because of the historical uncertainty surrounding its definition, or because until recently it was thought to be a marginal practice, no European language dictionary contains an entry for 'self-translation'. Not only does it confound definitions, self-translation escapes the ethical regime that applies to translation. While many authors translate themselves 'faithfully', producing a close rendering of their work's sense and form, some take the opportunity to extend or revise their project, or adapt it to a new readership. Studying this process offers fascinating insights into both authorship and translatorship; it reveals how individuals modulate their creative projects across different languages and cultures; it illuminates the context in which self-translators work, and the audience for whom they write. Research into literary self-translation has expanded considerably since the turn of the century. The practice is no longer associated exclusively with literary celebrities, such as Samuel Beckett or Vladimir Nabokov, or the many winners of the Nobel Prize for Literature who wrote their works in two languages, and which reinforced the perception that self-translators are a rare species of literary genius (Grutman,

2013). In Europe, self-translation has been shown to be an established practice with a history stretching back to at least the Middle Ages (Hokenson and Munson, 2007), and the collective bibliography of self-translation research lists more than 1,500 books, journal articles and book chapters documenting this practice (Gentes, 2020).

The emergence of self-translation research as a subdiscipline of translation studies has been surveyed by Anselmi (2012), Cordingley (2019), Grutman (2009a/2019), Grutman and Van Bolderen (2014) and others. Typologies of different forms of self-translator have been proposed by Recuenco Peñalver (2011) and Santoyo (2013b), their strategies explored in depth by Gentes (2017). This research has shown that, in the overwhelming majority of known cases, self-translation passes through at least one of the languages spoken in Europe. This chapter discusses the geopolitical reasons for this. It considers the power hierarchies within the network of the world's languages and the circulation of literary texts around the globe. It explores issues surrounding the transparency of self-translation, its avowal and recognition, the exclusivity of the 'self' of the self-translator, and to what extent their work with collaborators complicates the practice. It considers Eurocentrism as a factor in how self-translation is conceived, and the example of Chinese language self-translation. This leads to a critique of how self-translation has been used in debates in world literature studies as a concept to describe original writing that has the qualities of a translation and/or circulates in the globalized literary marketplace like a translation.

## 4.2 Self-Translation and the Global Language System

By the end of the twentieth century, a number of influential models emerged that described how languages interact within a global system where hierarchies between languages generate centrifugal dynamics that draw peripheral languages, their texts and speakers, towards more central ones (Calvet, 1999; Casanova, 1999; Heilbron, 1995, 1999; de Swaan, 2001). Many scholars of literary self-translation have drawn upon Casanova's discussion of dominant and dominating languages and the role this hierarchy plays in the choices that self-translators make. Especially pertinent is Casanova's discussion of the way in which individuals seek to legitimize themselves by establishing careers in the language of a dominant culture, a process she terms *littérisation*, defined as 'any operation – translation, self-translation, transcription, direct composition in the dominant language – by means of which a text from a literarily deprived country comes to be regarded as literary by the legitimate authorities' (Casanova, 2004 [1999], 136). Casanova sees this process enacted at both the global level, like the Bengali poet Rabindranath Tagore's transformation into an English writer and self-translator, and the regional level, when, for instance, the Swedish dramatist, writer and painter August Strindberg self-translated his early texts into French and even composed his celebrated 1897 *Inferno* directly in this tongue – only once Strindberg had secured his standing and reputation in the language of the highest literary prestige in nineteenth-century Europe did he return to composing texts in his native Swedish, delegating to others their translation into French. Casanova has in turn been criticized for her Eurocentric view of legitimation, which she equates with professional recognition within old-world centres of power.

Casanova's research is informed by Abram de Swaan's (2001) application of world-systems theory to the world's languages, which he synthesized in *Words of the World: The Global Language System* (2001). De Swaan harnesses statistics detailing the number of native speakers of a language and the multilinguals that learn and/or use it to determine its place in the 'galaxy' of world languages. This galaxy revolves around its central sun, surrounded by large planets, themselves encircled with moons. In this scheme, each language falls into at least one of four categories of varying centrality. Most distant is a *peripheral language*, spoken at the local level, like Māori in New Zealand. A *central language* is used by different ethnic or regional groups within a geographic region, like Indonesian across the islands of Indonesia, even if only for administrative purposes. A *supercentral language* has greater reach and may be used for transnational communication and/or specific practices, like religious observation (Arabic fulfils both). At the centre reigns the *hypercentral language*, a lingua franca used the world over, predominantly by non-native speakers for the purposes of business, science, culture and communication. While peripheral languages are estimated to make up some 90 per cent of the world's total language groups, they are spoken by only 10 per cent of the global population. At the centre of this galaxy today is English.

De Swaan's system is premised upon speakers who strive to become proficient in languages that will advance the success of their projects. Their actions create an overwhelmingly centripetal force, from periphery to centre. De Swaan estimates central languages to number around 200, while only a dozen languages qualify as supercentral (Arabic, Chinese, English, French, German, Hindi, Japanese, Malay, Portuguese, Russian, Spanish, Swahili) (de Swaan, 2020, p. 206). Speakers often skip a level of the language hierarchy to learn the global hyperlanguage, as soon as possible. Although the structure of this model is not descriptively controversial because it reflects statistical realities, the criteria for separating central from supercentral languages has provoked debate. Why, for instance, are Hindi and Japanese included but not Bengali and Korean?

Furthermore, the work of Johan Heilbron (1995, 1999) challenges the notion that the number of speakers of a languages should be the determiner of its centrality. He recognizes that international literary reputations are made or lost not through the relative size of an author's language community but through translation, that is, whether or not an author's work is exported. For Heilbron and Sapiro (2016), a language's centrality is reflected in its translation ledger: a language is more central when it exports more than it imports, when more books are translated out of it than into it. His notion of a world translation system reflects the market forces of global publishing rather than language learning, and it produces an image of geopolitical power relations that are even more asymmetrical than shown in De Swaan's model. An ever-increasing tide of books in English floods other language markets, within which English books are translated more than others, while an ever-diminishing number of foreign works are translated into the global hyperlanguage. Germain Barré's (2010) research into the 'world translation system' confirms de Swaan's portrait of the linguistic galaxy: if German and French have semi-central positions in the world translation system, all other languages languish in relative obscurity at the margins. Here, English is less the central sun that sustains life upon surrounding planets but 'a black hole devouring all languages that come within its reach' (de Swaan, 2010, p. 57).

Models of the global language or translation systems were introduced into the study of self-translation by Rainier Grutman (2009b, 2013). He drew particularly on De Swaan's notion of central-peripheral languages and Casanova's equation of dominating and dominated tongues when describing the prevailing 'verticality' of self-translation, its most common trajectory 'upwards' from dominated/peripheral languages and cultures to dominating/central ones. Self-translation that moves towards a global supercentral language he terms *supra-self-translation*, with inverse movement being *infra-self-translation* (Grutman, 2011). His research on language dynamics of the Iberian peninsula draws on the work of Santoyo (2005, 2010), Dasilva (2009, 2011), Manterola (2014) and others, describing a situation of near total *supra-self-translation*, where Galician, Basque or Catalan authors write in their regional tongue then self-translate into Castilian. Here, as elsewhere, *infra-self-translation* is extremely rare, while horizontal exchanges of self-translation between regional languages appear virtually non-existent (Grutman, 2016, p. 62). Furthermore, a self-translator's work may be classed as either *endogenous* when the bilingual author writes within a diglossic speech community (such as Latino self-translators in the United States) or *exogenous* when the author acquires bilingualism distinct from their speech community, surpassing the boundaries of that linguistic and cultural group (Grutman, 2013, p. 71). Grutman ties the verticality of the exchange to the question of the visibility of the translation and translator (Venuti, 1995). If the latter is the same person as the author, whose recognition increases the recognition of the (self-)translator, paradoxically this often comes at the expense of the translation's visibility, when the second version of a work is presented as an original with no, or only obscured, reference to its first version. Within the centralizing or vertical tropism that sees much self-translation move from more peripheral to more central languages, this occlusion reinforces the perception of the marginality of the first language's literary culture.

## 4.3 The Transparency of Self-Translation

The predominant verticality of self-translation means that this visibility of the 'translation' often reinforces the position of the dominating language at the expense of more fragile, marginal or dominated tongues. The situation can be stark in poetry translation, a genre that lends itself to bilingual editions with poems on facing pages. For commercial reasons, poets who write in a peripheral language and are proficient in a central language are often pressured by their publisher to produce bilingual editions. This has been said to have positive effects for the minority language, increasing its recognition for speakers of a dominating tongue, as Mark Gibeau (2013) finds in his study of Okinawan/Ryūkyūan-Japanese bilingual editions. Yet, for bilingual editions presenting Scots Gaelic and English poems, Corinna Krause (2013) argues that the presence of the dominating language means that the work in the minority language will only ever be perceived through the prism of the more powerful tongue, losing the particular qualities and unique coherence inherent to its first language expression. This, she argues, stymies the chance for the literary culture of the minority language to mature independently. For such reasons, the poet and novelist Christopher Whyte (2002, p. 67), who writes in Scots Gaelic, has said that 'self-translation has in my case always been done under duress. It has never been done with either pleasure or satisfaction.' These pressures exist for novelists also, as Manterola (2014) has documented in the case of Basque self-translators, whose publishers furthermore regularly present the self-translated novel as an 'original' when the paratexts neglect to communicate the existence of the work's minor-language predecessor.

Dasilva (2011) uses the metaphor of transparency when describing the degree to which a self-translated work is disclosed as such: if it is not clear from the physical work, its peritexts (cover, title and editorial pages) or its marketing that the work is a self-translation, it is defined as an 'opaque' or obscure self-translation – responsibility for which most often lies with the publishing house. The convention for transparent self-translation in English involves a declaration, usually a byline on the title page or the back cover, indicating that the work has been 'translated from [language] by the author', or a variant on this phrase. Importantly, this generates an expectation in the reader that the work is an accurate representation of its source, even though nothing prohibits an author from publishing an entirely new work under the same title as a previous text in a different language. Although this almost never occurs, it is common to find self-translation evoked ambiguously or not at all. Take the self-translated French edition of Camille Bordas's English novel *How to Behave in a Crowd*

(2017), entitled *Isidore et les autres* ([Isidore and the Others] 2018), which is marketed as a French novel and declared on the back cover to be 'écrit initialement en anglais par l'auteure' [first written in English by the author], circumventing the word 'translation' to affirm the independence of this version, and thus implying that the two works constitute a bilingual text of two equal parts, rather than an original and a translation. The back cover states that '*Isidore et les autres*, son troisième roman, a déjà été publié dans dix pays' [*Isidore et les autres*, her third novel, has already been published in ten countries], a claim apparently untroubled by the fact that it is *How to Behave in a Crowd* and not *Isidore et les autres* that has been published in ten countries. If publishers have commercial reasons to market their products as unique and original, self-translators have been known to claim an inverted order of composition for their texts, typically when establishing themselves as authors in a culture of greater literary prestige. One of the earliest documented cases of this was when the Spanish diplomat Martínez de la Rosa presented the French version of his 1830 *Aben Humeya* as the original, dissimulating the fact that he translated it from his original Spanish, a work now believed to be the first Spanish historical drama (Santoyo, 2006). An alternative strategy is pseudo-self-translation, when an author falsely presents their original as a self-translation, claiming that the work first emerged within a foreign culture, thus offering a (feigned) guarantee of the authenticity of its representation of a foreign subject (Santoyo, 2005, 2013a).

## 4.4 The Selves of Self-Translation: From Collaborative Self-Translation to Allograph Translation with Authorial Participation

The 'self' in the English term *self-translation* encourages reflection on the transformations of the individual during the writing process (Evangelista, 2013; Falceri, Gentes and Manterola, 2017). Collaborative self-translation, on the other hand, occurs when authors are the principal translators of their work but incorporate collaborators in their writing process. When the allograph (non-authorial) translator invites or is drawn to involve the author in his or her own translation, this comes under the umbrella of author–translator collaboration. In some cases, drawing a line between these two forms becomes complicated. Indeed, uncertainty about where allograph translation with authorial collaboration ends and authorial self-translation with collaboration begins has led collaborative self-translation to be considered a borderline case of self-translation (AUTOTRAD, 2007, p. 95). While collaborative self-translation might once have seemed a contradiction in terms, affirming at once the singular and the plural, more recently translation research has built upon literary scholarship that details how, throughout history, collaborative writing has routinely produced works attributed to a single author; this research debunks the Romantic ideal of authorship as solitary genius (Stillinger, 1991). Translation scholars have interrogated the assumption that translators should aspire to this model in order to achieve a comparable level of 'authority' over their text or to imbue it with their unique creativity (Cordingley and Frigau Manning, 2017b). Edited volumes have revealed the truly collaborative nature of myriad translations and self-translations attributed to one person only (Cordingley and Frigau Manning, 2017a; Hersant, 2020; Jansen and Wegener, 2013). The myth of literary authorship as inspired genius contributed to the long-held belief that the self-translator is a superlative case, redoubling this genius – early studies of Beckett (Fitch, 1988) or Nabokov (Grayson, 1977; Beaujour, 1989) establishing such prodigies as exemplars. Yet, as noted, research has shown the prevalence of self-translation in European languages since at least the Middle Ages, and the 'self' in self-translation need not imply a model of singular authorship; rather, self-translators, like other authors and translators, regularly work with peers (other writers, translators, editors), spouses and friends.

Definitions of this work have been discussed by Dasilva (2016, 2017), who argues that allograph translation with collaboration from the author should be excluded from what he terms 'semi-self-translation' (*semiauto-traducción*), the existence of which is confirmed by a single 'fundamental criterion', namely, the author's assumption of responsibility for the translation as witnessed in the paratexts (epitexts and peritexts). Yet, for as long as self-translation has been researched, inconsistencies have been discovered in such information. Indeed, not only do peritexts regularly misrepresent the reality of authorship, publishers often distort or occlude the true nature of a work's collaborative genesis (Manterola, 2013, p. 63, 2017; Anokhina, 2019, pp. 99–101). Manterola (2017) surveys the unstable terminology around collaborative self-translation and discusses a number of cases before concluding that there are as many potential configurations of collaboration as there are combinations of individuals participating. The study of collaborative self-translation has focused mainly on prominent authors, such as Beckett, Eco, Eliot, Nabokov and Ungaretti, while the only region where this phenomenon has received concerted attention is the Iberian peninsula, where texts almost always ascend vertically, from a minority to the majority tongue (Castilian or Portuguese).

Dasilva (2016, p. 26) identifies the most common forms of authorial collaboration on the rewriting of their work as: self-translation in *colla-boration with* an allograph translator, a relative or a spouse; self-translation that is *revised by* these parties; or allograph translation by any of these parties that is *revised by* the author. Belobarodova, Van Hulle and Verhulst (2021) use manuscripts, letters and other archival evidence to show that such categories may evolve over the course of a translation, with parties taking different degrees of responsibility for the translation at different times. Focusing on the work of Samuel Beckett, for whom manuscript evidence for some texts attests to how the collaborations unfolded, they show that the process often changed from one of allograph translation with the author's participation to one where the author took control, the translation becoming one best characterized as self-translation with assistance from an allograph translator, or self-translation *tout court*. Belobarodova, Van Hulle and Verhulst (2021) emphasize that the different forms of collaboration within the process of self-translation challenge any single categorization of the work. Indeed, it is not uncommon for self-translators to engage someone else to make a draft translation, often literal, of their work, which they use as a base from which to revise or rewrite their new version. Furthermore, complex discourses of power on the macro and micro levels intersect during the act of self-translation (Castro, Mainer and Skomorokhova, 2017).

## 4.5  Eurocentrism in Self-Translation Studies

Appeals have been made to internationalize or adopt a less 'Eurocentric' approach to the study of translation (Chan, 2004; Cheung, 2005, 2009; Hermans, 2006; Hung and Wakabayashi, 2005; Ricci and van der Putten, 2011; Rose, 2000; Susam-Sarajeva, 2002, 2017; Tymoczko, 2007; Wakabayashi and Kothari, 2009). However, some have challenged the very notion of Eurocentricism as a reductive generalization that homogenizes cultural difference and power differentials within this geographic region (Cronin, 1995, pp. 85–6; Flynn and van Doorslaer, 2011, p. 116; Delabastita, 2011, p. 154). Furthermore, Nam Fung Chang (2015) has offered a poignant critique of the patronizing claims, the contradictions and the cultural misrecognition on the part of many anti-Eurocentric Western scholars who claim to speak for those they believe to be oppressed by Western translation theory. And if the verticality or centrifugal dynamics of self-translation often lead it to gravitate towards one of the more 'central' languages spoken in Europe, this has engendered an inevitable Eurocentrism in the early days of self-translation studies itself, when scholars based in the West began to document the practice. Yet there is a need to look beyond this paradigm to discern revealing, if less typical, cases where self-translation does not conform to the pull towards the world's 'supercentral languages' but moves between or even towards peripheral languages, or is practised by globalized, de-territorialized authors who traverse geographic and cultural boundaries confounding any sense of a work's clearly defined trajectory from an imagined East to a notional West, or vice versa.

　　If knowledge of literary self-translation has vastly increased in recent times, a topographical survey of literary self-translation produces something resembling an early-colonial-era map of the world: certain areas of the globe are coloured by European occupation while others have only recently been sketched, and vast territories are left blank. Volumes have been written about hotspots of self-translation in Europe, notably the Iberian Peninsula (Dasilva, 2009; Gallén, Lafarga and Pegenaute, 2011; Manterola, 2014; Gallén and Ruiz Casanova, 2018), Italy (Rubio Árquez and D'Antuono, 2012) and France (Hokenson and Munson, 2007; Kippur, 2015; Puccini, 2015); surveys have been made of self-translation in Canada (Van Bolderen, 2014, 2021) and the Francophone world (Grutman, 2015, 2017); and attention has widened to Eastern Europe and the former Russian empire (Foscolo and Smorag-Goldberg, 2019), as well as Latin America (Bujaldón de Esteves, Bistué and Stocco, 2019). Many articles discuss self-translators from African nations and Central, East and South-East Asia, yet these regions are heavily under-represented in self-translation research, and only initial steps have been made to give a panoramic view of self-translation in each region. Research needs to take into account self-translation at different levels – local, regional, international – and consider the cultural and sociopolitical discourses that shape texts at each of these junctions.

Crucially, research into self-translation has not given a clear picture of its prevalence across regions of the world such as Africa, the Middle East, Asia and South-East Asia. The case of self-translation involving the Chinese language is a case in point. Martha Cheung (2005, p. 39) has argued that 'if Translation Studies is to break out of the cognitive boundaries set by Eurocentric views, or Sinocentric views, or, for that matter, any ossified views, what is needed is not just a new mindset but more material for study and for comparison'. The *Bibliography on Self-Translation* (Gentes, 2020) contains roughly one-fifth of the number of articles addressing self-translation in Chinese found in the China National Knowledge Infrastructure (CNKI) database, the most comprehensive database of research articles published in Chinese, the Airiti Chinese-language database and the Taiwan Citation Index, which identifies relevant work published in Taiwan. Relatively few titles on Chinese-language self-translation have been communicated by researchers to the editor of the collaborative *Bibliography on Self-Translation*, and this research is not registered in general discussions of self-translation published in English-language handbooks or encyclopaediae (e.g., Anselmi, 2012; Cordingley, 2019; Grutman, 2009a (2nd ed. 2019), 2019; Grutman and Van Bolderen, 2014; Montini, 2012). There is a wealth of material on the celebrated Chinese-language self-translator Eileen Chang (Zhang Ailing), and other Chinese-language self-translators have attracted attention, particularly Republican-era self-translators such as Dai Wangshu, Hsiung Shih-I (Xiong Shiyi), Liang Zongdai, Bian Shilin and Lin Yutang, who, like Chang, spent significant amounts of time abroad. While regions such as Singapore (e.g., Lee, 2013) or groups of diasporic writers (Tsu, 2011) have received attention, there has been little effort by translation researchers to offer a comprehensive account of the phenomenon across the Chinese language or within any one Chinese-speaking region. It is unfortunate that one of the earliest general discussions of self-translation published in English, Joseph Shiu-ming Lau's (1995) entry in the *Encyclopaedia of Translation: Chinese–English / English–Chinese Translation*, has been overlooked by researchers writing in European languages for it discusses the practice of self-translation through a sketch of its history in Chinese. Eurocentrism in current research is by no means restricted to Chinese, for inroads need to be made to understand the specific dynamics of the practice in cultures using, for example, Arabic, Persian, Korean, Hebrew, Russian, Hindi, Swahili, Japanese and Indonesian. By gaining a deeper understanding of cases beyond the cultures or languages of Europe, self-translation research will better understand how variable degrees of cultural and linguistic proximity influence the choices that self-translators make, including the collaborations they form to achieve their goals.

## 4.6  World Literature and Questions of Narratology

Self-translation has emerged as a topic within world literature studies, a branch of literary criticism conducted mostly in English, which focuses on literature from parts of the world whose cultures are less visible to Western audiences because they have been overlooked by media and education curricula. World literature is largely a pedagogical construction, a category used within the academy to group texts outside the canon, from neglected, marginalized or dominated cultures. Proponents of world literature studies argue that diversifying the canon gives students a wider perspective on literary forms and challenges the outdated monolingual paradigm inherited from literature departments structured around national languages. Its critics bemoan the teaching of the 'world' through (English) translation, unlike teaching in comparative literature programmes, which require the learning of foreign languages and a more sustained, deeper engagement with cultural difference. Critics claim that exposing students to the world's cultures through translation pays lip service to cultures dominated by hegemonic (anglophone) economies, offering little to change the status quo (Apter, 2013).

Intervening in these debates, Rebecca Walkowitz (2015) conceptualizes 'world literature' aesthetics and market dynamics as 'self-translation', a version of what she terms 'born translated' literature. This is literature that has the qualities of a translation because the language of expression does not correspond with the language being spoken by characters in the text or is endemic to its setting or geographic location, or because the original text enters the global market contemporaneous with, or even after, its translation. Born translated works foreground translation as a theme and 'bring circulation into view' (Walkowitz, 2015, p. 31). Walkowitz employs 'self-translation' as a synonym for 'born translated' literature when she writes that 'self-translation involves pretending to write fiction in another tongue ...; presenting English-language works as translations of some other language, some other version of language, or some other medium ...; reflecting on English literature's debts to other languages and literary traditions ...; and inviting translators to regard themselves as authors and collaborators ...' (Walkowitz, 2015, p. 22). She argues that J. M. Coetzee's novel *Childhood of Jesus* is a self-translation because it 'pretends' to be written in a foreign tongue. This work's omniscient narrator describes action that occurs in an unlocated hispanophone context, and Walkowitz believes that this narrator is therefore acting like a self-translator. This raises questions of narratology, because either the reader knows that the voice belongs to a fictional narrator and assumes this narrator to be inventing dialogues in English (so he is not self-translating but inventing) or the reader suspends disbelief and imagines the narrator to be witnessing the action he describes (the narrator is a translator of foreign scenes and dialogues). For the reader to imagine that the narrator is both creating and translating, the reader would have to believe that the narrator is engaging in what is known as 'cognitive' or 'mental' self-translation (translating a discourse that exists in the mind). This, however, requires the reader to doubt the authenticity of the narrator: they would not suspend disbelief and assume the narrator to be an impartial commentator on the action; rather they would believe him to be metanarrator, a character of the text who invents the text and brings his composition to the foreground. Prototypically, the narrators of Samuel Beckett's novels exploit such bilingualism within their aesthetic of self-translation; Coetzee's narrator, however, does not, and there is no reason to imagine that he is anything other than an inventor of his narrative in English or the omniscient translator of scenes that exist independently of him. A greater obstacle to Walkowitz's theory is that, although Coetzee can read Spanish, he is not bilingual in Spanish to the degree that would allow him to be conducting cognitive self-translation, transferring this quality to his narrator. But, keeping the author aside, Walkowitz's model implies multilingual composition with a number of key premises. She assumes that for a bilingual Spanish-English author or narrator to compose in English a scene that occurs in Spanish involves an act of self-translation. This is a very monolingual view of bilingual consciousness; it implies that when a person moves between language contexts, s/he necessarily engages in a form of cognitive self-translation. However, sociolinguistic studies show that the inner speech of bilinguals adapts to context in a way that is commonly unconscious (Pavlenko, 2014, p. 211). Walkowitz's idea rests on her assumption that the narrator conducts inner speech in Spanish which he translates into English. Yet, research testifies that inner speech is subvocal talk that is primarily self-directed and occurs in an identifiable language code; it is not conscious translation or literary narration (Pavlenko, 2014, ch. 6). We have no way of knowing the relationship between the inner voice and the narrative voice of Coetzee's narrator, which, if he were a person, would be a unique equation among L1, L2 and other languages, his experience, education, duration of residence and immersion in a foreign language, personality and other factors. It is furthermore uncertain that Coetzee's narrator experiences multilingual consciousness in the way a human does, especially given that Coetzee himself is not bilingual in Spanish. But if the narrator stands metaphorically for a *self in translation*, he may represent a cultural mediator, not a textual translator. He may be said to be a metaphorical translator, but making him a self-translator weakens the metaphorical force of self-translation as a specific metaphor; it also means that vast quantities of literature would need to be incorporated into self-translation studies, including potentially every instance of travel writing where the author or narrator understands or learns the foreign language. Every Gulliver a self-translator!

Walkowitz (2015, p. 22) argues that J. M. Coetzee's *Childhood of Jesus* is 'self-translated from the perspective of book history' because it was published in Dutch translation before the English edition. There is no proof that this is an authorial strategy, though a sticker on the Dutch language edition claims it to be the first published edition. When a translation arrogates the place of an original, it is usually because it has gained status by moving into a literary language of greater currency. Coetzee's English *Childhood* will, however, always be regarded as the original; its composition in the global hyperlanguage will never be mistaken. To suggest that the English version is a 'self-translation' from the Dutch original in terms of book history occludes the painstaking labour of its translator, Peter Bergsma (Walkowitz does not discuss him). Certainly, Bergsma will never be taken for the author of *Childhood of Jesus*, and this definition of 'self-translation' appears to override the translator's agency and this Dutch translator's specific language choices and strategies. On the other hand, scholars of self-translation have unearthed a plethora of examples when a self-translation is published before the first version, and in literary translation studies and comparative literature studies there is a substantial body of work that discusses and theorizes the fictional representation of translation, from Beebee's discussion of 'transmesis', which explores 'the mimetic treatment of those "black-box" aspects of the translational process' in literature, and 'the question of how to represent multilingual realities in literature' (Beebee, 2012, p. 3), to studies of metafictional and metalinguistic multilingual texts (Delabastita, 2009; Delabastita and Grutman, 2005), to the ever-expanding corpus of studies of 'transfiction', writing that thematizes translation (for an overview, see Kaindl, 2014, 2018).

Walkowitz's idea of a self-translation is oriented more towards fiction as 'global literature' than 'world literature', and a work that is perhaps more suitable to the spirit of her research is Camille Bordas's *How To*

*Behave in a Crowd*, mentioned in Section 4.3. This novel, written by a young French author in English, but set in France, was published in 2017; her French translation appeared the following year. The novel's adolescent narrator, Isidore, gives a droll account of growing up in provincial France surrounded by overachieving siblings in a dysfunctional family. Yet his diction is disorientating because it is so heavily inflected with North American idioms and slang. From the very first page, when he refers to his penis as a 'wang' (p. 3), the reader experiences scenes of life in France through a North American filter. Some adaptation for comprehension is understandable; for instance, when a neighbour traverses metric frontiers, cooking her 'three pound' roast at 'three hundred and fifty degrees' (Bordas, 2017, p. 37). Yet many elements of the book have been localized; for instance, Isidore's public school has lockers (unlike French schools), the 'grades' correspond to the American system, and in an emergency he calls 911 (in France the numbers are 15, 17, 18 or 112).

Crucially, the narrator is a character in the events he describes, and his voice is diegetic, albeit in the form of memoir. His English expression of those memories may be said to be self-translation in that he engages in cognitive or mental self-translation when rendering his immaterial text of past experience, lived in French, into English. His process parallels that of the author, for the genesis of *How to Behave in a Crowd* began when, struggling with another work and living in the Unites States, Bordas decided to translate the debut of a work she had written in French, the story of Isidore, which amounted to no more than three or four pages. Once she had finished translating these pages into English she simply continued the story. Having arrived in the United States only a few years before and writing in a language she only began to master as a young adult, she sought the help of her American partner to revise her expression; she finished the novel, sent to it her publisher, and embarked on its French version two or three years later (Bordas, 2020). In France, the work of translators of American literature is commonly, and bafflingly, credited on the title page as 'Traduit de l'Américan', as if American were a language. *How to Behave in a Crowd*, on the other hand, can plausibly be said to have been 'Translated into American' (from the unknowable mental text of its French author). The narrator of *Isidore et les autres* appears, on the contrary, to be nothing other than a French boy expressing in French his memories of growing up in France. He would never be considered a self-translator were it not for the fact that the bibliographical history of his narrative begins with his English version.

If the chronology and the editorial description of the French edition suggest that the two versions constitute a bilingual text, the two books circulate in the global marketplace with near identical design (see Figures 4.1 and 4.2). The French version reproduces almost exactly the cover of the English text, albeit with the French title. This is not

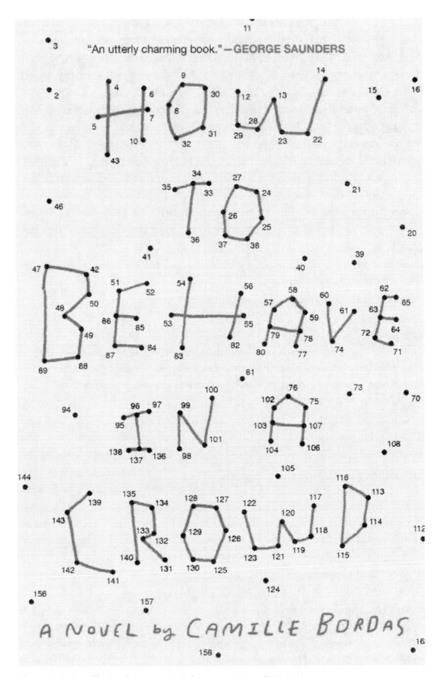

**Figure 4.1** Camille Bordas, *How to Behave in a Crowd* (2017)

uncommon when the same publishing house publishes a self-translated work in different languages (common in Spain), yet it is rare to see such similitude corroborated between two different publishers. These factors heighten the sense of a work that is 'born translated', for not only does the

**Figure 4.2** Camille Bordas, *Isidore et les autres* (2018)

English original read like a domesticated translation from French, but the material qualities of both editions reinforce the sense that they are localized versions of the same product.

## References

Anokhina, O. (2019). Cas limites d'autotraduction: cercle, spirale, chaos. In E. Hartmann and P. Hersant, eds., *Au miroir de la traduction: avant-texte, intratexte, paratexte*. Paris: Éditions des Archives Contemporaines, pp. 97–109.

Anselmi, S. (2012). *On Self-Translation: An Exploration in Self-Translators' Teloi and Strategies*. Milan: LED Edizioni Universitarie.

Apter, E. (2013). *Against World Literature: On the Politics of Untranslatability*. London: Verso.

AUTOTRAD. (2007). L'autotraduction littéraire comme domaine de recherche. *Atelier de traduction* **7**, 91–100.

Barré, G. (2010). La 'mondialisation' de la culture et la question de la diversité culturelle: étude des flux mondiaux de traductions entre 1979 et 2002. *Revista Hispana para el Análisis de Redes Sociales*, **18**(8), 183–217.

Bassnett, S. (2013). The self-translator as rewriter. In A. Cordingley, ed., *Self-Translation: Brokering Originality in Hybrid Culture*. London: Continuum, pp. 13–25.

Beaujour, E. K. (1989). *Alien Tongues: Bilingual Russian Writers of the 'First' Emigration*. Ithaca, NY: Cornell University Press.

Beebee, T. O. (2012). Transmesis: Inside Translation's Black Box. New York: Palgrave Macmillan.

Belobarodova, O., Van Hulle, D., and Verhulst, P. (2021). Reconstructing collaborative (self)translations from the archive: The case of Samuel Beckett. *Meta*, **66**(1).

Bordas, C. (2017). *How to Behave in a Crowd*. New York: Tim Duggan Books.

Bordas, C. (2018). *Isidore et les autres*. Paris: Editions incultes.

Bordas, C. (2020). Unpublished email interview with Anthony Cordingley (8 March).

Bujaldón de Esteves, L., Bistué, B., and Stocco, M., eds. (2019). *Literary Self-Translation in Hispanophone Contexts: La autotraducción literaria en contextos de habla hispana*. Cham, Switzerland: Palgrave Macmillan.

Calvet, L.-J. (1999). *Pour une écologie des langues du monde*. Paris: Pion.

Casanova, P. (1999). *La République mondiale des Lettres*. Paris: Seuil.

Casanova, P. (2004 [1999]). *The World Republic of Letters*, trans. Malcolm DeBevoise. Cambridge, MA: Harvard University Press.

Castro, O., Mainer, S., and Skomorokhova, S., eds. (2017). *Self-Translation and Power: Negotiating Identities in Multilingual European Contexts*. London: Palgrave Macmillan.

Chan, L. T.-h. (2004). *Twentieth-Century Chinese Translation Theory: Modes, Issues and Debates*. Amsterdam: John Benjamins.

Chang, N. F. (2015). Does 'translation' reflect a narrower concept than 'fanyi'? On the impact of Western theories on China and the concern about Eurocentrism. *Translation and Interpreting Studies*, **10**(2), 223–42.

Cheung, M. (2005). 'To translate' means 'to exchange'? A new interpretation of the earliest Chinese attempts to define translation ('fanyi'). *Target*, **17**(1), 27–48.

Cheung, M., ed. (2009). *Chinese Discourses on Translation: Positions and Perspectives*. Special issue of *The Translator*, 15(2).

Cordingley, A. (2019). Self-translation. In K. Washbourne and B. Van Wyke, eds., *Routledge Handbook of Literary Translation*. Oxford: Routledge, pp. 352–68.

Cordingley, A., and Frigau Manning, C., eds. (2017a). *Collaborative Translation: From the Renaissance to the Digital Age*. London: Bloomsbury.

Cordingley, A., and Frigau Manning, C. (2017b). What is collaborative translation? In A. Cordingley and C. Frigau Manning, eds., *Collaborative Translation: From the Renaissance to the Digital Age*. London: Bloomsbury, pp. 1–30.

Cronin, M. (1995). Altered states: Translation and minority languages. *TTR*, **8**(1), 85–103.

Dasilva, X. M. (2009). Autotraducirse en Galicia: ¿bilingüismo o diglosia? *Quaderns: Revista de Traducció*, **16**, 143–56.

Dasilva, X. M. (2011). La autotraducción transparente y las autotraducción opaca. In X. M. Dasilva and H. Tanqueiro, eds., *Aproximaciones a la autotraducción*. Vigo: Academia del Hispanismo, pp. 45–67.

Dasilva, X. M. (2016). En torno al concepto de semiautotraducción. *Quaderns: Revista de Traducció*, **23**, 15–35.

Dasilva, X. M. (2017). A semiautotradução: modalidade e variantes. *Cadernos de Tradução*, **37**(2), 229–44.

Delabastita, D. (2009). Fictional representations. In M. Baker and G. Saldanha, eds., *Routledge Encyclopedia of Translation Studies*. London: Routledge, pp. 109–12.

Delabastita, D. (2011). Continentalism and the invention of traditions in translation studies. *Translation and Interpreting Studies*, **6**(2), 142–56.

Delabastita, D., and Grutman, R. (2005). Introduction: Fictional representations of multilingualism and translation. In D. Delabastita and R. Grutman, eds., *Fictionalising Translation and Multilingualism*, special issue of *Linguistica Antverpiensia*, 4, 11–34.

De Swaan, A. (2001). *Words of the World: The Global Language System*. Cambridge: Polity Press.

De Swaan, A. (2010). Language systems. In N. Coupland, ed., *The Handbook of Language and Globalization*. Malden, MA: Wiley-Blackwell, pp. 69–89.

De Swaan, A. (2020). The unequal exchange of texts in the world language system. In C. B. Vigouroux and S. S. Mufwene, eds., *Bridging Linguistics and Economics*. Cambridge: Cambridge University Press, pp. 203–23.

Evangelista, E.-M. (2013). Writing in translation: A new self in a second language. In A. Cordingley, ed., *Self-Translation: Brokering Originality in Hybrid Culture*. London: Continuum, pp. 177–87.

Falceri, G., Gentes, E., and Manterola, E., eds. (2017). *Narrating the Self in Self-Translation*. Special issue of *Ticontre*, **7**.

Fitch, B. T. (1988). *Beckett and Babel: An Investigation into the State of the Bilingual Work*. Toronto: University of Toronto Press.

Flynn, P., and van Doorslaer, L. (2011). On constructing continental views on translation studies: An introduction. *Translation and Interpreting Studies*, **6**(2), 113–20.

Foscolo, A. L., and Smorag-Goldberg, M., eds. (2019). *Plurilinguisme et auto-traduction. Langue perdue, langue 'sauvée.'* Paris: Eur'Orbem.

Gallén, E., Lafarga, F., and Pegenaute, L., eds. (2011). *Traducción y autotraducción en las literaturas ibéricas*. Bern: Peter Lang.

Gallén, E., and Ruiz Casanova, J. F., eds. (2018). *Bilingüisme, autotraducció i literatura catalana*. Lleida: Punctum.

Gibeau, M. (2013). Indigenization and opacity: Self-translation in the Okinawan/Ryukyuan writings of Takara Ben and Medoruma Shun. In A. Cordingley, ed., *Self-Translation: Brokering Originality in Hybrid Culture*. London: Continuum, pp. 141–55.

Gentes, E. (2017). *(Un-)Sichtbarkeit der literarischen Selbstübersetzung in der romanischsprachigen Gegenwartsliteratur. Eine literatur- und übersetzungs-soziologische Annäherung*. Heinrich-Heine-Universität Düsseldorf. https://docserv.uni-duesseldorf.de/servlets/DerivateServlet/Derivate-45333/Gentes_Dissertation.lit_Selbst%C3%BCbersetzung.pdf.

Gentes, E. (2020). Bibliography: Autotraduzione/autotraducción/self-translation, XXXVIII ed. www.self-translation.blogspot.com.

Grayson, J. (1977). *Nabokov Translated: A Comparison of Nabokov's Russian and English Prose*. Oxford: Oxford University Press.

Grutman, R. (2009a). Self-translation. In M. Baker and G. Saldanha, eds., *Routledge Encyclopedia of Translation Studies*. 2nd ed. London: Routledge, pp. 257–60; (2019). 3rd ed. London: Routledge, pp. 514–18.

Grutman, R. (2009b). La autotraducción en la galaxia de las lenguas. *Quaderns: Revista de Traducció*, **16**, 123–34. http://ddd.uab.cat/pub/quaderns/11385790n16p123-2.pdf.

Grutman, R. (2011). Diglosia y autotraducción 'vertical' (en y fuera de España). In X. M. Dasilva and H. Tanqueiro, eds., *Aproximaciones a la autotraducción*. Vigo: Academia del Hispanismo, pp. 69–91.

Grutman, R. (2013). A sociological glance at self-translation and self-translators. In A. Cordingley, ed., *Self-Translation: Brokering Originality in Hybrid Culture*. London: Bloomsbury, pp. 63–80.

Grutman, R., and Van Bolderen, T. (2014). Self-translation. In S. Bermann and C. Porter, eds., *A Companion to Translation Studies*. West Sussex: Wiley-Blackwell, pp. 323–32.

Grutman, R. (2015). Francophonie et autotraduction. *Interfrancophonies*, **6**, 1–17.

Grutman, R. (2016). L'autotraduction, de la galerie de portraits à la galaxie des langues. In A. Ferraro and R. Grutman, eds., *L'autotraduction littéraire: perspectives théoriques*. Paris: Classiques Garnier, pp. 39–63.

Grutman, R. (2017). Babel in (spite of) Belgium: Patterns of self-translation in a bilingual country. In O. Castro, S. Mainer and S. Skomorokhova, eds.,

*Self-Translation and Power: Negotiating Identities in Multilingual European Contexts*. London: Palgrave Macmillan, pp. 25–49.

Heilbron, J. (1995). Mondialsering en transnationaal cultureel verkeer. *Amsterdams Sociologisch Tijdschrift*, **22**(1), 162–80.

Heilbron, J. (1999). Towards a sociology of translation: Book translations as a cultural world-system. *European Journal of Social Theory*, **2**(4), 429–44.

Heilbron, J., and Sapiro, G. (2016). Translation: Economic and sociological perspectives. In V. Ginsburg and S. Weber, eds., *The Palgrave Handbook of Economics and Language*. New York: Palgrave Macmillan.

Hermans, T., ed. (2006). *Translating Others*. 2 vols. Manchester: St Jerome.

Hersant, P., ed. (2020). *Traduire avec l'auteur*. Paris: Sorbonne Université Presses.

Hokenson, J., and Munson, M. (2007). *The Bilingual Text: History and Theory of Literary Self-Translation*. Manchester: St Jerome.

Hung, E., and Wakabayashi, J., eds. (2005). *Asian Translation Traditions*. Manchester: St Jerome.

Jansen, H., and Wegener, A., eds. (2013). *Authorial and Editorial Voices in Translation 1: Collaborative Relationships between Authors, Translators and Performers*. Montréal: Éditions québécoises de l'oeuvre.

Kaindl, K. (2014). Going fictional! Translators and interpreters in literature and film: An introduction. In K. Kaindl and K. Spitzl, eds., *Transfiction: Research into the Realities of Translation Fiction*. Amsterdam: John Benjamins, pp. 1–26.

Kaindl, K. (2018). Fictional representations. In L. D'hulst and Y. Gambier, eds., *A History of Modern Translation Knowledge*. Amsterdam: John Benjamins, pp. 51–6.

Kippur, S. (2015). *Writing It Twice: Self-Translation and the Making of a World Literature in French*. Evanston, IL: Northwestern University Press.

Krause, C. (2013). 'Why bother with the original?': Self-translation and Scottish Gaelic poetry. In A. Cordingley, ed., *Self-Translation: Brokering Originality in Hybrid Culture*. London: Continuum, pp. 127–40.

Lau, J. S.-m. (1995). Self-translation: Author as translator. In Chan S.-w. and D. E. Pollard, eds., *Encyclopaedia of Translation: Chinese–English/English–Chinese Translation*. Hong Kong: Chinese University Press, pp. 949–59.

Lee, T.-K. (2013). Translating anglophobia: Tensions and paradoxes of biliterate performances in Singapore. *Target: International Journal of Translation Studies*, **25**(2), 228–51.

López López-Gay, P. (2006). Lieu du sens dans l'(auto)traduction littéraire. In M. Lederer, ed., *Le sens en traduction*. Paris-Caen: Lettres Modernes Minard, pp. 215–23.

Manterola, E. (2011). La autotraducción en la literatura vasca. In X. M. Dasilva and H. Tanqueiro, eds., *Aproximaciones a la autotraducción*. Vigo: Academia del Hispanismo, pp. 111–40.

Manterola Agirrezabalaga, E. (2014). *Literatura vasca traducida*. Bern: Peter Lang.

Manterola Agirrezabalaga, E. (2015). La autotraducción en el contexto vasco: entre distancia interlingüística y la constitución de un campo literario nacional transfronterizo. *Glottopol*, **25**, 71–87.

Manterola Agirrezabalaga, E. (2017). Collaborative self-translation in a minority language: Power implications in the process, the actors and the literary systems involved. In O. Castro, S. Mainer and S. Skomorokhova, eds., *Self-Translation and Power: Negotiating Identities in Multilingual European Contexts*. London: Palgrave Macmillan, pp. 191–215.

Montini, Chiara. (2012). Self-translation. In Yves Gambier and Luc van Doorslaer, eds., *Handbook of Translation Studies*. Amsterdam: John Benjamins, pp. 306–8.

Oustinoff, M. (2001). *Bilinguisme d'écriture et auto–traduction: Julien Green, Samuel Beckett, Vladimir Nabokov*. Paris: L'Harmattan.

Pavlenko, A. (2014). *The Bilingual Mind and What It Tells Us about Language and Thought*. Cambridge: Cambridge University Press.

Puccini, P., ed. (2015). Regards croisés autour de l'autotraduction. Special issue of *Interfrancophonies*, **6**.

Recuenco Peñalver, M. (2011). Más allá de la traducción: La autotraducción. *Trans*, **15**, 193–208.

Ricci, R., and van der Putten, J., eds. (2011). *Translation in Asia: Theories, Practices, Histories*. Manchester: St Jerome.

Rose, M. G., ed. (2000). *Beyond the Western Tradition*. Binghamton: State University of New York Binghamton, Centre for Research in Translation.

Rubio Árquez, M., and D'Antuono, N., eds. (2012). *Autotraduzione. Teoria ed esempi fra Italia e Spagna (e oltre)*. Milano: LED dizioni Universitarie di Lettere Economia Diritto.

Santoyo, J.–C. (2005). Autotraducciones: Una perspectiva histórica. *Meta*, **50**(3), 858–67.

Santoyo, J.–C. (2006). Francisco Martínez de la Rosa, autor y traductor: Nueva visita a *Aben Humeya*. In F. Lafarga and L. Pegenaute, eds., *Traducción y traductores: Del Romanticismo al Realismo*. Bern/New York: Peter Lang, pp. 463–88.

Santoyo, J.–C. (2010). Autotraducciones intrapeninsulares: Motivos históricos, razones actuales. In E. Gallén, F. Lafarga and L. Pegenaute, eds., *Traducción y autotraducción en las literaturas ibéricas*. Bern: Peter Lang, pp. 365–80.

Santoyo, J.–C. (2013a). On mirrors, dynamics and self-translations. In A. Cordingley, ed., *Self-Translation: Brokering Originality in Hybrid Culture*. London: Continuum, pp. 27–38.

Santoyo, J.–C. (2013b). Autotraducción: ensayo de tipología. In P. Martino Alba, J. A. Albaladejo Martínez and M. Pulido, eds., *Al humanista, traductor y maestro Miguel Ángel Vega Cernuda*. Madrid: Dykinson, D.L., pp. 205–21.

Stillinger, J. (1991). *Multiple Authorship and the Myth of Solitary Genius*. Oxford: Oxford University Press.

Susam-Sarajeva, Ş. (2002). A 'multilingual' and 'international' translation studies? In T. Hermans, ed., *Crosscultural Transgressions: Research Models in Translation Studies II. Historical and Ideological Issues*. Manchester: St Jerome, pp. 193–207.

Susam-Sarajeva, Ş. (2017). In search of an 'international translation studies': Tracing *terceme* and *tercüme* in the blogosphere. *Translation Studies*, **10**(1), 69–86.

Tsu, J. (2011). *Sound and Script in Chinese Diaspora*. Cambridge, MA: Harvard University Press.

Tymoczko, M. (2007). *Enlarging Translation, Empowering Translators*. Manchester: St Jerome.

Van Bolderen, T. (2014). Huston, we have a problem . . .: (or what on earth is 'Canadian self-translation' supposed to mean?). *Tradução em Revista*, **16**, 83–94.

Van Bolderen, T. (2021). Literary self-translation and self-translators in Canada (1971–2016): A large-scale study. PhD dissertation. University of Ottawa. http://dx.doi.org/10.20381/ruor-26966.

Venuti, L. (1995). *The Translator's Invisibility: A History of Translation*. London: Routledge.

Wakabayashi, J., and Kothari, R., eds. (2009). *Decentering Translation Studies: India and Beyond*. Amsterdam: John Benjamins.

Walkowitz, R. L. (2015). *Born Translated: The Contemporary Novel in an Age of World Literature*. New York: Columbia University Press.

Whyte, C. (2002). Against self-translation. *Translation and Literature*, **11**(1), 64–71.

# 5

# Translated Text

Bergljot Behrens

## 5.1  Introduction: Translation in Society

Translation is of utmost importance for international communication and for the spread of knowledge and thought across cultures. In fact, it is fair to claim that no society can function smoothly without translation as an integral part of political, economic and cultural understanding across borders. Most people learn about world leaders' opinions through the way they are paraphrased in translation. We read instruction manuals in our native language versions. Readers of any foreign language author's work often receive the texts in a translated version. Translation is everywhere: in the press, in official documents, in police reports, in marketing as well as in everyday spoken discourse in multilingual environments.

So how do these texts come about and what characterizes them?

Formulaic texts in translation (e.g., weather forecasts) are pretty well taken care of by machine translation systems, and such systems can give the reader a hint of what almost any text is about, provided the terminology in the relevant language pair is available in the system. Yet anyone testing such systems on a piece of prose experiences amusing, if not frustrating, inadequacies, highlighting that human translators' sensitivity to fine-tuned meaning distinctions, morphology and syntax is still required for successful cross-linguistic understanding.

News from the world around us is often forwarded through target language paraphrases, in the words of the reporter. Interpreters rephrase utterances in real time in intercultural encounters. Written translations, however, often go through a reviewing process. Editors and copy-editors read the translator's draft, suggest amendments and correct spellings and other perceived errors.

The properties of translated text considered in this chapter are restricted to features of edited translations, texts we expect to be the result of well-founded premeditated choices. The chapter discusses the nature of translated text from a monolingual and a cross-linguistic perspective. Examples are offered to illuminate aspects of translated text and the concepts used to classify them. Section 5.2 describes general characteristics of translated text and Section 5.3 how the purpose of a translated text affects its wording. Section 5.4 discusses norm-governed aspects of translation products, in view of their sources as well as in comparison with first-written (original) text in the target language. It is divided into four subsections, each focusing on different aspects of norms. Section 5.5 considers the translator's and the author's impact on the final translation product, while Section 5.6 focuses on two translation strategies, foreignization and domestication, and applies this distinction to examples from multi-translations of literary canonical texts. Section 5.7 concludes the chapter, with a comment on translation universals.

## 5.2   The Characteristics of Translation

We know that every reader supplies any text with context triggered by the expressions used, and infers meanings from the propositions expressed, so the interpretation will depend on the reader to some extent. The translator is a reader who does their best to transfer to new readers the meanings they believe are intended by the author. It is usually expected that the words, phrases and sentences chosen for the target text have the potential to create in the target readership the same references, the same underlying senses, with the sensibilities and the sensitivities given access to by the original text, in its own linguistic and extra-linguistic context. This demands a fine-tuned awareness of lexical nuances, modality, idioms, syntax and discourse of both (or all) the languages involved, as well as the ability to identify with and access a multitude of registers.

A translation differs from other writings in that it is meant to communicate what somebody else has said or written. This is to be understood not as indirect speech or true paraphrase but as text transferred from one language into another 'on behalf of' the author of the original text. The author of the first-written text generally remains the author of the translation.

Putting into words what somebody else has already put into words and doing so in such a way as to produce a text whose authorship remains somebody else's carries with it significant responsibility. The translator pays service to the author, yet the translation has to meet the requirements of the target language and the target audience. While authors may not have a special readership in mind when they create their texts, translators will always have the target language readership in mind.

Furthermore, they may need to take the specific views and policies of their commissioners into account.

Target language requirements trigger syntactic and lexical changes in the rendering of the text. Responsibility towards the target audience motivates the translator to adapt formulations to make the text a good read. The translation must be idiomatically and stylistically adequate and acceptable, meaning that, often, the choice of syntax and lexis deviates from the closest possible form. A word-by-word translation, which may be used in a foreign language learning environment, is most often a less felicitous choice when communicating the source text message in the target language.

In ancient Rome, Cicero (106–43 BC) was perhaps the first to advise against a word-by-word translation (*non verbum pro verbo*) and to recommend a recreation of the style and its effect, the aesthetics of the target, taking the perspective of the orator. At this time in Roman literary circles, readers of translations were often well acquainted with the Greek source texts, and recreations of the Greek canon in Latin became demonstrations of pre-eminent rhetoric rather than linguistically truthful transfer of the source (Bassnett, 1980, pp. 43–5). The translator's production can be likened to a musician's interpretation of a musical score. No two pianists play Beethoven with the exact same intonation, and it is rare for any two translators to choose the same wording for any extended piece of text. The Latin translation of the Bible by Jerome (340–420) is a well-known example of non-literal translation. Non-correspondences between languages at the lexical level motivated what Jerome called a thought-for-thought translation, for which he was seriously criticized by his opponents, who knew previous translations from the Greek Septuagint. The unfamiliar wording of Jerome's Latin text was considered a tampering with the Word of God (Hayward, 1995, p. 102). The example demonstrates not only that translations vary in their relationship to their sources but that translators have employed different strategies with different effects on their readers. The negative responses to Jerome's Bible translation referred to here remain familiar today in reviews of re-translations of canonical texts.

## 5.3 The Purpose of a Translation Affects the Wording

The view that translations should be thought-based rather than word-based has been interpreted in a number of ways. Respect for the work a translator does has also varied. In our increasingly global societies, translation is ubiquitous, and interest in understanding the demands and challenges involved in this kind of language processing has entered the academic world. The concept of dynamic equivalence between source and target (Nida, 1964) was challenged in the early 1970s, when Hans Vermeer (1930–2010) suggested that the Skopos orientation (aim or purpose) led any translation action (Vermeer, 1989). From a Skopos perspective, the main aim is that the resulting text function adequately for its purpose. Evaluation of its relation to the source text, free or faithful, is less important than the purpose the text will serve, as determined by the people who commission the translation. Importantly, the purpose may be quite far removed from that of the source text, and the translation is successful only to the extent that it satisfies functional demands. Or, the purpose may be the same but, to meet target demands, major changes in the wording or presentation may be required. The concept of translation, according to this view, includes all sorts of adaptations, which means that the task becomes more of a target language functional writing process based on input from another text than the interlingual transfer of a content/thought set in the style of a foreign language author.

One example proffered by Skopos theorists came from marketing (Hönig and Kussmaul, 1984). Marketing principles can differ from culture to culture, and the goods to be promoted may be unknown to the target consumer. A marketing text will promote sales more successfully in the target market if it is formulated in accordance with the product's position in that culture and not with that of its source.

But is such an adapted text a translation? The view taken here is that a close translation of the source text is necessary although not sufficient for most translation tasks, and that the adaptation is the translator's authorship. There are problems with that view too, certainly, since there are borderline cases: classical novels have been adapted to suit younger readerships than were intended for the original, yet the author of the original remains the official author of such adaptations. Functionalists therefore make a distinction between equi-functional, hetero-functional and homologous translation (Nord, 1997). The warning 'Wet paint', for example, has a different, yet equi-functional wording 'Frisch gestrichen' (freshly painted) in German. Adaptations of fiction for adults into fiction for children, on the other hand, would be classified as hetero-functional, while translated fiction aiming at the same kind of readership in the source and target cultures is either homologous, having the same relative position, value or structure, or more documentary (Nord, 1997, pp. 48–51). The different functions clearly affect the text producer's artistic and linguistic freedom in formulating the target text.

Linguistic freedom is highly restricted in the translation of various types of official document. Official European Common Market Regulations, for example, appear in all the twenty-four official European languages. These texts are often written at the same time and compared during production to guarantee that they can have equal status as legal documents. Documents that are not legally binding appear in (at least) English, German and French, while urgent or short-lived information appears in just one language at first (https://europa.eu/european-union/index_en). Translations into other languages are considered secondary texts in legal terms. Still, target formulation is regulated by well-defined norms. Among them are full correspondence on sentence level, that is, full stop at the same point across the various language versions, and term by term translation, that is, no translation by description. Yet, the concept of norms is not always understood as regulations defined by those who commission the translation, or by the translator. Section 5.4 discusses translation as a norm-governed activity, based on close reading as well as quantitative corpus findings.

## 5.4  Translation Norms

Gideon Toury (1942–2016) observes that translation is a socio-cultural, and hence a norm-governed activity: translators follow certain conventions of language use and these conventions are triggered by the translation activity itself (Toury, 1995). Most importantly, he claims that they result in elements of language use that distinguish translated texts from non-translated text. The claim is not explicitly restricted to certain text types or certain language pairs, but his studies are based on literary prose and poetry in translation into Hebrew.

Rather than judging the relationship between the source text and the target text, as had been the trend in discussions prior to Toury's (1980, 1995) introduction of descriptive translation studies (DTS), research was now directed at uncovering translation norms, hypothesized to form a 'third code' (Frawley, 1984) and identified through a comparison of translated text and characteristics of first-written text in the same language.

The claim that translations realize an identifiable language norm led to a plea for quantitative DTS and became central for investigation into a number of phenomena across language pairs. The development and collection of electronic corpora of texts, including translations, made such studies possible. One of the earliest balanced, bi-directional corpora of source texts and their translations is the English-Norwegian Parallel Corpus (ENPC), initiated and developed in the early 1990s by Stig Johansson (1939–2010), of the University of Oslo (see www.hf.uio.no/ilos/english/services/knowledge-resources/omc/ENPCmanual.html); it was later expanded to include German and French. The corpus has been widely used as a source for comparative studies. It allows for contrastive research as well as monolingual comparative investigations (see, for example, papers in the journal *Languages in Contrast*). It has also inspired a number of researchers to build contrastive corpora in a number of languages along the same lines. The types of contrastive and parallel corpora, many of them built on attested translations, vary in size and design (see, for example, www.clarin.eu/resource-families/parallel-corpora).

Toury (1980, p. 130, 1995, p. 105), working in the pre-electronic corpus era, investigated the frequency of literary features in translated and non-translated Hebrew fiction. He hypothesized that binomials made up a marked category of translation into Hebrew. Binomials are near-synonymous conjoined phrases or lexical items. The meanings of the two are often so close that they refer to the same object or action. English examples include pairs like *law and order*, *lo and behold* and *prim and proper*. Toury's point is that many binomials, common and of high prestige in old, written Hebrew texts, have later fossilized into fixed expressions. The old texts were used as reservoirs for later texts, whether first-written texts or translations into Hebrew. In modern times, conjoint phrases of this kind grew out of fashion, and reliance on them declined. Yet, they were found to appear with much higher frequencies, whether in fossilized forms or in new combinations, in more peripheral literature, such as translations. The study gave strong support to Toury's hypothesis that norms of peripheral literature, such as translations, differ from norms of first-written, primary or central literature in a culture.

We learn from this that translated text can follow other norms than first-written texts in the same language. Norms are established through relative frequencies of defined features of language use in two modes of writing. Toury's example of binomials suggests that translation holds on to language norms that are more conservative than their parallels in first-written text.

Toury examined source texts only to the extent that he found aspects in the translations that he considered marked relative to original writings in the target language. While he insisted that the nature of translations could be identified irrespective of their origins, most subsequent studies have described translation phenomena based on a comparison with their sources. Chesterman (2004) suggested that translation be classified according to its nature, on the one hand, relative to the target language (T-universals) and, on the other, relative to its sources (S-universals). Only by studying translations relative to both perspectives can we get a comprehensive understanding of the nature of translated text. It should be noted here that extending the concept of translation norms to universals is rather bold and has been refuted by other translation scholars (see Section 5.7).

Source-oriented traits include matters such as closeness to the source, possible explicitation of cultural references and regionalization of social and geographical dialect, while target-oriented traits include matters of explicitness, standardization/normalization and atypical collocations (shining through) (see Sections 5.4.1–5.4.4). Translated text is also characterized by the translators' (in)visibility in the text, their perspectives and styles, an understanding of which requires recognition of the source author's linguistic habitus (see Section 5.5).

### 5.4.1  Explicitation and Explicitness as Translation Norms

Toury's hypothesis of translation as a separate textual norm has been investigated by a number of scholars internationally. Researchers working with different language pairs endorsed the idea and, with the development of larger parallel corpora, could compare features of first-written and translated texts. One finding, already discussed by Shoshana Blum-Kulka (1986), albeit in a contrastive comparison of source and target language texts (French–English), is that translated text is more explicit than original writing (the explicitation hypothesis). Øveras (1998) found strong support for explicitation in translated English and translated Norwegian based on the ENPC corpus. Olohan and Baker (2000) also found support for the hypothesis by comparing English sources and English translations. The relative explicitness of first-written and translated texts in the same language has also been demonstrated in a corpus-based German–English comparative study (Hansen-Schirra, Neumann and Steiner, 2012).

### 5.4.2   Normalization and Shining Through

While the above-mentioned studies based their findings on pure frequencies of features in first-written and translated texts, Teich (1999, 2012) refined the study of norms by considering first the relative frequency of similar forms in the source and the target languages respectively. Only with an insight into the way a structure is systematically used in the individual languages under comparison can we consider translation-mediated language. Teich hypothesizes that there are (at least) two characteristic traits of translated text: first, translations emphasize target language norms, that is, 'normal' structures in the target language will occur more frequently in translated text than in first-written texts in the same language. This trait is called *normalization*. In other words, normalization is a matter of levelling out the structure of the text rather than using fossilizing features, as was Toury's claim (see Section 5.4).

Teich's second hypothesis regards the relation between source and target language: providing that the same linguistic feature or structure exists in the two languages compared, but is more typical of the source language than of the target language, translations will have a higher frequency of those structures than original writing in the target language. This last trait is identified as *shining through*.

Teich tested her hypotheses by establishing the relative frequency of a particular structure in balanced corpora of original texts in German and English. For example, is the impersonal construction systematically more 'normal' in German than in English? If yes, then if it is even more frequent in German translation than in original German, it is a case of (over-)normalization. On the other hand, if it is more frequent in German than in English and occurs less frequently in translated German text than in originally produced German text of the same register and size, it is a case of shining through. Through this precise frequency analysis, Teich integrates systemic variation across languages in her study of translated text. She finds both types of translation norm in her data.

Features of shining through are not translation errors but mark translated text as having a strong link to the source language and culture. They identify the text as 'overt' translation in the sense of House (1997), that is, it has not gone through a thorough cultural filter, and thus invites the reader to orient themselves towards the author and the culture engrained in the original piece of work.

The concept of shining through is close to the concept of interference, and Toury presented the phenomenon as a *Law of Interference*: 'In translation, phenomena pertaining to the make-up of the source text tend to be transferred to the target text' (Toury, 1995, p. 275). Interference affects the text, but the effect does not have to be negative.

Normalization in Teich's sense only partly overlaps with Toury's *Law of Growing Standardization*: 'In translation, source text textemes tend to be converted into target language repertoremes' (Toury, 1995, pp. 267–8). A *repertoreme* is understood as a sign (word or expression) from an institutionalized repertoire. Standardization thus includes normalization, but Toury's concept is wider. The concept has also been applied in translation studies to discuss the translation of regional varieties of language in literature. In the following, we look first at lexical generalization, then at standardization of dialect and sociolect.

### 5.4.3 Levelling Out as a Translation Norm

Toury's norm of standardization entails that textual features in the source text will be modified, sometimes to the point of being ignored, in favour of more habitual options offered by the target repertoire. Baker (1996) refers to the same phenomenon using the term 'normalization' (cf. Teich, Section 5.4.2): a tendency to conform to the target language's typical patterns. (Over-)standardization can thus be considered a levelling out of the author's style.

Results from several studies have strengthened this hypothesis. Some studies relate to solutions based on typological or sociological differences among the languages and cultures represented. For example, a typological difference observed between Romance languages and English (Talmy, 2000) involves motion verbs and manner of motion. While English tends to encode the manner of motion in the verb itself, for example *swim*, and the path in a 'satellite' particle, for example *across*, Romance languages (verb-framed) tend to encode the path in the verb: cf. French *traverser* (cross), and possibly the manner of motion in an adverbial: à la nage (swimming).

This difference is not absolute, certainly, yet Slobin (2004) has provided empirical evidence that manner of motion is sometimes ignored in translation from English into the Romance languages, arguably for the very reason that it is not encoded in the verb itself, and thus representing a certain levelling out of the manner salience of the source. An example is chapter 6 of Tolkien's *The Hobbit*, which has twenty-six different types of manner verb. Translations into other satellite-framed languages (Germanic and Slavic languages) are on average quite close to English, while verb-framed language translations are down to an average of 17.2 types. When Tolkien uses 'He still wandered on', *wander* being a manner-of-motion verb and the path being expressed in the particle *on*, the French and the Portuguese translations have the path-oriented 'Il continua d'avancer', 'Continou avançando'. A satellite of manner is added in the French translation but in neither the Portuguese nor the Spanish version.

This kind of levelling out at the lexical level concerns fine-grained differences in co-referring expressions. However, the phenomenon does not always have a typological explanation. Some of the words chosen by the translator have a more general meaning than those used in the sources, that is, items with broader references tend to be selected. Halverson (2017) demonstrates that the general verb *get* in English is over-represented in translations from Norwegian, but this is not because the English language lacks more specific expressions to choose from. The explanation offered is cognitive: a prototype, that is, the most typical and salient expression for a semantic field (such as, the onset/change of possession) is more accessible in the cognitive processing of interlingual transfer and can account for the levelling out that is found to occur.

### 5.4.4   Standardization of Regional Varieties in Translation

Most language cultures have official national standards – Standard American English, Standard British English, Standard Arabic, etc. – and these language forms are used in most professional writing. In many text types, however, the use of sociolects and regional dialects is important for geographical and social reasons, and the transfer of such varieties into varieties of the target language runs the risk of being associated with particular dialect areas in the target culture and of creating a distance from the textual world of the original (Skogmo, 2015). Translators are therefore often advised to handle dialectal forms in their work with great care. Translators' dialectal repertoire may be limited, and whichever dialect/sociolect they may be familiar with may not fit the contexts associated with the source variety. Standardization may therefore be a 'safer' solution (Pym, 2015). Studies of language varieties in translated text are clear attestations that standardization or neutralization is a general norm (Leppihalme, 2000; Snell-Hornby, 2003; Englund Dimitrova, 2004; Soovik, 2006; Assis Rosa, 2012; Epstein, 2014; Skogmo, 2015). When varieties are attested, they more often show up in lexis than in morphosyntactic features. Different strategies have also been chosen for literary dialogues as compared with the narrators' voices. Neutralization of the narrator's voice may indeed result from a consideration of what matters to the new audience. Is the variety in the source relevant for the text itself, or is it a language-political comment on the society in which it appears (the source culture)? If the latter, the variety may be irrelevant to the target audience and neutralization may be well founded, yet the target readers will be unaware of the author's subversion strategies. If the former, on the other hand, neutralization deprives the reader of some of the characters' voices.

English is a multicultural language with a multitude of established colonial variants sometimes used to reflect multicultural environments in fictional prose. To mention but three relevant novels from different periods, the varieties used in Mark Twain's *The Adventures of Huckleberry Finn* (1884) or in Zadie Smith's *White Teeth* (2000), or in Alice Walker's *The Color Purple* (1982) are all central to the stories themselves. Yet any attempt to find parallels in translation runs the risk of failure. An exceptionally bold attempt, met with praise in the reviews, was the Norwegian translation of Alice Walker's novel (Rogde, 1984). The translator added a foreword in which he gave solid socio-cultural arguments for his choice of dialect and thus prepared the reader. The Norwegian translator of Zadie Smith's (2000/2001) novel, Sjøgren-Erichsen, on the other hand, attempted an immigrant version of Norwegian in some of the characters' voices and was harshly criticized in the reviews. An important consideration is that the varieties in *White Teeth* are relatively well-established varieties of Jamaican English, Indian English and North London English, while Norwegian had no corresponding well-established immigrant varieties that had been described in any systematic way at the time of the translation. The language varieties attempted in the target text simply did not reflect the voices of Smith's characters. The criticism led to public money being offered to translators to enable them to research minority cultures' way of expressing themselves in the language of their new homes.

## 5.5  Translators' and Authors' Voices in Translated Text

A major challenge in translating is to represent the original author's voice, understood as the author's or storyteller's presence in the text, recognized through her/his linguistic habitus. Boase-Beier (2006) discusses style in terms of an author's or a translator's *mind style*, a term originally taken from Fowler (1977).

The author's mind style is characterized by her/his choice of rhythm, tone, vocabulary and syntax. Since individual languages can be characterized by very different rhythms, and since their syntax differs and their vocabularies are not symmetric, transfer of voice is experienced as the most challenging task in literary translation. Translating a one-word expression into a two or three-word expression changes the explicitness of the text. Translating from a language like English, which has its determiner to the left of its noun, into a Scandinavian language, which expresses definiteness by a suffix on the noun, can cause rhythmical changes. The monosyllabic negator *not* has two morphemes *ne* and *pas* in French and a bisyllabic *ikke* in the Scandinavian languages. Such small differences among closely related languages clearly challenge the rhythmical transfer of texts. A parallel problem between English and Spanish or Italian is their differences in the placement of modifiers, as well as their typologically different intonation and stress patterns. Analyses of translated texts against their sources can thus take us from knowledge of marked tendencies in translated text to insights into the strategies used and the creativity applied in transferring the voice of the author.

Such comparisons can also help recognize a particular *translator's voice* (Hermans, 1996). Variations may even invite or explicitly mark different interpretations, as Malmkjær (2004) illustrates (see Section 5.5.1).

### 5.5.1  Multi-translation of Literary Canon: The Translator's Fingerprints

Malmkjær's (2003) analyses of a number of translations into English of the Danish fairy tales (1835–42) written by Hans Christian Andersen (1805–75) give examples to show that translators take different approaches to meeting their readers. One example is very telling:

> The following are two target versions of the same source sentence from *Nattergalen* (1844) (*The Nightingale*), in which Dulcken's version is introvert, only tentatively indicating a hearer, while Keigwin's version explicitly approaches a listener. The latter version also has an explicit storyteller advising the reader. The storyteller in the former version remains in the background, stating his opinion about the value of hearing the story.
>
> (DULCKEN, 1866):   'It happened a good many years ago, but that's just why it is worth while to hear the story, before it is forgotten.
> (KEIGWIN, 1976):   'The story I am going to tell you happened many years ago but that's just why you should hear it now, before it is forgotten.

It makes no sense to discuss the translators' fingerprints any further without checking with the source text. From that perspective, the more recent version marks the style of the most independent translator. The author's own sentence, with a gloss, demonstrates the closeness of Dulcken's version to the source, thus exemplifying the *invisible* translator:

> Det er nu mange Aar siden, men just derfor er det værd at høre Historien, før man glemmer den!

Gloss: It is now many years ago, but precisely therefore is it worth to hear the Story, before one forgets it!

Munday (2007) devotes a chapter to the many English translators of works by the Colombian Nobel Prize winner Gabriel García Márquez (1927–2014). Munday does not investigate multi-translations of the same works; rather, he compares the different translators' solutions to particular stylistic features across García Márquez's literary publications. While the author's two main (American-)English translators, Gregory Rabassa (1922–2016) and Edith Grossman, both follow the syntax of the author very closely, Grossman's translations differ from Rabassa's on the phraseological level (Munday, 2007, p. 108). She is more apt to retain Spanish words for various local references than to use more generalized or more descriptive target expressions. Examples are foodstuff references, such as *sancocho* (a particular type of soup or stew) or *masato* (a drink made from cassava root or rice), animal references such as *vicuña* (a relative of the llama) and local idioms such as *papeluchas* (scribbles on paper – worth nothing). Rabassa is more target culture oriented and can be very creative in finding local target language vocabulary (e.g., *hoodlums* (gangsters)) that mirrors local idiomaticity in the source. On the phraseological level, he also adapts target culture measures, like *litres* and *kilos* into *quarts* and *pounds* (Munday, 2007, p. 107). Comparisons of different translators' choices thus help us recognize the translator's fingerprints and realize that translated text to some extent ends up being a mix between the source author's and the translator's styles.

### 5.5.2 Authors' Relations to Translators and Their Translated Texts

Reaching a foreign language readership is important for an author's recognition and cultural capital. Yet s/he is often at the mercy of the translator, unable to judge the resulting text. For example, although Henrik Ibsen (1828–1906) was able to discuss translations of his plays with his German translators, he was completely at the mercy of his English translator, as well as his translators into French, since he did not master these languages. During his twenty-six years in Italy, he saw and commented on Italian stage performances of some of his – clearly domesticated – plays, which he responded to with disgust, but there is no correspondence indicating co-operation between him and his Italian translators, Alfredo Mazza, Pietro Galletti and Luigi Capuana (d'Amico, 2011, 2013).

More recently, however, co-operation between authors and their translators is not uncommon, particularly in the case of literary texts. Linguistic, social and cultural footprints in any literary text must be respected. This is equally relevant in all translation, yet it may be found more difficult in translation of texts between more distant cultures.

Authors who are concerned with this aspect of translation have sometimes either negotiated translation solutions with their translators or given specific directions on how to translate their work. For example, Umberto Eco (1932–2016) met with his translators to explain lexical and syntactic choices and discuss target language solutions (Eco, 2003).

J. R. R. Tolkien (1892–1973), on the other hand, found himself disliking the first draft translations of *The Lord of the Rings* into Dutch and into Swedish, by Max Schuchart and Åke Ohlmark, respectively (http://tolkien gateway.net). He objected, but was only partly successful in correcting the translations. As a linguist and German philologist, he had painstakingly used Anglo-Saxon–based vocabulary to avoid the Latin and early French influences on the language, and used the language he had reconstructed in his story-world. Because he was unhappy with the first Swedish translation, he wrote a guide to the names in his work, later revised in W. G. Hammond and C. Scull's (2005) *The Lord of the Rings: A Reader's Companion*. Re-translations have followed. Tolkien's Middle Earth fantasy appears in no fewer than thirty-eight languages. For reasons of aspects lost in the transfer, it has been re-translated several times into, for example, Russian, Swedish and Norwegian. There are to date no fewer than ten translations of Tolkien's work in Russian.

## 5.6 Source and Target Orientation as Translation Strategies

The perspectives on translation described and exemplified in Section 5.5 differ distinctly from the perspective taken by Toury. When we look at different translations of the same source, we are investigating individual translators' creative use of language rather than what can be uncovered as a special language of translation. Generalizations seen from this perspective answer questions on translators' creativity and on their working strategies. Retaining source text words and cultural-specific references is considered a foreignizing strategy, taking the reader to the (foreign) author rather than taking the author to the (domestic) reader. Schleiermacher's (1838) translation concept *Verfremdens* contrasts with *Einbürgerns*, foreignization versus domestication, respectively (Venuti, 2007).

Foreignization, the strategy strongly advocated by Venuti in his writings about translation, encompasses more than just borrowing or calquing source language words. Centrally, it relates to using expressions in the target language that individuate the source text author rather than using the well-established, standard idiomatic language of the target culture (domestication). Reviews of literature in translation, if they indicate any awareness of or pay any attention to the language of the translator at all, tend to comment on the idiomaticity, the natural flow of the target text. Current idiomaticity in the target language, however, can fail to transfer the aspects of language that unveil the identity and attitudes of the narrator and the individual characters as well as the geographical, political and social ambience(s) that surround them.

Words are signs. The words and sentence structures you use reflect the way you think and signal your personal and social self. Words and structures also carry with them their historical path, which resonates with the native reader. Authors who translate other authors sometimes do so to explore their own literary style. Edgar Allan Poe's (1845) poem *The Raven*, for example, has been translated several times into many languages by well-known authors. It is interesting to consider these translations in view of the translator's own style in the target text. Two translations of this poem exist in Norwegian, by two well-known authors. The tone in each translation is very different, and clearly mirrors the different styles of the two in their own writings. André Bjerke uses feminine end rhyme (rhyme on words that end with an unstressed syllable) and words with long front vowels, while Havard Rem uses more short vowel words and unvoiced consonants that have a harder, more masculine feel to them. The first two lines of the poem are given as an example:

Once upon a midnight dreary while I pondered, weak and weary,
Over many a quaint and curious volume of forgotten lore –

> BJERKE (1967):   En gang i en midnattstime, mens jeg svak og halvt
> i svime grublet over sære verkers visdom ingen kjenner
> mer,

Gloss: Once in a midnight hour, while I weak and halfway dozed
Mused over quaint works' wisdom that no one knows anymore

> REM (1985):   Engang svarte natten knuget der jeg matt og medtatt ruget
> På så mye gammel kunnskap ingen lenger regnet med –

Gloss: Once the black night clutched where I flat and exhausted brooded
Over so much old knowledge no one any longer counted on

The glosses demonstrate the different translations only partly. Wordings glossed as 'midnight hour' / 'black night' and 'weak and halfway dozed' / 'flat and exhausted' are adequate translations of 'midnight' and 'weak and weary' from a semantic point of view, but they sound different in the target, which affects the initial tone of the poem. Bjerke's translation parallels Poe's own assonance, while Rem's translation is rougher, darker and spookier, more direct. The masculine, dark tone of the short vowels and hard consonants in *svarte natten* ('the black night') and the hard alliteration and short vowel assonance of *matt og medtatt* ('flat and exhausted') in Rem's translation create an interesting contrast to Bjerke's version: note the slower energy *i en midnattstime* ('in a midnight hour') and *svak og halvt i svime* ('weak and halfway dozed') with their long vowel sounds. *Gruble* (musing over something), as in Bjerke's translation, is also gentler than *ruge* (brooding) in Rem's translation.

Similarly, the critic Jared Spears (Wikimedia Commons, October 2016) comments on Stephane Mallarmé's French translation of the poem (*Le Corbeau*) of 1875 that it, too, turns out spookier than the original, based on the words chosen:

> Une fois, par un minuit lugubre, tandis que je m'appesantissais, faible et fatigué
> Sur maint curieux et bizarre volume de savoir oublié –
> Gloss: Once, on a dismal midnight, as I lay heavy, weak and tired
> On many curious and bizarre volumes of forgotten knowledge –

Charles Baudelaire's translation (1871) is gentler: *mediter* does not have the presupposition of unrest that *appaiser* does, and a *bizarre* volume is spookier than a *precieux* one, certainly:

> Une fois, sur le minuit lugubre, pendant que je méditais, faible et fatigué,
> sur maint précieux et curieux volume d'une doctrine oubliée –
> Gloss: Once, on the gloomy midnight, while I was meditating, weak and tired,
> on many precious and curious volumes of a forgotten doctrine –

Generally, source text orientation has been the prime motivation for a number of re-translations. For example, recent English translations of Henrik Ibsen's social dramas (Penguin Classics, 2019, translated by Deborah Dawkin and Erik Skuggevik) have been made with this in mind (see the translators' note, pp. li–lii). One small example is the various characters' affective language, below represented by the character Mr Billing, an assistant at the local newspaper press in a small seaside town, in *Enemy of the People*. Billing keeps using the expression *Gud døde meg* (may God slay me), an oath not used by any of the other characters in the play, irrespective of class. The expression is marked: it is not in use in contemporary Norwegian. According to n-grams from the Norwegian National Library (see www.nb.no/sp_tjenester/beta/ngram_1), it had its highest frequency in Ibsen's day (although infrequent), with a sharp drop in 1904. The expression does not appear in any of today's Bible translations, but it appears to have its origin in the *Guds Ord* translation of the Old Testament, which went out of use in Norway after 1904 (the Bible was re-translated on a word-to-word basis from Danish into Norwegian in 1904; see the Norwegian Bible Society website, bibel.no). Mr Billing's use of the expression in Ibsen's play has several different translations in the various English editions. For instance, in the Ginn and Company American version from 1931, Billing replies to his newspaper editor in a comment on the style of Doctor Stockmann's letter to the press: *Strong? Well, strike me dead if he isn't crushing!* Note the omission of reference to God. His tone is much weaker and less amusing in the 1950 version by Rinehart and Co: *Hard? Bless my soul he's crushing.* The well-recognized translator James W. McFarlane, translating for Oxford University Press (1960), has chosen the contemporary variants *damned* and *By God* and in 1995 (Smith and Kraus, New Hampshire) Billing similarly uses current idiomatic language in English: *He's Goddamn devastating.* His curses in this 1995 version also vary throughout the same act (Act III), *God damn it!* and *My God!*, whereas Ibsen has actually humorously characterized Mr Billing by having him use the marked expression over and over again. The most recent translation of Ibsen's social dramas (2019), the Penguin Classics translation by Deborah Dawkin and Erik Skuggevik, mentioned earlier, leaves Billing with the expression *God strike me dead*, which is a near word-by-word translation of the source. The English expression is Biblical too, but it appears only in the *God's Word* translation (GW) (World Bible Publishers, 1995). As a curiosity, the phrase does appear in American fiction, albeit infrequently, particularly in 1920–40, but neither before nor later (Corpus of Historical American English, www.english-corpora.org/coha/). According to www.books-google.com/ngrams/, this English expression had its highest peak in 1899, with a sharp drop after 1925.

The translation choices presented here demonstrate different strategies adopted by the translators over the years. In Norway, a country publishing as much fiction in translation from other languages as first-written fiction, the literary translators' association has made source orientation its explicitly stated strategy (Eikli, 2019, personal communication). As for re-translations, Professor Tore Rem, the editor of the 2019 Penguin Classics translations of Ibsen's canonized dramas, states:

> It is worth remembering that the specialness of a writer can be lost if we take him for granted, if we domesticate him too strongly, if we assume that he is too much like us. This Penguin edition wants to contribute to opening Ibsen up, to establishing premises for fresh approaches, through capturing the strangeness of his language, the individuality of his plays, how they each create their own storyworlds, through making readers and audiences aware of the historical contexts of these texts and some of the most significant of the many choices made in the process of translation.
>
> (Rem, 2019, Introduction, p. xxxviii)

## 5.7 Concluding Remarks and a Note on Translation Universals

The previous sections have demonstrated that translated text is characterized as much by variation as by uniformity. Norms are followed, but different translators choose different strategies, which by themselves may imply different norms. Analyses of multi-translations indicate that no two translations of the same source look the same. Moreover, the translators' voices interact with the voices of the storytellers, no matter how much the translators testify to struggling to find the author's voice. Phenomena claimed to characterize translations, such as the norms discussed in Section 5.4 (but see also Baker, 1996 for an extended list), are not hard to find, irrespective of the language pair studied, but not all translations have all of them. Norms can be culture-specific, major language cultures approaching translation differently than minor language cultures. Norms are also found to change over time. The phenomena found to recur in translated text may be strategy specific or simply conventionalized usage, as we have seen. Further research to make the concept of foreignization more precise and operational would be useful for establishing working strategies over time and across language cultures. The variety demonstrated in the present chapter indicates that translation traits cannot be claimed to be universal (for this view, see also Malmkjær, 2012). Yet it has also been shown here that general traits repeat themselves across language pairs. One important effect of the quest for universal norms of translation is that translation research has reached an international readership and created a milieu for translation scholars that can only benefit the field. Research on potential universals has also contributed to establishing common concepts and a common ground for translation studies as an independent, identifiable field of research. Translation studies is still a young discipline, and we are still searching for and refining basic concepts that define this operation of transferring what someone else says into another language in the hope of bringing the message across with the same intended effect. Current studies indicate that translation has a common cognitive ground (e.g., Paradis, 2004; de Groot, 2014; Halverson, 2017). Cognitive psychology and cognitive linguistics have been applied to translation to explain general tendencies observed in translated text (Malmkjær, 2012). Questions of universality are therefore questions that can be answered not so much by the study of final translation products but by looking into the cognitive process of translation.

## References

Assis Rosa, A. (2012). Translating place: Linguistic variation in translation. Word and text. *Journal of Literary Studies and Linguistics*, **2**(2), 75–97.

Baker, M. (1996). Corpus-based translation studies: The challenges that lie ahead. In H. Somers, ed., *Terminology, LSP and Translation*. Amsterdam: John Benjamins, pp.175–86.

Bassnett, S. (1980). *Translation Studies*. London: Methuen.

Bjerke, A. (1967). Ravnen. In *Drømmen i en Drøm*. Oslo: Aschehoug, pp. 30–7.

Blum-Kulka, S. (1986). Shifts of cohesion and coherence in translation. Reprinted in L. Venuti, ed. (2001). *The Translation Studies Reader*. New York: Routledge, pp. 298–313 from J. House and S. Blum-Kulka, eds., *Interlingual and Intercultural Communication: Discourse and Cognition in Translation and Second Language Acquisition Studies*. Tübingen: Gunter Narr Verlag, pp. 17–35.

Boase Beier, J. (2006). *Stylistic Approaches to Translation*. Manchester: St Jerome.

Chesterman, A. (2004). Beyond the particular. In A. Mauranen and P. Kujamäkki, eds., *Translation Universals, Do They Exist?* Amsterdam: John Benjamins, pp. 33–49.

D'Amico, G. (2011). Marketing Ibsen: A study of the First Italian Reception, 1883–1891. *Ibsen Studies*, **11**(2), 145–75.

D'Amico, G. (2013). *Domesticating Ibsen for Italy*. PhD thesis. Università degli Studi di Torino.

De Groot, A. M. B. (2014). About phonological, grammatical, and semantic accents in bilinguals' language use and their cause. In L. Filipović and M. Pütz, eds., *Multilingual Cognition and Language Use: Processing and Typological Perspectives*. Amsterdam: John Benjamins, pp. 229–62.

Eco, U. (2003). *Mouse or Rat? Translation as Negotiation*. London: Weidenfeld and Nicolson.

Eikli, R. (2019). (Member of the Norwegian Translators' Association) Personal communication.

Englund Dimitrova, B. (2004). Orality, literacy, reproduction of discourse and the translation of dialect. In I. Helin, ed., *Dialektübersetzung und Dialekt in Multimedia*. Frankfurt am Main: Peter Lang, pp. 121–39.

Epstein, B. J. (2014). Are there blacks in Europe? How African-American characters are (or are not) translated. In B. J. Epstein, ed., *True North: Literary Translation in the Nordic Countries*. Newcastle upon Tyne: Cambridge Scholars Press, pp.84–98.

Frawley, W. (1984). *Translation, Literary, Linguistic and Philosophical Perspectives*. Newark: University of Delaware Press.

Fowler, R. (1977). *Linguistics and the Novel*. London: Routledge.

Halverson, S. L. (2017). Gravitational pull in translation: Testing a revised model. In G. de Sutter, M.-A. Lefer and I. Delaere, eds., *Empirical Translation Studies*. Berlin: de Gruyter, pp.9–46.

Hammond, W. G., and Scull, C. (2005). *The Lord of the Rings: A Reader's Companion*. London: Harper Collins.

Hansen-Schirra, S., Neumann, S., and Steiner, E. (2012). *Cross-Linguistic Corpora for the Study of Translations*. Berlin: de Gruyter.

Hayward, C. T. R. (1995). *St Jerome's Hebrew Questions on Genesis (translation)*. Oxford: Clarendon Press.

Hermans, T. (1996). The translator's voice in translated narrative. *Target*, **8** (1), 23–49.

Hönig, H., and Kussmaul, P. (1984). *Strategie der Übersetzung*. Tübingen: Gunter Narr.

House, J. (1997). *Translation Quality Assessment: A Model Re-visited*. Tübingen: Gunter Narr.

Leppihalme, R. (2000). The two faces of standardization: On the translation of regionalisms in literary dialogue. *The Translator*, **6**(2), 247–69.

Malmkjær, K. (2003). Et lingvistisk perspektiv på litterær oversettelse (from English: A linguistic perspective on literary translation. Trans. B. Behrens). In B. Behrens and B. Christensen, eds., *Oversettelse i teori og praksis*. Oslo: Novus, pp. 55–89.

Malmkjær, K. (2004). Translational stylistics. *Language and Literature*, **13**(1), 13–24.

Malmkjær, K. (2012). Translation universals. In K. Malmkjær and K. Windle, eds., *The Oxford Handbook of Translation Studies*, Online.

Munday, J. (2007). *Style and Ideology in Translation*. London: Routledge.

Nida, E. A. (1964). *Toward a Science of Translating*. Leiden: E. J. Brill.

Nord, C. (1997). *Translating as a Purposeful Activity*. Manchester: St Jerome.

Olohan, M., and Baker, M. (2000). Reporting that in translated English: Evidence for subconscious processes of explicitation? *Across Languages and Cultures*, **1**(2), 141–58.

Øverås, L. (1998). In search of the third code: An investigation of norms in literary translation. *Meta*, **43**(4), 571–88.

Paradis, M. (2004). *A Neurolinguistic Theory of Bilingualism*. Amsterdam: John Benjamins.

Poe, E. A. (1845). *The Raven*, full text available at www.poetryfoundation.org.

Pym, A. (2015). Translating as risk management. *Journal of Pragmatics*, **85**, 67–80.

Rem, H. (1985). Ravnen. In *Bak Dør på Gløtt*. Oslo: Cappelen, pp.39–45.

Rem, T. (2019). Introduction to *Henrik Ibsen. A Doll's House and Other Plays*. Harmondsworth: Penguin.

Rogde, I. (1984). Translator's preface to Alice Walker: *Fargen bortenfor* (*The Color Purple*). Oslo: Gyldendal.

Schleiermacher, F. (1838). Über die verschiedenen Methoden des Übersetzens. In *Sämtliche Werke*, vol. II. Berlin, pp.201–38.

Skogmo, S. F. (2015). *Marked Language in Norwegian Literary Text*. PhD dissertation, University of Oslo. Oslo: Akademika.

Slobin, D. I. (2004). Relating narrative events in translation. In D. Ravid and H. B. Shyldkrot, eds., *Perspectives on Language and Language Development: Essays in Honor of Ruth A. Berman*. Dordrecht: Kluwer.

Smith, Z. (2000/2001). *White Teeth / Hvite tenner*. Norwegian trans. by T. Sjøgren Erichsen. Oslo: Aschehough & Co.

Snell-Hornby, M. (2003). Re-creating the hybrid text: Postcolonial Indian writings and the European scene. *Linguistica Antwerpiensia. New Series*, **2**, 173–89.

Soovik, E.-R. (2006). Translating the translated: Arundhati Roy and Salman Rushdie in Estonian. In R. Granqvist, ed., *Writing Back in/and Translation*. Frankfurt am Main: Peter Lang, pp. 155–65.

Talmy, L. (2000). *Toward a Cognitive Semantics. Vol. II: Typology and Process in Concept Structuring*. Cambridge, MA: MIT Press.

Teich, E. (1999). System-oriented and text-oriented comparative linguistic research: Crosslinguistic variation in translation. *Languages in Contrast*, **2** (2), 187–210.

Teich, E. (2012). *Crosslinguistic Variation in System and Text*. Berlin: De Gruyter.

Toury, G. (1980). *In Search of a Theory of Translation*. Tel Aviv: Porter Institute.

Toury, G. (1995). *Descriptive Translation Studies and Beyond*. Amsterdam: John Benjamins.

Venuti, L. (2007). Translation, community and utopia. In L. Venuti, ed., *The Translation Studies Reader*. 2nd ed. London/New York: Routledge, pp. 482–502.

Vermeer, H. J. (1989). Skopos and commission in translational action. Trans. A. Chesterman. In L. Venuti, ed. (2000). *The Translation Studies Reader*. London: Routledge, pp.221–32.

Wikimedia Commons (October 2016). https://commons.wikimedia.org /wiki/File:Le_Corbeau_(The_Raven)_by_Edgar_Allan_Poe.

# Part II

## Translation in Society

# 6

# Translation and Translanguaging in (Post)multilingual Societies

Tong King Lee

## 6.1 Introduction

Translation and multilingualism are affiliated terms, though they are not always considered in tandem (Grutman, 2009, p. 182). The two terms point to different orders of things: multilingualism obtains where several languages coexist within a given space – cognitive, textual or social; translation is a linguistic or cultural intervention constituted by the concrete, semiotic act of turning a text composed in one language into a different language, although the term has increasingly been used as a convenient metaphor for cultural hybridity and other heteroglossic phenomena.

Translation and multilingualism intersect each other at different levels. On a cognitive level, proficiency in at least two languages is the requisite condition for translation: all professional translators must be bi- or multilingual and, more than that, bi- or multicultural. On the textual plane, multilingual writing presents notorious difficulties for the translator; this is especially so when one of the languages in the mix is the prospective target language, that is, the language to be translated into, thereby creating a paradoxical situation where 'the linguistic elements that signalled Otherness in the original run the risk of having their indexical meaning reversed and being read as "familiar" signs of Sameness [in the translation]' (Grutman, 2006, p. 22; see also Mezei, 1998; Lee, 2013, pp. 29–68).

This chapter discusses translation and multilingualism in connection with society. The relationship between translation and society is complex and multifaceted (see Tyulenev, 2014). Multilingualism puts a sociolinguistic spin on this relationship, bringing to the fore themes such as language ideology in multilingual regimes as embodied in translation-related policies; the impact of translators and translation in the transformation of cities; and the coupling of translation with the notion of translanguaging in superdiverse settings. The following sections will explore each of these in turn.

## 6.2  Translational Regimes

Multilingual regimes are territories where, by virtue of their demographic constitution, two or more languages lay claim to official language status. As sites of language ideological struggle, these territories often negotiate the relations between contesting languages via the institution of language policies, regulating whether and how languages can be used and translated into each other, 'by whom, in what way, in which geo-temporal, institutional framework' (Meylaerts, 2007, p. 298). It is in this sense that multilingual regimes are *linguistic territoriality regimes* (Meylaerts, 2011, p. 744). Further: in multilingual societies, language policy tends not to exist without a translation policy because 'determining the rules of language use presupposes determining the right to translation within a democratic society'; on this premise, linguistic territoriality regimes are also *translational regimes* (Meylaerts, 2011, p. 744).

Meylaerts (2011) sets out four prototypes of translational regime according to how different languages in a multilingual society are mediated through translation:

(1) *Complete institutional multilingualism*. This type of regime assigns multiple languages 'absolute institutional equality' (Meylaerts, 2011, p. 746), allowing people to access public services in their own language. This entails obligatory and multidirectional translation among all the relevant languages. A case in point is the EU's policy of translating all legislation and key policy documents into all its official languages. This policy is, however, based squarely on the notion of the nation-state, so that non-national languages, such as Catalan, Galician and Basque, are excluded.

(2) *Complete institutional monolingualism*. In contrast to (1), this type of regime selects one language as the language of governance and education; speakers of other, non-institutionalized languages are legally obliged to use the institutionalized language in accessing public services. Sustenance of such regimes requires 'a judicious combination of obliged and prohibited translation' (Meylaerts, 2011, p. 748), where translation from non-institutionalized languages *into* the institutionalized language is obligatory, while translation in the reverse direction is restricted or even prohibited. For example, the Comprehensive Immigration Reform Act (2006) of the United States that 'no person has a right, entitlement, or claim to have the Government of the

United States or any of its officials or representatives act, communicate, perform or provide services, or provide materials in any language other than English'; by way of this provision, US immigrants are legally deprived of the right to access translations from English into their languages.

(3) *Institutional monolingualism with limited translation into the minority languages.* This type of regime sits between the first two. As with the second regime, one language serves as the only working language for public services; however, a limited measure of translation is available in cases where 'specific legal dispositions condition the restricted presence of the minority language(s) in the public sphere or in certain institutions' (Meylaerts, 2011, p. 750). An example of this regime at work is the availability of Spanish versions of certain US government websites to cater for the sizeable Hispanic population in the country.

(4) *Institutional monolingualism combined with institutional multilingualism.* This type of regime adopts a two-tiered model that combines the first two regimes, with institutional multilingualism on a higher (e.g., federal) scale, and institutional monolingualism on a local (e.g., regional) scale. Exemplary of this model is Belgium, where the capital, Brussels, is bilingual, and the regions of Flanders (primarily Dutch-speaking) and Wallonia (primarily French-speaking) are monolingual. This creates 'monolingual institutional islands under a multilingual umbrella' (Meylaerts, 2011, p. 752), so that translation among official languages in monolingual municipalities either does not take place or is heavily regulated.

Meylaerts's framework demonstrates that, in multilingual regimes, translation operates within the legal-ideological structures of language policy and planning. Yet the institutional role of translation can be played out in more subtle ways.

Consider multilingual literary anthologies, which we might think of as a kind of discursive, 'soft' institution, as opposed to the 'hard' institutions of language policy and planning. Anthologies can be deployed to give structure to aspects of a culture (Essman and Frank, 1991, p. 67) by way of, for instance, projecting certain language values. This takes us from legal multilingualism to textual multilingualism, where the relations between anthologized texts written in different languages are organized by specific translation logics; the latter term refers to how translation 'moderates and negotiates language power relations by affording or depriving languages and their literatures of certain discursive properties, among which voice and visibility are prominent' (Lee, 2013, p. 109). Voice describes the capacity of a language to 'speak', hence to be audible, in a multilingual anthology; a language gains voice when it translates another language – thus 'speaking' on behalf of other languages – or otherwise stands untranslated, hence precluding other languages from

'speaking' in lieu of its own voice. Visibility refers to the corporeal existence of a language on the textual interface, that is, whether a language is
directly perceptible on the reading interface (page or screen), as either an
original language or a translating language. Hence, in the case where a text
in a multilingual anthology is translated but does not appear in its original
language, the latter's visibility is suppressed (Lee, 2013, p. 108).

On the basis of these parameters, we might advance four models to
understand how translation structures language power relations in multilingual anthologies (based on Lee, 2012):

(a) *Translating a non-hegemonic language into a hegemonic language, but not vice
versa.* In this model, texts written in languages that are less hegemonic
in terms of their demographics and symbolic capital are translated
into more hegemonic languages. The original texts may or may not
appear alongside their translations in the anthology. This direction of
translation increases the public exposure of texts composed in a non-
hegemonic language. Yet in the case where the original texts are
excluded, the visibility of the non-hegemonic language itself is suppressed. The latter language is also 'unvoiced' because it functions
only as a source (translated) language but never as a target (translating)
language.

(b) *Translating a hegemonic language into a non-hegemonic language, but not
vice versa.* Theoretically possible but not often seen in practice, this
model of translation reverses the directionality of the preceding
model by having a less dominant language translate its more
dominant counterpart. As this model affords the socially less privileged language greater visibility (the non-hegemonic language is
perceptible on the reading interface, but not the hegemonic language) and voice (the non-hegemonic language serves only as the
target language, while the hegemonic language offers itself up as
the source language), it has the potential to subvert established
language hierarchies.

(c) *Multidirectional translation.* This model differs from the first two by
positing a one-to-many, as opposed to a one-to-one, translation relation among languages: namely, non-hegemonic into hegemonic; hegemonic into non-hegemonic; non-hegemonic into non-hegemonic (and
where there is more than one hegemonic language, hegemonic into
hegemonic as well). There is a strong egalitarian ethos to this model, as
each language is translated into as well as out of, and all texts appear in
their original languages alongside their translations. This means that
each language represented in the multilingual anthology has an equal
measure of voice and visibility.

(d) *Non-translation.* On the other extreme end of the spectrum we have
non-translation, where all texts stand in their original language without being translated into each other. The absence of translation

silences the imperative to communicate across language borders, highlighting instead the autonomy of each language to speak for itself and only to its exclusive audience. There is something radical to this model in the context of multilingual anthologies, which are typically expected to bridge languages and cultures. A corollary of non-translation is the de-privileging of hegemonic languages, since non-hegemonic languages, prima facie, stand on an equal footing, projecting their own voice and visibility without the interference of translation.

In multilingual Singapore, for example, literary anthologies constitute an important platform for the performance of language identities. Translation, or the lack thereof, plays a crucial mediating role among the three ethnic languages – Chinese, Malay and Tamil, known locally as the mother-tongue languages (MTLs) – and the dominant English language, Singapore's de facto lingua franca (Lee, 2013, ch. 4). In the year 2000, the National Arts Council commissioned the publication of *Rhythms: A Singapore Millennial Anthology of Poetry*, a collection of 101 poems across the 4 official languages in Singapore. The volume adopts the model of multidirectional translation (Model (c) above), making available each poem in its original language and in each of the other three languages. The multicultural landscape evoked by such criss-crossing of languages is a kaleidoscopic and utopian one.

Further consider two anthologies published on the occasion of Singapore's golden jubilee celebrations in 2015: *Singathology: 50 New Works by Celebrated Singaporean Writers* and *SingaPoetry: An Anthology of Singapore Poems*. *Singathology* adopts Model (a) above, where each work written originally in one of the three MTLs is accompanied by an English translation; English-language works stand on their own without translation. In contrast, the corpus of eighty-two poems in *SingaPoetry* is neatly segmented along language lines without translation among them – an instantiation of Model (d).

The model of translation adopted in these anthologies may be based on the specific motivation behind each publication. *Singathology*, published under the aegis of Singapore's National Arts Council, has the commemorative function of marking the fiftieth anniversary of Singapore's establishment as a sovereign nation-state. Its language constellation is consonant with Singapore's much-prided policy of bilingual language education, according to which one is expected to be proficient in English and one MTL. Thus, in *Singathology*, the pivotal function of English as the only translating language is a discursive manifestation of its sociolinguistic role as an overarching medium transcending the ethnic-based MTLs.

*SingaPoetry*, on the other hand, is a literacy-based volume published by Singapore's National Library Board and conceived as part of the annual reading campaign *READ! Singapore* (see https://eresources.nlb.gov.sg/eReads/

MobileReads/details?uuid=8d6e0230-6960-4df6-8cf2-93ebc2d538d9). It can be suggested in this case that the model of non-translation is in line with the campaign's objective to promote reading among the population; the strong literacy motive here downplays the imperative to showcase cross-cultural communication and hence the imperative to translate. Having said this, some literacy-based anthologies have been designed along Model (a) and Model (c) (see Lee, 2013, ch. 4). The latter model seems to have become increasingly dominant in recent years, possibly owing to its egalitarian ethos and hence its potential to construct a dynamic and balanced relationship among the four official languages.

## 6.3  Translation and the City

The city has captured the imagination of translation studies scholars in recent years. As urban formations of social life, cities are evolving phenomena: they grow, morph and decline in specific time-spaces, with their histories and materialities sedimenting into cultural palimpsests. Cities are also heavily textualized, discursively constituted on a continual basis, and subject to layers of (re)semiotization. To the extent that language is at the very heart of a city's fabric, so that it is possible to speak of a city as being encapsulated in and represented by signs, cities *are* texts. And in respect of the numerous multilingual, superdiverse cities in this globalized age, could we not posit that cities-as-texts are also sites of translation enacting a 'conference of the tongues' (Hermans, 2014)?

While all cities are multilingual to some degree, 'dual cities' are most pertinent to the investigation of translation and multilingualism. Dual (or triple, quadruple) cities are urban spaces, both physical and imagined, that are linguistically divided by virtue of their history. To say that these cities are bi-/multilingual would be quite misleading. The notion of bi-/multilingualism conveys the impression of two or more languages in egalitarian coexistence; dual cities, however, are not merely linguistically plural and diverse but also hierarchically organized zones where relations between languages are 'active, directional and interactional' (Cronin and Simon, 2014, p. 119; Simon, 2012, p. 3). Such cities are therefore not simply bi- or multilingual but also, and more to our point, translational. This distinction is made clear by Simon (2016, p. 5, emphasis added):

> The translational city ... is a space of heightened language awareness where exchange is accelerated or blocked, facilitated or forced, questioned and critiqued. The translational city is of course a multilingual city, but *one viewed from the perspective of the movement and texture* in urban language life. Multilingualism points to pure diversity, the number of languages spoken, but translation speaks to *the relations of tension, interaction, rivalry, or convergence,* among them as well as the particular spaces they occupy in the city.

Within the notion of translational cities, translation often functions as a trope for either intercultural exchange or impasse. It has been turned into something of a catch-all term to encompass cultural phenomena characteristic of urban politico-semiotic spaces, such as the productive collision between 'the vernacular and the standard, the assimilated and the nonassimilated, the regional and the national, the global and the local, the general and the particular' (Pizzi, 2016, p. 45). This does not necessarily preclude the substantiveness of translation as a concrete, discursive practice; the metaphorical and literal facets of translation are coextensive and scalable with respect to multilingual cities.

Dual cities, as texts-in-translation, are eminently *readable* 'in the submerged languages of the past or in the rival languages of the present' (Simon, 2016, p. 5). One way of reading a city is to look into the layeredness of its appellation, which may fossilize key moments in its history. The city of Lviv in today's Western Ukraine, for example, was at different points in time called Leopolis, Lemberg, Lwów, and Lvov; the city's name is thus a translational palimpsest, a 'fragile cipher' (Simon, 2012, p. 15) recording its passage through successive domination by the Poles, Habsburgs, Russians, and Ukrainians (see Sywenky, 2014).

In a similar vein, Istabul's Beyoğlu was once upon a time called Pera – from the Greek *to pera* ('the other side' [of the old city]), a name immortalizing the district's Byzantine and Ottoman legacies. Seen as archaic for a long time, the historical name has been appropriated since the 1990s to signify a new cosmopolitan outlook; hence Demirkol-Ertürk and Paker's (2014) preferred use of Beyoğlu/Pera, which, with one slash, indicates both rupture and continuity between past and present, between old and new cosmopolitanisms. The strata of names accrued by a historical city owing to regime changes are symptomatic of the translational, where translation gets folded into the layered nominalizations of the territory in question. This is attested in several other examples, such as Vilna–Wilno–Vilnius; Czernowitz–Cernăuți–Chernivtsi; Pressburg–Pozsony–Presporak–Bratislava; and Danzig–Gdansk (Simon, 2016, p. 4).

The idea of readable cities leads to the fusing of translation with writing, where writers are turned into figurative translators (though they may also be working translators) who partake in modernist transformations of the cities they live in. They are cultural mediators whose practices of representation, transmission and transculturation (cf. Tymoczko, 2007) can include translation proper but also exceed it to encompass self-translation, retranslation, summary and parody (Meylaerts and Gonne, 2014, p. 137) – or even writing that eludes the source-target binary but is nonetheless governed by multilingual sensibilities.

For example, speaking of New Orleans, where translation is inherent in the city's francophone-anglophone divide, Malena (2014, p. 207) conceives of writers such as George Washington Cable, Alfred Mercier and Lafcadio

Hearn as 'performers of translation'. Their writings are translational in their probing into 'both the possibility and the negation of cultural transfer' (Malena, 2014, p. 205), and we observe how perspectives from translation studies and intercultural studies are merged in discussions about translational cities. Contrast this with Marshall's (2016, p. 197) emphasis on the dearth of English translations of French creole literature, hence his less optimistic conclusion that New Orleans is readable through the lens of translation 'only through a very elastic notion of space, and an extensive time lag'. The same city can thus give rise to different readings along a translational gradation, depending on whether one prefers to highlight cross-cultural negotiations or the lack thereof.

Translation has been applied to the understanding of geopolitical spaces that witness the traversal of territorial boundaries, as in the movement of migrants, refugees and exiles. Here, a reverse metaphorization is at work: etymologically, translation (from Latin *translatus*, perfect passive participle of *trānsferō* ('I transfer, convey')) denotes a 'carrying across' from one place to another. As figures in flux, migrants, refugees and exiles exemplify borders, which are dynamic fault-lines not necessarily congruent with territorial boundaries; therefore, it is no surprise that liminal geography has been a central site for the theorization of cultural translation (see, e.g., Bhabha, 1994) and, equally significantly, of the resistance to translation by the subaltern (Harel, 2016) or of the breakdown of translation under purist ideologies (e.g., restrictions on the use of French in Louisiana in the early twentieth century; see Marshall, 2016).

Itinerant figures such as migrants are, on one level, metaphorical embodiments of translation, experiencing with their bodies and minds the multiple dualities of disjunction (living in distinctive ethnic ghettos) versus dispersal (living across the city but remaining connected through digital communications); trace (physical signs registering ethnic cultures) versus link (virtual cultural networks); fixity (locale-based communication) versus nomadism (non-locale-based communication through mobile devices) (Cronin, 2016, p. 108). On another level, translation exists substantively in spaces inhabited by migrants; this involves not just the interlingual passage from migrant language to host language but also the intralingual processes of 'change, alteration, and mediation'. Digital technologies have made it easier to communicate virtually, and this further complicates the involvement of translation in migratory experiences, for example migrants' use of mobile translation apps and Skype interpreting, which enable them to be simultaneously absent from and present at their point of origin (Cronin, 2016, pp. 111–15).

The notion of the translational city prompts us to consider the city as *languaged space* – a space constituted through language practices, broadly defined – as well as how translation, in its various guises, is insinuated into urban spatial practices. Urban translating has been invoked in domains of representation beyond language-based texts, encompassing 'verbal or visual signs, graffiti, official architectures, marginal spaces, maps, installations, performances, or gardens' (Suchet and Mekdjian, 2016, p. 234). Here we witness the use of the term 'translation' widening, with its conventional semantic of transference assuming more diffuse meanings, including the circulation of words, symbols and narratives across cultural spaces without language borders necessarily being crossed (Baker, 2016, p. 7); the enactment of 'new situations and new modes of action' in urban spaces through graffiti, maps, installations and performances (Suchet and Mekdjian, 2016, p. 234); or the working through of all the city's textured heterogeneity with one's senses and body in city walks, or *flânerie* (see Furlani, 2016).

## 6.4 Translanguaging and Post-Multilingualism

Translation thrives not only at critical junctures of a city's historical-material transformation but also in the mundane intercultural moments of urban life. It is here that we can introduce the concept of translanguaging, which describes the flexible and creative deployment of resources to negotiate meanings and construct identities. Translanguaging happens within the movement between named languages but also between language varieties, between registers and between discourses. More crucially, it goes *beyond* language as such to incorporate, in tandem, all semiotic resources available in the circumstances (verbal, visual, aural-oral, olfactory, tactile, kinetic and so forth) to effect a multilingual, multimodal and multisensory process of making sense. In superdiverse urban contexts, this means working through the complex linguistic, discursive and cultural grids of the city by tapping into the full range of resources in one's repertoire – a virtual spectrum of linguistic and nonlinguistic resources drawn from different languages, language varieties, registers, discourses, modes and media at one's disposal.

So where do we locate translation in this? On this point, we have recourse to a large-scale AHRC-funded project conducted in the period 2014–18, titled 'Translation and Translanguaging: Investigating Linguistic and Cultural Transformations in Superdiverse Wards in Four UK Cities', or TLANG for short. TLANG (website, n.d.) defines translation as 'the negotiation of meaning through different modes (spoken/written/ visual/ gestural), where speakers have different proficiencies in a range of languages and varieties. When speakers do not share a common language they may rely on translation by professionals, friends or family, or by digital means. Such practices occur in "translation zones", and are at the cutting edge of translation and negotiation.' This is a sociolinguistic approach to translation, which takes the form of practices 'at the cutting edge of translation and negotiation', transcending the source-to-target and language-to-language schematic of translation, and thus shading into translanguaging. Translation, when coupled with translanguaging, therefore provides a more inclusive framework within which we can understand the semiotic dynamic of multilingual societies. From a translation-and-translanguaging perspective, people do not simply shuttle hither-and-thither *between* languages – although they can do that as the circumstances require; rather they reside *within* translation zones. Translation zones, a term popularized by Apter (2006), are not simply zones of interlingual translation; they are, rather, 'areas of intense inter-action across languages, spaces defined by an acute consciousness of cultural negotiations', serving as 'a nexus at which politics, poetics, linguistics, environment, history, economics, and mobility intersect' (Blackledge, Creese and Hu, 2018, p. 7).

On this view, translation zones form a continuum with translanguaging spaces (Li, 2018; Lee and Li, 2020), and also align with the idea of the translational city, as discussed earlier. Translation, in its interlingual, intralingual and intersemiotic facets, constitutes the to-and-fro exchanges characteristic of multilingual societies: at the same time, it partakes of translanguaging as holistic communication, converging languages, lan-guage varieties, registers, discourse, artefacts and bodies (Baynham and Lee, 2019), as well as users' personal histories; experiences and environ-ment; attitudes, beliefs and ideologies; cognitive and physical capacities 'into one coordinated and meaningful performance, and making it into a lived experience' (Li, 2018, p. 23).

Some illustrations from TLANG will demonstrate how translation fig-ures in this project. The following example, reported in Blackledge et al. (2018), took place in the Chinese Community Centre in Birmingham, UK. As part of the Centre's advocacy and advice services, Joanne provides translation support to members of the Chinese community in the city when they apply for social welfare benefits. Translation in this particular context is camouflaged as several procedures, including narrative repre-sentation, recontextualization, summary, negotiation, re-semiotization and so forth (Blackledge et al., 2018, ch. 2).

The applicant in this case was a certain X, who was applying for Personal Independence Payment on her husband's behalf. For this pur-pose, she had to fill in a form to furnish evidence of her husband's disability. Joanne's job was to translate the questions on the form into Mandarin Chinese for X and to translate X's responses from Mandarin Chinese into English to be written on the form. What Joanne effectively had to do involved the following (Blackledge et al., 2018, pp. 44–5, with minor amendments), which exceeds the bounds of what is normatively considered translation:

(a) translate the requirements of the form, and by extension the require-ments of the welfare benefits system;
(b) translate X's narrative from Mandarin Chinese to English;

(c)  translate X's extended narratives into abbreviated, summary versions;

(d)  re-semiotize the spoken narratives into the format required by the computer-based form; and

(e)  translate the re-semiotized English version of X's narratives into Mandarin Chinese.

In this list we see a range of processes that are broadly translational – a construct that eases translation into translanguaging, and vice versa. Among these, (b) and (e) come closest to a conventional understanding of translation. The rest involve summary translation, as in (c); interdiscursive mediation between the institution and the lay applicant, as in (a); and re-semiotization requiring changes in format as a text moves across media platforms, as in (d).

Let us turn to one concrete episode. One question on the form read: 'Tell us about whether you have difficulties with your speech, your hearing or your understanding of what is being said to you.' Instead of translating this head-on, Joanne first set the stage by recapitulating what they had done in the previous section and then introducing the next section: '[T]he following part will be the most important[;] it's about him [the client's husband] not being able to communicate' (translation from Mandarin). After X spoke about her husband's inability to remember names, Joanne followed up with this question, in Mandarin: 'So[,] for example[,] if he's here and I am talking[,] he won't know what I am talking about and he won't understand it?' (Blackledge et al., 2018, pp. 35–6). This effectively translates the gist of the question on the form with respect to 'your understanding of what is being said to you'. To this, X replies: '[U]m[,] can you say he'll understand it if it's about him' (Blackledge et al., 2018, p. 36). In a similar vein, Joanne unpacks the part of the question on 'difficulties with your speech' as follows (Blackledge et al., 2018, p. 38, in English translation with the Chinese transcript omitted):

J:  If someone talks to him[,] can he understand and join in the conversation?

X:  He won't say anything but just yee yee ey, yee yee ey[.]

J:  So he doesn't talk, just makes noises[?]

X:  He won't answer back each time we have an argument[,] he just makes funny noises to mock the way I talk to him[,] just like that he doesn't know how to quarrel with people[.]

As we can see here, an apparently straightforward question in English was stretched and unfolded circuitously over several conversational turns in Mandarin; and it was through this process that Joanne was able to translate the essence of the question to the client and translate the client's answer for the bureaucracy. We also see Joanne stepping beyond the role of the translator and taking on a more agentive role, explaining to X that certain points should be excluded from the form as they might work to her disadvantage (Blackledge et al., 2018, p. 38):

> J:    I think I'd better leave out the part that says I understand what people are saying if they are talking about me [note: this was X's response to the previous question] as it won't help you to score[.]
>
> X:    [I]t's just to say he knows if people are saying he's stupid[.]
>
> J:    [B]ecause this question is about communication and if you add this statement here[,] whoever reads it will think oh[,] so you actually can understand other people[,] what I mean is[.]

From this example, we see that the translator's challenge is not simply to overcome language barriers but also to plug gaps in registers and discourses. As such, Joanne's translation assignment was really an exercise in 'linguistic hospitality' (Blackledge et al., 2018, p. 34). All the questions on the form could easily have been translated into Mandarin, but, in order to elicit an accurate picture of the client's situation, Joanne had to do what I would describe as *translate incognito*, that is, sneak in a source text in fragments through translation by way of extended talk with the client. The principle of economy is irrelevant, as lots of scaffolding, redundancies, detours and small talk needed to be built in to bridge the register and discursive gap between bureaucracy (manifested by the English-language form) and the Mandarin-speaking client. The textual outcome would not conventionally be recognized as translation, although it does embed the source text (i.e., the question in the form) within a much longer stretch of text in the target language, effecting not transference on the face of the language but interlingual and interdiscursive communication for a particular purpose.

Another example, reported in Creese, Blackledge and Hu (2018, pp. 845–7), took place in a market, also in Birmingham. FC is a female customer, and KC and BJ are butchers. In this scene, a transaction involving the purchase of a meat product was undertaken between the primarily Cantonese-speaking FC and the English-speaking BJ through the mediation of KC. KC had several languages in his repertoire, strategically deploying one or more of them in his transactions according to the language proclivities of his customers. KC's language performance may be described as translanguaging inasmuch as it evidences a flexibility and contingency in his selection of language resources to fulfil specific communicative needs at particular moments of time.

1. BJ    hello. you want that one?
2. FC    ((xxxx))
3. BJ    you want all of it?
4. FC    ((to KC)) 哎,老細幫我叫佢切咁啲肥去 [hi, boss, please help tell him to cut off more fat]
6. KC    ((to BJ)) she want to take the fat off like the brown lady. That one.
7. BJ    yeah

8. KC   ((to BJ)) she want that one
      ((KC serves a male customer while BJ continues to serve the same female customer))
9. FC   mince, mince
10. BJ   ((to FC)) mince? mince, but no fat?
11. FC   yes. ((to KC)) 幫我斬小小肥就得㗎喇
      [please help me cut a little bit fat off, that's it]
13. KC   佢有嘛, 佢有幫你打碎, 佢知㗎喇, 同佢講㗎喇
      [he has done it, he has minced it for you. he knows, I have told him already.]
      ((KC is also serving a male customer))
15. FC   ((to BJ)) no no no, a little bit more
16. KC   ((to BJ)) take a little bit fat off, and then mince
17. BJ   yea. mince all of it, yea?
18. KC   ((to FC)) 係唔係全部打碎呀? [mince all of it?]
19. FC   打碎, 打碎 [mince it, mince it]
20. KC   全部? [all?]
21. FC   幫我切咁小小肥呀 [please help me cut a bit fat off]
22. KC   係呀, 係唔係呢兩㗎全部打㗎佢 [yes, both pieces need to be minced, right?]
23. FC   係呀, 切小小肥㗎幫我, 唔愛小小肥。 小小好喇, 唔好切咁多。 [yes, please help me cut a bit of fat off, I don't want a bit of the fat. only a bit off will do, do not cut too much]
26. BJ   ((to FC)) take a bit of fat off
27. KC   ((to BJ:)) take a little bit off ((chopping sound))
28. FC   ((to BJ:)) 㗎喇, 㗎喇 [enough enough]
29. KC   ((greeting a new customer:)) hello, no yellow today!
30. BJ   ((asking FC)) yea? and mince all of it? do you want it washed? wash? just washing yea?
32. KC   ((to a new group of customers)) Hello. 你们要点什么 <what you guys want to buy?>

On a microtextual level, we see a great deal of translation at work, with KC communicating FC's requests about how she wanted her meat to be cut to his assistant BJ, and also communicating BJ's questions back to FC (line 18). At three points (lines 9, 11, 15), FC attempted to bridge the language barrier herself with fragments of English, although for the most part she had to rely on KC.

KC's mediation, however, was not all strictly speaking translation: at line 13, he used Cantonese to reassure FC that her requests had been conveyed to BJ and that BJ knew exactly what she needed; at line 12, KC used Cantonese again to confirm with FC her request to mince both pieces of meat, without, however, translating this point for BJ; and at line 27, he instructed BJ to 'take a little bit [of fat] off', which did not translate any utterance in particular but rather affirmed FC's request as made throughout the conversation.

As with the previous example, what we are witnessing is the use of two languages not to effect a point-to-point correspondence but to iteratively negotiate difference and arrive at a common understanding, that is, remove a little bit of fat from the meat, with translation being subsumed into the whole process that is translanguaging.

Further, if we agree with Bauman (2000) that we are entering the age of liquid modernity, as characterized by the mobility and fluidity of texts, bodies and identities, we must consider whether multilingualism as a theoretical construct still sufficiently captures our language realities. Multilingualism, as pointed out earlier, points to the static co-presence of several languages within a space, be it cognitive, cultural, geopolitical or virtual. The contemporary world of communication, however, speaks more to Bauman's idea of liquidity, where language users are no longer confined by the language(s) they speak or write but are able to draw on heterogeneous repertoires comprising a mix of named languages, language varieties, registers, discourses and so forth. Moreover, there is increasing recognition that language is not solely utilitarian; it can be used performatively, for instance to satirize established discourses, to flaunt place-based identities, or simply to create light-hearted linguistic entertainment.

This situation heralds the age of post-multilingualism (Li, 2016), which takes us beyond the juxtaposition of two or more languages into complex discursive spaces, where language becomes a key instrument in performing liquid-modern subjectivities, creativities and criticalities and de-territorializes language usage from its institutions. Post-multilingualism embodies critical challenges, such as the tension between national languages and dialects, or the paradox sustained in the use of languages traditionally associated with cultural 'Others' to express the identities of 'Us' (Li, 2016, p. 19).

Post-multilingualism also means moving beyond multilingualism, even language as such, as a primary category in the organization of social experience. This opens up the possibility of thinking in terms of distributed language and spatial repertoires (Pennycook, 2018), where, instead of a human-centred notion of language, we think of communication as being constituted through spatially dispersed resources, including artefacts – compare with the mind-boggling idea of 'interartefactual translation' (Otsuji and Pennycook, 2021): processes by which objects change their meanings in relation to other objects within semiotic assemblages where human and language may play a mediating role.

Examples of language phenomena exhibiting post-multilingual tendencies include new Chinglish (English inflected with Chinese syntactical rules and used strategically to subvert dominant discourses through lexical coinage (Li, 2016)), Kongish (Hong Kong English inflected by Cantonese vocabulary and syntax) as used in satirical discourse, and Singlish (Singapore English) as used in strategic rather than vernacular settings.

 **Kongish Daily《港語日報》** shared a post.
6 May at 02:02 · ✪

性/別公義委員會 Gender and Sexual Justice in Action claim wah "Eat tofu" must hai women only....bcoz our society mainly use this expression on women wor...

Gum "raping" dou hai male only term la...although only a handful of unfortunately men been raped in our society je...

叫賣**臭豆腐**就是煽動男性
食女性**豆腐**，即使臭

✔ 香港政確

**Figure 6.1** A Facebook post from *Kongish Daily*

Figure 6.1 shows an example from Kongish Daily, a Facebook page that uses Kongish for social and political commentary. The two sentences in the post are typical of the kind of language used by Kongish Daily: 'Gender and Sexual Justice in Action claim wah "Eat Tofu" must hai women only ... bcoz our society mainly use this expression on women wor ... Gum raping dou hai male only term la ... although only a handful of unfortunately men been raped in our society je'.

The apparently English text is shot through with a strong dose of Cantonese, with the insertion of *wah* ('say'), *hai* (verb 'to be'), *wor* (interjection particle), *dou hai* ('is/are also'), *la* (sentence-final particle) and *je* (sentence-final particle). This is therefore a translational text in the sense that it is English *written through* Cantonese, or, better still, Cantonese masquerading as a (distorted) form of English. While vaguely comprehensible, the two 'English' sentences make complete sense only when mentally 'back-translated' into Cantonese, here a source language of sorts. This is trans-languaging at work, carrying with it a strong subversive potential, given that Hong Kong is a former colony of Britain, with its lingua franca Cantonese being degraded for the most part of its colonial history.

**Figure 6.2** An ecclesiastical artefact from Singapore

There is additionally an intercultural element: 'eat tofu' is a colloquial expression meaning 'to take sexual advantage of someone'; and the inter-semiotic reference to the picture of stinky tofu (Figure 6.1), a vernacular food commonly found in the streets of Hong Kong, cleverly turns the 'eat tofu' idiom back into its plebeian form, adding a layer of visual-verbal playfulness to the statement. All of this is undertaken as part of a critique: in this case, the editor is questioning whether the idiom 'eat tofu' should be associated exclusively with women. This is an example of how linguistic and other semiotic resources are put to creative and critical use by multilingual online communities; and how the constructs of translanguaging and translation might be employed in tandem to make sense of such phenomena.

Language can be subject to commodification in multilingual societies, often involving translation and translanguaging. Figure 6.2 shows an ecclesiastical artefact (a pin button) from Singapore, conceived as part of a series of merchandise subsuming Singlish into a Christian framework.

The expression *jiak buey liao* means 'can't finish eating' (suggesting an ample supply of food) in Hokkien, a dominant Chinese dialect in Singapore. Below this text, we see 'Jesus Feeds the Five Thousand', followed by a reference to Matthew 14:13–21. This evokes the Biblical story of Jesus turning two fish and five loaves of bread into more than enough food for his five thousand followers, with baskets of leftovers; this is visually supported by pictures of fish and bread on the pin button. The idea of abundance thus binds the expression *jiak buey liao* and the 'Jesus Feeds the Five Thousand' in a translational relationship, such that the one dialectically responds to the other without there being any lexical equivalence. This can be considered an instance of translanguaging inasmuch as the texts do not merely move across languages but also transgress registers (vernacular Hokkien versus Biblical English) and discourses (ordinary speech versus Biblical narrative).

## 6.5 Multilingualism sans Translation

Lastly, a balanced assessment of the role of translation in multilingual settings will need to contend with situations where translation may altogether be precluded; in other words, can multilingualism survive without translation? Indeed, the absence of translation can sometimes be theoretically more significant than its presence, especially in contexts where it is taken for granted.

Illustrative in this regard is Pennycook and Otsuji's (2015) study of the language dynamics of multilingual kitchens, where workers from different language backgrounds come together in a restricted space. The issue is what kind of language arrangement is necessary to get the work (cooking, serving, washing and so forth) done effectively. Conventional wisdom has it that if everyone spoke their own tongue, a Babelian scenario might ensue where interlingual communication breaks down (Pennycook and Otsuji, 2015, p. 68). Since Steiner (1975), a reference to Babel would almost automatically invoke translation as a solution in reconciling a plethora of tongues. Yet a prior question could be asked, and that is whether interlingual communication as such is indispensable; or: can a Babelian scenario be resolved in ways other than translation? For Pennycook and Otsuji (2015, p. 69), the divergence of tongues in multilingual kitchens need not always be mediated by a bridging medium, for '[m]ost of these workers have complex work and language trajectories, having picked up bits of other languages (and usually very functional bits) as they work their way through different kitchens'. The situation we have here is aptly described as multilingualism *sans* translation.

Without translation, how do people with different language backgrounds communicate without descending into chaos? Metrolingualism provides a way out of this multilingual quandary. Metrolingualism describes urban multilingualism in everyday settings, a form of 'quotidian translingual exchange that is part of how the city works, how language and identity are negotiated' (Pennycook and Otsuji, 2015, p. 10). It refers to a mode of thinking and researching communication in the city beyond the confines of language as we normally understand it, and hence bypasses translation as the exclusive mode of redemption from a Babelian situation. Metrolingualism posits that communication is achieved through dynamic interaction among linguistic and other semiotic resources (including artefacts), everyday activities (involving physical bodies) and spatial repertoires (an assemblage of discrete spaces). This line of thinking is in accord with translanguaging, and nuances what it means to be multilingual: 'The multilingual person is not someone who translates constantly from one language or cultural system into another, although translation is something multilingual subjects are able to do if needed. To be multilingual is above all to live in more than one language, *to be one for whom translation is unnecessary*' (Pratt, 2002, p. 35, emphasis added).

Thus, while all translators must be bi- or multilinguals, the reverse does not always hold true. Rather, translation remains an *option* for multilingual subjects; it is neither indispensable nor inevitable. This observation helps us move away from the default idea that translatability is a *sine qua non* in multilingual societies (and, therefore, that untranslatability is eminently undesirable). It has the potential to *de-fetishize translation* by having us come to terms with its inadequacy on higher theoretical grounds. As Pratt (2002, p. 35) argues, '[t]he image for multilingualism is not translation, perhaps, but *desdoblamiento* ("doubling"), a multiplying of the self. Translation is a deep but incomplete metaphor for the traffic in meaning. It is probably not in the long run an adequate basis for a theory of crosscultural meaning making and certainly not a substitute for such a theory.' What, then, does a theory of cross-cultural meaning look like? Given that (post-)multilingual societies are multifaceted, mobile and perennially evolving, can any single theoretical perspective capture the traffic in meaning for which translation is said to be 'a deep but incomplete metaphor'? I propose that a sufficient theory of cross-cultural meaning should, paradoxically, always be insufficient. Being truly multidisciplinary, it should remain a fluid discursive site capable of absorbing all relevant perspectives (some of which may still be on the horizon), including but not limited to those of urban studies, cultural geography, history, literature, sociology, architecture, translanguaging and translation. Translation dovetails into this intellectual constellation but does not constitute it.

## References

Apter, E. (2006). *The Translation Zone*. Princeton, NJ: Princeton University Press.

Baker, M. (2016). *Translation and Conflict: A Narrative Account*. Abingdon: Routledge.

Bauman, Z. (2000). *Liquid Modernity*. Cambridge: Polity.

Baynham, M., and Lee, T. K. (2019). *Translation and Translanguaging*. Abingdon: Routledge.

Bhabha, H. (1994). *The Location of Culture*. London: Routledge.

Blackledge, A., Creese, A., and Hu, R. (2018). Translating the City (WP.34), https://tlang754703143.files.wordpress.com/2018/08/translating-the-city.pdf.

Creese, A., Blackledge, A., and Hu, R. (2018). Translanguaging and translation: The construction of social difference across city spaces. *International Journal of Bilingual Education and Bilingualism*, **21**(7), 841–52.

Cronin, M. (2016). Digital Dublin: Translating the cybercity. In S. Simon, ed., *Speaking Memory: How Translation Shapes City Life*. Montreal: McGill-Queen's University Press, pp. 103–16.

Cronin, M., and Simon, S. (2014). Introduction: The city as translation zone. *Translation Studies*, **7**(2), 119–32.

Demirkol-Ertürk, Ş., and Paker, S. (2014). Beyoğlu/Pera as a translating site in Istanbul. *Translation Studies*, **7**(2), 170–85.

Essman, H., and Frank, A. P. (1991). Translation anthologies: An invitation to the curious and a case study. *Target*, **3**(1), 65–96.

Furlani, A. (2016). Montreal's third spaces on foot. In S. Simon, ed., *Speaking Memory: How Translation Shapes City Life*. Montreal: McGill-Queen's University Press, pp. 249–72.

Grutman, R. (2006). Refraction and recognition: Literary multilingualism in translation. *Target*, **18**(1), 17–47.

Grutman, R. (2009). Multilingualism. In M. Baker and G. Saldana, eds., *Routledge Encyclopedia of Translation Studies*. 2nd ed. Abingdon: Routledge, pp. 182–86.

Harel, S. (2016). Monolingualism and plural narratives: The translation of suffering in the language of the city. In S. Simon, ed., *Speaking Memory: How Translation Shapes City Life*. Montreal: McGill-Queen's University Press, pp. 117–41.

Hermans, T. (2014). *Conference of the Tongues*. Abingdon: Routledge.

Lee, T. K. (2012). Translation and language power relations in heterolingual anthologies of literature. *Babel*, **58**(4), 443–56.

Lee, T. K. (2013). *Translating the Multilingual City: Crosslingual Practices and Language Ideology*. Oxford: Peter Lang.

Lee, T. K., and Li, W. (2020). Translanguaging and momentarity in social interaction. In A. de Fina and A. Georgakopoulou, eds., *The Cambridge Handbook of Discourse Studies*. Cambridge: Cambridge University Press, pp. 394–416.

Li, W. (2016). New Chinglish and the post-multilingualism challenge: Translanguaging ELF in China. *Journal of English as a Lingua Franca*, **5**(1), 1–25.

Li, W. (2018). Translanguaging as a practical theory of language. *Applied Linguistics*, **39**(1), 9–30.

Malena, A. (2014). The city that shouldn't be: New Orleans. *Translation Studies*, **7**(2), 203–17.

Marshall, B. (2016). Linguistic zones of the French Atlantic. In S. Simon, ed., *Speaking Memory: How Translation Shapes City Life*. Montreal: McGill-Queen's University Press, pp. 191–204.

Meylaerts, R. (2007). 'La Belgique vivra-t-elle?' Language and translation ideological debates in Belgium (1919–1940). *The Translator*, **13**(2), 297–319.

Meylaerts, R. (2011). Translational justice in a multilingual world: An overview of translational regimes. *Meta*, **56**(4), 743–57.

Meylaerts, R., and Gonne, M. (2014). Transferring the city – Transgressing borders: Cultural mediators in Antwerp (1850–1930). *Translation Studies*, **7**(2), 133–51.

Mezei, K. (1998). Bilingualism and translation in/of Michèle Lalonde's Speak White. *The Translator*, **4**(2), 229–47.

Otsuji, E., and Pennycook, A. (2021). Interartefactual translation: Metrolingualism and resemiotization. In T. K. Lee, ed., *The Routledge Handbook of Translation and the City*. Abingdon: Routledge, pp. 59–76.

Pennycook, A. (2018). *Posthumanist Applied Linguistics*. Abingdon: Routledge.

Pennycook, A., and Otsuji, E. (2015). *Metrolingualism: Language in the City*. Abingdon: Routledge.

Pizzi, K. (2016). A modernist city resisting translation? Trieste between Slovenia and Italy. In S. Simon, ed., *Speaking Memory: How Translation Shapes City Life*. Montreal: McGill-Queen's University Press, pp. 45–57.

Pratt, M. L. (2002). The traffic in meaning: Translation, contagion, infiltration. *Profession*, **12**, 25–36.

Simon, S. (2012) *Cities in Translation: Intersections of Language and Memory*, Abingdon: Routledge.

Simon, S. (2016). Introduction. In S. Simon, ed., *Speaking Memory: How Translation Shapes City Life*. Montreal: McGill-Queen's University Press, pp.3–19.

Steiner, G. (1975). *After Babel: Aspects of Language and Translation*. London: Oxford University Press.

Suchet, M., and Mekdjian, S. (2016). Artivism as a form of urban translation: An indisciplinary hypothesis. In S. Simon, ed., *Speaking Memory: How Translation Shapes City Life*. Montreal: McGill-Queen's University Press, pp. 220–48.

Sywenky, I. (2014). (Re)constructing the urban palimpsest of Lemberg/Lwów/Lviv: A case study in the politics of cultural translation in East Central Europe. *Translation Studies*, **7**(2), 152–69.

TLANG website (n.d.) https://tlang.org.uk/.

Tymoczko, M. (2007). *Enlarging Translation, Empowering Translators*. Manchester: St Jerome.

Tyulenev, S. (2014). *Translation and Society: An Introduction*. Abingdon: Routledge.

# 7

# Less Translated Languages

Albert Branchadell

## 7.1 Introduction

Branchadell (2005) introduced the subject of less translated languages (LTLs) as a new field of inquiry – an idea that was generally applauded by reviewers and embraced by scholars (e.g., Brems, Réthelyi and van Kalmthout, 2017). Here, I review the concept and look at it from new angles. Firstly, I place LTLs in the wider context of the 'global constellation of languages' (de Swaan, 2001) and move it from the 'classic' field of literary translation (Heilbron, 2010; Casanova, 2010) to the emerging field of institutional translation (Koskinen, 2008). In the next sections I present four case studies to illustrate how translation and interpreting arrangements in selected institutional settings reinforce the same type of asymmetric power relations that prevail in the world language system.

## 7.2 The Concept

Prior to its use in translation studies (the journal *mTm*, which started in 2009, and d'Haen, Goerlandt and Sell (2015)), the notion of a 'minor language' existed in the field of linguistics. According to Stolz (2001, p. 218), if there are 6.5 billion people and 6,500 languages, 'the average speech-community of a presently spoken language has 1.0 million native speakers'. On this basis, 'languages with speaker populations above the average are major languages, whereas languages with speaker populations below the average belong to the class of minor languages'.

Although it may seem mechanical, this definition is much clearer than the one proposed in 2009 by the journal mTm, which is made in terms of non-defined concepts such as 'limited', 'intermediate' and 'unlimited' diffusion and which mixes diffusion with status:

> By the term minor language, we mean either a language of limited diffu-
> sion or one of intermediate diffusion compared to a major language or
> language of unlimited diffusion. By the term major language, we mean
> either a language of unlimited diffusion such as English, or a language that
> enjoys major status within a state where other, officially recognised minor
> languages are also spoken
>      (e.g. Finnish as an official language in Finland compared to Swedish).

In 2001, Stolz convincingly argued that minor languages 'do not correspond in a one-to-one relationship to the usual sociological categories of
linguistics'. While many minor languages are also endangered languages,
there are minor languages – Stolz mentioned Estonian, Luxembourgish
and Icelandic – that are not endangered. The same holds for the distinction between minor languages and minority languages. While many
minor languages are also minority languages, there are minor languages
that are not minority languages (Estonian, Luxembourgish and Icelandic
could be mentioned again) and there are minority languages that are not
minor languages (Stolz mentioned Chuvash in Russia, Occitan in France
and Low German in Germany, three minority languages whose speech-
communities are above the 1 million mark. To these one could add
Catalan, Galician and Basque in Spain, languages that we will discuss in
Section 7.5). Stolz was well aware of the relative nature of the category,
minority language, that we have observed in the *mTm* definition of
'minor'. As he put it, 'a language may be a minority language in state
X – German in Italy, Belgium, France, and Denmark – and at the same
time a majority language in state Y – German in Austria and Germany'. To
avoid misunderstandings, Branchadell (2011, p. 97) used the notion of
'absolute minority language' to refer to minority languages that are not
a majority language in any state.

Stolz (2001, p. 231) concluded that 'minor languages are a category of
their own based on demography. This category cuts across all other
categorizations of languages.' In the same vein, I contend that LTLs are
a category of their own based on translation. This category cuts across
the usual divide between major and minor languages. What is new in
this concept is that prominence of languages is not expressed in terms
of size (number of speakers) but rather in purely *translational* terms.
From this point of view, what turns a given language into an LTL is that
this language is comparatively less translated from (and/or less translated into) than other languages, irrespective of size.

A difference between LTLs and minor languages (or minority languages in the absolute sense) is that LTL is a context-relative notion.
To be or not to be a minor or an absolute minority language is a yes/no
question: it depends on whether a given language is above or under the
1 million mark (minor) or on whether the speakers of a given language
are fewer than the rest of a state's population (minority). Being an LTL

is a matter of degree (and is subject to evolution) and depends on the distribution of power across institutions. LTLs stand in the middle of a continuum ranging from NTLs (non-translated languages, e.g., languages that are neither the source nor the target of translation) to WTLs (widely translated languages) or even HTLs (hyper-translated languages). In this connection one has to look at the *direction* of translation as well. Languages can be less translated from but much translated into and vice versa.

These labels are intended to link this translation continuum to a general language hierarchy like that developed by de Swaan (2001). According to de Swaan (2001), languages are interconnected in a 'system' which consists of four levels defined according to their social role: at the lowest level are peripheral, typically 'minority', languages (98 per cent of the world's languages are included), which are satellites of central languages (some 100 languages, typically 'national' or state languages), whose speakers are connected to each other through a limited number of supercentral languages (thirteen very widely spoken languages like Arabic and Chinese), and above them sits English as *the* hyper-central language which is supposed to hold the entire system together.

Heilbron (2010) applied some of de Swaan's insights to (literary) translation. Looking at the global market for translations, he posited a 'world system of translation', a four-level structure in which he claimed that English occupies 'a sort of hypercentral position' (55 to 60 per cent of all translations). After English, German and French have a central position (a share of about 10 per cent each). In the third level or semi-central position are languages like Italian, Spanish and Russian (1 to 3 per cent of the world market). All the other languages of the world belong to the fourth level of 'peripheral' languages (less than 1 per cent of translations). What is striking in this structure is that peripheral status is independent of size: Arabic and Chinese – two *supercentral* languages in de Swaan's conception – count as peripheral despite their fairly large number of speakers.

Branchadell (2005) tried to connect the field of LTLs with the 'power turn' in translation studies. The issue of power is not alien to TS but has been largely confined to the field of *literary* translation. According to Dollerup (2002, p. 193), 'curiously enough, the discussion of "power" seems to have focused on literary translation, probably because most people concerned with translation theory are primarily interested in literary works'. In the face of this literary bias, Meylaerts (2018, p. 226) complained that 'in-depth research on the power issues involved in the politics of translation is still lacking'.

In response to these worries, this chapter explores power issues within the field of *institutional* translation *and interpreting*. According to Schäffner, Tcaciuc and Tesseur (2014, p. 493f.), 'there is widespread agreement among researchers (e.g. Kang, 2008; Koskinen, 2008; Mossop, 1988) that institutional translation is still rather unexplored and that empirical studies are missing'. In the following sections I endeavour to illustrate that institutional translation is a response to and paradoxically helps to maintain the same type of hierarchical structures that prevail in the 'global constellation of languages'. I examine the unbalanced translation (and interpreting) regimes of the United Nations (UN), a multilingual suprastate institution like the European Union (EU), a multilingual state (Spain) and a multilingual region within a multilingual state (Catalonia), using Spanish as a case in point.

## 7.3   The Unbalanced Translation Regime of the UN

The UN adopted official multilingualism in Resolution 2 of the General Assembly (1946), which provides that 'in all the organs of the United Nations, other than the International Court of Justice, Chinese, French, English, Russian and Spanish shall be the official languages, and English and French the working languages'. The General Assembly turned Spanish (1948), Russian (1968) and Chinese (1973) into working languages and admitted Arabic as both an official and a working language in 1973. No other official or working language has been added since, although a German Translation Section was established in 1974, which provides official German translations of UN documents.

UN regulations introduced a clear division between the reduced number of official and working languages and the rest of the world's languages. Some of the world's largest languages (with more than 100 million speakers), such as Japanese, Hindi, Malay and Portuguese, which are also 'supercentral' within de Swaan's system, share non-official status not only with 'central' but also with 'peripheral' languages, a class that includes all the minor languages of the world. In terms of translation within the UN system, all languages except the six official ones count as NTLs regardless of size.

To gauge the implementation of multilingualism in the UN system organizations, one can resort to the reports of the Joint Inspection Unit (JIU) of the UN system, which was established at the 21st session of the General Assembly (1966–7) as the only independent external oversight body of the UN system. The data provided by these reports might seem outdated: a telling circumstance is that the JU has not produced any report on the status of implementation of multilingualism in the UN system organizations after 2011 (Fall and Zhang, 2011).

These reports show that there is a divide between official and (mandated) working languages, which has no clear normative basis. Secondly, there is a divide between mandated working languages and de facto working languages. I want to explore the position of Spanish in this unbalanced situation.

Fall and Zhang (2011, p. 47) provided a list of official and (mandated) working languages of the secretariats of the UN system organizations (see Table 7.1). In the list, A stands for Arabic, C for Chinese, E for English, F for French, G for German, H for Hindi, I for Italian, P for Portuguese, R for Russian and S for Spanish; asterisks refer to issues of no concern here.

Commenting on this list, Fernández-Vítores (2014, p. 6) admits that it presents a rosy *de jure* situation. In many instances, Spanish-speaking delegates do not or cannot benefit from the status of Spanish as a working language and give in to the use of English either for budgetary reasons or in the name of 'functionality'.

Table 7.1 *List of official and (mandated) working languages of the secretariats of the UN system organizations*

| Organization | Official languages | Working languages? |
|---|---|---|
| UN Secretariat | ACEFRS | EF |
| UNE5CWA | AEF | AEF |
| UNESCAP | CEFR | EF |
| UNECLAC | EFS | EFS |
| UNBCA | AEF | AEF |
| UNECE | EFR | EFR |
| UNCTAD | ACEFRS | AEFS |
| UNDP | EFS | EFS |
| UNFPA | ACEFRS | EFS |
| UNICEF | ACEFRS | EFS |
| UNHCR | ACEFRS | EF |
| WFP | ACEFRS | E |
| UNEP | ACEFS | EFS |
| UN-Habitat | ACEFRS | EF |
| UNRWA | AE | E |
| UKODC | ACEFRS | EF |
| UNOPS | ACEFRS | EF |
| UjO | EFS | ACEFRSG |
| FAO* | ACEFRS | ACEFRS |
| UNESCO | ACEFRSHPI | EF |
| ICAO | ACEFRS | ACEFRS |
| WHO** | ACEFRS | ACEFRS |
| UPU | F | FE |
| ITU | ACEFRS | ACEFRS |
| WMO | ACEFRS | ACEFRS |
| IMO | ACEFRS | EFS |
| WIPO*** | | ACEFRS |
| UNIDO | ACEFRS | EF |
| UN WTO | ACEFRS | EFS |
| IAEA | ACEFRS | E |

Drawing on Kudryavtsev and Ouedraogo (2003, para. 35f.), who compare mandated working languages and de facto working languages as indicated by secretariats (see Table 7.2), Fernández-Vítores (2012, p. 94) notices that whereas Spanish is a mandated working language in twelve of sixteen secretariats, it is de facto used in just one (WIPO – OMPI in Spanish) and just 'occasionally'.

Observing interpretation services on the ground clearly shows that *de facto* multilingualism deviates from egalitarian expectations.

For this endeavour it is useful to resort to Gazzola's (2006, p. 405) three definitions of equality, adapted here for my own purposes. In the strictest sense, equality is achieved when delegates are guaranteed the right to speak and listen to their L1 and all languages are treated equally. In a less strict sense, equality is achieved when delegates are guaranteed the right to speak and listen to their L1 but languages are not treated equally (some use relay, others do not). In the least strict sense, equality is achieved when delegates are guaranteed the right to speak their L1 but not listen to it (there is an asymmetric interpretation regime). (Of course, the next point on the scale is sheer inequality, which is achieved when delegates are guaranteed neither the right to speak nor the right to listen to their L1.)

According to Kudryavtsev and Ouedraogo (2003, para. 39), 'official calendar meetings are conducted in general with simultaneous interpretation in the requested languages and informal meetings are provided with such services on an 'as-available' basis. However, for different reasons, full language services are not provided to all meetings attended by representatives of Member States.' Around 20 per cent of calendar meetings at the UN Headquarters were held *without* interpretation in the years 1994–2003. At the UN Office at Geneva, a little more than 50 per cent were held without interpretation. At Vienna, the percentage rocketed to 77 per cent in 2002–3.

As Kudryavtsev and Ouedraogo (2003, para. 40) point out, these data 'confirm that despite resolution 50/11 [see below] and other pertinent resolutions of the General Assembly calling for the respect of [sic] language parity, meetings held at the United Nations without interpretation … remain important in percentage terms'.

According to Fernández-Vítores (2014, p. 3 in the *formal* meetings foreseen for 2014, interpretation ranged from 97 and 95 per cent (English and French) to 79 per cent (Arabic and Chinese), with Spanish and Russian in the middle. Whereas inequalities are already visible in these data, when it comes to real use in *informal* meetings, asymmetry is even greater. According to a survey in the Geneva branch of the UN, in 2010 interpretation ranged from 98 per cent (English) and 87 per cent (French) to a mere 10 per cent (Russian), 7 per cent (Arabic) and 3 per cent (Chinese), with Spanish at 34 per cent.

Del Pino Romero (2014, p. 147) regrets that 'Spanish is treated as a second language category with respect to English and French'.

Table 7.2 Comparison between mandated working languages of the EU and de facto working languages

| Organization | Working language: | | Language: mostly used for | | |
| --- | --- | --- | --- | --- | --- |
| | Mandated | De facto | Intranets | Databases | Original texts of documents |
| United Nations | EF except for ECE*(EFR) ECLAC** (EFS) ESCWA*** (AEF) | | EF (Geneva) E (New York and other main duty stations) | E | E (76.5%) / F (12.8%) / ET (4.2%) / Other (6.5%) [UNOG**** in 2000] |
| ILO | EFS | | EFS | EFS | E (85 2%) F (13.3%) / S (1.5%) |
| FAO | ACEFS | | E | EFS | Out of 13,274,000 words sent for translation m 2002: E (97.34%) / S (1.47%) F (1.16%) / A (0.02%) |
| UNESCO | EF (Pans): either E or F or both (other duty stations) | | EF | | 1998: E (60.86%) / F (39.14%) 1999: E (64.09%) / F (35.91%) 2000: E (74.69%) / F (25.31%) |
| ICAO | ACEFRS | E | E | E | E (85%) / F (6%) / S (4%) / A C R (5%) |
| WHO | None | EF | E | E | |
| UPU | EF | EF | EF | EF | F (45%) / E (45%) / Others (10%) |
| ITU | EFS | EF | EF | EF | E (93%) |
| WMO | EFRS | EF | EF | E | E (97.4%) / A (1.7%) / R (0.2%) / Other (0.7%) |
| DviO | EFS | E | E | E | |

Table 7.2 *Continued*

| Organization | Working language: | | | Language: mostly used for | |
| --- | --- | --- | --- | --- | --- |
| | Mandated | De facto | Intranets | Databases | Original texts of documents |
| WIPO | ACEFRS + some P | Mainly EF + ACGJRS | EF | EF | E (57.5%) / EF (17.8%) / S (12.3%) / F (8.2%) / Other (4.2%) |
| UNIDO | | E | E | E | n/a |
| IAEA | None | E | E | E | E (68%) / R (14%) / S (8%) / F (4%) / A (3%) / G (2%) / C (0.4%) / Other (0.3%) |
| World Bant | | E | E | E | |
| IMF | E | | E | E | |
| IFAD | AEFS | | E | E | AEFS |

* ECE stands for Economic Commission for Europe.

** ECLAC stands for Economic Commission for Latin America and the Caribbean.

*** ESCWA stands for Economic and Social Commission for Western Asia.

**** UNOG stands for United Nations Office at Geneva.

His main complaint concerns indirect interpretation: owing to a shortage of Arabic, Chinese and Russian in the Spanish booth, when a delegate takes the floor in one of these languages, a Spanish interpreter rarely interprets his or her speech directly. On the other hand, when delegates take the floor in Spanish, there is often no direct interpretation into Arabic, Chinese and Russian.

But relay interpretation is not the only problem. Del Pino Romero (2014, p. 150) reports that owing to a shortage of interpreters from Chinese, it was decided that Chinese interpreters would work both into and out of their active language (retour). (The same thing happens, usually, with speeches delivered in Arabic.) In this way, in the interpretation from Chinese or Arabic, two practices are combined that according to him 'damage the quality of interpretation': (a) indirect interpretation and (b) interpretation into a B language, that is, a language that is not the interpreter's mother tongue. Of course, it may happen that, in order to avoid this problem, Spanish-speaking delegates prefer to listen directly to the Chinese > English or Chinese > French interpretation and/or that they prefer to take the floor in EN or FR instead of ES. Indirect interpretation and interpretation into a B language seem to be working *against* multilingualism.

In addition, it has to be remembered that owing to the limited number of official languages, many delegates must speak in a language other than their L1. This poses a special challenge because interpreters must be able to comprehend all sorts of accents, in addition to coping with standard issues of speed and style. As Baigorri and Travieso (2017, p. 54) point out, 'almost 50% of the delegates cannot use their mother tongue, but rather a foreign language, nowadays mostly English, with a cascade of consequences for end listeners and also for interpreters'.

The effects of English-dependency on Spanish, which have been observed for written translation (Hernández Francés, 2010; Barros Ochoa, 2001), are also an issue in interpretation. Fernández-Vítores (2012, p. 96) mentions that the use of a language as a pivot language can influence the style of target versions, 'which will probably incorporate structures and even vocabulary of that language and not of the original in which the speech is delivered'.

The lack of linguistic parity or equal treatment means that English (and, to a lesser extent, French) is used at the expense of other languages, in both formal and informal meetings. In the face of this, some effort to ensure equal treatment of languages in the UN system has been made.

On 20 July 1995, the representatives to the UN of several countries (mostly francophone ones) addressed a letter to the Secretary-General to request the inclusion in the agenda of the fiftieth session of the General Assembly of an additional item entitled 'Multilingualism'. In the explanatory memorandum to the letter, the representatives complained that the equal treatment accorded to the official and working languages of the UN was not respected in the different bodies with a variety of justifications (financial reasons, the unavailability of interpretation and translation services, the urgent nature of the work at hand and so on), and pointed specifically at the practice of holding 'informal' meetings without interpretation or circulating 'unofficial' documents in one language only, which in the long run would result in a virtually monolingual UN (Tafalla, 2010). This letter and the ensuing debate led the General Assembly to adopt its landmark resolution 50/11. Referring to multilingualism as the 'corollary' of the universality of the UN, the General Assembly regretted that unequal use is made in the UN of the different official languages and of the working languages of the Secretariat and noted that the principle of equality of the official languages was being called into question with increasing frequency by the holding of so-called low-cost informal meetings.

On 11 April 2001, the Permanent Representatives of Member States from Spanish-speaking countries and those from the group of Arab States sent separate letters to the Secretary-General to express the concerns of their respective language groups in relation to what they viewed as an unequal treatment of Spanish and Arabic compared to English. In July 2001, the Secretary-General, Kofi Annan, replied to these concerns in a letter addressed to the Mexican ambassador. Although he was 'personally interested' in making sure that information is disseminated on a multilingual basis, he also admitted that 'budgetary constraints' prevent the six official languages from being treated equally. The budgetary constraints cast doubt on the real effects of the 1995 and subsequent pro-multilingualism resolutions. Seventeen years after the landmark 1995 resolution, Fall and Zhang (2011, p. 4) admitted that, 'in the context of economic realities and financial constraints, the trend towards "monolingualism" is far from decreasing, with the "hegemonic" use of one language, English, over the other five United Nations languages, for the sake of pragmatism'.

## 7.4  The Unbalanced Translation Regime of the European Union

If multilingualism was once presented as a 'corollary' to UN universalism, multilingualism is one of the uncontroversial principles of the EU. In its endeavour to create 'an ever closer union among the peoples of Europe, in which decisions are taken as openly as possible and as closely as possible to the citizen' (Article 1 of the Treaty on European Union), it is paramount to give equal status to all EU languages so that everyone feels respected and included as a European citizen.

The fundamental EU statute regarding multilingualism is Regulation No. 1 determining the languages to be used by the European Economic Community. After successive enlargements (the last one in 2013), it now reads: 'The official languages and the working languages of the institutions of the Union shall be Bulgarian, Croatian, Czech, Danish, Dutch, English, Estonian, Finnish, French, German, Greek, Hungarian, Irish, Italian, Latvian, Lithuanian, Maltese, Polish, Portuguese, Romanian, Slovak, Slovenian, Spanish and Swedish.'

Regulation No. 1 ranks together hyper-central, supercentral, central and peripheral languages such as Maltese and Irish. As a matter of fact, Maltese and Irish are special cases. During the preparation for Malta's accession, it was realized that there were not enough translators or interpreters to turn Maltese into a full-fledged official language from the start. The Council decided that there would be a transitional period of three years to become a fully integrated language of the Union. As for Irish – the only EU language that is not spoken by a majority of the population in any member state – it was subject to a derogation lasting in principle until 2022, to ensure translation capacities for it equal to the other official languages so that it could become a full-fledged official language of the Union.

Leaving Maltese and Irish aside, the truth is that, despite Regulation No. 1, EU official and working languages are not on an equal footing throughout. As in the case of the UN, statutes permit that different EU bodies have different language regimes. Pursuant to Article 6 of Regulation No. 1, 'the institutions of the European Union may stipulate in their rules of procedure which of the languages are to be used in specific cases'. A case in point is that of the European Commission, where the term 'procedural languages' is used to refer to English, French and German, as these are the languages in which documents must be produced for the work of the College of Commissioners.

Behind the egalitarian façade of Article 1 of Regulation No. 1, reality reveals a truly hierarchical language system. The EU does not guarantee full multilingualism in all institutional settings. This is, of course, no real news. Every scholar who has dealt with European institutions is well aware of this. Coulmas (1991, p. 17) had little doubt that an 'actual inequality' exists despite 'the commitment to the equality of the EC's official languages'. Labrie (1993, pp. 143–4) noticed that 'bien que l'égalité des langues de travail soit assurée sur le plan juridique, plusieurs problèmes se posent sur le plan pratique' ('although equality of working languages is guaranteed from a legal point of view, several problems arise from a practical point of view'). Milian (2004) opposed 'l'égalité *de jure*' ('*de jure* equality') to 'l'inégalité *de facto*'('de facto inequality') Similarly, Ives (2004, p. 26) found many situations of 'de jure multilingualism' and 'de facto monolingualism', and Kraus (2008, p. 120) spoke of 'official' and 'real' multilingualism. According to Baaij (2012), one can speak of a discrepancy between principles and practicality: multilingualism is far from being an inherent element of the daily work of institutions, where English and French in the case of the Court of Justice of the European Union (CJEU) have become the main languages 'for practical reasons'.

In what follows I discuss data that illustrates that the theory of equality of all languages cannot be maintained in the field of interpretation.

The EU has three different interpreting services. The largest one – the Directorate General (DG) for Interpretation– is the European Commission's interpreting service, which also provides interpretation to the Council, the European Economic and Social Committee, the Committee of the Regions, the European Investment Bank and a number of European offices and agencies. The Parliament and the Court of Justice have their own interpreting services. In this section we will focus on DG Interpretation, which is the largest provider (70 per cent of all interpreting in 2003 according to the Court of Auditors' Special Report No. 5/2005), compared to the European Parliament (EP) and the Court of Justice inter-preting services (27 per cent and 3 per cent of all interpreting, respectively).

The SCIC's (Directorate-General for Interpretation's) Customer Satisfaction Survey (DG SCIC, 2018) provides telling data on the realities of interpretation. In 2017, a mere third of the respondents said that they listened to interpretation only into their mother language, and another third said that they always listened to interpretation into another language because interpretation into their mother tongue was not provided (DG SCIC, 2018; see Reithofer, 2018 for an analysis of 2015 data). Between 2015 and 2017, the number of participants who could listen to their mother tongue in both the Commission and the Council *declined*. Those who could not listen to interpretation into their mother tongue listened to EN (87 per cent), FR (3 per cent) and German (3 per cent).

The Survey asks why delegates do not always listen to interpretation into their mother tongue even though it is provided. In 2017, almost half of the respondents said that they understood the original (mostly English), 21 per cent said that they were more familiar with the subject in another language, and 11 per cent pointed to the need to report in another language.

Between 2015 and 2017, the number also *declined* of participants who spoke their native language (from 82 to 60 per cent) while the number who 'always' spoke another language (mostly English) rocketed from 7 to 21 per cent. Respondents quote familiarity with the subject and the belief that they would convey their message better if they used a more widely spoken language as the main reasons. Reithofer (2018, p. 123) believes that

> many delegates speak English because of an asymmetric interpreting regime, i.e. they can *speak* their L1, e.g. Danish ..., but cannot listen to it, since no Danish booth is provided or was requested. Thus, they often *listen*

to the English booth and then proceed to *speak* English when they take the floor, since they have been listening to English all day long.

It seems that, within the EU context, asymmetric interpretation deters multilingualism. It is no wonder that the first suggestion of the 2017 Survey was 'to provide more interpretation also for small languages'.

As in the UN, within the EU, lip-service resolutions have been passed which support multilingualism. On 20 January 1995, for instance, the EP reaffirmed 'its commitment to the equality of the official and the working languages of all the countries of the Union, which is a cornerstone of the concept of a European Union', and declared 'its determination to oppose any attempt to discriminate between the official and the working languages of the European Union'.

Dissatisfied with the treatment of Spanish in the EU institutions, the Spanish government has from time to time taken steps to enhance its status, in matters that crucially concern translation and interpreting.

In 1999, the Spanish Minister for Foreign Affairs, Abel Matutes, and his Italian colleague Lamberto Dini toyed with boycotting informal ministerial meetings in the midst of the Finnish–German 'language dispute' (Kraus, 2008, p. 130). Informal meetings at the time used English and French as working languages, but, under the Finnish presidency of the Council, the German government insisted on the right to use German as a conference language as well. An agreement was reached whereby in informal ministerial meetings there would be interpreting from German but not from the other working languages into German. Matutes and Dini argued that if German was included in the interpretation regime, Spanish (and Italian) must be included as well.

A second dispute arose six years later (Kraus, 2008, p. 130). In 2005, the European Commission allegedly proposed to keep a full interpretation regime for the Wednesday press conferences but to limit interpreting to English, French and German press conferences on other days. The Spanish and Italian governments objected to the proposal, which would put Spanish (and Italian) on a par with Maltese. As the conflict escalated, the Commission stepped back. The Spanish government had won the day, but in November that year it could not prevent the Commission from reducing the number of Spanish translators (Kraus, 2008, p. 131). According to Spanish sources, a 'strategic document' for the Directorate General for Translation advised a cut from 92 to 67 staff for Spanish, close to the number for Maltese (60 translators), far from English (122 translators) and French and German (126 translators each).

The most salient battle that Spain has fought against European decisions concerns the Unitary Patent Regulation. In 2010, the EU tried to adopt a single system to protect patents in the territory of all the member states. The idea was to make it possible for patents granted by the European Patent Office (EPO) to be valid throughout the EU. Among other advantages, this would cut translation costs. The EPO's language regime (English, French and German) would be applied to all patents and there would be no need to translate them into the official language of all states in which they were to be validated. Both the Spanish and the Italian governments opposed the proposal. The lack of consensus among member states regarding the language regime led to a decision adopted in 2011, whereby the Council authorized 'enhanced cooperation', with a view to creating the single European patent, among the remaining twenty-five member states. The two non-participating member states, Spain and Italy, challenged the regulation before the CJEU arguing that it discriminated against those patent applicants who did not normally use one of the three languages privileged in the regulation. The Court in *Spain and Italy v. Council* (Cases C-274/11 and C-295/11) dismissed the action. Later, Spain alone sought the annulment of the two regulations forming part of the 'unitary patent package'. In judgments in Case C-146/13 *Spain v. Parliament and Council* and Case C-147/13 *Spain v. Council*, the Court dismissed both of Spain's actions.

One battle that the Spanish government fought was not related to Spanish. In 1988, the devolved Parliament of Catalonia passed a resolution to seek official status for Catalan in European institutions. In reply to this, on 11 December 1990, the EP passed an unprecedented resolution in which the Council and the European Commission were asked to adopt measures in favour of Catalan short of official status, which included the publication in Catalan of the Community's treaties and basic texts. As late as 2002, the Commission confessed that 'it has not yet made an overall evaluation of the implementation of the resolution in question' (OJ C 160 E, 4 July 2002, p. 124). Responding to pressures from Catalan nationalist parties, on 13 December 2004, Spain sent a memorandum to the EU requesting that Catalan, Galician and Basque be awarded official status in the European institutions. The request was rejected as such, but the member states reached an agreement on the matter following a proposal made by the Luxemburg presidency. On 13 June 2005, the European Council decided that EU institutions can use official regional languages that are not official EU languages in a number of restricted circumstances (non-valid translation of acts, passive interpretation of speeches to a meeting of the Council and other EU institutions or bodies, and written communications to EU institutions and bodies, with the cost always met by the interested member state).

## 7.5 The Unbalanced Translation Regime of Spain

In Meylaerts's (2011, p. 745ff.) typology of translation regimes, the EU is classed as a clear case of 'complete institutional multilingualism with obligatory multidirectional translation in all languages for all'. As we have seen, this is true up to a certain point: there is no multidirectional interpretation in all languages in every European institution. In this section I want to step down from supra-state organizations like the EU to the state level. Rather than focusing on typical established institutional multilingualism in countries such as Belgium, Canada and Switzerland, I will deal with a country in which 'complete institutional monolingualism and non-translation' at the state level is evolving towards a degree of institutional multilingualism that crucially involves interpretation from regional languages in the Senate and translation into regional languages in the official gazette. How NTLs are striving to become (less) translated languages at the state level in countries like Spain is the topic of this section.

Pursuant to Article 3.1 of the Spanish Constitution, Spanish is the sole language of all state institutions, including the two-chamber Spanish Parliament in Madrid. This regime of complete institutional monolingualism was challenged in the 1990s by political representatives of the other languages of Spain (mostly Catalan and Basque). When the rules of procedure of the Spanish Senate were reformed in 1994, Catalan and Basque political parties succeeded in including the possibility of using languages other than the official state language in three circumstances. In later amendments of the rules (2005 and 2010), the possibilities for languages other than Spanish expanded slightly to enable senators to use these languages in writings to be registered and in the publication of legislative initiatives, in any meeting of the Committee of the Autonomous Communities, and in plenary sessions when motions are discussed. Even with this limited scope, these provisions required the creation of an interpretation service in the Senate.

The interpretation regime that was put in place is perfectly asymmetric with four passive languages (five if we add Valencian, a regional variety of Catalan) and just one active language: speeches can be delivered in Spanish, Catalan, Basque and Galician and interpretation is provided exclusively into Spanish.

With regard to languages other than Spanish, de la Serna (2014) reports the view of an interpreter according to whom many senators do not listen to the interpretation, 'sometimes because they understand the original, sometimes because they think they understand it, sometimes to show their opposition to the fact that several languages are spoken in the Senate'. Another interpreter said that some senators show 'a certain disdain' towards the interpretation service. Maybe for these reasons, delegates do not always seize the opportunity to use languages other than Spanish. In an early work on this matter, Branchadell (2007, p. 204) identified a Basque senator who consciously refrained from using Basque. In a questionnaire administered to Catalan interpreters, de la Serna (2014) included a question on a similar situation regarding a Catalan representative who chose to speak Spanish so that senators 'can save the earphones and listen to her'. An interpreter said that such situations were 'quite frequent'. Asymmetric interpretation seems to function as a deterrent of multilingualism in Spain as well. In the face of all this, it is not surprising that the majority of Senate interpreters are not convinced of their usefulness as facilitators of communication (de la Serna, 2014, p. 51).

Although the Spanish Constitution established Spanish as *the* official language of the State, it provided that the Constitution 'shall also be published in the other languages of Spain'. This was the first token of an official translation of a legislative text into non-official languages. A step further was taken in 1997, when the Royal Decree 498/1997 was passed as a response to previous Catalan initiatives. According to this Decree, legislative texts published in the official gazette 'can also be published in the other official languages of the different Autonomous Communities if their competent authorities decide so'. Pursuant to this Royal Decree, memoranda of understanding were signed for Catalan (1998), Galician (1998), Valencian (2000) and Basque (2011).

In spite of this important step, equality among Spain's languages was far from having been achieved. First, not all texts are translated into these languages. (It is worth noting that the memoranda of understanding (MoUs) themselves have never been translated.) Second, translations are not published on the same day as the Spanish original. In a 2008 amendment of the Catalan MoU, the goal was set to reduce delay to a maximum of seven natural days, with simultaneity on the horizon. The goal was attained between 2008 and 2012, but the delay increased in subsequent years to reach 29.14 natural days in 2017. Third, the translated texts are not authentic. And fourth, translations are not free. The autonomous governments have to bear 50 per cent of the cost of all translations (40 per cent in the case of Basque).

## 7.6  The Unbalanced Translation Regime of Catalonia

In this final section I want to examine the translation and interpreting regime of a *sub-state* polity like Catalonia, where Catalan plays a pivotal role with respect to Occitan (locally known as 'Aranese') and even to Spanish.

Aranese is spoken in the Aran Valley, a small territory of 620 square kilometres on the northern slope of the Pyrenees, bordering France. According to the 2018 population census, the population of the Aran Valley was 9,983 people. According to the 2018 Language Use Survey, Aranese was the 'initial language' (mother tongue) of 21.4 per cent of the Valley population and the 'usual language' of 19.7 per cent.

Despite its small size – around 2,000 'usual' speakers in a region of 7.5 million inhabitants – Aranese enjoys official status in Catalonia together with Spanish and Catalan.

The translation and interpreting regime of trilingual Catalonia is easy to describe: there is (almost) none. In the *Butlletí Oficial del Parlament de*

*Catalunya* (the *Official Bulletin of the Catalan Government*) texts are published in the original official language (mostly Catalan), with no translation whatsoever. The *Diari de Sessions del Parlament de Catalunya* (*Diary of the Sessions of the Catalan Government*) transcribes the speeches of delegates in the official language in which they were delivered (mostly Catalan), again with no translation.

For parliamentary sessions there is no interpretation service. The system proceeds on the assumption that Catalan, Spanish and Occitan are mutually intelligible. In any case, oral use of Occitan in Parliament is strictly anecdotal. During the 2017–21 term, just 1 out of 135 MPs was Aranese-speaking.

Law 2/2007, on the *Diari Oficial de la Generalitat de Catalunya* (the *Official Diary of the Government of Catalonia*), provides that the Catalan official gazette 'is published in Catalan and Spanish, and the regulations, provisions and acts that exclusively affect Aran are also published in Aranese'. Act 35/2010 on Occitan went one step further and provided that *all* laws passed by the Parliament of Catalonia are published in Occitan, which means 'translated from Catalan into Occitan'.

Within Catalonia's trilingual regime, some asymmetries stand out. Unlike laws in Catalan and Spanish, laws in Aranese are not published in the Spanish official gazette. On the other hand, there is no Occitan version of the Catalan official gazette. Finally, laws in Catalan and their Spanish translation are published simultaneously, whereas the Aranese translation is published with a significant delay.

Thanks to Catalan regulations, Occitan became an LTL instead of an NTL. And whereas little use is made of laws in Aranese among lawyers and politicians, their linguistic relevance is great. Fibla (2016) stresses that the seventy laws translated after 2010 constitute 'an important legislative corpus, unprecedented in Occitan, and which greatly contribute to the establishment of the Occitan legal language'. According to Fibla (2016), one of the problems that the Parliament encounters when translating laws into Aranese is 'the lack of a consolidated standard language model for Aranese'. A specific problem is that of specialized terminology and neologisms. Aranese is clearly an under-resourced language. On the other hand, Fibla also mentions the danger of too much Catalan-dependency of Aranese translations. This is the challenge: to create a standard Occitan language through intensive translation from Catalan.

## 7.7 Concluding Remarks

After reaffirming the concept of LTLs (Branchadell, 2005), in this chapter I presented four case studies to further illustrate it in the context of institutional translation and interpreting. A look at the UN system, the

EU institutions, the Spanish Parliament and the devolved Parliament of Catalonia in Spain shows (once again) how LTLs is a category that cuts across the usual divide between major and minor languages. In a given setting, major and minor languages can share the same fate with respect to their translation and interpreting opportunities.

Beyond the ascertainment of this fact, from the examination of these four cases some significant lessons about translation and interpreting can be drawn. Leaving classic issues aside like the role of translation in the development of languages, which aptly fits the case of Occitan in Spain, the most prominent insight concerns the role of translation and interpreting in fostering – or hindering – equality, democracy and linguistic justice at both the international and the domestic level (Meylaerts, 2011; Gazzola, Templin and Wickström, 2018).

Both the UN and the EU are committed to multilingualism and to equality among their respective official and working languages. Translation and interpreting are key elements in delivering on this commitment. We have seen that both the UN and the EU fail to fulfil their multilingual promises, as illustrated through the use of translation and interpreting in each case. In Gazzola's equality scale, the highest magnitude is never achieved (delegates can speak and listen to their L1 and all languages are treated equally). In many instances, delegates can speak and listen using their L1, but languages are not treated equally (relay is used); in many other instances, delegates can speak but not listen to their L1, and situations where no interpretation at all is provided are not exceptional. Generally speaking, the existing arrangements reinforce the role of English as a hyper-central language. When no interpretation is provided, affairs are conducted mostly in this language. When asymmetric interpretation is provided, it is never at the expense of English. And when full (relay) interpretation is provided, the pivot language is mostly English. Asymmetric and relay interpretation are deterrents to multilingualism: all too often delegates switch to the hyper-central language when they cannot listen to their L1 or when they are able to do so only through indirect interpretation.

The hyper-centrality of English has several consequences. One is that there is very little translation between other languages. In 1995, Carsten Quell warned about the dangers of EU enlargement: 'Mehr Länder, weniger Sprachen' ('more countries, fewer languages') was his motto. Now he could rephrase it in terms of translation: 'More languages, less translation' (or 'more translation from and into English'). For minor languages such as Irish and Maltese, the present arrangements in the EU paradoxically enhance their status as source and – above all – target languages of EU texts and favour their peripheral nature at the same time. The pivotal role of English – which is usually measured quantitatively – brings about 'side effects' on the *quality* of LTLs as well: a sort of language decay syndrome is emerging, caused by too much (and more and more non-native) translation and interpreting from English The linguistic side effects of translation-dependency have also been observed for other language pairs. Written Occitan in Catalonia, for instance, runs the risk of becoming an Occitanizing copy of Catalan.

These dangers notwithstanding, governments and other relevant political actors want their languages to be more and more translated. More often than not, what they seek is political prestige rather than easier communication, and the case of Catalan in Spain is a useful focus. Catalan interpreters in the Spanish Senate – where everybody is proficient in Spanish – might not be 'political pawns' but they do not seem to be 'facilitators of communication' either (de la Serna, 2014). The Catalan, Galician, Valencian and Basque regional governments keep paying for translations of the Spanish official gazette that few people read: they are published late, are not authentic and do not cover the entire gazette anyway.

This might be the final paradox: linguistic inequality breeds a desire for more translation, and what translation in the end does is to deepen linguistic inequality by legitimizing the existing language hierarchies, both at the international and at the domestic level.

# References

Baaij, J. W. (2012). The EU policy on institutional multilingualism: between principles and practicality. *International Journal of Language and Law*, **1**, 14–32.

Baigorri, J., and Travieso, C. (2017). Interpreting at the United Nations: The impact of external variables. The interpreters' view. *Clina: An Interdisciplinary Journal of Translation, Interpreting and Intercultural Communication*, **3**(2), 53–72.

Barros Ochoa, M. (2001). La traducción del español en la Organización de las Naciones Unidas (ONU). *In Actas del II Congreso Internacional de la Lengua Española. 'El español en la sociedad de la información'*. Madrid, Instituto Cervantes. Online.

Branchadell, A. (2005). Introduction: Less translated languages as a field of inquiry. In A. Branchadell and M. West, eds., *Less Translated Languages*. Amsterdam and Philadelphia: John Benjamins, pp.1–23.

Branchadell, A. (2007). La interpretació al Senat espanyol. *Quaderns. Revista de Traducció*, **14**, 197–205.

Branchadell, A. (2011). Minority languages and translation. In Y. Gambier and L. van Doorslaer, eds., *Handbook of Translation Studies. Volume 2.* Amsterdam and Philadelphia: John Benjamins, pp. 97–101.

Brems, E., Réthelyi, O., and van Kalmthout. T., eds. (2017). *Doing Double Dutch: The International Circulation of Literature from the Low Countries.* Leuven: Leuven University Press.

Casanova, P. (2010). Consecration and accumulation of literary capital: Translation as unequal exchange. In M. Baker, ed., *Critical Readings in Translation Studies*. London/New York: Routledge, pp. 285–303.

Coulmas, F., ed. (1991). *A Language Policy for the European Community: Prospects and Quandaries*. Berlin/New York: Mouton de Gruyter.

De la Serna, A. (2014). *Political Pawns or Essential Facilitators of Communication*. MA thesis, National University of Ireland, Galway.

Del Pino Romero, J. (2014). La interpretación al español en las Organizaciones Internacionales y la formación de intérpretes de conferencias de lengua española. In J. L. Mira, dir., *El Español lengua de comunicación profesional. Artículos seleccionados del V Congreso Internacional de Español para Fines Específicos*. Madrid: Ministerio de Educación, Cultura y Deporte.

de Swaan, A. (2001). *Words of the World: The Global Language System*. Cambridge: Polity Press.

DG SCIC. (2018). *SCIC Customer Satisfaction Survey 2017. Interpretation Services Nov–Dec 2017. Results & Conclusions*. PowerPoint presentation.

d'Haen, T., Goerlandt, I., and Sell, R. D. (2015). *Major versus Minor? Languages and Literatures in a Globalized World*. Amsterdam/Philadelphia: John Benjamins.

Dollerup, C. (2002). Translation and power at the European Union. *Current Writing: Text and Reception in South Africa*, **14**, 192–202.

Fall, L. P., and Zhang, Y. (2011). *Multilingualism in the United Nations System Organizations: Status of Implementation*. Geneva: United Nations. Doc. JIU/REP/2011/4.

Fernández-Vítores, D. (2012). El español en las relaciones y los foros internacionales. Los casos de la Unión Europea y las Naciones Unidas. In J. Rupérez and D. Fernández-Vítores, eds., *El español en las relaciones internacionales*. Barcelona: Ariel and Fundación Telefónica.

Fernández-Vítores, D. (2014). Spanish in the United Nations System. *Informes del Observatorio / Observatorio Reports*. Instituto Cervantes at the Faculty of Arts and Sciences of Harvard University.

Fibla, J. (2016). L'occità al Parlament de Catalunya: la Llei de l'occità, aranès a l'Aran. https://eapc.rld.blog.gencat.cat/tag/llengua-aranesa/.

Gazzola, M. (2006). Managing multilingualism in the European Union: Language policy evaluation for the European Parliament. *Language Policy*, **5**, 393–417.

Gazzola, M., Templin, T., and Wickström, B.-A., eds. (2018). *Language Policy and Linguistic Justice: Economic, Philosophical and Sociolinguistic Approaches*. Berlin: Springer.

Heilbron, J. (2010). Structure and dynamics of the world system of translation. UNESCO International Symposium 'Translation and Cultural Mediation', 22–23 February.

Hernández Francés, A. L. (2010). El español en las organizaciones internacionales. In *El español, lengua de traducción para la cooperación y el diálogo*,

*Actas del IV Congreso Internacional 'El español, lengua de traducción'*. Madrid: Esletra, pp. 191–5.

Ives, P. (2004). Language, representation, and suprastate democracy: Questions facing the European Union. In D. Laycock, ed., *Representation and Democratic Theory*. Vancouver: UBC Press, pp. 23–47.

Kang, J. H. (2008). Institutional translation. In M. Baker and G. Saldanha, eds., *Routledge Encyclopedia of Translation Studies*. 2nd ed. Abingdon: Routledge, pp. 141–5.

Koskinen, K. (2008). *Translating Institutions: An Ethnographic Study of EU Translation*. Manchester: St Jerome.

Kraus, P. (2008). *A Union of Diversity: Language, Identity and Polity-Building in Europe*. Cambridge: Cambridge University Press.

Kudryavtsev, E., and Ouedraogo, L. D. (2003). *Implementation of Multilingualism in the United Nations System*. Geneva: United Nations. Doc. JIU/REP/2002/11.

Labrie, N. (1993). *La construction linguistique de la Communauté européenne*. Paris: Champion.

Meylaerts, R. (2011). Translational justice in a multilingual world: An overview of translational regimes. *Meta*, **56**(4), 743–57.

Meylaerts, R. (2018). The politics of translation in multilingual states. In J. Evans and F. Fernandez, eds., *The Routledge Handbook of Translation and Politics*. London: Routledge, pp. 221–37.

Milian, A. (2004). Le régime juridique du multilinguisme dans l'Union européenne. Le mythe ou la réalité du principe d'égalité des langues. *Revue juridique Thémis*, **38**(1), 211–60.

Mossop, B. (1988). Translating institutions: A missing factor in translation theory. *TTR: traduction, terminologie, rédaction*, **1**(2), 65–71.

Quell, C. (1995). Die Europäische Union 1995 – Mehr Länder, weniger Sprachen? *Germanistische Mitteilungen*, **41**, 25–45.

Reithofer, K. (2018). Interpreting and multilingualism in the EU: Leave or remain? *CLINA: An Interdisciplinary Journal of Translation, Interpreting and Intercultural Communication*, **4**(1), 115–36.

Schäffner, C., Tcaciuc, L. S., and Tesseur, W. (2014). Translation practices in political institutions: A comparison of national, supranational, and non-governmental organisations. *Perspectives*, **22**(4), 493–510.

Stolz, T. (2001). Minor languages and the general linguistics (with special focus on Europe). In T. Stolz, ed., *Minor Languages of Europe: A Series of Lectures at the University of Bremen, April–July 2000*. Bochum: Universitätsverlag, pp. 211–42.

Tafalla, M. (2010). El multilingüismo en la Organización de las Naciones Unidas. *Revista de Llengua i Dret*, **53**, 137–62.

# 8

# The Translation Professions

Rakefet Sela-Sheffy

## 8.1 Introduction

The nature of translation as a profession has been a matter of concern of translation studies in recent decades. Scholars, themselves often actors in the field, are aware of the ambiguous status of this huge yet unregulated industry, and share the feeling that translation practices and the role of translators are misunderstood and underrated. Addressing the discrepancy between the importance of translation as an inter-culture mediation function and its unclear status as a profession, they elaborate on translators' qualifications and ethics with a view to assessing their agency or subservience in performing this work (e.g., Buzelin, 2014; Khalifa, 2014; Kinnunen and Koskinen, 2010; Simeoni, 1998; Wolf, 2007). With the sociological turn in translation theory, attention is increasingly devoted to the question of professionalization as a means of empowerment. It is largely agreed that translation should be regarded more seriously as a full-fledged profession. However, what does it mean? How is a profession, or professionalism, understood and what are its implications for the field of translation?

Sociological theory views professionalization as a mechanism of generating status and securing occupational autonomy. Occupations that are recognized as professions are considered the most trustworthy form of organized work, on a scale the other pole of which is nonprofessionalism or amateurism (Beegan and Atkinson, 2008; Stebbins, 1992). In the common (modern) view, professionalism is achieved by institutional means. Although this view has been challenged, it is still prevalent in discussions of many work contexts, including that of translation and interpreting.

Accounting for the multiplicity and ambiguity of professional logics and their different conceptual framings is vital for understanding the translation profession(s). In what follows, I will briefly introduce the complexity of the notions of profession and professionalism, and problematize the view of translation as a profession against this theoretical background. I will discuss different ways in which translation scholars and practitioners envision 'translation professionalism' and construct their professional world.

## 8.2 The Classical Notion of a Profession

Basically, 'profession' is about rebutting the image of an 'anyone can do it' occupation. The classical conceptualization of professions, developed in the early twentieth century, seeks to define clear measures, both abstract and technical, that mark out an occupation as a profession (Lester, 2015, Macdonald, 1999). These include a distinct body of knowledge and skills, usually associated with university education, formal rules and standards, and an ethical code, all of which control individuals' conduct. Accordingly, a profession is 'perceived to be about applying general, scientific knowledge to specific cases in rigorous and therefore routinized or institutionalized ways' (Noordegraaf, 2007, p. 765).

This mechanism is power driven. Historical accounts, focusing on Western capitalistic-bureaucratic society, describe professionalization as a process by which certain sectors, notably medicine and law, science and engineering, construct specialized knowledge required for a group of practices, thereby gaining monopoly over these practices (Abbott, 1988; Freidson, 2001; Larson, 1977; Sciulli, 2007). Salient elements here are restrictions on access to work and the social closure they guarantee. Workers, in this view, are constantly engaged in elaborating and codifying complex mental labour as their exclusive property. This requires self-reproduced occupational control (Brian, 1991) with sanctions on the acquisition and implementation of knowledge and skills by individuals. In specifying what one ought to know and do, this apparatus determines not only who is 'in' and who is 'out' but also the terms of inner competition and of gaining position within a professional sphere. The more inaccessible the knowledge, and the clearer the hierarchy it produces, the stronger the status of a profession.

Professions are thus about monopoly and autonomy. They secure boundaries and grant workers' independence vis-à-vis clients, authorities and various social actors. Yet, autonomy requires social legitimacy. For practitioners to gain the status of a self-governed profession, they must receive the approval and trust of the public. Professionals' rewards must be tied 'not only to occupational competence and workplace ethics but also to contemporaries' belief that their expert services are "of special importance for society and the common weal"' (Sciulli, 2007, p. 122). Professionals' struggle for power raises claims to moral influence, by which they play the role of modern elites (Larson, 1977; Scott, 2008). Accordingly, translators should have agency not only in determining the norms *of* their practice but also in setting cultural norms *through* their practice, in the same way that the medical profession determines notions of health and sickness (Freidson, 2001).

In the classical model, all this is achieved through institutional regulatory means, such as associations, formal training and certification systems, which set thresholds for entry to a profession and regulate its methods and ranks. Attempts to define the markers (or 'traits'; Ackroyd, 2016; Lester, 2015) by which an occupation can be crowned a 'full profession' usually mention full-time engagement, obligatory training and exams, titles and diplomas, and regulated procedures, conditions and wages. However, this static model hardly ever materializes fully in concrete cases, and its categories are debated.

## 8.3   How Is the Classical Model of Profession Manifest in the Realm of Translation?

In translation, monopoly and autonomy are not secured. The problem lies not in the demand for translation practices but in the demand for an expert workforce. To establish monopoly and authority, translators have to clarify the distinction between themselves and non-professionals and create belief in their special expertness (cf. Scott, 2008).

In practice, translators and interpreters constantly face competition from 'non-professional interpreters and translators' (NPIT; Antonini et al., 2017; Pérez-González and Susam-Saraeva, 2012) or from whoever is able to perform occasional translation in everyday circumstances, without committing themselves to standards or ethics, and without making it their career (whom David Katan (2011) calls 'cowboys'). The latter are identified by Brian Harris (1978) and Gideon Toury (2012 [1995]) as 'natural translators'. 'Natural translators' can be practically anyone, from secretaries in businesses, through students or other anonymous agents volunteering translations to the community (e.g., in digital media; Baños, 2019; Pym, Orrego-Carmona and Torres-Simón, 2016), to community members who help relatives or clients in encounters with officials (e.g., in health clinics, schools, banks, welfare services; Angelelli, 2010). All these people have the 'basic ability to translate', which amounts, according to Harris, to the 'innate verbal skill' of bilingualism 'within the limits of their mastery of the two languages' (Harris and Sherwood, 1978, p. 1).

In an attempt to identify translators' expertise beyond basic linguistic abilities, Toury (2012 [1995]) proposed a process by which 'a bilingual speaker becomes a translator'. He described a social-feedback process through which a person internalizes the cultural norms for producing adequate translation. From a different perspective, Bogusława Whyatt (2012), following others (e.g., Cronin, 2005; Kelly, 2005; Kiraly, 2005), discusses the cognitive development of a 'translator in the making'. In her view, a bilingual person who is regularly engaged in translating gradually accumulates and constructs a 'Knowledge Integration Network' (KIN). Both these theories conceptualize translating expertness as resulting from general socialization and cognitive processes, based on experience and self-reflection. Neither provides a clear account of translators' professional knowledge and competency.

In the classical view, indeterminate proficiency prevents autonomy in that it allegedly counteracts workers' authority to define the goals of work and make decisions. Translators and translation scholars often speak about translators' subordinate position and their 'being at the mercy of their clients' (Katan, 2011). The diversity of translation media, markets and work formats (i.e., salaried vs freelance) exacerbates this situation. Although translators and interpreters are not denied agency by definition (Khalifa, 2014; Kinnunen and Koskinen, 2010), the degree to which their authority is acknowledged varies according to the type of material they translate (e.g., literary vs business), contingent on clients' interest and policies, and is not inherent to their profession (Chriss, 2006; Drugan, 2013). In the traditional view of professions, this hampers the potential of translators to fulfil their culture-mediating role as transmitters and facilitators of knowledge and social norms.

It follows that it is critical for professional translators' material and symbolic rewards that they distinguish themselves from occasional 'language conduits'. The growing academic discourse about translation as a profession (Gouadec, 2007; also Drugan, 2013; Tyulenev, 2015) seeks to systematically 'describe and analyse the true world of professional specialized translation ... so that everyone should understand that quality in translation never comes cheap' (Gouadec, 2007, p. xiv). Yet, generally, scholars admit that the translation industry is too diverse, and proficiencies are too 'inconsistent', to comply with the rigid classical model.

First, as already mentioned, no distinct body of knowledge and skills defines translators' proficiency. While mastery of the languages one works with is taken for granted, it is widely agreed that this alone does not suffice to distinguish expert translation from other 'language jobs'. Nevertheless, in practice, translation education is very often connected with language classes, and theorization of translation proficiency is associated with language expertise (e.g., Cao, 1996; Snell-Hornby, 2002; Whyatt, 2012). Despite attempts to transcend the level of linguistic competency, no other concrete types of knowledge are listed as essential qualifications for translators and interpreters.

Second, indeterminacy also results from translators' weak specialization. Practices that are included under the notion of 'translation' are diverse and divided between written and oral translation, for which different skills are required. For example, interpreters need working memory capacity (Macnamara and Conway, 2016), whereas translators need technological and revision competence (Robert, Remael and Ureel, 2017). In recent decades, pressure is growing to professionalize interpreting in its own right, with the rise of interpreting studies as a distinct subdiscipline, with separate associations, and teaching and certification systems (e.g., Bajčić and Dobrić Basaneže, 2016; Furmanek, 2012; Pöchhacker, 2016; Setton and Guo-Liangliang, 2011). Nevertheless, many practitioners engage in various translating tasks, both written and oral, without facing sanctions (Drugan, 2013; Katan, 2011).

Moreover, the subfields in each of these spheres are defined by diverse classification principles – whether by content (e.g., business, technical, legal, medical, science or literary translation), by the source language (e.g., sign language interpreting) or by the media and venue (e.g., subtitling, conference interpreting), so that the required knowledge, skills and ethics vary with contents or techniques. However, except in specific sectors (e.g., legal and court translation (Monzó, 2011), conference interpreting (Duflou, 2016) or sign language interpreting (Grbić, 2010)), specialization is weak. Moreover, individuals often combine translation with other language jobs. In all these cases, practitioners move between different working spheres, subject to different market structures and worker–client rapports. Continuously operating as a heteronomous occupation (Bourdieu, 1996), many individual practitioners must have various skills and shift between ethical codes.

Third, all this has consequences for – and is reinforced by – the absence of systematic translation education. Obligatory training, a major means of regulation, is weak or entirely lacking. True, academization of translation studies has intensified since the 1970s and is gaining momentum worldwide, which is a typical marker of professionalization. Teaching often combines diploma programmes with theoretical learning, and interest in translation pedagogy has grown (Baer and Koby, 2003; Schäffner and Adab, 2000). However, this academic progress is ahead of market realities (Ali Abu-Ghararah, 2017; Dybiec-Gajer, 2014; Furmanek, 2012; King, 2017; Pym et al., 2012). Graduates of translation programmes do not necessarily become practitioners, and praxis is impacted by chance and opportunity. Attempts to cultivate an optimal professional profile for new candidates (e.g., Mizab and Bahloul, 2016; Sakwe, 2015; Viaggio, 1991) envision 'the good translator' but disregard evidence from the field. Practitioners, for their part, doubt the relevance of university learning and emphasize self-learning through experience (e.g., Katan, 2011; Sela-Sheffy, 2010; Setton and Guo-Liangliang, 2011).

Fourth, because of the above, closure is prevented. As Pym et al. (2012) indicate, except in the domain of sworn translators, practically anyone can offer translation services without legal sanctions. Pym et al.'s report relates to EU translators, but its conclusions hold in principle for many settings worldwide. In many cases, translators, mostly self-employed, constitute a part-time workforce, with neither formal trajectories and ranks nor standards of work and pay, often doing translation as a secondary job or as a second career after retirement. In other occupational spheres, quality, work conditions and tariffs are usually controlled by professional associations, which strive for legal status, whereas translator associations, despite their growing number (Furmanek, 2012; Pym et al., 2012), often operate as social clubs where membership is not obligatory (Pym, 2014). They are mostly dedicated to the 'professional development' of their members (related to linguistic expertise), rather than acting as efficient bodies fighting for union-type benefits and jurisdiction.

Given that none of the above-mentioned measures is consistently implemented, translation praxis can hardly be regarded as a 'full profession' in the classical sense (Tyulenev, 2015). For example, even in the Danish translation scene, which, according to Dam and Zethsen (2011, p. 979), is among 'the most well-organized and well-educated national [translation] markets in the world', translators are not confident in their professional status and influence (Dam and Zethsen, 2010, 2011, and elsewhere). Yet, in seeking explanations for this enigma, discussions usually proceed from the same fixed categories in the classical sense (Tyulenev, 2015), without questioning their validity, focusing on the tools and conditions that facilitate or obstruct their implementation.

## 8.4 Another View on Occupational Autonomy: The Symbolic Capital Hypothesis

However, sociologists have long called attention to inadequacies of the classical trait-oriented understanding of professions. They point at the dynamism of occupational configurations, on a continuum between rigidly regulated professions and loosely defined occupations, with many cases of blurred distinction between professionalism and amateurism (cf. Banfield, 2017; Nicey, 2016; Stebbins, 1992). Moreover, even in well-established professions, proficiencies are often indeterminate (Atkinson, Reid and Sheldrake, 1977). Praxis is not always consistent with formal rules since standards and boundaries are constantly reconfigured, and struggles occur between high-ranked and lesser-ranked proficiencies (e.g., between biomedical and alternative therapy (Barnes, 2003) or between legal and paralegal professionals (Lively, 2001)). Traditional professions weaken or dissolve, and new are created, whereas some professional domains remain interdependent even if institutional regulation is at play (e.g., nursing is continuously subordinate to the medical professions; Barton, Thome and Hoptroff, 1999).

In light of this dynamism, beyond its rational function, the deeper semiotic logic of 'professionalism' as a meaning-making and distinction mechanism is laid bare. This perspective was already proposed by Howard Becker (1970) who defined a profession as a 'folk symbol that serves to organize the way individuals think about themselves and society' (p. 92). In a different milieu, embracing the symbolic-economy conceptualization of Pierre Bourdieu and followers, Mirko Noordegraaf (2007) and others (Evetts, 2003; Fournier, 1999) think of work spheres as spaces of power tensions and status struggles, where stakes are negotiated and cannot be determined a priori. The very idea of professionalism is understood here as 'continuously at stake both within professional fields – where its legitimate substance is contested – and within the larger field of power' (Noordegraaf and Schinkel, 2011, p. 105). Accordingly, the classical notion of a profession, which Noordegraaf (2007) calls 'pure professionalism', is itself normative. Citing Fournier (1999) and Evetts (2003) (see also Elsaka, 2005), Noordegraaf (2007) shows how 'the appeal of professionalism' lies in its being a canonical image, imbued with ideology, which practitioners may mobilize to different degrees in different spheres depending on the symbolic capital it can generate. Some emerging or hybrid professions (e.g., managing (Noordegraaf and Schinkel, 2011), counselling (Hammond and Czyszczon, 2014) or public relations (Johansen, 2001)) aspire to 'pure professionalism' for enhancing closure and autonomy. However, this process is not linear.

Rather, hybridity is understood in this view as a common situation characterizing many professional settings (Noordegraaf, 2007), where versatility of actors and 'crossing boundaries' are inevitable for developing exclusive expertise. For example, in the information technology (IT) professions, multiple technical and non-technical competencies are simultaneously developed, requiring diverse resources and education paths (Bailey and Stefaniak, 2002). Fuzzy boundaries and versatility of actors are also the order of the day in the different subfields of translation and interpreting, as mentioned in Section 8.3. Colley and Guéry (2015) show, for instance, how public service interpreting is constructed through interactions with other professionals and with service receivers. In all of these cases, the notion of professionalism varies according to the symbolic benefits it generates.

Understanding 'professionalism' in terms of symbolic capital evokes Bourdieu's conceptualization of autonomy in culture-production fields. Bourdieu's analysis of autonomization deals with culture industries where institutional professionalization appears as inherently inappropriate, notably art and literature. In *The Rules of Art* (Bourdieu, 1996), he shows how social closure and autonomy are achieved in these spheres precisely by obscuring (rather than formalizing) quality standards and procedures, and prioritizing informal learning. As elaborated by Gisèle Sapiro (2019a and earlier), literary writers (and others doing 'creative jobs') constantly oscillate among different modes of action, operating mainly as 'intellectual workers' to whom the rigid model of a 'profession' does not apply. As amorphous as the forms and boundaries of their practice may appear, they are structured by the tacit rules of a symbolic market (Bourdieu, 1996; Sapiro, 2019b), which are no less effective than institutional ones. Being acquainted with these tacit rules is what frames practitioners' action and the ways they relate to one another and to clients.

This is what Bourdieu called 'the practical logic' by which social actors operate in all spheres of work and production. Professionality, in this perspective, is 'a feel for the game', namely, actors' intuitive, embodied compliance with an implied idea of 'best practice' (Stephens and Delamont, 2009). The focus thus shifts from profession as a structure to professionals, the actors, their sense making and dispositions to action, or their habitus (Bourdieu, 1990):

> Within a profession, the professional is not only educated in a technical sense. He or she is also socialized into a group as a member and really 'becomes' a professional in an embodied sense. Over time he or she will develop a socially constituted capacity to act and acquire a professional habitus, a set of dispositions that influences how he or she perceives, thinks and acts ... *Professional capital*, in other words, must be acquired in order to become professional.
>
> (Noordegraaf and Schinkel, 2011, p. 104, emphasis added)

While this holds for all occupational settings, in cases of weak or absent regulation, such as translation and interpreting, it constitutes the only form of professionalism. Apart from certain specialist niches, as mentioned earlier, translators' proficiency is negotiated within loose professional logics (Fournier, 1999) and is constructed mainly through social learning (Lave and Wenger, 1991; also Billett et al., 2018; cf. Toury, 2012). What makes translators a professional group is neither shared formal knowledge nor regulation but rather an *ethos*, internalized by individuals and embodied in their conduct, by which a member becomes 'one of us' (Bayerl, Horton and Jacobs, 2018).

## 8.5 Professional Identity as a Constitutive Element of Professions

By shifting attention from 'professions' as occupational structures to 'professionals' in the sense of workers' ethos and dispositions, the normativity of 'professionalism' is stressed, suggesting that there may be 'unprofessional professionals' or 'professional non-professionals' (Lively, 2001). In her study on paralegal workers, Kathryn Lively (2001) shows how, despite being classified as non-professionals, who are 'disrespected or asked to do things they believe fall outside their occupational domain'

(p. 363), these workers maintain professional status as individuals. By negotiating understandings of their fuzzy occupational requirements, they develop their own sense of professionalism. Moreover, coping with their inferiority, they avoid the rigid notion of professionalism associated with attorneys, to whom they are subordinate. A similar incongruity between 'a profession' and 'professionals' (though in different circumstances) is at play in the domain of translation. Studies on translators' job-perception show duality and manoeuvring between awareness of their ambiguous collective status as an occupation and their sense of professionality as individuals (Ruokonen and Mäkisalo, 2018; Sela-Sheffy, 2016).

Professionalism, in this view, is about 'ways to feel and act', rather than about structural traits. To be professional, one must develop a professional identity. More than the notion of habitus, the notion of identity emphasizes normativity and aspirations to recognition and gratifications (Sela-Sheffy, 2014). While the lens of habitus provides the dimension of consistency (of actors' disposition to action), the lens of identity provides the dimension of impression management and prestige (Goffman, 1959). Workers perform and modify professional personas to demonstrate their aptness and create distinction. The growing research on professional identity shows how practitioners tacitly construct their professionality by avowing images of 'the good worker' through their conduct and discourse (Van Mannen, 2010; Webb, 2016). Inspired by Goffman (1959) and the micro-sociological symbolic-interactionist tradition, these studies look at practitioners' identity work, in the sense of an 'individual projecting a particular image and ... others mirroring back and reinforcing (or not) that image as a legitimate identity' (DeRue and Ashford, 2010, p. 630; also Sveningsson and Alvesson, 2003). Thereby, workers establish their ideal persona (in Goffman's (1959) terminology), one that fits their understanding of 'the kind of a person one should be', to be recognized as a worthy worker.

Identity thus appears in itself as a crucial factor in constructing a profession (Barbour and Lammers, 2015; Brown and Coupland, 2015; Dent and Whitehead, 2002; Ibarra, 1999; Kyratsis et al., 2017; Pratt, Rockmann and Kaufmann, 2006). Personal attributes constitute major resources of the symbolic capital that endows practitioners with authority and credit. Identity studies have been conducted in various professional contexts, especially with regard to phases of transition or conflicts, for example, in analysing students' entry to their profession (Goldie, 2012), how experts adapt to new work spheres or how they deal with shifts in their career (e.g., Ibarra, 1999; Kyratsis et al., 2017; Pratt et al., 2006). However, studying professional identities is also potent in discussing how workers cope with status threats in settled situations (Brown and Coupland, 2015), especially in lower-ranked or under-institutionalized professions. Among these, translation is a typical case.

For translators and interpreters, a professional persona is not an auxiliary but a major means of establishing professional status. Since, beyond bilingualism, their knowledge and skills are undefined, their distinction from lay people lies only in personal dispositions and work ethos. Testimonies of translators and translation scholars suggest that it is not the linguistic competency as such but rather the value attributed to 'knowledge of languages' and 'acquaintance with foreign cultures', and one's love for and joy of translating, which make the difference. As scholars propose, translators' professionalism emerges from a process in which one starts translating and sees how it fits their inclinations. An inclination for languages is seen as part of a broader cluster of dispositions that make up the identity of 'the worthy translator'. According to popular guides to 'how to be a successful translator' (e.g., McKay, 2006 and a bulk of similar materials online) as well as translators' self-reflections, to be a translator one should have curiosity, open-mindedness, intellectualism and a desire for broad knowledge, ingenuity and resourcefulness, determination in facing challenges, thoroughness, versatility and multitasking:

> Translators and interpreters are voracious and omnivorous readers, ... in several languages, fiction and nonfiction, technical and humanistic subjects, anything and everything.
>
> They are hungry for real-world experience as well, through travel, living abroad ..., learning foreign languages and cultures .... [m]any translators were first professionals in other fields ... by necessity translators and interpreters carry a wealth of different 'selves' or 'personalities' around inside them, ready to be reconstructed on the computer screen whenever a new text arrives, or out into the airwaves whenever a new speaker steps up to the podium. (Robinson, 2012, p. 25)

Regardless of whether all practising translators equally share them, these personal characteristics are perceived as prerequisite.

This sense of a 'fitting persona' is exclusive in that, contrary to Harris's (1978) and Toury's (2012 [1995]) idea of 'the natural translator', it implies competencies that only certain individuals are endowed with. The professionality of these individuals lies in the mystique of giftedness (Subotnik and Jarvin, 2005), namely, in natural abilities and self-refinement that can be neither generated by systematic learning nor rationally formalized as rules. A 'translatorial professionality' develops in a person by virtue of this predisposition even if they have been trained for another career (as commonly happens). 'Professionalism' in this sense is closer to a calling, or a serious leisure (Stebbins, 1992), than to a standardized trained profession, in that one is emotionally invested in a certain type of work and finds in it self-fulfilment.

The symbolic capital accumulated thereby provides the rationale – and compensates – for structural 'drawbacks', such as amorphous education and career trajectories, or unregulated conditions and pay. In particular, identity-based symbolic capital provides moral justification for economic insecurity. Translators tend to demonstrate economic 'disinterestedness' (Bourdieu, 1983) and avoid discussing remuneration and other material expectations in describing their profession (Sela-Sheffy, 2010). Instead, they stress the non-material gratifications – satisfaction, freedom, interest, perfection or cultural impact – which they gain, at least in theory, from their work, so much so that addressing the issues of standardized knowledge and rewards would counter these actors' belief in the rules of the game in their field (or what Bourdieu (1990) called *illusio*; Colley and Guéry, 2015; Guanvic, 2005). Even if not each and every translator achieves these symbolic profits, in order to be a competent actor in this field one must believe in them and act accordingly.

## 8.6   The Tacit Structure of Translation as a Professional Field

Accentuating giftedness and economic 'disinterestedness' constitute an elitist ethics that defies the idea of democratically accessible trained proficiencies. Obviously, this ethos is not equally embraced in all the sectors of translation, and the extent to which it is embraced reflects hierarchical relations between them. Unsurprisingly, this ethos is championed by highbrow literary translators (Sela-Sheffy, 2008), who approach translation from the literary world, where translating is an addition to their functions as authors, critics, editors, lectors or university professors. As such, they derive their authority from their intellectual persona (cf. Allen and Bernofsky, 2013) and treat translation as an intellectual pursuit rather than paid work (Sela-Sheffy, 2008; cf. Sapiro, 2019a, about the writing professions). In proclaiming commitment to nothing but literary judgement, they establish an inverted ratio between professional credit and standardized rewards, as typical of art production spheres. The greater their literary reputation, the higher their gratifications, yet the stronger they hide matters of fees and wages. Similarly, their intellectual persona entails rejection of systematic training in favour of self-learning, in which methods are obscured by the notions of creativity and intuition.

The dozens of highbrow literary translators in every national market thus act in a hybrid professional configuration, at the intersection between translation and the literary spheres. In this hybrid space, their professional identity is shaped as individuals who are subject to the same 'stardom system' (Shumway, 1997; Sela-Sheffy, 2010), which defies standards in crowning literary virtuosos. Some attain the position of public intellectuals, whose role as culture taste-makers is acknowledged (Sela-Sheffy, 2008, 2010).

From the perspective of the translation profession, their hybrid situation grants highbrow literary translators authority and autonomy that are hardly matched by the other translation sectors. Unlike translators of popular or scientific literature, and far differently from the masses of rank-and-file translators and interpreters, star literary translators are allowed (and expected) to articulate their own work-ideology and style preferences. They usually have a say in translation policy and in selecting material for translating, and are able to negotiate with editors and to bargain their earnings and terms of work. Thereby, these translators have a share in what Bourdieu (1985) calls the small-scale space of cultural production, where producers (e.g., writers, translators) and consecrating agents (e.g., critics, academics, publishers) negotiate cultural values and images, jointly defining the agenda for their peers and for the public at large. Their literary fame and artist-like self-imaging provide the logic of distinction between them and all the other translators, whom they see as mere language conduits.

In a seemingly paradoxical way, in the most under-professionalized sphere of translation, where in theory work is entirely non-regulated, maximum control and autonomy are achieved – yet not collectively as an organized occupation. The individuals recognized as star literary translators have the strongest agency in navigating their own position and in exerting public influence, in extreme disproportion to their small number and volume of service in the translation industry (including in the wider literary translation market). This is supported by the disproportionate attention they gain from translation studies scholars. Consequently, the prestige of these individuals and the cultural role attributed to them in the public sphere are also recognized by their anonymous peers in the translation industry. Therefore, despite their claim to distinction, the persona of 'the good translator' they promote serves as a canonical model for the masses of translators aiming for recognition as professionals. Highbrow literary translators thus serve as the elite that determines the symbolic capital of this profession (Sela-Sheffy, 2016).

Rather than medium, contents or formats, the structuring principle of the translation professions lies in identity and ethos. The self-perception of rank-and-file translators is ambiguous. Away from the intellectual sphere, they operate as paid workers in the diverse service-oriented translation industries. Whether they are employees or self-employed, they must comply with their companies' or clients' goals and conditions of work (Katan, 2011; Ferreira-Alves, 2011). As mentioned, freelance translators, despite being independent and free to choose their type and volume of work, often work for more than one master, simultaneously subject to differentiated markets, without a common platform for establishing standards of expertise and self-control.

At the same time, as mentioned in Section 8.4, evidence shows that for the majority of translators and interpreters, the classical traits of professionalism seem irrelevant. Freelancers in particular build their reputation individually, highlighting experience rather than credentials (e.g., Antonini et al., 2017; Katan, 2011; Pérez-González and Susam-Saraeva,

2012; Setton and Guo-Liangliang, 2011), and often mistrust institutional tools such as training programmes and associations. Yet, these studies also reveal how, having neither organizational apparatus nor explicit ideology, rank-and-file translators communicate a professional persona. Although they downplay aspirations, their identity work draws on the idea that being a 'good translator' hinges on personal resources. Without outright denial of economic and pragmatic concerns, their 'tacit ideal of a professional self' (Webb, 2016) revolves around the symbolic gratifications that go with loosely structured working routines, such as individual freedom, personal advancement, creativity and intellectual interest, which they present as their prime motivation to work (Sela-Sheffy, 2010, 2016). Thereby they contest the rational logic of 'pure professionalism'. In short, although technically the masses of translators have no access to the intellectual industry, they tacitly avow the imagery that this industry produces, confirming thereby their share in the 'translation profession'.

## 8.7  Conclusion

The ambiguity of translation as a profession is usually discussed from an inside perspective, in which under-professionalization appears discordant with the momentous consequences of inter-cultural functions. From an external theoretical perspective on professions and professionalism, ambiguity is common in many occupational landscapes and is not exclusive to the translation occupation, nor is it understood as necessarily detrimental for the status of a profession. In essence, a profession is about monopoly and autonomy, in contrast to an 'anyone-can-do-it job'. In the canonical model, these functions are achieved by certain traits, notably expert knowledge and self-control, which are institutionally regulated. Yet, applying this model to the translation profession(s) either yields vague definitions of translation proficiencies or leads to the conclusion that translation is not a profession – which contradicts the conviction of many translators and interpreters.

In contrast, the recent conceptualization of professions disconnects the functions of monopoly and autonomy from their fulfilment through a specific organizational model, or certain 'traits'. Pointing at the diversity and dynamism of professional configurations, this theory sees professionalism as an ethos with which groups of workers create distinction. It highlights the semiotic normative aspect of this concept, as negotiated, rather than fixed, symbolic capital, in Bourdieu's terminology. Through this lens, ways of achieving occupational symbolic capital vary on a continuum between the canonical ideal of 'pure professionalism' and a loosely defined, *practical logic*, by which practitioners operate. Whereas the former is endorsed in certain prestigious professions, the latter is a fundamental dynamics in every professional sphere.

Not only does 'pure professionalism' entail ideology that may or may not be avowed; in certain occupational domains the gratifications it provides actually clash with the tacit rules adhered to by actors. The focus thus shifts from 'profession' as a structure to *professionals*, as actors. Translators' self-perception reflects their negotiation of norms and rules through their conduct and discourse. Their *identity work* calibrates action according to 'the worthy translator' *persona*, which grants them legitimation and recognition as professionals regardless of regulation.

The incongruity between these two models of professionalism is most typically expressed in the art and intellectual jobs where the symbolic value of giftedness and disinterestedness outweighs that of standardized expert knowledge and institutional control. In such domains, with neither titles and ranks nor regulated methods and pay, the distinction between 'professionals' and 'amateurs' is blurred. In the translation industry, this situation is typical of highbrow literary translators whose professionality is determined by their literary persona. However, for the most part, in this huge and diverse industry, translation and interpreting constitute paid work, which actors do for a living. Nevertheless, even rank-and-file translators show little interest in 'pure professionalism' in its classical sense. Since no exclusive knowledge or skills define their expertise (linguistic competency, the only prerequisite, is shared by all other language jobs, and bilingualism does not mark professionals out from 'natural translators'), their professionality lies in personal dispositions and ethos. Translators' reputation as professionals, as opposed to occasional 'language conduits', builds on dedication to work and self-refinement of natural inclinations – intuition and creativity, broad knowledge and passion for languages and cultures – rather than on formal training and credentials. In short, to be a recognized translator, one must have a 'translator identity'.

It is professional identity, and not measurable parameters, which provides the structuring principle and hierarchy of the translation profession. The most distinct 'translator persona' is constructed by highbrow literary translators who operate at the intersection between the literary and the translation industries. Only in this hybrid space is translators' roles as cultural mediators publicly acknowledged, and their status as intellectual workers fully recognized. While, in the literary sphere, these translators usually act in various capacities, their action in the translation field – unlike that of the masses of 'ordinary' translators and interpreters – is confined to translating highbrow literature. In this domain they serve as an elite that sets the tacit logic of professionality that lends meaning and value to the diverse translatorial practices and unites them as a 'profession'. Given their special position and public image as individuals, their intellectual persona provides the symbolic capital by which all the actors, including those who operate away from the intellectual industry, are recognized as professionals.

# References

Abbott, A. (1988). *The System of Professions: An Essay on the Division of Expert Labor*. Chicago/London: University of Chicago Press.

Ackroyd, S. (2016). Sociological and organisational theories of professions and professionalism. In M. Dent et al., eds., *The Routledge Companion to the Professions and Professionalism*. Routledge Handbooks Online, available at www.routledgehandbooks.com/citation?doi=10.4324/9781315779447.ch1.

Ali Abu-Ghararah, B. (2017). The gap between translator training and the translation industry in Saudi Arabia. *Arab World English Journal for Translation & Literary Studies*, **1**(4), 107–18.

Allen, E., and Bernofsky, S. (2013). *In Translation. Translators on Their Work and What It Means*. New York: Columbia University Press.

Angelelli, C. V. (2010). A professional ideology in the making: Bilingual youngsters interpreting for their communities and the notion of (no) choice. *Translation & Interpreting Studies*, **5**(1), 94–108.

Antonini, R., Cirillo, L., Rossato, L., and Torresi, I., eds. (2017). *Non-professional Interpreting and Translation: State of the Art and Future of an Emerging Field of Research*. Amsterdam: John Benjamins.

Atkinson, P., Reid, M., and Sheldrake, P. (1977). Medical mystique. *Sociology of Work and Occupations*, **4**(3), 243–80.

Baer, B. J., and Koby, G. S., eds. (2003). *Beyond the Ivory Tower: Rethinking Translation Pedagogy*. Amsterdam: John Benjamins.

Bailey, J. L., and Stefaniak, G. (2002). Preparing the information technology workforce for the new millennium. *ACM SIGCPR Computer Personnel*, **20** (4). https://dl.acm.org/doi/abs/10.1145/571475.571476.

Bajčić, M., and Dobrić Basaneže, K., eds. (2016). *Towards the Professionalization of Legal Translators and Court Interpreters in the EU*. Cambridge: Cambridge Scholars.

Banfield, J. (2017). Amateur, professional and proto-practices: A contribution to 'the proficiency debate'. *AREA*, **49**(2), 130–6.

Baños, R. (2019). Fandubbing across time and space. In I. Ranzato and S. Zanotti, eds., *Reassessing Dubbing: Historical Approaches and Current Trends*. Amsterdam: John Benjamins, pp. 146–67.

Barbour, J. B., and Lammers, J. C. (2015). Measuring professional identity: A review of the literature and a multilevel confirmatory factor analysis of professional identity constructs. *Journal of Professions and Organization*, **2** (1), 38–60.

Barnes, L. L. (2003). The acupuncture wars: The professionalizing of American acupuncture – A view from Massachusetts. *Medical Anthropology*, **22**, 261–301.

Barton, T. D., Thome, R., and Hoptroff, M. (1999). The nurse practitioner: Redefining occupational boundaries?. *International Journal of Nursing Studies*, **36**, 57–63.

Bayerl, P. S., Horton, K. E., and Jacobs, G. (2018). How do we describe our professional selves? Investigating collective identity configurations across professions. *Journal of Vocational Behavior*, **107**, 168–81.

Becker, H. (1970). The Nature of a Profession. In H. Becker, *Sociological Work: Method and Substance*. Chicago: Aldine, 87–103.

Beegan, G., and Atkinson, P. (2008). Professionalism, Amateurism and the Boundaries of Design. *Journal of Design History*, **21**(4), 305–13.

Billett, S., Harteis, C., and Gruber, H. (2018). Developing occupational expertise through everyday work activities and interaction. In *Cambridge Handbook of Expertise and Expert Performance*, Ericsson, K. A., Hoffman R. R., Kozbelt, A. and Williams, A. M. eds. Cambridge: Cambridge University Press, 105–26.

Bourdieu, P. (1983). The field of cultural production, or: The economic world reversed. *Poetics* **12**, 311–56.

Bourdieu, P. (1985). The market of symbolic goods. *Poetics*, **14**, 13–44.

Bourdieu, P. (1990 [1980]). *The Logic of Practice*. Cambridge: Polity Press.

Bourdieu, P. (1996 [1992]). *Rules of Art: Genesis and Structure of the Literary Field*. Stanford, CA: Stanford University Press.

Brian, D. (1991). Practical knowledge and occupational control: The professionalization of architecture in the United States. *Sociological Forum*, **6** (2), 239–68.

Brown, A. D., and Coupland, C. (2015). Identity Threats, Identity Work and Elite Professionals. *Organization Studies*, **35**(10), 1285–1313.

Buzelin, H. (2014). How devoted can translators be?: Revisiting the subservience hypothesis. *Target*, **26**(1), 63–97.

Cao, D. (1996). Towards a model of translation proficiency. *Target*, **8**(2), 325–40.

Chriss, R. (2006). *Translation as a Profession*. Morrisville: Lulu.Com

Colley, H., and Guéry, F. (2015). Understanding new hybrid professions: Bourdieu, illusio and the case of public service interpreters. *Cambridge Journal of Education*, **45**(1), 113–31.

Cronin, M. (2005). Deschooling translation. In: *Training for the New Millennium*, Tennent, M. (ed.), Amsterdam: John Benjamins, 249–65.

Dam, H. V., and Zethsen, K. K. (2010). Translator status: Helpers and opponents in the ongoing battle of an emerging profession. *Target*, **22** (2), 194–211.

Dam, H. V., and Zethsen, K. K. (2011). Status of professional business translators on the Danish market: A comparative study of company, agency and freelance translators. *Meta*, **56**(4), 976–97.

Dent, M., and Whitehead, S. (eds.) (2002). *Managing Professional Identities: Knowledge, Performativity and the 'New' Professional*. London: Routledge.

DeRue, D. S. and Ashford, S. J. (2010). Who will lead and who will follow? A social process of leadership identity construction in organizations. *Academy of Management Review*, **35**(4), 627–47.

Drugan, J. (2013). *Quality in Professional Translation*. London: Bloomsbury.

Duflou, V. (2016). *Be(com)ing a Conference Interpreter: An Ethnography of EU Interpreters as a Professional Community*. Amsterdam: John Benjamins.

Dybiec-Gajer, J. (2014). Going professional: Challenges and opportunities for the contemporary translator educators. In M. Piotrowska and S. Tyupa, eds., in *TRAlinea*. Special issue: *Challenges in Translation Pedagogy*. Available at www.intralinea.org/specials/article/2104.

Elsaka, N. (2005). New Zealand journalists and the appeal of 'professionalism' as a model of organization: An historical analysis. *Journalism Studies*, **6**(1), 73–86.

Evetts, J. (2003). The sociological analysis of professionalism: Occupational change in the modern world. *International Sociology*, **18**(2), 395–415.

Ferreira-Alves, F. (2011). Job perceptions, identity-building and interpersonal relations among translators as a professional group in northern Portugal. *ILCEA: Revue de l'Institut des langues et cultures d'Europe, Amérique, Afrique, Asie et Australie*, **14**, 1–15.

Fournier, V. (1999). The appeal to 'professionalism' as a disciplinary mechanism. *Sociological Review*, **47**(2), 280–307.

Freidson, E. (2001). *Professionalism: The Third Logic*. Cambridge: Polity Press.

Furmanek, O. (2012). Professionalization of interpreters. In C. A. Chapelle, ed., *The Encyclopedia of Applied Linguistics*. Hoboken, NJ: John Wiley and Sons, pp. 1–8.

Goffman, E. (1959). *The Presentation of Self in Everyday Life*. New York: Anchor Books.

Goldie, J. (2012). The formation of professional identity in medical students: Considerations for educators. *Medical Teacher*, **34**(9), e641–8.

Gouadec, D. (2007). *Translation as a Profession*. Amsterdam: John Benjamins.

Grbić, N. (2010). 'Boundary work' as a concept for studying professionalization processes in the interpreting field. *Translation & Interpreting Studies*, **5**(1), 109–23.

Gouanvic, J.-M. (2005). A Bourdieusian Theory of Translation, or the Coincidence of Practical Instances'. The Translator, **11**(2), 147–166.

Hammond, C., and Czyszczon, G. (2014). Home-based family counseling: An emerging field in need of professionalization. *Family Journal*, **22**(1), 56–61.

Harris, B. (1978). The difference between natural and professional translation. *Canadian Modern Language Review*, **34**(3), 417–27.

Harris, B., and Sherwood, B. (1978). Translating as an innate skill. In D. Gerver and W. Sinaiko, eds., *Language Interpretation and Communication*. New York: Plenum, pp. 155–70.

Ibarra, H. (1999). Provisional selves: Experimenting with image and identity in professional adaptation. *Administrative Science Quarterly*, **44**(4), 764.

Johansen, P. (2001). Professionalisation, building respectability, and the birth of the Canadian Public Relations Society. *Journalism Studies*, **2**(1), 55–71.

Katan, D. (2011). Occupation or profession: A survey of the translators' world. In R. Sela-Sheffy and M. Shlesinger, eds., *Profession, Identity and Status: Translators and Interpreters as an Occupational Group*. Amsterdam: Benjamins, pp. 65–88.

Kelly, D. (2005). *A Handbook for Translator Trainers*. Manchester: St Jerome.

Khalifa, A. W., ed. (2014). *Translators Have Their Say? Translation and the Power of Agency*. Zurich: LIT Verlag.

King, H. (2017). Translator education programs and the translation labour market: Linear career progression or a touch of chaos? *T & I Review*, **7**, 133–51.

Kinnunen, T., and Koskinen, K., eds. (2010). *Translators' Agency*. Tampere, Finland: Tampere University Press.

Kiraly, D. (2005). Project-based learning: A case for situated translation. *Meta*, **50**(4), 1098–1111.

Kyratsis, Y., Atun, R., Phillips, N., Tracey, P., and George, G. (2017). Health systems in transition: Professional identity work in the context of shifting institutional logics. *Academy of Management Journal*, **60**(2), 610–41.

Larson, M. S. (1977). *The Rise of Professionalism*. Berkeley: University of California Press.

Lave, J., and Wenger, E. (1991). *Situated Learning: Legitimate Peripheral Participation*. Cambridge: Cambridge University Press.

Lester, S. (2015). On professions and being professional. Available at http://devmts.org.uk/profnal.pdf.

Lively, K. J. (2001). Occupational claims to professionalism: The case of paralegals. *Symbolic Interaction*, **24**(3), 343–65.

Macdonald, K. (1999). *The Sociology of the Professions*. London: Sage.

Macnamara, B. N., and Conway, A. R. A. (2016). Working memory capacity as a predictor of simultaneous language interpreting performance. *Journal of Applied Research in Memory and Cognition*, **5**(4), 434–44.

McKay, C. (2006). *How to Succeed as a Freelance Translator*. Boulder, CO: Two Rat Press and Translatewrite, Inc.

Mizab, M., and Bahloul, A. (2016). The Integration of professional translators' 21st century profile in teaching translation at Batna University. *Arab World English Journal*, **3**, 187–209.

Monzó, E. (2011). Legal and translational occupations in Spain: Regulation and specialization in jurisdictional struggles. In R. Sela-Sheffy and M. Shlesinger, eds., *Identity and Status in the Translational Professions*. Amsterdam: John Benjamins, pp. 11–30.

Nicey, J. (2016). Semi-professional amateurs. In T. Witschge, C. W. Anderson, D. Domingo and A. Hermida, eds., *The SAGE Handbook of Digital Journalism*. London: Sage, pp. 222–35.

Noordegraaf, M. (2007). From 'pure' to 'hybrid' professionalism: Present-day professionalism in ambiguous public domains. *Administration & Society*, **39**(6), 761–85.

Noordegraaf, M., and Schinkel, W. (2011). Professional capital contested: A Bourdieusian analysis of conflicts between professionals and managers. *Comparative Sociology*, **10**, 97–125.

Pérez-González, L., and Susam-Saraeva, S. (2012). Non-professionals translating and interpreting participatory and engaged perspectives. *The Translator*, **18**(2), 149–65.

Pöchhacker, F. (2016). *Introducing Interpreting Studies*. London: Routledge.

Pratt, M. G., Rockmann, K. W., and Kaufmann, J. B. (2006). Constructing professional identity: The role of work and identity learning cycles in the customization of identity among medical residents. *Academy of Management Journal*, **49**(2), 235–62.

Pym, A. (2014). Translator associations – from gatekeepers to communities. *Target*, **26**(3), 466–91.

Pym, A., Grin, F., Sfreddo, C., and Chan, A. L. J. (2012). *The Status of The Translation Profession in the European Union*. Report to Europe Direct (Studies on Translation and Multilingualism) 7/2012, The European Commission.

Pym, A., Orrego-Carmona, D., and Torres-Simón, E. (2016). Status and technology in the professionalisation of translators: Market disorder and the return of hierarchy. *Journal of Specialised Translation*, **25**, 33–53.

Robert, I. S., Remael, A., and Ureel, J. J. J. (2017). Towards a model of translation revision competence. *The Interpreter and Translator Trainer*, **11**(1), 1–19. Available at https://doi.org/10.1080/1750399X.2016.1198183.

Robinson, D. (2012). *Becoming a Translator: An Introduction to the Theory and Practice of Translation*. Abingdon/New York: Routledge.

Ruokonen, M., and Mäkisalo, J. (2018). Middling-status profession, high-status work: Finnish translators' status perceptions in the light of their backgrounds, working conditions and job satisfaction. *Translation and Interpreting*, **10**(1), 1–17.

Sakwe, G. M. (2015). The standard profile of the 21st century translator and its impact on translator training. *International Journal of English Language & Translation Studies*, **3**(3), 86–104.

Sapiro, G. (2019a). The writing profession in France: Between symbolic and professional recognition. *French Cultural Studies*, **30**(2), 105–20.

Sapiro, G. (2019b). Rethinking the concept of autonomy for the sociology of symbolic goods. *Biens symboliques [Symbolic Goods]*, **4**. Available at https://revue.biens-symboliques.net/334.

Schäffner C., and Adab, B., eds. (2000). *Developing Translation Competence*. Amsterdam: John Benjamins.

Sciulli, D. (2007). Professions before professionalism. *European Journal of Sociology*, **48**(1), 121–47.

Scott, W. R. (2008). Lords of the dance: Professionals as institutional agents. *Organization Studies*, **29**(2), 219–38.

Sela-Sheffy, R. (2008). The translators' personae: Marketing translatorial images as pursuit of capital. *Meta*, **LIII**(3), 609–22.

Sela-Sheffy, R. (2010). 'Stars' or 'professionals': The imagined vocation and exclusive knowledge of translators in Israel. In O. D. Fouces and E. Monzó, eds., *MonTI 2: Applied Sociology in Translation Studies / Sociologia aplicada a la traducció*. Alicante: Publicaciones de la Universidad de Alicante, pp. 131–52.

Sela-Sheffy, R. (2014). Translators' identity work: Introducing micro-sociological theory of identity to the discussion of translators' habitus. In G. M. Vorderobermeier, ed., *Remapping Habitus in Translation Studies*. Amsterdam: Rodopi, pp. 43–55.

Sela-Sheffy, R. (2016). Elite and non-elite translator manpower: The non-professionalized culture in the translation field in Israel. In K. Koskinen and H. V. Dam (eds.) *The Translation Profession: Centers and Peripheries* [= *Journal of Specialised Translation*, **25**], 54–73.

Setton, R., and Guo-Liangliang, A. (2011). Attitudes to role, status and professional identity in interpreters and translators with Chinese in Shanghai and Taipei. In R. Sela-Sheffy and M. Shlesinger, eds., *Identity and Status in the Translational Professions*. Amsterdam: John Benjamins, pp. 89–117.

Shumway, D. R. (1997). The star system in literary studies. *PMLA*, **112**(1), 85–100.

Simeoni, D. (1998). The pivotal status of the translator's habitus. *Target*, **10**, 1–39.

Snell-Hornby, M. (2002). Back to square one? On the troubled relationship between translation studies and linguistics. *Logos and Language*, **3**(1), 21–30.

Stebbins, R. A. (1992). *Amateurs, Professionals, and Serious Leisure*. Montreal: McGill-Queen's University Press.

Stephens, N., and Delamont, S. (2009). They start to get malicia': Teaching tacit and technical knowledge. *British Journal of Sociology of Education*, **30**(5), 537–48.

Subotnik, R. F., and Jarvin, L. (2005). Beyond expertise. In R. J. Sternberg and J. E. Davidson, eds., *Conceptions of Giftedness: Sociocultural Perspectives*. Cambridge: Cambridge University Press, pp. 343–57.

Sveningsson, S., and Alvesson, M. (2003). Managing managerial identities: Organizational fragmentation, discourse and identity struggle. *Human Relations*, **56**(10), 1163–93.

Toury, G. (2012 [1995]). A bilingual speaker becomes a translator: A tentative developmental model. In G. Toury, *Descriptive Translation Studies and Beyond*. Amsterdam: John Benjamins, pp. 241–58.

Tyulenev, S. (2015). Towards theorising translation as an occupation. *Asia Pacific Translation and Intercultural Studies*, **2**(1), 15–29.

Van Mannen, J. (2010). Identity work and control in occupational communities. In S. B. Sitkin, L. B. Cardinal and K. Bijlsma-Frankema, eds., *Organizational Control*. Cambridge: Cambridge University Press, pp. 111–66.

Viaggio, S. (1991). Translators and interpreters: Professionals or shoe-makers? Unpublished paper, presented at the annual meeting of the 1st International Language Conference, Elsinore, Denmark.

Webb, S. A. (2016). Professional identity and social work. In M. Dent, I. L. Bourgeault, J.-L. Denis and E. Kuhlmann, eds., *The Routledge Companion to the Professions and Professionalism*. London: Routledge, pp. 355–70.

Whyatt, B. (2012). *Translation as a Human Skill: From Predisposition to Expertise*. Poznań: Wydział Anglistyki, Adam Mickiewicz University. Available at www.academia.edu/14900302/Translation_as_a_human_skill._From _predisposition_to_expertise?email_work_card=view-paper.

Wolf, M. (2007). The female state of the art: Women in the 'translation field'. In A. Pym, M. Shlesinger and Z. Jettmarová, eds., *Sociocultural Aspects of Translating and Interpreting*. Amsterdam: John Benjamins, pp. 129–41.

# 9

# Translation Studies and Public Policy

Gabriel González Núñez

## 9.1 Understanding Public Policy

The way in which people live has evolved over time, and, from the beginning of the nineteenth century, change has come about in an increasingly rapid manner, affecting everything from how we produce our goods to what we eat. Two characteristics of this acceleration in the rate of change are particularly relevant for the topic of this chapter. One is that individuals crowd together more than before. Because we live longer and healthier lives, population density increases, and as cities become hubs for resources, they grow exponentially. By 2050, it is estimated that 68 per cent of the world's population will live in urban areas, and by then the world is expected to have at least forty-three megacities – cities whose population exceeds 10 million inhabitants (UN Population Division, 2018, p. 2). The other characteristic is that mobility is much more robust than before. As the technical means to move quickly across great distances become available, people tend more frequently to move away from the places where they were born. As worldwide poverty decreases, obtaining access to such means of transportation allows for constant intra- and international migration. In 2017, the worldwide number of international migrants reached an estimated 258 million (UN Population Division, 2017, p. 1).

In that context, the need to organize public spaces is readily apparent. If increasingly densely populated societies are to avoid descending into anarchy, they must resolve basic questions such as: How do we get water and similar vital necessities to everyone? What is the best way to promote basic skills in the population? What happens when an individual becomes ill? How do we manage life-threatening emergencies? Importantly in terms of this chapter: How do we communicate? Dealing with these issues requires the work of many agents. Indeed, the challenges of organizing public spaces make co-ordinated action a necessity, and, in modern societies, this co-ordinated action is deployed through policy – more specifically, through public policy. In other words, the modern body politic utilizes public policy as the instrument through which it organizes itself.

The concept of public policy has been identified in several ways. Perhaps the simplest understanding is that '[p]ublic policy is whatever governments choose to do or not do' (Dye, 2002, p. 1). This includes obvious actions, such as levying taxes and organizing bureaucracies, but it also includes, for example, distributing benefits and regulating behaviour (Dye, 2002, p. 1). A more nuanced definition sees public policy as 'an officially expressed intention backed by a sanction, which can be a reward or a punishment' (Lowi et al., 2017, p. 612). Such officially expressed intentions take the form of laws, rules, orders and so on (Lowi et al., 2017, p. 612). Well-known types of public policy include economic policy, education policy, foreign policy, health-care policy and social policy. Public policy can also encompass cultural policy, language policy and translation policy. This last type of policy has, not surprisingly, garnered the attention of scholars in the field of translation studies, as will be shown in this chapter.

Studying any kind of public policy means approaching an extremely complex object. Its complexity stems from the high number of actors involved, the very lengthy process its development requires, the battles often fought over sometimes very technical issues, and the not-always-civil debates that arise over the issues at stake (Sabatier, 2007, pp. 3–4). Owing to its complexity, scholars often rely on models, or simplified understandings, of policy. At this point one might remember that 'all models are wrong, but some are useful' (Box and Draper, 1989, p. 424). In other words, these models are tools for understanding some aspect of public policy in a useful way through simplification of reality, and they may be informed by specific theoretical perspectives. For example, policy may be understood through a Marxist or a capitalist theory. The Marxist perspective sees the decisions made by the most economically powerful social classes as the primary driver of policy, while a capitalist perspective argues that natural forces of supply and demand, if unfettered, will shape policy (Turner et al., 2018, p. 401). Whatever theory informs the model, it is helpful to bear in mind that models are not intended to provide the comprehensive 'truth' about policy. Rather, they are useful tools in thinking about the object of study.

To help think about policy generally, Thomas Dye summarizes several conceptual models: the institutional model views public policy as the output of government institutions (Dye, 2002, pp. 12–14); the process model views public policy as the result of political activity (Dye, 2002, pp. 14–16); the rational model views public policy as an effort by governments to obtain 'maximum social gain' (Dye, 2002, pp. 16–19); the incremental model views public policy as the 'continuation of past government activities with only incremental modifications' (Dye, 2002, pp. 19–21); the group model sees public policy as the equilibrium among different groups that are in constant struggle (Dye, 2002, p. 23); the elite model sees public policy as a manifestation of 'the preferences and values of a governing elite' (Dye, 2002, pp. 23–5); the public choice model sees public policy as 'collective decision making by self-interested individuals' (Dye, 2002, pp. 25–7); and the game-theory model sees public policy as the result of rational choices made by actors in competitive, interdependent situations (Dye, 2002, pp. 27–9). There are other models, of course, that also highlight different elements of the concept of public policy, but this list serves to exemplify just how rich and varied the models can be. They all have limitations but are nonetheless useful in their own ways, as will be shown here.

A glimpse at the general policy models just mentioned reveals that the government, broadly understood, seems to be involved one way or another. This is the case because these are models of *public* policy, and the term 'public' is often used as a synonym for 'government', especially as government activity has the potential to affect most or all people in a territory. That does not mean that only a given government is capable of *having* policy. Organizations of all types can also formulate and implement their own policies. Consider the work of Stephen Caldas (2012), who has explored language policy in the domain of the family, including the raising of bilingual children. In turn, Wine Tesseur (2017) has explored translation policy in Amnesty International, an international non-governmental organization. As these two examples illustrate, any organization can make policy for itself, but only the government can make policy that aims to organize an entire territory or subsection thereof.

Thus, matters of public policy inevitably involve the government. Admittedly, the intensity of government involvement may vary, from a laissez-faire kind of approach to highly regulated methods of direct intervention. Whatever the approach may be, public policy is the attempt to manage and, ideally, fix the problems that arise in organizing highly complex societies such as those that characterize the twenty-first century. With that general understanding in mind, Section 9.2 will address the exact role that translation and interpreting can play in managing specific social problems.

## 9.2 Translation and Interpreting as a Response to Problems in Society

When dealing with public policy, the object of study is ultimately the co-ordination of action in order to respond to identified needs in society. Thus, the study of translation in public policy is the study of whether and how translation and interpreting are deployed to deal with social problems. In this regard, research into public policy is research into problem-solving on a social scale. Anthony Pym (2002, p. 5) has argued that translation scholars should focus on 'the problems that are most important, in the sense that they concern disagreement and debate between different social groups'. Focusing on matters of translation (which in this chapter includes interpreting) and public policy amounts to focusing on precisely such 'most important' of problems.

A starting point is understanding what is meant by the term 'social needs'. In an introductory text on social welfare and public policy, Nick Manning (2011, p. 21) indicates that a 'social need' can be defined as a need that affects different social groups to varying degrees and with different distributions. For example, the need to access the justice system might be seen as a social need because it affects different groups differently. A group of Indigenous Peruvians from the jungle who speak only Aguaruna (*awajún*) and who need to access the Spanish-speaking court system have a social need. This need affects them differently than it does a group of Spanish-speaking Peruvians born and raised in Lima. The need to access the courts might be the same, but the inability of the Aguaruna speakers to communicate effectively in Spanish will affect them in a way that situates them differently than groups of Lima-based Spanish speakers.

A social need becomes a 'social problem' when society, or a segment thereof, perceives the need as a shared problem (Manning, 2011, p. 22). The fact that Aguaruna speakers are unable to access the Peruvian court system in Spanish might not be deemed a social problem until a segment of society perceives this as a problem that affects everyone. For example, if the authorities wish to put several Aguaruna speakers on trial while guaranteeing the fundamental right to a fair trial, they are faced with a problem: proceedings cannot be held in Aguaruna because the state lacks the human and material resources to do this, but if proceedings are held in Spanish, Aguaruna speakers cannot participate and are thus unfairly tried. A social problem has been identified. At this point, solutions will be proposed. In the actual trial of the Aguaruna speakers being used as an example here, the solution was to recruit and train court interpreters specifically for this trial (see Howard, de Pedro Ricoy and Andrade Ciudad, 2018, pp. 31–3).

Of course, the solutions proposed for social problems will depend a great deal on the value judgement made about the problem itself (Manning, 2011, p. 23). In Peru, speakers of indigenous languages had been put on trial before, but it was not until a high-profile case (a deadly clash between indigenous groups and the police) that '[t]he need for legislation was brought to a head' (Howard et al., 2018, p. 31). In terms of the present chapter, this begs the question of which specific social problems are to be addressed by public policies through translation and interpreting. While value judgements are inevitably involved, some broad, basic needs can be identified. Inasmuch as democracy has slowly become consolidated as the most common political system for organizing modern states, one may begin by inquiring about the most basic needs of democratic societies. Arguably, at the core of the democratic exercise is the aspiration to function as a society through dialogue and consensus-building. As early as 1762, Jean-Jacques Rousseau (1712–78) argued that free societies need to have a common language because citizens must be able to communicate with each other (Dobel, 1986, p. 654). Since then, scholars have stressed that the ability to communicate, the ability of citizens to speak with one another, is a key characteristic of a functioning democracy (e.g., Kymlicka, 2001, p. 26). While scholars do not necessarily agree that communication must necessarily take place in one language only (e.g., Réaume, 2003, p. 253), they tend to agree that communication should take place. Thus, a basic social need in a modern, democratic society is the ability of citizens to talk to each other.

Where there are needs, the potential for problems exists. A relevant observation will suffice to illustrate this: in most modern societies – particularly in light of the increasing size of cities and the ongoing rates of migration – some individuals will simply face language barriers when trying to talk to each other. In the United States, for example, more than 350 languages are spoken, and nearly 9 per cent of the population '[s]peak English less than "very well"' (see tables at US Census Bureau, 2015). The inability of some individuals to communicate effectively with the rest of the population becomes a social problem when a segment of society decides that this is something that affects the whole of society negatively. For example, if roughly 25 million residents of the United States were unable to access the laws, communicate with public authorities, and become informed of public debate, the democratic model itself would be called into question because millions would be excluded from it. In addition, a wide range of injustices would occur, ranging from unequal opportunities to lack of access to the judiciary, all of which would be problematic in a society that aims to have a vigorous democracy.

In public policy, once a social problem has been identified, solutions are proposed. In a democratic society where not everyone can communicate effectively with each other, several solutions are possible. The solution that might come to mind most easily is that everyone should speak the same language. This solution echoes the oft-quoted belief of the liberal philosopher John Stuart Mill (1806–73) that '[a]mong a people without fellow-feeling, especially if they read and speak different languages, the united public opinion, necessary to the working of representative government, cannot exist' (Mill, 1861, p. 289). If one assumes, as Mill does, that representative government cannot exist when people speak different languages, then in order to have a democratic society everyone must speak a single language. This understanding can lead to requirements that individuals be monolingual in a single language or that they at least speak in a common language. As Helder de Schutter (2017, p. 20) points out, such views of language lead to proposed solutions whereby policy 'seeks to inculcate citizens with a shared language'. Such a public policy would in practice necessitate, for example, that the government establish or promote centres where individuals learn the common language.

A problem with this proposed solution is that making everyone in society speak the same language is nearly impossible in practice. It may be possible in small societies, but in large territories where the population measures tens or hundreds of millions, such a policy objective cannot be fully realized without employing coercive measures that are anathema to democratic principles. One of the reasons this is so difficult to achieve is linked to migration. As stated earlier, in the modern world, people move, including across language boundaries. This implies that some societies continually receive speakers of many languages. Faced with this reality, a number of societies have opted for policies that promote language acquisition but nonetheless provide translation and interpreting services that allow some individuals to access certain services in their own language. For example, this is the case in the United States, where the language of the federal government is English but translation and interpreting is regularly deployed by different agencies to provide access across language barriers (see González Núñez, 2017, pp. 155–8). Choices as to what, for whom, and when to translate/interpret become in themselves policy questions that are handled at different levels of government (see González Núñez, 2016b). This exemplifies translation and interpreting as a remedial, temporary measure for individuals who have not acquired the ability to communicate effectively in the language of the majority. In such situations, 'the existence of translation is [viewed as] a regrettable state of affairs only justifiable as a temporary absence of shared knowledge of a shared language' (de Schutter, 2017, p. 21).

Another basic social problem linked to language may arise when a group that can communicate in the language of the state has traditionally spoken a different language. The problem in this scenario is not that some members of society cannot speak to each other but rather that one group feels marginalized precisely because it is being made to speak the other group's language. From the onset, the proposed solution of making everyone speak the same language *is* the social problem. In this case, other types of solution may be proposed. The possible solutions are many, and, as no two societies are identical, they will vary depending on a wide range of specific circumstances. Some examples of proposed solutions include Paraguay's nominal recognition of Guarani as an official language while mostly maintaining Spanish as the language of the state and Canada's bilingual regime where individuals may communicate with the authorities in any of the two official languages, English and French. In the case of policies where the recognition of the minority language leads to bilingual service provision, translation (and to some extent interpreting) serves as a practical tool in their implementation. When such policies are adopted, 'translation can be justified as a way of honouring the identity associated with the target language of translation' (de Schutter, 2017, p. XX).

The basic social problems that arise in terms of language are broadly described here. It is useful to bear in mind that each society has its unique language combinations, history and demographics. In some societies, problems may arise mostly in terms of new minority languages, that is, those spoken by immigrants. In other societies, problems may arise mostly in connection with old minority languages, that is, those spoken by historical minorities. In yet others, issues may revolve around both language groups or, to make matters even more complicated, the distinction between old and new minority languages may not always be easily made (see, e.g., González Núñez, 2016c, 2017). Observing this reality, Reine Meylaerts (2011) argues that language regimes in multilingual societies may be developed under four prototypical models. Such regimes are, in essence, the implementation of public policy aimed at broadly addressing social problems associated with language difference. Meylaerts proposes that these regimes are the following:

> 1) at one end of the continuum, multilingualism with obligatory multi-directional translation in all languages for all; 2) at the other end of the continuum, complete institutional monolingualism with obligatory translation into the official language and non-translation into the minority languages combined; 3) an intermediate prototype of institutional monolingualism combined with occasional (and often temporary) translation in well-defined situations, in anticipation of minorities' learning of the majority language; 4) in some specific cases, a combination of prototype one and two: institutional monolingualism at the lower level and institutional multilingualism with multidirectional mandatory translation at the superior (e.g., federal) level or vice versa. The first case applies to Belgium and Canada. The second case applies to the UK, which is largely monolingual at the central level, while e.g., Wales is bilingual.
>
> (Meylaerts, 2017, pp. 46–7)

All of these prototypical models require, in order to be sustained, the deployment of translation and interpreting. This means that translation, including interpreting, plays a role in co-ordinating action to respond to social problems where language is a component. These problems may manifest themselves differently in different situations. For example, a hospital in London may need to provide services to patients in tens of languages, while a hotline in Brownsville (on the United States border with Mexico) may get calls in only two languages, with more calls in Spanish than in English. Research into the public policies adopted to deal with these problems offers scholars the opportunity to engage with social issues that affect crucially the lives of many people in contemporary societies. There are many different ways in which researchers can study these problems. Section 9.3 discusses how translation studies scholars have approached public policy matters.

## 9.3   Approaching Public Policy in Translation Studies

For translation scholars, several approaches to public policy have shown to be fruitful. These include considering the policies themselves, the agents involved, and the complex interactions that are observed. Different methods can be applied, including the methods of the social sciences.

One approach understands public policy in terms of some of the conceptual models described in Section 9.1. Such models help operationalize policy by allowing for observation and measurement of specific variables. This helps gather data that can be analysed in order to arrive at useful conclusions. An example of how this might be done in translation studies is provided by Jim Hlavac et al. (2018). In seeking to account for the provision in Australia of translation and interpreting services, Hlavac et al. (2018, pp. 62–4) lean on conceptual models of policy formulation developed within policy studies. Having discussed several models (the Stages (Heuristic) model, the Institutional Rational Choice Framework, the Punctuated-Equilibrium Framework and the Advocacy Coalition Framework), they select the Multiple Streams Framework for their analysis. As they explain it, this model

> seeks to describe policy-making as a complex set of interactions with multiple actors, often with competing and unpredictable objectives in a surrounding environment that may be ambiguous or diffuse. The framework centers on three streams of actors or processes: the *problem stream*, the *politics stream*, and the *policy stream*. The three streams are regarded as existing in parallel within the policy-making environment until they are 'coupled', that is, joined together when propitious circumstances called *policy windows* open and when *policy entrepreneurs*, the actors who take advantage of the policy windows, place the idea on the decision-making agenda.                                        (Hlavac et al., 2018, p. 63)

With this framework in place, they describe the development of translation and interpreting services in Australia, from the 1970s to the present. They identify the problem stream, the politics stream and the policy stream as these developed, including the opening of a policy window within which specific policy entrepreneurs acted (Hlavac et al., 2018, pp. 67–71). This method allows Hlavac et al. to reach useful conclusions, such as that 'activities, protagonists and conditions coalesced [in Australia] to bring about a national policy, multiculturalism, that after its adoption then became a macro-level policy that found representation in policy formulation for most government-funded services', including those relevant to translation and interpreting (Hlavac et al., 2018, p. 82). In other words, translation policy emerged as a result of the development of a larger policy in favour of multiculturalism.

This approach is, of course, not the only possible way to consider public policy in translation studies. Employing policy models as tools for analysis allows the casting of a very broad net that can catch a varying range of elements for analysis, depending on the model of choice. Narrower scopes may be adopted as well, for example considering specific actors involved in the development of policy. When early policy researchers considered actors in the policy process, they often focused on government institutions. They tended to see political actors as separate from the rest of society who were bound by obligations and responsibilities and who belonged to organizational structures that provided specific outcomes (see March and Olsen, 1984, p. 735). These views evolved over time, and the role of institutions in policy formulation and development came to be questioned. Eventually 'formally organized social institutions [came] to be portrayed simply as arenas within which political behavior, driven by more fundamental factors, occur[ed]' (March and Olsen, 1984, p. 734). In short, institutions were relegated to the background because analysis focused on individual choices and specific forces exerted. In time, this new view came to be questioned too, and a more recent understanding of political actors turned the focus back on institutions, postulating that '[i]nstitutions seem to be neither neutral reflections of exogenous environmental forces nor neutral arenas for the performances of individuals driven by exogenous preferences and expectations' (March and Olsen, 1984, p. 732). Thus, when looking at public policy actors, researchers do well to take into account institutions, as these are key actors in the development of policy that cannot easily be dismissed.

Scholars in translation studies have considered the role of translation in institutions for some time. Articles exploring the relationship between translation and institutions have appeared in, for example, the *Routledge Encyclopedia of Translation Studies* (Kang, 2009), the *Handbook of Translation Studies* (Koskinen, 2011) and the *Routledge Handbook of Translation and Politics* (Schäffner, 2018). Koskinen (2008, p. 17) argues that institutions exist at three different levels: abstract (e.g., religion), formal (e.g., the Catholic Church) and concrete (e.g., local Catholic parishes). Methodologically, research into institutions and translation can fruitfully be carried out as the researcher moves from the abstract to the concrete, especially if the research question has to do with the common concern of translator agency (see Schäffner, 2018, pp. 216–17).

However, when considering matters of public policy, concerns about translators and their agency are but a piece of a much larger puzzle. They are to some extent individual performances that often play out in institutions that are powerful policy actors in their own right. For this reason, focusing too narrowly on translators and interpreters themselves risks missing the big policy questions, including general policy objectives and whether these are effectively reached on a large scale. A broader scope that considers the role of the institutions themselves in policy development, implementation and evaluation can be useful in understanding the extent to which public policy creates translation (including interpreting) and for what purposes. For example, in an earlier study I have argued (González Núñez, 2016b) that institutional concerns for non-discrimination and recognition are two related policy interests that, through a complex interplay of management, practice and beliefs, have resulted in some democratic societies providing translation and interpreting as a matter of public policy.

Concerns relating to modelling of public policy development, including the role of institutions as key agents in such development, have led time and again to an awareness of the degree of complexity found in public policy (e.g., Morçöl, 2010). Indeed, public policy implies 'an extremely complex set of elements that interact over time' (Sabatier, 2007, p. 3), and it should come as no surprise that concepts of what has been termed 'complexity theory' have been applied to policy studies at least since the late 1980s (e.g., Kiel, 1989). As Jack Meek (2010, p. 1) argues, researching policy by borrowing from this paradigm offers 'attractive insights about behavior that helps [sic] address the limitations of rationally based policy and administrative logics that have guided much of our efforts in these areas of inquiry'.

In turn, translation scholars have also begun to take notice of the value of the concepts of complexity for their own field. In their edited volume *Complexity Thinking in Translation Studies*, Kobus Marais and Meylaerts (2019, pp. 2–3) invite scholars to conceptualize complexity as part of their models and theories. Methodologically, complexity offers challenges for translation scholars because there is no consensus as to how to approach it (Marais and Meylaerts, 2019, p. 14), but the conceptual advantages include the ability to study systems that have complex traits such as non-linearity, emergence and self-organization. Consequently, translation scholars who research policy are working with complexity paradigms as well. For example, Meylaerts (2017) applies complexity theory's concepts of non-linearity, complex causation, self-organization and emergence to Belgium's nineteenth-century language policies in terms of translation. This allows her to conclude that while 'we could understand Belgian language and translation policy in the 19th century as a linear evolution towards a more equal representation of the Flemish language and people in the public domain', it could also be understood as 'a myriad of sometimes contradictory and unequally applied language and translation rules, practices and beliefs' (Meylaerts, 2017, pp. 56–7). Other approaches are also possible (e.g., Li, forthcoming) because complexity theory offers powerful conceptual tools for analysing policy issues.

There are many methodological approaches to choose from besides those described in this chapter. Whatever the approach may be, translation scholars can benefit from remembering that their study of public policy will be most helpful if it deals with problems that are pressing in society. Take, for example, the policy question raised in Section 9.2, namely, how to best allow people to talk to each other in a democratic society. In practical terms, this social problem can arise when immigrants to a country arrive with limited skills in the language of the state. This is a complex social problem. It involves many different agents who interact over time and who have different interests. The solutions these agents propose are sometimes in conflict and are, therefore, fertile ground for political controversy. Some believe that translation and language acquisition can coexist as policy measures to help individuals communicate in a given society (e.g., Little, 2010, pp. 31–2). Their solution is to provide opportunities for both. Others, however, have been very vocal in their view that a public policy that promotes translation in accessing services is a policy that encourages individuals to *not* acquire the state's language of choice and thus undermines society's strength. This argument was made by the United Kingdom's then Secretary of State for Communities and Local Government, Eric Pickles (2013), when he stated to Parliament: 'Stopping the automatic use of translation and interpretation services into foreign languages will provide further incentive for all migrant communities to learn English, which is the basis for an individual's ability to progress in British society'. This proposed solution is a sink-or-swim approach: in terms of language, people should be allowed to 'sink' so that they have an incentive to 'swim'.

These kinds of politically charged controversies are often high on rhetoric and low on data, which opens a window for translation scholars to provide helpful insights. For example, Pokorn and Čibej (2018, p. 111) address 'claims in public debate and political discourse that the access to translation and interpreting services provided by the state reduces the incentive of recent immigrants to learn the dominant language of the host country and consequently hampers their linguistic and social inclusion'. Using questionnaires and interviews, they investigated the attitude of asylum seekers in Slovenia towards Slovene, the common language of their host country, and the effect that having access to interpreting had on their attitude. They learnt that asylum seekers in Slovenia, even when they rely on interpreters for interacting with the government, 'are all aware of the importance of learning the dominant language of the host country and express a wish to learn it' (Pokorn and Čibej, 2018, p. 123). In other words, the study provides empirical evidence that translation services for immigrants do not cause people to not want to learn the language of their host state. This makes sense intuitively as well – people have incentives to learn the language of their host society that go beyond communicating with the authorities.

In sum, the study of public policy in terms of translation and interpreting can be carried out through different methodological approaches.

These include the use of models developed in policy studies to understand how policy develops. In such studies, institutions emerge as key players, and the consideration of their role in developing public policy, including translation policies, can also be helpful in terms of understanding why translation and interpreting is deployed as a policy tool when and where it is. Because policy development is so complex, there are valuable insights to be gained by adopting concepts from complexity theory. The exact method to be used in these approaches will vary depending on the research questions.

These are not the only places from which helpful methodological and conceptual tools may be derived, of course. The field of language policy, for instance, provides the tools to develop concepts of translation policy, translation management and translation belief as a way to research translation policy (see González Núñez, 2016a). Whatever the approach may be, in matters of public policy, research is valuable as it deals with real-world problems that affect real people. In this regard, there is much that can still be addressed in translation studies. Section 9.4 will suggest some largely unexplored, promising avenues of research.

## 9.4   Future Avenues of Policy Research for Translation Scholars

The study of translation and interpreting in public policy offers many viable avenues of research. Several of these have been explored in this chapter, and studies such as those are likely to continue to be carried out fruitfully. One might imagine, for example, studies that consider the proposal and implementation of language and translation policies in different territories. In this sense, there remains largely unexplored ground, specifically in the developing world. In other words, in the future one might hope to see such studies becoming more geographically diverse. Currently, the geographical scope of published studies is mostly focused on Australia (e.g., Hlavac et al., 2018), Belgium (e.g., Meylaerts, 2017), Canada (e.g., Abraham and Fiola, 2006), Spain (Diaz Fouces, 2004), Switzerland (Grin, 1998), the United Kingdom (e.g., González Núñez, 2016b), the United States (Córdoba Serrano, 2016) and the European Union (Ginsburgh and Weber, 2011), that is, it is strongly focused on Europe, North America and countries with strong ties to what might be called the 'Western' tradition. For the most part, these are studies into the use of translation and interpreting in wealthy states. This may simply be the result of these areas investing in research. The European Union, for example, has provided generous funding through programmes such as the Marie Skłodowska-Curie Actions.

Even so, future research might purposely and helpfully look beyond the territories that have traditionally been the focus of study. This would include research in places like Mexico and Paraguay, Cameroon and Equatorial Guinea, or China and India. Such countries offer specific scenarios that can proffer a richer understanding of how policy can be proposed and implemented in attempts to deal with social problems that differ from those found in Europe. For example, in a special issue of the *International Journal of the Sociology of Language* (Córdoba Serrano and Diaz Fouces, 2018), two articles move beyond the traditional geographies. Rosaleen Howard, Raquel de Pedro Ricoy and Luis Andrade Ciudad (2018) provide a brief overview of the legal framework relative to translation and interpreting in indigenous languages in Bolivia, Colombia, Ecuador, Mexico and Paraguay before focusing on a case study in Peru. Nanette Gottlieb (2018) surveys the provision of translated information for foreign residents in Japan, where the national government is beginning to acknowledge diversity within its borders. Studies such as these are a welcome contribution to a body of knowledge with much potential for expansion.

These studies, owing to the context-specific nature of public policy, tend to be case studies, and one way for research in this vein to move forward would be to undertake a greater number of comparative studies, especially between territories that have been studied in the past and newer frontiers. Comparative studies encourage the development of better policies by showing how similar problems are approached in different contexts (Heidenheimer, Heclo and Adams, 2005, pp. 13–14). Many comparative studies already exist (e.g., González Núñez, 2017), but scholars might nonetheless benefit from comparisons between, for example, how Mexico deals with indigenous languages in the judiciary versus how Spain deals with traditional minority languages in the judiciary. How are indigenous groups in Mexico and traditional minority groups in Spain equally and differently situated? What are the language-related social needs and problems that arise, and what are the similarities and differences between how these affect the two groups? What solutions have been proposed and implemented? Have the implemented solutions enabled policy objectives to be achieved? Were increasing numbers of international comparative studies to be carried out, researchers might form a more comprehensive picture of the role of translation and interpreting in public policy.

Studies into public policy carried out by translation scholars tend to be skilful at identifying the problems that arise and at describing the policies devised to respond to those problems. However, policy evaluation largely remains a blind spot for translation studies. This area is relevant because policy-making is an ongoing cycle of policy proposal, implementation, evaluation and consequent adjustment (Hlavac et al., 2018, p. 62, after Jenkins, 1978). Thus, when considering the role of translation and interpreting in public policy, the evaluation of language and translation policies is a key element in appraising to what extent the policies as implemented reach their intended goals. This appraisal is helpful in the formulation of better policies.

Despite this, studies into language and translation policy rarely engage in matters of policy evaluation. A notable exception is Michele Gazzola and François Grin's (2017) paper on the evaluation of comparative language and translation policies. Gazzola and Grin do not shy away from policy evaluation (see, e.g., Gazzola, 2014) because they are economists whose field of research is the economics of language (on this topic, see Grin, 2003). Thus, they are equipped with the tools to evaluate public policy, which translation scholars often lack. This is not to say that translation scholars are unable to address policy evaluation, but they may benefit from collaborating with colleagues in other disciplines, including economics and political science.

Whatever the case may be, the study of translation in public policy involves engaging in situations in which different groups in society disagree about key issues. In order for translation studies scholars to enter such arenas, highlight social problems, explore the proposed and implemented solutions and evaluate whether the objectives to those solutions are met, they need to develop an understanding of public policy and of the role of translation and interpreting as deployed in public policy. Methodologically, this can be approached in different ways, depending on specific research questions. Ultimately, this is done to better inform scholars, policymakers and the public at large about how we actually respond and how we should respond collectively to some of the challenges faced in a world where people are increasingly mobile and cities are growing increasingly larger, with all the linguistic implications of that reality. Acquisition and dissemination of knowledge in this field could impact the lives of millions of people across the planet and is therefore research worth engaging in.

## References

Abraham, D., and Fiola, M. A. (2006). Making the case for community interpreting in health care: From needs assessment to risk management. *Linguistica Antverpiensia, New Series*, **5**, 189–202.

Box, G. E. P., and Draper, N. R. (1989). *Empirical Model-Building and Response Surfaces*. New York: Wiley & Sons.

Caldas, S. J. (2012). Language policy in the family. In B. Spolsky, ed., *The Cambridge Handbook of Language Policy*. Cambridge: Cambridge University Press, pp. 351–73.

Córdoba Serrano, M. S. (2016). Translation policies and community translation: The U.S., a case study. *New Voices in Translation Studies*, **14**, 122–63.

Córdoba Serrano, M. S., and Diaz Fouces, O., eds. (2018). *International Journal of the Sociology of Language*, **251**.

De Schutter, H. (2017). Translational justice: Between equality and privation. In G. González Núñez and R. Meylaerts, eds., *Translation and Public Policy: Interdisciplinary Perspectives and Case Studies*. Abingdon-on-Thames: Routledge pp. 15–31.

Diaz Fouces, O. (2004). Políticas de traducción en Cataluña y Galicia. Paper presented at the 5th Symposium on Translation, Terminology and Interpretation in Cuba and Canada, Havana, Cuba.

Dobel, J. P. (1986). The role of language in Rousseau's political thought. *Polity*, **18**(4), 638–58.

Dye, T. R. (2002). *Understanding Public Policy*. 10th ed. Upper Saddle, NJ: Prentice Hall.

Gazzola, M. (2014). *The Evaluation of Language Regimes*. Amsterdam: John Benjamins.

Gazzola, M., and Grin, F. (2017). Comparative language policy and evaluation: Criteria, indicators and implications for translation policy. In G. González Núñez and R. Meylaerts, eds., *Translation and Public Policy: Interdisciplinary Perspectives and Case Studies*. Abingdon-on-Thames: Routledge, pp. 83–116.

Ginsburgh, V., and Weber, S. (2011). *How Many Languages Do We Need? The Economics of Linguistic Diversity*. Princeton, NJ: Princeton University Press.

González Núñez, G. (2016a). On translation policy. *Target*, **28**(1), 87–109.

González Núñez, G. (2016b). *Translating in Linguistically Diverse Societies: Translation Policy in the United Kingdom*. Amsterdam: John Benjamins.

González Núñez, G. (2016c). Translation policy in a linguistically diverse world. *Journal on Ethnopolitics and Minority Issues in Europe*, **15**(1), 1–18.

González Núñez, G. (2017). Law and translation at the U.S.–Mexico border: Translation policy in a diglossic setting. In G. González Núñez and R. Meylaerts, eds., *Translation and Public Policy: Interdisciplinary Perspectives and Case Studies*. Abingdon-on-Thames: Routledge, pp. 152–70.

Gottlieb, N. (2018). Multilingual information for foreign residents in Japan: A survey of government initiatives. *International Journal of the Sociology of Language*, **251**, 131–49.

Grin, F. (1998). Language policy in multilingual Switzerland: Overview and recent developments. Paper presented at Cicle de confèrencies sobre política lingüística, Barcelona, Spain.

Grin, F. (2003). Language planning and economics. *Current Issues in Language Planning*, **4**(1), 1–66.

Heidenheimer, A. J., Heclo, C., and Adams, C. T. (2005). The politics of social choice. In B. Bushouse and H. J. Wiarda, eds., *Comparative Public Policy, vol. VI of Comparative Politics: Critical Concepts in Political Science*. Abingdon-on-Thames: Routledge, pp. 13–35.

Hlavac, J., Gentile, A., Orlando, M., Zucchi, E., and Pappas, A. (2018). Translation as a sub-set of public and social policy and a consequence of multiculturalism: The provision of translation and interpreting services in Australia. *International Journal of the Sociology of Language*, **251**, 55–88.

Howard, R., de Pedro Ricoy, R., and Andrade Ciudad, L. (2018). Translation policy and indigenous languages in Hispanic Latin America. *International Journal of the Sociology of Language*, **251**, 19–36.

Jenkins, W. (1978). *Policy Analysis: A Political and Organisational Perspective*. London: M. Robertson.

Kang, J.-H. (2009). Institutional translation. In M. Baker and G. Saldanha, eds., *Routledge Encyclopedia of Translation Studies*. 2nd ed. Abingdon-on-Thames: Routledge, pp. 141–5.

Kiel, D. L. (1989). Nonequilibrium theory and implications for public administration. *Public Administration Review*, **49**(6), 544–51.

Koskinen, K. (2008). *Translating Institutions: An Ethnographic Study of the EU*. Manchester: St Jerome.

Koskinen, K. (2011). Institutional translation. In Y. Gambier and L. van Doorslaer, eds., *Handbook of Translation Studies*, vol. 2. Amsterdam: John Benjamins, pp. 54–60.

Kymlicka, W. (2001). *Politics in the Vernacular: Nationalism, Multiculturalism and Citizenship*. Oxford: Oxford University.

Li, S. (forthcoming). The complexity of a translation policy: Interpreting for ethnic linguistic minorities in China's local courtrooms. In B. Nouws, H. van Gerwen and M. Bourguignon, eds., *Translation Policies in Legal and Institutional Settings*. Leuven: Leuven University Press.

Little, D. (2010). *The Linguistic Integration of Adult Migrants Intergovernmental Conference*. Report. Strasbourg: Language Policy Unit.

Lowi, T. J., Ginsberg, B., Shepsle, K. A., and Ansolabehere, S. (2017). *American Government: Power and Purpose*. 14th ed. New York: W. W. Norton & Company.

Manning, N. (2011). Social needs, social problems, and social welfare and well-being. In P. Alcock, M. May and S. Wright, eds., *The Student's Companion to Social Policy*. 4th ed. Hoboken, NJ: Wiley-Blackwell, p. 19–25.

Marais, K., and Meylaerts, R. (2019). *Complexity Thinking in Translation Studies: Methodological Considerations*. Abingdon-on-Thames: Routledge.

March, J. G., and Olsen, J. P. (1984). The new institutionalism: Organizational factors in political life. *American Political Science Review*, **78**(3), 734–49.

Meek, J. W. (2010). Complexity theory for public administration and policy. *E:CO*, **12**(1), 1–4.

Meylaerts, R. (2011). Translational justice in a multilingual world: An overview of translational regimes. *Meta*, **56**(4), 743–57.

Meylaerts, R. (2017). Studying language and translation policies in Belgium: What can we learn from a complexity theory approach? *Parallèles*, **29**(1), 45–59.

Mill, J. S. (1861). *Considerations on Representative Government*. London: Parker, Son, and Bourn.

Morçöl, G. (2010). Issues in reconceptualizing public policy from the perspective of complexity theory. *E:CO*, **12**(1), 52–60.

Pickles, E. (2013). Translation into foreign languages. www.gov.uk/government/speeches/translation-into-foreign-languages.

Pokorn, N. K., and Čibej, J. (2018). Interpreting and linguistic inclusion – friends or foes? Results from a field study. *The Translator*, **24**(2), 111–27.

Pym, A. (2002). Translation studies as social problem-solving. usuaris.tinet.cat/apym/on-line/research_methods/thessaloniki.pdf.

Réaume, D. G. (2003). Official-language rights: Intrinsic value and the protection of difference. In W. Kymlicka and W. Norman, eds., *Citizenship in Diverse Societies*. New York: Oxford University, pp. 245–72.

Rousseau, J.-J. (1762). *Du contrat social; ou, Principes du droit politique*. Amsterdam: Chez Marc Michel Rey.

Sabatier, P. A. (2007). The need for better theories. In P. A. Sabatier, ed., *Theories of the Policy Process*. Cambridge, MA: Westview Press, pp. 1–17.

Schäffner, C. (2018). Institutional translation. In F. Fernández and J. Evans, eds., *Routledge Handbook of Translation and Politics*. London: Routledge, pp. 204–20.

Tesseur, W. (2017). Incorporating translation into sociolinguistic research: Translation policy in an international non-governmental organization. *Journal of Sociolinguistics*, **21**(5), 629–49.

Turner, C., Bresler, R., Friedrich, R., Karlesky, J., and Stephenson Jr., D. (2018). *Introduction to American Government*. 9th ed. Redding, CA: BVT Publishing.

UN Population Division (2017). *International Migration Report 2017*. www.un.org/en/development/desa/population/migration/publications/migrationreport/docs/MigrationReport2017.pdf.

UN Population Division (2018). *World Urbanizations Prospect 2018: Key Facts*. population.un.org/wup/Publications/Files/WUP2018-KeyFacts.pdf.

US Census Bureau (2015). *Detailed Languages Spoken at Home and Ability to Speak English for the Population 5 Years and Over: 2009–2013*. www.census.gov/data/tables/2013/demo/2009–2013-lang-tables.html.

# 10

# Translator Associations and Networks

Julie McDonough Dolmaya

## 10.1 Overview of Translator Networks and Associations

As Risku and Dickinson (2009) note, translation is typically 'a solitary profession', which means that translators can benefit from being able to collaborate, share knowledge with and learn from one another (Risku and Dickinson, 2009, p. 57). Associations and networks are a means through which this collaboration, communication and sharing can be accomplished.

In its broadest sense, a network is a concept used to represent the connectivity inherent in complex relationships and organizational structures (Folaron and Buzelin, 2007, p. 606). Various categories of network exist, but the common element in all of them is connection – a sliding scale of 'degrees of connectedness and relationships through space and time' (Folaron and Buzelin, 2007, p. 606). We might, for instance, study technological networks, or the connections among the computer systems used by translators collaborating via online translation platforms. Or we might study lexical and semantic networks. Halverson's (2003, p. 205) work has explored schematic networks, or networks comprising the connections between the various senses associated with a lexical or grammatical item. In a similar vein, Campbell (2000) has studied 'choice networks', the general network of translation decisions, which researchers infer by studying source and target texts, and which they can use to identify the mental process used to create a translation.

The type of network that Risku and Dickinson (2009) were alluding to, and which will be of interest to us here, is the social network, or that comprising translators (or translation agencies) and other actors, either human or organizational. More specifically, this chapter will discuss how translators share, exchange and use information 'within networks of communication that relay interconnected groups of people' (Folaron,

2010, p. 231). Our approach will be based on social network analysis, which studies sets of actors (individuals, corporate or collective social units) and the relation(s) among them (e.g., interactions, movements, physical connections, biological relationships, transfers of material resources) (Wasserman and Faust, 1994, pp. 18–20).

## 10.2  Associations versus Networks

While all associations are networks, not all networks are associations. To qualify as a network, a grouping need only comprise a set of actors, such as translators, connected to one another through a set of ties, such as inter-actions in an online forum. By contrast, as Pym (2014, p. 467) notes in his study of 217 translator associations, a legal framework of some kind regulates professional associations, which may also use terms such as 'order' or 'union' to refer to themselves (see Pym, 2014 and Pym et al., 2012 for examples); networks do not have to have such a formal frame-work. Another difference between professional associations and networks more generally is that professional associations function as regulatory agencies: Greenwood, Suddaby and Hinings (2002) argue that the members of professional associations have three functions: (1) to develop a common understanding of 'reasonable conduct and the behavioural dues of mem-bership' (Greenwood et al., 2002, p. 61), to determine the range of activities over which members can claim exclusive jurisdiction and to specify who has the authority to practise these activities within the jurisdiction and how they may do so (Greenwood et al., 2002, p. 62); (2) to act as represen-tative agencies, a way for the professional community to represent them-selves to others both within and outside of their field (Greenwood et al., 2002, p. 62); and (3) to help monitor compliance with expected norms and to sanction members who fail to meet these standards (Greenwood et al., 2002, p. 62). Thus, professional associations can play both conservative and reforming roles, shifting between defending the status quo and attempting to effect change in the profession (Greenwood et al., 2002, p. 62).

Pym (2014) has discussed the tension between conservativism and reform in the context of professional translator associations. He offers examples of an association in Spain that seems to have been created in response to the dissatisfaction of some members with the larger, more well established, generalist professional associations, and he argues that the younger association, which is better able to leverage a range of information and communication technologies, offers services and inter-action possibilities 'that seem beyond the reach of the association of 7,000 older members' (Pym, 2014, p. 479). In a similar vein, he discusses an international association established because the founders disagreed with a regional association about who should have authority to practise translation: the international association argues that not all professional translators can have degrees in translation and that this association will accept translators as members based on their years of experience rather than their formal education. By doing so, Pym (2014, p. 480) argues, the international association offers 'strong signals of status to people who would otherwise not have access to such symbolic capital'. In Pym's view, now that more translation programs exist around the world, translators are not seeking a professional association that merely acts as a gatekeeper, or authority over who can practice the profession: instead, they are seeking associations that can (also) offer interaction with peers, up-to-date-information, professional development opportunities and access to clients. Associations that cannot adapt to these demands will find their members and potential members seeking out other associations, forming new ones or instead joining collaborative online networks (Pym, 2014, p. 483).

## **10.3** Types of Networks

Translation networks can be categorized in various ways – according to the actors in the network, their interests, the admission requirements and so on. McDonough (2007) proposed a categorization based on the primary common interest shared by the members of the network. Four types of networks emerge on this basis: profession-oriented, practice-oriented, education-oriented and research-oriented.

Profession-oriented translation networks are composed of actors who share a common interest in promoting translation as a professional activity. Their interest lies less with the act of translation than with the activities, events, challenges and other issues that are related to the profession, such as defending the rights of translators, enhancing the status of translation in society and improving working conditions for translators (McDonough, 2007, p. 796). Associations that offer professional certification exams to test the competencies of translators fall into this category, and the certification process within these organizations has been of interest to several translation studies researchers, including Chan (2010), Koby and Melby (2013) and Hlavac (2013).

While some profession-oriented networks offer a certification process, not all do. Some, such as a professional association of literary translators, do not certify their members but do engage in other profession-oriented activities such as offering professional development workshops, awarding prizes to recognize professional skill and organizing networking events for translators to connect with one another. Examples of the wide range of activities and interests of professional translator associations can be found in Pym (2014).

Practice-oriented networks are organized around a common interest in the actual performance or process of translation-related activities (McDonough, 2007, p. 797). The actors in these networks usually engage in activities such as discussing marketing strategies, exchanging terminological problems, or offering and bidding for translation contracts. A growing body of research examining different aspects of practice-oriented translation networks exists. Some of this research focuses specifically on how online translation networks function: Plassard (2007) has highlighted how translators have used electronic mailing lists to discuss translation problems with one another; Risku and Dickinson (2009) have surveyed members of the online network ProZ.com to discover why they belong to the network; while McDonough (2007) has studied how members of online practice-oriented networks interact with one another. Other research has explored literary and publication networks and the process through which works of literature are selected for translation (Buzelin, 2006; Córdoba Serrano, 2010). Finally, some work has focused more specifically on practice-oriented networks with an activist agenda (Baker, 2013; Boéri, 2008); these networks will be discussed in more detail in Section 10.4.

In education-oriented networks, the common interest is translation pedagogy, shared by actors such as university professors and academic institutions (McDonough, 2007, p. 797). This type of translation network has not been extensively studied by translation studies scholars, although networks of translation (studies) programmes, such as the International Doctorate in Translation Studies and the European Masters in Translation, have recently been discussed, respectively, by Gambier, Schäffner and Meylaerts (2019) and Torres-Simón and Pym (2019).

Finally, research-oriented networks focus on translation as a field of study, examining translation studies, intercultural studies, translation technologies, comparative literature and related subjects (McDonough, 2007, p. 798). While some networks may be composed of researchers carrying out a specific project, others can be focused on helping researchers to keep in touch with one another, organizing conferences, awarding prizes recognizing exceptional research and so on (McDonough, 2007, p. 798). These networks have received less attention from translation studies scholars; nonetheless, some studies do exist. Pym (2006) has discussed research-oriented networks when considering the political organization of the field of translation studies, while Castro-Prieto and Olvera-Lobo (2007) have combined social network analysis with citation analysis to study the relationships among authors of terminology articles published in nine terminology and translation studies journals from 1967 to 2001. They discovered that only 12 per cent of authors had a regular presence in the network (i.e., had authored more than three articles), and that only 1 per cent of authors in the sample had a high number of citations.

As McDonough (2007, p. 798) acknowledges, although each of the four network categories has a defining characteristic – namely, a shared interest in the profession, practice, teaching or study of translation – many networks will fall between categories. For instance, the practice-oriented translation network described by Thelen (2005) also has an educational focus since it consists of students working in a simulated translation agency, under the supervision of instructors. And Pym (2014, pp. 485–6) argues that some online translation marketplaces (which would fall into the practice-oriented network category) have begun to adopt various gatekeeping functions, such as administering translation exams, that have traditionally been performed by professional associations (or profession-oriented networks), thus blurring the lines between the two types of networks. So, while some networks may be best described by just one category when the defining common interest is largely of one type, other networks are described as belonging to more than one category when several types of common interest are prominent within the network.

McDonough (2007) also notes a number of variables that can affect the structure and composition of translation networks: sub-focus, shared values, geographic location, membership requirements and computer mediation. To these, we might add legal frameworks to help distinguish between networks and associations.

First, within each category of network, members may be linked not just by a broad common interest in the profession, practice, teaching or study of translation but also by more specific sub-focuses, namely: language combination(s), such as French to Spanish translation; text type(s), such as poetry or advertisements; translation-related profession(s), such as interpreting, subtitling, or software localization; and subject fields(s), such as law or insurance.

Second, the actors in the network may share a set of values, beliefs or principles related to their common interest. Both Gambier (2007) and Baker (2013) describe several such networks, including those whose translation work is in support of an anti-war agenda, and those whose work is intended to support political change.

Third, the networks can be geographically dispersed to varying degrees: in some translation networks, members may reside primarily in the same country (or even the same city) or work/volunteer for a single institution or company, while in others, members may not be concentrated in the same geographic area and the network can be considered international.

Fourth, some networks have virtually no membership requirements, while others are very restrictive: McDonough (2007, p. 802) notes that various online, practice-oriented networks have no membership requirements other than an internet connection; Thomson-Wohlgemuth (2004, p. 505), by contrast, mentions that mid twentieth century East German translators who sought to apply for membership of the translators' branch of the Writers' Association had to submit samples of their work, including at least one translated book of world literature and three to four other books. Note also that some networks can comprise individuals only, while others might (exclusively) include organizations, companies, departments or other organizational units.

Fifth, the extent to which the interactions among members are computer mediated will vary from one network to another, with international networks typically relying heavily on computer-assisted methods such as videoconferencing, email or web platforms to communicate. Researchers who have studied how members interact in largely online practice-oriented translation networks include Risku and Dickinson (2009), Plassard (2007) and Yu (2019).

Finally, the network may have a legal framework officially establishing it as a trade union, professional association or other, similar type of organization, or it may be more informally constituted – for example an online discussion group. Any of the four categories of network can be an association, although the focus of existing translation studies research on translation associations has largely been profession oriented. Pym (2014) is a rare example of a work that exclusively examines translator associations (rather than networks more broadly or activities of professional associations, such as certification); however, professional associations are also discussed to some extent in Chan (2010), Pym et al. (2012), Hlavac (2013) and Ruokonen (2013).

## 10.4   Activities of Translator Networks

As suggested in Section 10.3, and by Pym (2014, pp. 468, 482), the actors in translation networks engage in a variety of activities, including awarding prizes, organizing conferences and other networking events, disseminating news, advocating or lobbying on behalf of translators, acting as job markets, using translation to support various causes, engaging in collaborative translation activities, providing professional development and certification and developing codes of ethics. Several of these activities have received attention from translation studies researchers, and so they will be discussed in more detail. Activities that are particular to just one kind of translation network (e.g., engaging in research in a research-oriented network or doing translation in a practice-oriented network) will not be discussed here because examples were offered in Section 10.3.

### 10.4.1   Advocacy and Visibility for Translators

Translators tend to view their profession as having fairly low status (Ruokonen, 2013, p. 331); therefore, translation networks sometimes act as advocates for translators, attempting to improve the visibility of the profession among both the general public and translators themselves.

Ruokonen (2013) offers a helpful survey of recent research on translator status, with a section specifically discussing the strategies and actions that translator associations or authorities have adopted to try to change the status of the profession (Ruokonen, 2013, pp. 335–6).

Thomson-Wohlgemuth (2004) describes a case in East Germany where a professional organization was established in the early 1950s to help improve translator status. Translators were integrated into the Writers' Association as 'recreating authors' (Thomson-Wohlgemuth, 2004, p. 504), and, as Thomson-Wohlgemuth argues, being backed by a powerful organization like the Writers' Association meant that translators received greater support for their work and saw improvements to their financial position and professional status during the existence of the German Democratic Republic (Thomson-Wohlgemuth, 2004, p. 504).

As discussed more fully in Section 10.4.5, Lambert (2018) takes a more negative view of one aspect of the visibility-related activities that translator networks engage in. He has argued that professional translator associations develop codes of ethics in part to enhance the status of the profession in the eyes of the general public, and to serve as 'status symbols' that will add an air of authority and professionalism (Lambert, 2018, p. 285) to profession- and practice-oriented networks. In this case, the efforts are not focused on improving the visibility of translation, depicting it as a profession that involves 'reworking' texts; instead, these efforts provide 'a carefully curated—and false—image of the process of translation and the profile of the translators working in their name' because they give the unrealistic impression that translators can be totally objective, neutral conduits (Lambert, 2018, p. 281).

## 10.4.2  Activism for Other Causes

Networks of translators who are linked by their support for a particular cause are fairly widespread and have attracted attention from a number of researchers. Baker (2013, p. 26) suggests that activist communities of translators can be distinguished based on the kinds of text they translate and the venue for these translations. The first type consists of actors who select, translate and disseminate texts via websites and mailing lists, while the second consists of actors who work within the community or collective forums to interpret at specific events (Baker, 2013, p. 26). While Baker uses the term 'community' to refer to these groups, they might also be classified as networks, given that they consist of actors linked to one another through shared exchanges; indeed, several of the groups that Baker studies describe themselves as networks either in their names or on their websites (cf. Baker, 2013, p. 26). To date, translation studies research has investigated both of the types of networks that Baker describes.

Gambier (2007) discusses several networks that fall into the two categories, though most are of the first type. He argues that the activist networks he has studied are committed to certain values (Gambier, 2007, p. 660), and he discusses several examples, including one network from the early 2000s consisting of translators coming together not to translate but to express their disapproval of the war in Iraq under George Bush's administration (Gambier, 2007, p. 661). He also discusses the network Tlaxacala, which focuses on translating under-represented voices (Gambier, 2007, p. 662), and ECOS, a network based in Granada, Spain, that offers translation and interpreting services to non-governmental organizations (NGOs) with limited resources, and works to support human rights (Gambier, 2007, p. 663). On the basis of his overview of these networks, Gambier concludes that when they have a strong sense of political engagement and use translation or interpreting to resist and fight against political decisions, and so on, they do not also engage in selling or buying services: their goal is to defend and promote a position (Gambier, 2007, p. 669).

Boéri (2008) focuses largely on the second type of network in her narrative analysis of a controversy that arose in 2005, after the World Social Forum decided not to use professional conference interpreting services as it had in previous years but rather to rely on Babels, a network of volunteers, for its translation and interpreting needs. Wolf (2010) also discusses the Babels controversy, but from a sociological perspective. She raises a point that is particularly relevant to the study of networks with an activist agenda: like many social movements, Babels should not be considered a space where members collaborate harmoniously, since internal disagreements can and do occur (Wolf, 2010, p. 40). As Wolf asserts, when conflicts arise because a network is involved in 'intensive transnational cooperation', its members will have different interpretations and ideas about what the appropriate collective approach should be, resulting in disagreements within the network (Wolf, 2010, p. 40). This point has not been extensively explored in translation studies research; however it would be relevant not only to activist networks but to others as well: examining the points of tension that exist in translation networks would help us to better understand how and why translators collaborate.

### 10.4.3   Job Markets

Pym (2014, pp. 468, 476) suggests that professional translator associations function in part as job markets because they enable potential clients to contact association members. In his study of more than 200 professional translator associations, Pym (2014, p. 483) concludes that because there are many translator training programmes, 'vast numbers of trained translators are seeking more than an exclusive club' when they join a professional association. In return for their membership fees, they expect services such as professional development, peer-to-peer interaction and access to clients (Pym (2014, p. 483).

Job markets are not a feature limited to only profession-oriented networks. Kushner (2013, p. 1242) discusses the job market aspect of practice-oriented translation networks such as ProZ.com, arguing that they act as 'digital matchmakers', connecting clients with contingent, geographically distributed and entrepreneurial translators, while also collecting fees from these freelance translators and thereby 'injecting a new mediating layer into the translation economy'. It is worth noting, however, that sites like ProZ.com typically have both free and paid membership plans, which means that fees are not always collected from freelancers who want to connect with clients. Translators who do pay the membership fees, though, receive various benefits, including enhanced status within the network, as Pym et al. (2016, p. 38) discuss.

Kushner (2013, pp. 1250–1) argues that unless an online marketplace like ProZ.com is able to balance a steady flow of paying freelance translation suppliers with a steady flow of paying translation clients, the business model breaks down. His research is particularly relevant for further studies of the economics of the translation industry.

Pym et al. (2016) also discuss ProZ.com, but they focus more specifically on translator status within the network, arguing that higher status is associated with better job opportunities. Status in the ProZ.com network is achieved through membership level (paying members have better positions in the directory), by contributing to the community (via discussion forums, for instance), by posting client feedback on a translator's profile page, and by proving that a ProZ.com member also belongs to a professional translator association (Pym et al., 2016, p. 39). This multi-faceted way of signalling status, Pym et al. (2016, p. 41) argue, is a way to generate internal trust among the translators who belong to the network and external trust from prospective clients, helping to 'restore some degree of order to the online marketplace'.

### 10.4.4  Certification

Certification – also called *accreditation* in some countries (Hlavac, 2013, p. 35) – is an activity often found in profession-oriented networks, given that the common interest in such networks is enhancing the status of the profession: Gouadec (2007, p. 247) and Hlavac (2013, p. 33) note that certification is seen as a way to promote quality assurance within the translation industry, protecting service users and providing benchmarks for translators to achieve. However, not all profession-oriented networks offer certification: Pym (2014, pp. 471–2) offers helpful examples of literary translator associations that recognize members based not on exams and degrees but rather on whether they have published literary translations. Moreover, networks that are not profession-oriented can also offer some sort of certification process: Pym (2014, p. 485) notes that some practice-oriented networks, such as ProZ.com, have recently begun to offer their own certification processes as a way for members to distinguish themselves within the community. Gouadec (2007, p. 248) mentions that software vendors can also offer certification for users of their products, while Hlavac (2013, pp. 36–7) discusses examples of government organizations that administer and conduct the certification process.

Both individual translators and translation companies can seek certification, in some cases from international bodies, such as the International Organization for Standardization (ISO), and in others from professional translator associations and/or practice-oriented networks (Gouadec, 2007, pp. 247–8; Pym, 2014; Hlavac, 2013; Kushner, 2013, p. 1251). Indeed, profession-oriented networks are now involved in the drafting process of industry standards: Hlavac (2013, p. 34) offers examples of profession-oriented networks that have participated in the technical committees that develop ISO specifications.

The features of certification tests vary widely from one country to another, according to Hlavac's (2013) study of twenty-one professional translator associations. Most include formal examinations with general and/or specialist components, and about half have a required minimum education level, minimum experience level and minimum age. Fewer than half involve a language proficiency test or training prior to the test (Hlavac, 2013, pp. 38–9), which Hlavac argues is because the role of the organizations that are responsible for certification is to certify rather than train.

In general, research on translator certification has focused on two aspects: whether certification offers benefits to members, and how the testing process can be validated. On the first topic, Chan (2010) used a survey conducted with project managers, directors or owners of seventy translation companies to assess the perceived benefits of certification. Respondents generally agreed that translator certification would increase respect from co-workers and that certified translators were more committed to their careers and enhanced the image of the profession. However, there was less agreement about whether certification led to higher pay or being hired by translation firms. Nor did respondents typically feel that certified translators had better language proficiency and subject knowledge than non-certified translators. Bowker (2004), who studied 301 advertisements for translation-related jobs in Canada, came to similar conclusions. She found that fewer than half of the job postings required that applicants be certified by a professional association (Bowker, 2004, p. 968) and argued that this seemed to indicate that certification was not highly valued in Canada – at least at the time. By contrast, in their research on translator status in Iran, Kafi, Khoshsaligheh and Hashemi (2018) conducted eleven interviews with translation scholars, professional translators, project managers and publishers, and one of the points that was raised by nearly half of interviewees was that an accreditation test should be a requirement for those who wanted to work as a professional translator in Iran, illustrating that, in that country, certification exams are seen as enhancing the status of the profession.

Pym et al. (2012, p. 4), in their report for the European Commission and Directorate-General for Translation, note that the status of translators is in a state of flux and that some status-signalling mechanisms, including certification, are inefficient, particularly since 'online translator–client portals' (or practice-oriented networks) have started to develop new certification processes. They recommend that an international, standardized status-signalling process be developed – one that, among other things, will ensure that qualifications and certifications are recognized internationally and clearly understood by employers, and one that does not rely on academic degrees alone (Pym et al., 2012, pp. 4–5). Hlavac (2013, p. 58) echoes this goal, arguing that translator associations should aim to agree on 'common and desirable features' that should be required of certified translators and interpreters to help ensure that certification standards are equivalent and comparable on an international level.

As for the validation of certification testing, Koby and Melby (2013) have discussed how certification exams could be strengthened. After surveying 1,453 members of a professional translator association about the certification process and the knowledge, skills and abilities required by professional translators, Koby and Melby compared the survey results with existing research on translator competence. They recommended that all certification programmes be tested for validity by first determining what knowledge, skills and abilities are required by translators in a given region and then comparing these requirements with the knowledge, skills and abilities measured by the programme (Koby and Melby, 2013, p. 207). Clifford (2005) has focused more particularly on interpreter certification exams and reported on the results of an experiment that tests interpreter comprehension of a source language message. He has suggested that even though the experimental test was able to assess comprehension successfully, interpreters would likely resist the proposed approach because it involved a written component, rather than something more obviously related to interpreting performance (Clifford, 2005, p. 127). For this reason, among others, Clifford did not recommend incorporating the experimental test into certification exams (Clifford, 2005, p. 127).

### 10.4.5   Codes of Ethics and Practice in Translator Networks

As translator networks are built on connections of shared interests, and may also be based on shared values, codes of ethics are frequently established by these networks. Like certification processes, codes of ethics are a common element of profession-oriented networks; however, such codes can be found in any type of translation network. Lambert (2018, p. 270), for instance, mentions that translator agencies (or practice-oriented networks) occasionally have codes of ethics for their translators to follow, and although no research seems to specifically study ethics in research-oriented or education-oriented translation networks, it is certainly feasible that such networks could establish codes of practice that members could follow: as Baker (2011, p. 284) argues, many translation scholars and practitioners view codes of ethics as 'the reference point for ethical behaviour in the field'.

A number of scholars have discussed the codes of ethics in professional associations, placing particular emphasis on the shortcomings of existing codes. McDonough Dolmaya (2011) studied the codes of ethics of seventeen profession-oriented translation networks, comparing the principles in the codes to determine which values were most important to these professional networks. Then, to help determine whether and how the codes of ethics could be applied to practical translation problems, McDonough Dolmaya (2011) studied the discussion forum postings in a practice-oriented translation network and compared the problems with the guidelines offered in the codes of ethics. McDonough Dolmaya's (2011) research highlighted various shortcomings in the codes of ethics – namely, that the most common principles are those that apply to many professions, rather than to translation in particular, and that when codes do address factors that are particular to translation, such as accuracy and working languages, they sometimes conflict with one another and do not provide clear guidelines for translators to follow (McDonough Dolmaya, 2011, p. 45). In particular, the codes at that time did not address the ethical use of translation technology (McDonough Dolmaya, 2011, p. 45). In a later study, Lambert (2018) was particularly critical of the accuracy and impartiality clauses in codes of ethics, noting that the existing codes are not designed to teach translators ethical behaviour but rather to achieve political goals, namely, presenting to the public an image of translation as an objective activity and reinforcing a translation association or agency's professional status (Lambert, 2018, p. 278). Lambert urged researchers to explore the role that codes of ethics play in 'enhancing an organization's standing' (Lambert, 2018, p. 279) and suggested that codes could be revised to depict translation as an 'active, multi-faceted activity' – one that requires knowledgeable expertise and judgement and inevitably involves a degree of textual manipulation based on the translator's interpretation of the source text message (Lambert, 2018, p. 285).

While most of the existing research examines codes of ethics in profession-oriented networks, some work focuses on codes of ethics as they apply to practice-oriented networks. Drugan (2011) concentrated on networks comprising largely non-professional translators participating in online, collaborative translation projects. To do so, she compared the codes of practice of twenty-four professional translator associations with similar types of code (e.g., charters, guiding principles, by-laws, policies and community guidelines) in twenty non-professional translator groups. Drugan's comparison revealed that the two sets of codes (professional associations and non-professional practice-oriented networks) had different priorities. Shared values and goals were more highly prioritized, and penalties for not respecting the code were more explicit in the codes of the practice-oriented networks. Confidentiality and competence, the most important features of professional codes, were given less (or no) visibility in the non-professional codes (Drugan, 2011, pp. 117–18).

## 10.5  Future Directions

A considerable body of research examines various topics related to translation networks and professional translator associations. Nonetheless, some areas remain under-explored. These include the function, composition and goals of education- and research-oriented translation networks: to date, little research has compared the role these networks play in the dissemination and production of research, in the development of translation curriculums, and so on. Moreover, although codes of ethics have been discussed by several scholars, most of the emphasis has been on codes within profession-oriented networks, and not on codes of practice or by-laws of practice-, research- and education-oriented translation networks. It would be helpful to compare the codes across the different types of network, as this would help identify ways to revise existing professional codes of ethics to address the shortcomings identified by McDonough Dolmaya (2011), Lambert (2018) and others.

Second, researchers have studied many of the activities of translation networks, as discussed already, but some have been largely overlooked so far. Prizes, which are often awarded by translation networks, do not appear to have been of great interest to translation studies researchers, particularly when the prizes are related to activities other than literary translation. Questions that could be of interest include: what non-literary translation-related activities are considered prize-worthy? What are the profiles of prize winners? How do prizes contribute to the discussion around translator status (cf. Ruokonen, 2013; Lambert, 2018; Dam and Zethsen, 2009)?

Finally, given recent publications addressing the ecological footprint generated by translation technologies (e.g., Cronin, 2017), researchers could turn their attention to computer mediation in translation networks and examine the environmental impact of online and offline participation in networks and networking events, such as conferences, workshops and certification exams.

# References

Baker, M. (2011). *In Other Words: A Coursebook on Translation*. London: Routledge.

Baker, M. (2013). Translation as an alternative space for political action. *Social Movement Studies*, **12**(1), 23–47. https://doi.org/10.1080/14742837 .2012.685624.

Boéri, J. (2008). A narrative account of the Babels vs. Naumann controversy: Competing perspectives on activism in conference Interpreting. *The Translator*, **14**(1), 21–50. https://doi.org/10.1080/13556509 .2008.10799248.

Bowker, L. (2004). What does it take to work in the translation profession in Canada in the 21st century? Exploring a database of job advertisements. *Meta: Journal des Traducteurs*, **49**(4), 960. https://doi.org/10 .7202/009804ar.

Buzelin, H. (2006). Independent publisher in the networks of translation. *TTR: Traduction, Terminologie, Rédaction*, **19**(1), 135–73. https://doi.org/10 .7202/016663ar.

Campbell, S. (2000). Choice network analysis in translation research. In M. Olohan, ed., *Intercultural Faultlines: Research Models in Translation Studies: V. 1: Textual and Cognitive Aspects*. London: Routledge, pp. 29–42.

Castro-Prieto, M., and Olvera Lobo, M. (2007). Panorama intelectual de la terminología a través del análisis de redes sociales. *Meta: Journal des Traducteurs*, **52**(4), 816. https://doi.org/10.7202/017698ar.

Chan, A. Lung Jan. (2010). Perceived benefits of translator certification to stakeholders in the translation profession: A survey of vendor managers. *Across Languages and Cultures*, **11**(1), 93–113.

Clifford, A. (2005). Psychometric validation and interpreter certification. *Interpreting*, **7**(1), 97–131.

Córdoba Serrano, M. (2010). Translation as a measure of literary domina- tion: The case of Quebec literature translated in Spain (1975–2004). *MonTi: Monografías de Traducción e Interpretación*, **2**, 249–81. https://doi .org/10.6035/MonTI.2010.2.12.

Cronin, M. (2017). *Eco-translation: Translation and Ecology in the Age of the Anthropocene*. London: Routledge.

Dam, H. V., and Zethsen, K. K. (2009). Who said low status? A study on factors affecting the perception of translator status. *Journal of Specialised Translation*, **12**, 2–36.

Drugan, J. (2011). Translation ethics Wikified: How far do professional codes of ethics and practice apply to non-professionally produced translation? *Linguistica Antverpiensia*, **10**, 111–30.

Drugan, J. (2017). Ethics and social responsibility in practice: Interpreters and translators engaging with and beyond the professions. *The Translator*, **23**(2), 126–42. https://doi.org/10.1080/13556509 .2017.1281204.

Folaron, D. (2010). Networking and volunteer translators. In Y. Gambier and L. van Doorslaer, eds., *Handbook of Translation Studies*. Amsterdam: John Benjamins, pp. 231–4. https://doi.org/10.1075/hts.1.net1.

Folaron, D., and Buzelin, H. (2007). Introduction: Connecting translation and network studies. *Meta: Journal des Traducteurs*, **52**(4), 605–42. https://doi.org/10.7202/017689ar.

Gambier, Y. (2007). Réseaux de traducteurs/interprètes bénévoles. *Meta: Journal des Traducteurs*, **52**(4), 658–72.

Gambier, Y., Schäffner, C., and Meylaerts, R. (2019). Doctoral training in translation studies: Challenges and opportunities. In D. B. Sawyer, F. Austermühl and V. Enríquez Raído, eds., *The Evolving Curriculum in Interpreter and Translator Education*. Amsterdam: John Benjamins, pp. 99–118.

Gouadec, D. (2007). *Translation as a Profession*. Amsterdam: John Benjamins.

Greenwood, R., Suddaby, R., and Hinings, C. (2002). Theorizing change: The role of professional associations in the transformation of institutionalized fields. *Academy of Management Journal*, **45**(1), 58–80.

Halverson, S. (2003). The cognitive basis of translation universals. *Target*, **15**(2), 197–241. https://doi.org/10.1075/target.15.2.02hal.

Hlavac, J. (2013). A cross-national overview of translator and interpreter certification procedures. *Translation and Interpreting*, **5**(1), 32–65.

Kafi, M., Khoshsaligheh, M., and Hashemi, M. (2018). Translation profession in Iran: Current challenges and future prospects. *The Translator*, **24**(1), 89–103. https://doi.org/10.1080/13556509.2017.1297693.

Koby, G., and Melby, A. (2013). Certification and job task analysis (JTA): Establishing validity of translator certification examinations. *Translation and Interpreting*, **5**(1), 174–210.

Kushner, S. (2013). The freelance translation machine: Algorithmic culture and the invisible industry. *New Media and Society*, **15**(8), 1241–58. https://doi.org/10.1177/1461444812469597.

Lambert, J. (2018). How ethical are codes of ethics? Using illusions of neutrality to sell translations. *Journal of Specialised Translation*, **30**, 269–90.

McDonough, J. (2007). How do language professionals organize themselves? An overview of translation networks. *Meta*, **52**(4), 793–815.

McDonough Dolmaya, J. (2011). Moral ambiguity: Some shortcomings of professional codes of ethics for translators. *Journal of Specialised Translation*, **15**, 28–49.

Plassard, F. (2007). La traduction face aux nouvelles pratiques en réseaux. *Meta: Journal des Traducteurs*, **52**(4), 643–57. https://doi.org/10.7202/017690ar.

Pym, A. (2006). Globalization and the politics of translation studies. *Meta: Journal des Traducteurs*, **51**(4), 744–57. https://doi.org/10.7202/014339ar.

Pym, A. (2014). Translator associations: From gatekeepers to communities. *Target*, **26**(3), 466–91.

Pym, A., Grin, F., Sfeddo, C., and Chan, A. (2012). *The Status of the Translation Profession in the European Union: Final Report*. Luxembourg: Publications Office of the European Parliament. https://termcoord.eu/wp-content/uploads/2013/08/The_status_of_the_translation_profession_in_the_European_Union.pdf.

Pym, A., Orrego-Carmona, D. and Torres-Simón, E. (2016). Status and Technology in the Professionalisation of Translators. Market Disorder and the Return of Hierarchy. Journal of Specialised Translation, no. 25: 33–53.

Risku, H., and Dickinson, A. (2009). Translators as networkers: The role of virtual communities. *HERMES – Journal of Language and Communication in Business*, **42**, 49–70. https://doi.org/10.7146/hjlcb.v22i42.96846.

Ruokonen, M. (2013). Studying translator status: Three points of view. In M. Eronen and M. Roda-Risberg, eds., *Point of View as Challenge: Vakki Symposium XXXIII*. Vaasa: VAKKI Publications 2, pp. 327–38.

Thelen, M. (2005). Going European: A plea for building a network of simulated translation bureaus. In M. Forstner and H. Lee-Jahnke, eds., *CIUTI-Forum Paris 2005: Regards sur les aspects culturels de la communication*. Frankfurt am Main: Peter Lang, pp. 219–36.

Thomson-Wohlgemuth, G. (2004). A Socialist approach to translation: A way forward? *Meta: Journal des Traducteurs*, **49**(3), 498–510. https://doi.org/10.7202/009375ar.

Torres-Simón, E., and Pym, A. (2019). European masters in translation: A comparative study. In D. B. Sawyer, F. Austermühl and V. E. Raído, eds., *The Evolving Curriculum in Interpreter and Translator Education*. Amsterdam: John Benjamins, pp. 75–98.

Wasserman, S., and Faust, K. (1994). *Social Network Analysis: Methods and Applications*. Cambridge: Cambridge University Press.

Wolf, M. (2010). Translation 'going social'? Challenges to the (Ivory) Tower of Babel. *MonTi: Monografías de Traducción e Interpretación*, **2**, 29–46. https://doi.org/10.6035/MonTI.2010.2.2.

Yu, C. (2019). Negotiating identity roles during the process of online collaborative translation: An ethnographic approach. *Translation Studies*, **12**(2), 231–52.

# Part III

# Translation in Company

# 11

# Translation and Comparative Literature

Xiaofan Amy Li

## 11.1 Introduction

Translation has played a vital role in comparative literature since its beginnings as a discipline. Posnett (1886, p. 48) cites Shelley's view that translating poetry is as futile as 'cast[ing] a violet into a crucible [to] discover the formal principle of its colour and odour'. More than a century later, Apter (2006, p. xi) declares that 'global translation is another name for comparative literature'. These views illustrate critical divergences and changing attitudes over time. Indeed, debates about translation have shaped both comparative literature and theories of literary translation. In this chapter, I offer historical reflections and examine current scholarship to cast light on the relation between translation and comparative literature and the polemics this relation has sparked. I argue for a diversified view of translation and comparative literature that acknowledges not one but many conceptualizations of their interrelations.

## 11.2 Histories

Comparatists in Europe and North America broadly agree on how the relation between comparative literature and translation has evolved from neglect and antagonism to recognition and collaboration. In the early days of comparative literature, translations were 'suppressed' (Bermann, 2009, p. 437), seen through but not looked at in their own right, since comparatists preferred to study texts in the original languages. This disregard for translation became increasingly untenable as comparative literature expanded beyond the familiar European languages and literatures to include 'Chinese, Japanese, Sanskrit, Arabic', as highlighted in Greene's 1975 (in Bernheimer, 1995, p. 30) State of the Discipline Report for the American Comparative Literature Association. Consequently, comparatists' reliance on translations had to be acknowledged, albeit reluctantly. Nevertheless, with the translational turn in comparative literature in the 1990s championed by Bassnett (1993) and world literature posited as the new comparative literature in the global age, translation was established as integral to comparative literature. For translation is crucial to transnational literary circulation, as summarized by Damrosch's (2003, p. 281) dictum: 'World Literature is writing that gains in translation.' This is the well-known story of translation and comparative literature.

An alternative story emphasizes the role of the Oriental Renaissance in the birth of comparative literature in Europe, and considers translation and comparative literature beyond Europe, for example in East Asia. These perspectives do not so much reject the accepted narrative as revise and expand it by arguing for a more prominent role of translation and recognizing multiple histories of translation's relation to comparative literature. In what follows, I pivot my discussion on the nineteenth-century origins of comparative literature, before highlighting two subsequent turning points: the post-war emergence of translation studies as an independent discipline; and the rise of world literature since 2000.

## 11.3  Origins in Europe

The multiple origins of comparative literature refract its relation to translation in different contexts. Competing narratives have posited as its inception Noël and de la Place's (1816) first use of the term in 1816; Goethe's 1827 discussions of *Weltliteratur*; 1877 in Central Europe (Saussy, 2006, p. 6); and 1933 in Istanbul (Apter, 2006, p. 41). Nevertheless, regardless of precisely when and where comparative literature emerged, translation played a significant role. Beside the nineteenth-century rise of European nation-states, which provided the rationale for comparing literatures to explore national characteristics, the translation of Asian texts and its accompanying philological practices defined the emergence of comparative literature in Europe.

European translations of Chinese, Indian and Persian texts in the eighteenth and nineteenth centuries fostered a new comparative consciousness among nineteenth-century scholars, who increasingly felt compelled to make cross-cultural comparisons. These grew increasingly systematic and intense within burgeoning disciplines such as comparative literature, oriental studies, philology and religious studies. Quinet's (1841, p. 117) *De la renaissance orientale* articulates this phenomenal influx of Asian literature and thought and the promise they held out to European scholars: not only new knowledge but also 'une forme nouvelle de l'humanité' ('a new form of humanity'). Highlighting scholarly excitement about discovering Asia's rich traditions, Quinet (1841, pp. 116–17, 128) cites translations of Persian and Sanskrit texts by orientalists Anquetil-Duperron and William Jones, envisages new possibilities of comparing 'Orpheus to Vyasa' or 'Sophocles to Kalidasa' and discerns 'Asiatic' influence on Goethe's writings.

Quinet's remarks reflect the impact of a host of translations of Asian literature made by missionaries, philologists, orientalists and colonial administrators. Some translations became highly influential. Abel-Rémusat's *Iu-kiao-li: ou Les deux cousines (Iu-kiao-li: or the two cousins*, 1826), translated from the seventeenth-century Chinese novel *Yujiaoli*, is especially important for the nineteenth-century French reception of Chinese literature and comparative literary awareness. Significantly, Abel-Rémusat (1826) adds a description proposing literary comparison to his translator's preface: 'où se trouve un parallèle des romans de la Chine et de ceux de l'Europe' ('presenting a parallel between Chinese and European novels'). He emphasizes that European readers should learn about China by reading 'les véritables romans chinois' ('real Chinese novels') (Abel-Rémusat, 1826, p. 42) such as his own in direct translation instead of eighteenth-century counterfeit Chinese texts composed by 'prétendus Chinois' ('fake Chinese writers') (Abel-Rémusat, 1826, p. 40) who were in fact Frenchmen. Translating Asian texts, therefore, went hand-in-hand with the rise of oriental studies, cross-cultural comparatism and awareness of engaging with the Other on a deeper level. This was also manifest in other translational projects around this time: for example Wilkins's 1785 translation of the *Bhagavad-Gita*, 'estimated to have been re-translated into English about 300 times since then' (Trivedi, 2018, p. 18); Jones's 1789 translation of Kalidasa's classical Sanskrit play *Shakuntala,* which enthralled European readers as it was quickly translated from Jones's English translation into German (1791), French (1803) and Italian (1815) and received with particular fervour by German Romantics including Schlegel, Schiller, Novalis, Herder and Goethe (Culp, 2018); and Wilson's 1813 translation of Kalidasa's poem *Meghadūta*, which made its way to Goethe's shelf (Wilhelm, 1961, p. 397) and formed part of Wilson's translations of Sanskrit literature lauded by Posnett (1886, p. 314) as examples of 'World-Literature'.

Quinet's (1841) declaration of the Oriental Renaissance encapsulated what had been ongoing for decades and heralded what was forthcoming, for translations and studies of Asian texts intensified after his publication. In particular, FitzGerald's (1859) *Rubáiyát of Omar Khayyám* became a 'cult' English-language poem (Yohannan, 1971) and almost synonymous with Persian poetry in Victorian Britain. Julien's (1842) first translation of the *Daodejing* marked the beginnings of French sinological explorations of

Daoism and extensive attempts to categorize – albeit unsatisfactorily – classical Chinese texts into European genres of philosophy, religion or *belles lettres*, grappling with the familiar problem in comparative literature of not finding equivalent genres across cultures. Finally, Gautier's (1867) French translations of classical Chinese poetry in *Le livre de jade* (*The Book of Jade*) were highly regarded by Parnassian and symbolist poets and inspired German figures including Böhm, Bethge and Mahler (Yu, 2007). These translations are as much part of the Oriental Renaissance as they are the crucial link between translation and early comparative literature. It is no accident that Goethe (and Eckermann, 1875, pp. 210–11) mentions his appreciation of Persian poetry and a 'Chinese novel' (according to O'Bell (2018), Thoms's English translation *Chinese Courtship* of 1842) – both read in translation – in his conversation with Eckermann before proclaiming the advent of world literature. The Oriental Renaissance is not of exclusive interest to historians of European orientalism and indologists but should be acknowledged as a defining factor in translation's relation to comparative literature at the latter's very inception.

The second way in which translation enabled the rise of comparative literature is through the central role translation played in philology. Philology combined translation and textual exegeses (Turner, 2015) and provided the foundations of comparative literature (Damrosch, 2020, p. 13). Notably, nineteenth-century philology was stimulated by the translation of Asian texts. Besides Jones's (1786) declaration of Sanskrit's commonality with Greek and Latin, foundational to Indo-European linguistics, Abel-Rémusat's correspondence (1821–31) with Humboldt discussing the nature of the Chinese language is a critical juncture in comparative philology. In relation to translation and the theorization of the comparative method, two things stand out in this correspondence: both writers refer to translations of classical Chinese expressions and phrases to argue about the linguistic characteristics of Chinese; and both attempt to compare Chinese with Indo-European inflectional languages, especially Greek, Latin and Sanskrit. Specifically, Abel-Rémusat (in Humboldt, 1827, p. 115) attempts to produce 'une traduction toute littérale' ('a completely literal translation') that expresses the original Chinese 'enchaînement des propositions' ('sequence of propositions') that characterizes classical Chinese literary style as 'soutenu, périodique et symétrique' ('formal, serial and symmetrical'). For Humboldt (cited in Rousseau and Thouard, 1999, pp. 16, 53), the absence of inflection in Chinese means that it juxtaposes ideas directly, so readers must rely on the context and 'la pensée pure' ('pure thought') to understand a Chinese text. Chinese writing is thus 'philosophical' (Humboldt, 1827, p. 83). On Humboldt's comparative scale of languages, where inflected languages represent a higher level of abstraction and are therefore superior to non-inflected languages (Rousseau and Thouard, 1999, p. 14), Chinese is inferior but exceptional because its lack of grammatical categories reinforces its ideational and intellectual power. Abel-Rémusat disagrees, arguing that Chinese is not that different from other languages, and affirms the hypothesis that 'toutes les langues peuvent être considérées comme étant au même niveau' ('all languages can be considered to be on a par') (Rousseau and Thouard, 1999, p. 120). These comparative philological discussions include the lines of thought that would inform later discussions in comparative literature: the difficulty of translating literary style; the problematic use of comparison to assert cultural superiority or inferiority; and the perceived ideographic nature of Chinese, which inspired twentieth-century poets from Pound and Michaux to Haroldo de Campos. Thinking through the translation of classical Chinese into European languages made Abel-Rémusat and Humboldt recognize the challenge of radical difference which Chinese presented. Their attempts to address this challenge accelerated comparative philological developments, which provided the primary conditions for comparative literature.

In sum, translations and philological explorations of Asian texts were as important to the birth of comparative literature in nineteenth-century Europe as the rise of modern European nation-states and European continentalism. The Oriental Renaissance was a game-changer that broadened the scope of available texts and how literature was read. Rather than translation being suppressed in the early days of comparative literature, it was comparative literary awareness that went unacknowledged in nineteenth-century translation because writers, orientalists and philologists engaging with translation did not see themselves as doing comparative literature, even though they were doing the work that comparatists do.

## 11.4   Origin Stories in East Asia

Turning to East Asia, mass translations of Western texts, starting from the late nineteenth century, preceded the establishment of comparative literature as a discipline but enabled Japanese and Chinese scholars to swiftly learn about Western literature and thought, especially nineteenth-century novels, and Darwinian and Marxist theories. As translation was recognized as being essential to modernity, it permeated modern Japanese and Chinese literatures and scholarship. Indeed, modern Japan and China are cultures of translation (Levy, 2008; Hill, 2012). The amount of late nineteenth- to early twentieth-century East Asian translations of European texts far exceeded that of contemporaneous European translations of Asian texts. Modern Japanese and Chinese writers and translators also learnt English and European languages more eagerly than European and American writers learnt Japanese and Chinese, which remains true today. They felt compelled to do this after realizing that Europe and America were more powerful and that translating Western texts was a direct means to acquire Western knowledge and employ it to modernize Japan and

China. This meant that in Japan and China, comparative literature focused on comparisons between Japan or China and the West rather than North–South or inter-Asian comparisons. The reliance on translations was also second nature instead of something that elicited scholarly anxiety.

Comparative literature developed earlier in Japan than in China or Korea. Around 1889, Tsubouchi Shōyō started teaching Posnett's (1886) *Comparative Literature* at Waseda University, marking the beginning of the term *hikaku bungaku* ('comparison literature') in Japanese scholarly discussions (Aldridge and Kamei, 1972, p. 149). As Yoshikawa (2017) and Cho (2017) observe, besides Western literature, much Western scholarship on comparative literature was translated into Japanese and shaped the direction of Japanese comparatists' research considerably. From the 1930s to the post-war era, Japanese translations of Tieghem's 1931 *La Littérature comparée* (in 1943) and Moulton's 1911 *World Literature and Its Place in General Culture* (in 1934) appeared; founding members of the Japanese Comparative Literature Association (established in 1948) like Nakajima Kenzō and Kobayashi Tadashi advocated the study of historical influences between literatures (Nakajima, 1958). The French school's emphasis on 'rapports des faits' ('factual relations') was widely accepted by Japanese comparatists and was termed *eikyō kenkyū* ('influence research'). The study of literary translation was firmly established within *eikyō kenkyū*, since translation is a typical example of influence. In 1967, however, the Japanese translation of Wellek and Warren's (1942) *Theory of Literature* introduced the American school of comparative literature with its critical theory–based and cultural studies–oriented approaches, which led Japanese comparatists to see alternatives to *eikyō kenkyū*. Another fact supporting the centrality of translation to Japanese comparative literature is that many Japanese comparatists are also literary translators and scholars of translation. For instance, Nakajima translated Baudelaire, Valéry and Gide; Shimada Kinji, the first professor of comparative literature at Tokyo University, translated Robert Louis Stevenson, Byron and Poe, and wrote a monograph entitled *Hon'yaku bungaku* (*Translated Literature*) (Shimada, 1951). Japanese is one of the most translated-into languages when it comes to literature, and the evolution of Japanese comparative literature is inseparable from translation.

The translation of Western literatures and scholarship also conditioned the emergence of Chinese comparative literature, with some notable differences from the Japanese case. Firstly, Chinese translators and comparatists were as much concerned about producing mass translations of Chinese texts into Western languages, especially English, for an international readership as they were about producing large-scale Chinese translations of Western texts; however, there seemed to be no strong drive to translate Japanese literature for the Western Other in Japanese comparative literature. Late nineteenth-century Chinese intellectuals' encounter with the concept of a world literature that transcended national and linguistic borders gave rise to the concern that Chinese literature should be part of this canon. As Tsu (2010, p. 294) discusses, the diplomat Chen Jitong strongly advocated (see Shi Hu, 1998, p. 617) the 'participation of [Chinese literature] in World Literature' ('要參加世界的文學'), to be realized through 'translation en masse. Not only should we translate foreign masterpieces into Chinese, our important literary works must also all be translated into foreign languages' ('非提倡大規模的翻譯不可, 不但他們的名作要多譯進來, 我們的重要作品, 也須全譯出去'). Similarly, Chen's near contemporary Liang Qichao (1902/1989, p. 70) enthusiastically wrote that he was glad to be born in an era when 'various kinds of literature across the world [could] be imported' into China ('將世界各派的文學盡量輸入'). Liang also compared classical Chinese poetics with European Romanticism and translated a Japanese novel, as he considered the translation of Japanese and Western literatures into Chinese crucial to China's political and cultural transformation. Although neither Chen nor Liang saw themselves as comparatists, they engaged intensively with cross-cultural comparisons and identified translation as the essential means of cultural importation and exportation, foreshadowing contemporary views of world literature as literature that circulates outside its place of origin. Secondly, as in the Japanese case, the development of Chinese comparative literature in the formal sense was mediated by translation, in terms of both translated texts and translators-as-comparatists. The first use of the term 'comparative literature' dates to 1904 when the scholar Huang Ren (1904/2015) referred to Posnett (1886). By the 1920s to 1930s, after decades of Chinese translations of Western literature, courses on comparative literature were taught at the National Tsinghua University by Wu Mi and I. A. Richards; and in 1936 the poet Dai Wangshu translated Tieghem's 1931 *La Littérature comparée*. Notably, pioneering Chinese comparatists all studied in Western universities and actively translated literature: Wu studied at Harvard; Dai at Lyon; Ji Xianlin studied at Göttingen; Qian Zhongshu studied at Oxford and Paris. These comparatists are figures of cultural translation as their personal and academic experience of linguistic and cultural difference translated into their comparative work. Finally, although comparative literature and translational activities in China were stunted between the 1940s and the 1970s owing to sociopolitical turbulence, translations of foreign literatures restarted in 1979 after the Cultural Revolution. Huang Long's 1988 *Translatology* (翻譯學) was the first key text on translation studies in China. Against this new translational boom and academic interest in translation studies proper, comparative literature was firmly reestablished as an academic discipline in China, with the foundation of the Chinese Comparative Literature Association in 1985.

In both Europe and East Asia, translation enabled the development of comparative literature, and the East–West relation was pivotal. Major differences are, firstly, that in Europe there was less recognition of translation's connection to comparative literature by translators and comparatists; in Japan and China, this connection was emphatically recognized and translation and comparative literature were practised conjointly. Secondly, the temporality of translation's relation to comparative literature differed widely. Nineteenth-century European translators and scholars focused on Asian antiquities and were barely interested in the living present of Asian cultures and their emerging modern literatures. This produced a hybrid vertical temporality combining Asian antiquities with European modernity in translation and literary criticism. In contrast, late nineteenth- to early twentieth-century East Asian translators were less interested in Graeco-Roman classics but focused on modern Western texts since the Enlightenment because these writings were seen to contain the knowledge and science that produced European modernity. Thirdly, the preference for reading literature in the original language and the depreciation of translation existed in comparative literature as practised in Europe and North America well into the twentieth century, whereas in Japanese and Chinese comparative literature, there was no aversion to reading Japanese and Chinese translations. One reason may be that East Asian scholars already acknowledged the translatedness of their modern literature and scholarship. Another possible reason is that they felt no anxiety about perpetuating linguistic hegemony by reading Chinese or Japanese translations, whereas Anglo-American comparatists were concerned about reinforcing monolingualism by reading foreign literatures all in English translation.

In the evolution of translation's relation to comparative literature, the single most important event since the emergence of comparative literature was the establishment of translation studies as a discipline after the publication of Holmes's 1972/1988 foundational paper. Hereafter, research on translation was distinguished from and no longer subordinate to literary studies and linguistics. The asserted independence of translation studies prompted comparatists to rethink translation and question assumptions about the derivative nature and insignificance of literary translations compared to original texts. Simultaneously, from the 1960s to the 1980s, comparative literature in North America became increasingly engulfed by critical theory and interdisciplinary analyses of non-literary artefacts such as film and media, leading some comparatists to bemoan the absence of literature proper and deepening monolingualism in the discipline (Remak, 2002). Given these parallel developments of translation studies and comparative literature in the post-war era, the translational turn in comparative literature hailed by Bassnett (1993) was a logical conclusion. Translation studies brought back attention to the close reading of literary texts, a welcome return after the heyday of critical theory. Since this new departure point, translation and comparative literature have grown increasingly intertwined. After 2000, world literature has become an updated version of comparative literature, so discussions about translation and comparative literature are often formulated as 'translation and world literature', which is the title of Bassnett's (2018) edited volume.

## 11.5  Theories and Debates

Comparatists have scrutinized both key terms of their discipline's name: 'comparative' and 'literature'. Exploring translation in relation to these two components will provide insight into the specific contribution that comparative literature has made to the theorization of translation. Firstly, since translation engages with linguistic and cultural alterity, comparatists have always thought of translation as a cross-cultural comparative practice and a negotiation of difference. Subsequently, positing comparability/translatability versus incomparability/untranslatability as opposite ends of a spectrum expresses two fundamentally different attitudes: different cultures and languages are mutually intelligible to some extent and everything is comparable, so everything is translatable; or, some things are incommensurable and therefore untranslatable. As untranslatability has been debated with fervour since Cassin's (2004) *Dictionnaire des intraduisibles*, I examine untranslatability as incomparability here.

Comparative literature celebrates difference. Unsurprisingly, therefore, comparatists and world literature scholars are interested in untranslatability, which embodies irreducible alterity. Untranslatability is an extension of comparatists' preference for foreignization over domestication in translation, from Venuti (2008) to Bellos (2011) and Apter (2013). Foreignization reflects comparative literature's emphasis on recognizing the Other in its own right. When stretched to an extreme, foreignization becomes the championing of untranslatability and incomparability. The argument for untranslatability generally takes one of three forms. The first is a cliché represented by Frost's aphorism that 'poetry is what is lost in translation', leading to claims (e.g., Perloff's (2004)) about the untranslatability of poetry. I call this the aesthetic argument. It has been extensively examined and criticized, for instance by Robinson (2010, p. 82), who observes that the untranslatable aspects of poetry – for example individual style, sound, specific temporality – are also found in other genres that are considered translatable. The second approach, which I call the semantic argument, is more productive in generating world literature debates. This refers to Cassin's (2004, p. xvii) paradoxical definition of untranslatables not as expressions that 'ne soient pas traduit[e]s et ne puissent pas l'être' ('are not and cannot be translated') but as 'ce qu'on ne cesse pas de (ne pas) traduire' ('what one does not cease to (not) translate'). Untranslatables like *logos* or *Dasein* infinitely fail to be translated because they are infinitely translatable, or infinitely to-be-translated. The third is the ethical argument, originating from post-colonial literary criticism and Levinasian philosophy of radical alterity, and represented by Spivak, Apter and

Lezra. Spivak (1993/2009, p. 201) warns about the 'risks' of translation doing imperial and gendered 'violence' to the Other, reiterating the enduring objection to translation that sees it as reappropriation. Apter and Lezra continue this line of thought by upholding untranslatables as signs of linguistic and philosophical diversity, the 'non-reproducible' (Lezra, 2017, p. 7) in an age of digital reproduction. Apter (2013, p. 3) sees untranslatability as 'speed bumps' to the smoothing of difficult and specific foreign expressions and literatures into reader-friendly English ('Globish') translations that facilitate capitalist circulation. Translatability is thus exchangeability and universal comparability, the commerce of literature that destroys linguistic, aesthetic and ontological singularity. So untranslatables are 'proof of the manner in which some concepts or structures mean, in comparative literature, a limit of "commensurability"' (Terian, 2013, p. 54).

These arguments for untranslatability are not really about the feasibility of translation on a linguistic level but about fully respecting the Other's singularity and difference. Nevertheless, world literature criticism on untranslatability is predominantly about untranslatability *into English* rather than untranslatability into local languages like Korean, Japanese or Hindi. Will the aesthetics and ethics of untranslatability as incomparability be the same when the local translates the global, the weak translates the powerful? Following Mundt's (2018) argument about Eurocentrism in untranslatability discourses, I propose that the championing of untranslatability is primarily a critical gesture against global Americanization. This anxiety about the power asymmetry between (American) English as the international language and local languages is treated extensively in Minae Mizumura's (1995) novel 私小説 *From Left to Right* (*Shishōsetsu* (transliteration of the Japanese part of the title)), an 'I-novel', which is a confessional genre in modern Japanese literature. I cite the original Japanese script to show Mizumura's deliberate typographical and linguistic contrast between Japanese and English. *Shishōsetsu* is a self-reflexive literary exposition of untranslatability in relation to anglophone-centrism. *Shishōsetsu* not only has a bilingual format where English expressions are scattered throughout the Japanese text but is also printed according to Western conventions horizontally 'from left to right', departing from the established Japanese typography where the text runs vertically from right to left. The strangeness of reading *Shishōsetsu* as a Japanese reader is observed by the artist Nakazawa (2015, p. 133), who picked up the novel when staying in New York 'to escape from unfamiliar English communication for a while and read something in Japanese' ('英語でのやりとりから逃れ、久びさに日本語で読本でもしよう'), only to find it affirming the imported (from Western literatures) nature of modern Japanese writing. Nevertheless, the translatedness of *Shishōsetsu* paradoxically constitutes its untranslatability into English. An English translation would render invisible the jarringness of *Shishōsetsu*'s deliberate typographical change.

Translating the text's contrasts between the material form of Japanese *kanji* and their English romanizations is also a challenge, as when 'Minae と Nanae turn into 美苗 and 奈苗' (Mizumura, 1995, p. 40; 'Inside, ... was a world where ... our names were written not "Nanae" and "Minae" but the familiar 奈苗 and 美苗' (translation by Carpenter (2015), extract at www.thewhitereview.org/fiction/an-i-novel-from-left-to-right/). As Mizumura (2003, p. 5) states, although *Shishōsetsu* can be translated into other languages, '[t]he only language into which it would be impossible to translate [*Shishōsetsu*] would be English. If we leave the English sentences as they are, how are we to replicate the bilingual form in the translation?' *Shishōsetsu*'s untranslatability into English is later theoretically articulated in Mizumura's (2015) argument for the uniqueness of Japanese and its irreducibility to English. Writing in Japanese is therefore active resistance to the anglophone hegemony – read Americanization – that is impoverishing literary diversity today. By positing untranslatability into English as the rejection of commensuration to American culture, *Shishōsetsu* represents the refusal (or failure?) to Americanize and exemplifies world literature in *non-translation*.

Ironically, in 2021, Carpenter did publish an English translation, *An I-Novel*, so *Shishōsetsu* is not untranslatable after all. But this facilitates my reading of *Shishōsetsu* as a test-case that reveals both the merits and the limits of understanding untranslatability as incomparability. It is one of the early texts proposing untranslatability as resistance to anglophone-centrism, before comparative literature scholars such as Apter (2013), Mufti (2016) and Samoyault (2020) explicitly made the connection. Tellingly, Mizumura's views did not gain attention outside Japan and Japanologist circles until her works (especially *Fall of Language*) were translated into English. The time lag between the novel's original publication date, 1995, and its 2021 publication in translation confirms Mizumura's view that writing in Japanese is a self-limiting decision. Conversely, we can read *Shishōsetsu* as a counter-example to untranslatability that shows us classic pitfalls in comparative critical thinking. Firstly, linguistically and philosophically, the concept of untranslatability does not hold water and has been debunked on multiple occasions (e.g., Domínguez, Saussy and Villanueva, 2015, p. 83; Malmkjær, 2018). Simply put, if something can be explained by language then it can also be translated. That *Shishōsetsu* has finally been translated is completely unsurprising. And Mizumura's question of 'translating' into English her original English expressions is not a new or unsolvable problem for translators. Bellos (2011, p. 205) discusses it in the case of re-translating into French portions of *War and Peace* that are originally in French; Saussy (2017, pp. 15–16) mentions the same problem in translating French patisserie names in *Ulysses* back into French. One could object that this is beside the point because untranslatability discourses in comparative literature have never been about the feasibility of translation or the philosophy of language; they are about incomparability.

But the incomparability thesis has also been thoroughly debunked since Detienne's (2000) *Comparer l'incomparable* and more recently in Gagné, Goldhill and Lloyd (2018): the question 'How do you know if something is incomparable unless you have already compared it to something else?' logically entails 'How do you know if something is untranslatable unless you have already applied translation to it?'. Finally, what is missing in *Shishōsetsu* is the question of the untranslatability of English *into Japanese*. Probably this is not even a question for Mizumura (2018/19, p. 7), since she explicitly recognizes 'the possibility of translation as the very condition of modern Japanese literature' – that is, translation from Western languages and genres into Japanese. The strange absence of considering what untranslatability looks like when it involves a non-European target language suggests that assertions of the untranslatable Other are another version of Eurocentrism that condemns the Other to remain local and untranslatable into English, whereas English (along with other major European languages) is universal and translatable into non-European languages. This parallels the fact that Western theories are typically applied to study non-Western literatures (Dutton, 2012), whereas non-Western theories are almost never applied to Western literatures. Until the untranslatability of English or French into languages like Japanese or Tamil is properly examined, ethical arguments for untranslatability into English risk being self-defeating Othering acts.

As for translation and the 'literature' part of comparative literature, the first issue concerns translation's relation to literary monolingualism and multilingualism. For critics and writers anxious about anglophone-centric world literature, translation typically means monolingualism because literatures across the world are increasingly read not in the original language but in English translation, since English is the primary international language. Moreover, even writers using other languages are increasingly writing in a dulled translationese, as Snyder (2017) warns. As early as 1899, Brandes (1899, p. 25) observed that writers of minor languages are 'positioned most disadvantageously' in the 'universal struggle for world renown'. Access to the cultural capital of a dominant language by either writing in it or being translated into it is key to a writer's world recognition, as Casanova (1999) observes. Nevertheless, recent research suggests that we should remain sceptical of claims about translation's subservience to anglophone monolingualism. First, Casanova (2015, pp. 16–17) herself concedes that 'la traduction [peut] être conçue ... comme une forme de résistance ... à la domination linguistique' ('translation can be considered a form of resistance to linguistic dominance') because translation into English gives value to under-recognized minor literatures. Second, English is already a 'translingua franca' (Pennycook, 2010, p. 685) and a 'multilingua franca' (Jenkins, 2017, p. 601). Kirkpatrick and Wang (2020, p. 196) argue convincingly that 'English is [now] an Asian language'. English is neither the property of British and North American native speakers nor necessarily the vector of Anglo-American cultures and values. English is diversified in global multilingual contexts, which shows that language is not a bounded system and there is no real monolingual–multilingual binary. Third, when texts written in or translated into English cannot correspond straightforwardly to a nation-state or ethnic group, they do not gain a worldwide readership. Racial, national and cultural stereotypes determine literary marketability and international recognition more than language. For instance, who reads anglophone Hong Kongese, Singaporean and Macanese (i.e., of Macao) literatures, other than their local readers and a small bunch of sinophone studies scholars? Mizumura's (2015, p. 174) view that access to international readership requires mainly a sell-out of one's local language to English overlooks anglophone literatures that have fallen between the cracks of national and ethnic categories.

Rather than yoke translation with (non-existent) anglophone monolingualism, we may think of translation as multiplying a text's linguistic and cultural richness. If we see a literary work as a body of texts including all its translations instead of only the singular original work, then translation creates multilingual literature. This understanding underpins the Arts and Humanities Research Council funded Prismatic Jane Eyre Project initiated in 2016 at Oxford University, which examines *Jane Eyre*'s hundreds of refractions, via translation, into diverse languages and new contexts (https:// prismaticjaneeyre.org/). The metaphor of a prism for translation, expounded by Reynolds (2020), shifts the rhetoric about translation from loss to proliferation. The multiplying effects of translation push comparative literature's transnational agenda even further, for the multilingual translations and afterlives of a text are proof that literature is not owned by any single country, culture, ethnic group or language that may be posited as its origins. Given several similar projects on multilingual world literature with translation as a major research strand, for example Multilingual Locals and Significant Geographies (Mulosige) at SOAS, University of London (http://mulosige.soas.ac.uk/) and World Literatures: Cosmopolitan and Vernacular Dynamics at Stockholm University, Sweden (https://worldlit.se /about/), understanding of translation and comparative literature beyond anglophone-centrism and facile enunciations about translational loss can only deepen.

The second issue in translation's relation to literature involves the conceptualization of translation in comparative literature as an ongoing process rather than an end product; as a condition inherent in literary production and comparative criticism instead of an external and posthumous application to the original text. Paraphrasing Klein (2018, p. 232), is translation something done *to* the original text or is it rather done *through* the original text? Since Walkowitz's (2015) *Born Translated*, the answer is a resounding 'yes' to the latter. Comparatists have shifted from thinking of translation as a text that reproduces semantic invariants and replaces the original text – the view which Venuti (2019) calls 'instrumentalism' and rejects – to translation as co-emergent with the original text's production and reception. Walkowitz (2015, pp. 3–4) examines original 'born-translated' fiction that employs translational strategies in its creation, so that translation is 'medium and origin rather than … afterthought'; Emmerich (2017, pp. 2, 4) draws attention to translation as 'a form of translingual editing' that 'decide[s] … what the "source text" *is*'. The translated text is no longer the end of translational activity but a link in the participatory literary process called translation, involving writers, editors, translators, readers and critics.

For literary production, this means rethinking translation as creative (re) writing instead of secondary copying. Exophonic, multilingual and migrant literatures have proved particularly rich areas in which to explore creative translation, as shown by numerous discussions of Tawada Yōko, who writes bilingually in Japanese and German; Sino-French writers François Cheng and Shan Sa; or poet Hsia Yü (2007), who employed machine translation to produce her Chinese–English bilingual anthology *Pink Noise*. Besides *Shishōsetsu*, which is certainly a novel born-through-translation, contemporary French poet Michèle Métail's works offer another example of writing that embodies an inherent translational logic. Métail's (2000) *64 poèmes du ciel et de la terre* (*64 Poems of Heaven and Earth*) can be read as a translational recreation of the early Chinese divinatory text *Yijing*. Métail presents sixty-four poems, each of six short lines, intentionally written to correspond to the *Yijing*'s sixty-four hexagrams, each composed of six horizontal lines. Each poem is matched with a photograph of the same landscape at La Châgne, France, showing half sky, half land, and taken at different times of the day and in different seasons. The *Yijing*'s cosmological triad of heaven–earth–man is translated into Métail's photographed landscape, which is 'comme un ideogramme chinois' ('like a Chinese ideogram') (Métail, 2000, n.p.) that encapsulates the two poles of heaven and earth while implying human presence through the photographer (Métail herself). The landscape's transformations from dawn to dusk, spring to winter, accompanied by Métail's riddle-like poems where expressions about movement abound ('rotation', 'convergent', 'chancelant'), reflect the *Yijing*'s central tenet that everything is flux. Métail's transposition of a symbol-based divinatory manual into her French image-poem is a linguistic, intermedial and cross-genre translational move. Moreover, the reader is prompted to read *64 poèmes* translationally and comparatively with the *Yijing*'s hexagrams and their line statements, which shed light on the sequence of Métail's poems.

While understanding translation as part of the creative writing process is illuminating, two areas require further exploration. First: rather than elevating translation to the creative work that authors of original texts do – and therefore depreciating all translation that is perceived as insufficiently creative – we should rethink what creativity means. The Romantic understanding of creativity as the reflection of individual genius and absolute originality has been fundamentally challenged by our end-lessly reappropriative digital cultures, as Goldsmith's (2011) proposal of 'uncreative writing' indicates. Following Russell's (1935, p. 12) definition of productive work as 'altering the position of matter at or near the earth's surface relatively to other such matter', Graeber (2018) observes that most creative work is in fact the reorganization of existing elements. Moreover, Malmkjær (2020, p. 28) maintains that creative work always involves some copying, and that creativity can be 'trained', not simply stemming from born genius. Rather than originality *ex nihilo*, we may understand transla-tion and creative writing as work of the same nature: reorganizing and reformulating materials, and involving some imitation. Echoing Goldsmith's suggestion, Małecka and Marecki (2018) propose the notion of 'uncreative translation', where using machine translation in literary translation should not be discredited. Second: outside comparative litera-ture and inter-European language translation, many translators – espe-cially those working with premodern Asian texts – do not think of their work as creative rewriting and still cherish translational fidelity, although what fidelity means can vary. Among sinologists in early China studies and Sanskritists who regularly translate literary and philosophical texts as part of their groundwork, I have not met a single scholar who sees their translational work as creative. Or, some would question the notion of 'creativity' and how it applies to non-European literatures before assessing their translations. One eminent Sanskritist at Oxford even told me that fidelity is the primary goal in Indological translation. For them, clarifying what the source text means via translation is of utmost importance, so they value philologically precise translations and spot mistranslations keenly. Unfortunately, sinologists and Sanskritists seldom write self-reflexively about their translational processes. But comparatists and lit-erary critics studying translation will benefit from paying more attention to translational practices in premodern Asian studies.

Besides shedding light on literary production, the processual under-standing of translation has methodological implications for comparative criticism. Indeed, the embedded translatedness of born-translated litera-ture theoretically parallels the inherent comparativity of a single literary work discussed in recent scholarship. As Larsen (2015, p. 318) argues, 'comparativity' in comparative literature no longer needs to emerge from the comparison of two or more texts (or *comparanda*) from different nations but is already inherent in a single text that potentially engages with 'several textual and cultural contexts'. It is therefore possible to read a single text or author as world literature – Orhan Pamuk, Amitav Ghosh or Ouyang Jianghe – because their works are already transcultural. Translation is part of the comparativity of literature that travels through different contexts. Further to simply studying translation from compara-tive perspectives, Scott (2018) proposes a 'phenomenology of reading' (p. 132) where the translational act generates a new comparatism that is 'constant experimentation *with* the text', not about 'national authors and national languages, but … perceptual migrations and nomadism' (p. 110). Much contemporary scholarship thus sees translation as latent in comparative criticism and vice versa, so that translation is a critical perspective that creates new comparative possibilities. For instance, Bloomfield and Schilling (2016) take this translation-with-comparison approach by considering the writing constraints proposed by *L'Ouvroir de littérature potentielle* ('Workshop of Potential Literature', OuLiPo) and translation in each other's light. Why not read Queneau's (1947) *Exercices de style* as self-translations? Understood thus, translation is constrained writing, whereas Oulipian writing is profoundly translational.

## 11.6  Conclusion

Critical developments in translation studies and comparative literature in the twentieth and twenty-first centuries strongly suggest that translation will remain a substantial dimension of comparative literature. Several areas promise growth: firstly, crisis translation in relation to world literature studies focusing on global risks and crises, especially given the surging recent interest in literatures about precarity, public health, environmental degradation and racism; secondly, intralingual translation and intracultural comparisons, as monolithic conceptions of language and cultural entities are breaking down in a contemporary world where everything and everyone is more likely to be transcultural than monolingual or monocultural; and thirdly, research on oral literatures – especially in African contexts – and their translations, as Gikandi (2011), Haring (2012) and Bandia (2017) indicate. Intermedial translation in performative and visual art contexts is another possible area of closer interaction with comparative criticism on intermediality.

Although translation and comparative literature have not always had a collaborative relation, their intersection has sparked crucial disciplinary developments and new understandings of translation, comparison, and literature. I propose a global and comparative view of translation's relation to comparative literature, in light of increasing convergences owing to global transculturation and world literature.

## References

Abel-Rémusat, J.-P. (1826). *Iu-kiao-li, ou Les deux cousines [Yujiaoli, or Two Cousins]*. Paris: Moutardier.

Aldridge, O., and Kamei, S. (1972). Problems and vistas of comparative literature in Japan and the United States. *Mosaic*, **5**(4), 149–63.

Apter, E. (2006). *The Translation Zone*. Princeton, NJ: Princeton University Press.

Apter, E. (2013). *Against World Literature*. London: Verso.

Bandia, P., ed. (2017). *Orality and Translation*. London: Routledge.

Bassnett, S. (1993). *Comparative Literature*. Oxford: Blackwell.

Bassnett, S., ed. (2018). *Translation and World Literature*. New York: Routledge.

Bellos, D. (2011). *Is That a Fish in Your Ear?* London: Penguin.

Bermann, S. (2009). Working in the And Zone: Comparative Literature and Translation. *Comparative Literature*, **61**(4), 432–46.

Bernheimer, C., ed. (1995). *Comparative Literature in an Age of Multiculturalism*. Baltimore: Johns Hopkins University Press.

Bloomfield, C., and Schilling, D., eds. (2016). *Translating Constrained Literature*, Special Issue, *MLN*, **131**(4): 839–1001.

Brandes, G. (1899). World literature. In T. d'Haen, C. Domínguez and M. Rosendahl Thomsen, eds., *World Literature: A Reader*. London: Routledge, pp. 23–7.

Carpenter, J. W. (2015). See Mizumura, M. (1995).

Casanova, P. (1999). *La République mondiale des lettres [The World Republic of Letters]*. Paris: Seuil.

Casanova, P. (2015). *La Langue mondiale [The Global Language]*. Paris: Seuil.

Cassin, B., ed. (2004). *Vocabulaire européen des philosophies: Dictionnaire des intraduisibles [Dictionary of Untranslatables: A Philosophical Lexicon]*. Paris: Seuil.

Chen, J. (1998). 附錄: 曾先生答書 [Appendix: Letter to Mr Zeng]. In Hu Shi, 胡適文集 [*Collected Works of Hu Shi*], 12 vols. Beijing: Beijing daxue, vol. **4**, pp. 614–22.

Cho, K. (2017). A 'New Study' with 70 years' history. *Revista Brasileira de Literatura Comparada*, **30**, 91–7.

Culp, A. (2018). *Shakuntala*'s storytellers: Translation and performance in the age of world literature (1789–1912). *Theatre Journal*, **70**, 133–52.

Damrosch, D. (2003). *What Is World Literature?* Princeton, NJ: Princeton University Press.

Damrosch, D. (2020). *Comparing the Literatures*, Princeton, NJ: Princeton University Press.

Detienne, M. (2000). *Comparer l'incomparable [Comparing the Incomparable]*. Paris: Seuil.

Domínguez, C., Saussy, H., and Villanueva, D. (2015). *Introducing Comparative Literature*. London: Routledge.

Dutton, M. (2012). Lead us not into translation. *Transtext(e)s Transcultures* [online], 7. Available at https://journals.openedition.org/transtexts/458.

Emmerich, K. (2017). *Literary Translation and the Making of Originals*. London: Bloomsbury.

FitzGerald, E. (1859). *Rubáiyát of Omar Khayyám, the astronomer-poet of Persia*. London: Bernard Quaritch.

Gagné, R., Goldhill, S., and Lloyd, G., eds. (2018). *Regimes of Comparatism*. Leiden: Brill.

Gautier, J. (1867). *Le livre de jade [The Book of Jade]*. Paris: Alphonse Lemerre.

Gikandi, S. (2011). Contested grammars. In A. Behdad and D. Thomas, eds., *A Companion to Comparative Literature*. Oxford: Blackwell, pp. 254–72.

Goethe, J. W. von, and Eckermann, J.-P. (1875). *Conversations of Goethe with Eckermann and Soret*. Translated by John Oxenford. London: George Bell and Sons.

Goldsmith, K. (2011). *Uncreative Writing*. New York: Columbia University Press.

Graeber, D. (2018). Collège de France seminar 'The Revolt of the Caring Classes', 22 March 2018. www.college-de-france.fr/site/grandes-conferences/David-Graeber.htm.

Greene, T. (1975). A report on standards. In C. Bernheimer, ed. (1995). *Comparative Literature in an Age of Multiculturalism*. Baltimore: Johns Hopkins University Press, pp. 28–38.

Haring, L. (2012). Translating African oral literature in global contexts. *The Global South*, **5**(2), 7–20.

Hill, M. G. (2012). *Lin Shu, Inc.: Translation and the Making of Modern Chinese Culture*. New York: Oxford University Press.

Holmes, J. S. (1972/1988). The name and nature of translation studies. In J. S. Holmes (1988). *Translated! Papers on Literary Translation and Translation Studies*. Amsterdam: Rodopi, pp. 66–80.

Hsia, Y. (2007). *Pink Noise*=粉紅色噪. Taipei: Garden City.

Huang, L. (1988). 翻譯學 *[Translatology]*. Nanjing: Jiangsu jiaoyu chubanshe.

Huang, R. (1904/2015). 中國文學史 *[History of Chinese Literature]*. Suzhou: Suzhou University Press.

Humboldt, W. von. (1827). *Lettre à M. Abel-Rémusat [Letter to M. Abel-Rémusat]*. Paris: Dondey-Dupré.

Jenkins, J. (2017). The future of English as a lingua franca? In J. Jenkins, W. Baker and M. Dewey, eds., *Routledge Handbook of English as a Lingua Franca*. Abingdon, UK: Routledge, pp. 594–605.

Jones, W. (1786). Third anniversary discourse. In Lord Teignmouth, ed. (2013). *The Works of Sir William Jones*. Cambridge: Cambridge University Press, vol. **3**, pp. 24–46.

Jones, W. (1789). *Sacontalá, or The Fatal Ring*. Calcutta: n.pub.

Julien, S. (1842). *Le Livre de la voie et de la vertu [The Book of the Way and Virtue]*. Paris: Imprimerie Royale.

Kirkpatrick, A., and Wang, L. (2020). *Is English an Asian Language?* Cambridge: Cambridge University Press.

Klein, L. (2018). *The Organization of Distance*. Leiden: Brill.

Larsen, S. E. (2015). From comparatism to comparativity. *Interfaces*, **1**, 318–47.

Levy, I. (2008). Introduction: Modern Japan and the trialectics of translation. *Review of Japanese Culture and Society*, **20**, 1–14.

Lezra, J. (2017). *Untranslating Machines*. London: Rowman and Littlefield.

Liang, Q. (1902/1989). 喫冰室合集·文集之四十三 *[Combined Works of the Ice-Drinking Room: No. 43]*. Beijing: Zhonghua shuju.

Małecka, A., and Marecki, P. (2018). Literary experiments with automatic translation. In I. Kalla, P. Poniatowska and D. Michułka, eds., *On the Fringes of Literature and Digital Media Culture*. Leiden: Brill, pp. 77–88.

Malmkjær, K. (2018). On the (im)possibility of untranslatability. In D. Large, M. Akashi, W. Józwikowska and E. Rose, eds., *Untranslatability*. New York: Routledge, pp. 41–9.

Malmkjær, K. (2020). *Translation and Creativity*. London: Routledge.

Métail, M. (2000). *64 poèmes du ciel et de la terre [64 Poems of Heaven and Earth]*. Saint-Benoît-du-Sault: Tarabuste.

Mizumura, M. (1995). 私小説 *from Left to Right [An I-Novel]*. Tokyo: Shinshōsha. Extract translated by J. Winters Carpenter (2015). Available at www.thewhitereview.org/fiction/an-i-novel-from-left-to-right/.

Mizumura, M. (2003). Writing sample. *International Writing Program Archive of Residents' Work*, **76**, 1–24.

Mizumura, M. (2015). *The Fall of Language in the Age of English*. Translated by M. Yoshihara and J. Winters Carpenter. New York: Columbia University Press.

Mizumura, M. (2018/19). On translation. *The Serving Library Annual*, 1–8. Available at www.servinglibrary.org/journal/14/on-translation.

Moulton, R. (1911). *World Literature and Its Place in General Culture*. New York: Macmillan.

Mufti, A. R. (2016). *Forget English! Orientalisms and World Literatures*. Cambridge, MA: Harvard University Press.

Mundt, K. (2018). Against the 'Un-' in untranslatability. In D. Large, M. Akashi, W. Józwikowska and E. Rose, eds., *Untranslatability*. New York: Routledge, pp. 64–79.

Nakajima, K. (1958). 影響の測定 [The measurement of influence]. 比較文学 *[Comparative Literature]*, 1, 1–16.

Nakazawa, H. (2015). 現代美術史日本篇 *1945–2014 [Art History: Japan 1945–2014]*. 3rd ed. Tokyo: Art Diver.

Noël, F.-J.-M., and de la Place, F. (1816). *Cours de littérature comparée [Lessons in Comparative Literature]*. Paris: Le Normant.

O'Bell, L. (2018). Chinese novels, scholarly errors and Goethe's concept of world literature. *Publications of the English Goethe Society*, **87**(2), 64–80.

Pennycook, A. (2010). The future of Englishes. In A. Kirkpatrick, ed., *The Routledge Handbook of World Englishes*. London: Routledge, pp. 673–88.

Perloff, M. (2004). *Differentials*. Tuscaloosa: University of Alabama Press.

Posnett, H. M. (1886). *Comparative Literature*. London: Kegan Paul.

Queneau, R. (1947). *Exercices de style [Exercises in Style]*. Paris: Gallimard.

Quinet, E. (1841). De la renaissance orientale. *Revue des Deux Mondes*, quatrième série, **28**(1), 112–30.

Remak, H. (2002). Origins and evolution of comparative literature and its interdisciplinary studies. *Neohelicon*, **XXIX**(1), 245–50.

Reynolds, M., ed. (2020). *Prismatic Translation*. Cambridge: Legenda.

Robinson, P. (2010). *Poetry and Translation*. Liverpool: Liverpool University Press.

Rousseau, J., and Thouard, D., eds. (1999). *Lettres édifiantes et curieuses sur la langue chinoise, Humboldt/Rémusat (1821–1831) [Edifying and curious letters on the Chinese language, Humbold/ Rémusat (1821–1831)*. Villeneuve-d'Ascq: Presses Universitaires du Septentrion.

Russell, B. (1935). *In Praise of Idleness and Other Essays*. London: George Allen and Unwin.

Samoyault, T. (2020). *Traduction et violence [Translation and Violence]*. Paris: Seuil.

Saussy, H. (2006). Exquisite cadavers stitched from fresh nightmares. In H. Saussy, ed., *Comparative Literature in an Age of Globalization*. Baltimore: Johns Hopkins University Press, pp. 3–42.

Saussy, H. (2017). *Translation as Citation*. Oxford: Oxford University Press.

Scott, C. (2018). *The Work of Literary Translation*. Cambridge: Cambridge University Press.

Shimada, K. (1951). 翻訳文学 *[Translated Literature]*. Tokyo: Shibundō.

Spivak, G. C. (1993/2009). *Outside in the Teaching Machine*. New York: Routledge.

Snyder, S. (2017). The Murakami effect. Available at https://lithub.com/the-murakami-effect/.

Terian, A. (2013). The incomparable as uninterpretable. *World Literature Studies*, **2**, 52–63.

Tieghem, P. van. (1931). *La Littérature comparée*. Paris: Armand Colin.

Trivedi, H. (2018). Translation and world literature: The Indian context. In S. Bassnett, ed., *Translation and World Literature*. New York: Routledge, pp. 15–28.

Tsu, J. (2010). Getting ideas about world literature in China. *Comparative Literature Studies*, **47**(3), 290–317.

Turner, J. (2015). *Philology*. Princeton, NJ: Princeton University Press.

Venuti, L. (2008). *The Translator's Invisibility*. 2nd ed. London: Routledge.

Venuti, L. (2019). *Contra Instrumentalism*. Lincoln: University of Nebraska Press.

Walkowitz, R. (2015). *Born Translated*. New York: Columbia University Press.

Wellek, R., and Warren, A. (1942). *Theory of Literature*. New York: Harcourt.

Wilhelm, F. (1961). The German response to Indian culture. *Journal of the American Oriental Society*, **81**(4), 395–405.

Wilkins, C. (1785). *The Bhagvaat-Geeta*. London: C. Nourse.

Wilson, H. (1813). *The mégha dúta*. Calcutta: Hindoostanee Press.

Yohannan, J. (1971). The Fin de Siècle Cult of FitzGerald's Rubáiyát of Omar Khayyám. *Review of National Literatures*, **2**, 74–91.

Yoshikawa, J. (2017). La littérature comparée au Japon [Comparative literature in Japan]. *Revue de littérature comparée [Review of Comparative
Literature]*, **XCI**(2), 136–44.

Yu, P. (2007). 'Your Alabaster in This Porcelain': Judith Gautier's *Le livre de
jade*. PMLA, **122**(2), 464–82.

# 12

# Translation and Linguistics

Hanting Pan and Meifang Zhang

## 12.1 Introduction

Ever since Roman Jakobson (1896–1982) published his seminal paper 'On linguistic aspects of translation' in 1959, linguistics has played a pivotal role in translation studies (TS). Jakobson (1959) classified translation into three types according to the relationships between the source text and the target text: intralingual translation, interlingual translation and intersemiotic translation. Intralingual translation is akin to paraphrasing insofar as the language of the two texts is the same. Interlingual translation is translation between two different written language systems, which has been the major interest of TS. The issues of linguistic meaning and equivalence still remain core in linguistic approaches to TS including contrastive linguistics, computational linguistics, functional linguistics and discourse analytic approaches, whereas the more recent multimodal approach has aroused interests in intersemiotic translation, which is translation between two different types of sign system – for example, between the music of Prokofiev's *Peter and the Wolf* (1936) and the narrations by André Previn and David Bowie.

## 12.2 Translation and Early Modern Linguistics

In the mid-twentieth century, the development of modern linguistics entered a stage of 'expansion and diversification' (Howatt, 2013, p. xxviii). In addition to the three mainstream approaches in linguistics, that is, structuralism, functionalism and generativism, research on other subfields such as contrastive linguistics, computational linguistics, semantics and pragmatics also became popular.

Given the complexity and breadth of linguistics and its long tradition of interplay with TS, this chapter will probe the relationship between translation and linguistics, discuss the development of linguistic approaches to translation since around 1960 and examine the relationship between linguistics and translation, as well as presenting suggestions about how the relationship might develop in the future. Our foci are: (1) the linguistic theories and concepts that have been applied to TS; (2) the way in which these linguistic theories and concepts have informed the development of TS; and (3) what the relationship between TS and linguistics might be in the future. To address these topics, we will make reference to a bibliometric survey by Zhang et al. (2015) on discourse analysis and translation and include more recent developments within linguistics that have been applied to translation research, in particular multimodal discourse analysis. In what follows, the interplay between translation and linguistics will be addressed in terms of the three stages, namely the engagement of early modern linguistics, the engagement of discourse analysis, and the engagement of multimodality theory in translation.

It is commonplace to trace the formation of modern European linguistics back to the structuralist account of language provided by Ferdinand de Saussure (1857–1913), although the work through which Saussure's linguistics is mainly known (Saussure, 1916/1983) was written by his colleagues at the University of Geneva Charles Bally and Albert Séchehaye on the basis of Saussure's lectures and his students' notes on these. Saussure transformed 'philology' into 'linguistics', stressing the importance of the scientific study of language. Gradually, both linguists and translation scholars came to identify translation and translation studies as potential areas for the application of linguistic methodology. Key linguistic concepts and issues were borrowed to define translation, interpret translation activities and construct translation theories with the aim of establishing TS as a science. At this stage, two concepts played vital roles in the theory of translation. One was 'equivalence' and the other was 'meaning'.

### 12.2.1 Equivalence

Jakobson (1959) examines the key issues of linguistic meaning and equivalence in interlingual translation. Jakobson follows Saussure's theory of language that distinguishes between the linguistic system (*langue*) and instances of language in use (*parole*). Central to the theory of *langue* is the relation between the 'signifier' (the spoken and written signal) and the 'signified' (the concept) which together creates the linguistic 'sign' that is arbitrary or unmotivated (Saussure 1916/1983, pp. 67–9). Jakobson stresses that it is possible to understand what is signified by a word without actually seeing or experiencing the thing. In other words, it is possible for one to interpret the linguistic sign that belongs to a different linguistic system. Jakobson then moves on to discuss the issue of equivalence in meaning between words in different languages. In his view (Jakobson, 1959, p. 233), 'on the level of interlingual translation, there is ordinarily no full equivalence between code-units, while messages may serve as adequate interpretations of alien code-units or messages'. Thus, translation 'from one language into another substitutes messages in one language not for separate code-units but for entire messages in some other language' and therefore 'involves two equivalent messages in two different codes' (Jakobson, 1959, p. 234). Jakobson further argues that 'equivalence in difference is the cardinal problem of language and the pivotal concern of linguistics' and that translating activities 'must be kept under constant scrutiny by linguistic science' (Jakobson, 1959, p. 233). This strongly linguistic concept of equivalence was, as Hatim and Munday (2019, p. 123) comment, 'to occupy translation theorists for several decades afterwards'. One of the prominent works on the question of equivalence in meaning is that of Eugene Nida (1914–2011) who addressed the issue with a new 'scientific' approach.

Unlike Jakobson, whose background is in structuralism, Nida 'takes as his starting point Chomsky's more cognitivist, generative view of language' (Malmkjær, 2005, p. 9); in particular, he believes that Chomsky's work on syntactic structure provides the translator with a technique for decoding the source text (ST) and a procedure for encoding the target text (TT) (Nida, 1964, p. 60). His concern is to set out translation procedures and principles, particularly his 'principles of correspondence', and he posits 'two different types of equivalence', namely 'formal equivalence' and 'dynamic equivalence' (Nida, 1964, p. 159). According to Nida (1964, p. 165), a formal-equivalence translation is oriented towards the source text and 'designed to reveal as much as possible of the form and content of the original message'. The formal elements include: (1) grammatical units, (2) consistency in word usage, and (3) meanings in terms of the source context (Nida, 1964, p. 165). A dynamic-equivalence translation, on the other hand, is intended to provide the 'closest natural equivalent to the source-language message' (Nida, 1964, p. 166). He further explains that the term 'natural' points towards the receptor language, and a dynamic-equivalence translation 'is directed primarily towards equivalence of response rather than equivalence of form' (Nida, 1964, p. 166). However, both formal equivalence and dynamic equivalence present difficulties in practice. This is because formal equivalence is an ideal, but it is often not appropriate or even achievable in actual situations of communication. On the other hand, the receptor response, which is the cornerstone of 'dynamic equivalence', is subjective and hard to measure. In Nida's later work, he changed the controversial term 'dynamic equivalence' to 'functional equivalence' (Nida and Waard, 1986), but the definition of the terms remains basically the same and the new term does not change his theory of translation equivalence.

Although Nida aligns himself with linguistics, his 'fundamental measure of translation equivalence is reader response' (Malmkjær, 2005, p. 9), whereas 'the most systematic attempt in English at the wholesale interpretation of translation theory in terms of a linguistic theory is probably that of John Catford (1917–2009)' (Malmkjær, 2005, p. 7). Catford (1965) devotes a chapter to discussing translation equivalence, which he regards as an empirical phenomenon that can be discovered by a comparison between source language (SL) texts and target language (TL) texts with the assistance of a native speaker of the language of the translation (who also knows the language of the source text, of course). Catford (1965) proposes two types of equivalence between items of language, namely textual equivalence and formal correspondence. A textual equivalent is defined as 'any TL text or portion of text which is observed ... to be the equivalent of a given SL text or portion of text' (Catford, 1965, p. 27). A formal correspondent, on the other hand, 'is any TL category ... which can be said to occupy, as nearly as possible, the "same" place in the "economy" of the TL as the given SL category occupies in the SL' (Catford, 1965, p. 27). These definitions show that Catford attaches great importance to 'form' and his theory of translation equivalence is rule-based. Following the discussion of the two types of equivalence, Catford (1965, p. 31) defines a 'translation rule' as 'an extrapolation of the probability values of textual translation equivalence' and suggests that translation rules may be operational instructions to be applied in machine translation, which he calls 'translation-algorithms'. Catford's theory of translation equivalence, particularly formal correspondence, is therefore of great interest to example and statistics-based machine translation and translation memory systems. However, the examples used by Catford to illustrate the two kinds of equivalence are decontextualized, which makes it difficult to apply his approach to communicative events that are context-dependent.

Unlike Catford, whose focus is on the clause and sentence, the German linguist Otto Kade (1927–80) seeks to establish types of equivalence relations at the lexical level, particularly in the area of terminology. Kade (1968) contends that total equivalence, that is, 'where one SL unit exactly corresponds to one TL unit, and these units being interchangeable in any context' (Schäffner and Wiesemann, 2001, p. 7), is applicable only to numbers, proper names and terminology. Other types of equivalence at the lexical level include diversification (one-to-many equivalence), neutralization (many-to-one equivalence), approximative equivalence (one-to-part-of-one equivalence) and zero (or nil) equivalence. Kade (1968, p. 202) notes the influence of context, stressing that different receivers of a text may respond differently to it and that the intention of the originator of the text is unlikely to match its effect completely.

Although the linguistic perspective on equivalence has made an important contribution to the scientification of TS, it has been criticized by adherents of 'the cultural school' of TS for presenting an 'illusion of symmetry' between languages (Snell-Hornby, 1988, p. 22). In addition, Koller (1979/1992, pp. 98, 233) argues, from the perspective of the nature of translation, that translation activity is parole, language in use, and cannot be analysed from the angle of langue, language as system (Saussure, 1916/1983).

## 12.2.2  Meaning

Meaning is one of the key concepts in linguistics. The study and theory of meaning is referred to as 'semantics', in the same way that the study and theory of language structure can be referred to as 'grammar' or 'syntax'. The original use of 'semantics' can be traced back to the French linguist Michel Bréal (1832–1915) who launched the word in an article in 1883 in the annual of a society for Greek studies and published the full book *Essai de Sémantique* in 1897, which was regarded as a landmark in language study, especially in the study of meaning (Read, 1948, p. 79). In another influential work on the study of meaning, C. K. Ogden and I. A. Richards (1923) prefer the term 'science of symbolism' over 'semantics' and regard the 'net result' of Bréal's work as 'disappointing' owing to 'the constant resort to loose metaphor' and 'the hypostatization of leading terms' (Ogden and Richards, 1923, pp. 2–3). Despite the difference of opinion, both Bréal (1897) and Ogden and Richards (1923) agree on the importance of meaning to the study of language and have influenced younger linguists, for example Leech (1974) and Lyons (1977), to use the term 'Semantics' in the titles of their books.

The issue of meaning is equally significant to TS. Like linguists (see Leech, 1974, pp. 9–12), translation scholars are interested in identifying various categories of meaning. Nida (1964, pp. 57, 70), divides meaning into linguistic meaning (i.e., meanings of grammatical constructions), referential meaning (i.e., dictionary meanings) and emotive meaning (i.e., connotative meanings). Newmark (1981, pp. 26–7) categorizes meaning as grammatical meaning which attaches to grammatical units such as a sentence, a clause or a word-group, and lexical meaning which 'starts where grammatical meaning finishes: it is referential and precise, and has to be considered both outside and within the context'. According to Nida (1982, pp. 10–11), to translate is to translate meaning. A similar observation is made by Newmark (1981, p. 26), who says that 'the translation theorist is concerned from start to finish with meaning'.

Nida's theory of meaning is influenced by general linguistics, semantics and pragmatics. According to Nida (1964, p. 70), referential meaning arises primarily from 'the cultural context identified in the utterance', while emotive meaning relates to 'the responses of the participants in the communicative act'. Referential meaning is also known as dictionary meaning, that is, the referents identified in terms of field or context. Emotive meaning can be understood as native speakers' '"feeling" for the appropriateness of words in certain types of linguistic and cultural contexts' (Nida 1964, p. 70). Nida's discussion of meaning, in particular referential meaning and emotive meaning, provides the theoretical foundation for his distinction between 'dynamic equivalence' and 'formal equivalence', and makes 'response equivalence' one of the important indicators for measuring translation quality. In Nida's later work, he further specifies the scope of 'translating meaning': 'Translating meaning implies translating the total significance of a message in terms of both its lexical or propositional content and its rhetorical significance' (Nida, 1982, p. 11). As a result, evaluating the adequacy of a translation requires a complete analysis of meaning, from the lexical level to the discourse level, of both the source text and the target text.

Catford (1965) also considers meaning an essential concept in a theory of translation. Following Firth (1957), Catford (1965, p. 35) defines meaning as 'a property of a language' and 'the total network of relations entered into by any linguistic form'. The relations include formal relations and contextual relations. Formal relations are 'relations between one formal item and others in the same language', a variety of which constitute a form's formal meaning. Contextual relations are the relationships of grammatical or lexical items to linguistically relevant situational elements which constitute the contextual meaning of the relevant linguistic form (Catford, 1965, pp. 35–6). Based on this view, meanings of 'SL items and TL items can rarely be the same, and meaning transference from SL to TL is impossible' (Catford, 1965, p. 36).

Larson (1984) agrees with Nida that translation is meaning-based. According to her (Larson, 1984, p. 3), translation consists of transferring the meaning of the SL into the receptor language. In the process of translation, only the form changes while the meaning remains constant. In short, meaning has priority over form in translation.

### 12.2.3  Summary

From the preceding discussion we can see that early modern linguistics played an important part in the scientification of TS as a discipline. Key concepts such as equivalence and meaning were used to define translation and form the theoretical foundation of TS. In the linguistic approach to translation, keywords in linguistics, including 'message', 'code' and 'form', are repeatedly mentioned. However, at the early stage of the encounter between linguistics and the study of translation, the main research focus remained below the clausal level and focused on words and sentences. The situation changed as linguistics entered a new stage, in particular with the emergence and popularization of discourse analysis.

## 12.3   Translation and Discourse Analysis

Around the 1970s, a new focus emerged in linguistic research which has come to be known as discourse analysis (DA). There are two main conceptions of this new object of study. One takes a more linguistic view and sees discourse as 'the layer of meaning which is tied to situations of language use and located beyond the structural and semantic affordances of a language system' (Slembrouck, 2013, p. 135). Representative proponents of this view include Michael Halliday (1925–2018), Ruqaiya Hasan (1931–2015) and Michael Hoey (1948–2021). Another views language use, 'often in combination with other forms of semiotic behaviour', from the perspective of 'social practice' in context (Slembrouck, 2013, p. 135). A prime example of this direction is critical discourse analysis (CDA) (e.g., Fairclough, 1992; Wodak, 1996) which aims to relate situated language use, power and ideology (Slembrouck, 2013, p. 135). Despite the different emphasis, the two directions arrive at the same focus on language use and social context.

In 1990, Hatim and Mason published their book *Discourse and the Translator*, which has been considered the first influential endeavour to articulate the discourse perspective in translation. Since then, DA has been gaining increasing attention in TS. Key concepts in DA such as context, function and communication have been introduced to TS and integrated into the TS theoretical system.

### 12.3.1   Context

The influence on meaning of context was highlighted by the anthropologist Bronislaw Malinowski (1884–1942) who referred to the context of text production and reception as 'context of situation' and the socio-cultural background of the speaker as 'context of culture' (Malinowski, 1923). According to Malinowski (1923), context is key to the interpretation of a message. Against this background, J. R. Firth (1890–1960), the first professor of linguistics in Britain and the originator of the so-called London School of Linguistics, developed the concept of meaning as 'function in context' (Firth, 1957), which became a central influence on the systemic functional linguistics (SFL) developed by Michael Halliday, which relates language form and language function to context from a socio-cultural perspective.

In the linguistic turn of TS, context also plays an essential role in broadening the research territory of the linguistic approach to TS. For example, on the basis of SFL, Hatim and Mason (1990, p. 58) map the 'three dimensions of context', namely communicative transaction, pragmatic action and semiotic interaction, and suggest potential areas for investigation along with the three dimensions. Communicative transaction concerns the context of situation, which is mainly presented by user and use analysis, including the analysis of idiolect, dialect and register. Register covers the three aspects of discourse: field, tenor and mode. Pragmatic action includes speech acts, implicatures, presuppositions and text acts. Semiotic interaction treats linguistic recourses such as word, text, discourse and genre as signs. Hatim and Mason (1990) also take into account the context of culture that is beyond textual analysis and this leads to the discussion of culture, ideology and power.

House's influential work on translation quality assessment (TQA) (House, 1997, 2015) falls into the dimension of communicative transaction as the model adopts register analysis as its core analytical part. In this model, the scholar analyses and compares the register of the source text and the target text and arrives at a translation quality report based on the results of the comparison. The design of House's TQA model is influenced by the Hallidayan model of language (Halliday, 1978, 1985), which 'sees meaning in the writer's linguistic choices and, through a detailed grammar, systematically relates these choices to the text's function in a wider sociocultural framework' (Munday, 2016, p. 143). In Halliday's model, the linguistic choices (i.e., lexico-grammar), the aims of the communication (i.e., genre) and the socio-cultural framework (i.e., context) interact, and the direction of influence is illustrated by Munday with an inverted pyramid (see figure 6.1 in Munday, 2016, p. 143): On the top of the pyramid is the socio-cultural environment (or context), which partially conditions the genre 'understood in SFL as the conventional text type that is associated with a specific communicative function' and through the conditioning of genre determines register. The variables of register (i.e., field, tenor and mode) are associated with the three strands of meaning (or 'discourse semantics', i.e., ideational, interpersonal and textual meaning) which are formed by the choices of lexico-grammar (at the bottom of the inverted pyramid) in the text. House's model largely follows the hierarchy of the Hallidayan model and incorporates register analysis as the main body of the framework. With the purpose of assessing translation quality, the analytical procedure is as follows: (1) producing the source text (ST) register profiling; (2) adding the ST genre description; (3) making a 'statement of function' for the ST; (4) undertaking the same descriptive process on the target text (TT); (5) comparing the TT profile with the ST profile; (6) making 'a statement of quality'; and (7) categorizing the translation into 'overt translation' or 'covert translation' (House, 2015). In addition, House uses the term 'individual textual function', indicating the production of a 'statement of function' for ST and TT respectively. This 'textual function' in fact falls within the scope of 'context', which conditions or influences the production of ST and TT and can partly explain the differences between them, which is an important consideration for TQA.

The dimension of pragmatic action is rooted in pragmatics, 'the study of the relations between language and its context of utterance' (Hatim and

Mason, 1990, p. 59). The introduction of pragmatics to TS offers a selection of analytical tools for conducting textual analysis on translated works and helps the translator to remain aware of the intended purposes of a communication act and to foresee possible responses by the target audience. Scholars who work with this dimension usually focus on the process of contextualization and recontextualization in translation (see Baker, 2006; House, 2006). For instance, House (2006, p. 356) re-examines the relationship between text and context and argues that a theory of translation as recontextualization can be defined as 'taking a text out of its original frame and context and placing it within a new set of relationships and culturally-conditioned expectations'.

The dimension of semiotic interaction is based on semiotic theory. Hatim and Mason argue that the primary task of translation is to deal with signs and to preserve semiotic, as well as other pragmatic and communicative, properties which signs display (Hatim and Mason, 1990, p. 69). Word, text, discourse and genre are all signs. The exchanges among signs are constrained by 'the interplay between values yielded by a given field of discourse and the pragmatic action intended'. Hatim and Mason (1990, pp. 69–74) describe the process of intersemiotic transfer with an illustration of the hierarchical relationship among text, discourse and genre, in which social occasions at the top of the hierarchy are reflected in genre that is expressed in discourse realized in text. This hierarchical relationship is also articulated in the Hallidayan model we introduced in the previous paragraph. The Hallidayan model is known for taking the socio-semiotic approach to language study and has been adopted by a number of translation scholars as a discourse analytical tool in their studies with a focus on a variety of topic areas such as textual scale and translation units, cohesion in translation, thematic and information structure in translation, transitivity in translation, modality in translation, intertextuality, as well as appraisal and translator attitudes (Zhang et al., 2015). Textual scale includes a hierarchy of grammatical units including word, clause, sentence and text, which can be discussed in relation to the appropriate selection of translation units (e.g., Zhu, 2004). Cohesion is created by the linguistic devices by which the speaker can signal the experiential and interpersonal coherence of the text (Thompson, 2004, p. 179). It is important to text organization and therefore discussed by translation scholars. For instance, Baker (1992, pp. 180–215) devotes a chapter to explaining how cohesion works in translation through a set of cohesive devices which include reference, substitution, ellipsis, conjunction and lexical cohesion. Thematic and information structure in translation also concerns text organization. Thematic structure includes two segments of a clause, that is, theme and rheme, while information structure includes two segments of a message, that is, given and new. Both thematic structure and information structure are features of the context. They are different in that thematic structure is speaker-oriented while information structure is hearer-oriented (Baker, 1992, pp. 119–59). In thematic structure, theme is the 'point of departure of the message' or 'that which locates and orients the clause within its context' (Halliday and Matthiessen, 2004, pp. 64). In information structure, the given segment conveys information which the speaker regards as already known to the hearer and the new segment conveys information that the speaker wishes to convey to the hearer (Baker, 1992, pp. 144–5). Transitivity theory is often applied to the investigation of translational shifts. For instance, Calzada Pérez (2001) studies transitivity shifts in translation and their connection to ideological issues. Intertextuality is 'the way we relate textual occurrences to each other and recognize them as signs which evoke whole areas of our previous textual experience', through which 'texts are recognized in terms of their dependence on other relevant texts' (Hatim and Mason, 1990, p. 120). It can be applied to explaining the relationship between the ST and the TT (e.g., Farahzad, 2009). The topic of appraisal and the translator's attitudes then concerns the interpersonal relationship in translation. Appraisal theory was developed by Martin and White (2005), based on the interpersonal function of the Hallidayan SFL, for the analysis of evaluation in predominantly educational and journalistic texts in English, and it has been used in translation research for identifying 'critical points' of translator intervention and shift of values in the TT (Munday, 2018, p 305).

Although different topic areas may focus on different linguistic aspects in translation, the discussion in the end cannot avoid including reference to the socio-cultural context. Studying translation in context then becomes an important research paradigm of the discourse analytical approach to TS.

## 12.3.2 Function and Communication

The concepts of 'function' and 'communication' are indispensable to each other in DA in that DA views language use as communication and aims to study language in use in relation to language functions and contexts. The earliest systematic thinking about language function can be traced back to Karl Bühler (1879–1963), who belonged to the Prague Circle that inherited Saussurean structuralism. According to Bühler (1934), the function of language is threefold: the relation between the sign (i.e., language) and the world (i.e., context) points to the 'representational' or 'informative' function of language; the relation between the sign and the speaker points to the 'expressive' function of language; and the relation between the sign and the hearer points to the 'appellative' function of language. Bühler's tripartite division of language functions later influenced both Jakobson and Halliday and further influenced a group of TS scholars taking functional approaches to TS.

Capturing the essence of Bühler's categorization, Halliday (1973) proposes three language metafunctions – the ideational, the interpersonal and the textual – which are realized by the lexico-grammar in the text. For example, the ideational function can be manifested by transitivity, the interpersonal function by mood and modality, and the textual function by thematic structure and cohesion. The lexico-grammar forms the basis of SFL, which sees meaning in the writer's linguistic choices and systematically relates these choices to a wider socio-cultural framework. The three language metafunctions can be illustrated by the three basic questions that we can ask about language: (1) What is said? (2) What are the relationships between the speakers? and (3) How should an expression be formed? The three questions can be instantiated in translation as follows: (1) What is translated? (2) What are the relationships among the author, the translator and the receiver? and (3) How should the text be translated? Each question can be answered through the analysis of the lexico-grammar in relation to the relevant metafunction. Hallidayan functionalism in TS is represented by a number of scholars such as Mona Baker, Basil Hatim, Roger T. Bell, Juliane House and Jeremy Munday. For instance, House (1997) applies register analysis in her TQA model; Bell (1991) applies discourse semantics to analyse the elements in the communication process of translation; Baker (1992/2011) applies thematic structure and cohesion theory to guide the translator through the process of textual organization; Munday (2012) applies the interpersonal function, in particular in appraisal theory, to uncover 'critical points' of the translator's decision-making.

More recent work taking the Hallidayan functional approach also pays attention to ideology and power as advocated by scholars engaged in CDA. The CDA model, in particular Fairclough's (1992, 1995, 2001) three-dimensional model, is based on the power of description and explanation of SFL and shares its basic assumptions about textual functions with SFL. With reference to the CDA framework, Calzada Pérez (2001) proposes a threefold analytical methodology consisting of description, ideological explanation and perlocutionary exploration of texts. She analyses European Parliament speech translations and focuses on transitivity shifts and their connection to ideological issues. Munday (2007) investigates the ideology of individual translators and examines what is meant by 'ideology' and how it is treated in translation studies, where it has primarily been linked to manipulation and power relations. Valdeón (2005, 2008) in particular applies Fairclough's three-dimensional model to investigate the ideology of the BBC Spanish service. The theoretical model is also borrowed and adapted in the study of institutional discourse translation (Zhang and Pan, 2015) and gaming discourse translation (Pan and Zhang, 2016).

Another influential application of Bühler's categorization of language functions to TS is the German functionalism pioneered by Katharina Reiss (1923–2018), who proposed three major text types in relation to Bühler's three language functions, namely 'informative texts', 'expressive texts' and 'operative texts'. She tried to establish a correlation between text type and translation method for the purpose of working out a scientific and systematic translation assessment model based on the functional relationship between the ST and the TT (Reiss, 1977/1989). Reiss's text typology was developed by Christiane Nord who further classified Reiss's 'operative text' (in Nord's term 'appellative text') into three sub-types, namely 'direct appellative', 'indirect appellative' and 'poetic appellative' texts (Nord, 1997/2001, pp. 42–3). Nord also proposed a translation-oriented text analysis model highlighting the text function and communicative purpose in the context of the TL (Nord, 1997/2001). Her text analysis model aims to provide translation students with a model of ST analysis that is applicable to all text types and translation situations. The model is based on a functional concept to 'enable translators to understand the function of elements or features observed in the content and structure of the source text' and to 'choose the translation strategies suitable for the intended purpose of the particular translation they are working on' (Nord, 2005, p. 1).

Although the concept of 'function' of the German school of functionalism and that of Halliday's SFL derive from the same source, namely Bühler's tripartite division of language functions, there are some differences between them. One major difference is that in the functionalist approaches that have been developed with an orientation towards translator training, the application of the functional concepts 'set out from the hypothesis that the decisive factor in translation was the dominant communicative function of the source text' (Nord, 1997/2001, p. 39). In contrast, the Hallidayan model of DA is geared to the study of language in communication, and it 'sees meaning in the writer's linguistic choices and systematically relates these choices to a wider sociocultural framework' (Munday, 2012, p. 137). Despite the differences, the Hallidayan functional framework and German functionalism share some basic assumptions, including viewing language as a means of communication, emphasizing socio-cultural and physiological factors, and regarding semantic, pragmatic and functional patterning as central, as well as analysing texts in relation to their contexts. Overall, the introduction of 'function' and 'communication' to TS has revolutionized our understanding of translation and extensively enlarged the research scope of TS.

### 12.3.3 Summary

Unlike the stage of borrowing modern linguistic theories to build TS into a scientific and independent discipline, the encounter of TS with DA invites more diverse perspectives on translation research and is more concerned with the relationship between the translated text and the socio-cultural context that conditions its production and reception. Key concepts in DA such as 'context', 'function' and 'communication' have been introduced to TS and included in definitions of translation. Both DA and TS are by nature interdisciplinary and therefore continue to absorb new insights from recent developments in other disciplines. With the advent of the digital era, discourse analytical approaches to TS have moved towards a multimodal stage.

## 12.4  Translation and Multimodality

Multimodality, as the name suggests, focuses on communication involving more than one mode. In Zhang et al. (2015), multimodality is placed in the dimension of semiotic interaction in Hatim and Mason's (1990) map of context. Within the framework of DA, multimodality or multimodal discourse analysis originates in the 1980s when multimodal social semiotics (MSS) emerged as a branch of semiotics that sought 'to understand how people communicate in specific social settings' (Boria and Tomalin, 2020, p. 12). An influential theory of multimodality, MSS is rooted in the work of Michael Halliday, in particular in his monographs *Language as Social Semiotic* (1978) and *An Introduction to Functional Grammar* (1985). According to Halliday (1978, p. 2), language should be interpreted 'within a sociocultural context, in which the culture itself is interpreted in semiotic terms'. This observation echoes Jakobson's (1959) definition of intersemiotic translation in which verbal signs are interpreted by means of non-verbal signs, so the tripartite categorization of translation by Jakobson can be considered an early attempt to conceptualize translation in multimodal terms.

Following Jakobson's 'intersemiotic translation', Toury (1986, p. 1128) expands the concept of translation to include the transfer between non-verbal signs that belong to different semiotic systems. He differentiates between two types of translation, namely intrasemiotic translation and intersemiotic translation. Intrasemiotic translation is further divided into 'intrasystemic translation' corresponding to Jakobson's 'intralingual translation' and 'intersystemic translation' corresponding to Jakobson's 'interlingual translation'. Given that Jakobson did not further elaborate on the transfer from non-verbal signs to verbal signs, Gorlée (2010, p. 58) suggests that the categorization of translation should take into consideration the concept of multimodality. Kaindl (2013, p. 261) therefore proposes a more detailed model of translation categorization based on the concepts of mode, media and culture. In this model, Kaindl differentiates between 'intramodal translation' and 'intermodal translation' and between 'intramedia translation' and 'intermedia translation'. These sets of classification can be further differentiated as either 'intracultural' or 'transcultural'. In Kaindl's model, 'mode' and 'media' are different but overlapping categories. Mode can be realized by the medium, for example language becomes written words through the medium of writing, and becomes sound through the medium of speech. In translation, both 'mode' and 'media' should be taken into consideration. Kaindl's categorization of translation thus expands Jakobson's tripart categorization and contributes to a more accurate positioning of some translation phenomena that used to be difficult to define. In this view, translation is no longer only a textual activity. Instead, it is an act of communication involving mode, media and culture, or, in Kress and van Leeuwen's (2001) terms, 'transcultural multi-modal communication'. As Kress and van Leeuwen (2001, p. 21) argue, multimodal interaction has always been the 'normal state of human communication', and this is one of the underlying convictions that has guided MSS research from the very beginning (Boria and Tomalin, 2020, p. 13). Reynolds (2020) further claims that language itself is, and has always been, inherently multimodal, and that, 'therefore, even "language-centred" translation practices need to engage with, and account for, the multimodal dimension' (Boria and Tomalin, 2020, p. 199). In other words, the concept of translation needs to be informed by a theory of multimodality.

Paralleling its engagement with the conceptualization and categorization of translation, multimodality was also introduced to TS as a methodological tool to analyse translations of particular text types, such as audiovisual translations, advertising translations, game translations, webpage translations and picture-book translations. Among the aforementioned text types, audiovisual translation has been discussed most extensively since the 1990s. It could be considered the first subfield in TS to engage with multimodality and it emerged as the primary focus for multimodal studies of translation (Diaz-Cintas, 2009, p. 3). Currently, the research field of audiovisual translation has expanded to include all forms of translation that use any media (or format) to edit programmes, including subtitling, dubbing, interpreting, revoicing, simultaneous interpreting, living subtitles, surtitling for opera and theatre and so on (Orero, 2004, pp. vii–viii). The field also includes research topics such as subtitling for the deaf and hard of hearing and audio description for the blind and partially sighted. The influence of audiovisual translation is so profound that it is easy to form the impression that multimodality refers only to audiovisual phenomena, whereas, in fact, audiovisual translation constitutes merely a single manifestation of multimodality in translation (Boria and Tomalin, 2020, p. 5). Apart from audiovisual translation, advertising translation also requires visual analysis and has been an important point of engagement with multimodal theories, for example when visual grammar is applied to analyse TV advertisements (Millán-Varela, 2004). Interpreting, a traditional field in TS, also resorts to multimodal theories to deal with non-verbal elements such as facial expression and gestures that might affect the communication process (see Rennert, 2008). New text types such as game translation (e.g., O'Hagan, 2007) and experimental literary translation (e.g., Lee, 2012), which emerged alongside the development of multimodality, have also received theoretical support from insights derived from studies of multimodality. As fewer and fewer texts are monomodal in the digital era, multimodality-related concerns can be expected to be of interest in an increasing number of TS subfields.

In sum, TS engages with multimodality in two major ways. One is in conceptualizing TS with insights from theories of multimodality, including using the concept of 'multimodality' in the definition and categorization of translation. Another is using theories of multimodality in the analysis of translations, including translations of multimodal text types. The introduction of the concept of multimodality to TS has influenced our understanding of translation and widened the scope of TS considerably.

## 12.5  Future Developments

The above review of major developments in linguistic approaches to TS evidences the continuous expansion of the research field. It is conceivable that in years to come linguistics will continue to play an important role not only in descriptive translation studies but also in applied translation studies. Figure 12.1 suggests some potential future research themes and subthemes in TS.

This categorization by Zhang et al. (2015), based on Hatim and Mason's (1990, p. 58) 'three dimensions of context', not only suggests a three-level categorization of subthemes within the discourse analytical approach to TS but also expands it to include the extralinguistic context of culture and specific themes or sub-themes, such as power and ideology, which are rarely included in linguistic approaches. Also worthy of note are new themes, or an old concept if we recall Jakobson's (1959) categorization of 'intersemiotic translation', that have received increasing attention in TS: semiotics.

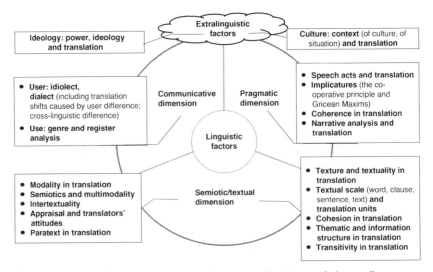

**Figure 12.1** Categorization of research in discourse analysis in translation studies

According to Malmkjær (2010, p. 477), semiotics, which 'derived from Ferdinand de Saussure's coinage of sémiologie', 'is most often loosely defined as "the study of signs" or "the theory of signs"' and a sign 'is a meaningful unit which is interpreted by sign-users as "standing for" something other than itself'. The semiotic features in paratexts, digital media and other types of text are likely to continue to interest researchers because human communication is conducted through signs and sign systems.

Possible developments in TS in the coming decades are likely to include the following. First, with the increasing demand of corpus-based studies to make translation research more empirically grounded, the most traditional sector of linguistics, namely contrastive linguistics, is likely to continue to offer useful theoretical insights and methods for building corpora and for quantitative research. Second, textual analysis is likely to continue to capture the attention of translation researchers. As argued by Malmkjær (2003, 2004), without close attention to the language of texts and their translations, a translational stylistics cannot exist. Malmkjær (2005, p. 16) also suggests that 'after decades devoted to examining translational phenomena from the points of view of a number of "studies" (e.g. cultural; post-colonial; gender) and "isms" (e.g. Marx-; femin-; colonial-; sex-) we should be able to carry out such close textual analysis in enlightened ways'. Third, multimodal theories and approaches are likely to continue to thrive with the new media continuing to transform translation practice and cause theory to revisit and embrace new concepts. Fourth, complementary interdisciplinary methodologies may be developed to deal with the analysis of 'big data', that is, large sets of quantitative data, which are rapidly accessible but which present scholars with considerable challenges related to close critical analysis of the texts and paratexts in their socio-cultural environment.

## 12.6 Conclusion

This chapter has focused on the role of linguistics in the development of TS. It has revisited three stages of linguistic influences on the rapidly growing area of TS, namely the influences of early modern linguistics, of DA, and of multimodality scholarship. With the benefit of the fruits of linguistic development and those of related fields, TS as an academic research area has expanded considerably since the middle of the twenty-first century to become an interdiscipline in which linguistics can be expected to continue to play an important part.

Acknowledgements: The authors are indebted to Professor Kirsten Malmkjær for her invaluable comments and suggestions. This work is supported by the Philosophy and Social Sciences Planning Project of Zhuhai City [2021YBA055].

## References

Baker, M. (1992/2011). *In Other Words: A Coursebook on Translation*. New York: Routledge.

Baker, M. (2006). Contextualization in translator and interpreter-mediated events. *Journal of Pragmatics*, **38**(26), 321–37.

Bell, R. (1991). *Translation and Translating: Theory and Practice*. London: Longman.

Bréal, M. (1897). *Essai de Sémantique*. Paris: Hachette Collection.

Boria, M., and Tomalin, M. (2020). Introduction. In M. Boria, Á. Carreres, M. Noriega-Sánchez and M. Tomalin, eds., *Translation and Multimodality: Beyond Words*. London: Routledge, pp. 1–23.

Bühler, K. (1934). *Sprachtheorie: Die Darstellungsfunktion der Sprache*. Jena: G. Fischer.

Calzada Pérez, M. (2001). A three-level methodology for descriptive-explanatory translation studies. *Target*, **13**(2), 203–39.

Catford, J. (1965). *A Linguistic Theory of Translation*. London: Oxford University Press.

Díaz-Cintas, J. (2009). *New Trends in Audiovisual Translation*. Clevedon, UK: Multilingual Matters.

Fairclough, N. (1992). *Discourse and Social Change*. Oxford: Blackwell.

Fairclough, N. (1995). *Critical Discourse Analysis: The Critical Study of Language*. London: Longman.

Fairclough, N. (2001). *Language and Power*. 2nd ed. London: Longman.

Farahzad, F. (2009). Translation as an intertextual practice. *Perspectives: Studies in Translatology*, **16**(3–4), 125–31.

Firth, J. (1957). *Papers in Linguistics 1934–1951*. London: Oxford University Press.

Gorlée, D. (2010). Metacreations. *Applied Semiotics*, **24**(9), 54–67.

Halliday, M. (1973). *Explorations in the Functions of Language*. London: Edward Arnold.

Halliday, M. (1978). *Language as Social Semiotic: The Social Interpretation of Language and Meaning*. London: Edward Arnold.

Halliday, M. (1985). *An Introduction to Functional Grammar*. London: Edward Arnold.

Halliday, M. A. K., and Matthiessen, C. (2004). *An Introduction to Functional Grammar*. 3rd rev. ed. London: Edward Arnold.

Hatim, B., and Mason, I. (1990). *Discourse and the Translator*. London: Longman.

Hatim, B., and Munday, J. (2019). *Translation: An advanced Resource Book for Students*. 2nd ed. London: Routledge.

House, J. (1997). *Translation Quality Assessment: A Model Revisited*. Tübingen: G. Narr.

House, J. (2006). Text and context in translation. *Journal of Pragmatics*, **38** (26): 338–58.

House, J. (2015). *Translation Quality Assessment: Past and Present*. London: Routledge.

Howatt, T. (2013). Introduction. In K. Malmkjær, ed., *The Routledge Linguistics Encyclopedia*. 3rd ed. Abingdon: Routledge, pp. xxiii–xxxvii.

Jakobson, R. (1959). On linguistic aspects of translation. In R. Brower, ed., *On Translation*. Cambridge, MA: Harvard University Press, pp. 232–9.

Kade, O. (1968). *Zufall und Gesetzmäßigkeit in der Übersetzung*. Leipzig: VEB.

Kaindl, K. (2013). Multimodality in translation. In C. Millán and F. Bartrina, eds., *The Routledge Handbook of Translation Studies*. London: Routledge, pp. 257–70.

Koller, W. (1979/1992). *Einführung in die Übersetzungswissenschaft*. Heidelberg: Quelle und Meyer.

Kress, G., and van Leeuwen, T. (2001). *Multimodal Discourse: The Modes and Media of Contemporary Communication*. London: Hodder Education.

Larson, M. (1984). *Meaning-Based Translation: A Guide to Cross-Language Equivalence*. Oxford: University Press of America.

Lee, T. (2012). Performing multimodality: Literary translation, intersemioticity and technology. *Perspectives: Studies in Translatology*, **21**(1), 245–56.

Leech, G. (1974). *Semantics*. Harmondsworth: Penguin Books.

Lyons, J. (1977). *Semantics*. Cambridge: Cambridge University Press.

Malinowski, B. (1923). The problem of meaning in primitive languages. In C. Ogden and I. Richards, eds., *The Meaning of Meaning: A Study of the Influence of Language upon Thought and the Science of Symbolism*. London: Kegan Paul, Trench, Trubner.

Malmkjær, K. (2003). What happened to God and the angels: An exercise in translational stylistics. *Target*, **15**, 39–62.

Malmkjær, K. (2004). Translational stylistics. *Language and Literature*, **13**, 13–24.

Malmkjær, K. (2005). Translation and linguistics. *Perspectives: Studies in Translatology*, **13**(1), 5–20.

Malmkjær, K. (2010). *The Linguistic Encyclopedia*, 3rd ed. London/New York: Routledge.

Martin, J. R., and White, P. R. R. (2005). *The Language of Evaluation: Appraisal in English*. Basingstoke: Palgrave Macmillan.

Millán-Varela, C. (2014). Exploring advertising in a global context: Food for thought. *The Translator*, **10**, 245–67.

Munday, J. (2007). Translation and ideology: A textual approach. *The Translator*, **13**(2), 195–217.

Munday, J. (2012). *Evaluation in Translation: Critical Points in Translator Decision-Making*. London: Routledge.

Munday, J. (2016). *Introducing Translation Studies: Theories and Applications*. London: Routledge.

Munday, J. (2018). Translation analysis. In L. D'hulst and Y. Gambier, eds., *A History of Modern Translation Knowledge: Sources, Concepts, Effects*. Amsterdam: John Benjamins, pp. 301–8.

Newmark, P. (1981). *Approaches to Translation*. Hemel Hempstead: Prentice Hall.

Nida, E. (1964). *Toward a Science of Translating*. Leiden: E. J. Brill.

Nida, E. (1982). *Translating Meaning*. California: English Language Institute.

Nida, E., and Waard, J. (1986). *From One Language to Another: Functional Equivalence in Bible Translation*. New York: Thomas Nelson.

Nord, C. (1997/2001). *Translating as a Purposeful Activity: Functionalist Approaches Explained*. Manchester: St Jerome. (2001. Shanghai: Shanghai Foreign Language Education Press.)

Nord, C. (2005). *Text Analysis in Translation: Theory, Methodology and Didactic Application of a Model for Translation-Oriented Text Analysis*. 2nd ed. Amsterdam: Rodopi.

Ogden, C. K., and Richards, I. A. (1923). *The Meaning of Meaning*. New York: Mariner Books.

O'Hagan, M. (2007). Video games as a new domain for translation research: From translating text to translating experience. *Revista Tradumatica*, **5**.

Orero, P. (2004). Audiovisual translation: A new dynamic umbrella. In P. Orero, ed., *Topics in Audiovisual Translation*. Amsterdam: John Benjamins, pp. vii–xiii.

Pan, H., and Zhang, M. (2016). Translating for a healthier gaming industry: Keywords and translation of the Macao gaming discourse. *Translation Spaces*, **5**(2), 163–80.

Read, A. W. (1948). An account of the word 'Semantics'. *Word*, **4**(2), 78–97.

Reiss, K. (1977/1989). Text types, translation types and translation assessment, trans. A. Chesterman. In A. Chesterman, ed., *Readings in Translation Theory*. Helsinki: Oy Finn Lectura Ab., pp. 105–15.

Rennert, S. (2008). Visual input in simultaneous interpreting. *Meta*, **53**(1), 204–17.

Reynolds, M. (2020). Translating 'I': Dante, literariness and the inherent multimodality of language. In M. Boria, Á. Carreres, M. Noriega-Sánchez and M. Tomalin, eds., *Translation and Multimodality: Beyond Words*. London: Routledge, pp. 117–33.

Saussure, F. (1916/1983). *Course in General Linguistics*, trans. W. Baskin. London: Fontana/Collins.

Schäffner, C., and Wiesemann, U. (2001). *Annotated Texts for Translation: English–German: Functionalist Approaches*. Clevedon, UK: Multilingual Matters.

Slembrouck, S. (2013). Discourse analysis. In K. Malmkjær, ed., *The Routledge Linguistics Encyclopedia*. 3rd ed. Abingdon: Routledge.

Snell-Hornby, M. (1988). *Translation Studies: An Integrated Approach*. Amsterdam: John Benjamins.

Thompson, G. (2004). *Introducing Functional Grammar*. 2nd ed. London: Hodder Education Publishers.

Toury, G. (1986). Translation. In T. Sebeok, ed., *Encyclopedic Dictionary of Semiotics*, vol. 2. Berlin: Mouton de Gruyter, pp. 1107–24.

Valdeón, R. (2005). The 'translated' Spanish service to the BBC. *Across Languages and Cultures*, **6**(2), 195–220.

Valdeón, R. (2008). Anomalous news translation: Selective appropriation of themes and texts in the Internet. *Babel*, **54**(4), 299–326.

Wodak, R. (1996). *Disorders of Discourse*. London: Longman.

Zhang, M., and Pan, H. (2015). Institutional power in and behind discourse: A case study of SARS notices and their translations used in Macao. *Special Issue of Target: Discourse and Translation*, **27**(3), 387–405.

Zhang, M., Pan, H., Chen, X., and Luo, T. (2015). Mapping discourse analysis in translation studies via bibliometrics: A survey of journal publications. *Perspectives: Studies in Translatology*, **23**(2), 223–39.

Zhu, C. (2004). Repetition and signification: A study of textual accountability and perlocutionary effect in literary translation. *Target*, **16**(2), 227–52.

# 13

# Translation
# and Philosophy

Duncan Large

It goes without saying that philosophy lives on in translation
and that translation survives even philosophy.

(A. Benjamin, 1989, p. 85)

## 13.1 Introduction: Original Translating and Multilingual Philosophy

In this chapter I will begin by arguing for the central importance of
translation to philosophy, which is 'born translated' and constantly
renews itself through translation, even if it has often resisted this recognition. I will then consider some of the leading philosophical accounts of
translation (Section 13.2), focusing on the question of untranslatability,
before considering complementary ways in which translation studies as
a discipline has been exercised by philosophical questions (Section 13.3),
especially concerning translation equivalence (Section 13.3.1) and the
ethical duty of the translator (Section 13.3.2). Two final sections examine
some of the purposes met by translations of philosophical texts
(Section 13.4) and some of the practical issues involved in translating
philosophical texts by canonical German philosophers (Kant, Hegel,
Nietzsche, Heidegger) into English (Section 13.5).

Philosophy has always had a somewhat uneasy relation to translation. It
is customary to be suspicious of translations, but philosophers have often
gone further and been suspicious of language itself, viewing language and
thought as in tension with each other. There is a long tradition of philosophers regretting the 'Fall' of pre-linguistic thought into language, and the
real-world imprecisions and ambiguities with which that is associated,
instead fantasizing about dispensing with (natural) language altogether.
Such was the impulse behind Leibniz's 'alphabet of human thought', his

universal pictographic language the *characteristica universalis* (Mates, 1986, pp. 183–8), and it was behind Frege's project to develop a stripped-down ideography or *Begriffsschrift*. Indeed, Frege goes so far as to describe it as one of the tasks of philosophy 'to break the domination of words over the human mind' (Frege, 1879, p. vi). Nor is this just a Western concern – Julian Baggini writes, for instance, of '[t]he mistrust of language in Daoism' (Baggini, 2018, p. 28). But philosophy is not just concepts: it cannot be 'cleansed' of the taint of language because it inhabits, precisely, the nexus of language and thought. Whether one seeks to celebrate or regret it, the relation between these two is at the heart of philosophical enquiry; philosophy is the study of what Andy Clark calls the 'wordful mind' (Clark, 2006, pp. 373–4).

Philosophy cannot be thought (of) without language, but neither language nor philosophy itself can be thought of without translation. The relations among language, thought and object (referent) have been formulated as translational in a number of philosophical and linguistic traditions. Clark describes Jerry Fodor's 'language of thought hypothesis' (Fodor, 1975) as a '"Pure Translation" view of language' (Clark, 2006, p. 370), but this has historic roots. Jonathan Bennett locates a 'translation view of language' in Locke: 'wishing to share with you something in my mind, I translate it into the public medium of articulate sounds; you hear the objective, interpersonal noises that I make, and retranslate them back into something in your mind; and so communication is complete' (Bennett, 1971, pp. 1–2). Likewise, Nietzsche's early theory of language makes much of the 'metaphorical' relations underlying concept formation: 'To begin with, a nerve stimulus is transferred [*übertragen*] into an image: first metaphor. The image, in turn, is imitated in a sound: second metaphor. And each time there is a complete overleaping of one sphere, right into the middle of an entirely new and different one' (Nietzsche, 1979, p. 82). Philosophy's besetting (original) sin is the imprecision of words (they are not rigid designators), and that arises out of original metaphorical displacements which are a kind of translation – after all, etymologically speaking *trans-lation* is itself merely a translation of *metaphor*. Philosophy can be viewed as *underwritten* by translation in these senses, then: *original translation* is at the heart of language and thus, by extension, philosophy. Heidegger stresses this aspect of what Roman Jakobson called intralingual translation (Jakobson, 2012, p. 127): 'we are also already constantly translating our own language, our native tongue, into its genuine word [*eigenes Wort*]. To speak and to say is in itself a translation .... In every dialogue and in every soliloquy an original translating [*ursprüngliches Übersetzen*] holds sway' (Heidegger, 1992, p. 12). A strong translational reading of human communication such as George Steiner expounds in his classic of translation theory *After Babel* (Steiner, 1992, p. 49) would claim that any kind of philosophical exegesis or interpretation in turn involves further translational steps. In other words, the interpretation of philosophical texts is tantamount to the translation of philosophical texts, especially if they are written in an older form of the language. Meanings change, and they may not be precise in the first place because of the ambiguity inherent in language, so any work of philosophy in a single language needs exegesis and interpretation (i.e., translating into other equivalent meanings): that is simply the nature of philosophical enquiry.

In these respects (original translation in language; interpretation as translation), philosophy is suffused with the translational. But this is the case in more concrete ways, as well. Western philosophy bootstraps itself into existence in ancient Greece, and in ancient Greek, when the first philosophical technical terms arise out of the redesignation of otherwise common words, such as when 'the Milesians asked for the φύσις [phusis (nature)] of all things' (Burnet, 1914, p. 27), and they set in train a succession of further translations: φύσις becomes *natura* becomes *nature*, etc. Our philosophical vocabulary has come down to us through chains of translations in this way.

Just like the contemporary novel in Rebecca L. Walkowitz's resonant formulation, then, philosophy is 'born translated' (Walkowitz, 2015) and constantly renews itself through translation. Across the history of philosophy we encounter pinch points when philosophy has transplanted itself to a new locale, and philosophical vocabularies have been created through translation: even if they are not overtly multilingual, all philosophical texts are multilingual in subtle ways because so many of the concepts they use have their origins in other-language philosophical traditions. Lucretius and Cicero created Latin philosophical vocabulary out of imported Greek materials in the first century BCE (Kaimio, 1979). Montaigne may have been 'the last native speaker of Latin' (Wheeler, 2013), but to view his extensive use of Latin quotations in his (otherwise mostly) French-language *Essais* is to see a vernacular philosophy gradually grafting itself onto classical precedents. 'Witcraft' emerges in English likewise in the sixteenth century (Rée, 2019; cf. Rosen, 2019), not least because Francis Bacon takes his cue from Montaigne's hybrid technique and does the same in (mostly) English with his 1597 *Essays*, thereby at the same time also translating the essay as form into English. It is ironic that the philosopher who did more than any other to establish French as a vernacular language fit for philosophy, Descartes, is now best known for a phrase which is not the one he used in the 1637 French-language *Discours de la méthode* ('je pense, donc je suis') but rather its Latin translation, 'cogito ergo sum', by his friend Étienne de Courcelles (Descartes, 1644, pp. 558–9). For Jonathan Rée, the cogito is 'surely one of the most famous products ever of the translator's hidden hand' (Rée, 2001, p. 249; cf. Young, 2014, p. 41). Furthermore, if we look beyond the mainstream of Western philosophy, smaller languages have been even more reliant on translation and on borrowing from the main traditions to establish themselves: translations of Greek and German philosophy into Romanian, for example, far outweigh the translations in the other direction.

Translated philosophical terms take on a new life in the receiving language, and it is soon forgotten that they were imported: like most such linguistic imports, they take on the character of the receiving language and become productive in turn, generating new modes of philosophical enquiry. But the philosophical word-hoard is being constantly renewed. Terms get borrowed from different philosophical traditions and assimilated into a European vernacular as loan-words (e.g., Schopenhauer with *nirvana*, *sansara* and other Sanskrit vocabulary from Buddhism). Even well-established terms become problematized and *re-translated*. For example, Heidegger turns the Greek ἀλήθεια [*aletheia* (truth; disclosure)] into *Unverborgenheit* or 'unconcealment', a more 'original' concept of truth, and he objects to its Latin translation as *veritas* (truth) (Wrathall, 2011). And, of course, new philosophical terms get invented which the Greeks did not know about – but in such cases they are usually either assembled from classical components (e.g., Lenin's эмпириокритицизм [empiriocriticism]) or (as at the birth of Western philosophy) 'borrowed' from everyday vocabulary all over again and given a new definition. An example of the latter is the term *emergence*, which may date back as a concept to the definition of the whole as more than the sum of its parts in Aristotle's *Metaphysics* (Book H 1045a 8–10), although the modern term was coined by G. H. Lewes only in 1875 (Lewes, 1875, p. 369).

Much philosophy ends up in this way covertly multilingual; another similar instance is when bi- or multilingual philosophers write two or more versions of the same text, a phenomenon that Walkowitz calls 'pre-emptive translation' (Walkowitz, 2015, p. 11). Some philosophers have gone, and continue to go, to great lengths to write their philosophy in a language other than their native one, especially when exiled from their native country. Examples here include Karl Marx writing and publishing in English and French or, a century later, Theodor Adorno, Hannah Arendt and Ludwig Wittgenstein writing in English, while Walter Benjamin, Cornelius Castoriadis and Julia Kristeva wrote in French (see Large, 2014). We are used to internationally prominent philosophers like Foucault and Derrida lecturing in English; in our own time philosophers from Karl-Otto Apel to Slavoj Žižek have written original philosophy in English – which is to acknowledge that English is currently the lingua franca of international philosophical debate. There will be some native speakers of any lingua franca, but otherwise philosophers are translating themselves before they even publish their work and engage in discussions about it.

As in international science, the world language is currently English, but 'twas not ever thus. The first lingua franca of philosophy was, of course, Greek; Latin held sway for a millennium and a half, then a relatively brief diversification into European vernaculars (especially French) during the early modern period and Enlightenment led to the swift ascendancy of German from the turn of the nineteenth century. The reputation of philosophy teaching in Berlin, in particular, ensured that, from the time of Hegel in the 1820s until World War II, what is now known as the Humboldt University acted as a magnet for generations of the world's brightest philosophical talents (de Berg and Large, 2012, pp. 1–2). But it is still an oversimplification to speak of, say, 'German-language philosophy' or the 'Anglo-American philosophy' that is currently in the ascendancy. All philosophical works are at least implicitly multilingual, as we have seen, but even modern philosophers are often explicitly multilingual, too. For example, Schopenhauer quoted gobbets of Latin, Nietzsche frequently dropped in snippets of French, and Heidegger quoted reams of Greek. This is of course a challenge for the reader, who may be reliant on translations of foreign-language quotations given either by the original author or by an obliging editor. In short, there is no escaping the fact that philosophy is a multilingual activity, and to be a competent philosopher one needs either to learn the other languages and/or to read philosophical texts in translation. As Rée puts it:

> You would be hard pressed to find a work of philosophy that is completely monolingual. No other discipline is so dependent on translations, and every philosophical library contains an impressive proportion of works by foreigners. A history of philosophy that aimed to be comprehensive would have to deal with a dozen or more linguistic traditions, each reverberating in its own way with words and works that are foreign to it.
>
> (Rée, 2019, p. 8)

## 13.2 Philosophical Accounts of Translation, and Untranslatability

Rée's work is particularly receptive to translation, and thereby typical of more recent philosophy in the continental tradition (Derrida, 1985; A. Benjamin, 1989; Gadamer, 1989; Sallis, 2002; Ricœur, 2006; Young, 2014). But this philosophical interest in the question of translation is relatively recent, and Anthony Pym finds a shocking lack of engagement by philosophers in translation theory: 'Western philosophy has no traditional discourse on translation' (Pym, 2007, p. 25). Given philosophy's intimate relation to translation, it is not surprising that philosophy has provided various accounts of what is at stake in the translation process. What is surprising is that it should not have provided more of them.

Historically, the most significant philosophical contribution to translation theory has been to argue that translation is impossible. Translation emerges as a problem for philosophy at the turn of the nineteenth century, and immediately it emerges as a serious, potentially insuperable problem – the problem of untranslatability. The German Romantics were interested generally in the notion of radical idiosyncrasy (most notably in the concept of genius); on the cultural level this leads to a recognition of the particularity of cultures and of cultural expression linked to language use. As a result, as Wilhelm von Humboldt remarks in the introduction to his 1816 translation of Aeschylus's *Agamemnon*: 'This kind of work is untranslatable because of its peculiar nature' (Lefevere, 1992a, p. 135). In the nineteenth century, European cultures were becoming increasingly interested in their linguistic histories from the perspective of nascent nationalism, but as Pym points out, using Humboldt as his example: 'if languages had different worldviews, translation in any ideal sense must be impossible' (Pym, 2007, p. 26). Such a pessimistic view of the potential for translation to adequately convey philosophical concepts led Schopenhauer in mid-century to resist translation and instead advocate learning foreign languages as the best way to engage with foreign-language philosophical traditions (Schopenhauer, 1992, p. 33).

It is but a small step from concepts of genius and peculiarity to a radical cognitive relativism with which we are perhaps more familiar in its twentieth-century guise as the so-called 'Sapir-Whorf hypothesis'. Within translation studies, the more pertinent mid-twentieth-century contribution is from Willard van Ormand Quine in his 1959 essay 'Meaning and Translation'. Quine focuses on what he calls the 'indeterminacy of translation' (because of indeterminacy of meaning in the first place, or 'indeterminacy of reference'), and uses the example of the (invented) foreign word 'gavagai', which is uttered when a native speaker points at a rabbit. A linguist trying to understand the language has to decide whether the native speaker's utterance means 'rabbit', 'undetached rabbit parts' or 'rabbit stage' (Quine, 1959, pp. 153–4) or (if superstitious) 'it will rain tonight' (cf. Malmkjær, 2019; Roth, 2019).

There have been a number of responses to this kind of approach, though: more pragmatic responses to the question of untranslatability take the view that translation must be possible because, as Paul Ricœur puts it, '*there is translation*' (Ricœur, 2006, p. 32) or, as George Steiner argues, '[w]e *do* translate intra- and interlingually and have done so since the beginning of human history. The defence of translation has the immense advantage of abundant, vulgar fact' (Steiner, 1992, p. 264). More recently, the American philosopher Donald Davidson introduced the concept of 'radical interpretation' to counter Quine's radical indeterminacy of meaning (Davidson, 1973). Davidson acts as an antidote to the putatively paralysing effect of the notion of untranslatability, allowing Kirsten Malmkjær to argue: 'The philosophy of translation shows us that translation is always possible' (Malmkjær, 2010, p. 216). Or as Lawrence Venuti (2019, p. x) puts it:

STOP asserting that any text is untranslatable.

START realizing that every text is translatable because every text can be interpreted.

Nor is it just modern theory that tells us this. If we go back to the early nineteenth century, another German Romantic, Friedrich Schleiermacher, confronts the question of untranslatability in his important 1813 lecture 'On the Different Methods of Translating' (Schleiermacher, 2012). The great Plato translator is enough of a pragmatist to allow that translation is possible, but recognizes that it requires a certain kind of approach that is now known (following Venuti) as 'foreignising' – in other words, respecting the foreignness of the source text and if necessary deforming the target text, its lexis and syntax, in order to make the reader do some work to acquire meaning ('bring the reader to the author', as Schleiermacher puts it).

The most important recent contribution to the debate on untranslatability is Barbara Cassin's *Dictionary of Untranslatables* (Cassin, 2014). Cassin is clearly drawing on Derrida's understanding of translation as impossible but necessary, caught in a double bind (Davis, 2001, p. 67). In her Introduction, Cassin describes 'untranslatables' as '*symptoms* of difference': 'To speak of *untranslatables* in no way implies that the terms in question, or the expressions, the syntactical or grammatical turns, are not and cannot be translated: the untranslatable is rather what one keeps on (not) translating [*l'intraduisible, c'est plutôt ce qu'on ne cesse pas de (ne pas) traduire]'* (Cassin, 2014, p. xvii). Cassin brings the untranslatability debate full circle, back to the Romantics' recognition that translation happens and has to happen, but that untranslatability lurks on the horizon as a spur to the translator's creativity.

## 13.3  Philosophical Translation Studies

The whole thematization of untranslatability arises out of an ontological question regarding the status of the translated text and its relation to the original. This question has an associated epistemological anxiety about the degradation of knowledge with translation: what gets 'lost in translation' is the original meaning, since no translation can hope to provide an equivalent for it. One philosophical way of putting this would be to say that translations are not analytic propositions but synthetic ones (since not even one language is ever a self-referential closed system, never mind two). Languages work differently from one another, and make different resources available for the translator to choose between, so that even a dictionary definition is never a one-to-one correspondence. Translation is inevitably a trade-off, then, but is meaning therefore inevitably lost in translation? Translation makes you aware of the linguistic ground of philosophical statements (which many branches of philosophy like to occlude) and leads to a pluralization and proliferation of meanings: univocal precision is lost (if it was ever there in the first place). Philosophy in elegiac mode likes to emphasize what is lost, but we need to recognize translation *gain* as well.

### 13.3.1 Equivalence

Initial attempts to counter these anxieties about equivalence of meaning (expressed in the philosophical arena by Quine and others) were made within the nascent field of translation studies from the late 1950s. Roman Jakobson's influential 1959 essay 'Linguistic Aspects of Translation' is centrally concerned with semantic equivalence, claiming: 'Equivalence in difference is the cardinal problem of language and the pivotal concern of linguistics' (Jakobson, 2012, p. 127). Jakobson moves confidently to the upbeat universal assertion: 'All cognitive experience and its classification is conveyable in any existing language' (Jakobson, 2012, p. 128), even if the conclusion of his short article is haunted by the spectre of untranslatability in the case of a literary genre that exceeds his scheme, namely poetry, in the case of which 'only creative transposition is possible' (Jakobson, 2012, p. 131). In the following decade, such a concern with creative transposition led J. C. Catford to formulate equivalence in terms of the 'shifts' that are involved in any translation activity (Catford, 1965, pp. 73–82), and Eugene A. Nida to pluralize 'equivalence' itself, introducing a distinction between (source-oriented) 'formal equivalence' and (target-oriented) 'dynamic equivalence', thus problematizing the key notion that had underlain so many centuries of translation theory (Nida, 1964, pp. 156–92). Dynamic equivalence, with its emphasis on a text's (equivalent) effect on the receiving culture, in turn paved the way for other functionalist translation theories such as Reiss and Vermeer's *skopos* theory that would substitute adequacy for equivalence as the prime criterion for translation quality (Nord, 1997).

Modern translation theory has moved away from the source-oriented, equivalence-focused thinking prompted by the linguistic turn in translation studies of the mid-twentieth century, and emphasizes instead its disseminative, 'prismatic' potential (Reynolds, 2019). If we recognize that not just any translation but any act of reading is an interpretation, then we can instead celebrate the hermeneutic potential that translation unlocks. As Clive Scott argues: 'Translation begins in equivalence, but is itself the very process of superseding equivalence, of setting language on the move' (Scott, 2012a, p. 13f.). In recent translation theory, the most vocal champion of this hermeneutic potential has been Venuti, who dismisses the great majority of previous translation theory as having sold short translation's great hermeneutic achievement by 'instrumentalising' it (Venuti, 2019).

### 13.3.2 Ethics

Another key area of philosophical interest within contemporary translation studies relates to the ethical duty of the translator. This has been a concern ever since classical times, with Horace already setting up the model of the *fidus interpres* (faithful interpreter) in his poem *Ars poetica*, 133ff. (see Kelly, 1979). 'Faithfulness' raises the question of 'faithful to whom or what?', and over the course of translation history there has been a wide variety of answers to that question, but nowhere has this sense of the paramouncy of fidelity been stronger than in the case of the faithful scripture translator feeling a sense of ethical duty to the ultimate source text author, God. This anxiety is evident in the great Bible translator St Jerome's Letter to Pammachius: 'If I translate word for word I produce nonsense, but if I have to change something in the order of the words or their sound I could be accused of failing in my duties [*officio*] as a translator' (Lefevere, 1992a, p. 48). Construals of the translator's ethical duty of faithfulness have included fidelity not only to the source text author and originating culture but also to the text (its 'letter' or its 'spirit' or its 'truth'), to the source language – including what Walter Benjamin calls 'pure language' (W. Benjamin, 2012, p. 82) – to the reader and to the target-language cultural context.

Such conceptions easily open the translator up to moral censure, for the other side of these coins is always the proverbial 'faithlessness' of the translator, the purported betrayal encapsulated in the Italian adage *traduttore, traditore* (translator, traitor) and the French 'belles infidèles'. Again, this mistrust dates back centuries, at least as far as Joachim du Bellay, writing in 1549 of 'those who really deserve to be called traitors, rather than translators, since they betray the authors they try to make known, robbing them of their glory and, at the same time, seducing ignorant readers by showing them black instead of white' (Lefevere, 1992a, p. 22). The conception of the translator as transgressor is given a Christian twist by Erasmus, writing to William Warham in 1506: 'I prefer to sin [*peccare*] through excessive scrupulousness rather than through excessive licence since I am a novice in translation' (Lefevere, 1992a, p. 60). Nor is this just idle rhetoric, for over the centuries the question of the translator's duty of faithfulness in the religious context has revealed the stakes at times to be tragically high, leading to the execution of translators (such as the Frenchman Étienne Dolet) who were perceived as falling foul. Contemporary translators have sought to reclaim and 'own' the 'unfaithful' designation with memoirs such as Gregory Rabassa's (2005) *If This Be Treason* and Mark Polizzotti's (2018) *Sympathy for the Traitor* (cf. Spitzer, 2020), but, to this day, the stakes for translators in some situations remain unacceptably high. In 1991, in the wake of the issuing of a *fatwah* on Salman Rushdie's *The Satanic Verses*, the book's Italian translator Ettore Capriolo was attacked and seriously wounded, while its Japanese translator Hitoshi Igarashi was stabbed to death.

As the field of applied ethics has itself expanded rapidly within contemporary philosophy, this has been matched by a rapid diversification in the ethical roles ascribed to the translator in contemporary translation theory. Especially since the 'cultural turn' of the 1990s (Bassnett and Lefevere,

1990; Lefevere, 1992b), translation scholars have drawn on varieties of social and political theory in order to place questions of ideology and power relations at the heart of translation theory. Investigations into censorship and other political interventions in translation history have broadened out to concerns with translation and cultural memory, including translation and the Holocaust (Boase-Beier, 2015; Davies, 2018), or the translator in conflict situations. Initial work from a feminist perspective in the 1980s has opened up translation studies to a wide array of gender-informed perspectives that have more recently encompassed gay/queer and transgender translation (Rose, 2021). Post-colonial translation theory, with its enquiries into how best to resist English-language hegemony and the oppression of language minorities through translation, has led in several important directions simultaneously, including: debates surrounding the role of translated literature in the rise of world literature studies (Apter, 2013) and the relation between translation and globalization more generally; and concern for indigenous and less translated languages, and for diversity in translation more generally. The latter came strikingly to the fore in early 2021 when prizewinning Dutch (white, non-binary) writer Marieke Lucas Rijneveld withdrew from translating the Black activist poet of the Biden Inauguration Amanda Gorman in response to the considerable opposition caused by their appointment.

Two exemplary translation theorists of the contemporary period whose work has been impelled by ethical concerns over several decades are the American Lawrence Venuti and the Irishman Michael Cronin. Already in his breakthrough 1995 work *The Translator's Invisibility*, Venuti was stressing: 'The terms "domestication" and "foreignisation" indicate fundamentally *ethical* attitudes towards a foreign text and culture, ethical effects produced by the choice of a text for translation and by the strategy devised to translate it' (Venuti, 2018, p. 19). Venuti's 1998 book *The Scandals of Translation* was subtitled *Towards an Ethics of Difference*, and his more recent work on hermeneutic versus instrumental translation retains a strongly ethical thrust (Venuti, 2019). Likewise the work of Michael Cronin, from his initial post-colonial intervention on *Translating Ireland* (Cronin, 1996) to more recent books on *Translation and Globalization* (Cronin, 2003) and *Eco-translation* (Cronin, 2017). Even a theory like *skopos* theory has fundamentally ethical implications – 'what we are talking about is no less than the ethos of the translator' argues its instigator Hans J. Vermeer (2012, p. 201) – and the recent development that is 'translator studies', which highlights the translator's subjectivity and positionality, is no less ethical in its intent (see Kaindl, Kolb and Schlager, 2021).

Contemporary translation studies features a rich array of scholars working in various ways at the interface of translation and philosophy, mobilizing the resources of philosophy in the interest of a deeper understanding of the translation process. Kirsten Malmkjær's (2020) *Translation and Creativity* derives its premises from Kant's aesthetics, while prolific

American theorist Douglas Robinson has drawn on a wide range of philosophical models, from Chinese philosophy (Robinson, 2015) to Deleuze and Guattari (Robinson, 2019). One of the most remarkable and ambitious projects in the philosophy of translation currently underway is that of the British scholar Clive Scott, who draws explicitly on Merleau-Ponty in order to distance himself from the hermeneutic tradition with his conception of 'translationwork' as representing the phenomenology of reading (Scott, 2012b, p. 1). Scott's credo is set out in the preface to his 2014 book *Translating Apollinaire*:

> I have in view not a (another) *theory* of translation but rather a *philosophy* of translation; that is to say, I do not want to develop methodologies based on putative translational functions or objectives; I want to imagine what translation is as a form of knowledge, as an existential undertaking, as an adventure in perception, as a mode of engaging with the world; I want to understand by what concepts translation should be animated.
>
> (Scott, 2014, p. xvii)

## 13.4  Translations of Philosophical Texts

Philosophical texts have been translated for a wide variety of purposes (see Large, 2019). Foremost is the desire to learn from a foreign philosophical culture and perhaps regenerate an indigenous one that is perceived as being in need of catching up to a more advanced (enlightened, sophisticated) tradition. Such cultural advocacy and exchange may be undertaken in a spirit of disinterested curiosity and selfless enthusiasm, but equally it may be undertaken from a desire to raid and conquer (as Nietzsche suspected – see Nietzsche, 2012, p. 67). Historically, there have been marked asymmetries in directions of travel, favouring translation out of the principal languages of Western philosophy – Greek, Latin, French, German, English – into other vernaculars, so there is an urgent need to decolonize the history of philosophy through translations in the opposite direction.

We assume nowadays that the translation of any cultural product is prompted in the first instance by a desire to share it with those who are unable to access it because they lack the language in which it is written. This was by no means always the case (nor is it now – Scott, for example, assumes a bilingual reader). In the classical period, the earliest translations from Greek into Latin were appreciated by bilingual readers, and it is clear, for example, from Cicero's remarks on his translation of Greek speeches into Latin that he coins new words in Latin in order to be appreciated for his stylistic invention by a bilingual Roman audience (Lefevere, 1992a, pp. 46–7). Bilingual publication continues to this day – notable examples (notable because of their significant impact on the receiving philosophical culture) have included G. E. M. Anscombe's German/English edition of

Wittgenstein's *Philosophical Investigations* (Wittgenstein, 1953) and Angèle Kremer-Marietti's German/French edition of Nietzsche's unpublished early philosophical notebooks (Nietzsche, 1969). Loeb Classical Library bilingual editions of Greek and Roman philosophical texts have been available for more than a century, helping monoglot and would-be bilingual students access classics of ancient thought. Nor do you need a full-blown bilingual edition, either, in order to appreciate the source language as you read a translation: often individual words or phrases from the source language will be included in parentheses, notes or glossaries to help orientate the reader and reduce their absolute reliance on the translated text. Translation can be undertaken for linguistic reasons, then – both to aid in learning the original language and out of a concomitant desire to develop and enrich the target (receptor) language through innovation.

Because of the specialist demands of philosophy translation (much philosophy is technical, most philosophy is conceptually demanding), most translators of philosophy have been philosophers themselves. In many cases, first-rank philosophers have cut their teeth on translation projects – like Anscombe translating Wittgenstein, Gayatri Chakravorty Spivak translating Derrida (Derrida, 2016) or Alberto Toscano translating Alain Badiou – and gained an invaluable philosophical apprenticeship through translating, or self-translating (see Large, 2014). Cases of top professional translators of philosophy being situated outside the academy – like Shaun Whiteside translating Nietzsche or Kate Briggs translating Barthes (Briggs, 2017) – are relatively rare. Philosophy translations are often carried out by professional academics, for teaching purposes, as a way of elucidating and interpreting the philosophy (in addition to any paratextual editorial apparatus). Unsurprisingly, as a result, philosophy translation has lagged behind translations of poetry or prose fiction in adventurousness: in general it has been conservative and risk-averse, tending to prioritize terminological precision and consistency above all else, and focused on conveying the source text meaning as accurately as possible (encouraging close translation with an emphasis on equivalence). Mass-market series like Oxford World's Classics, Penguin Classics or Hackett make translated philosophy easily affordable, but with rare exceptions these are not bestsellers and it is a niche market, so publishers are not expecting fireworks from a translator.

## 13.5 Translating Philosophical Texts

In this final section I want to consider *how* philosophical texts have been translated, and we need to begin by differentiating 'philosophical texts' because this is a broad field. Most laypeople might associate philosophy with a certain kind of rigorous conceptual language, as personified in the British celebrity philosopher C. E. M. Joad, who would generally begin responding to a question on the wartime discussion programme *The Brains Trust* with the catchphrase 'It all depends on what you mean by . . .'. But the language of philosophy encompasses the full gamut from propositional logic to technical terminology to conceptual language to Platonic dialogues to poetry. Philosophical language is where philosophy and literature intersect, and the language of philosophy is at least as varied as the language of the Bible.

This raises the question: what makes philosophy translation distinctive? What is it that is specific to philosophical texts that causes problems for translators? The short answer is that it is the literary features (metaphors, ambiguities, rhetorical structures) that cause the problems; the technical (and, above all, logical) terms are not, for the most part, what cause the problems when translating philosophy. Kant's philosophy is notorious for its technical terms like, for example, 'transcendental unity of apperception' in the *First Critique*, but the difficulty here is not a translation one because the English translator has simply calqued the German source ('die "transzendentale Einheit" der Apperzeption') and displaced the comprehension difficulty onto the reader. As a general rule, the more technical the term, the more likely it is that there will be a one-to-one correspondence in the target language. In this case, Kant was inventing a new philosophical vocabulary in German, so it is hardly surprising that his translator (the nineteen-year-old John Meiklejohn) did something similar in English (Kant, 1855). With Hegel's *Phänomenologie des Geistes* (1807), the more rebarbative first term of the title is actually the easy part to translate, and it is the ordinary-language second term that has proved the shibboleth. In the philosophical context, the choice in English translation has come down to two meanings: *Phenomenology of Mind*, used by J. B. Baillie as the title for his 1910 translation, and *Phenomenology of Spirit*, used by A. V. Miller (1977) and the two more recent translators Michael Inwood (2018) and Terry Pinkard (2018). Clearly these two meanings are very different, and the difference between them is summarized from a contemporary perspective by Paul Redding: '"Geist" can be translated as either "mind" or "spirit", but the latter, allowing a more cultural sense, as in the phrase "spirit of the age" ("Zeitgeist"), seems a more suitable rendering for the title' (Redding, 1997).

In the case of another key Hegelian term, *Aufhebung*, the translation problem again lies in its ambiguity, but that is more pronounced since even just in the philosophical context it can be translated variously as 'raising', 'relieving', 'cancellation' and 'abolition'. The ambiguity is deliberate on Hegel's part (one might say that the word is irretrievably ambiguous), and with such ambiguous language the philosophy translator faces the same problem as the poetry translator. Ideally you want a plurality of translations (of perspectives on the work), since any one translation will inevitably emphasize only particular features and downplay or even occlude others, and, indeed, generations of translators have rung the changes on Hegel's wordplay (which is what it is). One translation choice is not to translate the term at all but to use *Aufhebung* in the original German as a technical term in the target language, and this has achieved some currency – in the same way that Nietzsche's term *Übermensch* is often found untranslated these days rather than rendered as 'overman' or (now definitely beyond the pale) 'superman'. Hegel's *Aufhebung* is now generally rendered with *sublation* – in other words, as with Meiklejohn's *apperception* it is rendered with a neologism which in turn becomes a kind of shorthand for all the senses of the word that are wrapped up in the original German. The danger with such an approach, though, is that it technicizes Hegel's vocabulary where the German word is actually much more straightforward and (also) has an ordinary language meaning of 'pick something up'.

An example of neologism from my own translation practice is in the opening chapter of Nietzsche's (1998 [1888]) late text *Twilight of the Idols*, where he gives us a rhetorical question in the voice of a dentist: '"Wie viel hatte ehemals das Gewissen zu beissen? welche guten Zähne hatte es? – Und heute? woran fehlt es?" – Frage eines Zahnarztes.' You could translate the initial question literally as 'How much did the conscience have to bite on in former times?'. However, the whole aphorism is a pun on the German for 'remorse' or 'pangs of conscience', *Gewissensbisse* (literally, 'conscience-bites'). Elsewhere, Nietzsche (1996, p. 63) makes this clearer by a reference to '*morsus conscientiae*', the Latin term from which the German and the English derive (cf. James Joyce's reference to the 'Agenbite of inwit' in the first chapter of his *Ulysses*). This is hardly a very serviceable reference for the modern translator to exploit, though, so I ended up creating a neologism of my own, following the rule of thumb to compensate for translation loss wherever you can: '"How many remorsels did the conscience have to bite on in former times? what good teeth did it have? – And today? what's missing?" – a dentist's question' (Nietzsche, 1998, p. 8).

Ultimately not all that much was at stake in that passage, but the same could not be said of my final example. When Heidegger's *Beiträge zur Philosophie (Vom Ereignis)* was first published in Germany in 1989, it was acclaimed as his most important work after *Being and Time*. By this stage in his development (1936–8), Heidegger was doing a great deal of his philosophy through paying attention to language, and specifically etymology, deliberately mobilizing the hidden resonances of otherwise everyday terms like *Ereignis* (event) and (in this case) activating the normally dormant sense of *eigen-* (own) that it contains. Heidegger turns every word potentially into a pun, exploiting ambiguity in a radical way that resembles not so much Joyce's *Ulysses* as his *Finnegans Wake*. An English translation of Heidegger's text, by Parvis Emad and Kenneth Maly, appeared in 1999 as *Contributions to Philosophy: From Enowning* (Heidegger, 1999), but such a would-be Heideggerian translation of Heidegger was too much for even English-speaking Heideggerians to swallow, and a new, more conservative translation was eventually commissioned from Richard Rojcewicz and Daniela Vallega-Neu, appearing in 2012 as *Contributions to Philosophy (Of the Event)* (Heidegger, 2012). In cases like this, you want, if possible, as a translator to match ambiguity with ambiguity, pun with pun (as I tried to do with the Nietzsche), but often this is strictly impossible, and it becomes more so the greater the distance there is between the source and the target languages. In my example of 'remorsel', that pun was available in English because the English vocabulary is derived from the Latin (on which the German is basically a gloss), but such a move is just not possible if you are translating into a radically unrelated language like Xhosa or Chinese.

Both English translations of Heidegger's *Beiträge* are still in print, and we are privileged to have both from which to triangulate Heidegger's uncommonly inventive linguistic practice. Such instances are where philosophy and poetry intersect: you cannot just rule out the linguistic substrate as a 'taint' and take the view that philosophy ends at the point where poetry begins. Philosophers like Nietzsche and Heidegger make a mockery of any attempt to somehow hive off conceptual language, to set up a prophylactic *cordon sanitaire* between philosophy and literature in order to argue that conceptual language is peculiarly philosophical and hence peculiarly untranslatable. No, as both demonstrate so expertly, when characterizing philosophical language, one needs to give full force to both terms, for it is philosophy but it is also a language like any other, and it is the gift of translation to make this peculiarly apparent.

## References

Apter, E. (2013). *Against World Literature: On the Politics of Untranslatability*. London: Verso.

Baggini, J. (2018). *How the World Thinks: A Global History of Philosophy*. London: Granta.

Bassnett, S., and Lefevere, A. (1990). *Translation, History and Culture*. London: Pinter.

Benjamin, A. (1989). *Translation and the Nature of Philosophy: A New Theory of Words*. London: Routledge.

Benjamin, W. (2012). The translator's task, trans. S. Rendall. In L. Venuti, ed., *The Translation Studies Reader*. 3rd ed. London: Routledge, pp. 75–83.

Bennett, J. (1971). *Locke, Berkeley, Hume: Central Themes*. Oxford: Oxford University Press.

Boase-Beier, J. (2015). *Translating the Poetry of the Holocaust: Translation, Style and the Reader*. London: Bloomsbury.

Briggs, K. (2017). *This Little Art*. London: Fitzcarraldo.

Burnet, J. (1914). *Greek Philosophy, 1: Thales to Plato*. London: Macmillan.

Cassin, B., ed. (2014). *Dictionary of Untranslatables: A Philosophical Lexicon*, trans. S. Rendall et al. Princeton, NJ: Princeton University Press.

Catford, J. C. (1965). *A Linguistic Theory of Translation: An Essay in Applied Linguistics*. Oxford: Oxford University Press.

Clark, A. (2006). Language, embodiment, and the cognitive niche. *Trends in Cognitive Sciences*, **10**(8), 370–4.

Cronin, M. (1996). *Translating Ireland: Translation, Languages, Cultures*. Cork: Cork University Press.

Cronin, M. (2003). *Translation and Globalization*. London: Routledge.

Cronin, M. (2017). *Eco-translation: Translation and Ecology in the Age of the Anthropocene*. London: Routledge.

Davidson, D. (1973). Radical interpretation. *Dialectica*, **27**, 313–28; reprinted in (1984) *Inquiries into Truth and Interpretation*. Oxford: Clarendon Press, pp. 125–39.

Davies, P. (2018). *Witness between Languages: The Translation of Holocaust Testimonies in Context*. Rochester, NY: Camden House.

Davis, K. (2001). *Deconstruction and Translation*. Manchester: St Jerome.

de Berg, H., and Large, D. (2012). *Modern German Thought from Kant to Habermas: An Annotated German-Language Reader*. Rochester, NY: Camden House.

Derrida, J. (1985). Des Tours de Babel, trans. J. F. Graham, in J. F. Graham, ed., *Difference in Translation*. Ithaca, NY: Cornell University Press, pp. 165–207.

Derrida, J. (2016). *Of Grammatology: Fortieth Anniversary Edition*, trans. G. C. Spivak. Baltimore, MD: Johns Hopkins University Press.

Descartes, R. (1644) *Specimina Philosophiae seu Dissertatio de Methodo, ex Gallico translata, et ab auctore perlecta, variisque in locis emendata*, trans. E. de Courcelles. In *Oeuvres de Descartes*, vol. 6. Amsterdam.

Fodor, J. A. (1975). *The Language of Thought*. New York: Crowell.

Frege, G. (1879). *Begriffsschrift, eine der arithmetischen nachgebildete Formelsprache des reinen Denkens*. Halle: Louis Nebert.

Gadamer, H.-G. (1989). Lesen ist wie Übersetzen. In W. Eckel and J. J. Köllhofer, eds., *Michael Hamburger: Dichter und Übersetzer*. Frankfurt/Main: Peter Lang, pp. 117–24.

Hegel, G. W. F. (1910). *The Phenomenology of Mind*, trans. J. B. Baillie. London: Swan Sonnenschein.

Hegel, G. W. F. (1977). *Phenomenology of Spirit*, trans. A. V. Miller. Oxford: Clarendon Press.

Hegel, G. W. F. (2018a). *The Phenomenology of Spirit*, trans. M. J. Inwood. Oxford: Oxford University Press.

Hegel, G. W. F. (2018b). *The Phenomenology of Spirit*, trans. T. Pinkard. Cambridge: Cambridge University Press.

Heidegger, M. (1992). *Parmenides*, trans. A. Schuwer and R. Rojcewitz. Bloomington: Indiana University Press.

Heidegger, M. (1999). *Contributions to Philosophy: From Enowning*, trans. P. Emad and K. Maly. Bloomington: Indiana University Press.

Heidegger, M. (2012). *Contributions to Philosophy (Of the Event)*, trans. R. Rojcewicz and D. Vallega-Neu. Bloomington: Indiana University Press.

Jakobson, R. (2012). On linguistic aspects of translation. In L. Venuti, ed., *The Translation Studies Reader*. 3rd ed. London: Routledge, pp. 126–31.

Kaimio, J. (1979). *The Romans and the Greek Language*. Helsinki: Societas Scientiarum Fennica.

Kaindl, K., Kolb, W. and Schlager, D. (2021). *Literary Translator Studies*. Amsterdam: John Benjamins.

Kant, I. (1855). *Critique of Pure Reason*, trans. J. M. D. Meiklejohn. London: Henry G. Bohn.

Kelly, L. G. (1979). Rights and Duties: 'Fidus Interpres'? In *The True Interpreter: A History of Translation Theory and Practice in the West*. Oxford: Basil Blackwell, pp. 205–18.

Large, D. (2014). On the Work of Philosopher-Translators. In J. Boase-Beier, A. Fawcett and P. Wilson, eds., *Literary Translation: Redrawing the Boundaries*. Basingstoke: Palgrave Macmillan, pp. 182–203.

Large, D. (2019). The translation of philosophical texts. In P. Rawling and P. Wilson, eds., *The Routledge Handbook of Translation and Philosophy*. London: Routledge, pp. 307–23.

Lefevere, A. (1992a). *Translation / History / Culture: A Sourcebook*. London: Routledge.

Lefevere, A. (1992b). *Translation, Rewriting, and the Manipulation of Literary Fame*. London: Routledge.

Lewes, G. H. (1875). *Problems of Life and Mind. First Series: The Foundations of a Creed. 2*. Boston: Osgood.

Malmkjær, K. (2010). The nature, place and role of a philosophy of translation in translation studies. In R. Hyde Parker, K. L. Guadarrama García and A. Fawcett, eds., *Translation: Theory and Practice in Dialogue*. London: Continuum, pp. 201–18.

Malmkjær, K. (2019). On the (im)possibility of untranslatability. In D. Large, M. Akashi, W. Józwikowska and E. Rose, eds., *Untranslatability: Interdisciplinary Perspectives*. London: Routledge, pp. 41–9.

Malmkjær, K. (2020). *Translation and Creativity*. London: Routledge.

Mates, B. (1986). *The Philosophy of Leibniz: Metaphysics and Language*. New York: Oxford University Press.

Nida, E. A. (1964). *Toward a Science of Translating: With Special Reference to Principles and Procedures Involved in Bible Translating*. Leiden: Brill.

Nietzsche, F. (1969). *Das Philosophenbuch: theoretische Studien / Le livre du philosophe: études théorétiques*, ed. and trans. A. Kremer-Marietti. Paris: Aubier-Flammarion.

Nietzsche, F. (1979). *Philosophy and Truth: Selections from Nietzsche's Notebooks of the Early 1870s*, ed. and trans. D. Breazeale. Atlantic Highlands, NJ: Humanities Press International.

Nietzsche, F. (1996). *On the Genealogy of Morals*, trans. D. Smith. Oxford: Oxford University Press.

Nietzsche, F. (1998 [1888]). *Twilight of the Idols*, trans. D. Large. Oxford: Oxford University Press.

Nietzsche, F. (2012). Translations. In L. Venuti, ed., *The Translation Studies Reader*. 3rd ed. London: Routledge, pp. 67–8.

Nord, C. (1997). *Translating as a Purposeful Activity: Functionalist Approaches Explained*. Manchester: St Jerome.

Polizzotti, M. (2018). *Sympathy for the Traitor: A Translation Manifesto*. Cambridge: MIT Press.

Pym, A. (2007). Philosophy and translation. In P. Kuhiwczak and K. Littau, eds., *A Companion to Translation Studies*. Clevedon, UK: Multilingual Matters, pp. 24–44.

Quine, W. van O. (1959). Meaning and translation. In R. A. Brower, ed., *On Translation*. Cambridge, MA: Harvard University Press, pp. 148–72.

Rabassa, G. (2005). *If This Be Treason: Translation and Its Dyscontents. A Memoir*. New York: New Directions.

Redding, P. (1997). Georg Wilhelm Friedrich Hegel. In *Stanford Encyclopedia of Philosophy*, https://plato.stanford.edu/entries/hegel/.

Rée, J. (2001). The translation of philosophy. *New Literary History*, **32**(2), 223–57.

Rée, J. (2019). *Witcraft: The Invention of Philosophy in English*. London: Allen Lane.

Reynolds, M., ed. (2019). *Prismatic Translation*. Cambridge: MHRA.

Ricœur, P. (2006). *On Translation*, trans. E. Brennan. London: Routledge.

Robinson, D. (2015). *The Dao of Translation: An East–West Dialogue*. London: Routledge.

Robinson, D. (2019). *Transgender, Translation, Translingual Address*. London: Bloomsbury.

Rose, E. (2021). *Translating Trans Identity: (Re)Writing Undecidable Texts and Bodies*. London: Routledge.

Rosen, M. (2019). Word of Mouth: Philosophy in English, BBC Radio 4, 12 August, www.bbc.co.uk/programmes/m0007bd0.

Roth, P. A. (2019). Quine. In P. Rawling and P. Wilson, eds., *The Routledge Handbook of Translation and Philosophy*. London: Routledge, pp. 104–21.

Sallis, J. (2002). *On Translation*. Bloomington: Indiana University Press.

Schleiermacher, F. (2012). On the different methods of translating, trans. S. Bernofsky. In L. Venuti, ed., *The Translation Studies Reader*. 3rd ed. London: Routledge, pp. 43–63.

Schopenhauer, A. (1992). On language and words. In R. Schulte and J. Biguenet, eds., *Theories of Translation: An Anthology of Essays from Dryden to Derrida*. Chicago: University of Chicago Press, pp. 32–5.

Scott, C. (2012a). *Literary Translation and the Rediscovery of Reading*. Cambridge: Cambridge University Press.

Scott, C. (2012b). *Translating the Perception of Text: Literary Translation and Phenomenology*. Leeds: MHRA.

Scott, C. (2014). *Translating Apollinaire*. Exeter: University of Exeter Press.

Spitzer, D. M., ed. (2020). *Philosophy's Treason: Studies in Philosophy and Translation*. Wilmington, DE: Vernon Press.

Steiner, G. (1992). *After Babel: Aspects of Language and Translation*. 2nd ed. Oxford: Oxford University Press.

Venuti, L. (1998). *The Scandals of Translation: Towards an Ethics of Difference*. London: Routledge.

Venuti, L. (2018). *The Translator's Invisibility: A History of Translation*. 3rd ed. London: Routledge.

Venuti, L. (2019). *Contra Instrumentalism: A Translation Polemic*. Lincoln: University of Nebraska Press.

Vermeer, H. J. (2012). Skopos and commission in translation theory, trans. A. Chesterman. In L. Venuti, ed., *The Translation Studies Reader*. 3rd ed. London: Routledge, pp. 191–202.

Walkowitz, R. L. (2015). *Born Translated: The Contemporary Novel in an Age of World Literature*. New York: Columbia University Press.

Wheeler, G. (2013). Michel de Montaigne: The last native speaker of Latin? In *Language Teaching through the Ages*. New York: Routledge, pp. 56–58.

Wittgenstein, L. (1953). *Philosophical Investigations*, trans. G. E. M. Anscombe. Oxford: Basil Blackwell.

Wrathall, M. A. (2011). *Heidegger and Unconcealment: Truth, Language, and History*. New York: Cambridge University Press.

Young, R. J. C. (2014). Philosophy in translation. In S. Bermann and C. Porter, eds., *A Companion to Translation Studies*. Chichester: Wiley Blackwell, pp. 41–53.

# 14

# Translation, Gender and Sexuality

Brian James Baer

## 14.1 Introduction

Issues of gender and sexuality started to be addressed in translation studies in a serious and sustained way in the 1980s, during the so-called Cultural Turn, when the field began to move away from traditional linguistics-based approaches. Informed by feminist theory as well as the minority rights and independence movements of the time, and often inspired by specific translation projects, scholars in translation studies and other fields first explored translation's relationship to issues of gender and, later, sexuality. While, historically, issues of gender and sexuality have been thoroughly entangled – consider Karl Heinrich Ulrichs's (1864) construal of the male homosexual, or invert, as having a woman's soul trapped in a man's body or Otto Weininger's (1903, part 1, ch. III) contention that the greater the gender differences between a man and a woman, the more intense their sexual attraction will be – contemporary queer perspectives, especially since the advent of transgender studies, see a deep heteronormative bias in those entanglements and argue that gender identity is in no way determinant of sexual orientation and vice versa. So, while both topics will be addressed in this chapter, given their historical entanglement in Western sexology and popular culture, they will be treated in separate sections, which also reflects their different research trajectories within translation studies. At the same time, we recognize that there are deep theoretical and political connections between gender and sexuality. For example, research in both fields continues to be grounded in shared theoretical perspectives, such as a Foucauldian understanding of the discursive construction of identities and Judith Butler's (1990) non-essentialist conception of gender and sexual

identities as 'performative', asserted through the reiteration of certain signifying gestures and practices. Similarly, on a political level, progressivist
movements organized around issues of gender and sexuality in the Global
North are often characterized as liberatory or emancipatory. Another point
of intersection is in the realm of transfiction, or fictional representations of
translators and translation, in which issues of gender and sexuality are often
entangled (see Arrojo, 2005; Parker, 2005).

## 14.2  Translation and Gender

By the mid-1990s, enough scholarship had accumulated on the subject of
gender and translation to warrant two book-length treatments of the topic,
Simon (1996) and von Flotow (1997). That scholarship is activist, promoting interventionist translation strategies to address (and redress) gender
inequities in standard languages and literary canons; descriptive, documenting the historical work and working conditions of female translators;
and theoretical or meta-analytical, considering, among other things, the
'gendered metaphorics' of translation discourse. After surveying the current research within those discrete but intersecting categories, the chapter
will discuss emerging themes and future directions. I use the term feminist
in a general way to refer to any attempt to expose, resist or redress the
violence and injustice perpetuated against women-identified subjects by
patriarchal attitudes and institutions.

## 14.3  Towards a Feminist Translation Practice

A number of intersecting circumstances led to the first serious and sustained theoretical engagement with issues of gender and translation,
which arose in Canada in the 1980s among scholar-practitioners such as
Susanne de Lotbinière-Harwood and Barbara Godard. That theorizing was
shaped by contemporary currents in sociopolitical thought that focused
on the politics of language, such as: new directions in feminist thought,
specifically among French feminist writers who challenged the patriarchal
bias of standard language; the Québécois independence movement, which
sought to protect Québécois from the hegemony of English and to distinguish it from metropolitan French – which is why translations of
Shakespeare into *joual*, a distinct urban dialect of French Canada, took on
political significance at the time (see Brisset, 1996). Simultaneously, those
involved in the Black Rights movement in the United States were seeking
to reframe language use among Blacks outside the hierarchical dichotomy
of standard/substandard by renaming Black vernacular 'Ebonics' and
rethinking its relationship to the White idiom as one of translation (see
Jordan, [1972] 1989). By exposing the gender, racial and class bias reflected

in the norms and standards of most 'national' languages, these social and political movements challenged the idea that language was a neutral instrument of representation, which problematized traditional models of signification and, by extension, translation.

Informed by Lacanian psychoanalysis and Derridean deconstruction, French feminist writers, such as Hélène Cixous, Luce Irigaray and Julia Kristeva, produced profound critiques of gender in language and of gender as a language. Cixous, for example, argued that within a symbolic order centred by the Phallus, 'the female unconscious is less repressed, less radically separated from the consciousness (since the threat of castration, which creates repression, has already been carried out)' (Klages, 2012, p. 26). Because 'woman' is always already decentred in that symbolic order, she is closer to the real and 'therefore freer to move and create' (Klages, 2012, p. 27). She refers to this as an 'écriture feminine', or 'feminine/female writing', which has been critiqued as essentialist. Cixous's interest in transgressive writing practices led her to focus on authors who have 'strangered their own language' (Cixous, 1996–7, p. 8).

The theorizing on the relationship between gender and translation that these critiques of language inspired often emerged out of specific translation projects. For example, the writings of the Canadian translation scholars were closely tied to their translations of French feminist writers mentioned already, and of feminist-informed literary works by Québécois writers such as Nicole Brossard, France Théoret, Madeleine Gagnon and Louky Bersianik. The translation of these texts, which were characterized by dense word play and complex, non-standard syntax, pushed the Canadian translators to experiment with language in order to do to the English language what the French feminists were doing to French, while also challenging the separation of source and target languages through code-switching and multilingual writing (see Lotbinière-Harwood, 1991). Although born in practice, theorization quickly moved beyond the confines of any one project, as evidenced in the steady stream of theoretical writings outlining a feminist translation practice (see Godard, 1990; von Flotow, 1991; Massardier-Kenney, 1997; Dépêche, 2002; Fisher, 2010).

The other conceptual basis for a feminist translation practice was the notion that translation was not simply a form of literary work available to women when original writing was largely unthinkable but had long been conceived within the Western cultural imaginary in gendered terms, as laid out by Lori Chamberlain (1988) in the essay 'The Metaphorics of Translation'. If translation is construed as female, hence imitative and 're-productive', while 'original' writing is construed as male, hence 'productive', then a counter-patriarchal translation practice would reject notions of servility and fidelity in favour of a more expansive and creative understanding of translator agency. Chamberlain's argument is widely cited and continues to be interrogated, challenged, refined and extended (see Arrojo,

1994, 2005; Godoyal, 2013; Littau, 2000; Shread, 2008; Wallace, 2002). The notions of 'hijacking' (von Flotow, 1991) and 'womanhandling' (Godard, 1990) texts in translation were introduced at this time to challenge these social and textual hierarchies, construing female translatorial interventions as a form of political activism and resistance to patriarchy. Notable in this regard is Lotbinière-Harwood's (1991) engagement with the phrase *les belles infidèles*, which refers to the notion that translations, like women, can be either beautiful or faithful but not both, rewriting it as a feminist translation credo: *re-belle et infidèle* [rebellious and unfaithful]; her use of the hyphen does not eliminate the possibility that these translations could be beautiful, thereby undercutting the exclusive binaries of the original utterance. Also relevant here are debates in the 1980s and 1990s over creating more inclusive, gender-neutral translations of the Judeo-Christian Bible (see Gifford, 1985). The energy and sophistication of these feminist writings on translations led Vidal (1998, p. 201) to declare in the late 1990s that 'neither "woman" nor "translation" constitute now (sic) spaces of subordination, but, much to the contrary, alternative sources of textual/sexual power' (Santaemilia, 2011, p. 16).

The US-based scholar-practitioners Carol Maier and Suzanne Jill Levine worked mostly with Latin American male authors, 'translating machismo', as von Flotow (1997, p. 25) put it, which shaped the direction of their theorizing on the subject of translation and gender. Levine (1991, p. 1) saw her creative solutions as a 'subversive' expression of female translatorial agency, a way to 'make the translator's presence (traditionally invisible) visible and comprehensible'. Maier, on the other hand, acknowledged the challenge of rendering misogynist language and images while ultimately deciding to address her concerns in paratexts rather than in the translation itself (Maier, 1984, 1985), putting forward her conception of herself as a 'woman-informed' translator and, later, as 'an intervenient being' (Maier, 2007. While intervening in the translation to erase or downplay patriarchal or misogynistic aspects of a source text might have the salutary effect of removing such discourse from circulation, it might also have the more ambivalent effect of whitewashing an author's work or reputation and obscuring the reality of gender bias. Rosemary Arrojo (1999) offered a more pointed critique of such translatorial interventions by showing that womanhandling is not always a feminist challenge to patriarchal authority when viewed through the lens of post-colonial asymmetries. Arrojo analyses Hélène Cixous's translation of Brazilian novelist Clarice Lispector. Cixous's approach to the text, which included omitting and altering sections, demonstrates, Arrojo argues, the privilege and arrogance of scholars and translators from the Global North in their treatment of women writers from the Global South.

Another interesting project that raises questions related to a feminist translation practice is the anthology of translated abolitionist texts by francophone women writers in the late eighteenth and early nineteenth centuries: *Translating Slavery: Gender and Race in French Women's Writing, 1783–1823* (Kadish and Massardier-Kenney, 1994). The volume is distinctly hybrid, containing both original texts and English translations, accompanied by commentary by the translators, all of whom are women. The volume, as Kadish states in the introduction, attempts to treat 'the complex interrelationships that exist among [translation, gender, and race]' (Kadish and Massardier-Kenney, 1994, p. 1), recognizing that the women authors translated in the volume, who were white and privileged, speak for and about women of colour. And so, while these women were politically engaged, they also displayed the class-based and racial-based prejudices of their time. These thorny issues highlight the layering of forms of privilege and oppression, which has been theorized as intersectionality (see Crenshaw, 1989). This is noted by the only translator of colour in the volume, Sharon Bell, who discusses her experience translating the voice of de Staël's Mirza, who is Black; her discomfort led her 'to soften the [rhetorical] excesses' in Mirza in order to 'valorize her speech' (Kadish and Massardier-Kenney, 1994, p. 175).

## 14.4  Translation and Transnational Feminism

The issues raised by the volume *Translating Slavery* and by Arrojo's critique of Cixous's translations of Lispector serve as a kind of harbinger for the activist writing on gender and translation that would appear more than a decade later, writing that would be informed by new currents in post-colonial scholarship. Walter Mignolo (2000), Dipesh Chakrabarty (2000) and Santos (2018) challenged the universalizing claims of northern theory and the attendant marginalization of epistemologies of the Global South. That post-colonial critique as it relates to gender theory led to the emergence of transnational feminist studies, which is the organizing framework for the volume *Scattered Hegemonies: Postmodernity and Transnational Feminist Practices* (Grewal and Kaplan, 1994). While focusing on 'the operations of transnational culture' (Grewal and Kaplan, 1994, p. 7) and calling for 'the inclusion of hitherto marginalized voices' (p. 5), however, the volume treats issues of translation only peripherally.

If transnational feminist studies initially ignored translation, scholarship on gender and translation produced within translation studies was slow to expand its focus beyond Western Europe and Anglo-America to confront the post-colonial asymmetries shaping the circulation of gender knowledge. This is evident in the special issue of *Monti* edited by José Santaemilia and Louise von Flotow (2011). The 'small yet growing geography' (Santaemilia, 2011, p. 16) represented in the issue includes Russia, Spain, Galicia, Catalonia and Turkey, while in the collected volume *Translating Women* (von Flotow, 2011), only three of the fifteen chapters treat texts produced outside the Global North. So, progress in widening the geographic coverage of studies related to women was slow until the full integration of translation into transnational feminist studies occurred.

While Gayatri Spivak framed the problem of translating woman authors across post-colonial asymmetries as early as 1993, in her seminal essay 'The Politics of Translation' (Spivak, 1993), it would take over a decade before translation would be thoroughly incorporated into transnational feminist studies and for translation studies to expand the geographic scope of its gender-related research. One sees a marked increase in the geographic range of research on gender and translation in Larkosh (2011b): most of the seven chapters treat post-colonial contexts and one addresses the topic of race. We see it too in Yu (2015), which analyses the translation and reception of two key feminist texts in contemporary China, and in the collected volumes by Alvarez et al. (2014) and Castro and Ergun (2017). Outside translation studies, a profound engagement with translation in the context of transnational feminist research is Nagar (2014, p. 15), which proposes 'different forms of feminist engagement to grapple with questions of location, power, translation, and representation'.

In these works, activist interventions are targeted at resisting the geo-politics of knowledge that marginalizes gender writings from the Global South, or treats it as ethnographic data, while universalizing writings from the Global North. For many of these scholars, collaboration is promoted as an effective and more egalitarian means of producing and circulating gender knowledge (Nagar, 2014), and translation itself is posited as a form of 'collaborative authorship' (Uman and Belén, 2007). Levine (1991) coins the term 'closelaboration', although she largely ignores the post-colonial asymmetries shaping those relationships. Reimóndez (2017), on the other hand, advocates for more collaborative translation projects not only between hegemonic and non-hegemonic communities but also among non-hegemonic communities, and for more translator training courses in non-hegemonic languages to make that collaboration possible. That investment of time, effort and resources by scholars in the Global North to learn the languages of the Global South would result in greater polyphony in the field and would disrupt the unidirectional flow of knowl-edge from the Global North to the Global South, allowing ideas to travel 'in a more multi-directional fashion' (Reimóndez, 2017, p. 51).

## 14.5  Descriptive Studies of Translation and Gender

Descriptive studies of gender and translation work to recuperate histories of female literary and scholarly activity that have been obscured by the traditional optics in the field of literary studies, which privilege 'original' secular writing. Today, we have a rich and expanding body of research on woman translators in a variety of contexts. That research, however, continues to be dominated by case studies focusing on individual women translators or individual texts authored or translated by a woman, and the vast majority concern literary translation. A notable exception is Alison E. Martin's (2011) study of women translators of botanical texts in early-nineteenth-century Britain. Studies of gender in interpreting are also fairly rare (e.g., Orest Weber, Pascal Singy and Patrice Geux (2005) and Osman and Angelelli (2007)). Moreover, before the recent emergence of feminist translation studies, the overwhelming number of these studies were geographically confined to the Global North.

A significant body of research is dedicated to women translators in premodern Europe. While often treating individual women translators, these works typically take a broader sociological perspective on the question of gender and translation. In other words, they tend to inscribe these individual translators within their specific socio-historical moment and often treat them as a social group. Historical studies of this kind, such as Hannay (1985), were among the first scholarly works to treat the issue of gender and translation. Since then, a steady stream of historical studies have appeared focusing on women and translation, such as Goldberg (1997), Kronitiris (1997), Rosslyn (2000), Hayes (2009), White (2011), Uman (2012) and Goodrich (2014). For women in premodern Europe, translation offered one of the best opportunities for entry into the literary field, although translation at this time was not defined in opposition to 'original' writing, a distinction that would emerge in European cultures later and become deeply embedded in the cultural consciousness during the Romantic movement. In the premodern world, the true *authores* were the ancients, leaving contemporary writers the task of circulating, interpreting, imitating and translating them. The fact that Romantic notions of origins and originality continue to structure the nationalist framework for studying contemporary literature, alongside the Modernist privileging of secular writing and masculine pathos (see Rabaté, 2016), has left the creative work of premodern women translators, who translated mostly religious texts, at the margins of literary history. These historical studies, therefore, are important not only in recovering the contributions of these women translators but also in relativizing our notions of what constitutes literary value. Another noteworthy example of historical recovery is Delisle (2002), which highlights the translatorial work of women such as Anne Dacier and Eleanor Marx. Dacier was a seventh-century Frenchwoman who earned acclaim for her translations from Homer's *Iliad* and *Odyssey*, while Eleanor Marx was Karl Marx's daughter who translated Flaubert's *Madame Bovary* into English. Emily Apter (2013) dedicates a chapter to her.

These historical works tend to include thick descriptions of the social milieu in which these premodern women undertook their translation projects and so have a sociological dimension that is often lacking in case studies of contemporary women translators. For example, Michaela

Wolf (2005, pp. 19–21) offers an overview of the female translator's daily life in eighteenth-century Germany. True sociology-based studies of gender and translation, however, remain relatively rare, even following the so-called Sociological Turn in translation studies. Some examples include Cornelia Lauber's (1996) study of French translators; Lauber compiles sociological profiles of the translators with questions related to their gender, among other factors. Wolf's (2006) survey of women translators working in German-speaking countries for women's journals or book series is an example of a sociological study that focuses more specifically on issues of gender. Wolf (2002) examines the translation practice of female translators through the lens of their social networks. Another work that treats issues of gender and translation from a broader, empirical perspective is Brian James Baer's (2016) study of book reviews of translated works published in *The New York Times* in 1900, 1950 and 2000, which revealed striking gender disparities across all three corpora in terms of the source text authors, the translators and the reviewers.

Reception studies, too, offer a perspective on the issue of gender and translation that transcends the individual translator, while also recognizing her contribution. Exemplary in this regard is Sebnem Susam-Sarajeva (2006), which provides a comparative analysis of the reception of Hélène Cixous's work in the Anglo-American context and of Roland Barthes's work in the context of post-war Turkey. The work includes thick descriptions of the target contexts that shaped the reception of these authors' works. Qualitative analysis of the reception of these works, culled largely from reviews, is complemented by quantitative data on the translations – what works were translated and retranslated, and when?

## 14.6  Future Directions

As is evident from the overview provided so far, the volume of research treating issues of gender and translation has increased rapidly since the 1980s. However, that increase has not been accompanied by a broadening to include more sociological studies of women translators as a social group, more studies that involve the translation of non-literary works, and more studies that involve languages of the Global South. We have witnessed the most change, perhaps, in the last category mentioned, thanks to the emergence of transnational feminist translation studies. We might also anticipate greater reflection on the changes being wrought to traditional notions of production and reproduction with the continued advances in the sphere of new reproductive technologies (see Orloff, 2005) and in sex reassignment surgery, which may fundamentally alter the gendered metaphorics of translation, not to mention our understanding and experience of gender itself.

### 14.6.1 Sexuality and Translation

It is surprising that issues of sexuality and translation were not addressed in translation studies scholarship at the same time as issues of gender were first being raised, given the out-and-proud queer sexuality of James Holmes, one of the purported 'founders' of translation studies. True, some of the Canadian feminist scholar-practitioners, as well as Gloria Anzaldúa (2012 [1987]), connected gender and sexuality. With the former, this reflected second wave feminist writings on lesbianism as an escape from patriarchy, while with Anzaldúa, this was part of a broader project of queering her Chicana identity by rejecting 'that absolute despot duality'. Nevertheless, queer sexuality did not become a sustained object of study among translation scholars until after the millennium. Moreover, the study of translation and sexuality did not arise from practice, as much of the early theorizing on gender had. Nor did early research on translation and sexuality focus on historical case studies, as the sexuality of translators and authors of earlier times could not always be determined.

Much of the study of sexuality is divided between minoritarian perspectives, which promote an 'identity politics' approach, and queer perspectives, which are deeply critical of identity politics and the very concept of fixed and discrete sexual identities. The former perspectives I will refer to as 'gay' and the latter as 'queer', although the term 'queer' is often appropriated by minoritarian scholars as a synonym for 'gay', or as a non-normative sexual identity among others in the abbreviation LGBTIQ (lesbian, gay, bisexual, transgender, intersex and queer).

I will use the term 'homosexual' to refer to medical and legal conceptualizations, and the term 'gay' to index a modern, minoritarian identity and/or lifestyle. 'Same-sex desire' and 'queer' will be used to designate not only non-normative sexualities in premodern contexts and contexts outside the Global North, which it would be anachronistic or colonizing to label 'gay', but also sexual subjects within the Global North who reject or resist the label 'gay'. That being said, much interesting work is being done in Global Sexuality Studies, in particular, in the context of Latin America, demonstrating that even when terms from the Global North are 'borrowed', they are often re-signified and repurposed (see, for example, Ochoa's (2008) concept of *loca-lización*).

### 14.6.2 Laying the Foundations

Keith Harvey in many respects laid the foundations for the study of translation and sexuality. Harvey began his professional career as a sociolinguist, studying 'camp' talk, or the idiom that developed within US-based 'gay' communities. This research led to the publication of Harvey and Shalom (1997) and Harvey (2002). Harvey's major contribution to translation studies came when he investigated the treatment of camp talk in translation, focusing on the translation of US 'gay' literature into French. This would become Harvey's (2003a) magnum opus, and it is important in at least two ways. First, it contributed to our understanding of the global circulation of queer knowledge, showing that 'camp' talk was consistently tamped down or omitted in French translations, not because there was no French version of it but because it was perceived as minoritarian, which did not correspond to the concept of a universal French identity. Bruno Perreau (2016) supports Harvey's findings, although he does not mention Harvey's work. Second, by connecting translatorial decisions to larger cultural dispositions, rather than subjecting them to some kind of prescriptive evaluation as right or wrong, Harvey offered a compelling model for the integration of translation into a range of fields across the humanities seeking to transnationalize their perspective. As Harvey (2003a, p. 4) put it succinctly in the introduction, '[t]ranslations are not mere tokens of the commerce between cultural spaces. They have inscribed within their very texture *the problematic of the crossing*' (italics in the original). Other seminal works by Harvey include his 2003 study of the bindings of gay fictional texts translated from American English into French in the late 1970s, construing the bindings as registering 'the reservations of the receiving culture faced with American difference while also opening up small, contestatory spaces for the productive intrusion of the foreign' (Harveyb, 2003, p. 49).

### 14.6.3  An Emerging Body of Research

In some ways, Harvey was ahead of his time as it took almost ten years before the topic of sexuality and gender would produce a significant body of research. That said, scholars have made up for lost time with a steady and widening stream of publications on the topic appearing since 2010, including a special issue of the journal *In Other Words*, edited by B. J. Epstein (2010), dedicated to issues of translation and sexuality. Christopher Larkosh's (2011a) collected volume includes three chapters dealing with the translation of sexuality across languages and cultures. A special issue of the journal *Comparative Literature Studies*, edited by William J. Spurlin and dedicated to the gender and queer politics of translation, appeared in 2014 (Spurlin, 2014). Then came a volume edited by Heike Bauer (2015); a special issue of *Transgender Studies Quarterly*, titled *Translating Transgender*, edited by David Gramling and Aniruddha Dutta (2016); as well as a monograph by Héctor Domínquez Ruvalcaba (2016); a collected volume edited by B. J. Epstein and Robert Gillett (2017) and another edited by Brian James Baer and Klaus Kaindl (2018); a monograph by Douglas Robinson (2019); and Brian James Baer's 2020 monograph. (Santaemilia's 2005 volume, despite the inclusion of 'sex' in the title, overwhelmingly treats issues of gender.)

As with the study of gender and translation, most of the individual articles and chapters treat specific translators of texts, contributing to the broader project of historical recovery of work that has been doubly hidden from history – as queer-authored translations or translations of queer texts – and not only from standard national histories. Gay scholars, too, often ignore the contributions of translators. For example, Gregory Woods (1998) pays little attention to translations in his magisterial history of gay literature, dismissing Scott Moncrieff's translation of Proust in a footnote as a 'camp classic'. In this way scholars of gay literature display what Jasbir Puar (2007) has described as 'homonationalism', or a complicity with the heteronormative logic of the modern nation-state, with its privileging of 'original' writing. Also notable in the scholarship on translation and sexuality is the prominence of studies dealing with non-literary texts. This is no doubt a legacy of the enormous role played by 'scientific' (sexological) and legal texts in the modern discursive construction of homosexuality. Analysing the translation and non-translation of key sexological texts (see Bauer, 2015) as well as works of queer theory (see Baldo, 2018; Perreau, 2016) represents a significant subfield of research in the realm of translation and sexuality.

The three monographs mentioned above (those by Ruvalcaba (2016), Robinson (2019) and Baer (2020)), the first on the subject since Harvey (2003a), are important insofar as they represent a move beyond the individual case study to make larger arguments about various cultural and historical entanglements of translation and sexuality and to challenge them. Moreover, all are deeply influenced by post-colonial critiques of the modern heteronormative and monolingual nation-state. Ruvalcaba (2016, p. 1) examines Latin America through the multiple lenses of post-coloniality, translation and queer sexuality as a way to both expose the discursive violence of colonization while also provincializing the concept of queer, locating it 'in a specific geography and culture'. Ruvalcaba (2016, p. 167) construes coloniality as 'a form of reduction of the multiplicity to a binary heterosexual gender', which he studies through actual translations (understood in multiple senses, from interlingual to intralingual, including from oral to written) as well as through general processes of cultural interaction across colonial asymmetries, processes that are closer to Bhabha's concept of 'cultural translation' than to translation proper. Robinson's (2019) monograph also critiques the monolingual heterosexual nation-state through the concept of transgender. Beginning from Naoki Sakai's (1997) contention that the addressee of all translations in the modern world order, founded on individual monolingual nation-states, is monolingual, Robinson (2019) uses non-binary forms of address to imagine a new world order. He demonstrates this in regard to specific translation projects, or performances, exploring 'what happens to the imagination, to creativity, to critical thinking, to love and other affect, when you go beyond mandated boundaries' (Robinson, 2019, p. 200). Baer (2020) begins by tracing possible points of intersection between queer theory, with its unrelenting critique of identity and the binaries through which it is imagined, and translation studies, demonstrating, on the one hand, how queer theory might reinvigorate traditional models of translation and, on the other, what close attention to issues of translation can contribute to Global Sexuality Studies as it attempts to reconceptualize subaltern agency and to develop new models of exchange that avoid replicating 'the process of empire' (Said, 1989). Those chapters are followed by more targeted investigations of the role of translation in 'gay' anthologies, the translation of lyric poetry as a form of 'reparative reading' (as defined in Sedgwick, 2003) and the framing of queer life writing in translation, to explore the potential of translation to expose and address post-colonial asymmetries.

As with gender and translation, the work of scholars outside translation studies, namely historians, has contributed to our understanding of the historical relationship between women and translation, and the work of scholars in classical studies and in sexuality studies has contributed in significant ways to our understanding of the historical relationship between sexuality and translation. Works by scholars in classical studies have focused on the nineteen-century translations of Ancient Greek texts, in particular the works of Plato, which served as foundation texts for the modern gay rights movement. Notable in this regard are Linda Dowling (1994), Daniel Orrells (2011) and Gideon Nisbet (2013). In all three works, the authors pay close attention to issues of translation, modelling a philologically scrupulous incorporation of translation into historical research.

These works document how the rise of scientific historicism in the early part of the nineteenth century led to the first unabridged and non-bowdlerized translations of ancient texts, which had a profound influence on early gay rights pioneers in England, such as Edward Carpenter, John Addington Symonds and Oscar Wilde. Indeed, Symonds recounts in moving detail how reading Edward Carey's translation of Plato's *Symposium* and *Phaedrus* as a schoolboy led him to the epiphany that his same-sex desire need not be shameful. Wilde, it is believed, named his fictional hero Dorian Gray after Karl Müller's frank study of homosexuality among the ancient Dorians, *Die Dorier* (Müller, 1824). Wilde, who studied classics at Oxford, is likely to have encountered the English translation in the library of his tutor, Reverend Mahaffy. Queer men of that generation and of that social class were not only deeply influenced by the new translations of Ancient Greek texts, they themselves went on to translate both ancient and contemporary works dealing with matters of sex and sexuality. Carpenter, for example, translated sexological works from German and included many of his own translations in his 1902 anthology of friendship (Carpenter, 1902b). He also shamed other scholars for censoring their translations of sexually explicit works, calling such translations 'pious frauds'.

Issues of translation have also assumed a central place among historians of ancient Greece and Rome and of premodern European cultures. For example, much of the controversy surrounding John Boswell's (1994) historical study had to do with the translation of the disputed Latin word *desponsationis*, which Boswell renders as 'betrothal' but which previous translators had rendered as 'treaty'. Similarly, queer historian Carolyn Dinshaw (1999, pp. 11, 9) opens her seminal work with a discussion of the 'indeterminate' nature of many translation issues in premodern English texts, indeterminate owing not only to the asymmetry of languages but also to the fact that the meanings of the terms involved were often 'notoriously shifting'.

In the field of Global Sexuality Studies, scholars dealing with cultures outside the Global North have grappled with traditional models describing the circulation of queer knowledge, which tend to cast non-Western receivers or consumers as deluded, passive victims of cultural hegemony, hence replicating the power asymmetries they are critically analysing. Jon Binnie (2004, p. 68) offers a succinct reformulation of the agency of subaltern queers as 'deploying and re-working symbols and images associated with the global gay to help fight their own struggles for self-determination, rights and resistance to violence and the production of spaces and territories'. While Binnie does not acknowledge translation's role in those processes, other scholars in the field who are seeking 'new understandings of imbrication and transference' (Boellstorff, 2005, p. 5) have addressed translation and translation-related phenomena. Tom Boellstorff, for example, develops the concept of dubbing, which, he argues, 'provides a rubric for rethinking globalization without relying on biogenetic (and, arguably, heteronormative) metaphors like hybridity, creolization, and diaspora' (Boellstorff, 2005, p. 5). Dubbing is not, however, just a metaphor for Boellstorff; his interest in the phenomenon arose from a controversy that erupted in Indonesia in the late 1990s when dubbing was banned by the government 'on the grounds that if Westerners appeared to speak Indonesian in the mass media, Indonesians would no longer be able to tell where their culture ends and authentic Indonesian culture begins' (Boellstorff, 2005, p. 5). Also relevant here is the collected volume edited by Mesquita, Wiedlack and Lasthofer (2012), which traces the global circulation of queer theory and queer forms of activism in a way that complicates simple models of unidirectional flows from the metropole to the periphery. While translation is not discussed as part of the conceptual framing of the volume, several of the chapters address issues of interlingual translation.

### 14.6.4   Towards a Queer Translation Practice

There is far less writing dedicated to the elaboration or promotion of a queer translation practice than there is of a feminist translation practice.

One of the few examples is Aarón Lacayo's 2014 article which puts forward an 'ethics of irreducibility' that 'allows for thinking a new ontology of translation' (Lacayo, 2014, p. 226). The relative lack of such writings may be owing to the fact that queer translators took advantage of the translator's invisibility to circulate texts that were if not queer then open to queer reading (see Larkosh, 2007; Baer, 2011). Nevertheless, the central role played by translation in the gay rights movement has left various statements regarding translation that, when gathered together, may suggest the outlines of what might be called a queer translation practice.

For example, Carpenter's condemnation of the traditional censorship of (homo)sexual content, mentioned in Section 14.6.3, which was carried out through either excision, non-translation or heterosexualization (changing the gender of pronouns, for example), could be considered one aspect of an activist translation practice, characterized by a commitment to translate, as Carpenter (1902a, p. 22) put it, '*sans peur* and *sans reproche*' (without fear and without reproach). This would also include the 'correction' of older translations that had been subjected to censorship on moral or other grounds. We see a recent example of this in William Butcher's 1995 English retranslation of Jules Verne's *Around the World in Eighty Days*, which was based on extensive study of Verne's life and oeuvre and of the various versions of the novel preserved in archives. In the introduction to the translation, Butcher offers his interpretation of the work as an exploration of unconscious desire, expressed in, among other things, 'the brazen homosexual overtures [that] occur frequently between all three male characters' (Butcher, 1995, p. xxix). Butcher's 'thorough, explicative, scholarly, paratextual approaches', argues Keiran O'Driscoll (2009, p. 3), not only lend credence to his interpretation but also 'help to lend new depths of merit and professionalism to translation as an activity'. In his analysis of homoerotic passages in Melville's *Moby Dick*, Marc Démont (2018) proposes three distinct modes of translation, which he glosses as misrecognizing, minoritizing and queer; the last mode attempts to preserve the erotic ambiguity of the text. Other aspects of a queer translation practice can be found in introductions to transnational anthologies of same-sex literature, but especially in anthologies that deal with traditions outside the Global North, such as *Same-Sex Love in India* (Vanita and Kidwai, 2000). The editors of that volume note in the introduction that 'the quality of translation is crucial to this anthology' and that earlier 'bowdlerized translations have seriously biased scholars' understanding of several texts' (Vanita and Kidwai, 2000, p. xix). In order to address those concerns, they pay scrupulous attention to the translations: 'Translations from other languages have been executed by eminent scholars with whom we have worked closely, going over the translations word by word, trying to keep each translation as close to the letter and spirit of the original as possible and providing glosses, wherever needed, to contextualize particular words' (Vanita and Kidwai, 2000, p. xix). In addition to bowdlerization, we see scholarly critiques of the opposing phenomenon, the domestication of texts in translation to reflect contemporary 'gay' culture. Gregory Woods (1998, p. 9) for example, criticizes the translations of ancient Greek works in Stephen Coote's (1987) anthology of homosexual verse as overly domesticating, making the volume, in Woods's estimation, a work of 'skeptical' scholarship. Finally, like feminist translators, queer translation scholars have shown a distinct interest in multilingual writing that explores sexual and gender from outside the ontology of the modern nation state (see Larkosh 2011c, Spurlin 2016).

## 14.7 Future Directions

As with studies of translation and gender, research on sexuality and translation will, I hope, continue to develop transnational perspectives and treat contexts outside the Global North, tracing flows in both directions. In other words, it will pay attention not only to the flow of Western theory or classic texts of 'gay' literature from the Global North to the Global South but also to the appropriation of texts and concepts from the Global South through translation, and exploring translation within geographic regions, developing more complex models to better capture the unpredictability and messiness of the global circulation of sexual knowledge in translation. Future research projects along those lines might include transnational studies of key queer texts and authors, along the lines of Foster (2013) and Batchelor and Harding (2017). Writings on transgender will also continue to push queer theory into new directions and has already produced a body of work that challenges traditional models of gender, sexuality and translation in fundamental ways.

## References

Alvarez, S. E., de Lima Costa, C., Feliu, V., Hester, R., Klahn, N., and Thayer, M., eds. (2014). *Translocalities/Translocalidades: Feminist Politics of Translation in the Latin/a Américas*. Durham, NC: Duke University Press.

Anzaldúa, G. (2012 [1987]). *Borderlands, La Frontera: The New Mestiza*. 4th ed. San Francisco: Aunt Lute Books.

Apter, E. (2013). *Against World Literature: On the Politics of Untranslatability*. London: Verso.

Arrojo, R. (1994). Fidelity and the gendered translation. *TTR*, **7**(2), 147–64.

Arrojo, R. (1999). Interpretation as possessive love: Hélène Cixous, Clarice Lispector and the ambivalence of fidelity. In S. Bassnett and H. Trivedi, eds., *Post-Colonial Translation: Theory and Practice*. London: Routledge, pp. 141–61.

Arrojo, R. (2005). The gendering of fiction in translation: Translators, authors, and women/texts in Scliar and Calvino. In J. Santaemilia, ed., *Gender, Sex and Translation: The Manipulation of Identities*, pp. 81–95. Manchester: St Jerome.

Baer, B. J. (2011). Translating queer texts in Soviet Russia: A case study in productive censorship. *Translation Studies*, **4**(1), 21–40.

Baer, B. J. (2016). Translation criticism in newspaper reviews: The rise of readability. In M. Woods, ed., *Authorizing Translation*. IATIS Yearbook. London: Routledge, pp. 12–31.

Baer, B. J. (2020). *Queer Theory and Translation Studies: Language, Politics, Desire*. New York: Routledge.

Baer, B., and Kaindl, K., eds. (2018). *Queering Translation, Translating the Queer*. New York/London: Routledge.

Baldo, M. (2018). Queer translation as performative and affective un-doing: Translating Butler's 'undoing gender' in translation. In B. Baer and K. Kaindl, eds., *Queering Translation, Translating the Queer*. New York/London: Routledge, pp. 188–205.

Batchelor, K., and Harding, S., eds. (2017). *Translating Frantz Fanon across Continents and Languages*. London/New York: Routledge.

Bauer, H. (ed.) 2015. *Sexology and Translation. Cultural and Scientific Encounters across the Modern World*. Philadelphia, Rome, Tokyo: Temple University Press.

Binnie, J. (2004). *The Globalization of Sexuality*. London: Sage.

Boellstorff, T. (2005). *The Gay Archipelago: Sexuality and Nation in Indonesia*. Princeton, NJ: Princeton University Press.

Boswell, J. (1994). *Same-Sex Unions in Pre-modern Europe*. Oxford/New York: Villard Books.

Brisset, A. (1996). *A Sociocritique of Translation: Theatre and Alterity in Quebec, 1968–1988*. Toronto: University of Toronto Press.

Butcher, W. (1995). Introduction. In J. Verne, *Around the World in Eighty Days*. Oxford and New York: Oxford University Press, pp. vii–xxxi.

Butler, J. (1990). *Gender Trouble: Feminism and the Subversion of the Body*. New York: Routledge.

Carpenter, E. (1902a). *Love's Coming of Age*. Chicago, IL: Stockham.

Carpenter, E., ed. (1902b). *Ioläus: An Anthology of Friendship*. London: Swan Sonnenschein.

Castro, O., and Ergun, E. (2017). *Feminist Translation Studies: Local and Transnational Perspectives*. London: Routledge.

Chakrabarty, D. (2000). *Provincializing Europe: Postcolonial Thought and Historical Difference*. Princeton, NJ: Princeton University Press.

Chamberlain, L. (1988). Gender and the metaphorics of translation. *Signs*, **13**, 454–72.

Cixous, H. (1996–7). 'Guardian of language: An interview with Hélène Cixous (March 1996)', by Kathleen O'Grady. *Women's education des femmes*, **12**(4), 6–10.

Crenshaw, K. (1989) "Demarginalizing the Intersection of Race and Sex: A Black Feminist Critique of Antidiscrimination Doctrine, Feminist Theory and Antiracist Politics." *University of Chicago Legal Forum* 1989(1): 139–167.

Coote, S. 1983. *Penguin Book of Homosexual Verse*. Harmondsworth: Penguin.

Delisle, J. (2002). *Portraits de traductrices*. Ottawa: Presse de l'Université d'Ottawa.

Démont, M. (2018). On three modes of translating queer texts. In B. Baer and K. Kaindl, eds., *Queering Translation, Translating the Queer*. London/ New York: Routledge, pp. 157–71.

Dépêche, M.-F. (2002). La traduction féministe, hier et aujourd'hui. *Labrys: Études feminists*, **1**(2), 1–18.

Dinshaw, C. (1999). *Getting Medieval. Sexualities and Communities, Pre- and Postmodern*. Durham, NC/London: Duke University Press.

Dowling, L. (1994). *Hellenism and Homosexuality in Victorian Oxford*. Ithaca, NY/ London: Cornell University Press.

Epstein, B. J., ed. (2010). Special issue: Translating Queers/Queering Translation. *In Other Words*, **36** (Winter), 1–2.

Epstein, B. J., and Gillett, R., eds. (2017). *Queer in Translation*. London/ New York: Routledge.

Fisher, L. (2010). Theory and practice of feminist translation in the 21st century. In R. Hyde Parker, K. Guadarrama Garcia and A. Fawcett, eds., *Translation: Theory and Practice in Dialogue*. London: Continuum, pp. 67–84.

Foster, J. B. (2013). *Transnational Tolstoy: Between the West and the World*. New York/London: Bloomsbury.

Foucault, M. (1978). *The History of Sexuality. Volume I. An Introduction*, trans. R. Hurley. New York: Pantheon Books.

Gifford, C. de Swarte. (1985). American women and the Bible: The nature of the hermeneutical issue. In A. Y. Collins, ed., *Feminist Perspectives on Biblical Scholarship*. Chico, CA: Scholars Press, pp. 11–33.

Godard, B. (1990). Theorizing feminist discourse / translation. In S. Bassnett and A. Lefevere, eds., *Translation, History and Culture*. London: Pinter, pp. 87–96.

Godoyal, P. (2013). Metaphors, women and translation: From *les belles infidèles* to la frontera. *Gender and Language*, **7**(1), 98–116.

Goldberg, J. (1997). *Desiring Women Writing: English Renaissance Examples*. Stanford, CA: Stanford University Press.

Goodrich, J. (2014). *Faithful Translators: Authorship, Gender and Religion in Early Modern England*. Evanston, IL: Northwestern University Press.

Gramling, D. and Dutta, A. (eds.). 2016. Introduction to special issue *Translating Transgender*. *Transgender Studies Quarterly* 3(3–4): 333–356.

Grewal, I., and Kaplan, C., eds. (1994). *Scattered Hegemonies: Postmodernity and Transnational Feminist Practices*. Minneapolis: University of Minnesota Press.

Hannay, M. P., ed. (1985). *Silent but for the Word: Tudor Women as Patrons, Translators, and Writers of Religious Works*. Kent, OH: Kent State University Press.

Harvey, K. (2002). Camp talk and citationality: A queer take on 'authentic' and 'represented' utterance. *Journal of Pragmatics*, 34(9), 1145–65.

Harvey, K. (2003a). *Intercultural Movements: 'American Gay' in French Translation*. Manchester: St Jerome.

Harvey, K. (2003b). 'Events' and 'horizons': Reading ideology in the 'bindings' of translations. In M. Caldaza-Pérez, ed., *Apropos of Ideology*. London: Routledge, pp. 43–69.

Harvey, K., and Shalom, C., eds. (1997). *Language and Desire: Encoding Sex, Romance and Intimacy*. London: Routledge.

Hayes, J. C. (2009). *Translation, Subjectivity and Culture in France and England, 1600–1800*. Stanford, CA: Stanford University Press.

Jordan, J. ([1972]1989). White English/Black English: The politics of translation. In *Moving Towards Home: Political Essays*. London: Virago, pp. 29–40.

Kadish, D. Y., and Massardier-Kenney, F., eds. (1994). *Translating Slavery: Gender and Race in French Women's Writing, 1783–1823*. Kent, OH: Kent State University Press.

Klages, M. (2012). L'écriture feminine. In *Key Terms in Literary Theory*. New York/London: Bloomsbury, pp. 26–7.

Kronitiris, T. (1997). *Oppositional Voices: Women as Writers and Translators in the English Renaissance*. New York: Routledge.

Lacayo, A. (2014). A queer and embodied translation: Ethics of difference and erotics of difference. *Comparative Literature Studies*, **51**(2), 215–30.

Larkosh, C. (2007). The translator's closet: Editing identities in Argentine literary culture. *TTR*, **21**(2), 63–88.

Larkosh, C., ed. (2011a). *Re-engendering Translation: Transcultural Practice, Gender/Sexuality and the Politics of Alterity*. Manchester: St Jerome.

Larkosh, C. (2011b). Introduction: Re-engendering translation. In C. Larkosh, ed., *Re-engendering Translation: Transcultural Practice, Gender/Sexuality and the Politics of Alterity*. Manchester: St Jerome, pp. 1–10.

Larkosh, C. (2011c). Two in translation: The multilingual cartographies of Nestor Perlongher and Caio Fernando Abreu. In C. Larkosh, ed., *Re-engendering Translation: Transcultural Practice, Gender/Sexuality and the Politics of Alterity*. Manchester: St Jerome, pp. 72–90.

Lauber, C. (1996). *Selbsporträts: Zum soziologischen Profil von Literaturübersetzern aus dem Französischen*. Tubingen: Narr.

Levine, S. J. (1991). *The Subversive Scribe: Translating Latin American Fiction*. Saint Paul, MN: Graywolf Press.

Littau, K. (2000). Pandora's Tongues. *TTR*, **13**(1), 21–35.

Lotbinière-Harwood, S. de. (1991). *Re-belle et infidèle: la traduction comme pratique de réécriture au féminin*. Monréal/Québec: Les Éditions du Remue-Ménage.

Maier, C. (1984). Translation as performance: Three notes. *Translation Review*, **15**, 5–8.

Maier, C. (1985). A woman in translation, reflecting. *Translation Review*, **17**, 4–8.

Maier, C. (1996). Gender in/and literary translation (with F. Massardier-Kenney). In M. Gaddis Rose, ed., *Translation Horizons. Beyond the Boundaries of 'Translation Spectrum' (Translation Perspectives IX)*. Binghamton, NY: Center for Research in Translation, State University of New York Binghamton, pp. 243–68.

Martin, A. E. (2011). The voice of nature: British women translating botany in the early nineteenth century. In L. von Flotow, ed., *Translating Women*. Ottawa: University of Ottawa Press, pp. 11–35.

Massardier-Kenney, F. (1997). Towards a redefinition of feminist translation practice. *The Translator*, **3**(1), pp. 55–69.

Mesquita, S., Wiedlack, M. K., and Lasthofer, K., eds. (2012). *Import-Export-Transport: Queer Theory, Queer Critique and Activism in Motion*. Vienna: Zaglossus.

Mignolo, W. (2000). *Local Histories/Global Designs: Coloniality, Subaltern Knowledges, and Border Thinking*. Princeton, NJ: Princeton University Press.

Müller, O. K. (1824). *Die Dorier*. Breslau: Fr. Schneidewin.

Nagar, R. (2014). *Muddying the Waters: Coauthoring Feminisms across Scholarship and Activism*. Urbana: University of Illinois Press.

Nisbet, G. (2013). *Greek Epigram in Reception: J. A. Symonds, Oscar Wilde, and the Invention of Desire, 1805–1929*. Oxford: Oxford University Press.

Ochoa, M. (2008). Perverse citizenship: Divas, marginality, and participation in 'loca-lization'. *Women's Studies Quarterly*, **36**(3–4), 146–69.

O'Driscoll, K. (2009). Around the world in eighty gays: Retranslating Jules Verne from a queer perspective. CETRA Research Seminar in Translation Studies 2008, pp. 18–29.

Orloff, U. (2005). Who wrote this text and who cares? Translation, intentional 'parenthood' and new reproductive technologies. In J. Santaemilia, ed., *Gender, Sex and Translation: The Manipulation of Identities*. Manchester: St Jerome, pp. 149–60.

Orrells, D. (2011). *Classical Culture and Modern Masculinity*. Oxford: Oxford University Press.

Osman, G., and Angelelli, C. (2007). 'A crime in another language?' An analysis of the interpreter's role in the Yousry case. *Translation and Interpreting Studies*, **2**(1), 47–82.

Parker, E. (2005). Lost in translation: Gender and the figure of the translator in contemporary queer fiction. In D. Burnham and E. Giaccherini, eds., *The Poetics of Transubstantiation: From Theology to Metaphor*. Aldershot: Ashgate, pp. 118–25.

Perreau, B. (2016). *Queer Theory: The French Response*. Stanford, CA: Stanford University Press.

Puar, J. K. (2007). *Terrorist Assemblages: Homonationalism in Queer Times*. Durham, NC: Duke University Press.

Rabaté, J.-M. (2016). *The Pathos of Difference: Affects of the Moderns*. New York: Bloomsbury.

Reimóndez, M. (2017). We need to talk … to each other: On polyphony, postcolonial feminism and translation. In O. Castro and E. Ergun, eds., *Feminist Translation Studies: Local and Transnational Perspectives*. London: Routledge, pp. 42–55.

Robinson, D. 2019. *Transgender, Translation, Translingual Address*. New York and London: Bloomsbury.

Rosslyn, W. (2000). *Feats of Agreeable Usefulness: Translations by Russian Women, 1763–1825*. Fichtenwalde: Verlag F. K. Göpfert.

Ruvalcaba, H. D. 2016. *Translating the Queer. Body Politics and Transnational Conversations*. London: Zed Books.

Said, E. (1989). Representing the colonized: Anthropology's interlocutors. *Critical Inquiry*, **15**, 205–25.

Sakai, N. (1997). *Translation and Subjectivity: On 'Japan' and Cultural Nationalism*. Minneapolis: University of Minnesota Press.

Santaemilia, J., ed. (2005). *Gender, Sex and Translation: The Manipulation of Identities*. Manchester: St Jerome.

Santaemilia, J., and von Flotow, L., eds. (2011). *Woman and Translation: Geographies, Voices and Identities / Mujer y Traducción: Geografías, Voces e Identidades*. *MonTI*, **3**.

Santaemilia Ruiz, J. (2011). Introduction to woman and translation: Geographies, voices, identities. In J. Santaemilia and L. von Flotow, eds., *Woman and Translation: Geographies, Voices and Identities*. *MonTI*, **3**, 9–28.

Santos, B. de Sousa. (2018). *The End of the Cognitive Empire: The Coming of Age of Epistemologies of the South*. Durham, NC: Duke University Press.

Sedgwick, E. (2003). Paranoid reading and reparative reading, or, you're so paranoid, you probably think this essay is about you. In E. Sedgwick, *Touching Feeling: Affect, Pedagogy, Performativity*. Durham, NC/London: Duke University Press, pp. 123–51.

Shread, C. (2008). Metamorphosis or metramorphosis? Towards a feminist ethics of difference in translation. *TTR*, **20**(2), 213–42.

Simon, S. (1996). *Gender in Translation: Cultural Identity and the Politics of Transmission*. London: Routledge.

Spivak, G. (1993). The politics of translation. In G. Spivak, *Outside in the Teaching Machine*. London/New York: Routledge.

Spurlin, W. J., ed. (2014). Special issue of *Comparative Literature Studies*, 51(2) on the gender and queer politics of translation.

Spurlin, William. 2016. Contested Borders: Cultural Translation and Queer Politics in Contemporary Francophone Writing from the Maghreb. *Research in African Literatures* **47**(2): 104–120.

Susam-Sarajeva, S. (2006). *Theories on the Move: Translation's Role in the Travels of Literary Theories*. Amsterdam: Rodopi.

Ulrichs, K. H. (1864). *Forschungen über das Räthsel der mannmännlichen Liebe*. Leipzig: Heinrich Matthes.

Uman, D. (2012). *Women as Translators in Early Modern England*. Wilmington: University of Delaware Press.

Uman, D., and Bistué, B. (2007). Translation as collaborative authorship: Margaret Tyler's *The Mirror of Princely Deedes and Knighthood*. *Comparative Literature Studies*, **44**(3), 298–323.

Vanita, R., and Kidwai, S., eds. (2000). *Same-Sex Love in India*. New York: Palgrave.

Vidal, M. C. Áfrika (1998). *El futuro de la traducción: Últimas teorías, nuevas aplicaciones*. Valencia: Institució Alfons el Magnànim.

Von Flotow, L. (1991). Feminist translation. *TTR*, 4(2), 69–85.

Von Flotow, L. (1997). *Translation and Gender: Translating in the 'Era of Feminism'*. Manchester: St Jerome.

Von Flotow, L., ed. (2011). *Translating Women*. Ottawa: University of Ottawa Press.

Wallace, M. (2002). Writing the wrongs of literature: The figure of the feminist and post-colonialist translator. *Journal of the Midwest Modern Language Association*, **35**(2), 65–74.

Weber, O., Singy, P., and Geux, P. (2005). Gender and interpreting in the medical sphere: What is at stake? In J. Santaemilia, ed., *Gender, Sex and Translation: The Manipulation of Identities*. Manchester: St Jerome, pp. 137–47.

Weininger, O. (1903). *Geschlecht und Charakter: Eine prinzipielle Untersuchung*. Vienna: Wilhelm Braumüller Universitäts-Verlagsbuchhandlung Gesellschaft M.B.H.

White, M., ed. (2011). *English Women, Religion, and Textual Production, 1500–1625*. Farnham: Ashgate.

Wolf, M. (2002). Translation activity between culture, society and the individual: Towards a sociology of translation. In K. Harvey, ed., *CTIS Occasional Papers* 2, Manchester: UMIST, pp. 33–43.

Wolf, M. (2005). The creation of a 'Room of One's Own': Feminist translators as mediators between cultures and genders. In J. Santaemilia, ed., *Gender, Sex and Translation: The Manipulation of Identities*. Manchester: St Jerome, pp. 15–25.

Wolf, M. (2006). The female state of the art: Women in the 'translation field'. In A. Pym, M. Shlesinger and Z. Jettmarová, eds., *Sociocultural Aspects of Translating and Interpreting*. Amsterdam: John Benjamins, pp. 129–41.

Woods, G. (1998). *The History of Gay Literature: The Male Tradition*. New York: Columbia University Press.

Yu, Z. (2015). *Translating Feminism in China: Gender, Sexuality and Censorship*. London: Routledge.

# 15

# Translation and Education

Sara Laviosa

## 15.1 Introduction

In our increasingly globalized world, most communities are increasingly multilingual and most people are multilingual to some degree. Recognizing this, translation studies scholars and teachers are entering into a constructive dialogue with educational linguists and educators on common societal and pedagogical concerns that arise within a general multilingual paradigm. There is a need to understand 'the complexities of contemporary individual experiences in multi-layered communities', and deal with issues such as 'the language entitlement and education of all learners as social actors and global citizens in a complex world' (Conteh and Meier, 2014, p. 1). These important aspects of late-modern societies are engendering a shift in what is considered the norm in language use, language pedagogy, the discreteness of language varieties, and our under-standings of translation (Meylaerts, 2013), and the new paradigm is engendering a re-evaluation of reflexivity in language and intercultural education together with a rethinking of the traditional transmissionist model of learning in favour of a self-engaging, dialogic and holistic model that privileges the mutual exchange and co-construction of knowledge between teacher and students and among students themselves (cf. Byrd Clark and Dervin, 2014). Multilingual education entails a reappraisal of didactic translation (Cook, 2010; Tsagari and Floros, 2013; Laviosa, 2014a, 2014b) and of the role of the L1 (first language) in second language acquisition (SLA) studies (cf. Ellis and Shintani, 2014; Ortega, 2014). It also fosters translanguaging as a pedagogical model in bilingual education and in a variety of educational contexts where the school language is different from the learners' own languages (García and Li Wei, 2014; Li Wei, 2018). The dialogue between applied translation studies and educational linguistics is gradually extending the traditional boundaries of translation education and giving rise to an interdisciplinary area of enquiry that encompasses the training of would-be professional translators and translation teaching in other multilingual learning contexts. Against this background, this chapter examines the principles upheld by the 'multilingual turn' (Conteh and Meier, 2014; May, 2014) in educational linguistics and their influence on language education policies (cf. Council of Europe, 2001, 2018; MLA, 2007; ACARA, 2014a, 2014b). It explains how these tenets underpin novel teaching approaches and methods in translator education and discusses the relevance of translation in other multilingual learning contexts, before pointing to future directions in translation and translanguaging pedagogy.

## 15.2   The Multilingual Paradigm

At the turn of the century, educational linguistics established itself as a new disciplinary site for addressing critical language-related issues in education. With a focus on language learning and teaching, the field aims to forge close relationships among research, theory, policy and practice to produce 'knowledge that can give agency to educators, students, and families, and thus create streams of resistance and action that can affect change in arenas where education and language intersect' (Bigelow and Ensser-Kananen, 2015, p. 2). Educational linguists advocate multilingualism and equal linguistic human rights in instructional settings around the world. Premised on the tenet that learning is a collaborative, dialogic process between learners and teachers, the pedagogies put forward assert that learners bring diverse linguistic, cultural and other knowledge to their learning process, and teachers, students and peers are all partners in learning (Meier and Conteh, 2014, p. 293). The process of learning is considered cognitive and social as well as historical, cultural, emotional, kinaesthetic, interpersonal and moral. Language is conceived as a semiotic ecosystem within 'a complex network of complex systems that are interwoven amongst themselves as well as with all aspects of physical, social, and symbolic systems' (van Lier, 2004, p. 53). Language learning is assumed to require 'meaningful participation in human events', which involves 'perception, action and joint construction of meaning' (van Lier, 2004, pp. 52–3). In the classroom context, this language as action perspective means that learners engage in meaningful tasks as varied as projects, presentations and investigations. These activities engage students' interest and encourage language development through perception, interaction, planning, research, discussion and the co-construction of academic output.

The learner is seen as a person who engages in activities where they take control of the learning process and co-operate with the other members of the team. The teacher creates a learning environment that contextualizes language in a wide variety of interrelated meaning-making systems such as gestures, intonation, and social and cultural knowledge. In this collaborative learning environment, the teacher's role is to provide 'assistance, but only just enough and just in time (in the form of pedagogical scaffolding), taking the learner's developing skills and interests as the true driving force of the curriculum' (van Lier, 2004, pp. 223–4). The aim of such ecologically oriented pedagogy is to form students as multilingual individuals, 'sensitive to linguistic, cultural and, above all, semiotic diversity, and willing to engage with difference, that is, to grapple with differences in social, cultural, political and religious worldviews' (Kramsch, 2014, p. 305). It is a holistic, critical and self-reflexive pedagogy that integrates bilingual practices such as translation (Laviosa 2014a, 2018) and translanguaging (García and Li Wei, 2014; Li Wei, 2018) to raise cross-lingual and cross-cultural awareness and sensitivity, foster social values and develop learning strategies. As Kramsch (2009, p. 204) contends, all forms of translation (intralingual, interlingual and intersemiotic) have an important role to play in the advanced language classroom because translation is an effective means of exploring the relationship between different sign systems and the associations they evoke in the minds of hearers and readers.

The multilingual orientation enshrined in the ecological model of language learning and teaching is supported by SLA studies. From a psycholinguistic perspective, SLA research has shown that linguistic differences between the L1 and the L2 (second language) do not necessarily result in negative transfer, and that similarity can facilitate learning by speeding up acquisition (Ellis and Shintani, 2014, p. 245). From a social-psychological perspective informed by socio-cultural theory, as elaborated by Vygotsky (1978), the L1 is considered a semiotic tool for mediating thought through private/inner speech, and an affective cognitive tool for scaffolding L2 production (Ellis and Shintani, 2014, pp. 223, 242). From an intercultural perspective, the intercultural communicative competence (ICC) model presupposes that the language learner inhabits an intercultural space where they use the L1 and the L2 as mediating tools in order to construct and co-construct new meanings (Byram, 1997, 2008). From this stance, learning a second language means putting the individual's intracultural dynamic spaces into a new perspective 'through direct or mediated encounters with different social structures, cultural patterns, categories, conceptualizations, and conventions' (Witte, 2014, p. 245). Furthermore, '[t]his process opens up a new dimension of *intercultural* construction and blending of spaces, located on a continuum between the conceptualizations, values, and norms of discourses of the two (or more) cultures involved' (Witte, 2014, pp. 245–6, original emphasis). It follows that the learners' goal is not to achieve native-speaker mastery of the languages being learnt but rather to use both the L1 and the L2 as mediating tools to construct new meanings. As Byram, Porto and Yulita (2020, p. 47) explain, '[l]earners need an intercultural competence which enables them to interact with people of other languages and language groups, not a competence which implies that they identify with native speakers in such groups'.

As regards language policies, the Council of Europe endorses and promotes the multilingual vision of educational linguists inasmuch as it pursues the goal of forming plurilingual and intercultural individuals. Plurilingual competence is intended here as the capacity of an individual to use flexibly their single, interrelated, uneven and developing plurilinguistic repertoire by combining it with their general competences in order to accomplish a host of tasks involving more than one language. These tasks include code-switching, receptive bilingualism, calling upon a plurilinguistic repertoire to make sense of a text, recognizing words from a common international store in a new guise, mediating between individuals with no common language, bringing the whole of one's linguistic equipment into play and experimenting with alternative forms of expression.

The *Common European Framework of Reference for Languages* (CEFR) states:

> The learner does not simply acquire two distinct, unrelated ways of acting and communicating. The language learner becomes plurilingual and develops interculturality. The linguistic and cultural competences in respect of each language are modified by knowledge of the other and contribute to intercultural awareness, skills and know-how. They enable the individual to develop an enriched, more complex personality and an enhanced capacity for further language learning and greater openness to new cultural experiences. Learners are also enabled to mediate, through interpretation and translation, between speakers of the two languages concerned who cannot communicate directly.
>
> (Council of Europe, 2001, p. 43)

The concept of mediation in particular reappraises the use of the L1 in the language classroom and is elaborated in two documents. The first, quoted above, is the CEFR, where mediation, which involves providing 'for a third party a (re)formulation of a source text to which this third party does not have direct access', is recognized as occupying 'an important place in the normal linguistic functioning of our societies' (Council of Europe, 2001, p. 14). The second document is the CEFR *Companion Volume with New Descriptors* (Council of Europe, 2018), which contains a revised and more complex concept of mediation:

> In mediation, the user/learner acts as a social agent who creates bridges and helps to construct or convey meaning, sometimes within the same language, sometimes from one language to another (cross-linguistic mediation). The focus is on the role of language in processes like creating the

space and conditions for communicating and/or learning, collaborating to construct new meaning, encouraging others to construct or understand new meaning, and passing on new information in an appropriate form. The context can be social, pedagogic, cultural, linguistic or professional.
(Council of Europe, 2018, p. 103)

Mediation may happen within the same language (note-taking during a lecture or expressing a personal response to creative texts) or between languages (cross-linguistic mediation), that is, relaying specific information, explaining data, processing text in speech and writing or translating a written text in speech and writing (Council of Europe, 2018, pp. 106–16). Therefore, mediation involves different forms of translation and translanguaging, the latter being broadly defined as 'an action undertaken by plurilingual persons, where more than one language may be involved' (Council of Europe, 2018, p. 28). Further, the *Companion Volume* aims to contribute to the quality of inclusive education for all as well as the promotion of plurilingualism and pluriculturalism. To that end, it underscores the importance of mediation as a communicative language activity that fosters – alongside reception, production and interaction – plurilingual and pluricultural competence. It also identifies three types of mediation that are often combined:

- Mediating a text, which 'involves passing on to another person the content of a text to which they do not have access'.
- Mediating concepts, which 'refers to the process of facilitating access to knowledge and concepts for others'.
- Mediating communication, the aim of which is 'to facilitate understanding and to shape successful communication between users/learners who may have individual, sociocultural, sociolinguistic or intellectual differences in standpoint'. (Council of Europe, 2018, p. 104)

In accord with the principles informing the language education policies pursued by the Council of Europe are the recommendations made in the report issued in 2007 by the Ad Hoc Committee on Foreign Languages of the Modern Language Association of North America (MLA, 2007). In this programmatic document, interpretation and translation are integrated in the language curriculum: 'In the course of acquiring functional language abilities, students are taught critical language awareness, interpretation and translation, historical political consciousness, social sensibility, and aesthetic perception' (MLA, 2007, p. 4). The report also supports the teaching of translation as a skill in its own right, in the section on Continuing Priorities: 'Develop programs in translation and interpretation. There is a great unmet demand for translators and interpreters, and translation is an ideal context for developing translingual and transcultural abilities as an organizing principle of the language curriculum' (MLA, 2007, p. 9). Moreover, '[t]he idea of translingual and transcultural competence, in contrast [to seeking to replicate the competence of an educated native speaker], places value on the ability to operate between languages' and entails the capacity to reflect on the world and on ourselves through the lens of another language and culture (MLA, 2007, pp. 3–4).

Consonant with the principles upheld by the Council of Europe and the MLA, the new Australian Curriculum for languages (issued in 2014 by the Australian Curriculum, Assessment and Reporting Authority (ACARA)) adopts an intercultural orientation, and includes translation and interpreting as forms of intercultural mediation involving the analysis and understanding of language and culture as resources. At every level along the continuum from Foundation to Year 10, the content descriptions of the curriculum foreground the role of intercultural mediation in two ways: both as a reflection on the role of culture when relaying meaning from one language to another, and when creating texts in more than one language for diverse audiences (ACARA, 2014a, 2014b). As we have seen, educational linguistic principles and language education policies in the Western world converge in their appraisal of the role of the L1 in language learning and teaching together with the recognition that fostering plurilingualism and interculturality is of vital importance in our multilingual and culturally diverse late-modern societies. These recent developments have been taken up by translation studies scholars and integrated in their current pedagogic research and practice, to which I now turn.

## 15.3  Approaches and Methods in Translator Education

The present analysis of current pedagogies in translator education is premised on the general principle that the choices translators make are always informed, explicitly or implicitly, by a model or paradigm of translation, and so are the teaching approaches used to form would-be translators in undergraduate and graduate degree programmes. Translation models can be divided into two broad categories: instrumental and hermeneutic. The instrumental model represents translation as 'the reproduction or transfer of an invariant that is contained in or caused by the source text, whether its form, its meaning or its effect'. It assumes that 'translation can and should reproduce a stable form and meaning inherent in the source text without hindrance or without the interposition of any difference worth remarking'. It follows that the translator's task is to employ effective strategies aimed at maintaining formal, semantic or functional correspondences across the source and the target text. And in so doing, they remain invisible because the translation is considered to be 'effectively the source text' (Venuti, 2017, p. 6).

The metaphorical representation of translation as transfer purported by the instrumental model entails the inevitable loss of meaning when there are systemic or cultural asymmetries across the source and the target language. This assumption is clearly expressed by Isabella Vaj, the Italian translator of Khaled Hosseini's novels. In *Il cacciatore di storie*, the companion volume to *The Kite Runner* (translated into Italian as *Il cacciatore di aquiloni*), Vaj (2009, p. 37) explains the importance of the verb *run* in its double sense of 'run' and 'escape', and reflects on her own renderings of this verb throughout the novel:

> Sappiamo che nel traghettare un testo da una lingua e da una cultura a un'altra qualcosa va spesso smarrito sul fondo della barca: nell'usare due verbi italiani per tradurre un unico verbo inglese ['correre' e 'scappare'] si distrugge un *leitmotif* chiaramente importante per lo scrittore ma capita che talvolta qualcosa venga acquisito: il titolo *Il cacciatore di aquiloni* sembra più evocativo del termine tecnico *The Kite Runner*. Forse.

> (We know that in ferrying a text from one language and from one culture to another something often gets lost at the bottom of the boat: when two Italian verbs ['correre' and 'scappare'] are used to translate one English verb, a leitmotif which is clearly important to the author is destroyed, but sometimes something is gained too. The title *Il cacciatore di aquiloni* seems to be more evocative than the technical term *The Kite Runner*. Maybe.)

Premised on instrumentalist assumptions is also the following comment made by Mona Baker in her textbook *In Other Words: A Coursebook on Translation*:

> [A]s hard as one might try, it is impossible to reproduce networks of lexical cohesion in a target text which are identical to those of the source text. . . . Every time this happens, it introduces a subtle (or major) shift away from the lexical chains and associations of the source text. Significant shifts do occur, even in non-literary texts.          (Baker, 2018, p. 218)

Whereas the instrumental model purports the idea of translation as transfer and the inevitable loss of what is untranslatable, the hermeneutic model represents translation as

> an interpretive act that varies the form, meaning, and effect of the source text according to the intelligibilities and interests of the translating culture. The variation is inevitable, driven in the first place by the structural differences between languages and by the differences in values, beliefs, and representations between cultures. . . . The process involves, on the one hand, a loss of intricate relations between source-language features and source-culture contexts and, on the other hand, a gain of comparable relations between translating-language features and translating-language contexts.          (Venuti, 2017, p. 8)

An example of how the hermeneutic model may inform translator choices is *Pereira Declares* (1995), Patrick Creagh's translation of Antonio Tabucchi's novel *Sostiene Pereira* (1994), which is set in Portugal under the Salazar regime in the 1930s. In his translation, Creagh deliberately renders a number of expressions more colloquial in English than in standard spoken Italian: *taceva* is translated as *gagged*; *quattro uomini dall'aria sinistra* as *four shady-looking characters*; *stare con gli occhi aperti* as *keep your eyes peeled*; *un personaggio del regime* as *bigwig*; and *senza pigiama* as *in his birthday-suit* (Venuti, 2004, p. 485). Venuti contends that these shifts in register have the literary effect of associating Antonio Tabucchi's resistance novel with the English genre of political thrillers such as Graham Greene's *The Confidential Agent* (Greene, 1939, in Venuti, 2004, p. 486), which is set during the Spanish Civil War and portrays a more cautious liberalism compared with Tabucchi's portrayal of left-wing opposition to fascism. Venuti argues that the linguistic resemblances between Creagh's translation and Greene's novel at once highlight the ideological differences between the two authors and inscribe an English-language cultural history in the Italian novel (Venuti, 2004, p. 486).

By and large, the instrumental and hermeneutic paradigms underpin the pedagogies adopted in translator education, which are examined here using the framework elaborated by Jack Richards and Theodore Rodgers (2014) to describe a teaching method. Their model comprises three dimensions: approach, design and procedure. Approach is a set of principles informing the method. Design links approach with teaching procedures and is concerned with a) the method's general and specific objectives, b) the syllabus model, c) the types of learning activity advocated by the method, d) the role of learners, e) the role of teachers and f) the role of instructional material. Procedure describes how approach and design can be realized in actual classroom practices.

A typical translation pedagogy employed in translation studies degree programmes in Europe is illustrated by Maria González-Davies (2017). The teaching method she uses in the first, second and fourth years of the Degree in Translation and Interpreting as well as the one-year Master's Degree in Specialised Translation housed at the Universitat De Vic–Universitat Central De Catalunya is underpinned by the tenets of Vygotsky's (1978) socio-cultural theory of learning. Socio-cultural theory posits a dynamic interrelationship between intellectual and social development, two domains linked by language, which mediates social interaction and thought. Hence, the teaching–learning process is conceived as a social exchange in which shared meanings are built up through joint activity. This view emphasizes the constructive role of both learner and teacher in the collaborative classroom. The theories of translation informing González-Davies's method are the communicative approach and modern functionalism. Translation is viewed as a 'communicative process which takes place within a social context' (Hatim and Mason, 1990, p. 3) and seeks to relay the source text's function as well as preserve its effect on the target language readership. Functionalist theories underscore the role that the purpose of the translation assigned by the commissioner plays in the translator's decision-making process (Nord, 1997).

Within the broad target-oriented perspective advocated by this theoretical orientation, translator trainees are encouraged to develop the ability to make informed choices based on a specific translation brief, rather than complying with an abstract concept of equivalence based on a priori criteria such as linguistic accuracy and fluency. The linguistics-oriented and functionalist approach adopted by González-Davies is consonant with the instrumental model of translation since it presupposes the conceptualization of translation as transfer. The linguistic and pragmatic features that are carried across from the source to the target text are selected by the translator on the basis of a clear understanding of the brief, from which they can infer the requirements of the target situation so as to fulfil them as effectively as possible. Premised on these theoretical tenets, the design of the social constructivist, communicative and functionalist method devised by González-Davies involves undertaking a variety of graded activities, tasks and group projects based on narrative, descriptive and persuasive texts.

Activities are brief, concrete exercises that help students practise specific points. Tasks are chains of activities with the same overall aim. Projects are multicompetence assignments 'that enable students to engage in pedagogical and professional activities and tasks while working together on an authentic end product' (González-Davies, 2017, p. 73). The goal of this pedagogy is to educate competent, reflective, self-confident, self-reliant and responsible professionals who are capable of working effectively both individually and collaboratively with the other members of the team. These objectives are in line with three of the five areas of competence put forward in the *European Master's in Translation Competence Framework 2017*, namely language and culture (transcultural and sociolinguistic awareness and communicative skills); translation (strategic, methodological and thematic competence); personal and interpersonal (time planning and management, teamwork, responsible use of social media, self-evaluation and collaborative learning). The other two areas of competence described in the framework are: technology (tools and applications); and service provision (implementation of translation and language services in a professional context) (Toudic and Krause, 2017, pp. 6–11).

As regards the roles of teachers and learners, students take an active, participatory role as learners and peer-evaluators. The teacher assumes the multifarious role of: a) project co-ordinator; b) native speaker informant; c) guide in providing feedback on complex problems that are beyond the students' capacities. The role of instructional material is to hone practical skills as well as encourage theoretical reflection on problems of non-equivalence at different levels of linguistic analysis and effective translation strategies to deal with them. So, procedure entails activities and group discussions grounded on a set of readings assigned at key stages of the syllabus. In sum, González-Davies's method exemplifies the functionalist, social constructivist and linguistics-oriented translation pedagogy that is widely applied in non-literary translator education in the Western world.

Instead, literary translation degree programmes tend to favour the hermeneutic model. An eminent example is offered by the pedagogy elaborated by Maria Tymoczko (2007) for the teaching of literary translation in the Master of Arts in Translation and Interpreting Studies at the University of Massachusetts, Amherst. Tymoczko's method embraces a holistic approach to translating culture, which is underpinned by an enlarged notion of translation. Translation is viewed as a form of three modes of cultural exchange, namely representation, transmission (or transfer) and transculturation. As a form of representation, translation can create an image that resembles or reproduces an idea, viewpoint, value, fact or argument. As a form of transmission, translation typically relays, to various extents, the content, language, function or form of the source text. Transculturation is the exchange of cultural characteristics from one cultural group to another.

From this perspective, Tymoczko puts forward an enlarged notion of meaning that goes beyond conceptualizations focusing on semantics, and 'includes meaning that the translator as reader brings to the process of translation, including any contextual, material, or functional meaning presupposed' (Tymoczko, 2007, pp. 283–4). Moreover, meanings emerge when the translator becomes the writer of the translated text (Tymoczko, 2007, p. 285), hence translators can be creators rather than merely carriers of meaning. In order that students become aware of their role as meaning makers, Tymoczko proposes to engage them in the translation of a short text into whatever language they wish, using whatever strategy they consider best. The task may be undertaken in class or it may be assigned as homework to be prepared for the next class, where the translations are shared with the rest of the group. Some background information about the language and culture of the source text may be given beforehand. Details about the rhyme scheme or the use of tropes may be provided in the case of a poem. After translating the text, the students make notes about their decision-making procedure, prompted by open questions that encourage them to reflect on the elements they attempted to capture in their translation and those they privileged when there were conflicts, pinpointing where and why they made specific choices. In the final part of the teaching session, students compare and discuss their renderings.

Tymoczko illustrates her pedagogy by examining a multilingual sample of students' translations of a very short poem in medieval Irish, probably dating from the ninth century. The poem was taken from Gerard Murphy's *Early Irish Lyrics* (Murphy, 1956, in Tymoczko, 2007, p. 266). The following text reproduces Tymoczko's (2007, p. 267) own gloss translation, which gives the lexical meanings of the individual words in the Irish syntactical order.

> the bird little
> has loosed whistle
> from point of beak
> pure-yellow
> it throws cry
> over Loch Laig
> blackbird from branch
> piled-yellow

Students received information about the linguistic, cultural and literary background of the poem. The five translations examined by Tymoczko were carried out in three languages, namely English, Spanish and Dholuo (a Nilo-Saharan language spoken by the Luo people in western Kenya, northern Uganda and southern Sudan). On the basis of Tymoczko's extra-textual commentary on the practice of bird augury in early Irish culture, some renderings identified the themes of prophecy, warning cries and the return of the season of war. In another version, the bird was associated with a religious representation, without specifying the type of signal it was sending. The translation into Dholuo relocated the poem to Kenya and the blackbird was replaced by the woodpecker, which is believed, there, to have the ability to foretell ominous events. Thanks to the knowledge of the Old Irish syllabic metre and rhyme scheme provided by Tymoczko's commentary, another translation privileged the sounds and metre of the poem, disregarding almost completely the semantic meaning. To produce a phonetic translation, the translator chose monosyllabic English words whose sounds correspond with those of the Irish words (Tymoczko, 2007, pp. 270–4).

The teaching method detailed above, which draws on the North American workshop approach (see Gentzler, 2001, pp. 5–36), is deemed most appropriate for raising awareness about the nature of meaning, which resides in text, context and intertexts, and 'is far more complex than the semantic meaning privileged in translation pedagogy' (Tymoczko, 2007, p. 275). It also shows the variability of meaning and how it is determined, constructed and created during the process of translation (Tymoczko, 2007, p. 276). Other suggested activities are the translation of the same piece of writing for different audiences, different registers or genres, followed by a group discussion about the practical implications of such a brief together with a reflection on cross-linguistic and cross-cultural problems and solutions. Tymoczko (2010) contends that, with this holistic pedagogic approach, translation theory is learnt subliminally, and students develop an experiential understanding of theoretical principles, not just a cognitive one.

## 15.4   Translation in Other Learning Contexts

Beyond the boundaries of translation studies, as they were drawn by James S. Holmes (1972/1988) in his outline of the discipline, pedagogic translation is now appraised in language degree programmes from four major perspectives in educational philosophy (Cook, 2010, pp. 109–12). From a technological educational perspective, in today's increasingly multilingual and multicultural societies, translation is a much needed skill for several reasons: personal (e.g., mixed marriages), educational (e.g., to pass a language exam), social (e.g., with immigrant communities) and professional (e.g., international communication). From a social reformist perspective, translation can promote liberal, humanist and democratic values because it facilitates language and cultural encounters together with an understanding and awareness of difference. From a humanistic educational perspective, translation is looked upon favourably by students as a form of bilingual instruction. Finally, from an academic perspective, instruction in translation involves transmitting knowledge and understanding of academic disciplines such as linguistics, contrastive linguistics and translation studies. In line with these general considerations, research undertaken in the field of TESOL has demonstrated the effectiveness of contrastive analysis and translation in learning vocabulary and grammar vis-à-vis other form-focused exercises (Vaezi and Mirzaei, 2007; Källkvist, 2008; Laufer and Girsai, 2008). Moreover, classroom-based survey studies of students' opinions have revealed that translation is valued because it helps uncover the differences and similarities among languages (Zhang and Pang, 2014), it poses an intellectual challenge, it instils confidence, it enhances language learning, it raises awareness of cultural differences and it gives learners a feeling of achievement (Whyatt 2009a, 2009b).

Also, research has shown that translation fosters student–teacher interaction. Using an ethnographic and experimental action approach, Marie Källkvist (2013) examined three groups of upper-intermediate undergraduate students of English at a Swedish university, where all three groups were taught a module on grammar and writing over a period of seventeen weeks. The first group undertook a mixture of tasks that included the translation of eight Swedish sentences into English. The second group carried out tasks that excluded translation. The third group was composed of language teacher trainees who performed a mixture of tasks that included translation. Student-initiated queries were more frequent when translation tasks were discussed, and the issues addressed were more varied as they concerned not only features of L2 grammar, lexis and phraseology but also cross-lingual equivalence. As Källkvist (2013, p. 129) explains, the composition task need not consider the relationship between the source and the target text, hence 'fewer matters gave rise to student comments and questions'. Within the same line of enquiry, Sio Wai Lo

(2016, 2019) carried out a longitudinal study involving L1 Chinese students of English majoring in public administration. Her investigation shows that Chinese–English translation tasks facilitate classroom discussions and enhance linguistic competence significantly more than essay writing in English. Källkvist's and Lo's findings lend support to the use of translation as an additional activity in the language classroom since it enhances lexical and grammatical accuracy, and diversifies the range of skills developed through language learning.

Moving from theory and research to practice, translation studies scholars have developed translation-oriented pedagogies they implement in the undergraduate and graduate language classroom. Two examples of such pedagogies are provided by Laviosa (2014) and González-Davies (2018). The method put forward by Laviosa (2014a, pp. 90–106) is named 'holistic pedagogic translation' and is used with L1 Italian students of English in the second year of the Master's Degree in Modern Languages and Literatures at the University of Bari, Italy. The approach is underpinned by: Tymoczko's (2007) enlarged notion of translation as representation, transmission and transculturation; Kramsch's (2009) notion of language as symbolic representation, action and power; and the view that language learning is a holistic experience that empowers the multilingual individual 'to see him/herself through his/her own embodied history and subjectivity and through the history and subjectivity of others' (Kramsch and Whiteside, 2008, p. 668). Based on these tenets, the design of holistic pedagogic translation involves the contrastive stylistic analysis and holistic cultural translation of literary and poetic texts presented in different modalities – written, spoken and multimodal – to sensitize learners to the meaning expressed by form in its various manifestations. The goal of this pedagogy is to hone translingual and transcultural abilities and form multilingual individuals 'sensitive to linguistic, cultural, and above all, semiotic diversity, and willing to engage with difference' (Kramsch, 2014, p. 305). Learning is dialogic, collaborative, participatory and self-engaging. The teacher is a facilitator in the educational process, and creates a learning environment that contextualizes language in a variety of interrelated meaning-making systems: verbal, visual, acoustic. The learner is seen as a person who co-operates with other members of the team and is able to master 'the linguistic code well enough to be able to assume responsibility for one's linguistic choices and to respond appropriately to the choices made by others' (Kramsch, 2014, p. 305).

As regards procedure, the syllabus is organized into teaching units, each requiring five hours of seminar time. Each unit is composed of: a) an introduction; b) explanation of linguistic concepts; c) illustrative examples from literary and poetic texts; d) a discussion of the translation challenges and opportunities arising from the lexical, grammatical, stylistic and cultural differences between English and Italian; e) translation tasks into and out of English; f) a summary of the main points to remember; and g) further reading. The pace of the lesson is not fast, which enables students to absorb the teaching content cognitively and emotionally. 'Each learner with his or her biography, interests and strivings is regarded … as a uniquely heteroglossic author, crafting new worlds of meaning in his or her dialogic encounters with the foreign text' (Laviosa, 2014a, p. 58). Different forms of translation are practised across codes, modalities and genres in order to improve both the L2 and the L1, and engage critically with the social and cultural views they signify. Congruent with Tymoczko's holistic approach and Kramsch's ecological orientation, Laviosa's proposed pedagogy espouses the hermeneutic model of translation.

The teaching method put forward by González-Davies (2018) is framed within the plurilingual perspective advocated by the Council of Europe. The approach is called the Integrated Plurilingual Approach (IPA) and is currently used with bilingual Catalan and Spanish undergraduate learners of English at the University Ramon Llull, Barcelona. The approach adopts the notion of translation as a form of mediation alongside other practices such as 'participating in an oral discussion involving several languages, interpreting a cultural phenomenon in relation to another culture' (Council of Europe, 2001, p. 175). Translation is therefore viewed as a skill that is integrated with reading, writing, speaking, listening as well as vocabulary and grammar development in order to hone plurilingual communicative competence (PCC). This encompasses ICC and is defined as 'an appropriate use of natural, plurilingual practices (e.g., translation, code-switching or an informed use of the L1) to advance interlinguistic and intercultural communication' (González-Davies, 2018, p. 2). In turn, ICC is intended as 'the ability to work within more than one culture efficiently and to bridge cultures by foregrounding the study of "ways of thinking and doing" of the members of a community and by noticing similarities as well as differences' (González-Davies, 2018, p. 5).

The pedagogic approach espouses social constructivist principles and upholds translation 'as an efficient (planned and unplanned) translanguaging scaffolding strategy' in the learning process (González-Davies, 2018, p. 2). Translation is conceived as a 'dynamic process of communication' (Hatim and Mason, 1990, p. 223), and the activities and projects carried out in class involve student–student and teacher–students interactions aimed at raising awareness of the learning process itself. To this end, noticing, understanding, deciding and justifying are key actions that enhance teacher and student agency as well as reflective action and respect for diversity in a collaborative learning environment. More specifically, noticing involves sensitizing students to resemblances, differences and connections between languages, thus fostering metalinguistic competence. Understanding entails building on previous knowledge to construct new meanings. Deciding involves making informed choices. Justifying means explaining the reasons for choosing a particular solution to a given problem (González-Davies, 2018, p. 6). The activity reported below on solving mistranslations exemplifies these key actions and reveals the underlying instrumental model of translation adopted in this pedagogy:

> Once the teacher has presented examples of authentic mistranslations, the students are asked to search for other mistranslations in the streets, in newspapers, in ads, subtitles or dubbing, translated books and so on. They have a week to do so. Then, the mistranslations are pooled in groups and three are chosen to be shared with the rest of the class.
>
> The groups then carry out a four-stage activity: (1) Students spot (i.e., 'notice') the mistranslation; (2) They work out the origin of the mistranslation (i.e., 'understand') (e.g., semantic or syntactic calque, cultural gap and so on); (3) They translate it appropriately using resources, and applying creative and critical thinking (i.e., 'decide'); and (4) Each group presents their work and give reasons for their final translations (i.e., 'justify'). A discussion ensues.                                    (González-Davies, 2018, p. 7)

Another learning context where translation is appraised by educational linguists is bilingual education, which integrates content and language learning and uses two languages as media of instruction and assessment. In this educational setting, translation is used as one of several teacher-initiated activities that scaffold learning and develop translanguaging abilities (Garcia and Li Wei, 2014, pp. 119–25). Translation, together with reading, writing, comparing and listening to multilingual texts, fulfils a wide range of goals. These include: differentiating among students' levels and adapting instruction to different types of student in multilingual classrooms, for example those who are bilingual, those who are monolingual and those who are emergent bilinguals; developing and extending new knowledge, critical thinking and critical consciousness; interrogating linguistic inequality; disrupting linguistic hierarchies and social structures. In practice, pedagogic translanguaging might involve, for example, the teacher introducing new words and their definitions, followed by students translating the definitions into their home languages. The teacher would allow a student who finds it difficult to say something in the L2 during a presentation to ask a classmate to translate it; the student then repeats the translated utterance (Garcia and Li Wei, 2014, p. 124).

## 15.5 Conclusions and Future Directions

The positive dialogue translation studies that scholars and educationalists are engaging in within the multilingual paradigm are expanding the field of translation studies and narrowing the gulf between pedagogic translation and translator training in higher education. The former aims to enact and foster plurilingualism and interculturality, while the latter aims to develop specific skills that consolidate and enhance the employability of graduates of master's degrees in translation. Among these abilities, the area of language and culture, which encompasses general or language-specific linguistic, sociolinguistic, cultural and transcultural knowledge and skills, is the basis and driving force for advanced professional translation competence (Toudic and Krause, 2017). It is also the envisioned goal of degree programmes in modern languages (cf. MLA, 2007). By the end of their three- or four-year BA Hons degree programme, graduates in modern languages will have achieved an advanced level of linguistic proficiency in at least two languages. At this level, which corresponds to C1 of the CEFR, students will be able to provide fluent spoken translations into the L1 of complex texts written in the L2 and the L3 on a wide range of general and specialized topics, capturing most nuances (Council of Europe, 2018, p. 114). This ability is a prerequisite for gaining access to a master's degree course in translation in two working languages in Europe.

The constructive dialogue between applied translation studies and educational linguistics is unlocking the potential of translation as a pedagogic approach that can be adopted effectively in multilingual learning contexts as varied as degree programmes in modern languages, TESOL, bilingual education, content-based instruction (CBI), English as a medium of instruction (EMI), and content and language integrated learning (CLIL). The novel and forward-looking collaboration between translation scholars and educationalists is giving rise to a transdisciplinary area of study where pedagogy is viewed as a form of cultural translational work that hosts unfamiliarity and strangeness, and translation is viewed as a form of learning, especially learning to live within the plurality of languages and with their incompatibility (Thompson, 2019). This inclusive stance constitutes the general premise of a recent collective volume edited by the German educationalists Nicolas Engel and Stefan Köngeter (2019), *Übersetzung: Über die Möglichkeit, Pädagogik anders zu denken* (The Possibility of Thinking about Pedagogy in a Different Way). The aim of this editorial initiative is to share theoretical insights and pedagogic practices across the boundaries of translation studies and educational philosophy. Looking to the future, the broad vision put forward in this volume, which conceptualizes pedagogy as translation and translation as pedagogy, will no doubt bear fruit in terms of further innovative scholarly endeavours and wide-ranging practical applications in the teaching of cross-curricular and interdisciplinary subjects in primary, secondary and higher education.

# References

ACARA (Australian Curriculum, Assessment and Reporting Authority) (2014a). *The Australian Curriculum: Languages – French – Years F-10 sequence,* version 7.3. Available at http://docs.acara.edu.au/resources/French_-_Sequence_of_Content.pdf.

ACARA (Australian Curriculum, Assessment and Reporting Authority) (2014b). *The Australian Curriculum: Languages – Italian –Years F-10 sequence*, version 7.3. Available at http://docs.acara.edu.au/resources/Italian_-_Sequence_of_Content.pdf.

Baker, M. (2018). *In Other Words: A Coursebook on Translation*. 3rd ed. London: Routledge.

Bigelow, M., and Ennser-Kananen, J. (2015). Introduction: The advocacy turn of educational linguistics. In M. Bigelow and J. Ennser-Kananen, eds., *The Routledge Handbook of Educational Linguistics*. London: Routledge, pp. 1–5.

Byram, M. (1997). *Teaching and Assessing Intercultural Communicative Competence*. Clevedon, UK: Multilingual Matters.

Byram, M. (2008). *From Foreign Language Education to Education of Intercultural Citizenship: Essays and Reflections*. Clevedon, UK: Multilingual Matters.

Byram, M., Porto, M., and Yulita, L. (2020). Education for intercultural citizenship. In S. Laviosa and M. González-Davies, eds., *The Routledge Handbook of Translation and Education*. London: Routledge.

Byrd Clark, J. S., and Dervin, F., eds. (2014). *Reflexivity in Language and Intercultural Education: Rethinking Multilingualism and Interculturality*. London: Routledge.

Conteh, J., and Meier, G. (2014). Introduction. In J. Conteh and G. Meier, eds., *The Multilingual Turn in Languages Education: Opportunities and Challenges*. Clevedon, UK: Multilingual Matters, pp. 1–14.

Cook, G. (2010). *Translation in Language Teaching: An Argument for Reassessment*. Cambridge: Cambridge University Press.

Council of Europe (2001). *Common European Framework of Reference for Languages: Learning, Teaching, Assessment*. Strasbourg: Council of Europe Publishing. Available at www.coe.int/t/dg4/linguistic/cadre1_en.asp.

Council of Europe (2018). *Common European Framework of Reference for Languages: Learning, Teaching, Assessment. Companion Volume with New Descriptors* [online]. Strasbourg: Council of Europe Publishing. Available at https://rm.coe.int/cefr-companion-volume-with-new-descriptors-2018/1680787989.

Ellis, R., and Shintani, N. (2014). *Exploring Language Pedagogy through Second Language Acquisition Research*. London: Routledge.

Engel, N., and Köngeter, S., eds. (2019). *Übersetzung: Über die Möglichkeit, Pädagogik anders zu denken*. Wiesbaden: Springer VS.

García, O., and Li Wei (2014). *Translanguaging: Language, Bilingualism and Education*. London: Palgrave Macmillan.

Gentzler, E. (2001). *Contemporary Translation Theories*. 2nd ed. Clevedon, UK: Multilingual Matters.

González-Davies, M. (2017). A collaborative pedagogy for translation. In L. Venuti, ed., *Teaching Translation: Programs, Courses, Pedagogies*. London: Routledge, pp. 71–8.

González-Davies, M. (2018). The use of translation in an integrated plurilingual approach to language learning: Teacher strategies and best practices. *Journal of Spanish Language Teaching*. Available at https://doi.org/10.1080/23247797.2017.1407168.

Hatim, B., and Mason, I. (1990). *Discourse and the Translator*. London: Routledge.

Holmes, J. S. (1972/1988). The name and nature of translation studies. In J. S. Holmes, *Translated! Papers on Literary Translation and Translation Studies*. Amsterdam: Rodopi, pp. 66–80.

Källkvist, M. (2008). L1–L2 translation versus no translation: A longitudinal study of focus on forms within a meaning-focused curriculum. In L. Ortega and H. Byrnes, eds., *The Longitudinal Study of Advanced L2 Capacities*. London: Routledge, pp. 182–202.

Källkvist, M. (2013). The engaging nature of translation: A nexus analysis of student–teacher interaction. In D. Tsagari and G. Floros, eds., *Translation in Language Teaching and Assessment*. Newcastle upon Tyne: Cambridge Scholars Publishing, pp. 115–33.

Kramsch, C. (2009). *The Multilingual Subject: What Foreign Language Learners Say about Their Experience and Why It Matters*. Oxford: Oxford University Press.

Kramsch, C. (2014). Teaching foreign languages in an era of globalization: Introduction. *Modern Language Journal*, **98**(1), pp. 296–311.

Kramsch, C., and Whiteside, A. (2008). Language ecology in multilingual settings: Towards a theory of symbolic competence. *Applied Linguistics*, **29**(4), pp. 645–71.

Laufer, B., and Girsai, N. (2008). Form-focused instruction in second language vocabulary learning: A case for contrastive analysis and translation. *Applied Linguistics*, **29**(4), pp. 694–716.

Laviosa, S. (2014a). *Translation and Language Education: Pedagogic Approaches Explored*. London: Routledge.

Laviosa, S., ed. (2014b). *Translation in the Language Classroom: Theory, Research and Practice*. Special issue of *The Interpreter and Translator Trainer*, 8(1).

Laviosa, S. (2018). Cultural translation in language teaching. In S.-A. Harding and O. Carbonell Cortés, eds., *The Routledge Handbook of Translation and Culture*. London: Routledge, pp. 574–90.

Li Wei (2018). Translanguaging as a practical theory of language. *Applied Linguistics*, **39**(1), pp. 9–30.

Lo, S. W. (2016). Using translation in L2 classrooms: An empirical study on non-language major students' engagement in class discussions and improvement in language usage. Unpublished PhD thesis, Department of Modern Languages, University of Leicester.

Lo, S. W. (2019). Translation for communicative purposes: Engendering class discussions with L1–L2 translation tasks. *Translation and Translanguaging in Multilingual Contexts*, **5**(2), pp. 185–209.

May, S., ed. (2014). *The Multilingual Turn: Implications for SLA, TESOL and Bilingual Education*. London: Routledge.

Meier, G., and Conteh, J. (2014). Conclusion: The multilingual turn in languages education. In J. Conteh and G. Meier, eds., *The Multilingual Turn in Languages Education: Opportunities and Challenges*. Clevedon, UK: Multilingual Matters, pp. 292–9.

Meylaerts, R. (2013). Multilingualism as a challenge for translation studies. In C. Millán and F. Bartrina, eds., *The Routledge Handbook of Translation Studies*. London: Routledge, pp. 519–33.

MLA Ad Hoc Committee on Foreign Languages (2007). *Foreign Languages and Higher Education: New Structures for a Changed World*. Available at www.mla.org/flreport.

Nord, C. (1997). *Translating as a Purposeful Activity: Functionalist Approaches Explained*. Manchester: St Jerome.

Ortega, L. (2014). Ways forward for a bi/multilingual turn in SLA. In J. Conteh and G. Meier, eds., *The Multilingual Turn in Languages Education: Opportunities and Challenges*. Clevedon: Multilingual Matters, pp. 32–53.

Richards, J. C., and Rodgers, T. S. (2014). *Approaches and Methods in Language Teaching*. 3rd ed. Cambridge: Cambridge University Press.

Toudic, D., and Krause, A. (2017). (on behalf of the EMT Board) *European Master's in Translation Competence Framework 2017*. Available at https://ec.europa.eu/info/sites/info/files/emt_competence_fwk_2017_en_web.pdf.

Thompson, C. (2019). Philosophy of education and *pragma* of translation. In N. Engel and S. Köngeter, eds., *Übersetzung: Über die Möglichkeit, Pädagogik anders zu denken*. Wiesbaden: Springer VS, pp. 21–37.

Tsagari, D., and Floros, G., eds. (2013). *Translation in Language Teaching and Assessment*. Newcastle upon Tyne: Cambridge Scholars Publishing.

Tymoczko, M. (2007). *Enlarging Translation, Empowering Translators*. Manchester: St Jerome.

Tymoczko, M. (2010). Theory and translation studies education. Seminar given at Aston University, Birmingham, UK, 9 March.

Vaezi, S., and Mirzaei, M. (2007). The effect of using translation from L1 to L2 as a teaching technique on the improvement of EFL learners' linguistic accuracy – focus on form. *Humanising Language Teaching*, **9** (5), September. Available at http://old.hltmag.co.uk/sep07/mart03.htm.

Vaj, I. (2009). *Il cacciatore di storie. Un viaggio nel mondo dell'autore de Il cacciatore di aquiloni*. Milano: Piemme.

van Lier, L. (2004). *The Ecology and Semiotics of Language Learning: A Sociocultural Perspective*. Boston: Kluwer Academic Publishers.

Venuti, L. (2004). Translation, community, utopia. In L. Venuti, ed., *The Translation Studies Reader*. 2nd ed. London: Routledge, pp. 482–502.

Venuti, L. (2017). Introduction: Translation, interpretation, and the humanities. In L. Venuti, ed., *Teaching Translation: Programs, Courses, Pedagogies*. London: Routledge, pp. 1–14.

Vygotsky, L. S. (1978). *Mind in Society: The Development of Higher Psychological Processes*, trans. Michael Cole. Cambridge, MA: Harvard University Press.

Whyatt, B. (2009a). Translating as a way of improving language control in the mind of the L2 learner: Assets, requirements and challenges of translation tasks. In A. Witte, T. Harden and A. Ramos de Oliveira Harden, eds., *Translation in Second Language Learning and Teaching*. Bern: Peter Lang, pp. 181–202.

Whyatt, B. (2009b). Building L2 communicative confidence through interlingual tasks: Towards function-focused L2 learning. In M. Dynel, ed., *Advances in Discourse Approaches*. Newcastle upon Tyne: Cambridge Scholars Publishing, pp. 365–88.

Witte, A. (2014). *Blending Spaces: Mediating and Assessing Intercultural Competence in the L2 Classroom*. New York: Plenum Press.

Zhang, J., and Pang, Y. (2014). Mirroring, reformulation and functional translation: A complementary TEFL model for advanced learners. In S. Laviosa, ed., *Translation in the Language Classroom: Theory, Research and Practice*. Special issue of *The Interpreter and Translator Trainer*, **8**(1), pp. 52–69.

# Part IV

## Translation in Practice: Factual Genres

# 16

# Translating Technical Texts

Maeve Olohan

## 16.1 Technical Texts and Technical Communication

In delimiting the scope of this chapter, I take my cue from its position within the *Handbook*, in a section on translating factual genres, alongside contributions on translating non-literary prose, legal texts, medical texts and news. Beyond the distinction made between factual and non-factual, this organization of content may reflect the consideration of specialized text as a superordinate concept, with specific domains of specialization as subordinate concepts, for example medical, legal, financial, scientific, technical texts. This conceptualization of different domains of specialization is commonly applied to translation too, leading to a broad understanding of technical translation as the translation of texts concerned with or related to the domain of technology. However, since technology figures in so many of today's practices, there is substantial overlap between technical and other specialized domains; consider, among others, the subdomains of medical or legal informatics, lawtech (technologies that support the delivery of legal services) or fintech (technologies that support the delivery of financial services). We might therefore make an intuitive judgement about the extent to which a text is concerned with technical, medical or legal content and categorize accordingly. There is also a tendency to bundle technical translation with scientific translation, recognizing some commonalities in topics or approaches, while also acknowledging differences (Byrne, 2012; Olohan, 2016).

The concept of text may also be understood in different ways, depending on the theoretical starting point (see Rogers, 2015, pp. 59–70 for an outline of possible approaches). In many commercial translation contexts, reference is made instead to 'content', which is no less slippery theoretically but perhaps serves to emphasize particular aspects. First, verbal and non-verbal semiotic resources may be combined in communicating technical content; consider the central role of graphics, and increasingly video, in technical communication settings. Second, such technical content may not exhibit prototypical features of linear (verbal) text; for example, strings of menu items in software interfaces or entries in product catalogues may deviate markedly from standards of textuality such as cohesion and coherence. Third, technical content may not be produced through traditional authoring practices. For example, in a practice known as topic-based authoring, technical documentation is produced by retrieving different topic-based chunks or snippets of content that have previously been written, defined (through coding of elements and content using mark-up language), stored in that standardized format and then retrieved for reuse (Lanier, 2018). Thus, a user manual published as a PDF may traditionally have been authored as a linear narrative but is now likely to be a modular assembly of numerous pieces of topic-based content, some of which could also be used in online help files, or even in a marketing brochure. Additionally, a single source of content may be used to produce a range of output types for different media or publishing channels, for example for print, website or mobile application (app). Responsive design delivers dynamic formatting so that the content can be viewed optimally, regardless of the platform on which it is published. However, like topic-based authoring, this practice of single-source authoring can have an impact on decisions about what information to communicate and how (Lanier, 2018).

Rather than consider further how a technical text might be defined and delimited, it may be more productive to focus our attention on the practices in which technical content figures. From a practice-theoretical perspective, the social realm is conceptualized as a 'nexus' or 'plenum' of practices (Schatzki, 2001, p. 2, 2016, p. 6). Thus, to understand the nature of one practice, we can investigate both how it is constituted and how it connects with other practices. As indicated above, technical communication involves authoring practices of various kinds, and it is helpful to consider the practice of technical translation as being closely connected to those practices of technical authoring, as is done in Maylath and St Amant's (2019) guide to translation and localization in technical communication. Generally speaking, before technical content is translated into target languages (TLs), it is first produced in the source language (SL). Even if assembled in modular fashion, the content that is used to produce technical specifications, product descriptions, instruction guides, user manuals, software user interfaces, help files, etc. is usually first created by technical authors.

The practices of technical authoring and technical translation are connected in various other ways, beyond their temporal sequencing. If we understand practices as organized human activities that are constituted by a range of elements (Reckwitz, 2002; Shove, Pantzar and Watson, 2012), we may note that these practices of technical authoring and technical translation share some of the materials that are used, the competences that are required and the motivations that drive the practice. For example, the content management systems that are used by authors in monolingual settings are also deployed to organize multilingual, localized content. Thus, the technical know-how enabling authors and translators to work with and contribute to these systems is among a range of competences that are shared. Translators work interlingually and technical authors monolingually, but both practices also require know-how that is related to technology, language and communication. Examples of shared competences can be seen in discussions of how controlled languages are used in technical communication and translation (O'Brien, 2019; Musacchio, 2019) or how usability testing (e.g., Quesenbery, 2003; Alexander, 2013) has been applied to technical translation (Byrne, 2006). In addition, scholars (Risku, 2004; Gnecchi et al., 2011; Vandepitte et al., 2016) address the convergence of technical communication and technical translation in professional training.

Another connection between these authoring and translating practices relates to their teleologies; they share a common end. Drawing on the concept of genre, this end can be described as producing technical content that functions as 'communicative vehicles for the achievement of goals' (Swales, 1990, p. 46). The notion of genre encapsulates the way in which a 'recognizable communicative event [is] characterized by a set of communicative purpose(s)' (Bhatia, 1993, p. 13). The communicative event is structured and conventionalized, and thus is 'identified and mutually understood by the members of the professional or academic community in which it regularly occurs' (Bhatia, 1993, p. 13). Both technical authoring and technical translation aim at producing content that will fulfil identifiable communicative purposes for their respective discourse communities. Thus, one scholarly approach to technical content is to examine it as a set of genres. We tend to refer to genres such as technical data sheets, user manuals, software interfaces, online help, standard operating procedures, among many others, although these are more accurately considered as labels for textual formats that have become established as ways of using language for particular communicative purposes. This focus on genre is helpful in describing and explaining the challenges faced by technical translators (see, for example, Byrne, 2012; Olohan, 2016; Scarpa, 2020) as they familiarize themselves with these genres and make translation choices. Thus, part of this approach is to consider closely the features of the content that is authored, translated, disseminated, read and acted upon. Through their translation decisions, translators aim to use text-internal resources to fulfil communicative purposes, thus enabling the translated text to function as part of communicative events that occur within professional communities.

A genre-focused approach also requires us to consider text-external factors, namely, to understand discursive practices as being constituent parts of professional practices (Bhatia, 2008, 2016). Bhatia also highlights substantial gaps in our understanding of how genres interact and appropriate text-external resources from one another. This notion of interdiscursivity has been explored in interlingual settings (for example in Salö and Hanell's (2014) study of how a Swedish computer scientist performs 'unprecedented genres' in Swedish by drawing on prior linguistic practices in both Swedish and English) and, to a limited extent, in legal translation settings (e.g., Scott, 2018). For translation studies, it would be instructive to research those professional contexts in which translated technical content is used, and to examine the ways in which translations figure in those professional practices wherever they take place, in software development and industrial manufacturing, in laboratories and research centres, in diverse installation and operation settings and so on. This situatedness is largely unexplored in technical translation scholarship to date, but it offers an avenue for future research, particularly when informed by a practice-theoretical approach to translation (Olohan, 2021). Section 16.2 sets the scene by highlighting the sectors of professional activity in which technical translation is prevalent.

## 16.2 Language Services and Technical Translation

Market research companies CSA Research, Slator and Nimdzi produce regular reports on the language services sector, drawing on survey data, interviews and reports of business activities from language service providers (LSPs). The reports, when accessible, can provide useful insights into the language services landscape and the contexts for which technical content is translated today. Here we consider this global translation activity from two perspectives. In this section we first identify the domains, known as verticals, in which language services for technical content are in demand; this also provides an insight into frequently encountered professional genres. In Section 16.3, we then examine the key characteristics of how LSPs and translators operate in their sector.

The demand for translation of technical content can be gauged from *The Slator 2019 Language Industry Market Report* (Faes, 2019), which divides the market into ten verticals. Four verticals each account for 10 to 13 per cent of the market; they are technology, travel and retail, professional services, and engineering and manufacturing. Translation activities in these verticals are focused on software, user interfaces, technical documentation, technical manuals as well as marketing materials, advertising, product descriptions, websites, customer service, and regulatory and legal content. Much of the translation performed here is closely connected with other practices of internationalization and localization, and a large proportion of the work can be considered technical.

Another three verticals each account for 5 to 8 per cent of the market; they are life sciences, financial services, and aerospace and defence. Much of the content translated for these verticals is also technical, comprising manuals, technical documents and clinical trial documentation, alongside legal, regulatory, research and marketing content.

The largest vertical, accounting for almost a quarter of the overall market, is the public sector. This includes the interpreting and translation that is done for international organizations, like the European Union, and governments, administrations and authorities at regional, national and local levels. Translators and interpreters in public service settings often work with content related to health care, military, legal or immigration matters, and some of this material addresses technical themes. For example, the translation services provider Global Language Translation and Consulting (GLTaC, n.d.) is contracted to supply translation services to the US Army, and its translations include technical content in the form of training material, field manuals and vehicle maintenance manuals. It is also not uncommon for multiple subject domains to be addressed in material translated for national or international organizations; for example, the European Commission Recommendation 2020/518 is a non-binding legal instrument setting out a common EU approach to the use of technology and data to combat and exit from the Covid-19 crisis. In twenty-three language versions, this text, with an indisputable legal significance, tackles technical themes of epidemiological surveillance and monitoring, data protection, anonymization and aggregation, the use of medical devices, and the interoperability of mobile applications.

The two final verticals presented in the Slator report are media, accounting for almost 10 per cent, and gaming, the smallest vertical at 2.5 per cent in 2019. In both cases, voice-over, dubbing and subtitling practices dominate, and the core fictional genres are games, films and series, discussed elsewhere in this *Handbook*. However, it is worth noting that some translated media content is also technical, including audiovisual content used in marketing, advertising, training and education for technical products and services.

The verticals identified by Slator are reflected to a large extent in a European survey of LSPs and individual professional translators for the same period (ELIA et al., 2019). Almost all of the activities of individual translators fit within twelve verticals, and technical content dominates in several of these. They are in descending order of size: legal, government, other industrial, media, finance, travel, life sciences, automotive, food, consumer electronics, telecommunications and ICT (information and communications technology). The LSPs report similar levels of activity in those verticals, with small variations in significance depending on whether the LSP generated annual revenues lower or in excess of EUR

250 K. The verticals of travel, food and other industrial are more important for companies with smaller revenues, while life sciences, automotive, consumer electronics and telecommunications are more important for larger LSPs.

Another way of considering which verticals are most significant for technical translation is to identify the sectors of industry or companies whose internet presence is most multilingual, since the maintenance of multilingual websites and social networks by global companies and brands usually requires translation to play a significant role. CSA Research's *Global Website Assessment Index*, based on a study of more than 2,800 of the world's most prominent websites (Sargent and Lommel, 2019), identified automotive, computer and electronics, and consumer goods as the top three most multilingual verticals in 2019. CSA Research used a more fine-grained categorization of verticals (thirty-seven compared to Slator's ten), but it is clear that there is some general agreement between each of these different approaches to identifying key verticals for translation, and these include verticals in which technical texts of various professional genres play a central role.

## 16.3  Performing Technical Translation

How do LSPs and translators operate in this technical content landscape? Most language services are outsourced by commissioners to LSPs. Most LSPs, in turn, outsource translation, revision, interpreting, localization, subtitling, etc. to freelance linguists. Thus, translators of technical content generally operate as freelancers, often via the intermediation of an LSP which, in turn, manages translation projects that are often complex and involve multiple languages. Drawing on market analysis, it is possible to distinguish among different kinds of LSP in terms of their market and strategic positioning.

The aforementioned Slator report (Faes, 2019) divides the language services sector into four segments by annual revenue. The top 10 per cent comprise the five largest LSPs of the world (as constituted before RWS acquired SDL), called super-agencies, with revenues of more than USD 200 m (Transperfect, Lionbridge, LanguageLine, SDL and RWS). These companies operate globally in more than one vertical. The next 12 per cent generate more than USD 25 m and are labelled leader LSPs. In most cases, they have a strong regional presence. The next 5 per cent are the challenger LSPs, generating between USD 8 m and USD 25 m, often focused on specific verticals or a domestic/local market. The remaining 73 per cent comprise all other participants in the sector, including LSPs, language departments or units within organizations, and freelancers.

CSA Research organizes LSPs hierarchically into five categories (DePalma, 2020), based on LSPs' abilities to adapt to changing technologies and business practices, rather than on their annual revenue. At the bottom of DePalma's hierarchy are the 'language traditionalists'. These LSPs are described as not adapting easily, making minimal use of technology and not changing their business operations much over time. The 'process reengineers', by contrast, are more technologically aware than the traditionalists and have begun reinventing themselves in response to changes in technology and business practices, although they are not really exploiting artificial intelligence (AI) and big data. In the middle category are the 'data scientists'. These LSPs have automated more of their processes than the other two groups and have integrated machine translation into their workflows.

Taking joint top position in DePalma's hierarchy are two categories of LSP that are more specialized than the other LSPs. They are the 'knowledge processing outsourcers' and the 'global content strategists' and they are described as combining 'a powerful blend of technical, business skills and strategic vision'. The knowledge processing outsourcers have expertise that is specialized by vertical, service or content type, and their processes are heavily driven by machine learning and technology. An example may be seen in one of RWS's areas of activity, intellectual property (IP) services. RWS (n.d.) provides translation and other services across the IP life cycle, from research and development to patent filing and enforcement. The final group, the global content strategists, expertly manage content creation, processing analytics and intelligence in what DePalma calls an 'end-to-end information strategy'. For example, Lionbridge (n.d.) offers 'end-to-end technical content creation – in any format, in any language'. This includes technical writing, training and e-learning for company employees, computer-aided design and 3D modelling and media. These two categories of highly specialized global players overlap to a large extent with Slator's super-agencies and LSP leaders.

Both categorizations show both the diversity and the fragmentation of the language services sector. The practice of translating technical content varies in line with those vastly differing revenues and operational approaches. Detailed insights into practices in operations of smaller scales are offered by several recent studies. For example, Christensen and Schjoldager (2019) report on a study of-the life cycle of technical communication in a Danish medium-sized LSP, examining the relations between documentation and translation. Gonzales and Turner (2017) describe practices of technical translation, technical communication and design in the language services department of a non-profit community organization in the United States. Olohan (2018) considers the convergence of scientific translation and English-language scientific editing in an international research organization.

## 16.4 Working with Textual Content

We established in Sections 16.2 and 16.3 that a focus on communicative events and their purposes is helpful in producing effective technical content, including translations, for specific discourse communities. We also noted that some LSPs offer technical content management services that include both writing and translation. In this section we consider some key text-internal resources that are typically deployed to serve those specific communicative purposes. Scholarly contributions on technical or specialized translation are often centred on those features which can be seen as characteristic of languages for special purposes (Krein-Kühle, 2011; Byrne, 2012; Rogers, 2015; Olohan, 2016; Scarpa, 2020). We begin with terminology and then outline a selection of other textual and lexico-grammatical features.

Terminology usually refers to the collection of terms for a subject domain. One view of terminology (Antia et al. 2005; Cabré 2010) is based on the idea that a specialist subject domain is made up of objects with specific properties, and that those objects may be grouped into sets or classes of objects and conceptualized as units of knowledge. Those abstracted representations are known as concepts and they can be defined with reference to the characteristics that delimit them from other, related concepts. Concepts are referred to using specialized vocabulary labels known as terms. Standardization committees prescribe what terms are preferred for sets of agreed concepts. However, the work of standardization committees does not necessarily reflect the more complicated situation with which technical authors and translators are confronted. As Rogers (2015, p. 50) explains, authors' and translators' experience of terminology is more varied because it encompasses not only the terms used by academic experts but also the terms favoured by practitioners, hobbyists and lay users. In addition, the classic distinction between terms, conveying special meanings, and words, conveying general meanings, is often untenable in commercial contexts where an expression's significance for business operations may determine how 'special' it is (Rogers, 2015, p. 51).

Notwithstanding debates about how terms can be defined relative to other lexical features of texts, technical translators are expected to recognize and understand the terminological references to concepts in SL content and to communicate about those concepts in the TL using terms that will be recognizable to the TL discourse community. This requires translators to deal with numerous challenges that inevitably arise through contextual variations in terminological usage. This competence or know-how is among the elements that constitute the practice of technical translation; it extends beyond familiarity with bilingual or multilingual terminology and also encompasses conceptual understanding. Section 16.5 outlines how translators manage terminological resources.

Other characteristics of languages for special purposes may be classified in various ways. For example, Halliday, when considering the difficulties of scientific writing in English, notes that terms themselves are not difficult to master, but complexity arises because of the relations that terms have to one another (Halliday, 2004, p. 161). Writing about 'interlocking definitions', he looks at how clusters of related concepts tend to be referred to in texts and how terms are used to define other concepts, so that the reader is required to understand all of them at the same time. Technical concepts are often organized in taxonomies, and the nature of the relations that structure the taxonomy must also be understood by the reader (Halliday, 2004, p. 165). Moving from terms to 'technical grammar', Halliday notes that special expressions may be used in technical texts where grammatical structures are different from those used in general language; he gives the examples of risk being treated as an object so that someone can ask what *happens* to *risk*, or *smoking* being described as something that can *increase* (Halliday, 2004, p. 167).

High lexical density is another feature of scientific writing, and also relevant when considering technical content. This is the phenomenon of packing lexical items tightly into grammatical structures, usually into noun phrases, like *increasing lung cancer death rate* (Halliday, 2004, p. 168). The use of these nominal groups can introduce syntactic ambiguity because the relation between the different elements may not be clear, for example is *increasing lung cancer death rate* about how many people die from lung cancer or about how quickly people die from lung cancer?

Nominalization involves the replacement of one grammatical class, often a verb phrase or verbal group, by another grammatical class, in this case a noun phrase. This kind of replacement operation in general is what Halliday (2004) terms 'grammatical metaphor'. The most prevalent of these shifts is the use of nominalized forms to designate processes and qualities that might otherwise be expressed by verbs or adverbs. To quote one of Halliday's examples, *fire intensity has a profound effect on smoke injection* is a re-construal of what he describes as the congruent version, which would be something like *if (a) fire is intense it injects a lot more smoke* or *the more intense the fire, the more smoke it injects (into the atmosphere)* (Halliday, 2004, p. 28). Nominalization produces a higher level of lexical density and an economy of linguistic forms but also reflects a re-construal of experience. As experiences, processes or qualities are conveyed using a nominal group rather than a verbal one, the experience, process or quality is treated as a virtual entity. Linguistically, the nominalized form can serve as a subject and can be further modified. Conceptually, the virtual entity, thus abstracted, can be theorized and can participate in other relations and processes. As actors are often removed in conjunction with grammatical metaphor, an illusion of objectivity is created, alongside impressions of technicality, rationality or authority. As argued by Halliday (Halliday, 2004, p. 128), such features may be seen as signalling the discourse of experts. At the same time, processes and procedures lose their transparency, and personal accountability is diminished.

A final difficulty of scientific English discussed by Halliday (2004, p. 177) is that of semantic discontinuity, where writers make semantic leaps that a reader is expected to follow; this often entails readers having to work out whether something is new information or not, and how it relates logically to another piece of information. As Halliday suggests, these leaps may not pose difficulties for specialists but may, like other features outlined, serve to exclude those who are not considered part of that elite discourse community.

Another set of concepts that facilitate analysis of those interactional dimensions of texts is proposed by Hyland (e.g., 2000, 2005) under the umbrella label of 'metadiscourse', denoting the 'self-reflective expressions used to negotiate interactional meanings in a text, assisting the writer (or speaker) to express a viewpoint and engage with readers as members of a particular community' (Hyland, 2005, p. 37). The resources used by writers to organize their text and the readers' interaction with the information flow are grouped together as interactive resources (Hyland and Tse, 2004, p. 157). These include transition signals, that is, signals of topic change, or conjunctions and adverbials that signal the logical relations between ideas. They also include frame markers, that is, references to discourse sequences, as well as endophoric markers, referring to information in other parts of the text, and evidentials, referring to sources outside of the text (i.e., citations). Also performing this interactive function are code glosses, that is, reformulations or exemplifications. Other resources that signal writers' attitudes to the text and to readers, showing their stance and engagement, are categorized as interactional resources (Hyland and Tse, 2004, p. 157). These include hedges, boosters, attitude markers, engagement markers and self-mentions.

The use of these various resources is not merely stylistically motivated; rather, they are a means by which authors seek to fulfil certain communicative purposes with certain discourse communities. Variations across discourse communities mean that metadiscursive resources may be used differently to achieve similar communicative purposes; for example, authors of research articles in pure mathematics use less hedging than authors in many humanities disciplines, where conclusions are often offered as tentative or where alternative interpretations are invited (McGrath and Kuteeva, 2012). Patterns of usage of metadiscursive resources can also vary across languages (Vold, 2006; Pisanski Peterlin, 2008; Mur Dueñas, 2011).

Genre analysis, as established by Swales (1990, 2004) and exemplified widely in relation to the research article, as the prototypical genre of academic and scientific domains, also provides concepts that enable us to analyse how authors fulfil communicative purposes, for example through sequences of moves and sub-moves. A move is defined as a 'discoursal or rhetorical unit that performs a coherent communicative function in a written or spoken discourse' (Swales, 2004, p. 228). The widespread adoption of anglophone text-organizing conventions and patterns of moves in research articles has been acknowledged but also challenged (Swales, 1997; Bennett, 2007). There is also some recognition of how patterns of moves reflect different epistemologies across languages (see, for example, Martín Martín, 2003; Fakhri, 2004; Hirano, 2009) and across different academic disciplines and cultures (Samraj, 2005; Stoller and Robinson, 2013; Kanoksilapatham, 2015).

This selection of features is not exhaustive but rather indicative of how technical content may be analysed textually, particularly in relation to communicative purpose. As exemplified in Olohan (2016) and Scarpa (2020), these and other textual or syntactic features can require particular attention when translating various professional scientific and technical genres.

## 16.5 Technical Translation and Technologies

The practice of translating is constituted not just through fulfilment of certain communicative purposes but also through the deployment of specific materials, notably the human body and a range of tools, performing as infrastructures, devices and resources (Shove, 2017; Olohan, 2021). One of the stark differences between small LSPs and global players in the diverse language services landscape is likely to be in how technology is integrated into practices. In this section we narrow our focus to some of the technologies that participate prominently in technical translation practice, beginning with terminology management tools and moving to translation memory and machine translation. As noted, these may be combined with the kind of content management systems also used by clients and technical authors, or translation management systems that are predominantly deployed by LSPs and their project managers, and usually involve automation of certain business processes. Translation management systems are not discussed further here (see Heinish and Iacono, 2019 and Esselink, 2020 for more details). Similarly, a range of specialist tools have been designed to facilitate the management of software localization projects; these provide project management capabilities for the tasks of translators but also those of the software developers, engineers and testers whose focus is on the functionality of the localized software applications; see Roturier (2015) for details.

Terminology can be researched and managed monolingually or multilingually. The principles of terminology research and management have been set out in international standards, for example *ISO 704 Terminology work – Principles and methods* (British Standards Institution, 2010). In addition, organizations that deal with large-scale terminology management have also established standard procedures, and many examples of their terminology work are available for consultation. For example, the termbase of the Translation Bureau of Canada, Termium Plus, is freely available to consult (Government of Canada 2009). The principles by which the

Bureau's terminology work is conducted were set out in Pavel and Nolet (2001).

Many other institutional termbases can be searched online and sometimes also downloaded; see, for example, the European Union's termbase, IATE (Interactive Terminology for Europe) (European Union, n.d.).

Alongside publicly available termbases and glossaries, technical translators often have at their disposal some client-specific or project-specific terminological resources. In addition, they may conduct their own research, for example using term extraction tools to identify term candidates in the technical content they are translating and to assist in finding terminological equivalents in TL content. Typical term extraction tools that are bundled with computer-assisted translation (CAT) software or corpus-query tools seek to identify terms automatically in text by a variety of means and with varying degrees of success. MemoQ is an example of CAT software whose term extraction is based somewhat crudely on the length of term candidates (in number of characters and words) and the frequency with which they occur in the text (MemoQ, n.d.). Sketch Engine, by contrast, is corpus-query software that uses both statistical measures and linguistic information to identify term candidates. It compares a selected text (the focus corpus) with a reference corpus to produce lists of single-word items (keywords) and multi-word items that occur more frequently in the focus corpus than in the reference corpus (Sketch Engine, 2019). Frequency is normalized (per million words) for comparison. The rules of a language-specific term grammar are then applied to reduce the lists to those items that have the linguistic forms of term candidates in that language, for example including only nouns and noun phrases. Term candidates are then presented as lemmas, that is, in the base form, and the translator can proceed to judge the suitability of the proposed terms.

Translators have numerous options available for the storage, management and retrieval of terminology they have researched themselves or terms that have been provided by clients or shared by other translators. While a simple bilingual glossary might easily be compiled in a spreadsheet, more specific solutions that have been designed for translation work usually offer greater functionality and usability. These applications typically integrate with translation memory applications in a local or cloud-based CAT environment and they allow terms to be both retrieved and stored during the translation process. They start as an empty termbase to which translators or others add term entries, allowing a valuable terminological resource to be built up over time. Applications vary in the extent to which they permit or require full terminological entries to be compiled for concepts. Some cloud-based CAT tools with relatively limited terminological support simply store and retrieve SL and TL terms. Other applications encourage users to compile fuller term entries, including a definition of the concept, examples of the terms in use, sources, illustrations, etc.

Most applications offer sufficient flexibility to enable a translator to record the information they find most useful. The development and adoption in the 2000s of the TBX (TermBase eXchange) international format for terminology data was important in facilitating exchange of terminological data between users and applications.

The typical CAT environment has translation memory (TM) and a translation editor at its core and, increasingly, this is integrated with neural machine translation (NMT) engines via application programming interfaces (APIs). Thus, the TM software retrieves full or fuzzy matches from its database for segments of the source text that are sufficiently similar to source text segments already stored in memory. Similarity can range from 100 per cent matches to matches of, say, 70 per cent to 99 per cent; the level of acceptable similarity for fuzzy match retrieval can be set by the translator. The translator can then choose to leverage, that is, reuse, the already stored translation, with or without editing, or to ignore it. Matches are retrieved at the level of the segment, usually typographically delimited as a sentence, heading, bullet point, table cell, etc., but can also be searched at sub-segmental level.

Integration of MT with the TM can take various forms. Often (and particularly in early integrations) an MT suggestion would be generated for those segments for which there were no full or fuzzy TM matches (Zaretskaya, 2019). The logic is that even a fuzzy TM match is more useful to the translator than an MT suggestion, so the TM takes precedence and the MT suggestion is provided only where the TM can offer no assistance. However, where NMT engines have been specialized by domain/vertical and genre and the quality of the MT suggestions is high, the MT suggestion may be given priority over anything except a full TM match; thus, a fuzzy TM match may be considered inferior to the MT suggestion.

How TM and MT are integrated and how translators are expected to work with the technologies vary across use cases. Generally, translators will post-edit the MT suggestions, and edit TM matches, where applicable, to produce a translation of the requisite quality. Thus, in many settings, the focus of translator activity has shifted from translating from scratch to post-editing MT suggestions (Nunes Vieira, 2020). Translators working with interactive and adaptive MT systems have a slightly different role and involvement in translation production. In interactive systems (Läubli and Green, 2020), the MT suggestion is changed on the basis of what the user types, while adaptive MT systems also learn from the corrections made (Daems and Macken, 2019; Karimova, Simianer and Riezler, 2018). Other tools frequently used in a CAT environment, apart from terminology retrieval, include tools to perform quality assurance (QA) checks on the translation, both automatic and manual.

Research on the use of tools in professional translation practices is growing, both in laboratory settings and in translators' workplaces. Although predominantly concerned with tools use, many of these studies involve the practice of technical translation. They address questions related to the translator's experience from various angles, including physical and cognitive ergonomics (e.g., Ehrensberger-Dow and O'Brien, 2015; Ehrensberger-Dow and Hunziker Heeb, 2016; Ehrensberger-Dow and Massey, 2017), user needs and expectations (e.g., Moorkens and O'Brien, 2017; LeBlanc, 2017) and user preferences (e.g., Cadwell et al., 2016; García-Aragón and López-Rodríguez, 2017; Cadwell, O'Brien and Teixeira, 2018). These and other emerging strands of translation scholarship (Cronin, 2013, 2017; O'Hagan, 2016, 2020; Kenny, 2017a, 2017b; Olohan, 2021) are increasingly concerned with recontextualizing (technical) translation in the digital world by addressing material, discursive, economic, ecological and human-centred concerns. For the foreseeable future, translation studies is likely to continue to address questions pertaining to how the practice of translation 'shapes and is shaped by ongoing relationships with digital technologies' (Folaron, 2020, p. 204), ultimately leading to a better understanding of how 'the fortunes of translation are bound up with the fate of technology' (Cronin, 2020, p. 516).

## References

Alexander, K. P. (2013). The usability of print and online video instructions. *Technical Communication Quarterly*, **22**(3), 237–59. https://doi.org/10.1080/10572252.2013.775628.

Antia, B., Budin, G., Picht, H., Rogers, M., Schmitz, K.-D., and Wright, S. (2005). Shaping translation: A view from terminology research. *Meta*, **50**(4), https://doi.org/10.7202/019907ar.

Bennett, K. (2007). Epistemicide! The tale of a predatory discourse. *The Translator*, **13**(2), 151–69. https://doi.org/10.1080/13556509.2007.10799236.

Bhatia, V. K. (1993). *Analysing Genre: Language Use in Professional Settings*. London: Pearson Education Limited.

Bhatia, V. K. (2008). Genre analysis, ESP and professional practice. *English for Specific Purposes, Special Issue in Honor of John Swales*, **27**(2), 161–74. https://doi.org/10.1016/j.esp.2007.07.005.

Bhatia, V. K. (2016). *Critical Genre Analysis: Investigating Interdiscursive Performance in Professional Practice*. London: Taylor and Francis.

British Standards Institution. (2010). ISO 704:2010 Terminology Work – Principles and Methods. BSI Standards Limited.

Byrne, J. (2006). *Technical Translation: Usability Strategies for Translating Technical Documentation*. Dordrecht: Springer.

Byrne, J. (2012). *Scientific and Technical Translation Explained*. London: Routledge.

Cabré, T. (2010). Terminology and translation. In Y. Gambier and L. van Doorslaer, eds., *Handbook of Translation Studies: Volume 1*. Amsterdam: John Benjamins, pp. 356–65.

Cadwell, P., Castilho, S., O'Brien, S., and Mitchell, L. (2016). Human factors in machine translation and post-editing among institutional translators. *Translation Spaces*, **5**(2): 222–43. https://doi.org/10.1075/ts.5.2.04cad.

Cadwell, P., O'Brien, S., and Teixeira, C. S. C. (2018). Resistance and accommodation: Factors for the (non-)adoption of machine translation among professional translators. *Perspectives*, **26**(3), 301–21. https://doi.org/10.1080/0907676X.2017.1337210.

Christensen, T. P., and Schjoldager, A. (2019). Technical documentation and (technical) translation: A case study of work practices and concepts. In H. E. Jüngst, L. Link, K. Schubert and C. Zehrer, eds., *Challenging Boundaries: New Approaches to Specialized Communication*. Berlin: Frank and Timme GmbH, pp. 17–37.

Cronin, M. (2013). *Translation in the Digital Age*. London: Routledge.

Cronin, M. (2017). *Eco-translation: Translation and Ecology in the Age of the Anthropocene*. London: Routledge.

Cronin, M. (2020). Translation, technology and climate change. In M. O'Hagan, ed., *The Routledge Handbook of Translation and Technology*. London: Routledge, pp. 516–30.

Daems, J., and Macken, L. (2019). Interactive adaptive SMT versus interactive adaptive NMT: A user experience evaluation. *Machine Translation*, **33**(1), 117–34. https://doi.org/10.1007/s10590-019-09230-z.

DePalma, D. A. (2020). The end of the language industry as we know it? Presentation at the CSA research webinar, Cambridge, MA, 14 May.

Ehrensberger-Dow, M., and Hunziker Heeb, A. (2016). Investigating the ergonomics of a technologized translation workplace. In R. Muñoz Martín, ed., *Reembedding Translation Process Research*. Amsterdam: John Benjamins, pp. 69–88. https://doi.org/10.1075/btl.128.04ehr.

Ehrensberger-Dow, M., and Massey, G. (2017). Socio-technical issues in professional translation practice. *Translation Spaces*, **6**(1), 104–21. https://doi.org/10.1075/ts.6.1.06ehr.

Ehrensberger-Dow, M., and O'Brien, S. (2015). Ergonomics of the translation workplace: Potential for cognitive friction. *Translation Spaces*, **4**(1), 98–118. https://doi.org/10.1075/ts.4.1.05ehr.

ELIA, EMT, EUATC, FIT Europe, GALA, and LIND. (2019). 2019 Language Industry Survey – Expectations and Concerns of the European Language Industry.

Esselink, B. (2020). Multinational language service provider as user. In M. O'Hagan, ed., *The Routledge Handbook of Translation and Technology*. London: Routledge, pp. 109–26.

European Union. (n.d.). IATE. https://iate.europa.eu/home.

Faes, F. (2019). Slator 2019 Language Industry Market Report. Slator AG.

Fakhri, A. (2004). Rhetorical properties of Arabic research article introductions. *Journal of Pragmatics*, **36**(6), 1119–38. https://doi.org/10.1016/j.pragma.2003.11.002.

Folaron, D. (2020). Technology, technical translation and localization. In M. O'Hagan, ed., *The Routledge Handbook of Translation and Technology*. London: Routledge, pp. 203–19.

García-Aragón, A., and López-Rodríguez, C. I. (2017). Translators' needs and preferences in the design of specialized termino-lexicographic tools. In D. Kenny, ed., *Human Issues in Translation Technology*. London: Routledge, pp. 80–108.

GLTaC Inc. (n.d.). Military Translation. www.gltac.com/expertise/military-translation.

Gnecchi, M., Maylath, B., Mousten, B., Scarpa, F., and Vandepitte, S. (2011). Field convergence between technical writers and technical translators: Consequences for training institutions. *IEEE Transactions on Professional Communication*, **54**(2), 168–84. https://doi.org/10.1109/TPC.2011.2121750.

Gonzales, L., and Turner, H. N. (2017). Converging fields, expanding outcomes: Technical communication, translation, and design at a non-profit organization. *Technical Communication*, **64**(2), 126–40.

Government of Canada. (2009). TERMIUM Plus. Language Portal of Canada. 8 October 2009. www.btb.termiumplus.gc.ca/tpv2alpha/alpha-eng.html?lang=eng/.

Halliday, M.A.K. (2004). *The Language of Science*. Ed. J. J. Webster. London: Continuum.

Heinish, B., and Iacono, K. (2019). Attitudes of professional translators and translation studies towards order management and translator platforms. *JoSTrans – The Journal of Specialised Translation*, **32**, 61–89.

Hirano, E. (2009). Research article introductions in English for specific purposes: A comparison between Brazilian Portuguese and English. *English for Specific Purposes*, **28**(4), 240–50. https://doi.org/10.1016/j.esp.2009.02.001.

Hyland, K. (2000). *Disciplinary Discourses: Social Interactions in Academic Writing*. London: Longman.

Hyland, K. (2005). *Metadiscourse: Exploring Interaction in Writing*. London: Bloomsbury Publishing.

Hyland, K., and Tse, P. (2004). Metadiscourse in academic writing: A reappraisal. *Applied Linguistics*, **25**(2), 156–77. https://doi.org/10.1093/applin/25.2.156.

Kanoksilapatham, B. (2015). Distinguishing textual features characterizing structural variation in research articles across three engineering sub-discipline corpora. *English for Specific Purposes*, **37**, 74–86. https://doi.org/10.1016/j.esp.2014.06.008.

Karimova, S., Simianer, P., and Riezler, S. (2018). A user-study on online adaptation of neural machine translation to human post-edits. *Machine Translation*, **32**(4), 309–24. https://doi.org/10.1007/s10590-018-9224-8.

Kenny, D., ed. (2017a). *Human Issues in Translation Technology*. London: Routledge.

Kenny, D. (2017b). Introduction. In D. Kenny, ed., *Human Issues in Translation Technology*. London: Routledge, pp. 1–7.

Krein-Kühle, M. (2011). Register shifts in scientific and technical translation. *The Translator*, **17**(2), 391–413. https://doi.org/10.1080/13556509.2011.10799495.

Lanier, C. R. (2018). Toward understanding important workplace issues for technical communicators. *Technical Communication*, **65**(1), 66–84.

Läubli, S., and Green, S. (2020). Translation technology research and human-computer interaction (HCI). In M. O'Hagan, ed., *The Routledge Handbook of Translation and Technology*. London: Routledge, pp. 370–83.

LeBlanc, M. (2017). 'I can't get no satisfaction!' Should we blame translation technologies or shifting business practices? In D. Kenny, ed., *Human Issues in Translation Technology*. London: Routledge, pp. 45–62.

Lionbridge. (n.d.). Technical and Speciality Content Creation Services. www.lionbridge.com/what-we-do/content-creation-services.

Martín Martín, P. (2003). A genre analysis of English and Spanish research paper abstracts in experimental social sciences. *English for Specific Purposes*, **22**(1), 25–43.

Maylath, B., and St Amant, K. (2019). *Translation and Localization: A Guide for Technical and Professional Communicators*. London: Routledge.

McGrath, L., and Kuteeva, M. (2012). Stance and engagement in pure mathematics research articles: Linking discourse features to disciplinary practices. *English for Specific Purposes*, **31**(3), 161–73. https://doi.org/10.1016/j.esp.2011.11.002.

MemoQ. (n.d.). Extract Candidates (Term Extraction). Memoqdocs. https://docs.memoq.com/current/en/Places/extract-candidates.html.

Moorkens, J., and O'Brien, S. (2017). Assessing user interface needs of post-editors of machine translation. In D. Kenny, ed., *Human Issues in Translation Technology*. London: Routledge, pp. 109–30.

Mur Dueñas, P. (2011). An intercultural analysis of metadiscourse features in research articles written in English and in Spanish. *Journal of Pragmatics*, **43**(12), 3068–79. https://doi.org/10.1016/j.pragma.2011.05.002.

Musacchio, M. T. (2019). Quality in translation through 'controlled' writing, editing, and/or revising. In B. Maylath and K. St Amant, eds., *Translation and Localization: A Guide for Technical and Professional Communicators*. London: Routledge, pp. 89–110.

Nunes Vieira, L. (2020). Post-editing of machine translation. In M. O'Hagan, ed., *The Routledge Handbook of Translation and Technology*. London: Routledge, pp. 319–35.

O'Brien, S. (2019). Controlled language and writing for an international audience. In B. Maylath and K. St Amant, eds., *Translation and Localization: A Guide for Technical and Professional Communicators*. London: Routledge, pp. 65–88.

O'Hagan, M. (2016). Massively open translation: Unpacking the relationship between technology and translation in the 21st century. *International Journal of Communication*, **10**, 929–46.

O'Hagan, M. (2020). Introduction: Translation and technology: Disruptive entanglement of human and machine. In M. O'Hagan, ed., *The Routledge Handbook of Translation and Technology*. London: Routledge, pp. 1–18.

Olohan, M. (2016). *Scientific and Technical Translation*. London: Routledge.

Olohan, M. (2018). A practice-theory analysis of scientific editing by translators. *Alif: Journal of Comparative Poetics*, **38**, 298–328.

Olohan M. (2021). *Translation and Practice Theory*. London: Routledge.

Pavel, S., and Nolet, D. (2001). *Handbook of Terminology*. Ottawa: Canadian Government Publishing.

Pisanski Peterlin, A. (2008). Translating metadiscourse in research articles. *Across Languages and Cultures*, **9**(2), 205–18. https://doi.org/10.1556/Acr .9.2008.2.3.

Quesenbery, W. (2003). The five dimensions of usability. In M. J. Albers and M. B. Mazur, eds., *Content and Complexity: Information Design in Technical Communication*. Mahwah, NJ: Routledge, pp. 81–102.

Reckwitz, A. (2002). Toward a theory of social practices: A development in culturalist theorizing. *European Journal of Social Theory*, **5**(2), 243–63. https://doi.org/10.1177/13684310222225432.

Risku, H. (2004). Migrating from translation to technical communication and usability. In G. Hansen, K. Malmkjær and D. Gile, eds., *Claims, Changes and Challenges in Translation Studies: Selected Contributions from the EST Congress, Copenhagen 2001*. Amsterdam: John Benjamins, pp. 181–95.

Rogers, M. (2015). *Specialised Translation: Shedding the 'Non-Literary' Tag*. Basingstoke: Palgrave Macmillan.

Roturier, J. (2015). *Localizing Apps: A Practical Guide for Translators and Translation Students*. London: Routledge.

RWS. (n.d.). Intellectual Property Services. www.rws.com/solutions/intel lectual-property-services/.

Salö, L., and Hanell, L. (2014). Performance of unprecedented genres: Interdiscursivity in the writing practices of a Swedish researcher. *Language and Communication*, **37**(July), 12–28. https://doi.org/10.1016/j .langcom.2014.04.001.

Samraj, B. (2005). An exploration of a genre set: Research article abstracts and introductions in two disciplines. *English for Specific Purposes*, **24**(2), 141–56. https://doi.org/10.1016/j.esp.2002.10.001.

Sargent, B. B., and Lommel, A. (2019). The Global Website Assessment Index 2019. Cambridge, MA: CSA Research.

Scarpa, F. (2020). *Specialised Translation: Research and Professional Practice*. Basingstoke: Palgrave Macmillan.

Schatzki, T. R. (2001). Introduction: Practice theory. In T. R. Schatzki, K. Knorr-Cetina and E. von Savigny, eds., *The Practice Turn in Contemporary Theory*. London: Routledge, pp. 1–14.

Schatzki, T. R. (2016). Keeping track of large phenomena. *Geographische Zeitschrift*, **104**(1), 4–24.

Scott, J. (2018). Negotiation constraints on legal translation performance in an outsourced environment. In G. Tessuto, V. K. Bhatia and J. Engberg, eds., *Frameworks for Discursive Actions and Practices of the Law*. Newcastle upon Tyne: Cambridge Scholars Publishing, pp. 370–92.

Shove, E. (2017). Matters of practice. In A. Hui, T. Schatzki and E. Shove, eds., *The Nexus of Practices: Connections, Constellations, Practitioners*. London: Routledge, pp. 155–68.

Shove, E., Pantzar, M., and Watson, M. (2012). *The Dynamics of Social Practice*. London: SAGE.

Sketch Engine. (2019). Keywords and Term Extraction. Guide. www .sketchengine.eu/guide/keywords-and-term-extraction/.

Stoller, F. L., and Robinson, M. S. (2013). Chemistry journal articles: An interdisciplinary approach to move analysis with pedagogical aims. *English for Specific Purposes*, **32**(1), 45–57. https://doi.org/10.1016/j .esp.2012.09.001.

Swales, J. M. (1990). *Genre Analysis: English in Academic and Research Settings*. Cambridge: Cambridge University Press.

Swales, J. M. (1997). English as Tyrannosaurus Rex. *World Englishes*, **16**(3), 373–82.

Swales, J. M. (2004). *Research Genres: Explorations and Applications*. Cambridge: Cambridge University Press.

Vandepitte, S., Maylath, B., Mousten, B., Isohella, S., and Minacori, P. (2016). Multilateral collaboration between technical communicators and translator: A case study on new technologies and processes. *Journal of Specialised Translation*, **26**, 3–19.

Vold, E. T. (2006). Epistemic modality markers in research articles: A cross-linguistic and cross-disciplinary study. *International Journal of Applied Linguistics*, **16**(1), 61–87. https://doi.org/10.1111/j.1473-4192 .2006.00106.x.

Zaretskaya, A. (2019). Optimising the machine translation post-editing workflow. In *Proceedings of the Human-Informed Translation and Interpreting Technology Workshop (HiT-IT 2019)*. Varna, Bulgaria: Incoma Ltd, pp. 136–9. https://doi.org/10.26615/issn.2683-0078.2019_018.

# 17

# Translating Academic Texts

Krisztina Károly

## 17.1 Introduction

The translation of academic texts has received less attention in research (Franco Aixelá, 2004; Olohan, 2016; Pisanski Peterlin, 2008a) than other fields of non-literary translation (news translation, legal or business translation, etc.) even though translation has played an important role in the evolution of scientific thinking and international scholarly communication (Bennett, 2012; Wright and Wright, 1993). While a large number of contrastive studies are available on academic genres, only a few adopt a translational perspective. However, since the mid-1990s, interest in studying the translation of academic texts has grown as a result of the development of research methods within translation studies and the spread of English as the lingua franca of international scholarly communication.

As the topic is closely related to the evolution of science and stands at the interface of a number of disciplines, this chapter first presents the relationship between science and translation as well as the disciplinary perspectives on translating academic texts. The research methods applied to explore writers/translators working in diverse communicative situations and with different genres are also highlighted. The second part of the chapter offers a broad-based theoretical and empirical view of the translation of texts produced (1) in academic communication in formal education systems for academic purposes (e.g., textbooks, handbooks) and (2) in scholarly/disciplinary communication within the international research community for research purposes (e.g., research articles, monographs). Finally, the most important outcomes of research and their implications for translation and translator training are highlighted.

## 17.2 Translation and Science

### 17.2.1 Translation in the Practice and Discourse of Science

The evolution of science and conveying scientific knowledge via its various practices and discourses are fundamentally linked to translation. Scientists have always wanted to share their discoveries, and a succession of languages (Greek, Arabic, Latin, French, German, English) have been used to transmit scientific knowledge (Mendiluce-Cabrera and Bermúdez-Bausela, 2006, p. 446). Consequently, non-native speakers of these languages have needed to resort to translation for communication with members of the scholarly community in other cultures.

However, it is not merely communication that translation serves in the evolution of science. Translation scholars make significant contributions to the sociology and history of science, especially in the formation of discursive practices:

> Although science has been relatively neglected within translation studies, scholars of translation potentially have much to offer those who study the sociology and history of science. Translation scholars are well aware of the role that translation can play in hampering or propagating established discursive practices. Sociologists and historians of science tend to scrutinize agents (although sadly not often translators) and the power relations which influence them in their production of knowledge.
>
> (Meade, 2011, p. 226)

Olohan (2016) also emphasizes the role of translation in the performance of science and suggests ways of studying translation practices as integral components of scientific practices, 'in particular in relation to tools, technologies and sociotechnical developments in translation' (p. 5). She shows that there has been a shift in translation studies, too, in thinking about scientific translation. While in earlier times it primarily focused on the referential functions of scientific language 'without really recognizing that scientific ideas are constructed by scientists in certain ways to achieve certain rhetorical functions, and indeed that there are many different sciences, with different discourses for different addressees and different practices' (Olohan, 2016, p. 11), the imbalance has been redressed and the role of translation in the performance of science is better accommodated.

Translation has had a powerful influence on the construction of Western science too. Montgomery (2000, pp. 253–6) demonstrates that translation has been instrumental in the creation of astronomy in both the West and the East, in the formation of Arabic science, in the establishment of Latin as the lingua franca of science in the medieval world, in the evolution of modern science in the non-Western world and in making English the 'new Latin'.

Translation also plays a significant role in the creation and standardization of scientific terminology. Fuertes-Olivera and Pizarro-Sánchez (2002, p. 64) provide evidence of translators creating new linguistic metaphors which often become recognized scientific terms.

Finally, translation into or from the lingua franca has influenced patterns of thinking and shifts in the style of persuasion and in the establishment of new ways of organizing ideas, presenting arguments and ultimately a change of logic (Montgomery, 2000, p. 274).

### 17.2.2 Scientific Translation: Definition and Forms

Krein-Kühle (2011) defines scientific and technical translation as 'translation of expert-to-expert writing in the theoretical and applied fields of the natural sciences, engineering and technology' (p. 391). In this chapter, I use the term 'scientific translation' in a similarly broad sense to refer to the translation of expert-to-expert writing in the theoretical and applied fields of the natural and social sciences in communication for both research and academic purposes.

In this field, three main forms of translation may be identified:

(1) interlingual translation (or translation proper), for use by scholars who cannot read and/or write in certain relevant languages. The act of translation is virtually invisible as the (translated) texts (research articles, monographs, etc.) are read not as translations but as 'local' texts, exemplifying 'local' genres (Baumgarten, House and Probst, 2004, p. 84), and their translators are typically not overtly acknowledged (Franco Aixelá, 2004, p. 30; Pisanski Peterlin, 2008a, p. 207). Translations may be ordered from individual translators or from a translation agency. In either case, the actual translation is performed by individuals (trained translators or subject-matter specialists) or teams, often assisted by translation-specific software. Readers perceive a translation as the original. Therefore, adherence to target language norms, that is, taking a target-oriented approach (Toury, 1995), dominates and the acceptability of the translation is emphasized (Pisanski Peterlin, 2008a; Siepmann, 2006; Williams, 2004). Failure to comply with the rules and norms of the target culture may result in, for instance, the (translated) research article being rejected by the journal. This kind of translation is also referred to as covert (as opposed to overt) translation (House, 1997);

(2) self-translation (Bassnet, 2013; Rabacov, 2013) or auto translation (Grutman, 1998). Self-translators master the two languages, create their work in one language and then render it into the other (Grutman, 1998, p. 18);

(3) researchers writing their own papers in the relevant language (usually English), regardless of their proficiency (Snell-Hornby, 2007; Pisanski

Peterlin, 2008a), in an attempt to get published in English language international journals.

## 17.3 Disciplinary Perspectives

Because of the complex nature of academic translation, translation studies works with other disciplines such as science and technology studies (Bennett, 2012; Olohan, 2016), cognitive linguistics (especially Lakoff and Johnson's (1980) work on cognitive metaphor; Fuertes-Olivera and Pizarro-Sánchez, 2002), terminology studies (Rogers, 2012), text linguistics (Aksoy, 2001) and discourse analysis (Pisanski Peterlin, 2008a; Williams, 2004, 2005, 2006, 2007).

Within the science of text, relevant subfields include languages for specific purposes (LSP), English for academic purposes (EAP) (Jordan, 1997; Mayoral-Asensio, 2007), genre analysis (López-Arroyo and Méndez-Cendón, 2007), register studies (López-Arroyo and Roberts, 2017), contrastive rhetoric (for an overview, see Pilegaard, 1997), corpus linguistics (López-Rodríguez and Tercedor-Sánchez, 2008), critical discourse analysis (Bennett, 2006), English as a lingua franca (Agost, 2015; Baumgarten, House and Probst, 2004; Taviano, 2018; Franco Aixelá, 2004) and international English, 'the specialized language that non-native users of English need to acquire in order to be accepted by this community' (Mendiluce-Cabrera and Bermúdez-Bausela, 2006, p. 445).

## 17.4 Research Methods in the Study of Translating Academic Texts

The study of translating academic texts has gained new impetus with globalization and the rapid spread of English as the lingua franca of communication. From the 1990s, the field has been characterized by target-oriented contrastive research (Toury, 1995), aiming to identify features of translated language by comparing it with non-translated language produced in a target culture.

Researchers typically adopt a corpus-based methodology and corpus linguistic tools to test hypotheses about universal features of translation (e.g., explicitation (Jawad, 2014)), the translation of lexical elements (e.g., key words (Kemppanen, 2004) or jargon (Pilegaard, 1997)), textual features (e.g., metadiscourse (Pisanski Peterlin, 2008a)) or theme–rheme relations (Williams, 2004, 2006, 2007). Other techniques include:

- manual text analyses, drawing on discourse analysis – for example, Götz (2015) studied abstracts using Swales's 1990 and Hyland's 2005 frameworks, and Baumgarten, House and Probst (2004) used House's (1997) translation evaluation model, partly based on Halliday (1994);

- computer-based text analyses, using large corpora and computerized search techniques to provide quantitative evidence for or against hypotheses – for example, Kemppanen (2004) conducted a computer application of Firth's (1969) concept of key words to study the use of the Finnish word *ystävyys*/'friendship';
- interviews – for example, Muñoz-Miquel (2014, 2018) interviewed medical translators with different professional profiles – in-house translators, freelancers, etc.;
- focus groups to probe the findings of product-oriented analyses – for example, Brøgger (2017) explored the reasons given by medical translators for various translation choices;
- surveys – for example, Muñoz-Miquel (2018) used an online questionnaire, designed with the LimeSurvey management system;
- experimental designs – for example, Bowker (2016) conducted a pilot project in speed training;
- combined corpus and experimental study designs – for example, Jiménez-Crespo (2018) designed a preliminary corpus study complemented by an experimental one to reveal the reception of medical websites translated from English into Spanish in the United States, with instruments developed using corpus data.

Contrastive, empirical studies explore translators and writers working in different communicative situations. Comparisons (and consequently corpora) typically include source and target texts as well as translated and non-translated texts (i.e., originals in the target language) and are carefully designed to ensure validity and reliability. Williams (2004), for example, developed a model for target-oriented corpus-based contrastive analysis (CA) from Chesterman's (1998, p. 54) more general model for contrastive functional analysis. The model contains three steps: (1) linguistic data collection; (2) establishing criteria for comparison, defining linguistic variables and testing these statistically to obtain baseline data; and (3) contextual analysis. Williams found target-oriented quantitative CA applied to a sizeable corpus a fruitful approach as it provides solid empirical data and insights into the translation process that may later be applied in both translator training and practice.

For cross-linguistic studies, corpora can be parallel (i.e., consist of source texts and their corresponding target versions) or comparable (i.e., contain texts in two or more languages, collected according to identical criteria; López-Arroyo and Roberts, 2017, p. 115). However, the main criteria for corpus compilation, namely 'presenting proportion, genre, domain, and time' (McEnery and Xiao, 2007, p. 20), do not always guarantee a match between the sub-corpora in a comparable corpus. López-Arroyo and Roberts (2017), working with two corpora, show that 'even when the text selection criteria are refined, genre theory cannot always guarantee enough linguistic similarities between language for specific purposes (LSP) texts in different languages' (2017, p. 114).

Baumgarten, House and Probst (2004) work with three corpora: a translation corpus (original English texts and their German translations), a comparable corpus (English and German non-translated texts from the same genres with comparable topics, serving as a reference corpus) and a validation corpus. The last is used to validate the results of the text analyses from the translation corpus and the comparable corpus. It consists of translations from the same genres into the opposite direction, that is, from German into English, as well as translations from English into French and Spanish.

## 17.5  Research on Translating Texts for Academic and Research Purposes

Research on translating texts for academic and research purposes is abundant and varied in its focuses, so the present review is necessarily selective. It discusses research in relation to different language pairs (Section 17.5.1), genres (Section 17.5.2), disciplines (Section 17.5.3) and translation strategies (Section 17.5.4).

### 17.5.1  Language Pairs

Owing to the prevalence of English as the lingua franca of science and academia, a large amount of research explores translation involving English. Table 17.1 lists the language pairs that have received attention and the focuses of inquiry.

These studies indicate that the greatest challenges for translators result from differences in language structure (Bennett, 2011, p. 202), rhetorical and genre conventions, register differences, 'metaphorical conceptualizations' (Olohan and Salama-Carr, 2011, pp. 181–7) and interference (Bennett, 2011, p. 202).

### 17.5.2  Genre-Oriented Research

Research on genres is unbalanced; some genres receive considerable attention (e.g., the research article or the abstract), while others attract less interest (e.g., the call for paper or the case report).

Arntz (2001, pp. 203–4 in German; available in English in Krüger (2016)) developed an eleven-point scale for ranking scientific/technical genres according to their perceived difficulty and the knowledge required to benefit from the relevant texts (see Table 17.2). The scale ranks encyclopaedias and popular science texts at the lowest difficulty degree (I) and

Table 17.1 *Research on different language pairs*

| Languages | Source | Focus |
|---|---|---|
| English, French, German, Spanish, Russian | Franco Aixelá (2004) | - technical and scientific translation |
| English→Arabic | Al-Hassnawi (2007) | - scientific texts (vs literature) |
| | Hamdan and Natour (2014) | - scholarly publications (gender of cited authors) |
| | Jawad (2014) | - monographs (ST-oriented approach) |
| | Nasser (2014) | - scientific books |
| English–Brazilian Portuguese | Tack Erten (2012) | - academic calls for papers |
| English→Chinese | Xiangtao (2007) | - scientific textbooks |
| English–Danish | Pilegaard (1997) | - medical research articles |
| English→Dutch | Vandepitte, Vandenbussche and Algoet (2011) | - translations of Darwin |
| English–French | Hoorickx-Raucq (2005) | - scientific publications and TV documentaries |
| | Jooken and Rooryck (2011) | - philosophy texts |
| English→German | Gerzymisch-Arbogast (1993) | - economics textbooks |
| | Krüger (2016) | - Cologne Specialized Translation Corpus's scientific and technical sub-corpus (research reports, research articles) |
| | Stolze (2003) | - economics texts |
| English–Hungarian | Götz (2015) | - research article abstracts |
| English→Japanese | Meade (2011) | - role of translation in the development of engineering as a discipline in Japan |
| English→Persian | Farahzad (2003) | - texts on women's studies (manipulation in translation) |
| English–Polish | Pietrzak (2015) | - medical records |
| English–Spanish | Fuertes-Olivera and Pizarro-Sánchez (2002) | - economics manuals |
| | García Hidalgo and Dunham (1981); Mu oz-Miquel (2018); Jiménez-Crespo (2018) | - medical translation |
| | López-Arroyo and Méndez-Cendón (2007) | - medical research article abstracts |
| | Mendiluce-Cabrera and Bermúdez-Bausela (2006); Williams (2004, 2005, 2007) | - medical research articles |
| | Méndez-Cendón (2009) | - medical case reports |
| | López-Arroyo and Roberts (2017) | - scientific register and genres |
| | López-Rodríguez and Tercedor-Sánchez (2008) | - coastal engineering texts: corpora in teaching scientific translation |
| Arabic→Spanish | Gil-Bardají (2009) | - scientific texts |
| Arabic translation | Sharkas (2011) | - translated and original Arabic medical research articles |
| Finnish→English | Mauranen (1993) | - economics texts |

Table 17.1 *Continued*

| Languages | Source | Focus |
|---|---|---|
| | Tirkkonen-Condit (2001) | - grant applications |
| French→Arabic | Jacquemond (2015) | - social sciences texts (the case of Pierre Bourdieu) |
| French→English | Bowker (2016) | - scientific translator training |
| Galician→English | Fernández-Silva and Kerremans (2011) | - scientific articles on environment |
| German→English | Watt (1993) | - sentence-level translation strategies of simple and complex structures (numbers, clauses, etc.) |
| German→Spanish | Sánchez (2011) | - misogynist scientific treatise |
| Portuguese→English | Bennett (2006) | - texts on literary and cultural studies |
| | Bennett (2008, 2012) | - academic discourse |
| | Bennett (2011) | - technical discourse |
| Russian→Finnish | Kemppanen (2004) | - political history texts |
| Slovene→English | Pisanski Peterlin (2005, 2008a, 2008b, 2014) | - research articles |
| Turkish→English | Aksoy (2001) | - history books |

Symbols: → : translation direction; – : research both from and to the languages indicated.

standards, patents and application reports at the highest degree (XI). Research in translation studies is ranked mainly at degrees IV, VII, IX and X.

As Table 17.2 shows, research is most abundant on the research article (RA) genre and the medical field, and so I will concentrate on the outcomes of research pertaining to these areas (Section 17.5.2.1) and the genres that are connected to them: RA abstracts (Section 17.5.2.2), call for papers (Section 17.5.2.3) and grant applications (Section 17.5.2.4).

### 17.5.2.1 Translation of Research Articles

Pilegaard (1997) offers an overview of studies on the translation of medical research articles into Chinese, Danish, Dutch, French, German and Spanish. He reveals the challenges that translators of these articles face and suggests the following set of translation strategies, formulated as recommendations:

- Equivalence is to be sought at all levels – lexical, syntactic and textual.
- Lexico-syntactic and pragmatic modifications must be guided by genre- and culture-specific conventions 'at the levels of lexicon, word classes, verbal categories, syntactic functions, modality, relationships between sentences, and polarisation' (p. 180).
- Translator and source text author should work in close collaboration to strike a balance among the conventions of the (international/English)

Table 17.2 *Genres in translation studies (TS) research according to degree of technicality/difficulty (based on Arntz, 2001)*

| Degree | Genre(s) | Intended recipients | Required specialized knowledge | Examples of genres explored in TS |
|---|---|---|---|---|
| IV | introductory handbooks and introductory textbooks | persons interested in systematically presented basic knowledge | knowledge of scientific basics | - **medical records** (discharge summaries) (Pietrzak, 2015)<br>- **manuals on economics** (Fuertes-Olivera and Pizarro-Sánchez, 2002)<br>- **textbooks on science** (for primary and secondary education) (Xiangtao, 2007)<br>- **scientific multimedia** (Camara and Espasa, 2011)<br>- **academic transcripts and diplomas** (Mayoral-Asensio, 2003/2014) |
| VII | articles in learned journals | experts interested in very specific areas of a scientific/technical subfield | thorough theoretical and applied knowledge in a scientific/technical subfield | - **medical research articles** (Mendiluce-Cabrera and Bermúdez-Bausela, 2006; Pilegaard, 1997; Sharkas, 2011; Williams, 2004)<br>- **biomedical research articles** (Williams, 2005, 2007)<br>- **geography research articles** (Pisanski Peterlin, 2008a, 2008b)<br>- **medical abstracts** (López-Arroyo and Méndez-Cendón, 2007)<br>- **TS abstracts** (Götz, 2015)<br>- **call for papers** (Tack Erten, 2012) |
| IX | academic textbooks | students, scientists working in a scientific/technical subfield | thorough theoretical knowledge in science and technology | - **history textbooks** (Aksoy, 2001; Wright and Wright, 1993)<br>- **monographs** (Jawad, 2014) |
| X | research reports | scientists concerned with theoretical issues | complex and detailed theoretical knowledge | - **medical case reports** (Méndez-Cendón, 2009)<br>- **grant applications** (Tirkkonen-Condit, 2001) |

research article genre, the style demands of the journal in question and the idiosyncrasies of the author.

Sharkas (2011) investigates glossing, that is, the insertion of foreign terms next to their target text counterparts, in translated and original medical journal articles in Arabic. He finds that glossing is used frequently in both translated and original texts in the corpus; however, the ratios are smaller in original texts than in translations.

Abundant research is available on Spanish–English translation in the medical field. The greatest challenges that translators seem to face in this context involve transforming the discourse patterns of Spanish RAs into those of English RAs (Mendiluce-Cabrera and Bermúdez-Bausela, 2006, pp. 447–8). Mendiluce-Cabrera and Bermúdez-Bausela (2006) show that since the 1950s, scientific writing in the international context has developed a kind of compromise language between native and non-native users of English and since then native users tend to 'recognize the legitimate communicative status of a non-native use of English, that of International English' (p. 449). They also mention that a number of attempts have been made to create a more international version (p. 453), for example Basic English, Nuclear English and Controlled English, but suggest that today's lingua franca is International English (IE), 'characterized by simplified grammatical rules, a concise and clear structure avoiding ambiguity along with a fixed terminology, a lack of colloquialisms, slang or any other idiomatic variants' (Mendiluce-Cabrera and Bermúdez-Bausela, 2006, p. 453). They argue that 'the importance of reaching an international heterogeneous audience in Medicine results in "medical IE," an English variant that only exists in international medical research journals. Likewise, the economic interests of software localization result in a "neutral Spanish," a Spanish variant that only exists in our computers … or PCs' (Mendiluce-Cabrera and Bermúdez-Bausela, 2006, p. 453).

Williams (2004, 2005) explores the *Methods* and *Discussions* sections of medical research articles in English–Spanish translation. He uses a target-oriented contrastive analysis model to devise correction strategies that translators may apply to avoid unnatural texts and produce acceptable translations. In the case of the *Methods* section, Williams (2004) focuses on the theme–rheme structure and a subset of lexical items representing persons viewed as the object of clinical study. His corpus shows a number of statistically significant differences in the characterization of theme between the Spanish source texts and their English translations. The translations demonstrate information overload, an excess of person themes for all lexical categories, a different distribution of associated syntactic categories and discrepancies in the relative frequencies of the main lexical items. The results indicate a sentence-by-sentence translation process that imprints the thematic pattern of the source text on the target text. The changes recorded are typically syntactically motivated, super-ficial and have only local impact. Based on a contextual analysis, Williams (2004, pp. 99–100) identifies three thematic strategies that can bridge the gaps between sources and translations, namely postposition, redundancy and reduced information load. He argues that by these strategies all major excesses and deficits may be corrected in translations so that texts may be produced which conform to the target lexical, syntactic and thematic norms.

Williams (2005) explores the *Discussion* section of biomedical RAs and the semantic field of 'research' and 'researcher'. He reveals four points of contrast (pp. 156–7) between Anglo-American and Spanish discourse style, which are typically carried over into the Spanish translations. Anglo-American discourse

- is more impersonal;
- reflects a 'separatist' view of research, indicated by special tense use – aspects associated with performing the study and obtaining the data are described in the past tense (e.g., *The study showed* ...), while aspects referring to the act of writing or publication are expressed in the present time sequence (e.g., *This report describes* ...);
- works with moves (i.e., discourse functions such as claim, statement of result, comparing current with previous research; Williams, 2005, pp. 138–9) relating to tense, while in Spanish, moves relate to syntax;
- prefers unmarked themes for non-integral references in a reporting or projecting thematic frame, while Spanish texts tend to have marked adjunct themes in a non-reporting frame.

In other studies (e.g., Williams, 2007), based on corpus and contextual analyses, he proposes translation guidelines for potentially problematic lexical elements (e.g., for the verb 'observar' [literally, 'to observe']).

Pisanski Peterlin (2008a) explores the translation strategies relating to textual metadiscourse in research articles on geography, which organizes the contents of the discourse and structures the text at the macro level (e.g., *this paper argues, as mentioned above, to conclude*). She analyses English translations of Slovene geography articles and compares her findings to English-original research articles. She shows that not all of the metadis-course items of the original texts are translated (70 per cent were retained), while a significant number of items (e.g., *following* or *as follows*) are inserted in the translations. She also finds that the frequency of use of textual metadiscourse is twice as high in the English-original geography corpus as in the Slovene originals.

Considerable differences have also been observed between languages and cultures in the use of the thesis statement (Connor, 1996; Kaplan, 1966). Pisanski Peterlin's (2008b) corpus of thesis statements in Slovene geography research articles, their English translations, and English origi-nals shows that the thesis statement is used more frequently in original

English RAs than in original Slovene ones, and that the English translations correspond to the Slovene originals. She also investigates the position of the thesis statement in the three sub-corpora, identifying differences between the two sets of originals (English and Slovene) in this respect too, with the English translations resembling the Slovene originals. As in Williams's work referred to earlier, she notes changes made during translation from Slovene to English to create a better target language text.

### 17.5.2.2 Translation of Research Article Abstracts

López-Arroyo and Méndez-Cendón (2007) describe and compare the rhetorical and phraseological structures of medical RA abstracts in the field of diagnostic imaging, in English and Spanish. Their primary concern is to help translators, technical writers and English for specific (or special) purposes (ESP) students cope with challenges caused by differing discourse conventions (López-Arroyo and Méndez-Cendón, 2007, p. 503). Their focus is on the informative abstract, which is 'brief, accurate, objective, complete, and intelligible, and ... has to be presented in the same format [as] the RP [research paper] in order to facilitate the skimming of the RP' (p. 505) as opposed to the descriptive abstract, the main function of which is to help readers position RAs. They compare the English journal *Radiology* and the Spanish *Radiología* and find that the language in *Radiología*'s abstracts is less formulaic and more varied than that of *Radiology*'s abstracts and that lexical repetition thus occurs less frequently in *Radiología* than in *Radiology*. From a grammatical viewpoint, English frequently uses the passive voice in the simple past, while Spanish resorts to non-finite, verbless clauses. The 'telegraphic style' (p. 514) of *Radiología* makes its discourse more dynamic and involves the reader more than does the past tense used in English. The phraseological and rhetorical analyses indicate that Spanish authors do not always assume that the readers have the same level of expertise as they do. English authors, in contrast, use specific technical terms, with an abundance of premodification and complex noun phrases, implying that the audience has the same level of knowledge as they do. As far as the rhetorical organization is concerned, in *Radiology* the *Introduction, Methods, Results* and *Discussion* pattern is followed in compliance with the submission requirements, whereas authors publishing in *Radiología* do not follow these consistently. Furthermore, in the Spanish corpus, López-Arroyo and Méndez-Cendón (2007, pp. 514–15) found descriptive abstracts (12.7 per cent of the samples), although the guidelines specifically require informative abstracts.

Götz (2015) discusses abstracts published in translation studies journals. Using Swales's (1990) 'Create a Research Space' model and Hyland's (2004) theory of social interaction in research writing, she explores the rhetorical move structure of abstracts to reveal (1) whether it changes in Hungarian–English translation and (2) whether it differs in abstracts translated from

Hungarian into English and abstracts originally written in English. Contrary to expectations, her analyses show no significant difference between the Hungarian abstracts and their English translations, or between the translated English abstracts and the original English abstracts. However, the introduction move of the original English abstracts was more emphatic than that of the Hungarian and the translated English abstracts. She explains this with reference to the important role this move plays in positioning a study within international English language research.

### 17.5.2.3    Translation of Academic Call for Papers

Tack Erten's (2012) work on the translation of the call for paper (CFP) genre was motivated by the recognition that the greater the translator's awareness of how a particular genre operates at the cultural and textual levels in particular language pairs, the more likely it is that its translation achieves functional equivalence. Building on Halliday's (1994) systemic functional grammar, the study explores the similarities and differences in genre conventions in a small comparable corpus of CFPs in American English and Brazilian Portuguese. She shows that although CFPs in English and Portuguese are broadly similar, there are some pragmatic differences, and she formulates suggestions for translation strategies that will help to achieve functional equivalence:

- Make greater use of personalization.
- Avoid using or decrease use of a judgemental tone.
- Render group titles according to target text cultural norms.
- Mitigate imperatives.

### 17.5.2.4    Translation of Grant Applications

Tirkkonen-Condit (2001) focuses on project proposals submitted to the European Union (EU) by applicants with a Finnish L1 (first language) background. She argues that the rhetorical norm governing proposals written in English 'is close to the one prevailing in Anglo-American scientific rhetoric, especially as regards grant applications' (Tirkkonen-Condit, 2001, p. 261) whereas the Finnish rhetorical tradition

> is more implicit and impersonal. It starts from the background and tends to leave it to the reader to infer the aims of the project as well as the merits of the researchers. Praising oneself is felt to be impolite, and metatext is frowned upon as a sign of underestimating the reader's intelligence. The 'point' of the text tends to be left towards the end. ... Thus a Finnish applicant or a Finnish translator who is not aware of the rhetorical difference may end up producing an English text which is grammatically correct, but rhetorically deviant.    (Tirkkonen-Condit, 2001, p. 262)

While Tirkkonen-Condit notes that there are several target cultures in the EU context, she also points out that there exists a particular Euro-rhetoric.

Hence, the EU can be regarded as a target culture, with 'hybrid texts' (Schäffner and Adab, 2001, p. 169) which 'deviate from an established linguistic and rhetorical norm' (Tirkkonen-Condit, 2001, p. 263). Her study shows that the English-language texts produced by Finns are also hybrid. They merge the Finnish rhetorical norm, the intended target norm and the hybrid target norm (the EU-rhetoric).

### 17.5.3 Disciplinary Variation in Translating Academic Texts

Translation problems relating to different disciplines are typically caused by the fact that most translators are not scholars/scientists. The greater part of research is conducted on medical translation, but there is also work on the translation of texts on economics (Fuertes-Olivera and Pizarro-Sánchez, 2002; Stolze, 2003), women's studies (Farahzad, 2003), literary and cultural studies (Bennett, 2006), philosophy (Albert, 2000, 2001), social sciences (Collet, 2016; Jacquemond, 2015), political history (Kemppanen, 2004), engineering (Meade, 2011) and coastal engineering (López-Rodríguez and Tercedor-Sánchez, 2008).

Medical translation has been claimed to be 'the most universal and oldest field of scientific translation' (Fischbach, 1986, p.16) because of the universality of its subject (the human body), the role it has played in the construction and dissemination of medical knowledge (Muñoz-Miquel, 2018, p. 25), the variety and accessibility of its reference tools (textbooks, encyclopaedias, journals, physicians, librarians) and its terminological uniformity (at least in the Western languages, where its terminology is mostly of Latin and Greek origin). Nevertheless, as Pilegaard (1997, p. 163) discusses, medical translation faces challenges:

- English has replaced Latin as the language of international medical communication.
- Thousands of new terms and abbreviations are created annually.
- There is a lack of correspondence between certain concepts in different languages.
- Non-native speakers of English occasionally misuse the relevant technical vocabulary and jargon.

Translators are either medical/health professionals with language skills or translators with a linguistic or translation studies background. While most studies are based on personal experience, Muñoz-Miquel's (2018) work uses broader data to reveal what the academic and socio-professional profile of medical translators is, and explores whether there are any differences between translators with a linguistic background and those with a scientific or medical background in terms of their professional practice or training needs. She shows that translators with a linguistic background see their principal weaknesses in the conceptual and terminological aspects, while translators with a scientific/health-care background report having limitations when using technological tools or their mother tongue. Despite the differences, Muñoz-Miquel's (2018, p. 48) study provides evidence that medical translators share some stereotypical socio-professional features: they have ample experience in the field and work for a wide variety of customers, with many genres and documentation resources to solve medical translation problems.

The area of economics poses different kinds of challenge. Stolze (2003, p. 187), for example, demonstrates that one special problem in translating economics texts is 'vagueness' on various levels: pragmatic, semantic, terminological and conceptual (reflecting cultural differences). This may hamper understanding of the source text. The translator should therefore act as a 'co-author' and enhance their subject-specialist knowledge, including specialist ways of communication (Stolze, 2003, p. 202).

Fuertes-Olivera and Pizarro-Sánchez's (2002) corpus-based study focuses on a related problem, namely the translation of the terminological metaphor in economics texts. They show that some metaphors develop into technical terms and that this can cause translation problems. Using Lakoff's (1987) theory, they focus on metaphors for 'inflation' in English economics texts and their translation into Spanish. They argue that, when translating metaphors, 'translators must cope with rendering the same or similar metaphorical scenario to perform their function as terms and, at the same time, with preserving their aesthetic role, thus surprising, delighting and interesting interactants' (Fuertes-Olivera and Pizarro-Sánchez, 2002, p. 44). They conclude that translators should concentrate on maintaining metaphors' function for categorization and naming (i.e., their conceptual function) and for revitalizing concepts (i.e., their aesthetic function). Literal translation may be helpful in specialized texts not only because experts are familiar with literal renderings but also because it produces 'similarity-creating metaphors', a common method of spreading scientific knowledge and terminology. This highlights the contribution of translation to the construction of science and scientific thinking at large.

Collet's (2016) work relates to translation in the social sciences. She starts out from the assumption that social scientific texts possess features that can enhance or, conversely, impede a reader's ability to access their content. These are domain-specific lexis/terminology and conventional textual formats. Her study is based on a corpus of more than 200 semantic markers extracted from articles published in English or in French in the translation studies journal *Meta*. She examines one such feature, namely citation, and works with the assumption that a conventional textual format is a distinguishing characteristic of academic writing. The article offers a typology of semantic markers and shows that these markers can help the specialized translator during the pre-translation phase. Her analyses reveal that citations have multiple functions in specialized discourse. They

- acknowledge intellectual indebtedness;
- partake in the social construction of knowledge;
- enhance the text's overall persuasiveness;
- help to delineate the meaning of specific terms within the confines of the new text;
- acquire a dual dialogic quality, that is, they are oriented towards the writers of previous texts and also interact with the reader by responding to possible questions or to plausible needs for more precise semantic or conceptual information; and
- positively impact the overall readability of a text (written for a group of disciplinary 'insiders').

Farahzad (2003) studies English–Persian translation in the field of women's studies. He explores how and why translators manipulate texts and the reasons for manipulative shifts occurring in translation. The study involves ten female and ten male experienced English–Persian translators. Farahzad (2003) shows that, in this context, manipulation in translation is ideologically motivated: translators who deliberately do not render a lexical item or make syntactic changes in translation manipulate the contents of the source text in their translations in the same manner as those who unconsciously do so for ideological reasons. He therefore considers manipulation to be an interpretative strategy and claims that many target texts reflect such manipulation in the form of manipulative shifts (Farahzad, 2003, pp. 279–80).

Bennett (2006) investigates text extracts from essays on literary and cultural studies in English and in Portuguese. She finds that, despite surface-level similarities between genres in the two languages, the extracts reflect different worldviews: while the English texts reflect objective reality that can be observed, analysed and described, the Portuguese extracts do not. Secondly, while in the English texts information is transparent and easily accessible, in Portuguese it is less so. Finally, while the English authors work linearly and control sense tightly, the Portuguese authors are not unidirectional and reflect less control of the message, using ambiguity, paradoxes, analogical relations and complex syntax, which results in discourse that may seem chaotic to the English reader.

### 17.5.4 Translation Strategies in Academic Texts

A wide variety of strategies are used in the translation of academic texts. Table 17.3 summarizes the main research focuses and the kinds of topic explored in the literature. Seven main focuses may be identified: (1) explicitation and implicitation; (2) words and word combinations; (3) terminology; (4) information structuring, dynamics and

Table 17.3 *Research focuses in the study of strategies for translating academic texts*

| Research focus | Examples of research | Topic |
|---|---|---|
| explicitation/ implicitation | Jawad (2014) | - asymmetric explicitation |
| | Jiménez-Crespo (2018) | - translated medical websites |
| | Krüger (2016) | - degree of technicality vs. explicitation |
| words/word combinations | Krein-Kühle (2011) | - *have* and *be* as main verbs in English to German translation |
| | Williams (2007) | - the verb *observar* in English to Spanish translation |
| | Méndez-Cendón (2009) | - phraseological patterns |
| | Camara and Espasa (2011); Nasser (2014), Shuttleworth (2011) | - scientific metaphors |
| | Fuertes-Olivera and Pizarro-Sánchez (2002) | - terminological metaphor |
| | Kemppanen (2004) | - keywords and ideology |
| terminology | Rogers (2012) | - terminology |
| | López-Rodríguez and Tercedor-Sánchez (2008) | - terminological resources in coastal engineering |
| | Fernández-Silva and Kerremans (2011); Pilegaard (1997) | - jargon |
| information structuring | Williams (2004, 2005, 2006, 2007) | - theme–rheme structure, thematic progression and collocational patterns |
| text construction/ structuring | Pisanski Peterlin (2008a) | - textual metadiscourse |
| | López-Arroyo and Méndez-Cendón (2007) | - rhetorical and phraseological structures determining composition strategies |
| | Aksoy (2001) | - textuality in Turkish and Western cultures (translation model for history narratives based on the seven standards of textuality) |
| | Baumgarten, House and Probst (2004) | - textual norms (converging source and target norms) |
| | Jooken and Rooryck (2011) | - hedging devices |
| | Sharkas (2011) | - glossing to standardize terminology |
| | Nasser (2014) | - differences between scientific and literary texts |
| | Pietrzak (2015) | - style in English and Polish medical records |
| cultural issues | Gil-Bardají (2009) | - representations of cultures created by/via translation |
| | Hamdan and Natour (2014) | - gender of cited authors |
| | Kastberg (2007) | - cultural issues in technical texts |

Table 17.3 *Continued*

| Research focus | Examples of research | Topic |
| --- | --- | --- |
| ideology | Sánchez (2011) | - ideology and gender (discourse practices of women) |
| | Farahzad (2003) | - manipulation in Persian translation |

packaging; (5) (target) text construction and structuring; (6) cultural issues; and (7) ideology.

### 17.5.5 Conclusions and Implications for Translation and Translator Training

According to Stolze (2003, p. 187), English translations are ideally

- clear, explicit and unambiguous;
- concise;
- neutral;
- objective;
- standardized;
- faithful in information content to the source text;
- devoid of interpretation;
- devoid of features that would make them read as translations; and
- equivalent functionally at the textual level.

With this in mind, translator trainers should note that the ideal translator of academic texts is

- a disseminator of science across national and linguistic borders;
- instrumental in the construction of scientific discourse;
- able to recognize the characteristics of disciplines and specialist domains;
- highly communicatively competent in culture- and domain/discipline-specific discourse; but still
- invisible.

## References

Agost, R. (2015). Translation studies and the mirage of a lingua franca. *Perspectives: Studies in Translatology*, **23**(2), 249–64.

Aksoy, B. (2001). Aspects of textuality in translating a history book from Turkish into English. *Babel*, **47**(3), 193–204.

Albert, S. (2000). Filozófiai szövegek fordítása: 1. rész [The translation of philosophy discourse: Part 1]. *Fordítástudomány [Translation Studies]*, **2** (2), 5–23.

Albert, S. (2001). Filozófiai szövegek fordítása 2. rész [The translation of philosophy discourse: Part 2]. *Fordítástudomány [Translation Studies]*, **3** (1), 5–25.

Al-Hassnawi, A. (2007). Aspects of scientific translation: English into Arabic translation as a case study. Available at www.translationdirectory.com /article10.

Arntz, R. (2001). *Fachbezogene Mehrsprachigkeit in Recht und Technik*. Hildesheim: Olms.

Bassnett, S. (2013). The self-translator as rewriter. In A. Cordingley, ed., *Self-Translation: Brokering Originality in Hybrid Culture*. London/New York: Bloomsbury, pp. 13–25.

Baumgarten, N., House, J., and Probst, J. (2004). English as a *lingua franca* in covert translation processes. *The Translator*, **10**(1), 83–108.

Bennett, K. (2006). Critical language study and translation. The case of academic discourse. In J. F. Duarte, A. Assis Rosa and T. Seruya, eds., *Translation Studies at the Interface of Disciplines*. Amsterdam: John Benjamins, pp. 111–27.

Bennett, K. (2008). English academic discourse: Its hegemonic status and implications for translation. Unpublished doctoral dissertation. Universidade de Lisboa, Faculdade de Letras, Programa em Estudos Comparatistas.

Bennett, K. (2011). The scientific revolution and its repercussions on the translation of technical discourse. *The Translator*, **17**(2), 189–210.

Bennett, K. (2012). *English Academic Discourse: Hegemonic Status and Implications for Translation (with Particular Reference to Portuguese)*. Saarbrucken: Lambert Academic Publishing.

Bowker, L. (2016). The need for speed! Experimenting with 'speed training' in the scientific/technical translation classroom. *Meta*, **61**(Hors série), 22–36.

Brøgger, M. N. (2017). When translation competence is not enough: A focus group study of medical translators. *Meta*, **62**(2), 397–414.

Camara, L., and Espasa, E. (2011). The audio description of scientific multimedia. *The Translator*, **17**(2), 415–38.

Chesterman, A. (1998). Causes, translations, effects. *Target*, **10**(2), 201–30.

Collet, T. (2016). Intertextuality in specialised translation: Citations as semantic markers in social science. *Journal of Specialised Translation*, **26**, 72–95.

Connor, U. (1996). *Contrastive Rhetoric: Cross-Cultural Aspects of Second-Language Writing*. Cambridge: Cambridge University Press.

Farahzad, F. (2003). Manipulation in translation. *Perspectives: Studies in Translatology*, **11**(4), 269–81.

Fernández-Silva, S., and Kerremans, K. (2011). Terminological variation in source texts and translations: A pilot study. *Meta*, **56**(2), 318–35.

Firth, J. R. (1969) [1935, 1957]. The technique of semantics. In J. R. Firth, ed., *Papers in Linguistic Theory 1934–1951*. London: Oxford University Press, pp. 7–33.

Fischbach, H. (1986). Some anatomical and physiological aspects of medical translation: Lexical equivalence, ubiquitous references and universality of subject minimize misunderstanding and maximize transfer of meaning. *Meta*, **31**(1), 13–27.

Franco Aixelá, J. (2004). The study of technical and scientific translation: An examination of its historical development. *Journal of Specialised Translation*, **1**, 29–49.

Fuertes-Olivera, P. A., and Pizarro-Sánchez, I. (2002). Translation and 'similarity-creating metaphors' in specialized languages. *Target*, **14**(1), 43–73.

García Hidalgo, I., and Dunham, G. (1981). An experiment in English-Spanish automated translation of medical language data. *Methods of Information in Medicine*, **20**(1), 38–46.

Gerzymisch-Arbogast, H. (1993). Contrastive scientific and technical register as a translation problem. In S. E. Wright and L. D. Wright, eds., *Scientific and Technical Translation* Amsterdam: John Benjamins, pp. 21–52.

Gil-Bardají, A. (2009). Academic discourse and translation from Arabic: A case study from the Spanish tradition. *Babel*, **55**(4), 381–93.

Götz, A. (2015). Magyar és angol abstraktok retorikai szerkezetének elemzése [Analysis of the rhetorical structure of Hungarian and English abstracts]. *Fordítástudomány [Translation Studies]*, **17**(2), 88–116.

Grutman, R. (1998). Auto translation. In M. Baker, ed., *The Routledge Encyclopedia of Translation Studies*. London: Routledge, pp. 124–44.

Halliday, M. A. K. (1994). *An Introduction to Functional Grammar*. 2nd ed. London: Arnold.

Hamdan, J. M., and Natour, Y. S. (2014). Gender of cited authors: A problem for the English Arabic translation of scholarly research. *Babel*, **60**(3), 265–80.

Hoorickx-Raucq, I. (2005). Mediating the scientific text: A cultural approach to the discourse of science in some English and French publications and TV documentaries. *Journal of Specialised Translation*, 3, 97–108.

House, J. (1997). *Translation Quality Assessment: A Model Revisited*. Tübingen: Narr.

Hyland, K. (2004). *Disciplinary Discourses: Social Interactions in Academic Writing*. Ann Arbor: University of Michigan Press.

Hyland, K. (2005). *Metadiscourse*. London: Continuum.

Jacquemond, R. (2015). Translating social sciences into Arabic: The case of Pierre Bourdieu. *The Translator*, **21**(2), 189–209.

Jawad, H. (2014). Shifts in translating Jeremy Munday into Arabic: Asymmetric explicitation. *Across Languages and Cultures*, **15**(1), 51–66.

Jiménez-Crespo, M. A. (2018). Combining corpus and experimental studies: Insights into the reception of translated medical texts. *Journal of Specialised Translation*, **28**, 2–22.

Jooken, L., and Rooryck, G. (2011). The freedom of expressing one's ideas: Translating La Mettrie. *The Translator*, **17**(2), 233–54.

Jordan, R. R. (1997). *English for Academic Purposes. A Guide and Resource Book for Teachers*. Cambridge: Cambridge University Press.

Kaplan, R. B. (1966). Cultural thought patterns in intercultural education. *Language Learning*, **16**, 1–20.

Kastberg, P. (2007). Cultural issues facing the technical translator. *Journal of Specialised Translation*, **8**, 104–9.

Kemppanen, H. (2004). Keywords and ideology in translated history texts: A corpus-based analysis. *Across Languages and Cultures*, **5**(1), 89–106.

Krein-Kühle, M. (2011). Register shifts in scientific and technical translation: A corpus-in context study. *The Translator*, **17**(2), 391–414.

Krüger, Ralph (2016). The textual degree of technicality as a potential factor influencing the occurrence of explicitation in scientific and technical translation. *Journal of Specialised Translation*, **26**, 96–115.

Lakoff, G. (1987). *Women, Fire and Dangerous Things: What Categories Reveal About the Mind*. Chicago/London: University of Chicago Press.

Lakoff, G., and Johnson, M. (1980). *Metaphors We Live By*. Chicago/London: University of Chicago Press.

López-Arroyo, B., and Méndez-Cendón, B. (2007). Describing phraseological devices in medical abstracts: An English/Spanish contrastive analysis. *Meta*, **52**(3), 503–16.

López-Arroyo, B., and Roberts, R. P. (2017). Genre and register in comparable corpora: An English/Spanish contrastive analysis. *Meta*, **62**(1), 115–36.

López-Rodríguez, C. I., and Tercedor-Sánchez, M. I. (2008). Corpora and students' autonomy in scientific and technical translation training. *Journal of Specialised Translation*, **9**, 2–19.

Mauranen, A. (1993). Contrastive ESP rhetoric: Metatext in Finnish-English economics texts. *English for Specific Purposes*, **12**, 3–22.

Mayoral-Asensio, R. (2003/2014). *Translating Official Documents*. Manchester: St Jerome.

Mayoral-Asensio, R. (2007). Specialized translation: A concept in need of revision. *Babel*, **53**(1), 48–55.

McEnery, T. and Xiao, R. (2007): Parallel and comparable corpora: What are they up to? In G. Anderman and M. Rogers, eds., *Incorporating Corpora: Translation and the Linguist*. Clevedon, UK: Multilingual Matters, pp. 8–31.

Meade, R. (2011). Translation of a discipline: The fate of Rankine's engineering science in early Meiji-era Japan. *The Translator*, **17**(2), 211–32.

Méndez-Cendón, B. (2009). Combinatorial patterns in medical case reports: An English Spanish contrastive analysis. *Journal of Specialised Translation*, **11**, 169–85.

Mendiluce-Cabrera, G., and Bermúdez-Bausela, M. (2006). Sci-tech communication: Is there a process of internationalization in English and Spanish? *Meta*, **51**(3), 445–58.

Montgomery, S. L. (2000). *Science in Translation. Movements of Knowledge Through Cultures and Time*. Chicago: University of Chicago Press.

Muñoz-Miquel, A. (2014). El perfil y las competencias del traductor médico desde el punto de vista de los profesionales: una aproximación cualitativa. *Trans. Revista de Traductología*, **18**, 163–81.

Muñoz-Miquel, A. (2018). Differences between linguists and subject-matter experts in the medical translation practice: An empirical descriptive study with professional translators. *Target*, **30**(1), 24–52.

Nasser, L. A. (2014). The translation of English scientific metaphorical expressions into Arabic. *Adab Al-Rafidayn*, **70**, 25–42.

Olohan, M. (2016). Science, translation and the mangle: A performative conceptualization of scientific translation. *Meta*, **61**(Hors série), 5–21.

Olohan, M., and Salama-Carr, M. (2011). Translating science. *The Translator*, **17**(2), 179–88.

Pietrzak, P. (2015). Stylistic aspects of English and Polish medical records: Implications for translation. *Journal of Specialised Translation*, **23**, 316–32.

Pilegaard, M. (1997). Translation of medical research articles. In A. Trosborg, ed., *Text Typology and Translation*. Amsterdam: John Benjamins, pp. 159–84.

Pisanski Peterlin, A. (2005). Text-organising metatext in research articles: An English Slovene contrastive analysis. *English for Specific Purposes*, **25**, 307–19.

Pisanski Peterlin, A. (2008a), Translating metadiscourse in research articles. *Across Languages and Cultures*, **9**(2), 205–18.

Pisanski Peterlin, A. (2008b). The thesis statement in translations of academic discourse: An exploratory study. *Journal of Specialised Translation*, **10**.

Pisanski-Peterlin, A. (2014). Academic discourse in translation: Trainee translators' performance, experience and perception of rhetorical conventions. *English for Specific Purposes*, **36**, 60–73.

Rabacov, G. (2013). Self-translation as mediation between cultures. *Cultural and Linguistic Communication*, **3**(1), 66–9.

Rogers, M., guest ed. (2012). *Journal of Specialised Translation*, 18 Special issue on terminology, phraseology and translation.

Sánchez, D. (2011). Translating science: Contexts and contests. On the translation of a misogynist scientific treatise in early twentieth-century Spain. *The Translator*, **17**(2), 325–48.

Schäffner, C., and Adab, B. (2001). The idea of the hybrid text in translation: Contact as conflict. *Across Languages and Cultures*, **2**(2), 167–80.

Sharkas, H. (2011). The use of glossing in modern original scientific writing in Arabic: An influence of translation? *The Translator*, **17**(2), 369–90.

Shuttleworth, M. (2011). Translational behaviour at the frontiers of scientific knowledge: A multilingual investigation into popular science metaphor in translation. *The Translator*, **17**(2), 301–24.

Siepmann, D. (2006). Academic writing and culture: An overview of differences between English, French and German. *Meta*, **51**(1), 131–50.

Snell-Hornby, M. (2007). *The Turns of Translation Studies*. Amsterdam: John Benjamins.

Stolze, R. (2003). Vagueness in economic texts as a translation problem. *Across Languages and Cultures*, **4**(2), 187–203.

Swales, J. (1990). *Genre Analysis: English in Academic and Research Settings*. Cambridge: Cambridge University Press.

Tack Erten, S. (2012). Establishing norms for functional translations from Portuguese to English: The case of academic calls for papers. *Journal of Specialised Translation*, **17**, 207–23.

Taviano, S. (2018). ELF as a translational lingua franca: Reciprocal influences between ELF and translation. *The Translator*, **24**(3), 249–62.

Tirkkonen-Condit, S. (2001). EU project proposals as hybrid texts: Observations from a Finnish research project. *Across Languages and Cultures*, **2**(2), 261–4.

Toury, G. (1995). *Descriptive Translation Studies and Beyond*. Amsterdam/ Philadelphia: John Benjamins.

Vandepitte, S., Vandenbussche, L., and Algoet, B. (2011). Travelling certainties: Darwin's doubts and their Dutch translations. *The Translator*, **17**(2), 275–300.

Watt, R. K. (1993). The challenges of simplicity and complexity: German-English modes and interrelationships. In S. E. Wright and L. D. Wright, eds., *Scientific and Technical Translation*. Amsterdam: John Benjamins, pp. 53–68.

Williams, I. A. (2004). How to manage *patients* in English-Spanish translation: A target oriented contrastive approach to Methods. *Target*, **16**(1), 69–103.

Williams, I. A. (2005). Thematic items referring to research and researchers in the discussion section of Spanish biomedical articles and English-Spanish translations. *Babel*, **50**(2), 124–60.

Williams, I. A. (2006). Towards a target-oriented model of quantitative contrastive analysis in translation studies: An exploratory study of theme-rheme structure in Spanish-English biomedical research articles. *Languages in Contrast*, **6**(1), 1–45.

Williams, I. A. (2007). A corpus-based study of the verb *observer* in English-Spanish translations of biomedical research articles. *Target*, **19**(1), 85–103.

Wright, S. E., and Wright, L. D., eds. (1993). *Scientific and Technical Translation*. Amsterdam: John Benjamins.

Xiangtao, F. (2007). Scientific translation and its social functions: A descriptive-functional approach to scientific textbook translation in China. *Journal of Specialised Translation*, **7**(1), 42–73.

# 18

# Translating Medical Texts

Karen Korning Zethsen and Vicent Montalt

## 18.1   Introduction

In this chapter, we outline the long history of medical translation and present some of its characteristic features. We introduce the main genres and the very diverse target groups (e.g., experts or laymen) within the field and discuss the most important challenges faced by medical translators. The shift from the biomedical paradigm to patient-centredness and patient empowerment, which has gradually taken place since the late 1970s, has engendered a major increase in patients' and citizens' demands to understand information involving their own health. For this reason, the concept of intralingual translation (reformulation of a text in its original language) is crucial when expert–lay medical translation takes place, and we discuss the particular challenges involved in intralingual translation (often coupled with interlingual translation, which is what is usually understood as translation, namely, translating a text into a language other than the language it was originally written in) as a case in point. We also underline the importance of medical ethics in medical translation and draw the reader's attention to developments – such as translational medicine or narrative medicine – that may be relevant to medical translators.

Translation can be defined and classified in a variety of ways, mainly by field (legal, technical, medical, etc.), mode (written, audiovisual, oral, etc.), method (literal, communicative, etc.), agency (human, automatic, mixed) as well as by the nature and aims of the process (professional, philological, pedagogical, non-professional, etc.). Medical translation is a specific type of utilitarian translation designed mainly to achieve practical goals – rather than to produce texts to be read for pleasure. Medical translation is conceptually embedded in the fields of medicine, pharmacology, nursing, veterinary science and other disciplines linked to health care and the study of health, disease and illness, such as public health, molecular biology, genetics, psychiatry and psychology. It encompasses a rich and varied continuum of contexts, situations and genres, and shares a considerable number of key concepts, methods and resources with the different types of medical interpreting. As a utilitarian type of translation, its practical consequences are its main standard for quality. Undesired consequences owing to translation errors or inadequacies can put the well-being and lives of patients at risk as well as jeopardize the behaviour of health professionals making use of those translations. In current medical translation practice, English is the major source language because most biomedical research is published originally in this language, and then transferred intralingually and interlingually to clinical practice and education. From the point of view of biomedical research and its spread, English is also a relevant target language: researchers from all over the world seek to publish their scientific results in English to make them known to the international community of peers.

## 18.2  Historical Overview

Historically, translation has evolved hand in hand with technological developments, often in a mutually beneficial relationship. Archaeological evidence shows that medical translation has existed since the oldest writing technologies, that is, cuneiform writing on clay tablets in Ancient Mesopotamia, conventionally dated to 3200 BCE. According to the Cuneiform Digital Library Initiative, the earliest known medical text dates from the third dynasty of Ur (2000 BCE) and is written in Sumerian. Other early (fourteenth century BCE) Sumerian texts have been found at Hattusa (Boghazkeui), but it is not known if they were originally composed in Sumerian or copied and translated from Babylonian originals. Also of importance are the lexical sources for anatomical and disease terminology. These 'vocabularies' were often bilingual (Sumerian with an Akkadian translation) beginning from the Middle Babylonian period (Oppenheim, 1962, p. 247). One of these vocabularies in Sumerian, Ugaritic, Akkadian and Hurrian (languages spoken in Ancient Mesopotamia) dating around 1300 BCE and containing medical information in its pre-scientific form – together with other kinds of information in the areas of mathematics, agriculture or city administration – might well be the first written hint of medical translation.

Medical knowledge is cumulative, resulting from the addition and interweaving of successive authors, concepts, vocabularies, texts, traditions, languages, cultures and civilizations, which means that any historical accomplishment owes its success to previous contributions. Classical Greece is particularly relevant to translation because it was the cradle of authors and works that were translated and studied in subsequent centuries, Greek being for many centuries the lingua franca of science and medicine. One of the most important of those works is the *Corpus*

*Hippocraticum*, a collection of medical texts attributed to Hippocrates and other erudite scholars of his school of medical thought, and dating from the last decades of the fifth century BC and the first half of the fourth century BC.

Some 400 years later, Galen (129–c.210), who admired the Hippocratic work, maintained a critical independence from it. He placed the texts within his own system of interpretative categories. He used them and corrected them, almost always considering his opinions as the definitive ones. Galen considered himself to be the true heir of Hippocrates and produced a vast body of medical knowledge in Greek which, in its turn, would be further studied, altered, amplified and translated, giving rise to new knowledge beyond its original conceptual, linguistic and cultural boundaries. Greek medicine was conveyed to Rome by translators, many of them physicians (Fischbach, 1993, p. 96), such as Aulus Cornelius Celsus, who lived in the first century AD.

Translating neologisms was one of the main challenges that medical translators had – and have – to face. As early as the first century BCE, Lucretius (c.99 BC–c.55 BC) expressed it in eloquent terms in his didactic poem *De rerum natura* (*On the Nature of Things*): 'Nec me animi fallit Graiorum obscura reperta/difficile illustrare Latinis versibus esse,/multa novis verbis praesertim cum sit agendum/propter egestatem linguae et rerum novitatem …' (*Nor does it escape my mind that the dark discoveries of the Greeks/Are difficult to illuminate in Latin verses,/Principally since one must make many new words/Because of the poverty of the language and the novelty of things*).

In the ninth century AD, much of Galen's work was translated into Arabic at the House of Wisdom in Baghdad. Arab medicine during the Middle Ages was creative and innovative, and Arabic was, far and away, the leading language of the medieval period (Gordin, 2015). Arab scholars had an excellent knowledge of Greek medicine through translations but were not content to merely repeat its findings and conclusions. The task of translators went far beyond just translating. As the historian of medicine Emilie Savage-Smith (2004) has put it, 'in order to make the Greek tradition more accessible, understandable, and teachable, Islamic scholars ordered the vast and sometimes inconsistent Greco-Roman medical knowledge and made it more systematic by writing encyclopaedias and summaries'. In the eleventh century AD, Arabic translations were translated into Latin, together with the comments made by later Arab scholars. So, they innovated in concepts and vocabulary, and introduced new words. Unfortunately, many of them were lost owing to the fact that, from the Renaissance onwards, scientists tried to do without the medieval heritage as much as possible. Medical humanists of the fifteenth and sixteenth centuries saw the need to repeat the experiments and observations of the Greek physician and to make Latin translations directly from Greek texts. This renewal of the Galenic tradition in the European Renaissance through new translations is one of the fundamental elements in the configuration of modern scientific medicine.

Current medical terminology is a historical sediment of scientific medicine including terms from twenty-five centuries ago to those created much later (López Piñero and Terrada Ferrandis, 2005), mainly from Greek ('biosynthesis', 'cataract', 'diet', 'electrode', etc.) and Latin ('abort', 'addiction', 'cell', 'germ', etc.), but also from Arabic ('alcohol', 'aniline', 'alkalinity', 'caffeine', etc.) and vernacular languages such as Italian ('malaria', 'influenza', etc.) or, more recently, English ('parkinsonism', 'scanner', etc.). Greco-Latin predominance should not lead us to believe that medical terminology has an exclusively European origin, a confusion that favours ethnocentrism. American languages such as Guarani ('cocaine', 'guanine', etc.) or African ones such as Bantu ('chimpanzee', 'Ebola', etc.) have also contributed neologisms to medical language. Ethnocentric prejudice leads to the assumption that the only valid knowledge is modern European science, which is far from true both in historical and in present-day terms. The Indian healing system Ayurveda, Traditional Chinese Medicine, acupuncture and homeopathy are among other forms of medical knowledge and therapy that have traditionally coexisted with modern scientific medicine.

## 18.3   Features Specific to Medical Translation

Medical translation shares many features with any other kind of translation: it is a professional activity that involves understanding the source text, developing mental strategies, applying textual procedures or using information resources and technological tools. However, there are some characteristics that distinguish it from other types of translation (Montalt and González-Davies, 2007). Medical translation comprises the knowledge generated and used in all medical specialties, from anatomy and physiology to internal medicine to surgery or pharmacology. Each medical specialty has its own technical terminology. Concepts and terms for anatomical parts, functions of the body, diseases, syndromes, drugs, medical equipment and so forth are specific to medical translation. This medical knowledge accounts for a considerable part of what is communicated in the myriad situations in which medical translation may be required, covering not only communication among experts (i.e., researchers, clinicians) but also any kind of communicative interaction (oral, written or multimodal) that involves health professionals, patients, their relatives and the general public.

Regarding the users of medical translation, there is a great variety of possible addressees of the target texts – patients, health professionals, researchers, university students and teachers, hospital managers and technicians, manufacturers of medical devices, regulators and policymakers, media and the general public. Among the many settings in which communication and translation function in the biomedical and health-care sectors are running clinical trials, training health professionals, maintaining specific medical devices, disseminating biomedical research among specialists, transferring that research into clinical practice, making accessible to patients the information they need to be able to adhere to treatments and manage their therapeutic process, and circulating on the Internet and in other media information aimed at enabling the general public to prevent disease or to respond to crisis situations. These communicative situations are reflected in genres specific to medical translation such as clinical case reports and research articles published in international biomedical journals, clinical guidelines for clinicians, and informed consents and fact sheets for patients. As we will see in Section 18.4, these genres make specific demands on translators and are embedded in situations and interactions in which medical ethics regulate the communication among and the behaviour of participants.

## 18.4 Text Genres: Their Practical and Ethical Implications

Why be aware of genres and not only individual texts? Communication in medical and health-care contexts – hospitals, health centres, national and international governmental and non-governmental health organizations and so on – is highly institutionalized and routinized. Consider, for example, a research article, a clinical case report, an informed consent form or a patient information leaflet. In each of these examples, aspects such as structure, length, types of information provided, use of terminology, phraseological preferences, register, tenor and style are, to a certain extent, predetermined. In fact, the acceptability and the credibility of translations of texts belonging to these and other genres depend to a large extent on the observance of the conventions that govern them as acts of communication. Knowledge of the genres being translated can contribute to a better understanding of the information contained in the texts. Such knowledge enables the translator to anticipate certain types of information that conventionally appear in particular genres and thus reinforces the process of understanding. In addition, contrastive knowledge of the aspects of a given genre that differ between languages can enable a translator to deal sensitively with more or less subtle differences in register and style. Finally, knowledge of genres is essential in heterofunctional translation briefs in which the genre of the target text is different from that of the source text, or briefs in which the target text must include elements drawn from more than one genre.

In addition to the formal conventions governing the drafting and translation of texts, there are a number of basic ethical principles that affect both the process and the outcome of translation. Possibly the main and most relevant one is the need to ensure the veracity, accuracy and validity of the information contained in the target text, since the well-being and the health of the patients depend on them. That is why the role of verification is a frequently emphasized aspect (Montalt, Zethsen and Karwack, 2018). Another fundamental ethical principle in medical translation is confidentiality. Translators are obliged to respect the privacy of medical records, informed consent forms, and documentation for the development of new drugs or biomedical patents. Respect and empathy for specific groups of patients with disabilities, or for ethnic minorities, are essential in genres aimed at patients, such as a patient guide. An informed consent, given its legal nature and its possible consequences of shared responsibility, is based on the principle of clarity and comprehensibility so that the patient can sign the consent with assurances that he or she understands the risks that he or she is taking. In the case of a research article, the ethical principle that should govern the drafting and translation process is precision in the expression so that the experiment can be replicated and the argumentation can be followed in detail. In short, apart from the ethical principles shared by all genres, each particular genre is often governed by one or more ethical principles that affect the form and function of the text being translated.

## 18.5   From the Biomedical Model to the Biopsychosocial Model

Health communication, and with it medical translation, has been highly influenced by the paradigmatic shift which has gradually taken place within medicine since the late 1970s. Until then, the biomedical model dominated Western medicine and this model entailed that the body was more or less seen as a machine with parts that could be fixed. The biomedical approach has its origin in Louis Pasteur's germ theory from the late 1850s, which sought to explain all disease in biological terms and as biological defects. In Pasteur's time, the model made more sense than today as the germ theory laid the foundation for the elimination of the most frequent primary causes of death at the time, namely, infectious diseases such as tuberculosis, pneumonia, influenza and diarrhoea (Johnson, 2012). A more holistic approach to medicine was presented in 1977 by George Engel (1913–99) in his seminal paper 'The Need for a New Medical Model: A Challenge for Biomedicine' in which he proposed an alternative to the biomedical model, the biopsychosocial model. Engel (1977) saw the biomedical approach as reductionist and exclusionary in its attempt to explain everything from a biological point of view and in its lack of consideration of symptoms which could not be biologically explained. The biopsychosocial model, on the other hand, offers a holistic alternative, emphasizing patient-centred care and communication. As the name indicates, the model requires health-care professionals to attend simultaneously to the biological, psychological and social dimensions of illness. Engel furthermore advocated an approach which does not merely consider patients as objects but takes into consideration their subjective experiences in order not to dehumanize medicine or disempower patients. In other words, subjective experience is seen as an important contributor to diagnosis as well as general health care.

## 18.6 Patient Centredness and Patient Empowerment

A patient-centred approach to health care as described in Section 18.5 normally entails a certain amount of patient empowerment, and a fundamental requirement for patient empowerment is health literacy. Nutbeam (2000, p. 265) divides health literacy into three levels – namely, functional, interactive and critical – and a prerequisite for even the most basic functional health literacy level is, not surprisingly, that the patient understands all relevant communication, oral or in writing, directed at him or her. However, not all medical texts are accessible to laymen, in fact even texts aimed directly at this target group may often be very difficult to understand and this is where intralingual translation is needed.

### 18.6.1 Target Groups

Information about health, medication and so on is often potentially aimed at the entire population of a country and can therefore be described as mass communication. This means that it may be impossible for the author or translator of a text to obtain a clear picture of the target group. In such cases, it is advisable to write for the lowest common denominator. As a case in point, the Danish health authorities recommend writing so that the text would be understandable to a child of eleven to twelve years of age (Sundhedsstyrelsen, 2009). On the face of it, this may seem a very low common denominator. However, it is important to keep in mind that an entire population includes young people without much experience, old people who may not be as alert as they used to be, people with very little schooling, non-native speakers, people who suffer from dyslexia in varying degrees and so on. Even in well-educated countries, quite a number of citizens can be described as weak readers or even illiterate. To this should be added that the reading situation may be a stressful one. A parent who reads a patient information leaflet for child medication may not have slept for three nights, may be anxious and so on, and therefore not as quick to understand as usual.

### 18.6.2   Intralingual Translation

Though the practice has presumably existed since time immemorial, the term 'intralingual translation' comes from Roman Jakobson's tripartite division of translation into interlingual, intralingual and intersemiotic translation (Jakobson, 1959, p. 114). Intralingual translation is translation, or rewording, within one language; as Jakobson puts it, '[t]he intralingual translation of a word uses either another, more or less synonymous, word or resorts to a circumlocution' (Jakobson, 1959, p. 114). In many ways, intralingual translation makes use of the same translational micro-strategies as the more prototypical form of translation, interlingual trans-lation, or translation between two national languages (Zethsen, 2007, 2009; Whyatt, Kajzer-Wietrzny and Stachowiak, 2016). The difference between the two types of translation seems to be more a question of degree rather than kind (Zethsen, 2009; Ersland, 2014). Well-known translational strategies such as explicitation and omission are thus more common in intralingual translation than in interlingual translation as the *skopos* (or purpose) of intralingual translation often involves a degree of simplifica-tion (Zethsen, 2009, 2018).

### 18.6.3   Intralingual Medical Translation

When health professionals, or other experts for that matter, write about their field, they often use the expert syntax, lexis and so on, of which the genre normally avails itself, even when the projected reader is a layman. It is well known that it may be difficult for experts to gauge exactly at which linguistic and knowledge level they will be able to reach a layman audi-ence – a phenomenon which Hinds (1999, p. 205) refers to as *the curse of expertise*. To complicate matters further, within the medical field there are many genres aimed at a lay readership which have strong intertextual elements. They may, for example, need to relate in fairly strictly or even legally stipulated ways to other texts (so-called mandatory genres; see Askehave and Zethsen, 2003); this is true of patient information leaflets which must, by law, be closely related to the summary of product char-acteristics, which is an expert text. For these reasons, intralingual transla-tion is often relevant within the field of health communication.

Intralingual translation may be carried out on its own, for example if a medical expert text is to be reworded to make it accessible to a layman audience, but quite frequently intralingual translation takes place in com-bination with interlingual translation. This is the case when a medical translator is asked to translate a text from one language into another for a layman audience and notices that the source text would be too difficult for laymen. In such a situation, the translator would need to translate both inter- and intralingually, and the situation clearly places additional demands on the translator. It should also be pointed out that trained medical translators may over time become semi-experts themselves to the degree that they may lose some of their ability to gauge what a layman would understand and even turn a medical source text targeted at laymen into a more complicated target text because of their expert knowledge. In fact, studies have found that trained medical translators have a tendency to revert to expert medical language when they translate a medical text for a lay readership (Askehave and Zethsen, 2000; Nisbeth Jensen and Zethsen, 2012; Nisbeth Jensen, 2013).

## 18.7 Translating Medical Texts for Laymen in Practice: Some Useful Strategies

There is a reason why experts write as they do. Expert language is often economical and thus time-saving in the sense that fairly brief texts may contain much information and, perhaps most important of all, expert language generally has a very high degree of precision. Within an expert discourse community, the target group is often well known and well defined.

A layman target group, on the other hand, may of course be very diverse. In addition to some of the factors mentioned already, some well-educated laymen are familiar with Latin, and may be able to deduce the meaning of some medical terminology. Some laymen suffer from a chronic disease and have gradually become acquainted with the terminology of that particular disease, but know next to nothing about medical language in general; and yet others may not be able to read any medical texts at all. Some national languages (e.g., Spanish and English) are more Latin-based than others (such as German and the Nordic languages), and speakers of the more Latin-based languages may be able to figure out what a Latin word means, or the Latin word may be part of everyday language. In Nordic languages, in contrast, everyday language does not make use of Latin medical terminology, but it has doublets, that is, layman terms with Nordic roots and with no connection to Latin at all (for example, 'blindtarmsbetændelse' and 'appendicitis' both exist in Danish, the former being preferred in everyday parlance). This means that, in many cases, most people will literally not have a clue what a Latin word means, and it is crucial that everyday words are used (Zethsen, 2004).

The tools for making a text more lay-friendly are legion, but in the following we will focus on a discussion of some of the main micro-strategies available to the intralingual medical translator within the overall fields of terminology, syntax, sentence length, omission, explicitation, structure and graphics. The list is inspired by the findings of Askehave and Zethsen (2000, 2002, 2010, 2014; see also Nisbeth Jensen, 2015 and Muñoz-Miquel, Ezpeleta-Piorno and Saiz-Hontangas, 2018).

### 18.7.1   Expert Terminology

Officialeese, expert terminology and especially Latin-based vocabulary should generally be avoided and should be translated into layman vocabulary, if such an alternative exists, or be paraphrased. An exception could be made in connection with chronic illnesses, where some laymen may benefit from knowing selected expert terms so that they can undertake their own research. The expert term can then be provided in brackets after the layman term. The reason why expert terms in brackets should be carefully selected and not be a standard solution is that many laymen may not be able to assess whether the information in brackets is additional information or synonymous information. This is, for instance, the case if we write 'the injection should be given under the skin (subcutaneously)'. How can the layman reader know whether 'subcutaneously' is additional or synonymous information? This is especially true in connection with non-Latinate languages and in particular laymen who are not strong readers may be confused by such brackets, which furthermore typically lengthen noun phrases. In the case of 'subcutaneously', this expert term is simply not relevant to the patient in any way.

Also, the use of synonyms is generally not recommended. As the main *skopos* of the translation is understanding, stylistic variation is not important. If expressions such as 'women of child-bearing age' and 'fertile women' appear as synonyms in a medical text, layman readers may be confused and wonder whether there is a difference after all. Abbreviations should likewise be avoided as they will often be incomprehensible to the layman; even simple medical abbreviations may not be as logical to laymen as they are to experts who use them on a daily basis.

### 18.7.2   Syntax

In expert language, the agent is often not important, or it is obvious to the expert who the agent is. In some languages, it is therefore common to write specialized texts in the passive voice. However, laymen often need to know exactly who the agent is, especially in cases where they themselves are expected to do something. If a patient information leaflet for an asthma inhaler says that 'the pump on top of the inhaler should be pressed down three times before first usage' then the patient may be in doubt as to who should do this. In the same vein, nominalizations which are not part of everyday vocabulary should be avoided as they hide the agent in the same way and make it more difficult for the reader to process a sentence. Active voice, verbs instead of nouns and hence often the use of personal pronouns make it clear to the layman reader who should do what and may also make the text seem more involving and relevant.

Another characteristic of expert language is heavy premodification, which saves much space but which may be either time-consuming or very difficult for the layman reader to process, or both. If one lacks expert knowledge, it may be almost impossible to say what premodifies what in a heavy construction such as 'gastroscopically verified Helicobacter Pylori associated ulcer'. These premodifications should be dissolved into relative clauses instead.

### 18.7.3 Sentence Length

A long sentence is not necessarily a difficult sentence, but generally it is advisable to split sentences up by using more punctuation for a layman target group than when translating for experts. The main point is perhaps not so much the length of the sentence as such but whether too much information has been crammed into one sentence and whether it is organized within that sentence in such a way as to facilitate reading and comprehension.

### 18.7.4 Omission

Information which is not relevant to the layman reader should be omitted, but it goes without saying that the medical expert author of the text should be consulted before anything is left out. Expert language is often detailed to a degree which is not relevant to the layman reader; for instance, the customary precise description of the colour and form of a solution or pill in the summary of product characteristics such as 'white to off-white round, biconvex film-coated tablets' is not relevant to include in the patient information leaflet.

### 18.7.5 Explicitation

The phenomenon of presupposition plays an important role when translating intralingually from experts to laymen. In other words, what is absent from the text is as important as what is present. Again, it may be difficult for experts to gauge exactly what laymen know and do not know. Typically, the intralingual translator will have to use the strategy of explicitation to ensure that absent background information, which is obvious to the expert, is made explicit to help the layman reader. Presupposition is very common and its use in medical texts may be one of the main reasons why medical texts are often so inaccessible to laymen. Expert medical terms in themselves presuppose knowledge, but even expressions which are linguistically straightforward may presuppose important knowledge, as illustrated by this example from electronic hospital records accessible to the patient: 'We will take new blood tests today to see if he is heading the wrong way.' The patient may not necessarily know what 'the wrong way' entails. As is the case with omission, it is often advisable to consult the expert author of the text before explicitation if any doubts arise.

### 18.7.6  Structure and Graphics

As the default, it is common to retain the linearity of a source text in a translation. However, in connection with intralingual translation, even the structure of the text may have to be changed radically. First and foremost, some layman medical texts may be fairly long for legal reasons (see Askehave and Zethsen, 2003, on mandatory genres) and we have to assume that not all readers will read the entire text. This means that it is safest, and a good service to the reader, to provide the most important information first. Simple graphic tools such as bullets, sub-headlines (perhaps formulated as questions), emphasis and so on may also be used to make it easier for the layman reader to comprehend large amounts of information. Statistical information on, for example, the risk of side effects can be given by saying 'one in ten' or 'two out of a hundred', which many laymen find more illustrative than percentages. Pictograms are often seen in layman texts, but they are not always the best solution. Perhaps contrary to popular belief, there is much room for misinterpretation, and the interpretation of pictures is highly culture-sensitive; therefore, one must tread carefully.

When a medical text is translated intralingually, it is often changed more than we usually see in connection with interlingual translation. Sometimes it even has to be changed quite radically and translational micro-strategies such as omission and explicitation may be used to a much higher degree than is the case with interlingual translation (Zethsen, 2009). This means that intralingual translators have to rely on their very detailed interpretation of the text, but, since even the most skilled translators are rarely medical experts themselves, it is important to consult the author of the text if in doubt. Co-operation between the intralingual medical translator and medical experts is often the recipe for success. The subject of user-testing is beyond the scope of this chapter, but it is a very important tool to be used in cases where a translation is of particular importance. However, the many electronic readability tests available online, and much used, are typically very superficial and will give only a very general picture of the likely reception of a text among laymen. A readability test would, for example, typically give the same ratings to the same text regardless of whether it has been written forwards or backwards. Qualitative methods such as text analysis or a critical reading of one's own text with the target group in mind, coupled with interviews or tests with respondents who, if possible, also have to show that they can act in accordance with the text in cases where it contains instructions – for example on how to use an inhaler or the like – are generally more reliable and therefore safer to use.

## 18.8 Developments

There have been a number of developments and innovations in biomedical research and health care that require the attention of translators as experts in multilingual and multicultural communication. In particular, we refer to translational medicine, personalized medicine and narrative medicine.

Translational medicine (TM) aims to connect research and clinical application, either 'bench-to-bedside' or 'bedside-to-bench'. Bench-to-bedside refers to the use of research in clinical applications, while bedside-to-bench suggests that patient needs can inspire research. TM is a bidirectional process encompassing (a) bench-to-bedside factors aimed to increase the efficiency by which new therapeutic strategies developed through research are tested clinically; and (b) bedside-to-bench, that is, factors that provide feedback about applications of new treatments and how they can be improved. In this way, TM aims to facilitate the research and application of new therapies and medical procedures through the implementation of research results to health care and the transfer of clinical data to the field of research. Translators are in a good position to provide bridges between research and clinical practice, thereby promoting feedback between the two fields involved and facilitating translatability among the different stages – discovery, development, regulation and use (Montalt, 2017).

Personalized medicine (PM) starts from the assumptions that we are all unique, and that our health is determined by our inherent differences combined with our lifestyle and environment. Basically, personalized medicine is a move away from the idea that one size fits all. In personalized medicine, tailor-made prevention and treatment strategies for individuals and groups of individuals are adopted so that specific therapies that work for them are used. Personalized medicine encompasses all aspects of health care from health promotion to risk stratification and screening.

Narrative medicine (NM) is rooted in the idea that it is through stories that people make sense of themselves and the world. Patients tell (and, increasingly, publish) stories about their experiences, their illnesses, how their illnesses affect them, how they manage their illnesses, how they make decisions about their illnesses and so on. In addition, in a medical consultation, the primary information on which a diagnosis and treatment are based is provided by the patient, ideally in the form of a detailed story which the doctor listens to. From the point of view of the doctor, NM is the application of narrative ideas to the practice of medicine.

These three developments pose challenges and offer opportunities to medical translation and translators. Bridging the gaps between experts and non-experts communicating in different – and yet connected and interdependent – institutional settings – both inter- and intralingually – is complex because it often involves making complex decisions beyond the equi-functional paradigm of translation. Translating for highly defined groups of patients (like those found in PM) or even for individual patients in a relevant way means having detailed knowledge of their needs and expectations, as well as the material and emotional circumstances in which they process the information. Quite often, translators do not have empirical knowledge about the reading and communication process of specific groups of patients. Lack of both resources and established good practices for specific genres as well as control, assurance and measurement of text quality are among the main challenges that translators have to face in these emerging fields. TM, PM and NM can benefit from medical translation since it can facilitate the flow of information and knowledge in both intra- and interlingual contexts. Medical translation can also provide solutions for targeted groups of patients, tailoring health care culturally and linguistically.

## References

Askehave, I., and Zethsen, K. K. (2000). *The Patient Package Insert of the Future: (Report for the Danish Ministry of Health)*. Århus: Handelshøjskolen i Århus, Det erhvervssproglige fakultet.

Askehave, I., and Zethsen, K. K. (2002). Translating for laymen. *Perspectives: Studies in Translatology*, **10**(1), 15–29.

Askehave, I., and Zethsen, K. K. (2003). Communication barriers in public discourse: The patient package insert. *Information Design Journal*, **4**(1), 23–41.

Askehave, I., and Zethsen, K. K. (2010). PIL of the month: A study of best practice in EU patient information leaflets. *Journal of Applied Linguistics and Professional Practice*, **7**(1), 97–120.

Askehave, I., and Zethsen, K. K. (2014). A comparative analysis of the lay-friendliness of Danish EU patient information leaflets from 2000 to 2012. *Communication and Medicine*, **11**(3), 209–22. DOI: 10.1558/cam.v11i3.20700.

Engel, G. L. (1977). The need for a new medical model: A challenge for biomedicine. *Science*, **196**, 129–36.

Ersland, A. (2014). *Is Change Necessary? A Study of Norms and Translation Universals in Intralingual Translation*. MA thesis, University of Bergen, Norway.

Fischbach, H. (1993). Translation, the great pollinators of science: A brief flashback on medical translation. In S. E. Wright and L. D. Wright, eds., *Scientific and Technical Translation*, vol. VI. Amsterdam/Philadelphia: John Benjamins.

Gordin, M. D. (2015). *Scientific Babel: How Science Was Done Before and After Global English*. Chicago: University of Chicago Press.

Hinds, P. J. (1999). The curse of expertise: The effects of expertise and debiasing methods on predictions of novice performance. *Journal of Experimental Psychology: Applied*, **5**(2), 205–21.

Jakobson, R. (1959). On linguistic aspects of translation. In R. A. Brower, ed., *On Translation*. New York: Oxford University Press, pp. 232–9. Reprinted in L. Venuti, ed. (2012) *The Translation Studies Reader*. London: Routledge, pp. 126–31.

Johnson, S. B. (2012). Medicine's paradigm shift: An opportunity for psychology. *American Psychological Association, President's Column*, **43**(8), 5 www.apa.org/monitor/2012/09/pc.

López Piñero, J. M., and Terrada Ferrandis, M. L. (2005). *Introducción a la terminología médica*. Barcelona: Masson.

Montalt, V. (2017). Patient-centred translation and emerging trends in medicine and healthcare. *European Society for Translation Studies Newsletter*, **51**, 10–11.

Montalt, V., and González-Davies, M. (2007). *Medical Translation Step by Step: Learning by Drafting*. London: Routledge.

Montalt, V., Zethsen, K. K., and Karwack, W. (2018). Medical translation in the 21st century – challenges and trends. *MonTI*, **10**, 27–42.

Muñoz-Miquel, A., Ezpeleta-Piorno, P., and Saiz-Hontangas, P. (2018). Intralingual translation in healthcare settings: Strategies and proposals for medical translator training. In V. Montalt, K. Zethsen and W. Karwacka, eds. *Retos actuales y tendencias emergentes en traducción médica / Current challenges and emerging trends in medical translation. MonTI*, **10**, 177–204.

Nisbeth Jensen, M. (2013). *Translators of Patient Information Leaflets: Translation Experts or Expert Translators? A Mixed Methods Study of Lay-Friendliness*. Aarhus: Aarhus University, School of Business and Social Sciences. (PhD thesis).

Nisbeth Jensen, M. (2015). Optimising comprehensibility in interlingual translation: The need for intralingual translation. In K. Maksymski, S. Gutermuth and S. Hansen-Schirra, eds., *Translation and Comprehensibility*. Berlin: Frank and Timme, pp. 163–94.

Nisbeth Jensen, M., and Zethsen, K. K. (2012). Translation of patient information leaflets: Trained translators and pharmacists-cum-translators – a comparison. *Linguistica Antverpiensia. New Series*, **11**, 31–50.

Nutbeam, D. (2000). Health literacy as a public health goal: A challenge for contemporary health education and communication strategies into the 21st century contemporary health. *Health Promotion International*, **15**, 259–67. DOI: 10.1093/heapro/15.3.259.

Oppenheim, A. L. (1962). Mesopotamian medicine. *Bulletin of the History of Medicine*, **xxxvi**, 97–108.

Savage-Smith, E. (2004). Islamic medical manuscripts at the National Library of Medicine. www.nlm.nih.gov/hmd/arabic/med_islam.html.

Sundhedsstyrelsen. (2009). *Health literacy – Begrebet, konsekvenser og mulige interventioner* [Health literacy – The concept, consequences and possible interventions]. København: Sundhedsstyrelsen. www.sst.dk/da/udgivelser/2009/health-literacy—begrebet-konsekvenser-og-mulige-interventioner.

Whyatt, B., Kajzer-Wietrzny, M., and Stachowiak, K. (2016). Similar and different: Cognitive rhythm and effort in translation and paraphrasing. Special issue: *Language Processing in Translation. Poznan Studies in Contemporary Linguistics*, **52**(2), 175–208.

Zethsen, K. K. (2004). Latin-based terms: True or false friends? *Target*, **16**(1), 125–42. DOI: 10.1075/target.16.1.07zet.

Zethsen, K. K. (2007). Beyond translation proper – Extending the field of translation studies. *TTR: Traduction, Terminologie, Redaction*, **20**(1), 281–308.

Zethsen, K. K. (2009). Intralingual translation: An attempt at description. *Meta*, **54**(4), 795–812.

Zethsen, K. K. (2018). Access is not the same as understanding. Why intralingual translation is crucial in a world of information overload. *Across Languages and Cultures*, **19**(1), 79–98.

# 19

# Translating Legal Texts

Łucja Biel

## 19.1 Introduction

This chapter maps the field of legal translation practice, research and training, overviewing foundations, historical perspectives and later trends. It clarifies the fuzzy concepts of legal text, legal genre and legal translation. Legal translation is divided into intersystemic and intrasystemic translation, to account for different types of challenge, target text status and function, and translation approach. The chapter highlights developments in the field such as growing democratization and modernization of legal language, a reorientation of legal translation towards accessibility and functionalism, increasing professionalization and technologization of legal translators' work, as well as emancipation of legal translation studies as a methodologically mature and diverse field of research. The final section discusses legal translator training, outlining competences and innovations.

Legal translation is a subtype of specialized non-literary translation which, broadly speaking, involves the translation of legal texts. It can be defined, after Šarčević (1997, p. 55), as 'an act of communication within the mechanism of the law'. Because it requires cross-linguistic mediation in the field of law, legal translation is an interdiscipline at the intersection of translation studies, legal studies, linguistics and terminology. This chapter maps and describes legal translation through the lens of practice, research and training, focusing on the dynamism of the field.

## 19.2 Clearing the Ground: Legal Texts, Legal Genres and the Scope of Legal Translation

Law is a formalized system of rules that serve as a mechanism of social control (Harris, 2006, p. 2); therefore, it is essentially connected to language: 'law needs language' (de Groot, 1998, p. 21), 'law is a profession of words' (Mellinkoff, 1963, p. vii) and '[l]aw is language ... a profoundly linguistic institution' (Gibbons, 1999, p. 156). Language is used to draft, interpret, enforce and practise law, which is realized through a broad range of legal texts.

Prototypical legal genres include legislation, judgments, contracts, powers of attorney, articles of association, wills, legal opinions and academic books. They are in principle created by legal professionals, such as legislative drafters, judges, prosecutors, solicitors, barristers and notaries.

Legal genres may be further grouped into hierarchical systems of related genres (cf. Bazerman, 1994, p. 96). On the basis of their communicative purpose, Bhatia (2006) distinguishes primary from derived genres, positioning legislation among the primary genres since it lays the foundation for all legal practices. Derived genres subsume: (1) secondary genres connected with adjudication, which interpret the real world against the model world envisaged in legislation, such as judgments; (2) enabling (pedagogical) genres used by academia or the profession, for example textbooks, pleadings, memoranda; and (3) target genres such as contracts, affidavits and court case documents, which are both instruments and products of legal professionals' work (Bhatia, 2006, pp. 6–7). Šarčević (1997, p. 11) correlates the function of genre with legal effect, dividing genres into primarily prescriptive genres (legislation, contracts), hybrid genres which are primarily descriptive but also prescriptive (judicial and administrative decisions) and purely descriptive genres (textbooks, legal opinions). Cao (2007, p. 9) classifies legal genres into legislative texts, judicial texts, private legal texts and scholarly texts.

These traditional classifications do not account for a large group of peripheral genres. These include administrative documents, that is, certificates and school diplomas; press releases; oral genres such as cross-examination, out-of-court mediation and conference with counsel; and entertaining genres such as crime fiction and TV crime series (cf. Alcaraz Varó and Hughes, 2002, pp. 101–52). Some hybrid genres have emerged owing to technological developments, for example tweets on legal issues or a law firm's website. Peripheral genres tend to be intended for semi-experts and non-specialist audiences, for example consumers and citizens, and have attracted attention from both administration and academia owing to the growing democratization of legal language. These genres are adapted to a communicative purpose and tend to contain 'diluted' legal language (Biel, 2014, p. 20).

There is no consensus among scholars about the extent to which peripheral and even some core genres are legal texts, and the fuzziness of categorization of legal texts also applies to the category of legal translation. For Šarčević (1997, p. 9), a leading scholar in the field, legal texts cover only specialized communication between lawyers. This narrow view is questioned, for example, by Harvey (2002, p. 178) since it excludes many genres addressed to non-specialist audiences, such as contracts or judgments, which constitute the bulk of a legal translator's work. Harvey (2002, p. 178) and Cao (2007, p. 8) construe legal translation broadly on the basis of target text (TT) purpose and situational criteria, as 'the translation of texts used in law and legal settings' (Cao, 2007, p. 12), including texts used in court as 'part of the judicial process' (Harvey, 2002, p. 178), for example witness statements, medical reports or technical opinions (Cao, 2007, pp. 10–12). Prieto Ramos (2019, p. 33) considers the situational criterion too broad and excludes texts 'that contain no sign of legal language'. He identifies 'the minimum common denominator of legal texts' on the basis of three criteria: the presence of legal discourse, of legal theme and/or of legal function (Prieto Ramos, 2014, pp. 264–5). While it is convenient to impose a sharp boundary between legal and non-legal genres, in fact the boundary is fuzzy and the transition zone includes peripheral (semi-)legal, emergent and mixed genres where these criteria are represented to a lesser extent.

Different conceptualizations of the scope of legal translation are also triggered by overlaps with other types of translation which cover legal texts to some extent but foreground other aspects of translation. Most notably, legal translation partially overlaps with court translation, which also includes non-legal texts serving as documentary evidence in court. Court translation is subsumed under a broader category of official translation, also known as sworn translation and public service translation, where a translated text functions as an official document for administrative purposes (see Section 19.4.3). A related concept is community translation, which is provided for immigrants, temporary communities, indigenous populations and minorities, where translation empowers such communities by providing them with access to legal, administrative and other information (Taibi and Ozolins, 2016, pp. 1–3). Another overlap is with institutional translation, provided by and for supranational and international institutions, where legal genres are at the core of text production but which also covers a broad range of administrative genres (cf. Biel, 2019, pp. 29–31; Prieto Ramos, 2019).

## **19.3** Properties of Legal Discourse: Conservatism and Modernization

Legal language, a functional and professional variety of specialized language used in legal genres, is 'not monolithic' (Tiersma, 1999, p. 141) and covers a diverse range of discourses. It is sometimes pejoratively referred to as 'legalese' owing to its distinctive style, characterized by conceptual and syntactic complexity, formality, conservatism and formulaicity (cf.

Crystal and Davy, 1969, p. 194; Mattila, 2013, p. 108; Tiersma, 1999). The highest concentration of legalese is found in prototypical legal genres as opposed to expository or persuasive genres (Tiersma, 1999, p. 139) and 'judicial narrative' (Alcaraz Varó and Hughes, 2002, p. 21).

The central feature of legal discourse is terminology and phraseology. Legal concepts are 'crystallisations of legal rules' (Mattila, 2013, p. 137) and units of legal knowledge which are standardized and system-specific (Biel, 2014, pp. 39–41). Legal terms comprise purely technical terms limited to the domain of law, for example *subpoena, prosecutor*; semi-technical or mixed terms, that is, everyday lexemes which have acquired legal meaning through terminologization, for example *consideration, claim, complaint*; and everyday vocabulary, for example *section, subject matter* (Alcaraz Varó and Hughes, 2002, pp. 16–18). Legal phraseology is system-bound, restricted and relatively fixed (Biel, 2014, pp. 47–8).

Syntactically, legal language upholds 'the tradition of the long sentence' (Mellinkoff, 1963, p. 366), motivated by 'the desire to place all information on a particular topic into one self-contained unit' (Tiersma, 1999, p. 56). In consequence, the internal sentence structure is complex (Mattila, 2013, p. 121), with several levels of embedding through subordinated and co-ordinated clauses (Tiersma, 1999, p. 56). Other features – typically associated with the formal register and lack of clarity – include frequent use of nominalization with complex nominal groups, passive voice, impersonal constructions, multiple negation and complex prepositions; conditionals and deontic modality markers, for example *shall* in legislation and contracts; and rhetorical devices and epistemic modality in courtroom genres (cf. Mellinkoff, 1963; Crystal and Davy, 1969; Tiersma, 1999; Alcaraz Varó and Hughes, 2002). The formality of legal language iconically creates an impression of gravity 'to ensure respect for legal rules' (Mattila, 2013, p. 123). This impression is strengthened by the occasional use of archaisms retained in legal formula, for example *Now this deed witnesseth as follows*; Latinisms (e.g., *ex officio*); and text-navigating compound adverbials such as *hereby, hereinunder* and *thereby* (Alcaraz Varó and Hughes, 2002, p. 9).

Discursive conventions vary across genres and countries. For example, for historical reasons, legal English is tolerant of repetitions and redundancy, that is, doublets and triplets of synonyms which have become fixed expressions (Mellinkoff, 1963, p. 349), such as *terms and conditions* and *the contract made by and between*. Continental Europe's legal discourses avoid redundancy, which, if retained in translation, is confusing to lawyers (Mattila, 2013, p. 321). Another case in point is a degree of modernization of legal language with plain language regulations, for example in Sweden, Canada, Australia and the United States, which have affected legislation, judgments, government forms and consumer documents (Tiersma, 1999, pp. 214–20). Similar initiatives may be found in European Union (EU) law, which requires certain types of consumer information to be written 'in plain intelligible language'. Despite continued progress towards modernization, the clarity and readability of legal language remain an issue.

## 19.4 The Legal Translation Continuum: From Intersystemic to Intrasystemic Legal Translation

The main challenges faced by legal translators are: (1) language-specific – caused by cross-linguistic semantic, syntactic and pragmatic differences between legal discourses; (2) translation-process specific – relating to cognitive effort during simultaneous bilingual text processing by translators; and (3) legal-system specific – connected with the nature of the legal systems involved (Biel, 2014, p. 50).

Legal translation may be categorized according to a range of criteria, for example (1) legal genres or branches of law; (2) translation purposes, that is, legal translation for normative, informative and juridical purposes (Cao, 2007); (3) situational factors, namely, institutional translation and court/official translation; and (4) the type of legal systems involved. While all these factors affect the legal translator's decision-making process, its key determinant is the legal system: whether translation is *between* legal systems or *within* the legal system (Biel, 2017b, p. 78). Legal systems are versatile and so is legal translation. It can be conceptualized as a continuum with two extremes: intersystemic and intrasystemic translation, respectively (see Figure 19.1).

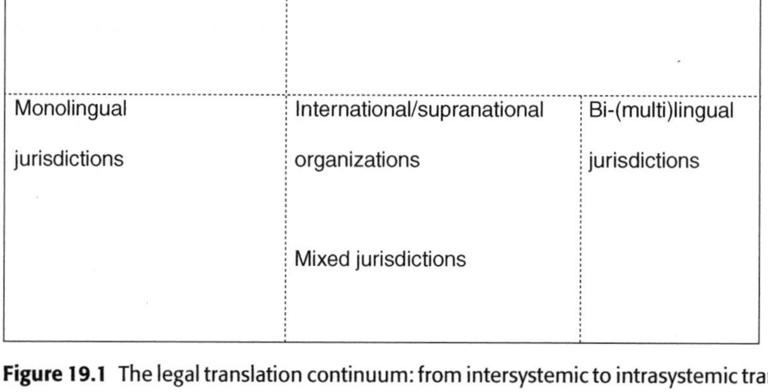

| Intersystemic translation | Intrasystemic translation | |
|---|---|---|
| between legal systems | within a legal system | |
| Monolingual jurisdictions | International/supranational organizations | Bi-(multi)lingual jurisdictions |
| | Mixed jurisdictions | |

**Figure 19.1** The legal translation continuum: from intersystemic to intrasystemic translation

### 19.4.1 Intersystemic Legal Translation

Intersystemic translation mediates between two legal systems: the source legal system where a legal text was drafted and the target legal system where a translation will be used; it is a translation 'from the source legal system into the target legal system' (Šarčević, 1997, p. 13) and from 'one legal language into another legal language' (de Groot, 1998, p. 23). Legal systems differ: they have their unique history, principles, conceptual structures and legal languages and they have been created by a particular nation. The degree of difficulty in intersystemic translation depends on asymmetries between legal systems (de Groot, 1987, p. 798). Conceptual differences are larger between systems from the common law tradition, a judge-made law shaped through precedents, for example the UK and the United States, and the civil law tradition based on Roman law and shaped through statutes, for example Germany, Spain and France (cf. Tetley, 2000). More affinities may be expected within the same family of legal systems and within the EU as a result of harmonization of laws.

The primary challenge in intersystemic translation is the incongruity of legal terminology owing to its system-bound nature (Šarčević, 1997, p. 232), resulting from its embedding in national legal systems and autonomy (de Groot, 1998, p. 22). Full equivalence is rare, 'elusive' and 'illusory' (Alcaraz Varó and Hughes, 2002, p. 23) and translators are often confronted with near, partial and zero equivalence. As a result, legal translation is imperfect by nature: it is a 'compromise' which 'will always fall short of the ideal' (Schroth, 1986, pp. 47–52).

Although owing to high litigation and other risks entailed by legal texts, 'precision is the order of the day' (Meredith, 1979, p. 67); faithfulness (fidelity) is not understood as word-for-word translation but is construed dynamically as 'an equivalent impact on the target reader' (Harvey, 2002, p. 180) through a translation 'that will be interpreted in the same way by legal professionals in the target legal system, as it would be in the original legal system' (Wolff, 2011). In the dominant receiver-oriented approach (Šarčević, 2000), also known as the functionalist approach (Garzone, 2000), the translator's task is to facilitate communication between the source text (ST) author and the TT recipients, albeit with precautions. Searching for optimal ways of approximating STs to recipients, translators are expected to draw on comparative law methods and compare the legal content of source language (SL) and target language (TL) concepts (de Groot, 1987, p. 797), more specifically, as recommended by Šarčević (1997, p. 237), by comparing *essentialia*, vital characteristics of legal concepts, and leaving aside additional characteristics – *accidentalia*. If the degree of incongruity is relatively small (Šarčević, 1997, p. 236), the ideal solution is a functional equivalent, also known as a natural or dynamic equivalent, which is a corresponding term in the target legal system (cf. Weston, 1991, p. 23; Alcaraz Varó and Hughes, 2002, pp. 178–9).

Other types of equivalent, for example descriptive equivalents, literal equivalents and borrowing, do not belong to the TL terminology and, hence, are legal neologisms from the perspective of the target system (de Groot, 1998, p. 25). The most domesticating, reader-friendly and proactive technique is a descriptive equivalent which explicates or explains the legal content of the SL concept by a paraphrase or modification of a TL term to bridge the recipient's knowledge gaps (Biel, 2009, p. 185). More foreignizing are literal equivalents, also known as formal equivalents, which are calques or loan translations, whose acceptability depends on semantic transparency (Weston, 1991, p. 25). Finally, a borrowing, that is, a transcription of a foreign term with or without some adaptations of spelling, 'admits defeat' (Weston, 1991, p. 26) because it is semantically opaque. This technique is rarely applied, and mainly for non-equivalent SL terms. Legal neologisms signal foreign frames of reference 'to maintain the reader's suspicion' (Schroth, 1986, p. 58), yet foreignizing techniques may also be associated with 'laziness or cowardice' rather than 'respect for cultural uniqueness' (Alcaraz Varó and Hughes, 2002, p. 155). Since, as a rule, translators use a mix of domesticating and foreignizing techniques depending on the degree of incongruity at the micro level and depending on genres and recipients, legal translation is inevitably a hybrid which accesses the ST through target knowledge structures (Biel, 2009, p. 187).

Preoccupation with accuracy may create tension with TL naturalness and readability, yet it is argued that professional legal translations 'can read as elegantly as any other' (Meredith, 1979, p. 54) and should be 'at least as readable and natural as their source predecessors' (Alcaraz Varó and Hughes, 2002, pp. 178–9). While foreignness is sometimes acceptable for non-equivalent terms and phraseology, other micro-level lexico-grammatical patterns are expected to be domesticated and fit TL conventions of a comparable target legal genre (cf. Monzó Nebot, 2008, p. 224) to facilitate recipients' TT processing.

### 19.4.2 Intrasystemic and Hybrid Legal Translation

Intrasystemic translation involves mediation within a legal system, most typically in bilingual and multilingual jurisdictions, such as Switzerland or Belgium, which promulgate their national law in more than one language. In such jurisdictions, law is multilingual: it is enacted in two or more authentic language versions. Intrasystemic translations, in particular of multilingual law, are authoritative, that is, equally valid from a legal point of view (Šarčević, 1997, p. 21); by contrast, intersystemic translations have only an informative value (Garzone, 2000, p. 6). Another fundamental difference is that, from the conceptual point of view, the ST and the TT in intrasystemic translation have the same frames of reference and the same background knowledge structures derived from the same legal system and sources of law.

More complex and hybrid set-ups include mixed jurisdictions and international and supranational organizations, which are placed closer to the centre of the legal translation continuum (see Figure 19.1). Mixed jurisdictions, such as Louisiana, Québec, South Africa, Scotland, Zimbabwe, Sri Lanka or Egypt, are based on two or more legal traditions or families, for example mixing civil law and common law traditions (Tetley, 2000, pp. 679, 684). Organizations such as the EU and the United Nations (UN) create supranational/international legal frameworks distinct from their members' laws. Key features of hybrid intrasystemic translation will be further illustrated with EU law, an extreme example of translated law.

The main challenge in EU translation is to ensure the uniform application and interpretation of EU multilingual law in all member states (Šarčević, 1997, p. 73). The EU, which currently comprises twenty-seven member states and twenty-four official languages, is a supranational organization with legal autonomy. EU law is enacted in twenty-four authentic language versions of equal status, all of which contribute to the meaning of a single legal instrument (Derlén, 2015, p. 62). EU law has supremacy over and is independent of member states' national laws (cf. Woods, Watson and Costa, 2017; Case 283/81 *Srl CILFIT* [1982]). Yet, although created at the supranational level, EU law is applied in and interacts with twenty-seven national legal systems (Kjær, 2007, p. 79), for example through directly binding regulations which become automatically incorporated into national legal systems or directives which are transposed, that is, localized into national legal languages (Biel, 2014, p. 59). Thus, whereas in principle EU legal translation is intrasystemic since its primary point of reference is EU supranational law, it has multiple – supranational and national – frames of reference due to recontextualization in the member states' legal systems. What adds to the difficulty is the politically complex and multi-stage drafting process tied up with translation, with the content being filtered back and forth through twenty-four official languages. This increases the risk of divergences among language versions. EU legal terminology tends to be formulated with neutralization techniques, at both the drafting and the translation stage: neologisms, terminologization of generic terms and adaptation of existing terms (cf. Mattila, 2013, pp. 157–8). Translation tends to be source-oriented, with preference for literal translation techniques (Koskinen, 2000, p. 54; Baaij, 2018). This creates EU hybrid translator-mediated legal languages – Eurolects – distinct from national legal languages.

### 19.4.3   Official Translation

Official translations are translations which 'meet the requirements to serve as legally valid instruments in a target country' (Mayoral Asensio, 2003, p. 1). Such requirements are regulated in domestic legislation and differ across countries. Official translation is rendered by translators diversely labelled around the world as public, official, sworn, certified, legal translators: *certified translator* (Canada), *traductor-intérprete jurado* (Spain), *allgemein beeideter und gerichtlich zertifizierter Dolmetscher* (Austria), *tłumacz przysięgły* (Poland), *auktoriserad translator* (Sweden), *traductor público* (Argentina), etc. The profession is regulated and protected. Eligibility criteria and accreditation models vary across countries, yet in most cases candidates are required to have a higher education diploma and a clean criminal record; they may be required to pass a state- or court-organized examination. Official translation may be less professionalized in the case of languages of limited diffusion, for example minor African or Asian languages (Taibi and Ozolins, 2016, p. 3). Countries which do not regulate official translation may introduce other solutions, including government-approved or tender-selected outsourcers, for example translation companies.

Official translators are authorized to provide translation and/or interpreting for juridical and administrative purposes, that is, for courts, prosecution, the police, registrars and other bodies; hence, they are jurilinguistic experts (Mayoral Asensio, 2003, p. 37). They translate judgments; witness statements; company registration documents; tender documentation; personal documents, that is, birth, marriage and death certificates; school diplomas; as well as non-legal texts such as medical examinations or technical reports which may be required by courts. Official translators assume liability for translation and with their signature and official seal, if applicable, they certify that the translation is accurate and was rendered in line with principles of professional ethics, such as impartiality, confidentiality and due diligence. This makes the translator visible. Official translations are more source-oriented, with priority given to formal fidelity to the ST, and the decision-making process has to balance within 'the administration's margins of acceptability' (Mayoral Asensio, 2003, p. 42).

## 19.5 Historical Perspectives on Legal Translation: Growing Accessibility and Functionalism

Legal translation has evolved towards greater accessibility, both formally and linguistically. For many centuries, law was linguistically inaccessible to common people. Throughout Europe, it was enacted and practised in Latin, the lingua franca of the Middle Ages, known by intellectual elites. In some countries, law was practised in invaders' or colonizers' languages. The lack of translation to the vernacular was a manifestation of power by limiting knowledge to a small group of lawyers. Referring to Norman French, the language of law and judicial proceedings in England after the Norman conquest, Mellinkoff (1963, p. 101) asks: 'What better way of preserving a professional monopoly than by locking up your trade secrets in the safe of an unknown tongue?' This started to change in the Renaissance with the growing interest in vernacular languages. From the late fifteenth century, English statutes were enacted in English, although French continued to be used in courts till the seventeenth century (Tiersma, 1999, pp. 35–6). Nowadays, the right to translation and interpretation during trial is regarded as a fundamental human right. In the EU it is regulated by Directive 2010/64/EU of the European Parliament and the Council of 20 October 2010 on the right to interpretation and translation in criminal proceedings, where the right of suspects and accused persons to gratis interpreting/translation if they do not understand the language of proceedings is an element of fair trial. The right to interpretation imposes an obligation to provide interpreting during police questioning, client–lawyer meetings and court hearings while the right to translation covers the translation of documents essential for defence (e.g., indictments or judgments).

Another development which increased the accessibility of legal discourse was a shift in approaches to legal translation owing to changing perceptions of STs, TTs and the translator's role. As synthesized by Šarčević (1997, p. 24), legal translation evolved from literalness towards functional approaches and went through phases from strictly literal, through literal and moderately literal, to near idiomatic and idiomatic approaches, and finally to co-drafting. The first known guidelines on legal translation are Emperor Justinian's directive permitting only a word-for-word translation of the fifth-century compilation of Roman law *Corpus juris civilis* into Greek as a 'means of preserving the letter of the law' (Šarčević, 1997, p. 24). In the early period, legal texts had a sacrosanct status similar to religious texts and their strictly literal rendering was a safeguard against heterodoxy (Šarčević, 1997, p. 25). It was not until the nineteenth century that more sensitivity to TL conventions could be observed, accompanied by a gradual domestication of legal translations to ensure enhanced comprehensibility (Šarčević, 1997, pp. 34–6). This shift was slower than in other types of translation. It started with the Swiss debate on the French translation of the Swiss Civil Code (*Schweizerisches Zivilgesetzbuch*) by Rossel, giving preference to the spirit over the letter of the law through idiomatic translation and foregrounding of comprehension issues (Šarčević, 1997, pp. 36–40). The next development was the Canadian practice of co-drafting (bilingual drafting) where translators have become part of drafting teams (Šarčević, 1997, pp. 42–6) and translations have evolved from literal to fully functional (Gémar, 2015, p. 491). The focus on communicative aspects of legal translation is supported by the growing awareness of the need for clarity in legal language.

Historically, translation was a source of new laws and social reforms, transferring foreign legal knowledge and transplanting legal concepts. For example, the French Civil Code (*Code Napoléon*, 1804) was introduced, with varied degrees of adaptation, in countries controlled or influenced by

France – Belgium, the Netherlands, Portugal, Spain, Switzerland, Poland, Romania, and some areas of Italy and Germany – and, in consequence, into their colonies in Africa and Latin America (Graziadei, 2006, pp. 450–1). The German Civil Code inspired the Japanese Civil Code, which in turn affected the Chinese and South Korean codes (Graziadei, 2006, p. 451). The nineteenth-century Ottoman Empire drafted its Penal Code (1858) on the basis of the translated French Penal Code to modernize and Westernize the country, '"translating" crimes and punishments' for a culturally distant society (Öner and Banu Karadağ, 2016, p. 323). This process may be referred to as 'lawmaking through translation' (Öner and Banu Karadağ, 2016, p. 333). As stressed by comparative lawyers, legal systems exist thanks to 'both original innovation and borrowing' (Graziadei, 2006, p. 474), which is mainly effected through translation. Legal translation has also triggered the development of hybrid specialized varieties of national languages, for example a Cypriot Greek legal variety as a result of translating English common law into Standard Modern Greek after Cyprus gained independence (Vlachopoulos, 2008), a Chinese legal variety for English common law in Hong Kong after 1997 (Chan, 2012) or Eurolects in the EU (Mori, 2018).

## 19.6 Legal Translation as a Market Practice: The Professionalization of Legal Translators

As an area of professional practice, legal translation is a premium sector of the translation industry which requires specialized competences and qualifications. Legal translators work in a range of settings which determine their profiles (Biel, 2011, p. 164; see also Borja Albi and Prieto Ramos, 2013). A large number of translators work as freelancers (independent contractors) for translation agencies or direct clients in the outsourced 'outstitutional' environment (cf. Scott, 2019). Other translators work as in-house translators employed in law firms, companies, public administration and international institutions. Some institutions require translators to have a legal background, for example the Court of Justice of the European Union, which employs lawyer-linguists as translators. Finally, some translators work as official translators for courts or the police (see Section 19.4.3).

Having published an umbrella standard for the provision of translation services, ISO 17100:2015 (ISO, 2015), the International Organization for Standardization has prepared the standard ISO 20771:2020 Legal translation – Requirements to specify competences and qualifications of legal translators and revisers, professional development and specific issues related to legal translation services, such as confidentiality, security and professional liability (ISO, 2020). A similar standard for legal interpreting

(20228:2019) was published in 2019 (ISO, 2019). The standards harmonize requirements and give translators a more professional image.

The growing professionalization of legal translators' work is attested by the increasing number of associations of legal translators and interpreters, for example the US NAJIT (National Association of Judiciary Interpreters and Translators), the Polish TEPIS (Society of Sworn and Specialized Translators), the Spanish APTIJ (Asociación Profesional de Traductores e Intérpretes Judicales y Jurados), the French EXPERTIJ (Experts et Traducteurs Interprètes Judicaires), as well as an umbrella organization for associations – EULITA (European Legal Interpreters and Translators Association). Their objectives include: to promote the recognition of legal translators' and interpreters' professional status; to safeguard their rights and monitor working conditions; to establish professional and ethical standards of practice; and to provide targeted continuous professional development (CPD).

## 19.7 Technologies and Resources for Legal Translators

Legal translators' work environment has been affected by information technology (IT) developments since the turn of the twenty-first century, becoming an integrated technology-rich environment where translation is accomplished through human–computer interaction (cf. O'Brien, 2012, p. 101). Key technologies which impact text processing include computer-assisted translation (CAT) tools (e.g., SDL Trados, memoQ), terminology management tools (e.g., SDL MultiTerm, QTerm) and machine translation systems (e.g., eTranslation, DeepL, GoogleTranslate). These are designed to increase productivity, enhance quality and reduce translation costs.

CAT tools identify and retrieve previously translated segments stored in the translation memory (TM), reusing previous work and maintaining the consistency of translation at the macro- and the micro-structural level. For example, EU translators are required to pre-translate an ST with the normative translation memory which contains repetitive translation units to be translated uniformly into all official languages. Examples of this would be *This Regulation shall be binding in its entirety* and *Having regard to the Treaty on ....* CAT tools enable more nuanced terminology work with term bases where translators manage terminology on an ad hoc basis and for a specific client. Quality assurance tools check terminological consistency in the TT and with existing documents. Concordance searches function as contextualized bilingual glossaries. Studies show that they are a preferred resource and that translators are reluctant to leave the CAT environment (Bundgaard and Christensen, 2019).

These changes in translators' research behaviour lead to a gradual replacement of paper dictionaries with electronic term bases and ontologies, preferably integrated with CAT tools. In the hierarchy of resources,

legislation is a primary source of terminological information and dictionaries are a secondary source (cf. Prieto Ramos, 2011, p. 15; Biel, 2017a,
p. 319). Bilingual dictionaries have long been criticized for having limited
functionality for translators owing to insufficient legal information in
entries and for decontextualization (de Groot and van Laer, 2006). This
was initially compensated for with search engines, peer-to-peer discussion
fora and social media groups for terminological support (Biel, 2008) and
subsequently with more sophisticated online and electronic termino-
graphic resources (see Mac Aodha, 2014 for developments in legal lexicography), for example the Inter-Active Terminology for Europe (IATE), the
EU's multilingual terminology database. Developments concern the content of terminological entries with translation-oriented entries ideally
based on comparative law methods, not only containing definitions but
also assessing the degree of equivalence and naming types of equivalent
(Bestué, 2019, pp. 140–1, 143). Another solution is a term ontology, that is,
a term management system which provides concepts, background information and documents needed to understand the ST and generate a TT
(Orozco and Sánchez-Gijón, 2011, p. 40). An area of terminography which
requires improvement owing to insufficient coverage is legal phraseology
(Buendía-Castro and Faber, 2018, p. 82).

More recent technologies use artificial intelligence (AI) to translate
legal texts automatically with machine translation (MT) systems. Major
progress was achieved with the advent of neural MT systems. This
change has been fast despite predictions that legal translation 'will
remain an essentially human activity, at least in the near future'
(Mattila, 2013, p. 22; Prieto Ramos, 2014, p. 271). The use of raw MT
output is still problematic and raises the question of admissibility and
liability for errors. To achieve an acceptable quality, raw MT output
requires post-editing by human translators. Its usability depends on
the availability of domain-restricted training data for a language pair.
For example, an engine trained with English–Spanish clinical trial
agreements may provide usable output for post-editing this type of
document. When integrated as a CAT feature, MT becomes another
resource, where MT suggestions follow TM matches. A study conducted
in 2015 by Cadwell et al. (2016, p. 235) shows that reasons why EU in-
house translators use MT include productivity gains, ergonomics of
reduced typing, 'inspiration, to kick-start the translation process, or
for new ideas' and for weaker source languages. On the other hand,
post-editing is connected with risks which are critical in legal translation, in particular information transfer errors (additions, omissions,
distortions), terminological inconsistency and reduced text coherence.
These issues may be difficult to spot owing to the fluency of MT output
and a lack of the ST/TT deep processing typical of from-scratch
translation.

## 19.8   Legal Translation Studies: Research Trends

Legal translation has become a vibrant subfield of translation studies and has emerged as a sub-discipline known as legal translation studies (LTS) and legal translation and interpreting (LTI, LIT). The development of LTS has been divided by Prieto Ramos (2014, pp. 268–72) into three phases: (1) the initial phase from the 1970s to the mid-1990s; (2) the catalytic stage from the mid-1990s to the mid-2000s; and (3) the consolidation and expansion phase since the mid-2000s.

The initial phase coincided with the emancipation of translation studies as a discipline and the pioneering Canadian scholarship proclaiming *jurilinguistique* [jurilinguistics] as a new field of study (Prieto Ramos, 2014, pp. 268–9). Positioned at the intersection of law, language and legal translation, *jurilinguistique* aimed at reflection on legal translation practice to enhance understanding of it (Gémar, 2005). Developments were also inspired from within comparative law, which shows high sensitivity to translation issues owing to the constant need to explain the contents of domestic or foreign legal systems in another language (de Groot, 1998, p. 22). The catalytic stage saw seminal monograph publications by Šarčević (1997), Borja Albi (2000), Alcaraz Varó and Hughes (2002), Cao (2007) and Bocquet (2008), with attempts at conceptualization and theorization about legal translation. The phase of consolidation and expansion heralded exponential growth of research activity around the world, evidenced by its volume, scale, geographical spread, and thematic and methodological diversification, embracing new methods and shifting from qualitative to quantitative and mixed approaches (Biel, 2018, pp. 26–7; Biel et al., 2019). LTS has become a more methodologically rigorous, diverse and mature field.

Adapting Saldanha and O'Brien's (2013, p. 5) focus on translations to legal translation (Biel, 2017b), research into legal translation can be modelled through five dimensions: (1) the context of text production; (2) participants; (3) the process; (4) the product; and (5) reception. Figure 19.2 shows dimensions of translations and their sample research components.

Research into the context of production includes the contextual and situational analysis of how STs are produced, for example legal drafting. It explores factors which impact translators' behaviour (cf. Saldanha and O'Brien, 2013, p. 205), for example institutional, legal, political, cultural and historical factors. It investigates other pre-production processes and circumstances, such as quality assurance procedures. This type of contextualization requires qualitative approaches, including genre analysis (critical) discourse analysis, observational studies and ethnography.

The dimension of participants covers various roles involved in translation: translators, lawyer-linguists, revisers, proofreaders and post-editors. It is inspired by sociology of translation and translator studies,

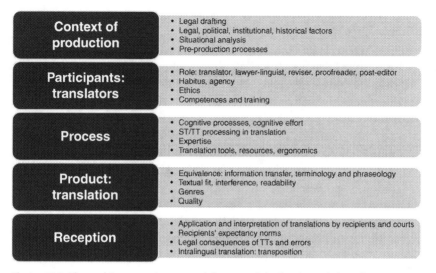

**Figure 19.2** The multi-perspective research framework for legal translation: dimensions and components
Source: Adapted from Biel (2017b).

which are interested in cultural aspects such as ideologies and ethics, and sociological factors such as networks, habitus and agency (Chesterman, 2017). This dimension also explores participants' competences and their development (see Section 19.9). A mix of quantitative and qualitative methods is used, for example surveys (Scott, 2019), indepth interviews, observational studies, workplace studies and ethnography (Koskinen, 2008).

Process research applies experimental methods, such as eye tracking, think aloud protocols and keystroke logging, in an effort to understand translators' cognitive processes when they translate, in particular how translators process the ST (cf. Griebel, 2021) and the TT and interact with resources and technologies. There is very little research on legal translation processing and it remains the largest gap in LTS.

Most research investigates the product, that is, translated, revised or post-edited texts. There are two key approaches: (1) the relation of equivalence between an ST and a TT; and (2) the relation of textual fit, that is, the naturalness of translations, established by comparing TTs to non-translated TL texts (cf. Biel, 2014). An important area of study is legal terminology and phraseology, including translation strategies and techniques. Other topics include the stylistic, syntactic and discursive dimensions of translations (contrastive genre analysis, diachronic/synchronic genre variation, studies of legal language for translation purposes, translation of selected lexico-grammatical patterns); quality assessment; and inverse translation. Qualitative, quantitative and mixed methods are used to study products, including comparative law methods (cf. Glanert,

2014), with a surge in the popularity of corpus methods since the early 2010s (Biel, 2018).

In the case of legal translation, reception should be singled out from Saldanha and O'Brien's (2013) category of the context of production and reception. Reception of translated legal texts includes their application and interpretation by direct recipients and courts (cf. Derlén, 2009; Paunio, 2013) and a study of legal consequences of translations. Another topic is intralingual translation, that is, the transposition of EU directives into national law. Reception is explored mainly with qualitative legal methods, although there is a need for experimental cognitive studies on how legal translation is processed by recipients.

These developments support a move beyond applied research towards empirically grounded theoretical reflection and modelling of legal translation (Biel, 2017b, p. 78). However, as argued by Gémar (2005), fundamental research is still a 'utopia' and legal translation lacks theoretical foundations. More consolidation is needed across disciplines (law, linguistics, translation studies), 'language-specific enclaves', for example English, French, Spanish, Chinese (Biel and Engberg, 2013, p. 2) and modes of provision to establish common ground with legal interpreting, where research tends to focus on cultural, ethical and interactional aspects, for example Hale (2004), Valero-Garcés and Martin (2008), Biernacka (2018), but still concerns legal texts.

## 19.9　Training of Legal Translators

The training of legal translators typically starts at Master's level, with modules devoted in whole or in part to legal translation, and continues as more flexible diploma courses, on-the-job training and CPD. A few programmes exclusively devoted to legal translation also exist, for example at the University of Geneva, the Open University of Hong Kong and the University of London. These offer interdisciplinary training based in languages faculties, and in some cases law faculties.

Legal translators' competences are generally similar to other specialized translators' competences but differ in the core translation competence. In the European Master's in Translation (EMT) model, this covers strategic, methodological and thematic sub-competences (Toudic and Krause, 2017). Most studies concern legal translators' thematic sub-competence, stressing the need for legal knowledge: knowledge of branches of law, terminology and phraseology, asymmetries between ST/TT legal systems, as well as basic legal skills of reasoning, legal problem solving, foreseeing text interpretation, drafting skills and comparative law analysis skills (Šarčević, 1997, pp. 113–14; de Groot, 1987, p. 798; Orozco and Sánchez-Gijón, 2011, pp. 25–6; Scarpa and Orlando, 2017). This list defines the ideal – but, as Šarčević (1997, pp. 113–14) observes, non-existent – legal translator; although legal translators do not need a lawyer's level of legal knowledge, they need to be able 'to situate the documents in their legal and procedural context' and construe ST/TT legal effects (Prieto Ramos, 2011, p. 13). Legal knowledge must be supplemented with textual competence – a sound knowledge of legal genres, comparative legal linguistics and contrastive rhetoric (Prieto Ramos, 2011, p. 13; Galán-Mañas, 2013; see Scarpa and Orlando, 2017 and ISO, 2020, p. 7 for other competences).

Trainers also focus on procedural knowledge connected with the strategic and methodological sub-competences which help integrate all competences. Prieto Ramos (2011, p. 14) proposes a sequence of steps to facilitate the decision-making process at the macro-textual level and quality control at the micro-textual level: (1) Skopos analysis and macro-contextualization to identify a legal system, branch of law and genre; (2) ST analysis to identify comprehension problems and to mine legal information; (3) transfer and TT production; and (4) TT checking as part of quality control. The second step should also subsume the development of research needs and identification of reliable information and parallel texts (Bestué and Orozco, 2016, p. 479). Considering technological advancements, it is necessary to integrate revision and post-editing skills in the training process.

In addition to work on competences and their acquisition, training literature discusses classroom methodologies, for example discourse analytical approaches (Way, 2016), epistemological approaches (Martínez Carrasco, 2017), professional realism (Biel, 2011) and the use of technologies to promote learner autonomy, for example corpora and e-learning platforms. Legal corpora are used as: (1) a translation aid to enhance the communicative aspects of legal translation by raising trainees' awareness of TL conventions; and (2) a socialization resource which reflects professional translators' problem solving and helps trainees develop critical-thinking skills (Biel, 2017a; Monzó Nebot, 2008). Other tools include debating fora on e-learning platforms as online communities, enhancing trainees' motivation to improve legal knowledge and raising their confidence (Bestué and Orozco, 2016, pp. 482–3).

Acknowledgement: This work was supported by the National Science Centre (NCN) under Grant 2014/14/E/HS2/00782.

# References

Alcaraz Varó, E., and Hughes, B. (2002). *Legal Translation Explained.* Manchester: St Jerome.

Baaij, C. J. W. (2018). *Legal Integration and Language Diversity: Rethinking Translation in EU Lawmaking.* New York: Oxford University Press.

Bazerman, C. (1994). Systems of genres and the enactment of social intentions. In A. Freedman and P. Medway, eds., *Genre and the New Rhetoric.* London: Taylor and Francis, pp. 79–101.

Bestué, C. (2019). A matter of justice: Integrating comparative law methods into the decision-making process in legal translation. In Ł. Biel, J. Engberg, R. M. Martín Ruano and V. Sosoni, eds., *Research Methods in Legal Translation and Interpreting: Crossing Methodological Boundaries*. London: Routledge, pp. 130–47.

Bestué, C., and Orozco, M. (2016). Online training in legal translation: Designing curricula for bilingual students. *Babel*, **62**(3), 470–94.

Bhatia, V. K. (2006). Legal genres. In K. Brown, ed., *Encyclopedia of Language and Linguistics*. Oxford: Elsevier, pp. 1–7.

Biel, Ł. (2008). Legal terminology in terminology in translation practice: Dictionaries, Googling or discussion forums? *SKASE Journal of Translation and Interpretation*, **3**, 22–38.

Biel, Ł. (2009). Organization of background knowledge structures in legal language and related translation problems. *Comparative Legilinguistics: International Journal for Legal Communication*, **1**, 176–89.

Biel, Ł. (2011). Professional realism in the legal translation classroom: Translation competence and translator competence. *Meta*, **56**(1), 162–78.

Biel, Ł. (2014). *Lost in the Eurofog: The Textual Fit of Translated Law*. Frankfurt am Main: Peter Lang.

Biel, Ł. (2017a). Enhancing the communicative dimension of legal translation: Comparable corpora in the research-informed classroom. *The Interpreter and Translator Trainer*, **11**(4), 316–36.

Biel, Ł. (2017b). Researching legal translation: A multi-perspective and mixed-method framework for legal translation. *Revista de Llengua i Dret [Journal of Language and Law]*, **68**, 76–88.

Biel, Ł. (2018). Corpora in institutional legal translation: Small steps and the big picture. In F. Prieto Ramos, ed., *Institutional Translation for International Governance: Enhancing Quality in Multilingual Legal Communication*. London: Bloomsbury, pp. 25–36.

Biel, Ł. (2019). Theoretical and methodological challenges in researching EU legal translation. In I. Simonnæs and M. Kristiansen, eds., *Legal Translation: Current Issues and Challenges in Research, Methods and Applications*. Berlin: Frank and Timme, pp. 25–40.

Biel, Ł., and Engberg, J. (2013). Research models and methods in legal translation. *Linguistica Antverpiensia, New Series – Themes in Translation Studies*, **12**, 1–11.

Biel, Ł., Engberg, J., Martín Ruano, R. M., and Sosoni, V., eds. (2019). *Research Methods in Legal Translation and Interpreting*. London: Routledge.

Biernacka, A. (2018). *Interpreter-Mediated Interactions of the Courtroom*. Berlin: Peter Lang.

Bocquet, C. (2008). *La traduction juridique: Fondement et méthode*. Brussels: De Boeck.

Borja Albi, A. (2000). *El texto jurídico inglés y su traducción al español*. Barcelona: Ariel.

Borja Albi, A., and Prieto Ramos, F., eds. (2013). *Legal Translation in Context: Professional Issues and Prospects*. Oxford: Peter Lang.

Buendía-Castro, M., and Faber, P. (2018). Online resources for phraseology-related problems in legal translation. In S. Goźdź-Roszkowski and G. Pontrandolfo, eds., *Phraseology in Legal and Institutional Settings*. London: Routledge, pp. 61–86.

Bundgaard, K., and Christensen, T. P. (2019). Is the concordance feature the new black? A workplace study of translators' interaction with translation resources while post-editing TM and MT matches. *Journal of Specialised Translation*, **31**, 14–37.

Cadwell, P., Castilho, S., O'Brien, S., and Mitchell, L. (2016). Human factors in machine translation and post-editing among institutional translators. *Translation Spaces*, **5**(2), 222–43.

Cao, D. (2007). *Translating Law*. Clevedon, UK: Multilingual Matters.

Chan, C. H.-Y. (2012). Bridging the gap between language and law: Translational issues in creating legal Chinese in Hong Kong. *Babel*, **58**(2), 127–44.

Chesterman, A. (2017). The name and nature of translator studies. *HERMES – Journal of Language and Communication in Business*, **22**(42), 13–22.

Crystal, D., and Davy, D. (1969). *Investigating English Style*. London: Longman.

De Groot, G.-R. (1987). The point of view of a comparative lawyer. *Les Cahiers de droit*, **28**(4), 793–812.

De Groot, G.-R. (1998). *Language and Law: Netherlands Report to the Fifteenth International Congress of Comparative Law*. Antwerp: Intersentia.

De Groot, G.-R., and van Laer, C. J. P. (2006). The dubious quality of legal dictionaries. *International Journal of Legal Information*, **34**, 65–86.

Derlén, M. (2009). *Multilingual Interpretation of European Community Law*. Alphen aan den Rijn: Kluwer Law International.

Derlén, M. (2015). A single text or a single meaning: Multilingual interpretation of EU legislation and CJEU case law in national courts. In S. Šarčević, ed., *Language and Culture in EU Law: Multidisciplinary Perspectives*. Farnham: Ashgate, pp. 53–72.

Galán-Mañas, A. (2013). Contrastive rhetoric in teaching how to translate legal texts. *Perspectives*, **21**(3), 311–28.

Garzone, G. (2000). Legal translation and functionalist approaches: A contradiction in terms? Actes du Colloque International 'La traduction juridique. Histoire, théorie(s) et pratique, 17–19.2.2000'. Geneva: University of Geneva, pp. 395–414.

Gémar, J.-C. (2005). De la traduction (juridique) à la jurilinguistique: Fonctions proactives du traductologue. *Meta*, **50**(4), 5–22.

Gémar, J.-C. (2015). De la traduction juridique à la jurilinguistique: La quête de l'équivalence. *Meta*, **60**(3), 476–93.

Gibbons, J. (1999). Language and the law. *Annual Review of Applied Linguistics*, **19**, 156–73.

Glanert, S., ed. (2014). *Comparative Law: Engaging Translation*. London: Routledge.

Graziadei, M. (2006). Comparative law as the study of transplants and receptions. In M. Reimann and R. Zimmermann, eds., *The Oxford Handbook of Comparative Law*. Oxford: Oxford University Press, pp. 441–76.

Griebel, C. (2021). Legal meta-comments in the think-aloud protocols of legal translators and lawyers: A qualitative analysis. *Target*, **33**(2), 183–206.

Hale, S. B. (2004). *The Discourse of Court Interpreting: Discourse Practices of the Law, the Witness and the Interpreter*. Amsterdam: John Benjamins.

Harris, P. (2006). *An Introduction to Law*. Cambridge: Cambridge University Press.

Harvey, M. (2002). What's so special about legal translation? *Meta*, **47**(2), 177–85.

ISO 2015. *ISO 17100:2015 Translation services – Requirements for translation services*. Geneva: International Organization for Standardization.

ISO 2019. *ISO 20228:2019 Interpreting services – Legal interpreting – Requirements*. Geneva: International Organization for Standardization.

ISO 2020. *ISO 20771:2020 Legal translation – Requirements*. Geneva: International Organization for Standardization.

Kjær, A. L. (2007). Legal translation in the European Union: A research field in need of a new approach. In K. Kredens and S. Goźdź-Roszkowski, eds., *Language and the Law: International Outlooks*. Frankfurt am Main: Peter Lang, pp. 69–95.

Koskinen, K. (2000). Institutional illusions: Translating in the EU Commission. *The Translator*, **6**(1), 49–65.

Koskinen, K. (2008). *Translating Institutions: An Ethnographic Study of EU Translation*. Manchester: St Jerome.

Mac Aodha, M., ed. (2014). *Legal Lexicography: A Comparative Perspective*. London: Routledge.

Martínez Carrasco, R. (2017). Epistemological Approaches to Legal Translation Education: A Situated Account. PhD dissertation, Universitat Jaume I.

Mattila, H. E. S. (2013). *Comparative Legal Linguistics: Language of Law, Latin and Modern Lingua Francas*. Aldershot: Ashgate.

Mayoral Asensio, R. (2003). *Translating Official Documents*. Manchester: St Jerome.

Mellinkoff, D. (1963). *The Language of the Law*. Boston: Little, Brown and Co.

Meredith, R. C. (1979). Some notes on English legal translation. *Meta*, **24**(1), 54–67.

Monzó Nebot, E. (2008). Corpus-based activities in legal translator training. *The Interpreter and Translator Trainer*, **2**(2), 221–52.

Mori, L., ed. (2018). *Observing Eurolects: Corpus Analysis of Linguistic Variation in EU Law*. Amsterdam: John Benjamins.

O'Brien, S. (2012). Translation as human–computer interaction. *Translation Spaces*, **1**(1), 101–22.

Öner, S., and Banu Karadağ, A. (2016). Lawmaking through translation: 'Translating' crimes and punishments. *Perspectives*, **24**(2), 319–38.

Orozco, M., and Sánchez-Gijón, P. (2011). New resources for legal translators. *Perspectives*, **19**, 25–44.

Paunio, E. (2013). *Legal Certainty in Multilingual EU Law: Language, Discourse and Reasoning at the European Court of Justice*. London: Routledge.

Prieto Ramos, F. (2011). Developing legal translation competence: An integrative process-oriented approach. *Comparative Legilinguistics: International Journal for Legal Communication*, **5**, 7–21.

Prieto Ramos, F. (2014). Legal translation studies as interdiscipline: Scope and evolution. *Meta*, **59**(2), 260–77.

Prieto Ramos, F. (2019). Implications of text categorisation for corpus-based legal translation research: The case of international institutional settings. In Ł. Biel, J. Engberg, R. M. Martín Ruano and V. Sosoni, eds., *Research Methods in Legal Translation and Interpreting: Crossing Methodological Boundaries*. London: Routledge, pp. 29–37.

Saldanha, G., and O'Brien, S. (2013). *Research Methodologies in Translation Studies*. London: Routledge.

Šarčević, S. (1997). *New Approach to Legal Translation*. The Hague: Kluwer Law International.

Šarčević, S. (2000). Legal translation and translation theory: A receiver-oriented approach. La traduction juridique: Histoire, théorie(s) et pratique [Legal Translation: History, Theory/ies, Practice]. Proceedings, Geneva, 17–19 February 2000. Bern/Geneva: ASTTI/ETI.

Scarpa, F., and Orlando, D. (2017). What it takes to do it right: An integrative EMT-based model for legal translation competence. *Journal of Specialised Translation*, **27**, 21–42.

Schroth, P. W. (1986). Legal translation. *American Journal of Comparative Law*, **34**, 47–65.

Scott, J. R. (2019). *Legal Translation Outsourced*. Oxford: Oxford University Press.

Taibi, M., and Ozolins, U. (2016). *Community Translation*. London: Bloomsbury Academic.

Tetley, W. (2000). Mixed jurisdictions: Common law v. civil law (codified and uncodified). *Louisiana Law Review*, **60**, 677–738.

Tiersma, P. M. (1999). *Legal Language*. Chicago: University of Chicago Press.

Toudic, D., and Krause, A., eds. (2017). *European Master's in Translation Competence Framework 2017*. Available at https://ec.europa.eu/info/sites/info/files/emt_competence_fwk_2017_en_web.pdf.

Valero-Garcés, C., and Martin, A., eds. (2008). *Crossing Borders in Community Interpreting: Definitions and Dilemmas*. Amsterdam: John Benjamins.

Vlachopoulos, S. (2008). Translating into a new LSP: The translation of laws in the Republic of Cyprus. *Target*, **20**(1), 103–14.

Way, C. (2016). The challenges and opportunities of legal translation and translator training in the 21st century. *International Journal of Communication*, **10**, 1009–29.

Weston, M. (1991). *An English Reader's Guide to the French Legal System*. New York: Berg.

Wolff, L. (2011). Legal translation. In K. Malmkjær and K. Windle, eds., *The Oxford Handbook of Translation Studies*. Oxford: Oxford University Press, pp. 228–42.

Woods, L., Watson, P., and Costa, M. (2017). *Steiner and Woods EU Law*. Oxford: Oxford University Press.

# 20

# Translating News

Lucile Davier

## 20.1  Introduction

Virtually every introduction to news writing (see e.g. Keeble, 2007 [1994]) mentions the five Ws of journalism, questions which help editors organize a news story and include all important information, and this chapter about translation in the media is also structured around them: *What* is news translation? *When* is news translated? *Who* translates news? *Where* is news translated? *How* is it translated? A sixth question (e.g., *Why* is translation used by media organizations?) is discussed in the conclusion only because it is left unanswered by many scholars.

## 20.2  What Is News Translation?

### 20.2.1  What Is News?

According to Catenaccio et al. (2011, p. 1844), the News, Text and Talk group of scholars from linguistics and neighbouring disciplines use the term 'news' 'to refer to a broad spectrum of journalistic activity . . . in any domain or technological modality (including radio, television, online news sites, and internet-based social media)'. This broad view seems particularly important at a time when convergence – or multi-platform journalism – impacts all media (see Section 20.3.2).

Etymologically, news 'is about novelty' and 'should be timely', but novelty is also 'a relative notion, which can be reframed as a short period of validity', write Catenaccio et al. (2011, p. 1844). This criterion of novelty is relativized by two phenomena. First, news with a particular impact can get integrated in the 'community's collective memories' (Catenaccio et al., 2011, p. 1844). Second, news is 'all about retelling' (Catenaccio et al., 2011, p. 1844), which implies the extraction of text from one discourse (decontextualization) and its reinsertion into another context (recontextualization) (Bauman and Briggs, 1990; Silverstein and Urban, 1996).

The aim of this section is not to discuss news values (Galtung and Ruge, 1965; Harcup and O'Neill, 2017) but to suggest that research on news writing and news translation needs to rely on a broad definition of news in order not to exclude important types of data. In other words, news consists of all the non-fictional output – written, oral and visual – produced by news outlets or other organizations.

### 20.2.2  Journalistic Translation Research

This subfield of translation studies is often referred to as 'news translation', but introductory chapters and literature reviews classify it under diverse headings: press translation (Bani, 2006), journalism and translation (van Doorslaer, 2010), news gathering and dissemination (Palmer, 2011), news translation (Holland, 2013), journalistic translation (Valdeón, 2015) or translation in news media (Schäffner, 2018).

Although news enjoys a prominent space in the teaching of translation (Seibel and Zambrana Kuhn, 2000; Li, 2006), professional translators have very little news to translate, with the exception of press releases in multilingual countries or organizations (Lavault-Olléon and Sauron, 2009).

However, Schäffner (2018, p. 328) has shown that publications in this subfield have significantly increased after 2010. In the *Translation Studies Bibliography* (Gambier and van Doorslaer, 2018), 26 per cent of the output indexed with the standardized keyword 'press' was written between 2010 and 2020 (approximately 50 per cent with 'news translation' in the title and 40 per cent with 'news translation' in the abstract). In the BITRA (Bibliography of Interpreting and Translation) database held at the University of Alicante, Spain, 40 per cent of records with the standardized keyword 'journalism' were published during the same period (approximately 50 per cent of publications with 'news translation' in the title or abstract). In other words, scholarly interest in news translation grew exponentially during this decade.

## 20.3  When Was News First Translated? How Long Will It Be?

The translation of news began with the birth of journalism, and the various transformations the media have undergone recently – including convergence and the development of social networks – do not seem to have affected the importance afforded this practice.

### 20.3.1  A Very Brief History of News Translation

Although news translation was slow to attract scholarly interest, translation is intimately linked to journalism, according to Valdeón (2015, p. 636).

Even prior to 1620, the *corantos*, weekly collections of news about the Thirty Years War published in Britain (Barnhurst and Nerone, 2009), mostly consisted of texts first published in other European countries and languages (Valdeón, 2015, p. 637), so it can be inferred that these publications mostly included translations and little national news (Valdeón, 2012, p. 853). In the seventeenth and eighteenth centuries, the French gazettes covered international and national political news and were 'composed of short texts' (McLaughlin, 2015, p. 560).

In the eighteenth century, the 'translational activity was not only limited to foreign news'; some periodicals 'also provided their readers with English versions of foreign fiction' (Valdeón, 2012, p. 854). The first English and Dutch daily newspapers also translated news originating from other European countries (Valdeón, 2015, p. 638), and in the nineteenth century in Latin America, press translations were a means of supporting either the colonial power or the movements of independence, depending on the authority behind a given media institution (Navarro, 2011, p. 87; Bastin, Navarro and Iturriza, 2012).

With the proliferation of the written press and the commodification of information, the first news agencies appeared in the mid-nineteenth century. It is telling that the Bureau Havas – the predecessor of AFP (Agence France-Presse, an international news agency with headquarters in Paris, France) – was created in 1832 as an agency 'which translated foreign newspapers for the French media' (Bielsa and Bassnett, 2009, p. 39). The press recruited many reporters and translators before the media companies began to employ foreign correspondents among others in the nineteenth century (Valdeón, 2012, p. 856; McLaughlin, 2015, p. 560) to cover conflicts (Bielsa and Bassnett, 2009, pp. 40–1). As the media outlets put more emphasis on journalistic experience than language knowledge, foreign correspondents had to rely on local translators and interpreters, as still happens today (Valdeón, 2012, p. 857).

Scholars investigating news translation from a historical point of view agree that although there was a considerable proportion of translations in the past (Bastin et al., 2012), it is 'difficult to trace ... the sources upon which these works were based in order to create comparable and parallel corpora' (Valdeón, 2015, p. 637), because the sources have disappeared or are difficult to access in libraries (Navarro, 2010, p. 40; McLaughlin, 2015). The majority of the press translations tackle political topics (Navarro, 2010, p. 40) and, as shown by several members of the HISTAL (History of Translation in Latin America) research group at the University of Montreal, journalists often used translations to comment on foreign news and support their ideological positions (Valdeón, 2015, p. 639). Navarro (2011, p. 97), who has examined translation strategies and techniques on the micro-textual level, has noted a clear preference for the strategy of appropriation, which is realized by techniques such as additions, deletions, comments and footnotes.

### 20.3.2  The Future of News Translation: Convergence

News translation may be as old as news itself, but it is unlikely to be outdated any time soon. The idea that English is replacing other vehicular languages on the Internet and in the media is misleading in this context (Nederveen Pieterse, 2015), as national and local news remains predominant, even in the American and British media, which are 'not "handicapped" by language barriers' (Quandt, 2008, p. 733). The media have taken a convergent turn since the beginning of the twenty-first century, and convergence – or multi-platform journalism – means that formerly distinct media are merging in the era of the Internet: print media have developed websites and social media accounts; radio stations have started to broadcast videos on their webpages; television channels also publish written stories on their websites.

Davier and Conway (2019) argue that journalistic translation scholars have not yet embraced this convergent turn and continue to structure their research around the distinctions formerly imposed by legacy media – such as newspapers, radio and television – although these distinctions are not very meaningful anymore. Their edited collection (Davier and Conway, 2019) is an attempt to fill this gap.

Convergence poses new research questions and new methodological challenges. First, the distinction between press translation and audiovisual translation no longer holds. Audiovisual material colonizes all media, which implies that translation scholars without previous training in video analysis need to update their methodological knowledge. Questions that were previously asked in connection with fictional works take on enhanced importance in news media (e.g., Does the voice-over match the image on the screen? Is the tone of the speaker adequately maintained in the subtitles?). Second, issues of live coverage in written form (Caimotto, 2019) radically change the conditions of translation and the means of collecting research data. Third, representations of the audiences have become considerably more realistic as journalists have acquired more efficient tools to measure the impact of a news story or receive feedback from their readers and listeners. Fourth, the presence of media on social networks multiplies the types of data available for researchers to examine.

In the case of social media, the fundamental change is similar: the aim of research is to understand how social networks help 'to reconfigure important aspects of the profession and the field' (Desjardins, 2017, p.5). Translation on media and social media can be conceptualized in the framework of non-professional translation (see Section 20.4.3).

In brief, the future of journalistic translation research is bright: translational phenomena still permeate the media. As Desjardins (2017, p. 123) puts it, translation has to be reframed 'in light of a hypervisual and multimodal era'.

## 20.4 Who Translates News?

### 20.4.1 Translators: In Rare Instances

Translators are thought to be the exception rather than the rule in newsrooms dealing with multilingual information. There is no quantitative information available to confirm this hypothesis, but it seems reasonable, given the scholarly knowledge collected in various cultural contexts (see Section 20.4.2). According to an informal survey by Lavault-Olléon and Sauron (2009, p. 5), in the French context, professional translators dedicate between zero and 5 per cent of their time to the translation of news items and while some specialized translators may translate up to 50 per cent of their time for technical magazines, such magazines are at the margin of journalism.

There is one exception to these observations: translators play an important role in news magazines that rely heavily on international translated news. These media outlets usually enjoy a strong scientific visibility. In Italy, for instance, *Internazionale* collaborated with freelance translators, who worked hand in hand with editors to produce target versions of news reports in foreign languages (Bani, 2006; Troqe and Fontanille, 2015; Manfredi, 2018). *Courrier international* followed the same working principle in France (Franjié, 2009), *Newsweek Hankuk Pan* in Korea (J.-H. Kang, 2007) and, to a lesser extent, *Spiegel International* in Germany (Schäffner, 2005).

A few news agencies, such as the IPS (Inter Press Service) that covers news from the Global South, hire translators directly (Bielsa and Bassnett, 2009, p. 82). In the Chinese context, several fieldwork studies have shown that *Cankao Xiaoxi*, the daily newspaper published by China's state newswire, relies on a team of translators (S.-j. Kang, 2011; Pan, 2014; Xia, 2016). Other studies show that other media outlets across the world need translators and interpreters, such as Formosa Television in Taiwan (Tsai, 2005) and the IRIB news agency in Iran (Hajmohammadi, 2005).

As argued in Section 20.2.2, press releases can also be the focus of studies of news translation. Press releases are pieces of institutional discourse that are distributed to the media and compete to attract journalists' attention (Jacobs, 1999, p. 2). According to Lavault-Olléon and Sauron (2009, p. 7), professional translators commonly translate press releases in the French and Swiss contexts, and press releases constitute a major source of information for media outlets (Jacobs, 1999), including news agencies (Davier, 2017). Tesseur (2012, p. 5) confirms that press releases are translated between '"major" languages such as German, Portuguese, Japanese and Russian' by professional translators at Amnesty International, whereas for 'smaller languages such as Dutch', translation 'is taken care of by local staff who were not trained in translation or by (mostly unprofessional) volunteers'.

Research still needs to establish what percentage of translators' activity is dedicated to press releases, which other stakeholders translate these texts, and how these translations are edited in an organization and, later, in a media outlet.

### 20.4.2 Journalists

The term 'news translation' can be slightly misleading to lay people, who would expect to find professional translators producing 'complete translation' of this type of text (Li, 2006). However, this interlingual practice is almost always undertaken by journalists, and these journalists refuse to be called 'translators', preferring terms such as 'international journalist' or 'bilingual journalist' (Schäffner, 2018, p. 332). Journalists may also use the verb 'to edit' instead of 'to translate' (Bielsa and Bassnett, 2009; Gambier, 2010), and interviews conducted by Davier (2014, p. 61) show how antipathetic agency journalists working in Switzerland are towards the word 'translation': translation is depicted in a negative light ninety-five times in approximately nineteen hours of transcribed recordings with twenty-seven journalists. The word 'translation' is rejected because translation is understood as a simple and complete transfer of information that does not involve adaptation to the target readership (Bielsa and Bassnett, 2009; Davier, 2014).

Even some international news magazines that visibly rely on translation (see Section 20.4.1) have favoured journalists for interlingual transfer. For example, in South Africa, van Rooyen (2018) writes that only multilingual journalists work in community radio stations. In Asia, the newsroom Buzzfeed Japan only has staff with an occupational background in journalism (Matsushita, 2019). In Europe, both *El País English Edition* (Valdeón, 2016) and *Spiegel International* (Schäffner, 2005, p. 158) have a small team of anglophone journalists who select and translate some stories, while they also report on other stories directly. In North America, Davier (2019b) observes that a daily newspaper operating in a bilingual area (*Le Droit*) does not employ translators, although it used to do so between the 1940s and the early 1960s (Tremblay, 1963, p. 205).

### 20.4.3 Non-professional Translation and Interpreting in the Media

Section 20.4.2 suggests that translation and interpreting in the media are non-professional activities. The vast majority of journalists are 'bilingual speakers' who have had 'no formal training in translation and who are often not remunerated for their work as an interpreter/translator' but are nonetheless performing 'linguistic and cultural mediation activities' (Antonini and Bucaria, 2016, p. 7).

However, Antonini and Bucaria (2016, pp. 9–10) warn against considering these players as wholly non-professional: 'non-professionals who interpret/translate in the media, in most cases, are unqualified having not received any training in this specific profession, however, this does not necessarily mean that they are incompetent as, over time, they can acquire expertise and competence in a specific area of interpreting/translation in the media'. In fact, Ghignoli and Torres Díaz (2016, p. 206) found that listeners preferred interpretations of a sports interview performed by journalism students to interpretations performed by interpreting students.

A growing number of scholars investigate the practices of journalists translating or interpreting as part of their job in the context of multilingual media (Davier, 2017; van Rooyen, 2018, 2019) or officially monolingual media (Gnach, 2013; Perrin, Ehrensberger-Dow and Zampa, 2017; Bouko, Standaert and Vandendaele, 2019; Davier, 2019b) or international news (Antonini, 2016; Caimotto, 2019; Matsushita, 2019).

This subfield of research is likely to develop further, notably with discussions around the issue of quality (are volunteers or professionals in other areas able to provide suitable translations, perhaps even to a higher standard than professional translators?). In the area of news, an exploratory study suggests that non-professional interpreting and translation may be more prominently discussed in the press than professional non-literary translation (Davier, 2019a).

## 20.5 Where Is News Translated?

### 20.5.1 In News Agencies

According to Bielsa and Bassnett (2009, p. 56), 'news agencies can be viewed as vast translation agencies, structurally designed to achieve fast and reliable translations of large amounts of information'.

Newswires are mainly B2B (business-to-business) media organizations (Lagneau, 2002, p. 59) with large networks of informants and offices scattered across the globe (or at least several regions) that deliver fast information to their clients, namely, other media that cannot keep (too many) correspondents. Nonetheless, communication scholars observe a growing trend to deliver news dispatches directly to the final customer, as Reuters does. There are global newswires (such as Reuters, AP (Associated Press) and AFP) and transnational newswires (such as the Spain-based EFE (the pronunciation of the letter F in Spanish; the import of the name is disputed)) or the German-based DPA (*Deutsche Presse-Agentur*); there are also national newswires such as the Swiss news agency ATS (*Agence télégraphique suisse*) or the Iranian state agency IRIB (Islamic Republic of Iran Broadcasting) (Boyd-Barrett and Rantanen, 1998).

Agency journalists mainly follow three guiding principles: accuracy of information is prioritized over faithfulness to a source text (García Suárez, 2005, pp. 175–6; Davier, 2012, p. 91); speed of production (Bielsa and Bassnett, 2009, p. 63; Davier, 2012, p. 92); and strong adaptation to the target readership (Bielsa and Bassnett, 2009, p. 101; Davier, 2012, p. 95). To maintain all these criteria at once, journalists strongly edit and transform the information they translate, which is why some authors use the term 'transediting' (see Section 20.6.2).

Most scholars who have investigated translation in news agencies have done so from an insider's perspective: Hursti worked as a journalist for Reuters in Finland and the Finnish news agency; García Suárez collaborated with the transnational Spanish EFE; and Hajmohammadi was a senior translator at IRIB. Other researchers have gained access to the hidden world of news agencies by means of fieldwork: Bielsa and Bassnett at AFP, Reuters and Inter Press Service (IPS); Davier at AFP and ATS; and McLaughlin at the Paris bureau of one of the three global news agencies. The study of translation in these contexts is key, as newswires are 'in many cases the first to approach and describe new realities' (Bielsa and Bassnett, 2009, p. 67) and disseminate their news dispatches to a great number of media organizations.

### 20.5.2   International News in Transnational and National Media

In the media landscape, transnational media are visible to translation studies researchers because they deliver their stories to the end customer directly, and openly display their multilingualism on their websites.

Although the phenomenon of convergence makes scholars question the distinctions among legacy media such as television, radio and newspapers (Davier and Conway, 2019), it is still useful to classify earlier examples from the literature.

For instance, authors have analysed the product or process of translation in the following television channels and networks: BBC (British Broadcasting Corporation) World (Valdeón, 2007; Cheesman and Nohl, 2010; Kadhim and Kader, 2010; Baumann, Gillespie and Sreberny, 2011); CNN (Cable News Network) and CNNenespañol (Cable News Network in Spanish) (Valdeón, 2005); Euronews (Valdeón, 2009); and France 24 (Falbo, 2017).

Others have examined news magazines or newspapers that target international readerships and make their texts available in several languages (Schäffner, 2018, p. 328), in studies such as the following: *Le Monde diplomatique* (Cortés Zaborras and Turci Domingo, 2005; Hernández Hernández, 2017); *El País English Edition* (Frías Arnés, 2005; Valdeón, 2016); *Newsweek's* Korean (J.-H. Kang, 2007), Arabic (Abdel-Hafiz, 2002) or Japanese editions (Barnard, 2000); *Spiegel International* (Schäffner, 2005); and *Cosmopolitan* (Chueasuai, 2013). Gambier (2010) and Schäffner (2018, p. 328) give further examples (*Times, Financial Times, National Geographic, American Science, Elle* and *People*) that have not yet been investigated under a translational lens.

There are also a few magazines targeting national audiences by publishing translations from foreign media, following the model of a press review. These media are popular among translation scholars because they usually provide a clear source of translated material, even if original texts may be cut. For instance, there are recent studies on the French *Courrier international* (Franjié, 2009), the Italian *Internazionale* (Bani, 2006; Troqe and Fontanille, 2015) and the Russian InoSMI (иноСМИ, derived from the Russian for 'foreign mass media') (Spiessens and Van Poucke, 2016).

Some national newspapers and magazines also 'include translations of texts which were initially published by newspapers in other countries' (Schäffner, 2018, p. 328), for instance the Spanish *El País* (Hernández Guerrero, 2012), the Italian *La Repubblica* (Caimotto, 2019) and the German *Spiegel* (Schäffner, 2008).

New media brands also exist in several language versions, such as Buzzfeed (Matsushita, 2019), HuffPost (Roumanos and Noblet, 2019) and Mediapart (Hernández Guerrero, 2017).

Two other cases are particularly prominent and visible in the circulation of international news (Bielsa, 2016): the work of foreign correspondents and the 'opinion pieces of distinguished commentators, most notably … public figures who have transcended both their original academic and disciplinary backgrounds as well as their national contexts' (Bielsa, 2016, p. 156). Bielsa (2016, p. 151) reminds us that 'it is our domestic journalists who are reporting on foreign news, so that we rarely get a foreign perspective on foreign news'. This situation poses a challenge to cultural translation 'by making the other falsely familiar' (Bielsa, 2016, p. 153).

### 20.5.3 National or Regional News in Multilingual Countries

The case of international news is perhaps the most obvious example of news translation, but media organizations operating in multilingual countries or regions also draw on information sources in several languages.

Bouko, Standaert and Vandendaele (2019) investigate the role of Dutch in the French-speaking Belgian public broadcaster RTBF (Radio-télévision belge francophone). Although they do not specifically focus on translation, they show that French-speaking journalists have to rely on sources in their second language, even if they do not consider themselves proficient in their second language. Jacobs and Tobback (2013) also investigate multilingual practices at RTBF and wonder whether 'the language that sources speak have an impact … on the way in which a news report is shaped by the journalist'.

Three studies illustrate the importance of translation in the Canadian public service broadcaster CBC (Canadian Broadcasting Corporation/Ici Radio-Canada) (Conway, 2011; Gendron, Conway and Davier, 2019), in daily newspapers of national importance (Gagnon, 2012) and in a regional daily newspaper based in the national capital region (Davier, 2019b).

In Finland, journalists who belong to the Swedish-speaking language minority regularly have to translate quotations or interviews conducted in their second language (Haapanen and Perrin, 2019).

Focusing on community radio stations, which play an important role in the dissemination of regional and local news in less wealthy areas of South Africa, van Rooyen (2018) shows that multilingualism permeates the practice of journalists based in the Free State province.

Gnach (2013) argues that multilingualism and translation form an integral part of the production of news in the French-speaking and the German-speaking service broadcasters in Switzerland, and, with a focus on the linguistics of news writing, Perrin (2013) describes situations where journalists have to translate news – or, more specifically, subtitle videos – for the same media outlets.

These case studies, conducted in different parts of the world, illustrate that news translation happens in a variety of contexts where reporters draw on sources in another language than their own, even for national or regional news. Although multilingual countries have been subject to most investigation because of their clearly stated language policies, journalism produced in migrant languages or minority languages that are not officially recognized merits further research.

## 20.6   How Is News Translated?

### 20.6.1   Gathering, Writing and Dissemination

News reports can be translated 'at various points in the overall process of news gathering and dissemination' (Palmer, 2011, p. 187). News gathering is the collection of information from a variety of journalistic sources, while news writing is the process by which the information is put into written or spoken shape (McKane, 2006). Information can then be disseminated – or circulated – in many different ways: directly to media consumers or indirectly to other media outlets (for news agencies); immediately on the outlet's webpage or social networks; or with a delay in a TV news bulletin and the print media.

Translation or interpreting can occur during the stage of news gathering. As research I conducted in 2016–17 in Canada shows, reporters may read information in their second language to gain an understanding of the background to an event; they may meet an informant – or a source – who speaks another language. Either they master the language of the documents and sources and accomplish this task without leaving recordable traces, as I witnessed in the Swiss (Davier, 2017) and Canadian (Davier, 2019b) contexts, or the reporters are 'unable to communicate directly with relevant sources of information', as is 'frequent in international reporting, where journalists employed by media from one nation work temporarily in another nation' (Palmer, 2011, p. 187). In these cases, journalists work with non-professional interpreters – also called 'fixers' (Castillo, 2015). Translation and interpreting occurring during news gathering tend to be invisible and are, therefore, understudied.

The most visible form of translation and interpreting happens at the stage of editing – or news writing (where 'writing' has to be understood in a broad multimodal sense). News stories usually combine information from a large number of sources. In an example drawn from my own research conducted at the Swiss national newswire (Davier, 2017), the editor attends a press conference in Germany and receives a press release in German; she has to translate elements from this material to put together a story in French. Reporters also routinely translate quotes obtained during an interview or a press conference or copied from an official report or a press release. Apart from situations in which the choice of a language is political (e.g., in federal politics in Canada (Gagnon, 2012)), translation usually goes unnoticed in written text (Davier, 2017, 2019a). In audiovisual material, however, translation takes the form of subtitles or voice-over and, thus, cannot be overlooked, which causes reporters to try to avoid it as far as possible, at least in the Canadian context (Davier, 2019b). According to my experience in the field, interpreting is confined to rare situations compared to other forms of translation. If practised, interpreting can be broadcast live, recorded or as podcast, whether in a studio, on location or in an editing room (Castillo, 2015).

Translation can also occur during the circulation or dissemination of information, as part of either the output or the reception of information. Media outlets do not regularly translate ready-made news before they circulate it, except for newswires in specific situations. For instance, several AFP reporters told me during in-depth interviews that the regional headquarters of the news agency may translate a story it considers newsworthy for another audience reading a transnational language, such as English or Spanish (Davier, 2017). Some media outlets have agreements with other institutions in other languages and buy stories and publish these in full or abridged form. However, these translations represent an exception in the daily production of news (see Section 20.4.2). In rare instances, news agencies receive dispatches that they choose to translate for their own clients. I observed that this happened in the international section of the Swiss national news agency, which received international stories in English that the reporters had to translate into German for their clients (Davier, 2017). Palmer (2011, p. 188) also names media-monitoring organizations, such as the BBC and the American OSC (Open Source Center), which need to translate news items before sending them to their clients.

Although translation and interpreting are most visible during the editing of a story, both activities can occur at all stages of journalism. Complete translations are the exception (Li, 2006), while it is very common that translational elements from several source texts are integrated into a story (Davier and van Doorslaer, 2018).

### 20.6.2  Localizing, Transediting or Translating the News

Until this point, the words 'translation' and 'interpreting' have not been problematized in this chapter. However, scholars have long argued whether 'news translation' can be seen as a form of 'translation'. Some researchers choose to use alternative terms such as localization, adaptation and transediting, while others argue that the translation concept is broad enough to encompass the various realities observed in the media.

Drawing on Pym (2004), Orengo (2005) suggests applying the term 'localization' – well known from the software, videogame and internet industry – to translation in the media landscape. He argues that global news is adapted or localized 'to come to terms with the national – and political – sensitivities of a people while meeting market requirements' (Orengo, 2005, p. 170) and to enhance their 'marketability' (2005, p. 175). Nevertheless, as argued by Orengo (2005, p. 184) himself, in the localization industry one single product is localized to a 'well[-]defined number of locales', whereas news spreads 'from often uncertain and not necessarily reliable sources to an indeterminate number of locales'. This is one reason why the concept of 'localization' does not seem to transfer well to the media context.

Some authors avoid theoretical discussions about the concepts they use; however, they opt for terms other than 'translation', probably as a way of implying that news translation goes beyond translation. For instance, Li (2006, p. 612) opposes 'complete translation' to 'selective trans-adaptation'; Frías Arnés (2005) uses the pair 'translation/adaptation' in Spanish to describe phenomena at play in *El País English Edition*.

Other scholars (e.g., Hursti, 2001; van Doorslaer, 2009; Chen, 2011; Caimotto, 2019) have adopted the term 'transediting', which was coined by Stetting (1989) and is meant to cover changes of all kinds made during translation. The use of this term is criticized by Bielsa and Bassnett (2009), Schäffner (2012) and Davier (2015). Bielsa and Bassnett (2009, p. 63) advise researchers against 'the somewhat artificial concept of transediting'. Schäffner (2012, p. 876) argues that changes made in the context of the media do not set news translation apart from other sub-genres of translation: 'as research in Translation Studies has shown, shifts at macro- and micro-level are an integral part of any translation process'. She believes that 'using "transnsediting" instead of "translation" would mean that "translation" continues to be understood in a narrower sense of a purely word-for-word transfer process' (Schäffner, 2012, p. 7881). For these reasons, I argue that broadening our understanding of translation is more fruitful than looking for alternative labels (Davier, 2015).

Toury's (1995) conception of translation as any activity labelled as translation does not help scholars, who witness interlingual practices that are not called translation in the field. However, a concept such as multilingualism (Grutman, 2009; Meylaerts, 2010) may be more suitable to give visibility to multilingual practices that are still understudied because they are deliberately not described as translation.

### 20.6.3 Translation Strategies

The debate concerning the labelling of news translation partly derives from considerations about the types of strategy or shift observable in the context of news translation: scholars often observe important changes between source text and target text (if source and target can be identified).

Three authors agree on the following general classification of shifts: reorganization, deletion, addition and substitution (Vuorinen, 1997; Hursti, 2001; Gambier, 2010). Subsequent categorizations propose only slight modifications. For example, Bani (2006) suggests cutting, explaining, generalizing and substituting; J.-H. Kang (2007) proposes omission, addition, generalization, particularization and re-perspectivization; Loupaki (2010) has literal translation, neutralization, omission, addition and explication. Based on earlier research, Schäffner (2018, p. 330) also adds the explicitation and specification of *realia*.

## 20.7 Conclusion

Answering the 5Ws gives a comprehensive overview of news translation, although this reality varies immensely from one cultural context to the other. It is not helpful to restrict journalistic translation research to a specific type of medium, a specific journalistic activity or a strict understanding of novelty. News translation remains open to different kinds of stakeholder, be they professional translators, journalists or amateurs. These professionals and non-professionals translate (even if they avoid the term 'translate' altogether) in international news but also less visibly in news agencies and in national and regional media outlets around the world. This translational practice can happen through various strategies at the stage of news writing (more obviously) but also during news gathering or even dissemination. Although one can say that news was almost born out of translation in the seventeenth century, news translation is more than alive in the era of globalization, convergence and social media. Some journalism handbooks argue that a sixth W – *Why?* – should be answered in a news report. This chapter has left the why questions open: Why is news translated? Because it is cheaper, faster and easier than producing news independently in another language? Because it forms an integral part of news reporting in a multilingual world? These are important questions that deserve detailed answers by way of individual case studies.

## References

Abdel-Hafiz, A.-S. (2002). Translating English journalistic texts into Arabic: Examples from the Arabic version of Newsweek. *International Journal of Translation*, **14**(1), 79–103.

Antonini, R. (2016). Non-professional media interpreting of radio interviews. In R. Antonini and C. Bucaria, eds., *Non-professional*

*Interpreting and Translation in the Media*. Frankfurt am Main: Peter Lang, pp. 149–71.

Antonini, R., and Bucaria, C. (2016). NPIT in the media: An overview of the field and main issues. In R. Antonini and C. Bucaria, eds., *Non-professional Interpreting and Translation in the Media*. Frankfurt am Main: Peter Lang, pp. 7–20.

Bani, S. (2006). An analysis of press translation process. In K. Conway and S. Bassnett, eds., *Translation in Global News: Proceedings of the Conference Held at the University of Warwick, 23 June 2006*. Coventry, UK: Centre for Translation and Comparative Cultural Studies, University of Warwick, pp. 35–46.

Barnard, C. (2000). The Tokaimura nuclear accident in Japanese *Newsweek*: Translation or censorship? *Japanese Studies*, **20**(3), 281–94. DOI https://doi.org/10.1080/713683786.

Barnhurst, K. G., and Nerone, J. (2009). Journalism history. In K. Wahl-Jorgensen and T. Hanitzsch, eds., *The Handbook of Journalism Studies*. New York: Routledge, pp. 17–23.

Bastin, G., Navarro, A., and Iturriza, M. G. (2012). La prensa independentista venezolana (1808–1822) desde la traducción. In G. Lillo and J. L. Urbina, eds., *De independencias y revoluciones*. Santiago de Chile: LOM Ediciones, pp. 193–213.

Bauman, R., and Briggs, C. L. (1990). Poetics and performance as critical perspectives on language and social life. *Annual Review of Anthropology*, **19**, 59–88.

Baumann, G., Gillespie, M., and Sreberny, A. (2011). Transcultural journalism and the politics of translation: Interrogating the BBC World Service. *Journalism*, **12**(2), 135–42. DOI https://doi.org/10.1177/1464884910388580.

Bielsa, E. (2016). *Cosmopolitanism and Translation: Investigations into the Experience of the Foreign*. London: Routledge.

Bielsa, E., and Bassnett, S. (2009). *Translation in Global News*. London: Routledge.

Bouko, C., Standaert, O., and Vandendaele, A. (2019). Being a journalist in a multilingual country: Representations of Dutch among Belgian French-speaking journalists. *Multilingua: Journal of Cross-Cultural and Interlanguage Communication*, **38**(3), 231–51. DOI https://doi.org/10.1515/multi-2018-0036.

Boyd-Barrett, O., and Rantanen, T. (1998). The globalization of news. In O. Boyd-Barrett and T. Rantanen, eds., *The Globalization of News*. London: Sage, pp. 1–18.

Caimotto, M. C. (2019). Transediting Trump: The inaugural speech reported in Italy. In L. Davier and K. Conway, eds., *Journalism and Translation in the Era of Convergence*. Amsterdam: John Benjamins, pp. 43–62.

Castillo, P. (2015). Interpreting for the mass media. In H. Mikkelson and R. Jourdenais, eds., *The Routledge Handbook of Interpreting*. London: Routledge, pp. 280–301.

Catenaccio, P., Cotter, C., De Smedt, M., Garzone, G., Jacobs, G., Macgilchrist, F., and Van Praet, E. (2011). Towards a linguistics of news production. *Journal of Pragmatics*, **43**, 1843–52. DOI https://doi.org/10.1016/j.pragma.2010.09.022.

Cheesman, T., and Nohl, A.-M. (2010). Many Voices, One BBC World Service? The 2008 US Elections, Gatekeeping and Trans-Editing. Working Paper Series, **20**, 1–18. Available at the Open University website www8.open.ac.uk/researchprojects/diasporas/files/diasporas/diasporas_working-paper-20.pdf.

Chen, Y.-M. (2011). The translator's subjectivity and its constraints in news transediting: A perspective of reception aesthetics. *Meta: Translators' Journal*, **56**(1), 119–44. DOI https://doi.org/10.7202/1003513ar.

Chueasuai, P. (2013). Translation shifts in multimodal texts: A case of the Thai version of *Cosmopolitan*. *Journal of Specialised Translation*, **20**, 107–21.

Conway, K. (2011). *Everyone Says No: Public Service Broadcasting and the Failure of Translation*. Montreal: McGill-Queen's University Press.

Cortés Zaborras, C., and Turci Domingo, I. (2005). La edición española de *Le Monde diplomatique*. In C. Cortés Zaborras and M. J. Hernández Guerrero, eds., *La traducción periodística*. Cuenca: Ediciones de la Universidad de Castilla-La Mancha, pp. 289–376.

Davier, L. (2012). Légitimité ou illégitimité de la traduction dans les agences de presse? *Forum: International Journal of Interpretation and Translation*, **10**(1), 79–114. DOI https://doi.org/10.1075/forum.10.1.05dav.

Davier, L. (2014). The paradoxical invisibility of translation in the highly multilingual context of news agencies. *Global Media and Communication*, **10**(1), 53–72. DOI https://doi.org/10.1177/1742766513513196.

Davier, L. (2015). 'Cultural translation' in news agencies? A plea to broaden the definition of translation. *Perspectives: Studies in Translation Theory and Practice*, **23**(4), 536–51. DOI https://doi.org/10.1080/0907676X.2015.1040036.

Davier, L. (2017). *Les enjeux de la traduction dans les agences de presse*, Lille: Presses Universitaires du Septentrion.

Davier, L. (2019a). Non-literary translation in Switzerland: Silence in print media. *Translation Spaces*, **8**(2), 257–79.

Davier, L. (2019b). Technological convergence threatening translation: The professional vision of francophone journalists in Canada. In L. Davier and K. Conway, eds., *Journalism and Translation in the Era of Convergence*. Amsterdam: John Benjamins, pp. 177–207.

Davier, L., and Conway, K. (2019). Introduction: Journalism and translation in the era of convergence. In L. Davier and K. Conway, eds., *Journalism and Translation in the Era of Convergence*. Amsterdam: John Benjamins, pp. 1–11.

Davier, L., and van Doorslaer, L. (2018). Translation without a source text: Methodological issues in news translation? *Across Languages and Cultures*, **19**(2), 241–58. DOI https://doi.org/10.1556/084.2018.19.2.6.

Desjardins, R. (2017). *Translation and Social Media: In Theory, in Training and in Professional Practice*. Basingstoke: Palgrave Macmillan.

Falbo, C. (2017). Les oraux des interprètes: un terrain particulier d'observation. *REPÈRES DORIF*, **12**. Available at www.dorif.it/ezine/ezine_printarti cle.php?id=338.

Franjié, L. (2009). Quand la traduction devient un moyen de communication orientée: le cas du *Courrier International* pendant la guerre du Liban de 2006. In M. Guidère, ed., *Traduction et communication orientée*. Paris: Le Manuscrit, pp. 61–86.

Frías Arnés, J. F. (2005). Traducción y periodismo: El País English Edition. *Puentes*, **5**, 39–46.

Gagnon, C. (2012). La visibilité de la traduction au Canada en journalisme politique: mythe ou réalité? *Meta: journal des traducteurs*, **57**(4), 943–59. DOI https://doi.org/10.7202/1021226ar.

Galtung, J., and Ruge, M. H. (1965). The structure of foreign news: The presentation of the Congo, Cuba and Cyprus crises in four Norwegian newspapers. *Journal of Peace Research*, **2**(1), 64–90. DOI https://doi.org/10 .1177/002234336500200104.

Gambier, Y. (2010). Media, information et traduction à l'ère de la mondialisation. In R. A. Valdéon, ed., *Translating Information*. Oviedo: Universidad de Oviedo, pp. 13–30.

Gambier, Y., and van Doorslaer, L., eds. (2018) *The Translation Studies Bibliography* (15th release). Amsterdam: John Benjamins. Available at www.benjamins.com/onlilne/tsb/.

García Suárez, P. (2005). Noticias de agencia: algunos problemas planteados en la traducción español-árabe. In C. Cortés Zaborras and M. J. Hernández Guerrero, eds., *La traducción periodística*. Cuenca: Ediciones de la Universidad de Castilla-La Mancha, pp. 175–97.

Gendron, P., Conway, K., and Davier, L. (2019). News translation on the Canadian Broadcasting Corporation's English and French websites. In L. Davier and K. Conway, eds. Amsterdam: John Benjamins, pp. 63–81.

Ghignoli, A., and Torres Díaz, M. G. (2016). Interpreting performed by professionals of other fields: The case of sports commentators. In R. Antonini and C. Bucaria, eds., *Non-professional Interpreting and Translation in the Media*. Frankfurt am Main: Peter Lang, pp. 193–208.

Gnach, A. (2013). *Produktion von Fernsehnachrichten: Unterschiede zwischen der deutsch- und französischsprachigen Schweiz*. Wiesbaden: Springer VS Verlag für Sozialwissenschaften.

Grutman, R. (2009). Multilingualism. In M. Baker and G. Saldanha, eds., *The Routledge Encyclopedia of Translation Studies*. Manchester: St Jerome, pp. 182–5.

Haapanen, L., and Perrin, D. (2019). Translingual quoting in journalism: Behind the scenes of Swiss television newsrooms. In L. Davier and K. Conway, eds., *Journalism and Translation in the Era of Convergence*. Amsterdam: John Benjamins, pp. 15–42.

Hajmohammadi, A. (2005). Translation evaluation in a news agency. *Perspectives: Studies in Translation Theory and Practice*, **13**(3), 215–24. DOI https://doi.org/10.1080/09076760508668993.

Harcup, T., and O'Neill, D. (2017). What is news? *Journalism Studies*, **18**(12), 1470–88. DOI https://doi.org/10.1080/1461670X.2016.1150193.

Hernández Guerrero, M. J. (2012). La traducción al servicio de una línea editorial: la primavera árabe en el diario El País. *Meta: Translators' Journal*, **57**(4), 960–76.

Hernández Guerrero, M. J. (2017). Translation in new independent online media: The case of Mediapart. *Perspectives: Studies in Translation Theory and Practice*, **25**(2), 294–307. DOI https://doi.org/10.1080/0907676X.2016.1213304.

Hernández Hernández, T. P. (2017). Translation, a hybrid form of capital: The translators of *Le Monde diplomatique* en español (1979–1988). *Perspectives: Studies in Translation Theory and Practice*, **25**(3), 509–20. DOI https://doi.org/10.1080/0907676X.2017.1285949.

Holland, R. (2013). News translation. In C. Millán and F. Bartrina, eds., *The Routledge Handbook of Translation Studies*. London: Routledge, pp. 332–46.

Hursti, K. (2001). An insider's view on transformation and transfer in international news communication: An English-Finnish perspective. *Electronic Journal of the Department of English at the University of Helsinki*, **1**, 1–11.

Jacobs, G. (1999). *Preformulating the News: An Analysis of the Metapragmatics of Press Releases*. Amsterdam: John Benjamins.

Jacobs, G., and Tobback, E. (2013). Is language a news value in Belgium? *Journalism Studies*, **14**(3), 407–22.

Kadhim, K. A., and Kader, M. (2010). Stylistic differences and message changes in the translation of English BBC political news into Arabic. *Jurnal [sic] Penterjemah*, **12**(1), 23–46.

Kang, J.-H. (2007). Recontextualization of news discourse: A case study of translation of news discourse on North Korea. *The Translator*, **13**(2), 219–42. DOI https://doi.org/10.1080/13556509.2007.10799239.

Kang, S.-j. (2011). Study on the edited translation of Korean news by Chinese news media. *Journal of Interpretation and Translation Research Institute*, **15**(1), 1–27.

Keeble, R. (2007 [1994]). *The Newspapers Handbook*. London: Routledge.

Lagneau, É. (2002). Le style agencier et ses déclinaisons thématiques: l'exemple des journalistes de l'Agence France-Presse. *Réseaux*, **111**, 58–100. DOI https://doi.org/10.3917/res.111.0058.

Lavault-Olléon, É., and Sauron, V. (2009). Journaliste et traducteur: deux métiers, deux réalités. *ILCEA*, **11**, 1–11.

Li, D. (2006). Translators as well as thinkers: Teaching of journalistic translation in Hong Kong. *Meta: Translators' Journal*, **51**(3), 611–19. DOI https://doi.org/10.7202/013566ar.

Loupaki, E. (2010). Investigating translators' strategies in rendering ideological conflict: The case of news translation. In C. Schäffner and

S. Bassnett, eds., *Political Discourse, Media and Translation*. Newcastle upon Tyne: Cambridge Scholars Publishing, pp. 55–75.

Manfredi, M. (2018). Investigating ideology in news features translated for two Italian media. *Across Languages and Cultures*, **19**(2), 185–203. DOI https://doi.org/10.1556/084.2018.19.2.3.

Matsushita, K. (2019). Globalization of the emerging media newsroom: Implications for translation and international news flow in the case of BuzzFeed Japan. In L. Davier and K. Conway, eds., *Journalism and Translation in the Era of Convergence*. Amsterdam: John Benjamins, pp. 135–53.

McKane, A. (2006). *News Writing*. London: Sage.

McLaughlin, M. (2015). News translation past and present: Silent witness and invisible intruder. *Perspectives: Studies in Translation Theory and Practice*, **23**(4), 552–69. DOI https://doi.org/10.1080/0907676X.2015.1015578.

Meylaerts, R. (2010). Multilingualism and translation. In Y. Gambier and L. van Doorslaer, eds., *Handbook of Translation Studies*. Amsterdam: John Benjamins, pp. 227–30.

Navarro, A. (2010). Las traducciones como fuentes para la prensa en el siglo XIX: el caso de la Gaceta de Caracas. *Íkala, revista de lenguaje y cultura*, **15**(24), 15–43.

Navarro, A. (2011). La *Gaceta de Caracas*, traduction et indépendance au XIX$^e$ siècle. *Meta: journal des traducteurs*, **56**(1), 81–100.

Nederveen Pieterse, J. (2015). *Globalization and Culture: Global Mélange*. 3rd ed. Lanham, MD: Rowman and Littlefield.

Orengo, A. (2005). Localising news: Translation and the 'global-national' dichotomy. *Language and Intercultural Communication*, **5**(2), 168–87. DOI https://doi.org/10.1080/1470847050866889.

Palmer, J. (2011). News gathering and dissemination. In M. Baker and G. Saldanha, eds., *The Routledge Encyclopedia of Translation Studies*. 2nd ed. London: Routledge, pp. 186–9.

Pan, L. (2014). Investigating institutional practice in news translation: An empirical study of a Chinese agency translating discourse on China. *Perspectives: Studies in Translation Theory and Practice*, **22**(4), 547–65. DOI https://doi.org/10.1080/0907676X.2014.948888.

Perrin, D. (2013). *The Linguistics of Newswriting*. Amsterdam: John Benjamins.

Perrin, D., Ehrensberger-Dow, M., and Zampa, M. (2017). Translation in the newsroom: Losing voices in multilingual newsflows. *Journal of Applied Journalism and Media Studies*, **6**(3), 463–83. DOI https://doi.org/10.1386/ajms.6.3.463_1.

Pym, A. (2004). *The Moving Text: Localization, Translation and Distribution*. Amsterdam: John Benjamins.

Quandt, T. (2008). (No) news on the world wide web? *Journalism Studies*, **9**(5), 717–38. DOI https://doi.org/10.1080/14616700802207664.

Roumanos, R., and Noblet, A. (2019). Framing terrorism in the U.S., French, and Arabic editions of HuffPost. In L. Davier and K. Conway, eds.,

*Journalism and Translation in the Era of Convergence*. Amsterdam: John Benjamins, pp. 107–32.

Schäffner, C. (2005). Bringing a German voice to English-speaking readers: *Spiegel International. Language and Intercultural Communication*, **5**(2), 154–67. DOI https://doi.org/10.1080/14708470508668891.

Schäffner, C. (2008). 'The Prime Minister said …': Voices in translated political texts. *Synaps: Fagspråk, Kommunikasjon, Kulturkunnskap*, **22**, 3–25.

Schäffner, C. (2012). Rethinking transediting. *Meta: Translators' Journal*, **54**(4), 866–83. DOI https://doi.org/10.7202/1021222ar.

Schäffner, C. (2018). Language, interpreting, and translation in news media. In K. Malmkjaer, ed., *The Routledge Handbook of Translation Studies and Linguistics*. London: Routledge, pp. 327–41.

Seibel, C., and Zambrana Kuhn, R. (2000). Los artículos de prensa en los ejercicios introductorios a la traducción económica. *Sendebar*, No. 10-11, 279–98.

Silverstein, M., and Urban, G. (1996). The natural history of discourse. In M. Silverstein and G. Urban, eds., *Natural Histories of Discourse*. Chicago: University of Chicago Press, pp. 1–17.

Spiessens, A., and Van Poucke, P. (2016). Translating news discourse on the Crimean crisis: Patterns of reframing on the Russian website InoSMI. *The Translator*, **22**(3), 319–39. DOI https://doi.org/10.1080/13556509.2016.1180570.

Stetting, K. (1989). Transediting: A new term for coping with the grey area between editing and translating. In G. E. A. Caie, ed., *Proceedings from the Fourth Nordic Conference for English Studies*. Copenhagen: University of Copenhagen, pp. 371–82.

Tesseur, W. (2012). Amnesty International's language strategy put into practice: A case study of the translation of press releases. In G. González Núñez, Y. Khaled and T. Voinova, eds., *Emerging Research in Translation Studies: Selected Papers of the CETRA Research Summer School 2012*, pp. 1–17.

Toury, G. (1995). *Descriptive Translation Studies and Beyond*. Amsterdam: John Benjamins.

Tremblay, L. (1963). *Entre deux livraisons*. Ottawa: Le Droit.

Troqe, R., and Fontanille, J. (2015). Who said it? Voices in news translation, from a semiotic perspective. *Semiotica*, **207**, 411–41. DOI https://doi.org/10.1515/sem-2015-0063.

Tsai, C. (2005). Inside the television newsroom: An insider's view of international news translation in Taiwan. *Language and Intercultural Communication*, **5**(2), 145–53. DOI https://doi.org/10.1080/14708470508668890.

Valdeón, R. A. (2005). The CNNenEspañol news. *Perspectives: Studies in Translation Theory and Practice*, **13**(4), 255–67. DOI https://doi.org/10.1080/09076760608668996.

Valdeón, R. A. (2007). Ideological independence or negative mediation: BBC Mundo and CNN en Español's (translated) reporting of Madrid's terrorist attacks. In M. Salama-Carr, ed., *Translating and Interpreting Conflict*. Amsterdam: Rodopi, pp. 99–118.

Valdeón, R. A. (2009). Euronews in translation: Constructing a European perspective for/of the world. *Forum: International Journal of Interpretation and Translation*, **7**(1), 123–53.

Valdeón, R. A. (2012). From the Dutch *corantos* to convergence journalism: The role of translation in news production. *Meta: Translators' Journal*, **57**(4), 850–65. DOI https://doi.org/10.7202/1021221ar.

Valdeón, R. A. (2015). Fifteen years of journalistic translation research and more. *Perspectives: Studies in Translation Theory and Practice*, **23**(4), 634–62. DOI https://doi.org/10.1080/0907676X.2015.1057187.

Valdeón, R. A. (2016). The construction of national images through news translation: Self-framing in *El País English Edition*. In L. van Doorslaer, P. Flynn and J. Leerssen, eds., *Interconnecting Translation Studies and Imagology*. Amsterdam: John Benjamins, pp. 219–37.

Van Doorslaer, L. (2009). How language and (non-)translation impact on media newsrooms: The case of newspapers in Belgium. *Perspectives: Studies in Translation Theory and Practice*, **17**(2), 83–92. DOI https://doi.org/10.1080/09076760903125051.

Van Doorslaer, L. (2010). Journalism and translation. In Y. Gambier and L. van Doorslaer, eds., *Handbook of Translation Studies*. Amsterdam: John Benjamins, pp. 180–4.

Van Rooyen, M. (2018). Investigating translation flows: Community radio news in South Africa. *Across Languages and Cultures*, **19**(2), 259–78. DOI https://doi.org/10.1556/084.2018.19.2.7

Van Rooyen, M. (2019). Tracing convergence in the translation of community radio news. In L. Davier and K. Conway, eds., *Journalism and Translation in the Era of Convergence*. Amsterdam: John Benjamins, pp. 155–76.

Vuorinen, E. (1997). News translation as gatekeeping. In M. Snell-Hornby, Z. Jettmarová and K. Kaindl, eds., *Translation as Intercultural Communication: Selected Papers from the EST Congress – Prague 1995*. Amsterdam: John Benjamins, pp. 161–71.

Xia, L. (2016). *News translation in Cankao Xiaoxi in China: Manipulation, institutionalisation, and power*. PhD thesis, University of Sydney. Available at http://hdl.handle.net/2123/15683.

# Part V

## Translation in Practice: Arts

# 21

# Translating for the Theatre

Geraldine Brodie

## 21.1 Introduction

Theatre translation is an applied form of translation that has connections with literary and poetry translation but is in fact hyperspecialized because, unlike the broader activity of drama translation, it is focused on a performed text and that text's users. The readers of translated theatrical texts encompass not only active consumers, such as theatre practitioners creatively engaged in the design and development phases of performance and actors who learn and reproduce the text either orally as dialogue or semiotically as movement, but also readers for reference purposes: audience members, theatre enthusiasts, academic researchers, teachers and students. Translated dramatic texts are increasingly frequently published and distributed via theatres and specialist publishing houses, but theatre translations may also be circulated only among the participants of a particular production and limited to a restricted readership while still being disseminated widely through performance. Translating for the theatre is therefore a specialist activity requiring linguistic and performance expertise and an understanding of the environment within which the eventual text will be performed. The specificities of this type of translation have had the effect of creating a subset of methodologies and terminologies recognizable from other branches of translation or text types but which in theatre have specialist applications. Furthermore, the nature of theatre practice and the progressive development of different forms of theatre-making influence the modes of creation of translated theatrical texts.

To demonstrate the specificity of translating for theatre, this chapter begins with an examination of the products of the theatre translation process, and their users. Detailing the physical forms of theatre translation provides background for a discussion of the variety of methods applied in translating for the theatre, contrasting, in particular, the direct translation of a source text to a target text by a specialist translator with the frequently found practice of commissioning an expert linguist to create a literal translation which is then used by a theatre practitioner to generate a text for performance. This leads to an examination of the theatrical terminologies relating to performed texts of plays initially composed in another language than that of the performers and prospective audience and the lack of consistency in equating such terms as translation, version, adaptation and other lexis with the processes actually taking place. The role of the translator in the theatrical environment is then considered, investigating the extent to which theatrical collaborative practices are reflected in theatre translation. The chapter ends with a discussion of the implications for theatre translation of relevant theories from the wider translation arena, focusing on retranslation and the application of adaptation theory and its extremes. I argue that although translating for the theatre is a specifically targeted practical activity, it nevertheless sheds light on broader issues around collaboration, performance and creativity in translation.

## 21.2  Translating for Target Users

When thinking about translating for the theatre, it is important to establish the specificities of this mode of practical translation, differentiating it from the more general conception of drama translation. Sirkku Aaltonen (2000, p. 33) recognizes that 'the double tie of dramatic texts to the literary and theatrical systems is present in the way "drama" is used to refer to both a written text and a theatrical performance'. Aaltonen's analysis identifies the overlaps but also the variations between literary and theatrical textual functions, where drama is the object of literary translation for readers whereas theatre translation is intended for performance. Given that this places focus on the targets for translated dramatic texts, it is helpful to consider practical illustrations of translated theatrical text users to understand the significance of translation for theatre before going on to consider the translation process in detail.

Janet Garton, herself both an academic and a translator (from Norwegian), discusses the guidelines she composed with her co-editors of a new series of English translations of the plays of Henrik Ibsen (1828–1906) for Penguin Books, which specifically addressed the 'conflict between … a reading and an acting edition'. Garton and her collaborators acknowledged that the translations they sought to commission for this series, intended primarily for students, academics and a more general readership, would 'pay closer attention to the original than do most modern acting editions. … Realistically considered, this will mean that this will not be a text which can without revision be performed on the contemporary stage.' A secondary aim for the series was that it could 'also function as the best "reference edition" for people from the theatre who are ... involved in producing one of the plays' (Garton, 2018, p. 292); this series is thus an example of the intersection of literary and theatrical systems discussed by Aaltonen. Significantly, the nature of the readership was systematically prioritized and the translators briefed accordingly.

In the event, the translators commissioned for the Penguin series were experienced in both drama and theatre translation; their curricula vitae display their ability to differentiate among literary systems and to target relevant audiences. Erik Skuggevik, for example, co-translator with Deborah Dawkin for Volumes 2 and 3, had previously translated Ibsen's *Ghosts* for production at the Octagon Theatre Bolton in 2009. His translation was reviewed by Andrew Liddle (2009) as 'sensitive, sinuous, ... the real star turn here', praising the 'impassioned and utterly realistic' dialogue. This assessment indicates Skuggevik's aptitude to create a script which supports the immediacy of performance. On the other hand, Garton's analysis of Dawkin and Skuggevik's annotation in explanatory notes of their translation decisions for *A Doll's House* in the Penguin series highlights the documentation of fine detail such as 'the breach of etiquette in using a familiar form of address' to inform a source-oriented readership (Garton, 2018, p. 301). These varying approaches reveal not only the differing translations required for theatre audiences and readers of drama but also the awareness and ability of translators of the necessity to tailor their product for its users. Another of the Penguin Ibsen translators, Anne-Marie Stanton-Ife, is acknowledged as the creator of the literal translation of *Hedda Gabler* used by the playwright Cordelia Lynn to write her modern adaptation, renamed *Hedda Tesman*. Lynn (2019, p. 7) notes the attention to Ibsen's 'structure, story, form, tone and symbolism' for which she would have drawn on Stanton-Ife's translation. In this case, Stanton-Ife addresses a third type of translation-user: the theatre practitioner creating a text for performance.

Such theatre practitioners, identifiable with Garton's 'people from the theatre' who might turn to the Penguin Ibsen for reference, are active users of specialist translations for theatre. In addition to playwrights such as Lynn who are writing new adaptations, a range of theatrical creative practitioners require translated theatre texts when commissioning and developing a production. Nicholas Hytner, the former artistic director of the Royal National Theatre (more usually referred to as the National Theatre) in London, describes the limitations of using extant translations as the basis of decision-making when commissioning plays from languages other than that of the target audience for production (and retranslation). Ibsen's *Kejser og Galilæer* (1873), first translated into English as *Emperor and Galilean* by William Archer (1856–1924), but never previously staged in English, was read through by a group of actors 'in turgid Victorian blank verse over a long day at the NT Studio' (Hytner, 2017, p. 195). The decision was made to commission a production in 2011 in the form of a new version by Ben Power based on a literal translation by Anne-Marie Stanton-Ife and Marie Wells, even though the read-through had prompted unintended laughter. Hytner's verdict on the resulting production was that it 'embraced the modernity of what Ibsen had to say about fundamentalism and totalitarianism, and at the same time gave its audience as lucid an account as possible of a play that it had never seen and would never see again' (Hytner, 2017, p. 195). This response indicates the difficulties of basing a commission on a translation intended for a different readership.

Theatre practitioners also use translations to make detailed production decisions. The director Katie Mitchell constructs her handbook for theatre directors around an extended case study of her production of *The Seagull* by Anton Chekhov (1860–1904) for the National Theatre in 2006. Although the final production was a performance of a new version by the playwright Martin Crimp based on a literal translation by Helen Rappaport, Mitchell uses an earlier 1986 translation by Michael Frayn to document her advance preparation for planning the production and directing rehearsals (Mitchell, 2009, p. 2). Frayn is a playwright but also a Russian-speaker, writing in a note to his published translations that his two principles are that 'each line should be what that particular character would have said at that particular moment if he had been a native English-speaker [and that] every line must be as immediately comprehensible as it was in the original' (Frayn, 1993, p. 357). However, Frayn provides detailed notes on the history and context of the plays, their literary allusions, how he solved specific translation and dramaturgical issues, and how to pronounce the Russian names. Mitchell's reference to Frayn's translation is an example of a practitioner using a published text for reference purposes. It is noteworthy that, although Frayn explicitly states that his translations 'are intended for production' (Frayn, 1993, p. 355), his text was used neither for the production nor as the source text for Crimp's new performance text. For a discussion of Martin Crimp's use of Helen Rappaport's translation, see Brodie (2018b). This is a further indication of the applied specificities of theatre translation and the targeted usage for translated dramatic texts.

Further, theatre practitioner users with specific requirements of translated texts are, of course, actors whose task is to learn and perform the lines in their scripts. A stage play, as the playwright David Edgar points out, is 'an art form squeezed into such narrow confines [of time and format that it] has built up a repertoire of conventions' (Edgar, 2009, p. xii). A theatre text must be capable of delivery by actors, but the construction of a play is the confluence of many elements (action, plot, structure, characterization, period and genre, for example) which underpin the spoken dialogue beyond the deliverability of the words. In theorizing translation for performance, the nature of this 'speakability' and – in relation to the text as a whole – the existence of a concept of 'performability' have been subjected to extended debate as to whether they are pre-inscribed in the source text and the extent to which it may be possible to reflect such qualities in a target translation. Silvia Bigliazzi, Peter Kofler and Paola Ambrosi rehearse this controversial debate, including Susan Bassnett's shifting position on the existence of a 'gestic text, or inner text that is read intuitively by actors' (Bassnett, 1998, p. 92), before reaching the conclusion that translation for performance 'means adjusting the language-body of the source text to the individual requirements of the target culture in a continuous encounter of actorial practices' (Bigliazzi, Kofler and Ambrosi, 2013, p. 9). The actor's embodiment thus 'exceed[s] the meaning of the verbal text at every single performance' (Bigliazzi et al., 2013, p. 9); nevertheless, writers and translators for theatre are generally acutely aware of actors as users of their texts.

The theatre practitioner and writer Lisa Goldman notes that 'actors do wonders to breathe life into dead drama' but emphasizes the need for playwrights to create living dialogue that is 'believable' in its artistic context (Goldman, 2012, p. 120). In constructing translated text to be spoken by an actor, theatre translators feel themselves to be under a similar obligation. May-Brit Akerholt records an example of translating for a specific performer renowned for an idiosyncratically emotional approach to his delivery: choosing 'a two- rather than a three-syllable word, or a "light" word instead of a "dark" one' in order to mitigate the already 'elaborate and intense' speeches of the source text (Akerholt, 2017, p. 26). This is the epitome of a targeted translation, where a particular actor's technique is reflected in the script, but Akerholt argues that the ensuing translated language 'becomes anchored in a specificity whose ultimate result is universality – perhaps because there is an authenticity which cannot otherwise be achieved?' (Akerholt, 2017, p. 25). Thus, writing performance into the translation by focusing on a specific user produces a text that more accurately represents the performance qualities of the original play. Kate Eaton demonstrates how this emphasis on actors as users of translation can be used to develop further elements of the text beyond the verbal through a collaborative rehearsal process in such a way that 'words may very well be adapted into movement, music, lighting, and sound' (Eaton, 2012, pp. 172–3). Eaton considers the rehearsal process a significant contributing feature for the outcome of the translation because it provides an opportunity to focus attention on the underlying nature of the source text while also finding a way to make the translation work for the actors who ultimately will be 'the ones exposed on stage' (Eaton, 2012, p. 181).

This vulnerability of the actors is a direct result of their appearance before a further body of translation users: the theatre audience. That audience is at the end of the user-chain and potentially the most populated user-group, arguably making it also the most significant. Certainly directors, actors, translators and other relevant theatre practitioners will take audience (and critical) reception into account when creating a translated production. Within the physical theatre, audiences experience a multi-sensory reception of a translated text. However, they may also become readers of a translated performance text, returning to the published text for subsequent review and possible comparative purposes. Certain English-speaking theatres now sell the text of a translated play alongside or in place of a theatre programme; the National and the Royal Court theatres in London even have their own bookshops within the theatre building. Specialists such as Nick Hern Books, theatre publishers and performing rights agents, or Oberon Books, independent performing arts publishers, prepare a newly translated text in advance for sale at the theatre from the opening night of the performance, usually including a note to the effect that the text went to press before the end of rehearsals and therefore may differ slightly from the performed play. The published text also records the date and place of the first production, lists the cast and creative artists and provides details of the copyright holder and the performing rights managers and agents (who may vary dependent on prospective amateur and professional performance and geographical region). This text therefore not only represents the performed translation but also creates a record of its physical production, demonstrating again the encompassing nature of theatre translation and the variety of potential users and readers of a translated theatre text.

## 21.3  Theatre Translation Methodology and Terminology

It is unsurprising, given the range of users, that there are also methodological variations in the practical translation of texts for theatre. Identifying the decision-makers and commissioners of theatre translations is instructive in establishing which approaches are taken to the practical translation of a dramatic text, as is an analysis of the training and occupational backgrounds of the translators themselves. The ensuing variations are reflected in the terminology used to describe the translation output, as I explain in this section.

The translation practices I describe are based on my research on the processes of translating theatrical texts into English for performance on stage in central London theatres (Brodie, 2018c). It is important to stress that the London context for theatre translation is not necessarily representative of translation practices in other languages and cultures. However, London is a global centre for theatre. In 2018, as an example, the box office report produced by the Society of London Theatre, representing some 50 theatres around central London, reported 18,708 performances of all genres of theatre (musicals, plays and other entertainment) with 15,548,154 attendances (Society of London Theatre, 2019). This volume and variety of productions in performance creates space for plays from a range of languages and cultures to be offered. Periodic snapshots I have captured of production listings in London indicate that there will regularly be around six to ten productions on stage based on plays originally composed in languages other than English. London theatre therefore provides a resource in which to examine different approaches to translating for the theatre.

The traditional concept of translation as an activity undertaken by an individual translator or team of specialist linguists tends not to apply in theatre. Section 21.2 demonstrated the significance of the performance element sought within translated theatre texts by theatre practitioners when creating a staged production. The translator is usually one member of a syndicate of users and developers who tease out that performance element; identifying the role of the translator in theatre therefore involves identifying the nature of the translator's engagement within the syndicate. I have co-opted the term 'syndicate' because I wish to convey a looser collection of participants than is suggested by the notion of 'team'. The theatre translator may work directly with other theatre practitioners – I examine collaborative translation further in Section 21.4 – but it is also possible that the translator of a theatre text will never come into contact with other theatre practitioners, or that the source language text created by the translator will not be the final text performed on stage. London theatre illustrates these, and more, variations.

Two basic distinctions can be made in theatre translation: a direct translation, where a translator who is familiar with the source language composes a text for performance, and an indirect translation, in which a theatre-maker who does not know or is not confident in the language of the original text writes a new performance script using a translation created by a language expert. If this latter text has been created expressly for such intermediate purposes, it is known in theatre circles as a 'literal translation' (see further Brodie, 2018a). This terminology should not, however, be associated with the more or less word-level translations, pejoratively named 'trots', 'cribs' or 'ponies', employed by 'target text authors' requiring a linguistic 'informant' (Washbourne, 2013, p. 613). Literal translations for theatrical use are specialist documents that provide their users with targeted information to assist in creating a performance text – and a performance. My analysis of Helen Rappaport's literal translation for Martin Crimp reveals her inclusion of contextual information, such as performance histories, translation publication history, the definitive source text, the playwright's dramatic and literary oeuvre, theatre conventions in the source culture, along with explanations of references to contemporary figures and literary allusions (Brodie, 2018b, pp. 214–15). Most significantly – and disruptively for the concept of literal translation as a simplistic activity and product – Rappaport documents the nuance of her translation decisions. One illustration is the line, 'I feel completely

shattered [broken to pieces]', in which she supports her choice of translation with a more literal transposition of the original Russian in square
brackets (Brodie, 2018b, p. 215). In my view, these theatrical literal translations could more accurately be named 'dramaturgical translations', recognizing their value, precision and significance within the theatre
translation process.

Acknowledging dramaturgy within translation activity also highlights the
role of the dramaturg more generally in theatrical artistic decisions.
According to Katalin Trencsényi, the work of dramaturgs is that of 'professionals engaged in a dynamic dialogue-relationship with a theatre-maker ...;
a collaborative, hermeneutical, facilitating role that is characterised by a high
level of communication' (Trencsényi, 2015, p. xxi). This activity can range
among archiving, critiquing, curating, drama developing, mentoring and
even actively translating. Cathy Turner and Synne Behrndt note that
a dramaturg allocated to a production can expect to be 'working with the
director in rehearsal, probably offering advice on textual changes, researching contextual information, offering comment on the evolving work' (Turner
and Behrndt, 2008, p. 7). This role may sometimes be filled by a freelance
professional dramaturg; some theatres outside the UK, such as Internationaal
Theater Amsterdam, include dramaturgs among their permanent staff, who
are also credited as translators in relevant productions. In larger UK theatres
these duties fall to theatre Literary Departments, but in a small theatre
company members of the creative team will combine dramaturgical research
with their directing and production tasks. Dramaturgical or literary input
relates not only to the development of a text for performance, however,
but also to the creation and selection of dramatic texts and performance.
The National Theatre's expansion of its Literary Department in 2015 to
become the New Work Department, leading all its artistic development
'including new play commissions, workshopping of devised projects, and
new treatments of classic texts' (National Theatre, 2019), signals the
important role of dramaturgy in programming and development of productions. With regard to translation, professional literary staff members
seek out, research and advise on potential plays to be translated (or
retranslated), translation methodology and the translator and writer to
be engaged. These overlapping activities demonstrate that translation
and dramaturgy are complementary functions that can on occasion be
accomplished by a single individual.

Ultimately, the decision as to how a translation should be approached
when staging a play from a language other than that of the actors and
audience falls to the artistic director of the producing theatre company.
The choice is likely to be influenced by both artistic and budgetary factors.
Most organizations, if they have the financial resources, wish to commission a bespoke translation, and this will clearly be necessary where the
play under consideration has not previously been translated into the
relevant language. Indeed, the question of how such a play emerges for

production is itself problematic, especially if it is written in a language lesser spoken among the receiving culture; in such circumstances, decision-makers have to rely on reports from contacts in the relevant source culture or find local speakers of the source language to review the text (see Aston and O'Thomas, 2015, pp. 39–41). The method of translation is therefore dependent to some extent on the availability of experts in the source language who have a reputation for composing performable text in the target language. Commissioners of translations for London theatre prioritize theatrical writing over linguistic ability; this is often the reason provided for opting for the indirect route through a literal translation, although the full decision-making process is more nuanced and depends on the identities and networks of the relevant theatre practitioners (see further Brodie, 2018c, ch. 4). Margherita Laera points to the 'lack of diversity in the British cultural system – from behind-the-scenes-workforce to artists, audiences, and reviewers' – that results in London theatre failing to represent the local range of languages and cultures on stage adequately (Laera, 2018, p. 384). Similarly, the variety of languages from which translations are regularly performed tends to be restricted to those of the dramatic canon (for example, French, German, Italian, Norwegian, Russian, Spanish and Swedish). The playwrights belonging to that canon are also disproportionately represented, as Gunilla Anderman notes in her description of Chekhov and Ibsen as 'honorary British dramatists' (Anderman, 2005, p. 8) (and as was evident from the examples I provided in my earlier discussion on the target users of translated texts). This focus on canonical texts in translation is not restricted to the British stage, however, as shown by recent studies of the 'wide panorama of Chekhovian inspirations' (Clayton and Meerzon, 2013, p. 2) and the global impact of performances of Ibsen's plays (Fischer-Lichte, Gronau and Weiler, 2011).

In London, the general pattern for translation methodology is that contemporary plays and those from less frequently represented languages are translated into English using the direct route, whereas new productions of older work by canonical dramatists are more likely to be written by English-speaking playwrights based on a literal translation. There are, however, abundant examples of deviation from this generalized rule. A connecting factor among all the individuals engaged in the translation process, however, is that they are specialist theatre practitioners. Playwrights who create performance texts based on literal translations are frequently seasoned adaptors of theatrical texts; this is true of the playwright Cordelia Lynn, mentioned already, whose *Hedda Tesman* ('after' Ibsen's *Hedda Gabler*) was produced at the Chichester Festival Theatre in 2019, and who also received a staging of her version of Chekhov's *Three Sisters* at the Almeida Theatre in London in the same year. Literal translators are frequently theatre specialists as well as linguists; Helen Rappaport, who has provided literal translations into

English for all of Chekhov's extant plays, is representative of other practitioners in this field who have additionally worked as actors. Direct translators combine their specialism in the source language with playwriting and adaptation. Christopher Hampton, for example, translates directly from French and German, and productions of his translations from both languages were represented on the London stage in 2019. These included the contemporary French playwright Florian Zeller's *The Son* first at the Kiln Theatre before moving to the Duke of York's, and his adaptation of the Austro-Hungarian playwright Ödön von Horváth's novel *Youth Without God* at the Coronet Theatre. Hampton is also a playwright and screenwriter. These illustrations give some indication of the circulation within the theatrical field of creative writing, translating and performing. They also demonstrate the blurring of the lines among these activities.

One effect of the hazy distinctions in translating for theatre is the lack of consistency in British theatrical terminologies relating to performed texts of plays initially composed in a language other than English. The playwright and adaptor Tanya Ronder rehearses some of the regularly used variants – 'translation, version, new version, free version, inspired by, taken from, after, adapted, co-adapted, loosely adapted' – before reaching the conclusion that 'the label is simply an agreement reached between writers, theatres, agents and estates ... it is a sliding scale of categories with no real absolutes' (Ronder, 2017, p. 203). In my view, this preponderance of terms demonstrates an effort on the part of the theatre industry to acknowledge the differing approaches to theatre translation and the range of practitioners and specialists participating in the production of a translated play. The all too frequent disappearance of the label 'translation', however, disguises the essential underpinning movement between languages. This has ethical consequences, as Margherita Laera underlines in her critique of translation in theatre: 'Only those translations that remark themselves *as translations* can do the work of uprooting and regrounding that is necessary to resist cultural narcissism' (Laera, 2019, p. 76, her emphasis). The strongly target-focused nature of translating for theatre, evident from commissioning to performance, runs the risk of reducing the source text and culture to symbolic representation (such as the ubiquity of the samovar in productions of period Russian plays). As I have suggested, theatre translation is a highly collective activity; the weighting of the contributions of the participants affects the balance between source and target in the performed translation. Investigating collaborative activity in theatre translation therefore sheds further light on the theatre translation process.

## 21.4   Collaborative Theatre and Translation

The explicitly collaborative nature of theatre and performance makes theatre translation distinctive among translation types and methodologies. The embodiment of text is an integral element of the performance process, which consequently feeds through to the translation process both during the preparation of the translation and then while rehearsing and modifying the translated text for performance. As I have suggested, a range of practitioners contribute to that embodiment. Many of these practitioners are also users of the text: directors, dramaturgs, design and production teams, actors. These practitioners may not contribute directly to the code-switching element of a translation, but they are potential co-producers to the extent that they influence the text selected. I gave examples earlier of translations that were written with specific actors in mind and of actors participating in the research and development of a translation. Moreover, directors and dramaturgs are party to these modifications inasmuch as they plan, direct and advise on the detailed trialling of text through rehearsal. Design and production teams may also request amendments to a performance text if needed to accommodate physical factors such as scene and lighting arrangements or moving actors on and off stage. Such alterations are more likely to involve cutting text or inserting stage directions, but they are still relevant to the performance element of the script.

Furthermore, theatre foregrounds an element of intersemiotic translation. Gay McAuley observes that '[a]ctors in rehearsal explore the text to find places where it is open to intervention, and the move, gesture, or action they choose then confers meaning upon the words in question' (McAuley, 1999, p. 225). Physical performance can thus be used to support the communication of a translated text, but it may also supplement or replace spoken text. McAuley asserts that 'in the theatre, speech becomes a spatial function: ... the meanings created by the words are shaped, even determined, by the spatial factors inherent in the performance reality' (McAuley, 1999, pp. 95–6). Theatre space and performance thus participate in the creation and communication of the performance text, which is itself only one element of the whole production: the *mise en scène*. The holistic nature of this crucial constituent of theatre, defined as the stage setting and 'all other related aspects of the spatial and temporal order of theatrical performance' (Postlewait, 2010, p. 396), indicates not only the extent of collaboration in creating performance but also the function of text as only one of a wider set of theatrical components. Theatre translation is shaped by these parameters. The translator is thus one of a number of theatre practitioners and theatrical roles contributing to the performed text.

However, the methods and timelines by which translators add their contribution to the collaborative activity around creating a performed translation vary considerably, as indeed do the contributions of other practitioners. One particularly co-operative theatrical form is devised theatre, which 'depends on the participation of all the producing group in all or most stages of the creative process' (Kershaw, 2010, p. 164). Such theatre practices seek to remove the hierarchies of theatre production, developing performance through rehearsal workshops in which actors and other creative practitioners (which might also include writers and translators) contribute to a performance formula that can be reproduced with regularity, although it may retain an element of improvisation and vary between performances. In such circumstances, the translator's input would include a higher level of immediacy than would usually be the case, although potentially less representation in the eventual performance, because the words spoken on stage may vary. In more traditional forms of production, where the script is prescribed, a translator is more likely to be active in the textual elements of a production rather than the action. Laera notes that '[a] large portion of makers in western theatre agree that it is best practice to produce a stage translation in a rehearsal context . . .. However, that is not always the case and many Europe-based companies rely on pre-existing translations' (Laera, 2019, p. 45–46). The extent of the translator's collaboration therefore depends to some extent on finances: whether a production's budget extends to commissioning a new translation and paying for the translator's time in rehearsal. In cases where there is an indirect translation, it is more likely to be the adapting playwright who attends rehearsal; the literal translator may well meet fellow performance artists only as a member of the audience on press night. Translation collaboration in such circumstances is a distant extension of the main collaborative activity for the production.

There is no doubt that the indirect translation route problematizes the concept of theatre translation as collaboration. Susanna Witt has concluded with regard to indirect translation practices unrelated to theatre that the notion of intermediate texts for translation is 'multifaceted and paradoxical. It . . . [relativizes] the very concept of translation, and, perhaps even more importantly, of the translator, continuously informing discourses of professionalization and status' (Witt, 2017, p. 178). In theatrical literal translation, translational input is sequential rather than concurrent and the balance of authority in the performed text shifts from the translating linguist to the adapting playwright, a shift that is perpetuated paratextually (in theatre publicity, programmes and published texts, for example) and often, by the granting of copyright to the adapting playwright, legally. Nevertheless, the key role of the literal translation in the transfer between languages points to the centrality of translation even in circumstances where the term 'translation' and the activity of the translator may be publicly overlooked. Examining the role of the translator within the wider scope of theatre translation activity prompts a reassessment of translation in relation to more extended forms of creative production.

## 21.5  Translation, Retranslation and Adaptation

A review of the vocabulary used to describe translated theatre texts provides a theoretical steer towards broader areas of translation theory, and suggests how theatre translation assists in an examination of the borders of translation. One of the most recurring terms attached to theatre texts that have been transferred from another language is 'adaptation', and, indeed, the connection between translation and adaptation in theatre is the subject of critical analysis and debate. Differing perceptions of adaptation and translation can mirror the 'belles infidèles' debate fundamental to translation studies since Gilles Ménage (1613–92) applied the term to the very free translations made of the classics by Nicolas Perrot d'Ablancourt (1606–64) (Giroud, 2010, p. 1216): is it possible to represent a translated text in a way that is both beautiful and faithful to its source? However, as Katja Krebs remarks in relation to the disciplines of translation studies and adaptation studies in the context of theatre and film, '[s]uch closely intertwined areas need to encounter each other's methodologies and perspectives .... Once it has become clear that we are dealing with converging agendas[,] ... the merging of ideas and the emergence of creative practices will challenge current assumptions and prejudices in terms of both adaptation and translation' (Krebs, 2015, p. 6). Theatre models of collaborative translation test the boundaries of adaptation and translation in their creative practices, although the weighting of the various roles within co-operative activity remains indistinct. Laurence Raw recognizes the problems in attempting to differentiate cognitively between the processes of adaptation and translation: 'If we view adaptation and translation as transformative acts involving individuals as well as the communities they inhabit ... it follows that any definition of either term would be perpetually subject to renegotiation' (Raw, 2017, p. 502). Even so, the theatre translation practices I describe are processes of negotiation and renegotiation; resolution is found in a visible act of communication: a performance.

In considering the relationship between translation and adaptation, it is pertinent to investigate whether there is a point at which extremities of adaptation become detached from translation. J. Douglas Clayton and Yana Meerzon argue that 'a dramatic adaptation rests somewhere between the actual translation of the play from one language into another ... and creating a new work inspired by the original', but conclude that 'no matter how close/far the target text deviates from its source, adaptation takes pleasure in masking and unmasking the presence of the original in the target text' (Clayton and Meerzon, 2013, pp. 7–8). This playfulness between the target and the source texts resonates particularly strongly in theatre and, in my view, creates a resilient link irrespective of the range of versions and extensions through which a translated play may traverse. Linda Hutcheon, in outlining a continuum model of adaptation travelling from literary translation at one end to 'expansions' such as sequels and prequels at the other, considers that this line has the 'advantage of offering a way to think about various responses to a prior story; it positions adaptations specifically as (re-)interpretations and (re-)creations' (Hutcheon, 2013, pp. 171–2). Thinking about the iterative quality of adaptation, and its consequence for translation, provides an opportunity to engage further with theoretical assessments of retranslation.

Theatre provides many illustrations of multiple translations of classic texts; ancient tragedy in English translation maintains 'a particularly strong presence in modern theatre' and the translation and adaptation of Greek and Latin plays is the subject of a distinct discipline: classical reception studies (see further Brodie and Cole, 2017, pp. 11–13). Translation studies' engagements with retranslation have tended to view translations in a linear relationship stemming from the original text with, on the one hand, Antoine Berman's (1990) hypothesis whereby each new translation moves closer to the source text and, on the other, Lawrence Venuti's (2004, pp. 32–3) concern that because retranslations 'call attention to their competing interpretation' with previous versions, they risk 'effacing the linguistic and cultural differences of the foreign text to serve a domestic cultural politics'. Françoise Massardier-Kenney, however, notes that 'a retranslation does not necessarily stem from a weakness, deficiency, inadequacy in previous translations or in the source text but from the often unacknowledged power of translation to constitute a text as literature and to make visible the process through which literature is constituted as such' (Massardier-Kenney, 2015, p. 73). In theatre, where retranslation is so frequent, and so varied in form and method, translation and retranslation are part of the creative exercise of theatre-making, with each new example offering a different perspective on the original play.

I would argue therefore that theatre employs translation as a tool to display the creative process of theatre-making. The problem is that this tool is itself an intricate mechanism comprising a range of components that should be more visibly named. The term 'adaptation' perhaps conveys the collective nature of the endeavour that is assembled in creating a piece of translated theatre, but it does not reflect the movement between languages that underpins the creative process. Laera (2019, p. 25) sees 'the difference between translation and adaptation as historically and socially determined, not as structural'. Greater advocacy for the term 'translation' among theatre-makers could deflect some of this predetermination. Jean Graham-Jones, herself a translator, scholar and theatre artist, considers that 'there always exists a spectrum of adaptation across which we translators and our collaborators range, and our approaches to translation vary as much as the works we translate' (Graham-Jones, 2017, p. 137). Graham-Jones therefore proposes the use of the adjective 'translational' to describe both artistic and scholarly theatrical work, not only as a way of acknowledging the always-present and always-fluid relationality in translation but also as a means of opening up the category of translation itself to consider not only the linguistic and cultural text – the playscript ... – but also other challenges faced in translating, translocating, and adapting a play to a different performance environment' (Graham-Jones, 2017, pp. 137–8).

Positioning translation more visibly in the theatre translation process remains a challenge, but a challenge that throws light on the role of translation and translators more widely, in theory and practice.

The close examination of translating for theatre reveals a complex system of activity with multiple participants, a range of resources and expertise and a variety of outputs and users. The constant factor within this structure is the element of performance, which is inscribed in the source text, the target text and the collaborative transformative process between the two. Participants in a theatre translation project have performance as their primary objective and, as I have discussed, even where a translated theatre text is published, it both echoes and records performance. The overlapping nature of the users and generators of a translated theatre text creates a network of agents contributing to the translation process, but it also blurs the lines among contributors and, consequently, among the component parts of the creation of a performed translation. The interlingual translator plays an essential part within the translation syndicate, but that role may be less visible and less synchronically collaborative than other practitioners'. This is most likely to be the case for literal translators even though, as I demonstrate, their contribution to the performance element takes both dramaturgical and translational forms. Theatre translation thus highlights the nature of translation within collaborative and intersemiotic contexts, and consequently the linkage of translation and adaptation. Detailed examination demonstrates that theatre translation is a creative activity pushing against boundaries of translation, retranslation and adaptation, but translation still needs to be foregrounded as a term, activity and concept within theatre and, accordingly, within communication more generally among genres, modes and cultures.

# References

Aaltonen, S. (2000). *Time-Sharing on Stage: Drama Translation in Theatre and Society*. Clevedon: Multilingual Matters.

Akerholt, M.-B. (2017). The Revolution of the Human Spirit, or 'There Must Be Trolls in What I Write'. In G. Brodie and E. Cole, eds., *Adapting Translation for the Stage*. Abingdon: Routledge, pp. 21–8.

Anderman, G. (2005). *Europe on Stage: Translation and Theatre*. London: Oberon.

Aston, E., and O'Thomas, M. (2015). *Royal Court: International*. Basingstoke: Palgrave Macmillan.

Bassnett, S. (1998). Still trapped in the labyrinth: Further reflections on translation and theatre. In S. Bassnett and A. Lefevere, eds., *Constructing Cultures*. Clevedon: Multilingual Matters, pp. 90–108.

Berman, A. (1990). La retraduction comme espace de la traduction. *Palimpsestes*, **4**, 1–8.

Bigliazzi, S., Kofler, P., and Ambrosi, P. (2013). Introduction. In S. Bigliazzi, P. Kofler and P. Ambrosi, eds., *Theatre Translation in Performance*. New York: Routledge, pp.1–26.

Brodie, G. (2018a). Indirect translation on the London stage: Terminology and (in)visibility. *Translation Studies*, **11**(3),333–48.

Brodie, G. (2018b). Performing the Literal: Translating Chekhov's *Seagull* for the stage. In J. Boase-Beier, L. Fisher and H. Furukawa, eds., *The Palgrave Handbook of Literary Translation*. Cham: Palgrave Macmillan, pp. 209–29.

Brodie, G. (2018c). *The Translator on Stage*. New York: Bloomsbury.

Brodie, G., and Cole, E. (2017). Introduction. In G. Brodie and E. Cole, eds., *Adapting Translation for the Stage*. Abingdon: Routledge, pp. 1–18.

Clayton, J. D., and Meerzon, Y. (2013). Introduction. The text and its mutations: On the objectives of the volume. In J. D. Clayton and Y. Meerzon, eds. *Adapting Chekhov: The Text and Its Mutations*. New York: Routledge, pp. 1–13.

Eaton, K. (2012). Turnips or sweet potatoes …? In L. Raw, ed., *Translation, Adaptation and Transformation*. London: Continuum, pp. 171–87.

Edgar, D. (2009). *How Plays Work*. London: Nick Hern.

Fischer-Lichte, E., Gronau, B., and Weiler, C., eds. (2011). *Global Ibsen: Performing Multiple Modernities*. New York: Routledge.

Frayn, M. (1993). A note on the translation. In *Anton Chekhov, Plays*. London: Bloomsbury Methuen Drama, pp. 355–78.

Garton, J. (2018). Ibsen for the twenty-first century. In J. Boase-Beier, L. Fisher and H. Furukawa, eds., *The Palgrave Handbook of Literary Translation*. Cham: Palgrave Macmillan, pp. 291–307.

Giroud, V. (2010). Translation. In M. F. Suarez and H. R. Woudhuysen, eds., *The Oxford Companion to the Book*, vol. 2. Oxford: Oxford University Press, pp. 1215–17.

Goldman, L. (2012). *The No Rules Handbook for Writers*. London: Oberon.

Graham-Jones, J. (2017). The critical and cultural fault lines of translation/adaptation in contemporary theatre. In G. Brodie and E. Cole, eds., *Adapting Translation for the Stage*. Abingdon: Routledge, pp. 137–43.

Hutcheon, L. (2013). *A Theory of Adaptation*. 2nd ed. Abingdon: Routledge.

Hytner, N. (2017). *Balancing Acts: Behind the Scenes at the National Theatre*. London: Vintage.

Kershaw, B. (2010). Devised theatre. In D. Kennedy, ed., *The Oxford Companion to Theatre and Performance*. Oxford: Oxford University Press, p. 164.

Krebs, K. (2015). Introduction. In K. Krebs, ed. *Translation and Adaptation in Theatre and Film*. New York: Routledge, pp. 1–10.

Laera, M. (2018). Performing heteroglossia: The Translating Theatre Project in London. *Modern Drama*, **61**(3), 380–410.

Laera, M. (2019). *Theatre and Translation*. London: Red Globe.

Liddle, A. (2009). Ghosts review at Octagon Bolton. *The Stage*, 2 November. www.thestage.co.uk/reviews/2009/ghosts-review-at-octagon-bolton/.

Lynn, C. (2019). *Hedda Tesman*, after Henrik Ibsen. London: Nick Hern.

Massardier-Kenney, F. (2015). Toward a rethinking of retranslation. *Translation Review*, **92**(1),73–85.

McAuley, G. (1999). *Space in Performance: Making Meaning in Theatre*. Ann Arbor: University of Michigan Press.

Mitchell, K. (2009). *The Director's Craft: A Handbook for the Theatre*. Abingdon: Routledge.

National Theatre. (2019). New Work Department. www.nationaltheatre .org.uk/about-the-national-theatre/new-work.

Postlewait, T. (2010). Mise-en-scène. In D. Kennedy, ed., *The Oxford Companion to Theatre and Performance*. Oxford: Oxford University Press, p. 396.

Raw, L. (2017), Aligning adaptation studies with translation studies. In T. Leitch, ed., *The Oxford Handbook of Adaptation Studies*. Oxford: Oxford University Press, pp. 494–508.

Ronder, T. (2017). The roaming art. In G. Brodie and E. Cole, eds., *Adapting Translation for the Stage*. Abingdon: Routledge, pp.203–5.

Society of London Theatre. (2019). 2018 Box Office figures released by Society of London Theatre and UK Theatre (1 March). https://solt.co.uk /about-london-theatre/press-office/2018-box-office-figures-released-by-society-of-london-theatre-and-uk-theatre/.

Trencsényi, K. (2015). *Dramaturgy in the Making*. London: Bloomsbury Methuen Drama.

Turner, C., and Behrndt, S. K. (2008). *Dramaturgy and Performance*. Basingstoke: Palgrave Macmillan.

Venuti, L. (2004). Retranslations: The creation of value. *Bucknell Review*, **47** (1), 25–38.

Washbourne, K. (2013). Nonlinear narratives: Paths of indirect and relay translation. *Meta*, **58**(3), 607–25.

Witt, S. (2017). Institutionalized intermediates: Conceptualizing Soviet practices of indirect literary translation. *Translation Studies*, **10**(2), 166–82.

# 22

# Audiovisual Translation

Serenella Zanotti

## 22.1 Audiovisual Translation

Audiovisual translation (AVT) has grown rapidly since the 2000s (Chaume, 2018a), a development that has gone hand in hand with a boom in audiovisual content production, enhanced by a proliferation of TV channels, online streaming platforms and social media. In an age dominated by technology and new forms of production and consumption, 'the notion of audiovisual translation needs to be wide enough to acknowledge and encompass the continuous changes that arise in the market, this way maintaining its validity as a theoretical concept', as suggested by Chaume (2019, p. 311).

The term *audiovisual* highlights the simultaneous presence of two channels of communication, the acoustic and the visual. In audiovisual texts, meaning is produced through the interaction of these channels and their different signifying codes (Chaume, 2004). In Chion's seminal definition, 'the reality of audiovisual combination' is 'that one perception influences the other and transforms it' (Chion, 1994, p. xxvi). As a consequence, despite the important role it plays in all audiovisual texts, the linguistic code is but one among many semiotic resources that are co-deployed (Chaume, 2004). Audiovisual texts are 'composite products' (Baldry and Thibault, 2006, p. 18) that are both multimodal and multimedial (Pérez-González, 2014a, p. 187). They are multimodal in that they deploy a variety of modes (sound, music, image and language) that are perceived and processed as a unified whole. They are multimedial in that they 'are made available via the synchronized use of multiple media' (Pérez-González, 2014a, p. 187), for example via a screen with multimedia technology.

Various terms have been used to denote this field of activity and study, reflecting changes in technology as well as evolving practices and conceptualizations of AVT. The terms *film dubbing* (Fodor, 1976) and *film translation* (Snell-Hornby, 1988) reflect an initial focus on the film medium, while *screen translation* (Mason, 1989), *multimedia translation* (Gambier and Gottlieb, 2001) and *multimodal translation* (Pérez-González, 2014b) were coined in connection with the rise of electronic and digital screen media. Other labels, such as *transadaptation* (Gambier, 2003), bring into focus the transformative nature of audiovisual translation, which has become 'the standard referent' (Díaz-Cintas and Remael, 2007, p. 15). This plethora of terms is indicative of the difficulty scholars have encountered 'in delineating the AVT domain' (Gambier, 2013, p. 46), owing to the changing nature of the media industry and the ensuing intrinsic dynamicity of the AVT sector. The term *constrained translation* was introduced by Titford (1982) and taken up by Mayoral, Kelly and Gallardo (1988) to account for the many restrictions imposed on the process of translation by the medium itself. It soon gained currency among AVT scholars (Zabalbeascoa, 1996; Chaume, 2019, p. 312) but also attracted criticism because of the negative connotations it carries (Díaz-Cintas and Remael, 2007, p. 11; Zabalbeascoa, 2008).

AVT encompasses the range of transfer methods used in dealing with both long-standing and emergent forms of multimodal and multimedia meaning-making practices. The linguistic and semiotic transfer that AVT involves can take the form of translation between languages (interlingual), as in the case of dubbing, interlingual subtitling and voice-over, or between modes within the same language (intralingual), as in subtitling for the deaf and hard of hearing and audio description for the blind (Gambier, 2013). Some scholars even regard film remakes as a form of translation falling within the realm of AVT (Evans, 2014).

Dubbing, interlingual subtitling and voice-over have traditionally been regarded as the dominant modalities (Gambier, 2003). More recently, other modalities have come to the forefront (Gambier, 2004), including subtitling for the deaf and hard of hearing (SDH), sign language interpreting, audio description, audio subtitling, live subtitling and surtitling for theatre and opera. Audio description, SDH and sign language interpreting facilitate 'media accessibility', a term traditionally employed to refer to AVT practices aiming to make media accessible to viewers with sensory impairment. Some scholars, however, advocate enlarging the concept of accessibility to include all forms of translation that facilitate access to audiovisual content, independently of whether the barrier is linguistic or sensory (Díaz-Cintas, 2005; Greco, 2019; Romero-Fresco, 2019). They argue for the more comprehensive term 'media accessibility'.

The importance of widening the notion of accessibility is a fundamental assumption of accessible filmmaking (Romero-Fresco, 2013, 2019). Accessible filmmaking promotes a holistic understanding of translation and accessibility, and seeks to integrate them into the film production process by establishing collaboration between the creative team and translators, whereas normally translation and accessibility are relegated to the distribution stage, generally outsourced and outside the control of the filmmaker. Notable exceptions are film directors such as Stanley Kubrick (Nornes, 2007; Zanotti, 2019).

This brings us to the question of 'the low status [that] audiovisual translation has had' within screen culture 'as a result [not only] of the "auteur" emphasis of film history' (O'Sullivan and Cornu, 2019a, p. 24) but also of 'the potent myth that film speaks a universal language that transcends linguistic and cultural difference' (Dwyer, 2017a, p. 3). As Gambier points out, AVT tends to be regarded as a 'problem' and is often conceptualized in terms of 'loss' 'rather than as a creative solution to the problems of international distribution' (Gambier, 2013, p. 45). This, at least, is the approach traditionally adopted by the film industry (Vasey, 1997). As Guillot points out, 'loss' has been 'a driving theme' (Guillot, 2019, p. 38) in AVT research – not surprisingly, perhaps, since looking at translation in terms of loss is a commonplace. This approach has been especially prominent in much academic work in the field of AVT, partly owing to the constrained nature of professional AVT practices and an over-emphasis on the shifts that occur in the transfer process. Contrary to this view, later research has stressed the capacity of translated audiovisual texts to generate meaning 'in their own terms' (Guillot, 2019, p. 39), thanks to the interaction of the linguistic component with the range of meaning-making resources that are woven into their semiotic fabric (Pérez-González, 2014a, p. 187), and lend themselves to manipulation during the translation process, yielding further layers of meaning by virtue of their semiotically complex composition (Ramière, 2010).

## 22.2  General AVT Modalities: Dubbing, Subtitling and Voice-Over

AVT modalities can be grouped into two large categories: captioning and revoicing (Chaume, 2019). Captioning involves the insertion of text onto the screen, in the form of either a translation into a target language or an intralingual adaptation of the dialogue and other verbal elements. Revoicing encapsulates a variety of oral translation methods, usually involving the addition of a voice track in a different language.

The three most common methods of translating the language of an audiovisual product, such as a film or television programme, are dubbing, subtitling and voice-over. The choice of mode is largely dependent on the target country and the medium used for distribution (cinema, television, DVD, streaming services, etc.). The film industry has traditionally divided world markets into dubbing, subtitling and voice-over territories, depending on a range of economic, social and historical factors. However, one of the effects of the digital revolution has been that the choice of modality is left in the hands of the viewer, particularly given the significant 'growth in globalized translation flows' (O'Sullivan, 2016, p. 265). The advent of streaming platforms has brought about significant changes in the AVT landscape, subtitling having gained ground in traditionally dubbing territories and dubbing being on the increase in exporting territories (i.e., Anglophone countries), where English-language dubbing is increasingly used as a strategy to broadcast non-English-language productions through video-on-demand platforms such as Netflix (Chaume, 2018b, p. 87; Ranzato and Zanotti, 2019).

Dubbing is a post-production process involving 'replacement of the original speech by a voice track which attempts to follow as closely as possible the timing, phrasing, and lip movement of the original dialogue' (Luyken et al., 1991, p. 311). It can be interlingual (between two languages) or intralingual (within the same language) – for example, from one variety of English to another (Dwyer, 2017b). It is the most expensive audiovisual transfer method and remains the preferred option in European countries with large linguistic communities (i.e., France, Italy, Germany and Spain). One of the main priorities of dubbing is compliance with synchronization norms, which prescribe that the translated text achieve some level of synchrony with the actors' mouth and body movements, and the duration of their utterances (Chaume, 2012, p. 15). However, as Chiaro (2009, p. 147) points out, 'dubbing is a language service that is consumed automatically and in a sense goes by unnoticed by audiences that are used to this modality', and reception studies have shown that audiences in dubbing countries exhibit viewing habits that allow for imperfect lip sync to pass unnoticed (Di Giovanni and Romero-Fresco, 2019). In fact, lip synchronization is considered essential only in connection with close-up shots (Herbst, 1994), and scholars emphasize the need to take into account other features of the filmic text such as those contributing to characterization or reflecting the director's artistic vision and style (Whitman-Linsen, 1992).

Dubbed language constitutes a major area of investigation within dubbing studies (Pavesi, 2005; Romero-Fresco, 2006). Much attention has been focused on 'dubbese' (Myers, 1973), a register specific to dubbed audiovisual products which distinguishes them from domestic productions. Among its defining features is a tendency to standardize linguistic variation and reduce interpersonal features, the presence of source-language interference and the 'repetitive use of formulae' (Pavesi, 2008, p. 81). The idiosyncratic conventions of dubbed language are subsumed under the label of 'prefabricated orality' (Baños-Piñero and Chaume, 2009). The language of dubbing aims at creating an 'illusion of authenticity' (Whitman-Linsen, 1992, p. 54) and naturalness (Romero-Fresco, 2006) obtained through a process of selection favouring a particular set of linguistic features that are systematically used as 'privileged carriers of orality' (Pavesi, 2008, p. 79). Recent studies have placed emphasis on the multimodal dimension of dubbing (Chaume, 2004; Pavesi, 2019b), particularly with reference to performance in terms of both voice (Bosseaux, 2015) and prosody (Sánchez Mompeán, 2019).

Voice-over, also called half-dubbing, involves superimposing a voice track in another language on an original voice track which remains fully audible at the beginning. The volume of the source dialogue is lowered and the translated voice track becomes acoustically prominent, with the original sound remaining audible in the background. Voice-over has been the standard method of screen translation in Russia, Poland and other former Soviet Union countries (Matamala, 2019). The translated text is narrated by one or more voices, which can be either male or female, depending on the country's tradition and on whether the genre is fictional or non-fictional (Szarkowska, 2009, p. 189). Voice-over is also employed in dubbing, subtitling and exporting territories for translating documentaries, interviews, reality shows and other types of audiovisual content which do not require lip synchronization (Franco, Matamala and Orero, 2010). According to Franco (2000, p. 236), voice-over 'provides a kind of "authenticity illusion" through the simultaneous presence of the original counterpart', and, compared to synchronized dubbing, voice-over is a cheaper and faster method. The process usually involves making a written translation which is delivered orally and recorded by one or more voice talents. Like dubbing, voice-over is subject to synchronization constraints. The original text often needs to be rephrased and condensed by reducing or omitting information in order for the translated text to fit into the time available. Rephrasing may be necessary to make it more comprehensible to the target audience through the deletion of dysfluencies, repetitions, false starts and the like, which characterize spontaneous spoken language (Matamala, 2019, p. 69). As shown by Darwish and Orero (2014), however, rephrasing may result in textual manipulation.

Other forms of revoicing include simultaneous interpreting at film festivals (Lecuona, 1994), narration and free-commentary. Narration is 'a kind of voice-over, where the translation has been summarized' (Chaume, 2012, p. 3), while free-commentary entails the manipulation of the translation for humoristic purposes, usually carried out by a comedian.

Subtitling is 'a translation practice that consists of presenting a written text, generally on the lower part of the screen', which aims to convey 'the original dialogue of the speakers, as well as the discursive elements that appear in the image (letters, inserts, graffiti, inscriptions, placards, and the like), and the information that is contained on the soundtrack (songs, voices off)' (Díaz-Cintas and Remael, 2007, p. 8). Subtitling is thus an additive form of translation as a written text is added to and interacts with the original multimodal text, generating effects of semiotic redundancy (Gottlieb, 2001). It is defined as 'diamesic translation' (Gottlieb, 2012, p. 23) in that it entails a shift from speech to writing, and as 'diagonal' translation (Gottlieb, 1994) in that it crosses over from the source-language spoken mode to the target-language written mode. As Kapsaskis (2019, p. 555) points out, subtitling 'is conceptualized as a mimetic process' that seeks to reproduce the dialogues and other verbal elements of the audiovisual text within the spatial and temporal constraints imposed by the medium, the reading speeds of viewers and the need to maintain synchronicity with the audio track and the film's editing (Ivarsson, 1992; de Linde and Kay, 1999). The outcome of this process is the creation of a new audiovisual text which differs from the source text in terms of both form and function (Kapsaskis, 2019, p. 555) but also in the way it communicates with its audience. As Messerli (2019, p. 546) argues, interlingual subtitles can be seen not just as a product of translation but also as 'textual agents' that 'structure and pre-process information, authorise and foreground meaning, and aestheticise and foreignise elements of the source text'. In other words, interlingual subtitles add to the multimodal meaning-making of the filmic text and achieve distinct communicative effects.

The languages of dubbing and subtitling have been described as 'idiosyncratic varieties' (Guillot, 2016). As Chaume (2019, p. 318) points out, however, very little research has been 'dedicated to the language of subtitling, that special register that, unlike dubbing, does not yet have a coined term, an equivalent expression to "dubbese"'. Linguistic approaches to subtitling have mainly focused on text reduction as a result of the strategies of condensation, reformulation and omission, and on the presentation and distribution of text on screen by means of segmentation and line breaks, as well as the related issues of legibility and readability (Gottlieb, 1992; Kovačič, 1996; Díaz-Cintas and Remael, 2007). A prominent theme in the literature is the impact that medial constraints have on the representation of the interpersonal dimension of film dialogue (Hatim and Mason, 1997; Pinto, 2010; McIntyre and Lugea, 2015). The process of linguistic condensation that is inherent to subtitling is seen as a major trigger of interlingual pragmatic shifts, which may affect characterization, film narrative and the representation of the foreign language and culture. However, as noted by Guillot (2012), the inevitable stylization of the subtitle text in comparison with the corresponding source text should be regarded as an asset rather than a deficit, for subtitles have the capacity 'to capitalise on their specificities to generate their own system of representation' thanks to 'the interdependence of linguistic choices and narrative/filmic structure' (Guillot, 2012, p. 485).

The fact that the target text is shown on screen in synchrony with the source-language multimodal complex creates opportunities for comparison on the part of viewers, which is why the notion of subtitling as 'vulnerable translation' (Díaz-Cintas, 2001) has been introduced. Moreover, viewers are made 'aware of the mediating role of subtitles, a fact which adds a level of self-reflectivity to the experience of viewing subtitled material' (Kapsaskis, 2019, p. 555), which in turn explains the emphasis on loss that characterizes both academic and non-academic discourse on subtitling (Guillot, 2012). On the other hand, in analysing subtitling as a form of cross-cultural mediation (Guillot, 2019), some scholars have emphasized 'the power of subtitling in the dissemination and entrenchment of certain concepts and realities in other cultural communities' (Díaz-Cintas, 2013, p. 278).

Since the silent film era, on-screen text has been an essential ingredient of cinema, whether in the form of intertitles (Dupré la Tour, 2005) or textual inserts such as letters, notes, cards, etc. Studies conducted on fan cultures and participatory practices have documented the emergence of alternative approaches which explore the semiotic potential of the written mode in ways that contrast with dominant subtitling conventions (Pérez-González, 2013). Formal experimentation with written titles is also prominent in commercial films and TV series, where the use of experimental and 'authorial titling' (Pérez-González, 2013, pp. 15–16) performs a number of dramatic functions. Professionally produced creative subtitles (McClarty, 2012), also called 'integrated titles' (Fox, 2016), experiment with font, size, colour, position, rhythm and other effects. They 'interact with the film's soundscape and *mise en scène*' (McClarty, 2012, p. 144) and are part of 'the typographic identity' of a film (Fox, 2016, p. 8). As Pérez-González (2020, p. 94) suggests, these developments point to 'changing subtitling aesthetics across media cultures'.

## 22.3  Media Accessibility

In the field of AVT, the term *media accessibility* is used to refer to a subdomain covering access to information and entertainment through audiovisual media. Originally, the concept of *accessibility* was mainly concerned with assistive forms of AVT such as SDH, sign language interpreting and audio description (Greco, 2019). With time, a broader conceptualization was proposed to expand the realm of media accessibility to both media and non-media content (Orero and Matamala, 2008), enlarging the concept to incorporate both sensory and linguistic barriers, with a radical shift in focus from disability to universal access (Greco, 2019).

SDH, also called 'closed captioning' in the United States and Canada, is primarily aimed at viewers with a hearing impairment or who are deaf, 'although it is equally useful for people with intellectual or learning difficulties or with a lesser command of the spoken language' (Neves, 2019, p. 83). The SDH user group is far from homogeneous, including people who are hard of hearing, people who are deaf but 'use an oral language as their mother tongue' and people who are deaf and use sign language as their first language (Neves, 2008, p. 129). This wide range of viewers have 'distinct profiles and needs' (Neves, 2008, p. 131) and may require different subtitling solutions in terms of reading speed, text reduction and encoding of acoustic information. According to Neves, the operations involved in SDH are best described in terms of 'transadaptation', which encapsulates 'the task of "translating" + "transferring" + "adapting" for the benefit of receivers with special needs' (Neves, 2008, p. 137).

Research on SDH has primarily focused on establishing standards (Romero-Fresco, 2015) and elaborating recommendations to improve subtitle quality (Neves, 2005). Much attention has been paid to enhancing readability and understanding (Bartoll and Martínez Tejerina, 2010), in an attempt to determine ideal reading speeds, text reduction strategies, visual presentation, and encoding of aural information (Neves, 2008). An enduring debate pervading research on SDH has focused on the choice between verbatim versus edited subtitles, that is, between subtitles that provide a complete transcription of speech and subtitles that offer a condensed version of on-screen dialogue to ensure greater readability (Neves, 2008). Eye-tracking research has shown the benefits of edited subtitles, but this seems to contrast with the preferences of deaf and hard-of-hearing viewers, who tend to favour verbatim captions (Szarkowska et al., 2011, p. 375). In fact, the findings of the European Commission's Digital Television for All (DTV4ALL) project show that hearing impaired audiences are alert to the loss of information that occurs in edited subtitles (Romero-Fresco, 2015, p. 348).

In the era of streaming platforms, the market for accessible audiovisual content around the globe is booming. AVT scholars pay increasing attention to interlingual SDH (Neves, 2009; Szarkowska, 2013; Bruti and Zanotti, 2018) and to the need to cater for different hearing-impaired audiences, including children (Zárate, 2010). One problem is that, while 'technology is contributing to the fragmentation of audiences and offering new opportunities for individual viewership and tailoring' (Neves, 2019, p. 88), most norms in use for SDH, such as the guidelines provided by regulatory bodies, service providers and broadcasters, are still those originally conceived for teletext on analogue television. In contrast, as Neves points out, technology has transformed the consumption of audiovisual content, allowing for a customized user experience that takes into account individual users' needs and preferences. In light of this, she advocates a terminological shift from SDH to 'enriched (responsive) subtitling' (Neves, 2019, p. 83), a non-discriminatory term denoting 'the incorporation of SDH standards as a subtitling variety to be made available to every viewer on demand' (Neves, 2019, p. 92).

Respeaking is the most common live subtitling method (Romero-Fresco, 2019). The subtitler/respeaker listens to the original soundtrack of a (live) programme or event and respeaks the audio input to a speech recognition software, which transforms it into subtitles that are broadcast in real time (Romero-Fresco, 2011, p. 1). Respeaking is usually intralingual and involves the inclusion of punctuation marks and specific features for the deaf and hard-of-hearing audience. Although respeakers are encouraged to produce verbatim subtitles that shadow the original soundtrack, the impact of high speech rates and various constraints imposes some degree of condensation leading to edited subtitles.

Surtitling and captioning for theatre and opera are used in live theatre or opera settings (Mateo, 2007; Secară, 2018, p. 130). Surtitles are 'a kind of caption displayed above the stage during a live performance, giving a written translation of the audible words' (Low, 2002, p. 97), while captions involve intralingual transfer providing information on the manner in which the lines are being delivered. Readability emerges as a central issue in both cases, as the limited time available to display the titles calls for textual presentation and translation that make the on-screen text easy to process (Orero and Matamala, 2008). Experimental and creative approaches to accessibility in the theatre have emerged, particularly in the UK, where 'pioneers in the field have been exploring the creative potential of these access elements in a way that enhances the work for all audience members, whilst making the show accessible to those with particular impairments' (Turnbull, 2019) in the context of the so-called 'aesthetics of access' or 'integrated access'.

Audio description (AD) provides access to films, TV shows, theatre performances, museums, art exhibitions and live events for people who are blind or partially sighted. In AD, visual information is rendered in the form of a verbal narration inserted when there is no dialogue or sound. AD can be pre-recorded and mixed with the soundtrack, as in cinemas, on TV and in audio guides; it is usually live in theatres, opera houses and museums. It is seen as a type of constrained translation because it must fit within the time constraints of the soundtrack and interact with the aural signifying codes of the source text (Fryer, 2019, p. 210).

Research in this area has primarily focused on AD guidelines in different cultural contexts, the nature of AD language, and audience reception. Several EU-funded projects have been devoted to investigating how cultural perspectives impact the perception of a film (Mazur and Kruger, 2012) and producing guidelines or recommendations through audience research (Remael, Reviers and Vercauteren, 2015). Given the limited time available for inserting descriptions between dialogues, audio describers need to select and verbalize visual elements that are narratively relevant. Eye tracking has been used to investigate the processing of audiovisual texts by sighted viewers (Kruger, 2012), while insights from narratology (Vercauteren, 2012) have proven relevant to studying how visual information is selected and which elements are to be prioritized in AD scripts. Methods and models originating in psycholinguistics have been used in research on audio description to explore cross-modal interaction, multisensory integration and visual perception (Fryer, 2019).

Other research has focused on specific aspects of the language of AD that set it apart from other registers (Taylor, 2015). According to Salway (2007, p. 154), AD scripts use 'a special language characterized by a preponderance of linguistic features that are idiosyncratic in comparison with everyday language'. Using a corpus-based approach to data collection, Salway's investigation of English AD language reveals a tendency to overuse concrete nouns and verbs that refer to material processes, including verbs that provide information about a character's current focus of attention or on interaction between characters (Salway, 2007, pp. 159–61). Corpus linguistic tools have been used to investigate the nature of audio described texts in different languages (Arma, 2011; Jiménez Hurtado and Soler Gallego, 2013; Reviers, Remael and Daelemans, 2015), showing how corpus analyses can contribute to our understanding of both idiosyncratic and universal features of AD language (Perego, 2019).

Another important research strand engages with identifying AD users' preferences, priorities and needs. Reception-centred research has been prominent in this field and has had considerable impact on the practice of AD (see Di Giovanni, 2018, for an overview). Besides investigating visually impaired people's perception of AD and providing empirical evidence for identifying best practices, reception research has also attempted to investigate the effects of AD on sighted viewers (Perego, 2019, p. 124).

## 22.4 Research Themes and Methods

Research models and methods informing scholarship in AVT studies range from micro-level textual analysis to macro-level contextual approaches and experimental and cognitive studies (see Pérez-González, 2014a; Chaume, 2018b; Di Giovanni and Gambier, 2018). Taking a broader perspective, Pérez-González (2014a, p. 141) distinguishes between *conceptual research*, 'i.e. studies that prioritize the exploration of ideas over the interrogation of data', and *empirical research*, which entails the use of corpus tools, archival approaches or experimental methods including gathering data through eye tracking, questionnaires, interviews, etc. While research on traditional AVT modes such as dubbing and subtitling has remained tied to equivalence-based notions of translation, with a strong focus on source text / target text shifts, 'an alternative understanding of translation as mediation' has been promoted in research on media accessibility (Pérez-González, 2014a, p. 141), which in turn has 'stimulated audience-based, empirical research even with reference to more traditional AV modalities' (Di Giovanni, 2018, p. 231).

The history of AVT remains a largely under-researched area (Chaume, 2019, p. 311), although it has spurred growing interest among AVT scholars since the 2000s (see, among others, Nornes, 2007; Mereu Keating, 2016; Cornu, 2014; O'Sullivan and Cornu, 2019a, 2019b). Little diachronic work exists on the norms of AVT in specific linguistic and geographical contexts (O'Sullivan and Cornu, 2019b), the viewing experiences of film audiences in the past or the implications of translation for the reception of films and television programmes through history (Zanotti, 2018). An extensive body of research directs attention to ideology, manipulation and censorship (see

Fawcett, 2003; Scandura, 2004; Chiaro, 2007; Díaz-Cintas, 2012; Wang and Zhang, 2016; Di Giovanni, 2017, among others) and to questions of gender in AVT (Baumgarten, 2005; Adamou and Knox, 2011; Feral, 2011; De Marco, 2012; Ranzato, 2012; von Flotow and Josephy-Hernández, 2019).

The representation of spoken discourse in translated audiovisual texts has been a productive field of investigation (Bruti, 2019). Corpus methods have been used to collect empirical data on translated film and television dialogue, with a view to observing regularities within and across languages (Salway, 2007; Valentini, 2008; Freddi and Pavesi, 2009; Baños, Bruti and Zanotti, 2013; Prieels et al., 2015; Pavesi, 2019a), while the possible applications of parallel subtitle corpora for machine translation are illustrated in Bywood et al. (2013). Looking at AVT from the perspective of cross-cultural pragmatics, linguistics-informed analyses have addressed the challenges posed by differences in communicative practices and preferences across languages and cultures (Bruti, 2009; Pinto, 2010; Desilla, 2014; Guillot, 2016; Guillot, Pavesi and Desilla, 2019). Multilingualism is one of the most intensely studied language-related topics and remains a major area of investigation (see O'Sullivan, 2011; De Higes-Andino, 2014; Şerban and Meylaerts, 2014; Chiaro, 2019, among others).

Experimental research has played a key role in our understanding of the cognitive processes involved in the processing of audiovisual content and in the development of approaches tailor-made to the preferences and needs of receivers (Di Giovanni and Gambier, 2018), and research on AVT increasingly draws on multimodality to investigate the meaning-making resources that are deployed in the polysemiotic fabric of audiovisual texts (Taylor, 2016; Pérez-González, 2020). Eye-tracking methods (Perego, 2012) are increasingly used in AVT studies, and scholars have begun to explore the impact of technological change on AVT, both diachronically and synchronically. The effects of the technologization of AVT in the digital era have gained a prominent place in research on AVT as awareness has grown of the challenges posed by on-demand services, cloud tools, machine translation and the centrality of the user experience (Georgakopoulou, 2019; Díaz-Cintas and Massidda, 2019), which is also a central concern for scholarship in the field of game localization (O'Hagan, 2019; Mangiron, 2018). Scholars working on co-creative, participatory practices such as fansubbing (Díaz-Cintas and Muñoz Sánchez, 2006; Pérez-González, 2013; Massidda, 2015; Orrego-Carmona, 2015; Jiménez-Crespo, 2017) and fandubbing (Baños, 2019) have shown the different instantiations and conceptualizations of fan AVT (Dwyer, 2019; Pérez-González, 2019b) – one of the most debated topics in AVT research (Pérez-González, 2014a) – in different cultural contexts, a phenomenon of great interest because of its ubiquity and 'in light of the demonstrated power of fans to redefine professional translation practices and audience expectations' (Pérez-González, 2019b, p. 176).

## 22.5  Conclusion

This chapter has provided an overview of AVT from more traditional transfer modes such as dubbing, subtitling and voice-over to translation modes that are used to enhance accessibility for people with sensory impairment. It has illustrated the medium-specific constraints, linguistic specificities and creative possibilities associated with each transfer mode, and research themes and methods informing scholarship in AVT studies have been outlined. By looking at AVT as a form of 'interlingual, inter-semiotic and intercultural mediation' (Pérez-González, 2019a, p. 3), this chapter has emphasized studies that, in promoting 'alternative modes of analysis' (Guillot, 2012), pose a challenge to discourses of loss, pointing to a change in perspective that turns towards what is gained in AVT.

## References

Adamou, C., and Knox, S. (2011). Transforming television drama through dubbing and subtitling: Sex and the cities. *Critical Studies in Television*, **6** (1), 1–21.

Arma, S. (2011). The language of filmic audio description: A corpus-based analysis of adjectives. Unpublished doctoral thesis, Università degli Studi di Napoli Federico II.

Baldry, A., and Thibault, P. J. (2006). *Multimodal Transcription and Text Analysis*. London: Equinox.

Baños, R. (2019). Fandubbing across time and space: From dubbing 'by fans for fans' to cyberdubbing. In I. Ranzato and S. Zanotti, eds., *Reassessing Dubbing: Historical Approaches and Current Trends*. Amsterdam/ Philadelphia: John Benjamins, pp. 146–67.

Baños, R., Bruti, S., and Zanotti, S. (2013). Corpus linguistics and audio-visual translation: In search of an integrated approach. *Perspectives: Studies in Translatology* **21**(4), 483–90.

Baños-Piñero, R., and Chaume, F. (2009). Prefabricated orality: A challenge in audiovisual translation. *InTRAlinea*. Special issue: *The Translation of Dialects in Multimedia*. www.intralinea.org/specials/article/PrefabricatedOrality.

Bartoll, E. and Martínez Tejerina, A. (2010). The positioning of subtitles for the deaf and hard of hearing. In A. Matamala and P. Orero, eds., *Listening to Subtitles: Subtitles for the Deaf and Hard of Hearing*. Bern: Peter Lang, pp. 69–86.

Baumgarten, N. (2005). On the women's service? Gender-conscious language in dubbed James Bond movies. In J. Santaemilia, ed., *Gender, Sex and Translation: The Manipulation of Identities*. Manchester: St Jerome, pp. 53–70.

Bosseaux, C. (2015). *Dubbing, Film and Performance: Uncanny Encounters*. Oxford: Peter Lang.

Bruti, S. (2009). The translation of compliments in subtitles. In J. Díaz Cintas, ed., *New Trends in Audiovisual Translation*, Clevedon, UK: Multilingual Matters, pp. 226–38.

Bruti, S. (2019). Spoken discourse and conversational interaction in audiovisual translation. In L. Pérez-González, ed., *The Routledge Handbook of Audiovisual Translation*. New York: Routledge, pp. 192–208.

Bruti, S., and Zanotti, S. (2018). Representations of stuttering in subtitling: A view from a corpus of English language films. In I. Ranzato and S. Zanotti, eds., *Linguistic and Cultural Representation in Audiovisual Translation*. New York/London: Routledge, pp. 228–62.

Bywood, L., Volk, M., Fishel, M., and Georgakopoulou, P. (2013). Parallel subtitle corpora and their applications in machine translation and translatology. In R. Baños Piñero, S. Bruti and S. Zanotti, eds., Corpus Linguistics and Audiovisual Translation: In Search of an Integrated Approach. Special issue of *Perspectives: Studies in Translatology*, **21**(4), 595–610.

Chaume, F. (2004). Film studies and translation studies: Two disciplines at stake in audiovisual translation. *Meta*, **49**(1), 12–24.

Chaume, F. (2012). *Audiovisual Translation: Dubbing*. Manchester: St Jerome.

Chaume, F. (2018a). Is audiovisual translation putting the concept of translation up against the ropes? *Journal of Specialised Translation*, **30** (September), 84–104.

Chaume, F. (2018b). An overview of audiovisual translation: Four methodological turns in a mature discipline. *Journal of Audiovisual Translation*, **1** (1), 40–63.

Chaume, F. (2019). Audiovisual translation. In R. Valdeón and Á. Vidal, eds., *The Routledge Handbook of Spanish Translation Studies*. London: Routledge, pp.311–50.

Chiaro, D. (2007). Not in front of the children? An analysis of sex on screen in Italy. *Linguistica Antverpiensa*, **6**. Available at https://lans.ua.ac.be/index.php/LANS-TTS/issue/view/10.

Chiaro, D. (2009). Issues in audiovisual translation. In J. Munday, ed., *The Routledge Companion to Translation Studies*. London: Routledge, pp. 141–65.

Chiaro, D. (2019). To Europe with love: Woody Allen's liquid society. In Irene Ranzato and Serenella Zanotti, eds., *Reassessing Dubbing: Historical Approaches and Current Trends*. Amsterdam/Philadelphia: John Benjamins, pp. 170–87.

Chion, M. (1994). *Audio-Vision: Sound on Screen*. New York: Columbia University Press.

Cornu, J.-F. (2014). *Le doublage et le sous-titrage. Histoire et esthétique*. Rennes: PUR.

Darwish, A., and Orero, P. (2014). Rhetorical dissonance of unsynchronized voices: Issues of voice-over in news broadcasts. *Babel*, **60**(2), 129–44.

De Higes-Andino, I. (2014). The translation of multilingual films: Modes, strategies, constraints and manipulation in the Spanish translations of *It's a free world . . ..* *Linguistica Antverpiensia, New Series. Themes in Translation Studies*, **13**, 211–31.

De Linde, Z., and Kay, N. (1999). *The Semiotics of Subtitling*. Manchester: St Jerome.

De Marco, M. (2012). *Audiovisual Translation Through a Gender Lens*. New York: Rodopi.

Desilla, L. (2014). Reading between the lines, seeing beyond the images: An empirical study on the comprehension of implicit film dialogue meaning across cultures. *The Translator*, **20**(2), 194–214.

Díaz-Cintas, J. (2001). *La traducción audiovisual: El subtitulado*. Salamanca: Almar.

Díaz-Cintas, J. (2005). Audiovisual translation today: A question of accessibility for all. *Translating Today*, **4** (July), 3–5.

Díaz-Cintas, J., ed. (2012). La manipulation de la traduction audiovisuelle [The manipulation of audiovisual translation]. *Meta*, **57**(2).

Díaz Cintas, J. (2013). Subtitling: Theory, practice and research. In C. Millán-Varela and F. Bartrina, eds., *The Routledge Handbook of Translation Studies*. London/New York: Routledge, pp. 285–99.

Díaz-Cintas, J., and Massidda, S. (2019). Technological advances in audiovisual translation. In M. O'Hagan, ed., *The Routledge Handbook of Translation and Technology*. London: Routledge, pp. 255–70.

Díaz-Cintas, J., and Muñoz Sánchez, P. (2006). Fansubs: Audiovisual translation in an amateur environment. *Journal of Specialised Translation*, **6**, 37–52.

Díaz-Cintas, J., and Remael, A. (2007). *Audiovisual Translation: Subtitling*. Manchester: St Jerome.

Di Giovanni, E. (2017). New imperialism in (re)translation: Disney in the Arab world. *Perspectives*, **25**(1), 4–17.

Di Giovanni, E. (2018). Audio description and reception-centred research. In E. Di Giovanni and Y. Gambier, eds., *Reception Studies and Audiovisual Translation*. Amsterdam/Philadelphia: John Benjamins, pp. 225–50.

Di Giovanni, E., and Gambier, Y., eds. (2018). *Reception Studies and Audiovisual Translation*. Amsterdam/Philadelphia: John Benjamins.

Di Giovanni, E., and Romero Fresco, P. (2019). Are we all together across languages? An eye tracking study of original and dubbed films. In I. Ranzato and S. Zanotti, eds., *Reassessing Dubbing: Historical Approaches and Current Trends*. Amsterdam: John Benjamins, pp. 127–44.

Dupré la Tour, C. (2005). Intertitles and titles. In R. Abel, ed., *Encyclopedia of Early Cinema*. New York: Routledge, pp. 326–31.

Dwyer, T. (2017a). *Speaking in Subtitles: Revaluing Screen Translation*. Edinburgh: Edinburgh University Press.

Dwyer, T. (2017b). Mad Max, accented English and same-language dubbing. In T. Whittaker and S. Wright, eds., *Locating the Voice in Film*. London: Oxford University Press, pp. 137–55.

Dwyer, T. (2019). Audiovisual translation and fandom. In L. Pérez-González, ed., *The Routledge Handbook of Audiovisual Translation*. New York: Routledge, pp. 436–52.

Evans, J. (2014). Film remakes, the black sheep of translation. *Translation Studies*, **7**(3), 300–14.

Fawcett, P. (2003). The manipulation of language and culture in film translation. In M. Calzada Pérez, ed., *Apropos of Ideology*. Manchester: St Jerome, pp. 145–63.

Feral, A.-L. (2011). Gender in audiovisual translation: Naturalizing feminine voices in the French Sex and the City. *European Journal of Women's Studies*, **18**(4), 391–407.

Fodor, I. (1976). *Film Dubbing: Phonetic, Semiotic, Esthetic and Psychological Aspects*. Hamburg: Helmut Buske.

Fox, W. (2016). Integrated titles – An improved viewing experience? A contrastive eye tracking study on traditional subtitles and integrated titles for Pablo Romero-Fresco's *Joining the Dots*. In S. Hansen-Schirra and S. Grucza, eds., *Eyetracking and Applied Linguistics*. Open Access Book Series Translation and Natural Language Processing, Berlin: Language Science Press, pp. 5–30.

Franco, E. (2000). Documentary film translation: A specific practice? In A. Chesterman, N. Gallardo and Y. Gambier, eds., *Translation in Context: Selected Contributions from the EST Congress*. Amsterdam: John Benjamins, pp. 233–42.

Franco, E., Matamala A., and Orero, P. (2010). *Voice-Over Translation: An Overview*. Bern: Peter Lang.

Freddi, M., and Pavesi, M., eds. (2009). *Analysing Audiovisual Dialogue: Linguistic and Translational Insights*. Bologna: Clueb.

Fryer, L. (2019). Psycholinguistics and perception in audiovisual translation. In L. Pérez-González, ed., *The Routledge Handbook of Audiovisual Translation Studies*. New York: Routledge, pp. 209–24.

Gambier, Y. (2003). Introduction. *The Translator*, **9**(2), 171–89.

Gambier, Y. (2004). Audiovisual translation: An evolving genre. *Meta*, **49**(1), 1–11.

Gambier, Y. (2013). The position of audiovisual translation studies. In C. Millán and F. Bartrina, eds., *The Routledge Handbook of Translation Studies*. London: Routledge, pp. 88–101.

Gambier, Y., and Gottlieb, H., eds. (2001). *(Multi)Media Translation: Concepts, Practices, and Research*. Amsterdam: John Benjamins.

Georgakopoulou, P. (2019). Technologization of audiovisual translation. In L. Pérez-González, ed., *The Routledge Handbook of Audiovisual Translation Studies*. New York: Routledge, pp. 516–39.

Gottlieb, H. (1992). Subtitling: A new university discipline. In C. Dollerup and A. Loddegaard, eds., *Teaching Translation and Interpreting 1: Training, Talent and Experience*. Amsterdam: John Benjamins, pp. 161–70.

Gottlieb, H. (1994). Subtitling: Diagonal translation. *Perspectives: Studies in Translatology*, **2**(1), 101–21.

Gottlieb, H. (2001). Texts, translation and subtitling – in theory, and in Denmark. In H. Holmboe and S. Isager, eds., *Translators and Translations: Greek–Danish*. Aarhus: University Press, pp. 149–87.

Gottlieb, H. (2012). Subtitles: Readable dialogue. In E. Perego, ed., *Eye-Tracking in Audiovisual Translation*. Rome: Aracne, pp. 37–81.

Greco, G. M. (2019). Accessibility studies: Abuses, misuses and the method of poetic design. In C. Stephanidis, ed., *HCII 2019*. Cham: Springer, pp. 15–27.

Guillot, M.-N. (2012). Stylization and representation in subtitles: Can less be more? *Perspectives: Studies in Translatology*, **20**(4), 479–94.

Guillot, M.-N. (2016). Cross-cultural pragmatics and audio-visual translation. *Target*, **28**(2), 288–301.

Guillot, M.-N. (2019). Subtitling on the cusp of its futures. In L. Pérez-González, ed., *The Routledge Handbook of Audiovisual Translation Studies*. New York/London: Routledge, pp. 31–46.

Guillot, M.-N., Pavesi, M., and Desilla, L. (2019). Audiovisual translation as cross-cultural mediation: What's the story? Special issue of *Multilingua*, **38**(5).

Hatim, B., and Mason, I. (1997). *The Translator as Communicator*. London: Routledge.

Herbst, T. (1994). *Linguistische Aspekte der Synchronisation von Fernsehserien: Phonetik, Textlinguistik, Übersetzungstheorie*. Tübingen: Niemeyer.

Ivarsson, J. (1992). *Subtitling for the Media: A Handbook of an Art*. Stockholm: Transedit.

Jiménez-Crespo, M. A. (2017). *Crowdsourcing and Online Collaborative Translations*. Amsterdam: John Benjamins.

Jiménez Hurtado, C., and Soler Gallego, S. (2013). Multimodality, translation and accessibility: A corpus-based study of audio description. In R. Baños Piñero, S. Bruti and S. Zanotti, eds., Corpus Linguistics and Audiovisual Translation: In Search of an Integrated Approach. Special Issue of *Perspectives: Studies in Translatology*, **21**(4), 577–94.

Kapsaskis, D. (2019). Subtitling, interlingual. In M. Baker and G. Saldanha, eds., *The Routledge Encyclopedia of Translation Studies*. London: Routledge, pp. 554–60.

Kovačič, I. (1996). Subtitling strategies: A flexible hierarchy of priorities. In C. Heiss and R. M. Bollettieri Bosinelli, eds., *Traduzione multimediale per il cinema, la televisione, la scena*. Bologna: Clueb, pp. 297–305.

Kruger, J. L. (2012). Making meaning in AVT: Eye tracking and viewer construction of narrative. *Perspectives*, **20**(1), 67–86.

Lecuona, L. (1994). Entre el doblaje y la subtitulación: la interpretación simultánea en el cine. In F. Eguíluz et al., eds., *Transvases culturales: literatura, cine, traducción*. Vitoria: Universidad del País Vasco, pp. 279–85.

Low, P. (2002). Surtitles for opera: A specialised translating task. *Babel*, **48** (2), 97–110.

Luyken, G.-M., Herbst, T., Langham-Brown, J., Reid, H., and Spinhof, H. (1991). *Overcoming Language Barriers in Television: Dubbing and Subtitling for the European Audience*. Manchester: European Institute for the Media.

Mangiron, C. (2018). Reception studies in game localisation: Taking stock. In E. Di Giovanni and Y. Gambier, eds., *Reception Studies and Audiovisual Translation*. Amsterdam:John Benjamins, pp. 277–96.

Massidda, S. (2015). *Audiovisual Translation in the Digital Age: The Italian Fansubbing Phenomenon*. London: Palgrave Macmillan.

Mason, I. (1989). Speaker meaning and reader meaning: Preserving coherence in screen translation. In R. Kölmel and J. Payne, eds., *Babel: The Cultural and Linguistic Barriers between Nations*. Aberdeen: Aberdeen University Press, pp. 13–24.

Matamala, A. (2019). Voice-over: Practice, research and future prospects. In L. Pérez-González, ed., *The Routledge Handbook of Audiovisual Translation Studies*. New York: Routledge, pp. 64–81.

Mateo, M. (2007). Surtitling nowadays: New uses, attitudes and developments. *Linguistica Antverpiensia*, **6**, 135–54.

Mayoral, R., Kelly, D., and Gallardo, N. (1988). Concept of constrained translation: Non-linguistic perspectives of translation. *Meta*, **33**(3), 356–67.

Mazur, I., and Kruger, J.-L., eds. (2012). *Pear Stories Description: Language Perception and Cognition across Cultures*. Special issue of *Perspectives: Studies in Translatology*, **20**(1).

McClarty, R. (2012). Towards a multidisciplinary approach in creative subtitling. In R. Agost, P. Orero and E. di Giovanni, eds., *Monographs in Translating and Interpreting (MonTI)*, **4**, 133–55.

McIntyre, D., and Lugea, J. (2015). The effects of deaf and hard-of-hearing subtitles on the characterisation process: A cognitive stylistic study of The Wire. *Perspectives: Studies in Translatology*, **23**(1), 62–88.

Mereu Keating, C. (2016). *The Politics of Dubbing: Film Censorship and State Intervention in the Translation of Foreign Cinema in Fascist Italy*. Oxford: Peter Lang.

Messerli, T. (2019). Subtitles and cinematic meaning-making: Interlingual subtitles as textual agents. *Multilingua*, **38**(5), 529–46.

Myers, L. (1973). The art of dubbing. *Filmmakers Newsletter*, **6**(6), 56–8.

Neves, J. (2005). *Audiovisual Translation: Subtitling for the Deaf and Hard-of-Hearing*. PhD Thesis, Roehampton University.

Neves, J. (2008). Ten fallacies about subtitling for the d/Deaf and the hard of hearing. *Journal of Specialised Translation*, **10**, 128–43.

Neves, J. (2009). Interlingual subtitling for the deaf and hard-of-hearing. In J. Díaz Cintas and G. Anderman, eds., *Audiovisual Translation: Language Transfer on Screen*. Basingstoke: Palgrave Macmillan, pp. 151–69.

Neves, J. (2019). Subtitling for deaf and hard of hearing audiences: Moving forward. In L. Pérez-González, ed., *The Routledge Handbook of Audiovisual Translation Studies*. New York: Routledge, pp. 82–95.

Nornes, A. M. (2007). *Cinema Babel: Translating Global Cinema*. Minneapolis: University of Minnesota Press.

O'Hagan, M. (2019). Game localization: A critical overview and implications for audiovisual translation. In L. Pérez-González, ed., *The Routledge Handbook of Audiovisual Translation Studies*. New York: Routledge, pp. 145–59.

Orero, P., and Matamala, A. (2008). Accessible opera: Overcoming linguistic and sensorial barriers. *Perspectives: Studies in Translatology*, **15**(4), 262–77.

Orrego-Carmona, D. (2015). The reception of (non)professional subtitling. Unpublished doctoral thesis. Tarragona: Universitat Rovira I Virgili.

O'Sullivan, C. (2011). *Translating Popular Film*. Basingstoke: Palgrave Macmillan.

O'Sullivan, C. (2016). Imagined spectators: The importance of policy for audiovisual translation research. *Target*, **28**(2), 261–75.

O'Sullivan, C., and Cornu, J.-F. (2019a). History of audiovisual translation. In L. Pérez-González, ed., *The Routledge Handbook of Audiovisual Translation Studies*. New York: Routledge, pp. 15–30.

O'Sullivan, C., and Cornu, J.-F., eds. (2019b). *The Translation of Films 1900–1950*. Oxford: Oxford University Press, pp. 1–23.

Pavesi, M. (2005). *La traduzione filmica. Tratti del parlato doppiato dall'inglese all'italiano*. Roma: Carocci.

Pavesi, M. (2008). Spoken language in film dubbing: Target language norms, interference and translational routines. In D. Chiaro, C. Heiss and C. Bucaria, eds., *Between Text and Image: Updating Research in Screen Translation*. Amsterdam: Benjamins, pp. 79–99.

Pavesi, M. (2019a). Corpus-based audiovisual translation studies: Ample room for development. In L. Pérez-González, ed., *The Routledge Handbook of Audiovisual Translation Studies*. New York: Routledge, pp. 315–33.

Pavesi, M. (2019b). Dubbing. In M. Baker and G. Saldanha, eds., *Routledge Encyclopedia of Translation Studies*. London: Routledge, pp. 156–61.

Perego, E., ed. (2012). *Eye Tracking in Audiovisual Translation*. Rome: Aracne.

Perego, E. (2019). Audio description: Evolving recommendations for usable, effective and enjoyable practices. In L. Pérez-González, ed., *The Routledge Handbook of Audiovisual Translation*. New York: Routledge, pp. 114–29.

Pérez-González, L. (2013). Co-creational subtitling in the digital media: Transformative and authorial practices. *International Journal of Cultural Studies*, **16**(1), 3–21.

Pérez-González, L. (2014a). *Audiovisual Translation: Theories, Methods and Issues*. New York: Routledge.

Pérez-Gonzélez, L. (2014b). Multimodality in translation and interpreting studies: Theoretical and methodological perspectives. In S. Bermann and

C. Porter, eds., *A Companion to Translation Studies*. Chichester, UK: Wiley-Blackwell, pp. 119–31.

Pérez-González, L. (2019a). Rewiring the circuitry of audiovisual translation: Introduction. In L. Pérez-González, ed., *The Routledge Handbook of Audiovisual Translation*. New York: Routledge, pp. 1–12.

Pérez-González, L. (2019b). Fan audiovisual translation. In M. Baker and G. Saldanha, eds., *The Routledge Encyclopedia of Translation Studies*. London: Routledge, pp. 172–7.

Pérez-González, L. (2020). From the 'cinema of attractions' to danmu: A multimodal-theory analysis of changing subtitling aesthetics across media cultures. In M. Boria, Á. Carreres, M. Noriega-Sánchez and M. Tomalin, eds., *Translation and Multimodality: Beyond Words*. London: Routledge, pp. 94–116.

Pinto, D. (2010). Lost in subtitle translations: The case of advice in the English subtitles of Spanish films. *Intercultural Pragmatics*, 7(2), 257–77.

Prieels, L., Delaere, I., Plevoets, K., and De Sutter, G. (2015). A corpus-based multivariate analysis of linguistic norm-adherence in audiovisual and written translation. *Across Languages and Cultures*, **16**(2), 209–31.

Ramière, N. (2010). Are you 'lost in translation' (when watching a foreign film)? Towards an alternative approach to judging audiovisual translation. *Australian Journal of French Studies*, **47**(1), 100–15.

Ranzato, I. (2012). Gayspeak and gay subjects in AVT. *Meta*, **57**(2), 369–84.

Ranzato, I., and Zanotti, S. (2019). The dubbing revolution. In I. Ranzato and S. Zanotti, eds., *Reassessing Dubbing: Historical Approaches and Current Trends*. Amsterdam/Philadelphia: John Benjamins, pp. 1–14.

Remael, A., Reviers, N., and Vercauteren, G. (2015). *Pictures Painted in Words: ADLAB Audio Description Guidelines*. Trieste: EUT.

Reviers, N., Remael, A., and Daelemans, W. (2015). The language of audio description in Dutch: Results of a corpus study. In A. Jankowska and A. Szarkowska, eds., *New Points of View on Audiovisual Translation and Accessibility*. Oxford: Peter Lang, pp. 167–89.

Romero-Fresco, P. (2006). The Spanish Dubbese: A case of (un)idiomatic friends. *Jostrans*, **6**, 134–52.

Romero-Fresco, P. (2011). *Subtitling through Speech Recognition: Respeaking*. London: Routledge.

Romero-Fresco, P. (2013). Accessible filmmaking: Joining the dots between audiovisual translation, accessibility and filmmaking. *Journal of Specialised Translation*, **20**, 201–23.

Romero-Fresco, P., ed. (2015). *The Reception of Subtitles for the Deaf and Hard of Hearing in Europe*. Bern: Peter Lang.

Romero-Fresco, P. (2019). *Accessible Filmmaking: Integrating Translation and Accessibility into the Filmmaking Process*. London: Routledge.

Salway, A. (2007). A corpus-based analysis of audio description. In J. Díaz Cintas, P. Orero and A. Remael, eds., *Media for All: Subtitling for the Deaf, Audio Description and Sign Language*. Amsterdam: Rodopi, pp. 151–74.

Sánchez Mompeán, S. (2019). *The Prosody of Dubbed Speech: Beyond the Character's Words.* Basingstoke: Palgrave.

Scandura, G. L. (2004). Sex, lies and TV: Censorship and subtitling. *Meta,* **49** (1), 125–34.

Secară, A. (2018). Surtitling and captioning for theatre and opera. In L. Pérez-González, ed., *The Routledge Handbook of Audiovisual Translation.* New York: Routledge, pp. 130–44.

Şerban, A., and Meylaerts, R., eds. (2014). *Multilingualism at the Cinema and on Stage: A Translation Perspective.* Special Issue of *Linguistica Antverpiensia,* 13.

Snell-Hornby, M. (1988). *Translation Studies: An Interdiscipline.* Amsterdam: John Benjamins.

Szarkowska, A. (2009). The audiovisual landscape in Poland at the dawn of the 21st century. In A. Goldstein and B. Golubović, eds., *Foreign Language Movies: Dubbing vs. Subtitling.* Hamburg: Verlag Dr. Kovač, pp. 185–201.

Szarkowska, A. (2013). Towards interlingual subtitling for the deaf and the hard of hearing. *Perspectives,* **21**(1), 68–81.

Szarkowska, A., Krejtz, I., Klyszejko, Z., and Wieczorek, A. (2011). Verbatim, standard, or edited? Reading patterns of different captioning styles among deaf, hard of hearing, and hearing viewers. *American Annals of the Deaf,* **156**(4), 363–78.

Taylor, C. (2015). The language of AD. In A. Remael, N. Reviers and G. Vercauteren, eds., *Pictures Painted in Words: ADLAB Audio Description Guidelines.* Trieste: EUT, pp. 48–51.

Taylor, C. (2016). The multimodal approach in audiovisual translation. *Target,* **28**(2), 222–36.

Titford, C. (1982). Subtitling: Constrained translation. *Lebende Sprachen,* **27** (3), 113–16.

Turnbull, J. (2019). The aesthetics of access. 28 January. Available at https:// disabilityarts.online/magazine/showcase/playlist-the-aesthetics-of-access/.

Valentini, C. (2008). Forlixt 1 – The Forlì corpus of screen translation: Exploring macrostructures. In D. Chiaro, C. Heiss and C. Bucaria, eds., *Between Text and Image: Updating Research in Screen Translation.* Amsterdam: John Benjamins, pp. 37–50.

Vasey, R. (1997). *The World According to Hollywood, 1918–1939.* Madison: University of Wisconsin Press.

Vercauteren, G. (2012). A narratological approach to content selection in audio description: Towards a strategy for the description of narratological time. *Monographs in Translating and Interpreting (MonTI),* **4**, 207–31.

Von Flotow, L., and Josephy-Hernández, D. (2019). Gender in audiovisual translation studies: Advocating for gender awareness. In L. Pérez-González, ed., *The Routledge Handbook of Audiovisual Translation.* New York: Routledge, pp. 296–311.

Wang, D., and Zhang, X. (2016). Ideological manipulation of controversial information: The unusual case of the Chinese-subtitled version of House of Cards. *Altre Modernità*, **1**, 1–20.

Whitman-Linsen, C. (1992). *Through the Dubbing Glass: The Synchronization of American Motion Pictures into German, French and Spanish*. Frankfurt am Main: Peter Lang.

Zabalbeascoa, P. (1996). Translating jokes for dubbed television situation comedies. *The Translator*, **2**(2), 235–57.

Zabalbeascoa, P. (2008). The nature of the audiovisual text and its parameters. In J. Díaz-Cintas, ed., *The Didactics of Audiovisual Translation*. Amsterdam: John Benjamins, pp. 21–37.

Zanotti, S. (2018). Historical approaches to AVT reception: Methods, issues and perspectives. In E. Di Giovanni and Y. Gambier, eds., *Reception Studies and Audiovisual Translation*. Amsterdam/New York: John Benjamins, pp. 133–56.

Zanotti, S. (2019). Investigating the genesis of translated films: A view from the Stanley Kubrick archive. *Perspectives: Studies in Translation Theory and Practice*, **27**(2), 201–17.

Zárate, S. (2010). Bridging the gap between deaf studies and AVT for deaf children. In J. Díaz Cintas, A. Matamala and J. Neves, eds., *New Insights into Audiovisual Translation and Media Accessibility: Media for All 2*. Amsterdam: Rodopi, pp. 159–73.

# 23

# Translating Literary Prose

Karen Seago

Literary prose covers an enormous variety of creative writing, ranging from children's literature, genre fiction (crime, science fiction, fantasy) and literary fiction to lyrical fiction, employing an extraordinary range of language from description to dialogue to lyrics or slang. In each, the relationship between meaning and form varies in its foregrounding of formal features, that is, in the extent to which the language used complies with or departs from the standard definition of prose as naturally flowing text without a formal metric structure, using ordinary grammar and normal patterns. While in literary fiction the rhetoricity of the text is considered essential to its purpose, genre fiction tends to be thought of as privileging plot over rhetorical effects with its focus on the 'what' rather than the 'how'. But both literary and genre texts tell stories which have believable and captivating characters, a convincing setting and absorbing themes. In addition, both are shaped by and explore – to a greater or lesser degree – the possibilities and limits of language whether these are rhetorical effects in literary fiction, language play in children's texts or language creation in science fiction or fantasy. These pose constraints for the translator whose creativity needs to negotiate literary and cultural frames of reference as well as the linguistic possibilities and limitations that shaped the source text and which need to be worked out and through in the target language.

Prose texts are therefore positioned on a sliding scale between the poles of rhetorical effect and story, showing features of each. The translation challenges posed by lyrical fiction will be very similar to those posed by poetry translation, except for the greater freedom in negotiating a less indissoluble relationship between meaning and form. In prose, literariness depends on 'prominence', on some linguistic features standing out in some way, generating enhanced meaning which encompasses what is said and what is not said but inferable. Genre fiction will rely less on such non-casual language; translation challenges involve rendering socio-cultural specificities and observing genre constraints.

In the interests of clarity, the following will address specific features in separate sections on translation strategies, rhetoricity and genre constraints, but any of the issues discussed may apply to any kind of literary prose.

## 23.1  Translation Strategies and General Concerns

In the translation of any text, the translator needs to decide whether to aim at maintaining language-specific and culturally specific features of the source text which may be strange to the target reader, or to produce a text which negotiates the linguistically and culturally foreign elements in such a way that they accommodate the target reader's horizon of expectation and understanding. These translation strategies are often referred to as domesticating and foreignizing (Venuti, 1995/2008), a somewhat misleading suggestion that a translation will be either target reader oriented or source author oriented. In fact, such a global strategy notwithstanding, in practice there will be a range of translation decisions spread across the spectrum but with an orientation towards one of the poles.

Typically, the greater the distance is between source and target, the greater and the more numerous will be the shifts, such as explaining, replacing or omitting cultural, historic or linguistic features, that need to be considered and managed. Distance can be linguistic, resulting in textual, rhetorical or pragmatic differences, or it can be cultural and temporal: translating between languages that have very different lexicons, syntax or morphology poses very obvious challenges. Japanese, for example, uses different language varieties depending on the speaker's status or gender and Arabic generates ambiguous compound nouns through letter affixation. The letter 'ب' (b in English) can convey the following meanings: through, in, by, for and at (Alkhatib and Shaalan, 2018, p. 153). Chinese does not explicitly specify gender, number or tense which compels the translator to make decisions leading to such diverse renderings as in the following examples, translations of the same source text, given by Yu Hou (2011, p. 99).

> At sight of Qin Zhong, Baohad felt quite eclipsed. (The Yangs, 2003, p. 207)

> When Bao-yu first set eyes on Qin Zhong it had been as though part of his soul had left him.                                            (Hawkes, 1973, p. 178)

> Since he had first glanced at Ch'in Chung, and seen what kind of person he was, he felt at heart as if he had lost something.        (Joly, 1892, p. 115)

But even in languages that are closely related, for example English and German, there are structural differences, requiring translatorial interpretation. In German, for example, it is very common to use modifiers as nouns. In the Grimm fairy tale 'Dornröschen' ('Sleeping Beauty'), the uninvited wise woman who curses the child in her anger is referred to as 'die dreizehnte' (the thirteenth), whereas among the nineteenth-century translations into English, only one opted for 'the thirteenth', while the majority added a noun, ranging from the unmarked 'thirteenth wise woman' to the marked, and highly preferred, 'the thirteenth fairy'. In the Grimms' mythic interpretation of fairy tales, the thirteenth is part of the community of wise women; in contrast, the English differentiates between the 'good' fairies and the 'evil' fairy. This aligns with a range of other changes introduced into the translations in the nineteenth century which adapt male and female representations in 'Sleeping Beauty' to promote desirable and objectionable behaviour for men and women.

Cultural differences cover an extremely wide field from apparently simple aspects such as modes of address or proper names, to food, social and cultural organizations, education, family relationships, government and the law, to name just a few. Translators need to decide whether their main aim is to produce a readable, smooth and easily comprehensible text or whether to maintain a text's foreignness, keeping, for example, idiomatic expressions and concepts, and cultural and social institutions. In the latter case, culturally specific associations and knowledge that the source text reader brings to the text need to be made explicit for the target reader in a way that does not distract from the flow of language or the narrative. Even with such an apparently simple feature as proper names, where there tends to be agreement that they cannot be substituted without relocating the narrative universe, many of the evoked meanings of names (gender, social class, regional provenance, whether the name is contemporary, old-fashioned or archaic) are lost and may become too foregrounded if explained. The Russian naming system is famously challenging with its use of first name, patronymic and last name plus intimate abbreviations of the first name. Variations such as Vasya or Vasyuk for Vasilisa, and Volodya, Volodka, Volodechka or Volya for Vladimir may not appear obviously related to the same character and may confuse a foreign reader or require greater effort. And as Bassnett (1980, p. 119) points out, 'it is of little use for the English reader to be given multiple variants of a name if he is not made aware of the function of those variants' which convey affectionate, patronizing or friendly relations between addresser and addressee.

The translator faces the difficult choice among making a culturally specific feature explicit, generalizing it or substituting it with a more domestic choice. The greater the distance between the languages and cultures, the greater the shift, resulting in too much explanation detracting from the literariness of the text if the foreign feature is retained, losing potentially text-relevant information if it is generalized or losing its cultural specificity if wholesale domestication choices lead to the potential substitution of another system of references in order to achieve comprehensibility. Reader-oriented translation approaches aim at readability and dynamic equivalence (Nida, 1964, p. 159), producing a text which works for the target reader in a similar way as the source text does for the source reader. It is, of course, difficult to identify with any certainty what particular literary effect is achieved for a reader, or different readers at different times in different environments. The danger of such an approach is that it may lead to the loss of cultural and linguistic specificity and, in extreme cases, to replication of the hegemonic relations between central and peripheral cultures and languages when the referents and literary models of the more powerful language replace culturally foreign words and rhetorical systems. Venuti (1995/2008, p. 2) famously identified the concept of fluency as the main criterion for Anglo-American reception of translated literature, while Spivak points out the loss of (gendered) Third World specificity in 'with-it translatese' where 'the literature by a woman in Palestine begins to resemble … something by a man in Taiwan' (Spivak, 2000, p. 400). Marilyn Booth discusses how, in the case of her consciously foreignizing translation of *Girls of Rhiyad*, which attempted to render the very wide range of religious, canonical, literary, vernacular and popular global variants of Arabic, the structural experimentation and use of local and global pop culture references were rejected in favour of an accessible, transparent and domesticated text, shaped to conform to the linguistic, stylistic and generic format of popular chick lit (Booth, 2008, p. 201). The following example demonstrates the smoothing out of language, omissions to conform to expectations of conduct and a Westernized choice of restaurant: 'After the mall, and a pretty satisfying number of innocent flirtatious exchanges, plus a few (a very few) that were not so innocent, the girls set their sights on the smart restaurant they had picked out for dinner' (Booth, 2008, p. 203). 'The girls made their way toward the elegant Italian restaurant they had picked out for dinner' (published translation Alsanea, 2007, p. 17).

It is not only in texts that are linguistically or culturally remote that the translator faces particularly difficult choices but also in dealing with temporal distance. When translating classical and older canonical texts, the translator needs to decide how to bridge the gap for a contemporary reader not familiar with historic references, words or customs. 'Academic' translations use lengthy notes, providing explanations and historical references, while reader-oriented translations avoid notes, which distract from the reading-pleasure, and instead update and adapt terminology and customs so that they are intelligible without lengthy explanations. Scarpa's (2015) discussion of the translation of food and food imagery in Shakespeare is a good example of the challenges posed by temporal distance and culturally specific items. Outdated terminology is often updated to modern usage, since it is also not accessible to modern English readers, but reference to food items or preparations which are unfamiliar to the target audience need to be adapted, especially if they are used as a simile: 'If ye pinch me like a pasty' in *All's Well That Ends Well* has been rendered into Italian using imagery generated by a different process of food preparation since neither 'pasty' nor 'pinching' have Italian equivalents. In addition, the translators have been successful in rendering the figurative meaning of the English by transferring it to the slightly more brutal process of 'making mincemeat of somebody' (Scarpa, 2015, p. 172). More difficult is the temporally specific usage of 'coffin' for pie crust, which cannot be updated without losing the crucially relevant second meaning of 'casket': the reference occurs at the point when Goth queen Tamora in *Titus Andronicus* is served a pie made of her two sons (Scarpa, 2015, p. 168). The extended web of connected meanings drawn from both food preparation and the cannibalistic intention further complicates rendering such a complex passage which the translators, in this case, recreated through new images and association with modern Italian culinary terms, although they often cannot be reproduced without introducing an entirely new system of references.

Literary translators balance the desire to create a piece of writing in the target language and culture which is as literary as the source text, with the need to comply with contemporary editorial policies, and the tastes and trends of the moment as manifested in publisher (and reader) expectations. This means that translations deploy contemporary idiom, syntax, references and style, making them socio-historical documents revealing much about the target culture and its political, social and literary values. In the following example, very different levels of formality are evident in the lexical and syntactic choices made in three translations of *The Brothers Karamazov* spanning the twentieth century (Dostoyevsky, 1912, 1970, 1990). These range from Garnett's antiquated and highly formal idiom in 1912, to MacAndrew's punchy and assertive tone in 1970, and Pevear and Volokhonsky's standard and formal renderings in 1990:

- '**How it came to pass** that an heiress ... could have married such a worthless puny weakling, as we all called him, I won't attempt to explain.' (Garnett – Dostoyevsky, 1912)
- '**Why** should a girl with a dowry ... marry such a worthless "freak" as they called him? I will not really attempt to explain.' (MacAndrew – Dostoyevsky, 1970)
- '**Precisely how it happened** that a girl with a dowry ... could have married such a worthless "runt" as everyone used to call him, I cannot begin to explain.' (Pevear and Volokhonsky – Dostoyevsky, 1990)

The three translations also demonstrate different interpretations of narrative rhetorical positioning: in Garnett's rendering, the speaker includes themselves in the condemnatory attitude displayed by the town ('as **we all** called him'), MacAndrew's is exclusive ('as **they** called him') and Pevear and Volokhonsky's is neutral with respect to narratorial distancing ('as

**everyone** used to call him'). This illustrates how translatorial choices interpret the source text; explaining, correcting, adapting and disambiguating, they often make it easier to read a work in translation than it is to read the original. Dodds cites Christopher Taylor's analysis of the translations of Joyce where it is evident that the translator has done much of the interpretative work for the reader, producing a far more readable text in Italian than it is in the original English (Dodds, 2015, p. 37). Professional (literary) translators work within the constraints imposed by the expectations of their publisher and readership and the tastes of the day. While the original is a static work of art, fixed in time, translations are 'dynamic, everchanging, interpretative and re-interpretative, ephemeral and only rarely of universal appeal' (Dodds, 2015, p. 41). For translated texts, such reinterpretation in re-translations is a measure of their continuing relevance for different reader communities, different times and different objectives.

## 23.2   Non-casual Language/Rhetoricity

Literariness in prose is characterized by its deviation from standard, expected or probable use, and covers phonological, syntactic, positional and semantic features as well as figures of speech. The literary translator will be listening and looking for evidence of such non-casual language, of patterns and echoes across the text and other extra-contextual associations which can point to a heightened meaning. The literary translator needs to convey these literary qualities as well as the content, doing it as unobtrusively as possible in order to generate an effect for the reader which carries across the literary force of the source text. This requires sensitivity to the various levels or features in the text, an understanding of the intended effects and how these may be achieved in a different language and culture and a different literary system. An author's characteristic patterns of deviation make up their style which will be evident across their range of literary output. In his book on translating style, Tim Parks gives the following excerpt typical of Lawrence's style (Parks, 2007, p. 10): 'In a few minutes the train was running through the disgrace of outspread London. Everybody in the carriage was on the alert, waiting to escape. At last they were under the huge arch of the station, in the tremendous shadow of the town. Birkin shut himself together – he was in now.'

Some of these features are the unusual collocations 'disgrace' with 'outspread London', the grammatically highly unusual 'shut himself together' as well as the underspecified 'everybody . . . was on the alert' and 'he was in now' requiring the reader to infer what the passengers are on the alert *for* and what the 'in' refers to. In translation, these lexical and grammatical non-conformities and uncertainties in meaning need to be maintained, offering similar cues for interpretation without closing down on potential sense and producing similar creative disruption. And if that is not possible, the translator needs to choose whether to make the inferable explicit, generalized, substituted or – in a didactic or academic translation – to explain, annotate or footnote. The Italian translation, for example, specifies that the passengers escape from 'the carriage' by adding 'dal convoglio' and normalizes the 'disgrace of outspread London' to 'squalid suburbs' thus losing the impression of an overwhelmingly oppressive and threatening city and introducing a different kind of value judgement. Lawrence's manipulation of the common sense English 'pull yourself together' as 'shut himself together' activates both the meaning of the standard expression and Lawrence's reworking of it so that they play off against each other, evoking Birkin's response of drawing on his resources in order to face the immensity of the city and then closing himself off from overwhelming contact (Parks, 2007, p. 14). German and English are closely related languages so the translator can draw on – and manipulate – a similar expression, 'sich zusammen**reissen**' as 'sich zusammen**schliessen**', which would generate a similar clash and productive meaning creation. This potential to reveal more is a key aspect of literary prose and if a particular feature of non-casual language use is part of an author's individual style, the translator also needs to be attentive to patterns across the text which need to be maintained if possible.

Awareness of the text as a whole is particularly relevant in the case of repetition of lexical items, recurrence of syntactic structures, and lexical chains where words from the same semantic field create continuities and establish connections among events, characters, settings and themes. In Jessica Cohen's translation of David Grossman's hybrid prose/drama *Falling out of Time*, the central theme of death is foregrounded by clustered repetition (six times) over two pages of the phrases 'he is dead' or 'the boy is dead' and seven times 'his death' (Grossman, 2014, pp. 105–6). The text further foregrounds the centrality of death by conjugating the noun 'We were deathened, you will be deatherized, they will be deathed' and creating new adjectives and verbs: 'Death is deathful.' 'Death will deathify, or is it deathened?' (Grossman, 2014, p. 94). These neologisms extending across word classes and manipulating morphologies thematize the omnipresence and omnipotence of death linguistically and will challenge languages with fewer resources for word creation and manipulation. Dense repetition in the space of one or two pages is far more obvious than meaningful occurrence over long stretches of text. Roy Youdale used corpus analysis to support his impression that the use of the word 'estallar' (burst, explode) in the novel *Gracias por el fuego* by Mario Benedetti was a stylistic device. It occurred only eight times, but context of use (scene-setting at the beginning of chapters and emotional climax at the end of chapters, linked to specific characters only) clearly indicated the relevance of this lexical item in developing the central theme of emotional and psychological pressure resulting in eruption, and shaped the translation decision for repetition over variation, discarding synonyms used in early drafts (Youdale, 2020, p. 163).

Repetition can contribute to the rhythm of a text, as for example in this description from *Of Mice and Men* where the enumeration of natural sounds and effects in paratactic clauses creates an effect of peace: 'The little evening breeze blew over the clearing and the leaves rustled and the wind waves flowed up the green pool. And the shouts of men sounded again, this time much closer than before' (Steinbeck, 1937/1994, p. 104). Joyce's rhythmical, monosyllabic prose, combined with alliteration, creates a musical yet sparse and exact register in *The Dead* (in *Dubliners*): 'Gabriel, leaning on his elbow, looked for a few moments unresentfully on her tangled hair and half-open mouth, listening to her deep-drawn breath. ... It hardly pained him now to think how poor a part he, her husband, had played in her life' (Joyce, quoted in Parks, 2005, p. 60). In this example, the first sentence consists of three clauses, each starting with the letter 'l', and concludes with the poetic compounding of 'deep-drawn' breath, while the second sentence begins with a strong, iambic rhythm, a prevalence of monosyllabic words and prominent use of the letters 'p' and 'h'. Parks shows how the Italian translation loses the alliteration in the first sentence, and normalizes the compound adjective into a standard phrase 'il suo respiro profondo' (her deep breathing); and while it is possible to maintain some of the alliterated 'p's, the one-syllabic rhythm is not available in a language whose vocabulary consists primarily of multi-syllabic items (Parks, 2005, pp. 60–2). The short extract from Joyce demonstrates that the different features working together in creating Joyce's distinctive tone cannot all be accommodated in a different linguistic system with very different resources. Translators need to be attentive to the constituting elements of the source text style, perhaps especially where their target language cannot produce a particular effect, and consider compensating by using different linguistic devices, perhaps at another point in the text. Harvey gives an example where the interplay of simple past and passé composé tenses in the French creates a sense of shock over the death of a girl working for the Resistance. In English, this shock needed to be generated using different, available, linguistic devices and was created by using a demonstrative pronoun and noun instead of the pronoun (this girl – *elle*), creating a pause through introducing punctuation and using the foreign word *résistante* (Harvey, 1998/2000, p. 39). While such shifting creates its own dangers of altering the source text themes or balance, it also recognizes the translator's creativity as a writer and points to the need to reinvent in translation, which Calvino sees as the only way of producing a faithful rendering (Calvino, quoted in Grossi, 2015, p. 202).

According to Calvino, 'the author's work is to force the language, to make it say something that the current language does not say' (quoted in Grossi, 2015, p. 201) and figurative language is one of the means by which the author pushes boundaries, creating ambiguity which invites the reader to engage with the text and create the meanings implied but not spelled out. Metaphors, in particular, require the reader to search for the meaning suggested by indirect language, images or statements which violate truth conditions (a weeping stone, for example). While there are conceptual and conventional metaphors which are shared across (some) languages, figurative language is often dependent on cultural context or language-specific structures. This is particularly the case with the creative metaphors typical in literary style, introducing vividness and colour and drawing on cultural connotations. In translating metaphors, the translator needs to work out the implied meanings or the image generated in order to provide cues for the reader of the target text to create a similar interpretation. However, there is a tendency in translation to spell out the implied meanings in metaphors and other figurative language. Othman Ahmad Abualadas discusses mostly conventional metaphors and similes in two Arabic translations of Hemingway's *A Farewell to Arms*, showing that, in the majority of cases, the translators explicitated the implied meaning in the figurative language, producing a text with far less ambiguity overall than the source text contained. In the following example, the translator spells out the implied meaning of the relationship between Henry and Catherine Barkley moving from friendship to romance/sexual liaison when the metaphor 'a dog in heat' is rendered as 'affection which a dog shows when having a lust' (Abualadas, 2019, p. 68).

| | |
|---|---|
| HEMINGWAY: | 'So you make progress with Miss Barkley?' 'We are friends.' 'You have that pleasant air of a dog in heat.' (ch. 5) |
| BAʿLBAKĪ: | tabdū ʿalā muḥyāka al-ʿudhūbatu allatī takūnu lil-kalbi ʿinda al-nazwa. (ch. 5, p. 41) |
| | [Gloss: Your face seems to show affection which a dog shows when having a lust] |

In the case of polysemous metaphors which activate different meanings, the translator may be forced to make a choice in prioritizing one over the other. A good example of the difficulties the translator faces is the extended use of machine metaphors for the hospital orderlies in *One Flew Over the Cuckoo's Nest*. One of these is their 'sliding movement' which generates meanings of both 'silent movement' and 'machine-like movement'. In the Dutch translation, 'sliding' is rendered with lexical items which only foreground the meaning of 'silently moving', which produces a dissonance in the portrayal of Big Nurse whose footsteps are loud and emphatic, and the description of him 'sliding' as 'silent' rather than 'machine-like' does not work. Dorst points out that to maintain the extended use of metaphor, choice of a Dutch verb which is used in relation to objects 'sliding' would have generated the polysemous meanings of the source text and would have maintained the machine metaphorics of the text overall (Dorst, 2019, p. 882).

An author will also show patterns of language typical of individual narrators or characters in individual books, creating a typical voice which may display standard, non-standard or idiosyncratic features. Such stylistic variation is evoked in regional and social dialects, swearing and informal language, lexical and syntactic errors and, in dialogue, the features typical of spoken language and diction. These contribute to characterization but are notoriously difficult to render. Attempting to evoke a regional dialect in another language involves either some degree of relocation by drawing on the repertoire of regional features in the target language, or attempting to signal the non-standard features in the source language by creating deviations in the target language. But this means that there will be loss of evoked meanings of social, regional or educational background, which contribute to generating vivid characters. As a result, non-standard language tends to be normalized in translation, although there are some attempts at reproducing vernacular forms in translation. Čerče, for example, discusses her own attempt to reconstruct Steinbeck's use of colloquial and highly informal vernacular used by Lennie and George in *Of Mice and Men* when translating into Slovene. She identifies typical features in the American English at phonological, grammatical and lexical levels and uses these as the principles for constructing similar deviations in the Slovene. At the phonological level, for example, she introduces sound omissions and dropping of end-consonants, 'creating' non-standard nč (nothing, standard nič), je blo (it was, standard je bilo) or zajc (rabbit, standard zajec); English grammatical deviations such as double negatives, incorrect verb forms and omission of personal pronouns posed problems because they were standard forms in Slovene and the translator compensated by violating grammatical rules in standard Slovene including using the plural form instead of the mandatory dual grammatical number, informal modes of address combining singular particle and plural auxiliary verb or incorrect imperatives. Steinbeck's use of slang, jargon and non-standard idioms was reproduced by drawing on a similar repertoire from spoken Slovene, a violation of literary norms, as are some of the stylistic devices of repetition of words, phrases and sentences (Čerče, 2017, pp. 75–6). To what extent a translator can recreate a source text's non-standard language varieties depends not only on the linguistic and stylistic resources available in the target language but also on whether or to what extent vernacular irregularities and colloquialisms in literary texts are acceptable to the target culture readership.

## 23.3  Constraints of Genre Fiction

The previous sections have focused primarily on the non-casual language and stylistic features of literary prose, the 'how something is said' rather than the themes and contents, the 'what is said'. But, as the introductory paragraph outlined, non-factual prose covers a very wide range of text forms and in the following sections I will be looking at what is typical in different genres, such as children's literature, crime fiction and speculative fiction (science fiction and fantasy). In these genres, the balance between the 'what' and the 'how' shifts towards the story, but many of the aspects discussed under rhetoricity in Section 23.2 are still present and often significant. Stories draw to a greater or lesser degree on features, beliefs, attitudes and conventions familiar to the reader; alternatively, the author creates a text world which generates its coherence within the text, as, for example, in fantasy or science fiction. But even in these genres, frames and references will have some cultural recognizability and therefore cultural specificity, and how to convey it, remains a challenge in translation. Non-casual language, voice and tone, as well as textual and contextual practical challenges such as capturing the cadence, rhythm and music of a text, are difficult and not always recognized. Children's literature, in particular, often plays with language and form; figurative language, selectional restrictions and humour are culturally specific and generate as many challenges as culture-specific references, items and associations. Stylistic variation is crucial in crime fiction where different idiolects differentiate regional and social background, and non-standard language in the form of swearing, lexical and syntactic errors and pronunciation are essential in creating dialogue. Indeterminacy, ambiguity, inference and implicatures are essential in generating clues and suspense; they rely on contextual understanding and may need to be explicitated. Intratextual associations, lexical chains and foregrounding or backgrounding of particular features need to be recognized as non-local features and maintained across the text. Linguistic creativity is essential in science fiction and fantasy where neologisms and neosemes (existing words with a new meaning) are the foundational components in the world building of these speculative genres. So, what is crucial in genre fiction is that stylistic devices are often deployed in the service of generic tropes; that is, specific genres impose specific constraints and pose additional concerns for the translator, at times to the extent that generic constraints override idiomaticity and naturalness in the target language.

## 23.4  Children's Literature

Children's literature, in particular, is subject to contextual constraints such as didactic aims or cultural norms, which may differ in the source and target environment. An example is the omission of sexual representations and actions in Chantal Wright's English translation, *The Pasta Detectives*, of Andreas Steinhöfel's *Rico, Oskar und die Tieferschatten*, where the German has a more relaxed attitude to teenage sex and mothers as sexual beings (Wright, 2019, online). In addition, children's literature covers a very wide variety of genres, from picture books to serial novels, and reader ages from preliterate to young adult, and crossover texts which are read by adults as well. Reader age will shape the vocabulary and complexity of syntactic structures as well as choice of topics; genre impacts on the presence of non-textual elements ranging from picture books where the text is subordinate to the images, to illustrated books where text and image interrelate, to chapter books where text is dominant with perhaps some illustrations, or none at all. But even in picture books where the language used may appear very simple, it is usually chosen with great care – to some extent, because books for preliterate children are read aloud and need to work prosodically. Alfred Lobel's (1970/2012) picture book *Frog and Toad Are Friends* is a good example to demonstrate the care in word choice, sentence length and rhythm all contributing to characterization, dramatic tension and interrelation with the images. 'Spring' is the very simple story of Frog running to see his friend Toad who is still hibernating in his dark, shut-up house. The text consists of very short, descriptive, declarative sentences and dialogue, and each passage appears on a single page, with an accompanying image on the second and third page (see Figure 23.1):

The reporting verbs are of particular interest here: Frog's emotional state, and excitable character, are conveyed in the variations of 'shouted', 'cried' and 'called', which contrast with Toad's repetitive 'said'. Frog's speech acts are emphatic and loud, escalating in intensity, while Toad's are neutral and entirely unmarked and his absence is further conveyed by him being identified as 'a voice' and 'the voice' only. In translation, the simplicity of this short passage needs to be maintained while the variations and repetition need to be carefully rendered. This may be a problem in languages which do not have such a varied repertoire of reporting verbs, or where the didactic demand of teaching appropriate and varied language use overrides the source text's stylistic choices. The didactic role of children's literature in children's language education also drives the

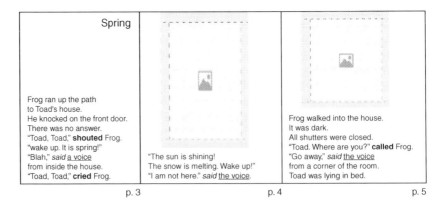

**Figure 23.1** Linguistic choice and characterization in Alfred Lobel's *Frog and Toad Are Friends* (1970/2012)

replacement of dialect, informal or colloquial usage into 'correct' standard language, for example in Swedish translations of *Huckleberry Finn* (Epstein, 2012).

Maurice Sendak's *Where the Wild Things Are* is another example of an apparently very simple illustrated text, telling the story of Max's imaginary journey, sailing to the island of the 'wild things' after he has been sent to bed without supper, and returning after he has become bored with being king of the rumpus and is missing his mother. The interrelationship of image and text conveying contrasting meanings is a central feature for translation in this and in other children's texts, and poses a range of problems. But here I wish to concentrate on the rhythm of the text which mimics in sentence length and inverted sentence sequencing the outward and return journey of the protagonist. The entire story consists of nine sentences spread over thirty-two pages, plus six image-only pages, showing the rumpus, the high point of Max's adventure: sentence length increases up to the text-free climax, then decreases into shorter, choppier sentences to finish on an extended, almost static, sentence in the safety of his bedroom with supper waiting. The reversal of outward and return journey is mirrored in a similar reversal of time periods (day – weeks – year / year – weeks – day) and sequencing (through night and day – through day into night). The German translation has not captured this rhythm and sequencing, not only losing a central aesthetic device but impacting on meaning as well.

Reading aloud is a key feature of literature aimed at preliterate children and those learning to read and I have already mentioned the performative requirements, the read-aloud-ability that translation of these texts needs to satisfy. This raises another crucial challenge in children's literature translation: the dual audience of adult reader and child listener both need to be addressed. Maintaining the adult reader's interest can be achieved through social or historical allusions or through humour or double-entendre beyond the child's understanding. Alluding to serious historical context, as, for example, with the question of the holocaust in *The Borrowers* (1952) which the adult reader will recognize in the persecution of the 'borrowers' by the 'human beans' and their potential extinction, does not necessarily pose linguistic problems but raises the question of historical and cultural frames of recognition in the target readership. Language play, on the other hand, may need to be shifted or recreated in some languages and is, in fact, often omitted with the translator opting for one meaning only. A good example is the opening of A. A. Milne's *Winnie the Pooh* which plays with – and articulates – the double perspective of adult and child knowledge through exploiting the literal and phrasal meaning of 'under the name' and plays with the different perceptions of time for adults and children:

> Once upon a time, a very long time ago now, about last Friday, Winnie-the-Pooh lived in a forest all by himself under the name of Sanders.

*('What does "under the name" mean?' asked Christopher Robin.*
*'It means he had the name over the door in gold letters and lived under it.' ...)*

(Milne, 1973, pp. 3–4)

Conveying the double meaning of 'under the name' may be a challenge, and the range of creative translation solutions, choosing another polysemous expression which fits the context, is further constrained by the illustration, showing Pooh sitting in front of his 'door' with a name sign over it.

## 23.5  Crime Fiction

Crime fiction draws on a wide range of linguistic resources creating clues, suspense and misdirection; it is also highly culturally specific in content, setting and characterization – definitions of what is a crime, the legal system, police ranks and authority cannot be transplanted to the target culture environment but need to be sufficiently transparent for the story to make sense. Characterization draws on description, behaviour and idiolect with deviations from the norm, or the expected, signalling potential clues and triggering (reader) suspicion. Explicitation of connotations or explanations of culturally specific features may foreground a feature too much or may slow up the narrative pace. The translator needs to be attentive to the smallest detail and may, at times, have to privilege accurate, literal choices over a smoothly idiomatic and natural-sounding text. In the German translation of Val McDermid's *The Wire in the Blood,* the idiomatic 'mit der linken Hand' (with the left hand) for the English 'with his free hand' excludes one of the potential suspects whose left hand is a prosthesis, unable to perform the attack described. This not only reduces ambiguity and therefore the puzzle-solving involvement of the reader, it also disrupts the text's believability since the excluded suspect turns out to be the perpetrator. Crime fiction draws on cohesive devices such as pronominal reference or lexical chains to conceal identities or suggest links between apparently disparate elements. Languages with gendered adjective, verb or noun endings have far fewer resources for rendering obscure entities such as 'the killer' or 'the perpetrator', a typical device in English crime. In Inge Löhnig's (2011) *So unselig schön* (so terribly beautiful), complex lexical chains throughout the text generate patterns, connecting apparently disparate people, places and four different narrative strands, slowly creating a web of associations which generates suspicions and suspense to include almost every character before it coheres into identifying the murderer. These lexical chains are drawn from several semantic fields including flowers, paintings, insects, physical features such as hair, pale skin, crystal and glass, and colours. Translating these with words which can function across a range of domains and different text forms, from poetry to pathology reports, is an almost impossible challenge for any language. In addition, it slowly emerges that the serial murderer is recreating a scene from a Baudelaire poem ('Une martyre' 'Die Märtyrerin' (The martyr) from *Les fleurs du mal*) and increasingly longer quotations from a German translation of this poem appear in the text; words and imagery from it are alluded to in descriptions of scenes or characters and occur even in newspaper articles and police reports, until the detective recognizes and finds the poem online. This creates a range of translation challenges: intra-textual allusions across the entire novel which need to be maintained, the quotations from the German translation which is, in fact, available on the Internet, and finding an English translation which is sufficiently close to the phrasing of the German translation so that the quotations can serve the same trigger effect as in the source text (Seago, 2014).

## 23.6  Speculative Fiction

Fantasy and science fiction create an alternate reality which deviates – to a greater or lesser degree – from the laws and conventions of physical and social reality. Evoking the unfamiliar, strange and new poses tremendous challenges for description, requiring new words and concepts to convey ways of being, thinking, acting and speaking that are divorced from the real world. While the world building in science fiction focuses on cognitive estrangement, extrapolating from the known to an 'other' in place (space) or time (the future), fantasy sidesteps into alternate worlds, existing in parallel in the fissures and underground places of the known world, or creating archaic societies in imagined realms of mythical beasts, sorcerers and magic. Both science fiction and fantasy rely heavily on neologisms and neosemes, but also draw on a repertoire of linguistic styles ranging from the archaic to the scientific. Rational discourse in science fiction extrapolates from known science in a plausible way, creating entirely new items such as Le Guin's famous 'ansible', an interstellar communication device, or Miéville's 'vespcams', flying micro-cameras. These are difficult to render and are often transferred, losing semantic echoes, as in the hypothesis that 'ansible' is a shortened 'answerable'. Where neologisms manipulate existing words such as *Star Trek*'s 'Borg', a shortened form of 'cyborg', and even more so if they draw on Latin or Greek forms, translation can recreate in the target language, using similar formation mechanisms such as adding, or replacing, prefixes to create 'psychohistory' or 'astrogation', blended words such as 'plasmetal' or 'Turingware'. Neologisms in fantasy often draw on older language varieties, such as Anglo-Saxon in English texts, using similar mechanisms to create runesmiths, riddlemasters or werelights or more modern slang-based 'fangbanger', all of which can be recreated in translation. Phonetic reductions such as 'BLDSKR' (bloodsucker) or language play such as 'Parisn't', 'Un Lun Dun' and 'Lost Angeles' require creative translation approaches similar to the challenges posed in poetry.

Language itself is often thematized in science fiction and fantasy; in science fiction, language change features as a natural development in the far future, or post-apocalyptic enforced reduction and deploys a move away from written conventions 'Him on 1 end of the spear', simplified or phonetic spelling 'ther', 'agen', 'tack ticks' and morphological simplification 'kilt' (killed), 'ternt' (turned). These may be recreated using target language phonological and morphological resources, but this is quite difficult in languages with phonetic spelling or very different morphologies. Fantasy draws on a range of linguistic styles to convey an-other world. Archaic language creates strangeness, an elsewhere and otherness as in Hope Hodgson's *The Night Land*: 'And a great and painful excitement came upon the people of the lesser pyramid; for the loneliness of the world pressed upon them; and it was to them alas as though we in this age called to a star across the abyss of space' (quoted in Gilman, 2012, p. 139).

Translating such formally elaborate, stylized language, set apart from the vernacular, drawing on features of the sacred, needs to evoke otherness without being banal or silly, or disambiguating vague lexis or syntax. Miéville's overloaded style with its Baroque excessiveness is a tour de force, testing the translator's creativity in maintaining a similarly sustained breaking of selectional restrictions between the inanimate and the animate, the animal and the sacred, and unremitting images drawn from physical and material 'wrongness':

> The river twists and turns to face the city. It looms suddenly, massive, stamped on the landscape. Its light wells up around the surrounds, the rock hills, like bruise-blood. Its dirty towers glow. I am debased. I am compelled to worship this extraordinary presence that has silted into existence at the conjunction of two rivers. It is a vast pollutant, a stench, a klaxon sounding. Fat chimneys retch dirt into the sky even now in the deep night. It is not the current which pulls us but the city itself, its weight sucks us in. Faint shouts, here and there the calls of beasts, the obscene clash and pounding from the factories as huge machines rut. Railways trace urban anatomy like protruding veins. Red brick and dark walls, squat churches like troglodytic things, ragged awnings flickering, cobbled mazes in the old town, culs-de-sac, sewers riddling the earth like secular sepulchres, a new landscape of wasteground, crushed stone, libraries fat with forgotten volumes, old hospitals, towerblocks, ships and metal claws that lift cargoes from the water.                    (Miéville, 2000, Loc 96)

## 23.7 Conclusion

Miéville's wildly creative prose is in stark contrast to the often clichéd and formulaic writing associated especially with fantasy but more generally with all genre fiction. Similarly, in crime fiction, Chandler and Simenon are known and valued for their distinctive style which contributes to a large extent to their popularity. So, while the language used in genre literature may at times be subject to generic constraints and comply with formulaic clichés, it nevertheless poses challenges in translation which require similar creative resources as the translation of literary rhetoricity. Both literary and genre texts need to tell an absorbing story with believable and captivating characters, a convincing setting and absorbing theme. Stories draw to a greater or lesser degree on features, beliefs, attitudes and conventions familiar to the reader; alternatively, the author creates a text world which generates its coherence within the text, as, for example, in fantasy or science fiction. But even in these genres, frames and references will have some cultural recognizability and, crucially, all writing is shaped by and explores the possibilities and limits of language. Figurative language, selectional restrictions, humour, allusions and quotations are culturally specific and generate as many challenges as culture-specific references, items and associations. Indeterminacy, ambiguity, inference and implicatures rely on contextual understanding and may need to be explicitated. Intratextual associations, lexical chains and foregrounding or backgrounding of particular features need to be recognized as non-local features and maintained across the text. All of these are present to a greater or lesser degree in the range of literary prose from lyrical fiction to popular genres. Translators of both literary and genre prose negotiate the desire to create a piece of writing in the target language and culture which is as literary as the source text while complying with contemporary editorial policies, and the tastes and trends of the moment as manifested in publisher (and reader) expectations.

## References

Abualadas, O. A. (2019). Systematic shifts in implicatures in two Arabic translations of Ernest Hemingway's A Farewell to Arms. *International Journal of Comparative Literature & Translation Studies*, **7**(3), pp. 65–73.

Alkhatib, M., and Shaalan, K. (2018). The key challenges for Arabic machine translation. In K. Shaalan, A. E. Hassanien and M. F. Tolba, eds., *Intelligent Natural Language Processing: Trends and Application*. New York: Springer Verlag, pp. 139–56.

Alsanea, R. (2007). *Girls of Riyadh*. Harmondsworth: Penguin.

Bassnett, S. (1980). *Translation Studies*. London: Methuen and Co. Ltd.

Booth, M. (2008). Translator v. author (2007) *Girls of Riyadh* go to New York. *Translation Studies*, **1**(2), 197–211.

Čerče, D. (2017). Between translation and transformation: Recreating Steinbeck's language in Of Mice and Men. *The Translator*, **23**(1), 67–82.

Dodds, J. M. (2015). Word or meaning? *Lingue Linguaggi*, **14**, 31–42.

Dorst, A. G. (2019). Translating metaphorical mind style: Machinery and ice metaphors in Ken Kesey's *One Flew over the Cuckoo's Nest*. *Perspectives*, **27**(6), 875–89.

Dostoyevsky, F. (1912). *The Brothers Karamazov: A Novel in Four Parts and an Epilogue*. Trans. Constance Garnett. New York: Macmillan.

Dostoyevsky, F. (1970). *The Brothers Karamazov*. Trans. Andrew H. MacAndrew. New York: Bantam.

Dostoyevsky, F. (1990). *The Brothers Karamazov*. Trans. Richard Pevear and Larissa Volokhonsky. San Francisco, CA: North Point Press.

Epstein, B. J. (2012). *Translating Expressive Language in Children's Literature*. Oxford: Peter Lang.

Gilman, G. (2012). The languages of the fantastic. In E. James and F. Mendlesohn, eds., *The Cambridge Companion to Fantasy Literature*. Cambridge: Cambridge University Press, pp. 134–46.

Grossi, G. (2015). Calvino and Weaver on translation: In theory and in practice. *Lingue Lingaggi*, **14**, 197–208.

Grossman, D. (2014). *Falling out of Time*. New York: Vintage Books.

Harvey, K. (1998/2000). Compensation. In M. Baker and K. Malmkjær, eds., *The Routledge Encyclopedia of Translation Studies*. New York: Routledge, pp. 37–40.

Hawkes, D. (1973). *The Story of the Stone (Vol. 1: The Golden Days)*. Harmondsworth: Penguin Books.

Joly, B. (1892–3). *Hung lou meng, or, The Dream of the Red Chamber, a Chinese Novel*. Hong Kong: Kelly & Walsh.

Lobel, A. (1970/2012). *Frog and Toad Are Friends*. London: Harper Collins.

Löhnig, I. (2011). *So unselig schön*. Berlin: Ullstein.

Miéville, C. (2000). *Perdido Street Station*. London: Pan Books.

Milne, A. A. (1926/1973). *Winnie-the-Pooh*. London: Egmont.

Nida, E. (1964). *Toward a Science of Translating: With Special Reference to Principles and Procedures Involved in Bible Translating*. Leiden: Brill.

Parks, T. (2007). *Translating Style, A Literary Approach to Translation, A Translation Approach to Literature*. Manchester: St Jerome.

Scarpa, F. (2015). 'Wit larded with malice': Translating Shakespeare's culinary language. *Lingue e Linguaggi*, **14**, 163–80.

Seago, K. (2014). Introduction and overview: Crime (fiction) in translation. *Journal of Specialised Translation*, **22**(July), pp. 2–14. www.jostrans.org/issue22/art_seago.pdf.

Spivak, G. (2000). The politics of translation. In L. Venuti, ed., *The Translation Studies Reader*. London: Routledge, pp. 397–416.

Steinbeck, J. (1937/1994). *Of Mice and Men*. New York: Penguin Books.

Venuti, L. (1995/2008). *The Translator's Invisibility: A History of Translation*. London: Routledge.

Wright, C. (2019). Literary translation workshop: Translating for children and young adults. https://warwick.ac.uk/fac/cross_fac/translation-at-warwick/events/ugtranslation/workshops/.

The Yangs [shortened form for Yang Xianyi and Gladys Yang] (2003). *A Dream of Red Mansions* (Chinese–English ed. Vol. 1, 2, 3, 4, 5). Beijing: Foreign Languages Press.

Youdale, R. (2020). *Using Computers in the Translation of Literary Style.* New York: Routledge.

Yu Hou (2011). *Nominalization in the Translation of Literary Prose from Chinese into English (Based on the Three English Versions of Hong Lou Meng).* PhD thesis, Macquarie University Sydney, Australia.

# 24

# Translating Poetry

Paschalis Nikolaou and Cecilia Rossi

## 24.1 A Brief History of Thought on Poetry Translation

How is poetry translation different from the translation of prose or theatrical texts? Even this basic, tripartite categorization has not been with us always, and we will begin with a discussion of what has been understood, across millennia, as poetic art.

Insofar as epic poetry is concerned, the act of translation was, in a sense, included in the variability of oral retelling. The role of reading is itself consequential, as Susan Bassnett (2011) reminds us – especially in what creative writers produce, which is 'to some extent a kind of translation, because that work will be the product that has emerged out of readings of other people's writing. Sometimes that rewriting will be unconscious, while at other times it will be a deliberate choice' (Bassnett, 2011, p. 164). Bassnett (2011, p. 164) notes that '[t]his is particularly the case with poetry, when words and images used by one poet are echoed in the work of another'. What is more, poetry and its translation may combine with other genres and production as a tradition evolves: Shakespeare's *Troilus and Cressida* also exists as a concatenation of Greek sources and later invention by medieval poets, including Chaucer's late-thirteenth-century *Troilus and Criseyde*.

We will start with some widely accepted parameters requiring adjustment when attempting interlinguistic transfer. T. S. Eliot (1965, p. 8) offered that 'genuine poetry can communicate before it is understood', while Edgar Alan Poe (1850, p. 1) spoke of the 'Rhythmical Creation of Beauty'. Implied in such aphorisms is a mode specific to the production and reading of poetic texts. Sylvia Plath (1962, p. 56) articulates this: 'If a poem is concentrated, a closed fist, then a novel is relaxed and expansive, an open hand.' There exists in poetry a tendency towards organization through cadence and patterning, as opposed to a focus on telling stories that span time and place, and involve several characters. Poetic expression also purports to remake aspects of language and invites a reconsideration of the automatisms of everyday speech: the concept of 'defamiliarization', *ostranenie*, reached us via the Russian formalists early in the previous century, but we encounter formulations of this understanding since Aristotle.

Yet when Cicero (46 BC) introduces Western thought to the possibilities of translation in *De optimo genere oratorum*, this coincides with a discussion of the benefits of rendering public speaking from Greek into Latin. Cicero realizes that such exercises energize one's verbal imagination. Douglas Robinson (1992, pp. 15–55) points out that classical concepts of translation also contrast with the medieval Church's taboo on 'free' or unauthorized translation through the often restrictive, 'ecclesiastical' translation theories of Jerome and Augustine. Nevertheless, classical Greece enters translation thought via the Romans, as we note when Pliny writes to Fuscus Sallinator some 150 years later that

> this kind of exercise develops in one a precision and richness of vocabulary, a wide range of metaphor, and power of exposition, and, moreover, imitation of the best models leads to a like aptitude for original composition. At the same time, any point which might have been overlooked by a reader cannot escape the eye of a translator. All this cultivates perception and critical sense. (Robinson, 1992, p. 35)

We sense in Pliny a use of translation that is markedly poetic, and leads to improvement of style and form. In *Ars Poetica* (circa 20 BC), Horace opines on the retelling of existing myths and legends, that 'hard task' of treating 'what is common in a way of your own'. His admonition not to 'render word for word as a slavish translator' (*nec verbum verbo curabis reddere fidus interpres*) presages the difficult balance ideally sought by literary translation: re-energizing the original while involving the translator as a person.

The need to orient oneself within this process is particularly keenly discussed around the translation of poetic texts; it is dramatically visible when two poets are involved. Ben Jonson (1572–1637) returned repeatedly to a translation of Horace's guide to writing in a lifelong engagement with the Roman poet. In Jonson, we encounter a sustained consideration of 'imitation' – with reference to Horace but also in Jonson's own account of the art of poetry:

> The third requisite in our poet, or maker, is imitation, to be able to convert the substance, or riches of another poet, to his own use. To make choice of one excellent man above the rest, and so to follow him, till he grow very he, or so like him as the copy may be mistaken for the principal ... not to imitate servilely, as Horace saith, and catch at vices, for virtue: but, to draw forth out of the best, and choicest flowers with the bee, and turn all into honey, work it into one relish, and savour: make our imitation sweet: observe how the best writers have imitated, and follow them. (Jonson, 1892 [1640–1], pp. 3057–73)

Reflections on the act mature further in Dryden, whose own understanding of Jonson (*and* Horace) is evident in his oft-cited theory of the 'three heads' that translation can be reduced to (preface to translation of *Ovid's Epistles* (1680); see Dryden, 1992, p. 17):

> First, that of metaphrase, or turning an author word by word, and line by line, from one language into another. Thus, or near this manner, was Horace his *Art of Poetry* translated by Ben. Johnson. The second way is that of paraphrase, or translation with latitude, where the author is kept in view by the translator, so as never to be lost, but his words are not so strictly followed as his sense; and that too is admitted to be amplified, but not altered. Such is Mr. Waller's translation of Virgil's Fourth *Æneid*. The third way is that of imitation, where the translator (if now he has not lost that name) assumes the liberty not only to vary from the words and sense, but to forsake them both as he sees occasion; and taking only some general hints from the original, to run division on the groundwork, as he pleases.

Dryden expounds on the latter as the most extreme, arbitrary practice, which moves beyond the limits of translation, in terms, however, that still recognize that it can be poetically productive, an empathic calculation of sensibility far from its original environs:

> I take imitation of an author, in their sense, to be an endeavour of a later poet to write like one who has written before him, on the same subject; that is, not to translate his words, or to be confined to his sense, but only to set him as a pattern, and to write, as he supposes that author would have done, had he lived in our age, and in our country.   (Dryden, 1992, p. 19)

Dryden's defence of the second approach is representative of the balance that needs to be struck as the translator is caught between contrary forces and commitments.

The translation of poetry underlies a large proportion of theory on the art, accumulating across centuries through introductions, afterwords and other paratextual statements. Especially with poets like Arnold, Cowley, Dryden and Pope,

> the translator's preface comes of age, firstly as a prose essay in which to announce new translation manifestos, but also as a new form of writing, linked to the work it precedes, both radical and artificial. For the first time since the classical age, seventeenth- and early eighteenth-century statements also sought to explore a new vocabulary for the task they undertook, while articulating a new awareness – and respect – for the poetic skills it demanded.                    (Balmer, 2013, p. 24)

The early twentieth century saw wide agreement on Ezra Pound's role as 'the first broadly influential writer since at least the seventeenth century to bestow upon translation, over and above merely so-called original composition, an explicitly and generative, rather than a derivative and supplementary role in the process of literary culture formation' (Yao, 2002, p. 2). Isolated incidents, singular experiments and idiosyncratic approaches to translation did appear in the intervening three centuries; however, with Pound, we witness translation in co-ordination with a literary movement.

What follows are the systematization and contributions of late-twentieth-century translation theory: though, despite the useful clarity some theorists offer in considering movements in the translation process, whether it is the series of *Factors in a Theory of Poetic Translating* proposed by Robert de Beaugrande (1978) or, a little earlier, George Steiner's (1992 [1975]) four-stage 'hermeneutic motion', the translator's mind houses occurrences that are far less linear and programmatic than most conceptions of the act would have us believe. An early categorization by James Holmes (1969) on the forms that verse translation may adopt remains helpful, charting a range from 'mimetic' tendencies to more 'analogical' approaches where the translator pursues a functional parallel to what exists in the poetic tradition of the original, to the 'organic' (understood as when semantic material is allowed to realize its own poetic shape as the process of translation progresses), to what is 'deviant/extraneous', where the original form or content does not suggest the resulting form of the translation, or 'metapoem'. More recently, scholars like Theo Hermans (2007) further examine the self-reflexive potency of poetry translation especially along with the present-ness of the translator in the text.

## 24.2 From Pound to the Present

Pound's is an appropriative understanding of translation whereby the (poet-)translator may prioritize and amplify aspects of the original. Steven Yao (2002, p. 6) reminds us that, for modernist writers following Pound, translation constituted 'an integral part of the Modernist program of cultural renewal, a crucially important mode of writing distinct from, yet fundamentally interconnected with, the more traditionally esteemed modes of poetry and prose fiction'. This renewal more explicitly relies on quotation of texts, aiming to reflect a modern consciousness that is increasingly contradictory and multi-lingual. Translation becomes a form of criticism, even as modernist translation sought to produce a poetry that would operate in the present, as Pound's repeated instruction to reject pseudo-archaism suggests. The first decades of the twentieth century echo in today's practices, in that translators more consciously appraise an analogous experience for the modern reader, instead of static definitions of fidelity. We sense this in the work of modern poet-translators like Josephine Balmer who likens herself to

> ... an abstract painter, who does very, very close, detailed studies, figura-
> tive studies, before approaching their abstract work. So I would start with
> a literal translation. Then on the facing page of my big note book I would
> write down all the points that I've read in commentaries that might help,
> because you are trying to excavate meaning from the text and obviously
> that meaning is not static – it's fluid ... it gives you as a writer and as
> a translator a way in to start working on the text and I think that without
> scholarship, obviously, you wouldn't be able to do that.
>
> (Balmer and Hardwick, 2010, p. 2)

There is a range of translational responses to ancient originals across Balmer's work, from her translations of Sappho (1992) or those antholo-gized in *Classical Women Poets* (Balmer, 1996), to her rearrangement and even subversion of classical authors. In *Chasing Catullus: Poems, Translations and Transgressions* (Balmer, 2004), instances of found poetry and versions or partial translations from classical poets are juxtaposed with Balmer's own work. In *The Word for Sorrow* (Balmer, 2009), elements of family history encounter testimonies of soldiers from the Gallipoli campaign as well as the story of Catullus's exile in the Roman outpost of Tomis: translation powerfully communicates the likeness of human experiences across mil-lennia. Balmer's (2017) thematizing of a lost original by Aeschylus in *The Paths of Survival* creates spaces where our memory, retrieval or processing of a literary text can be as powerful as its original content. Balmer's theoretical work, especially *Piecing Together the Fragments* (Balmer, 2013), further investigates examples of classical poetry inflecting later authors.

Following Pound, a sense of translation as experiment develops, which does not exclude non-poets from translating but necessitates a constant problematization of the act. Examples here suggest a range of ways in which the relationship between poetry and translation has been 'inscribed' in the century that follows Pound's *Cathay* (1915) proceeding from the notes and literals of Ernest Fellonosa, or Pound's 1911 version of the Anglo-Saxon *The Seafarer*, or his *Homage to Sextus Propertius* (1919), which adapts the first-century Roman elegist to include a reflection on the 'imbe-cility' of British Empire and the carnage surrounding the modern poet-translator, as World War I unfolds. Recent surveys of this field, such as Kozak and Hickman (2019), dedicate an entire group of essays to Poundian projects and the ways they show more liberal translation work coinciding with reception and personal literary preoccupation.

Among such refigurations is Christopher Logue's *War Music*, a forceful editing and re-energizing of Homer's *Iliad* (see Nikolaou, 2017, pp. 17–40). Following a radio version of rhapsody XIV (published as *Patrocleia*,1962), Logue produced several other 'instalments' between 1967 and 2005. We read of armies that hum like power station outflow cables, or warriors' shields with as many arrows as microphones on politicians' stands. Steiner (1992 [1975], p. 370) notes how the translator in a case like this 'may telescope time violently so as to produce a shock of contemporaneity ...

[and] can modernize not only to induce a feeling of immediacy but in order to advance his own cause as a writer'; Logue's end notes list anachronisms judiciously positioned across his text. In contrast, Simon Armitage sees no need for the extremes of anachronism – his *Odyssey* 'is not set on a housing estate in Salford' (Armitage, 2008 [2006], p. vi), though he points out that 'we should not be surprised if the *Odyssey* rings with echoes and resonances of our contemporary world. Such is the power and purpose of myth.' This suggests again how, in the wake of modernism, the act of reading visibly enters the translation. During the next decades, (classical) translation is constantly rethought and renamed: early on, Logue spoke of a work 'dependent on' the *Iliad*. Logue's (1995) *The Husbands* is 'an account' of Books 3 and 4; the next-to-last volume, published in 2003, is subtitled 'the first battle scenes of Homer's *Iliad* rewritten', while *Cold Calls* (2005) is '*War Music* continued'.

We have grown to acknowledge a poet's interest in translation, as evident in blurbs and endorsements; the back cover of Ted Hughes's rendering of Aeschylus's *The Oresteia* explains that his '"acting version" of the trilogy is itself a great performance, recasting the Greek original in light of one of the themes of Hughes's own poetry, that of the survivor's guilt and remorse and need to grasp at significance after a death in the family' (Aeschylus, trans. Ted Hughes, 2000). But the posthumous publication of *Selected Translations* (Hughes, 2006) also highlights Hughes's long-term commitment to the art, from the dissident poetry of János Pilinszky, to rendering the Hebrew of Yehuda Amichai, to Pushkin's 'The Prophet', the last poem Hughes worked on. Hughes's sometimes-literalistic approach, and statements that he did little more than 'install some pace and rhythm' to the notes he was handed, belie a detailed and arduous process. Between a starting point which bears striking similarity to Logue's, namely 'Everyman's Odyssey' (1960) and later emblematic works, such as the accessible and popular *Tales from Ovid* (1997), perhaps Hughes's most important contribution is his co-founding, in 1965 with Daniel Weissbort, of the journal *Modern Poetry in Translation*. Hughes writes in 1982 that, from the start, he and Weissbort 'had a general notion of making familiar to English readers the whole range of contemporary possibilities in poetry – in so far as translation can convey any idea of such things. We weren't beyond the hope of influencing our own writers in a productive way' (Hughes, 2006, p. 204). Several other journals, such as *Agni*, *Exchanges*, *Metamorphoses* and *Asymptote*, adopt a similarly committed stance to the publication of translations, and dedicated publishers also exist, for instance Istros Books, Arc Publications or Banipal. Given the much smaller and specialized audience that reads poetry (and even less, translated poetry), the activity is often further encouraged through sponsored grants, bursaries, even state-funded publication programmes and beyond the state level even, as with the European Commission's 'Creative Europe' initiative for the translation and promotion of literary works.

An engagement with translating often points to a narrative of the poet as person. Seamus Heaney considers *Beowulf* to be part of his 'voice-right' as he recalls Joseph Brodsky who 'once said that poets' biographies are present in the sounds they make' (Heaney, 1999, p. xxiii). Heaney defines an 'erotics of composition' as that 'prereflective excitation and orientation, some sense that your own little verse-craft can dock safe and sound at the big quay of the language. And this is as true for translators as it is for poets attempting original work' (Heaney, 1999, p. xxvi). For Heaney (1999, especially pp. xxiv–xxviii), roots of words resurfacing in Irish speech allowed him to connect with the language of the original; favourite words, used in his own poetry, also surface in drafts of his translation (see Heaney, 1999/2000, p. 29). There are other instances of translation as indirect autobiography as well – a posthumously published version of book XI of the *Aeneid* (Heaney, 2016) originates in work that started three decades earlier, after the death of Heaney's father.

As already seen, classical writing has consistently offered paths into translation as experiment. More recently, Anne Carson's work is a particularly prescient example, from her assertive investigation of textual absences in *If Not, Winter: Fragments of Sappho* (Carson, 2003), to her composite, 'non foundational' *An Oresteia* (Carson, 2009) which collates works on the myth cycle by Aeschylus, Sophocles and Euripides, charting developments in theme and stagecraft, to her poignant, autobiographical interrogation of a poem by Catullus through exhaustive translation in *Nox* (Carson, 2010), or the dialogue with the illustrations and handwriting that defines a retold Sophocles in *Antigonick* (Carson, 2012). Such radical realignments would be difficult to contemplate before Pound. The same applies to the poetic sensibility that infuses Carson's paratexts, directing solutions to translational problems or amplifying ancient content through interstitial use of textual genres or referencing modern art (for instance, the paintings of Francis Bacon, our complex relationship with the photographic image). Modernist precedent is apparent in the ways in which boundaries between critical function and poetic expression sometimes come into question, how the translating act manifestly leads to further verse, as in Carson's (2015) note to her translation of *Bakkhai* (pp. 7–12; 'i wish i were two dogs then i could play with me').

Poetic translation also means formal invention: Alice Oswald's version of the *Iliad* is a prime example. *Memorial* (Oswald, 2011) starts as an image of its title: a list, eight pages long, of capitalized names. Then these become surrounded by a simple structure of stanza and twice-told simile. In alternating those Homeric similes that convey manifold transformations in the natural world with the names and brief glimpses of soldiers on the battlefield, Oswald (2011, p. 2) also consciously combines two modes: 'my "biographies" are paraphrases of the Greek, my similes are translations', she notes in her Introduction. This contributes to a condensed, 'bipolar' poem that also depends on 'the thematic amplification that epic simile conveys.

Oswald uses it in the spirit of Homer as a tool of contrast set apart from narrative structure' (Rosenthal, 2013, n.p.).

In different ways, the rearrangements of Homer by Logue and Oswald deploy translation to remind us of the history and culture behind any literary value posited later; of how the actuality and true cost of war becomes dimmed by the artifice of poetic language – and by the subsequent layers of faithful translation. Oswald has also performed and recited *Memorial*, intensifying a sense of returning to a preliterate, oral tradition; and to an experience comparable to that of ancient audiences. Beyond subtitling *Memorial* as 'excavation' of the *Iliad*, Oswald (2011, p. 2) noted that her aim was 'translucence rather than translation'. Such conscious renaming of the act characteristically comes after modernism. In *Nobody* (Oswald, 2019), 'a collage of water-stories, taken mostly from the *Odyssey*' as her publisher describes it, Oswald's rhythm and reasoning recall the very element surrounding Odysseus for most of his journey.

## 24.3 Poetry and (Un)translatability

We have seen that for the modernist poets after Pound, translation constituted a 'crucially important mode of writing'. In the anthology *Poem into Poem* (1970), Steiner intimates that 'poetic translation is not only a living spark, a flow of energy between past and present and between cultures … poetic translation plays a unique role inside the translator's own speech. It drives inward' (p. 27). Later commentators confirm this 'inward drive'. Marilyn Gaddis Rose, for instance, argues that translating brings us 'into the literary work in the usual sense of immersion and identification'. (Gaddis Rose, 1997, p. 2). Somatic understandings of translation emerge in the work of Douglas Robinson (especially 2001) and even form aspects of 'habitus' orientations in translation theory, which is also the bedrock of some later, sociological approaches. According to Robinson (1991, p. 260), '[t]ranslators' personal experiences – emotions, motivations, attitudes, associations – are not only allowable in the formation of a working [translation], they are indispensable'. But, most importantly, we consistently observe this sense in accounts of the experience of translators, often expressed in terms of bodily responses, or in a language of possession or metempsychosis. Kate Briggs in *This Little Art* simply affirms that 'I read with my body, I read and move to translate with my body, and my body is not the same as yours' (Briggs, 2017, p. 107). This recalls Clive Scott's view of translation as a phenomenological process, 'in-textual' (as opposed to 'post-textual' or interpretative). For Scott, reading is 'the process of activating the text' (Scott, 2000, p. 184) through which 'the reader actualises or embodies her individual experience of the text' (Scott, 2012, p. 2).

Another translation theorist, Rosemary Waldrop, has emphasized that she does not deal dispassionately with a text but with another 'aesthetic personality'; the translator's first task in this context is to 'find the genetic code of the work . . . to get from the surface to the seed which, in our terms, would mean getting close to the nucleus of creative energy that is at the beginning of the poem' (Waldrop, 1989, p. 43).

Indeed, publications such as *Translation and Creativity: Perspectives on Creative Writing and Translation Studies*, edited by Eugenia Loffredo and Manuela Perteghella, and *The Translator as Writer*, edited by Susan Bassnett and Peter Bush, both published in 2006, as well as *Translating Selves: Experience and Identity between Languages and Literatures* (2008), edited by Paschalis Nikolaou and Maria-Venetia Kyritsi, helped shift the focus of attention further to the translator's subjectivity and creativity, which is paramount in challenging commonly held assumptions about the untranslatability of poetry. Mireille Gansel recounts her first experience of translation and the possibilities it offered when she encountered the existence of four different words in Hungarian to express a concept related to 'beloved'. She says, in Ros Schwartz's English words, '[t]hose four words opened up another world, another language that would one day be born within my own language – and the conviction that no word that speaks of what is human is untranslatable' (Gansel, 2017/18, p. 4).

Untranslatability poses challenges not only at the linguistic level, that is, with the words in one language expressing seemingly 'untranslatable' concepts, but also at a textual level, in the impossibility of separating form and content, particularly felt in poetic discourse. This understanding is axiomatic, more than it is absolute: for there may be stretches of poetic prose that will be denser, and more literary, than a given poem. Edith Grossman in *Why Translation Matters*, for example, refers to artful prose (Grossman, 2010, p. 92) and likens it to poetry. The sense is further compounded by the compactness of most poetic expression: rhythm and musicality, imagery and sound associations occur in a usually very limited space that likely disables prospects of replicating the same effects without veering towards exegesis and elongation. Distances between cultures and time periods notwithstanding, any translation process that addresses such texts will, at the very least, discover that the syntactic, lexical and formal choices that achieved certain aesthetic effects and emotional responses in the reader of the original must somehow rebalance, recombine. The translator is faced with a series of questions: to what purpose and emphasis should these elements be recombined? To intimate what the original meant for its intended audience, in an approach that will likely sacrifice poeticity for clarity (often using commentary)? Or towards a poem in the target language that underlines literariness even if it means that the source poem will be more 'freely translated'? This dilemma has haunted translation theory since Cicero, but in environs of poetry the stakes are highest, and the textual results (as well as accounts describing them) more proclamatory and intense. In poetry, the contrast is more pronounced between a theory that nearly forbids the undertaking or enumerates defeats, and a practice that is both fruitful and profuse. It serves to explain the range of strategies we encounter, from Roman Jakobson's assertion that only 'creative transposition' is possible when it comes to poetry, to the severe literalism of Nabokov's (2004, pp. 115–27) *Eugene Onegin*, where never-ending paratext supports a re-articulation from the Russian. At the same time, the difficulty and extremes described above testify to experiments – less often instigated in prose translation – and to such outliers as Celia and Louis Zukofsky's homophonic *Catullus* (Zukofsky and Zukofsky, 1969). Such translation may variously repurpose or resituate its original, rather than reattempt that once-existing balance of form and content.

Some translation theorists have reached towards hybrid projects. Susan Bassnett's dialogue with the poetry of Alejandra Pizarnik in *Exchanging Lives* (Bassnett and Pizarnik, 2002) includes a bilingual presentation of short poems from the Argentinian poet's collection *Árbol de Diana* (Pizarnik, 1962), followed by the titular section, in which she juxtaposes a personal selection of poems by Pizarnik with her own, thus illustrating distinctions as well as a connection gradually forming between poet and translator. The third part presents poems that, Bassnett explains, 'I would never have written had I not been inspired by the task of translating Pizarnik. The experience of freeing Pizarnik's poetry and recreating it in English helped me free my own poetry' (Bassnett and Pizarnik, 2002, p. 9). In a 'postscript', Bassnett arrives at a rendering of a three-line poem totalling six words of which three are 'alejandra'; but the preceding alchemy of voices necessitates the poet's name being replaced by 'susan' and 'susanna' (Bassnett and Pizarnik, 2002, p. 84). The very structure of *Exchanging Lives* tells the story of translational encounter and illustrates what Bassnett describes as a 'dialogic metaphor', which foregrounds translation as an empowering form of writing that fosters reflexivity and creativity (see Bassnett, 2006, and Kadiu, 2019).

The original formulation in Spanish of Pizarnik's poem 'Sólo un nombre' on which Bassnett's postcript is based further illustrates the interconnectedness of poetic form and meaning: this three-line poem is *doing what it says*:

> Sólo un nombre
>
> alejandra alejandra
>   debajo estoy yo
>     alejandra         *(Pizarnik, 2000, p. 65)*

> Just a name
>
> alejandra alejandra
>   beneath I am me
>     alejandra         *(Rossi, 2019, p. 29)*

Rossi (2007) argues that 'just a name' is not just about a name. Pizarnik was called 'Flora', known as 'Blímele' among the Eastern European Jewish immigrants who settled in a suburb of Buenos Aires in the 1930s, and then chose to call herself 'Alejandra'. The poet and critic Tamara Kamenszain (2000) claims that the repetition of 'alejandra alejandra' is already the start of versification, as it joins the two names (through the aspiration of the final and first 'a') to produce a heptasyllable, which acts as the girl's christening as poet. The poem becomes a new place where the poet rises into being: *debajo estoy yo*: the poet lies below, underwriting every signature of the one who is in the world. Yet, this poetic christening also functions as an epitaph, as hinted at by *debajo estoy yo*. This is precisely how Belarusian poet Valzhyna Mort (2020, p. 52) reads this poem in *The Poetry Review*: '[w]hat I observe and learn in Pizarnik's work is her visionary ability to see the dead-other in herself'. Indeed, Mort links Pizarnik's narrow escape from death from the Rovno ghetto to Marianne Hirsch's (2012) concept of postmemory; an insistent thematic concern with death becomes emblematic of a generation's trauma while 'Pizarnik's memory is a memory of a would-have-been life' (Mort, 2020, p. 51).

But the poem also presents a mirror image of the persona through the way in which the first person singular pronoun *yo* is placed after the verb *estar* (to be) conjugated to *estoy*: est**oy yo.** Given Pizarnik's thematic concerns with mirrors, with the splitting of the self, this mirror effect is no coincidence but an example of the close bond between form and meaning in poetry, and of iconicity (see Boase-Beier, 2020, pp. 119–20). There is no way of recreating this effect totally in English, but Rossi's translation of this line 'beneath I am me' is an attempt at doing so, and an improvement on her previous version: 'it's me underneath' (Rossi, 2010, p. 10) in which she hinted at the duality of the persona expressed through the introduction of the objective pronoun and reproduced the assonance in the repetition of the /o/ sound in the source text, by the repetition of the /iː/ sound (in 'me' and 'underneath').

Bassnett is not the first to remind us of the proximities of theorizing poetry translation with its practice: James Holmes was himself a celebrated translator from the Dutch, among others of Martinus Nijhoff's (2010 [1934]) modernist poem *Awater*, itself considered a response to T. S. Eliot's *The Waste Land*. And Lawrence Venuti, introducing his 2009 translation of Ernest Farrés's 2006 collection *Edward Hopper* (Farrés, 2009), only a few years after its appearance in Catalan, links us with his own theoretical bend, as he translates into 'the globally hegemonic language' (p. xi), especially given that the original itself avoids Spanish in favour of the poet's native tongue. 'Bearing witness' to Catalan literature and its value, this necessarily bilingual edition sees the translating act as one of 'linguistic and cultural ecology' (Farrés, 2009, p. xii).

Not least through these constant connections to scholarship, translation of poetry is a highly creative activity. Indeed, as Boase-Beier (2011, p. 53) puts it, 'it is impossible to conceive of translation, or any other sort of writing, as merely reproducing or representing without creative interference'. Worth citing also is Kirsten Malmkjær's (2020) *Translation and Creativity*, which provides a comprehensive study of the role of creativity in all translation processes.

## 24.4   Forms and Influences: Translation and the Circulation of Poetry

In this section we will look at how anthologies of translated poetry and retranslations of classical poems create a space where fossilized notions and attitudes towards translated poetry can be contested.

*Sappho through English Poetry* (Jay and Lewis, 1996) is an illuminating anthology of the sensibility of an ancient poet as it courses through anglophone writers; it covers nearly half a millennium but also includes varied expressions of influence, tellingly split into 'Versions: Translations and Imitations' and 'Representations: Myths, Meditations and Travesties'. Stuart Gillespie's (2011) *English Translation and Classical Reception: Towards a New Literary History* has examined the prevalence of classical authors within modern poetry, and the difficulty in locating cut-off points between translation, imitation and more transgressive practices – just as we detect it in the sections devised by Jay and Lewis. When it comes to poetry practitioners, any intended work of salvage might approximate tribute, reimagining or recontextualizing. Take 'Third Epitaph', which closes the anthology by Jay and Lewis; in fact, this is not a version of Sappho but is drawn from Pierre Louÿs's *Chanson de Bilitis*, appearing in French in 1894, purporting to be a translation from the ancient Greek of a contemporary of Sappho, the Cypriot courtesan Bilitis. So, in this case, Olga Broumas and Jane Miller essentially translate *imitations* of Sappho, their source text already a pseudo-translation. The practice is not new; the example better known is James Macpherson's fictitious translation of 'The Poems of Ossian' from 1760 onwards.

Of course, one need not start from such special cases to grasp the widening of poetic genres via the practising of translation. Traditional forms often originate from the structure and speech patterns of a given language, become established in a place and time, then spread: the economies of the Japanese haiku, the argument and resolution that comes to us with the fourteen lines of the Italian sonnet, the logic of interwoven quatrains defining the Malaysian pantoum – all now belong to world poetry. Further, poetry translation is often sanctioned as a mode of cultural rescue-work, publishing and delineating a community's identity; an anthology of poems from the Uyghur Autonomous Region may double as political action; to translate Aboriginal or Black Australian poets is to record and transmit the expression of a largely oral culture. Whenever such attempts occur, there is the risk of appropriation, that simultaneous voicing and silencing that often defines evolving dynamics between minor and major languages. Sentiments of wonder can easily veer into views of superiority (FitzGerald's classic rendering of the *Rubáiyát of Omar Khayyám*, published in 1859, was inspired by a sense that 'these Persians *do* want a little *Art* to shape them' (see FitzGerald, 1980, p. 261)).

On occasion, this idea of dialogue is poignantly encapsulated. Introducing *Volta: A Multilingual Anthology*, where one of his own poems is relayed into ninety-two languages, Richard Berengarten (2009) is very much aware of a theme that inhabits the original:

> the setting and take-off point for the poem 'Volta' is an evening walk, a promenade, in a Greek seaside town, as the sun is setting on the horizon. That is: a self-turning, as day is turning into night and as light is evening itself out into darkness. The act of poetic translation too is a 'volta'. And translation involves a turning that is at least double, for it consists of both a return and a departure.                                (Berengarten, 2009, n.p.)

The source of 'Volta' is itself of import – belonging as it does to the sequence of poems *Black Light: Poems in Memory of George Seferis* (Berengarten, 1995 [1983]) resulting from Berengarten's brief stay in Greece and subsequent close relationship with its culture, as well as his sustained reading of one of its key twentieth-century poets. Such a publication confirms the fellowship and inspiration that occur as poets read, then write about, or translate, each other. The Greek poet Nasos Vayenas further conveys this sense: 'In translating poetry the original is the experience, and the process of translation is the poetic act' (Vayenas, 2010, p. 131). Another, longer aphorism is particularly persuasive in describing those workings of influence alongside translation:

> A meaningful theory of influence cannot be formulated if it is not supported by a meaningful theory of translation, because influence between two poets who write in different languages necessitates translation. In the last resort, the things that influence a poet are not lines in the original language, but those of the original transported into the poet's own language. No poet can take a poetic image from a foreign poet unless that image is put into words first, unless a rhythm of one's own language is instilled into it. Whether a poet will appropriate the lines of a foreign poem depends on how the lines of that poem sound within the fabric and rhythms of the poet's own language. This does not mean that foreign influence necessitates a written translation. Each influence depends on there being a translation, whether this takes on paper, or in the poet's mind.
>
> (If the translation of poetry is an art, and if poetic influence requires translation, then such influence does not undermine originality. A foreign poet's text is raw material for a poet, just as is any other.)
>
> (Vayenas, 2010, p. 131f.)

Vayenas's own output is resplendent with instances of such work; especially notable is his translating of three poems by Gavin Ewart alongside
seven of his own original poems in a 1997 edition because it both serves to
introduce the British poet to Greek readers and simultaneously reveals
how integral Ewart's sardonic tone and examinations of pretentious behaviour and even methods of alluding to, or parodying, other poets have
been to Vayenas's own early work.

Such linkages and dialogues between poetic voices and translational
modes are documented in anthologies and selections. Well known is the
example of Robert Lowell (1958), whose *Imitations*, by his own admission,
'should be first read as a sequence, one voice running through many
personalities, contrasts and repetitions'. More recently, in *Adaptations*,
Derek Mahon (2006) defends 'the imaginative, recreative (and recrea-
tional)' practice of the title, and notes in his introduction that the effort
of 'making the original read like a poem in English[] is an equally venerable
tradition' to that of properly translating: poets 'use it to keep the engine
ticking over. Impertinence or poetic license, the mode has been around too
long to need excuses' (Mahon, 2006, p. 11). Christopher Reid (2003) breaks
down the workings of influence even more clearly and portrays the essential dialogue between poets in the title of his book *For and After*. Containing
poems dedicated to fellow poets, or versions ranging from Horace to
Leopardi and Tsvetayeva, the volume witnesses the boundaries between
the two intentions collapsing. Projects like *For and After* or, more recently,
*Into English: Poems, Translations, Commentaries* (Collins and Prufer, 2017) more
broadly communicate the twin impulses behind many collections of
poetry that also house works of translation: to record formative experiences of literature, while turning back one's maturing voice onto the
influences that partly made it what it is. Many poets have reflected on
such undertakings, with often strong opinions, as in the case of Don
Paterson, at the end of *Orpheus: A Version of Rilke*: 'if we are not prepared
to make a choice between honoring the word or the spirit, we are likely to
come away with nothing. Or, perhaps between method and goal: in translation, the integrity of the means justifies the end; in the version, the
integrity of the end justifies the means' (Paterson, 2006, p. 81). It is not
just critical comment that is stimulated but creative ideas too. Paterson
then includes a meditative prose parable (itself 'after Nicanor Parra') in *40
Sonnets* (Paterson, 2015) titled 'The Version'.

Retranslation redirects attention to the original. For instance, introducing her own rendering of *The Odyssey*, Emily Wilson reminds us of the
ways in which gender is situated in translation theories and aphorisms,
and how '[t]he gendered metaphor of the "faithful" translation, whose
worth is always secondary to that of a male-authored original, acquires
a particular edge in the context of a translation by a woman of *The Odyssey*,
a poem that is deeply invested in female fidelity and male dominance'
(Wilson, 2018, p. 86). She locates ways in which translation, of epic poetry

in this case, can remain a powerful mode of implicit criticism: 'Unlike many modern translators, I have avoided describing the Cyclops with words such as "savage," which carry with them the legacy of early modern and modern forms of colonialism – a legacy that is, of course, anachronistic in the world of *The Odyssey*' (Wilson, 2018, p. 88).

Efforts at foregrounding the translation process have yielded volumes of translated poetry in which approaches to translation are highlighted in paratexts which are themselves innovative ways of presenting the traditional translator's 'introduction' or 'note'. In the 2016 anthology *Currently & Emotion*, Sophie Collins presents the reader with an enticing collection of translated poems: 'all of the texts in this book have been included for their potential to challenge dominant perceptions of poetry translation, whether due to the source texts from which they derive (in terms of their coming from under-represented languages and cultures) or through the kinds of strategies applied' (Collins, 2016, p. 20). Among the poems are, for example, interlingual renderings of Chaucer's tales by Caroline Bergvall and versions by Don Mee Choi of Korean folktales extracted from her collection *The Morning News Is Exciting* (Choi, 2010). These examples are emblematic of the anthology's concerns: to present experiments in poetry translation to challenge the fixedness of language and national identity. Indeed, the fluidity of language, and of national borders, is brought to the surface: 'But do we need a second language to translate?' asks Erín Moure. The answer is simply that '[w]e always already speak a second language: we call it our mother tongue. Our first language is not this tongue; it is silence, the silence before speaking . . . .] All of us, though, retain that language in our body, in our ability to feel fear, uncertainty, passion . . .' (Moure, 2016 [2013], p. 29).

In her translations of Dutch poet Lieke Marsman (2019), Collins goes a step further in presenting her translation approach in the form of a letter to her author and friend: 'Translator's Note: Dear Lieke'. This space allows her to challenge the idea of 'fidelity' by proposing 'intimacy':

> As a proposal for a new ideal of translation, 'intimacy' began with the observation that, while 'fidelity' implies the presence of a primary source of power, 'intimacy' indicates a mutual, consensual and willing exchange between two or more subjects without referencing (an) authority at all. And so intimacy is about developing a sincere engagement with the source text, author and culture, about 'getting close'.          (Collins, 2019, p. 50)

Collins's citation of the work of Gayatri Chakravorty Spivak on critical intimacy follows: it is the foundation for the development of her own concept of 'intimacy' but it is also, in the case of Collins's translations of Marsman's poems, a further instance of how closely a translator reads: '[intimacy] seemed a particularly fitting model for your work, Lieke', says Collins (2019, p. 53), 'because there is a deep intimacy in the way *you* seek to connect with *your* audience'.

# Bibliography

Aeschylus. (2000). *The Oresteia: A New Translation by Ted Hughes*. New York: Farrar, Straus and Giroux.

Armitage, S. (2008 [2006]). Introduction. In *The Odyssey: A Dramatic Retelling of Homer's Epic*. New York: W.W. Norton & Company, pp. v–vi.

Balmer, J. (1996). *Classical Women Poets*. Newcastle upon Tyne: Bloodaxe Books.

Balmer, J. (2004). *Chasing Catullus: Poems, Translations and Transgressions*. Newcastle upon Tyne: Bloodaxe Books.

Balmer. J. (2009). *The Word for Sorrow*. Cambridge: Salt.

Balmer, J. (2013). *Piecing Together the Fragments: Translating Classical Verse, Creating Contemporary Poetry*. Oxford: Oxford University Press.

Balmer, J. (2017). *The Paths of Survival*. Bristol: Shearsman Books.

Balmer, J., and Hardwick, L. (2010). Josephine Balmer, Poet and Translator, in Interview with Lorna Hardwick (Oxford, 17 May 2010). *Practitioners' Voices in Classical Reception Studies* 2, 1–10. Available at www.open.ac.uk/arts/research/pvcrs/2010/balmer.Bassnett, S. (2006). Writing and translating. In S. Bassentt and P. Bush, eds., *The Translator as Writer*. London: Continuum, pp. 173–83.

Bassnett S. (2011). The power of poetry. In *Reflections on Translation*. Clevedon, UK: Multilingual Matters, pp. 164–8.

Bassnett, S., and Bush, P., eds. (2006). *The Translator as Writer*. London: Continuum.

Bassnett, S., and Pizarnik, A. (2002). *Exchanging Lives: Poems and Translations*. Leeds: Peepal Tree.

Berengarten, R. (1995 [1983]). *Black Light: Poems in Memory of George Seferis*, 3rd ed. Norwich: The King of Hearts.

Berengarten, R. (2009). Border/lines: An introduction. *International Literary Quarterly*, 9 [Volta: A Multilingual Anthology]. Available at http://interlitq .org/issue9/berengarten/job.php.

Boase-Beier, J. (2011). *A Critical Introduction to Translation Studies*. London: Continuum.

Boase-Beier, J. (2020 [2006]). *Translation and Style*. 2nd ed. London/New York: Routledge.

Briggs, K. (2017). *This Little Art*. London: Fitzcarraldo Editions.

Carson, A. (2003). *If Not, Winter: Fragments of Sappho*. London: Virago.

Carson, A., trans. (2009). *An Oresteia*. New York: Faber and Faber.

Carson, A. (2010). *Nox*. New York: New Directions.

Carson, A. (2012). *Antigonick*. Tarset, Northumberland: Bloodaxe Books.

Carson, A. (2015). 'i wish i were two dogs then i could play with me'. In *Euripides, Bakkhai: A New Version by Anne Carson*. New York: New Directions, pp. 7–12.

Choi, D. M. (2010). *The Morning News Is Exciting*. Indiana: Action Books.

Collins, S., ed. (2016). *Currently & Emotion: Translations*. London: Test Centre.

Collins, S. (2019). Translator's note: Dear Lieke. In L. Marsman, *The Following Scan Will Last Five Minutes*. Liverpool: Liverpool University Press, pp. 41–53.

Collins, M., and Prufer, K., eds. (2017). *Into English: Poems, Translations, Commentaries*. Minneapolis, MN: Graywolf Press.

De Beaugrande, R. (1978). *Factors in a Theory of Poetic Translating*. Assen: Van Gorcum.

Dryden, J. (1992). On translation. In R. Schulte and J. Biguenet, eds., *Theories of Translation: An Anthology of Essays from Dryden to Derrida*. Chicago: University of Chicago Press, pp. 17–31.

Eliot, T. S. (1965). *Dante*. 2nd ed. London: Faber and Faber.

Farrés, E. (2009). *Edward Hopper*, trans. L. Venuti. Minneapolis, MN: Graywolf Press.

FitzGerald, E. (1980). *The Letters of Edward FitzGerald*, eds. A. M. Terhune and A. B. Terhune, 4 vols. Princeton, NJ: Princeton University Press.

Gaddis Rose, M. (1997). *Translation and Literary Criticism: Translation as Analysis*. Manchester: St Jerome.

Gansel, M. (2017/18). *Translation as Transhumance*, trans. R. Schwartz. London: Les Fugitives.

Gillespie, S. (2011). *English Translation and Classical Reception: Towards a New Literary History*. Malden, MA: Wiley-Blackwell.

Grossman, E. (2010). *Why Translation Matters*. New Haven, CT: Yale University Press.

Heaney, S. (1999). Introduction. In *Beowulf: A New Translation*. London: Faber and Faber, pp. ix–xxx.

Heaney, S. (1999/2000). Fretwork: On translating Beowulf. *In Other Words*, **13–14**, 23–33.

Heaney, S. (2016). *Aeneid: Book VI*. London: Faber and Faber.

Hermans, T. (2007). *The Conference of the Tongues*. Manchester: St Jerome.

Hirsch, M. (2012). *The Generation of Postmemory: Writing and Visual Culture after the Holocaust*. New York: Columbia University Press.

Holmes, J. (1969). Forms and verse translation and the translation of verse form. *Babel*, **15**(4), 195–201.

Hughes, T. (2006). *Selected Translations*. London: Faber and Faber.

Jay, P., and Lewis, C., eds. (1996). *Sappho through English Poetry*. London: Anvil Press Poetry.

Jonson, B. (1892 [1640–1]). *Discoveries Made upon Men and Matter and Some Poems*. London: Cassell and Company.

Kadiu, S. (2019). *Reflective Translation Studies: Translation and Critical Reflection*. London: UCL Press.

Kamenzsain, T. (2000). *Historias de amor y otros ensayos sobre poesía*. Buenos Aires: Paidós.

Kozak, L., and Hickman, M., eds. (2019). *The Classics in Modernist Translation*. London: Bloomsbury Academic.

Loffredo, E., and Perteghella, M., eds. (2006). *Translation and Creativity: Perspectives on Creative Writing and Translation Studies*. London: Continuum.

Logue, C. (1962). *Patrocleia*. London: Scorpion Press.

Logue, C. (1995). *The Husbands: An Account of Books 3 and 4 of Homer's* Iliad. New York: Farrar, Straus and Giroux.

Logue, C. (2003). *All Day Permanent Red: The First Battle Scenes of Homer's* Iliad *Rewritten*. New York: Farrar, Straus and Giroux.

Logue, C. (2005). *Cold Calls: War Music Continued*. London: Faber and Faber.

Lowell, R. (1990 [1958]). *Imitations*. New York: Farrar, Straus and Giroux.

Mahon, D. (2006). *Adaptations*. Loughcrew: The Gallery Press.

Malmkjær, K. (2020). *Translation and Creativity*. London: Routledge.

Mort, V. (2020). Be a comfort for the dead little girls. *Poetry Review*, **110**(3), 48–53.

Moure, E. (2016 [2013]). But do we need a second language to translate? In S. Collins, ed., *Currently & Emotion: Translations*. London: Test Centre.

Nabokov, V. (2004). Onegin in English. In L. Venuti, ed., *The Translation Studies Reader*. 2nd ed. London/New York: Routledge, pp. 115–27.

Nijhoff, M. (2010 [1934]). *Awater*. Ed. T. Möhlmann, trans. D. Cokmer, J. S. Holmes and D. van der Vaat. London: Anvil Press Poetry.

Nikolaou, P. (2017). 'The *Iliad* suits you': Christopher Logue's Homer – from *Patrocleia* (1962) to the posthumous edition of *War Music*. In *The Return of Pytheas: Scenes from British and Greek Poetry in Dialogue*. Bristol: Shearsman Books, pp. 17–40.

Nikolaou, P., and Kyritsi, M.-V., eds. (2008). *Translating Selves: Experience and Identity between Languages and Literatures*. London: Continuum.

Oswald, A. (2011). *Memorial*. London: Faber and Faber.

Oswald, A. (2019). *Nobody: A Hymn to the Sea*. London: Jonathan Cape.

Paterson, D. (2006). Fourteen Notes on the Version. In *Orpheus: A Version of Rilke's* Die Sonette an Orpheus. London: Faber and Faber, pp. 73–84.

Paterson, D. (2015). *40 Sonnets*. London: Faber and Faber.

Pizarnik, A. (1962). *Árbol de Diana*. Buenos Aires: Sur.

Pizarnik, A. (2000). *Poesía completa*. Barcelona: Lumen.

Plath, S. (2000 [1962/1977]). A comparison. In *Johnny Panic and the Bible of Dreams: Short Stories, Prose and Diary Excerpts*. London: Harper Perennial, pp. 56–8.

Poe, E. (1850). The poetic principle. *Home Journal*, **36**(238), 31 August, 1 (col. 3).

Reid, C. (2003). *For and After*. London: Faber and Faber.

Robinson, D. (1991). *The Translator's Turn*. Baltimore/London: Johns Hopkins University Press.

Robinson, D. (1992). Classical theories of translation from Cicero to Aulus Gellius. *TcT*, **7**, 15–55.

Robinson, D. (2001). *Who Translates? Translator Subjectivities Beyond Reason*. Albany, NY: State University of New York Press.

Rosenthal, M. (2013) Alice Oswald's Memorial and the reinvention of translation. *Kenyon Review* (Fall). Available at https://kenyonreview.org/kr-online-issue/2013-fall/selections/memorial-by-alice-oswald-738439/.

Rossi, C. (2007). Translating the translation of subjectivity. In F. J. Mackintosh and K. Posso, eds., *Árbol de Alejandra: Pizarnik Reassessed*. Woodbridge: Tamesis, pp. 130–47.

Rossi, C., trans. (2010). *Selected Poems of Alejandra Pizarnik*. Hove: Waterloo Press.

Rossi, C., trans. (2019). *The Last Innocence and the Lost Adventures* by Alejandra Pizarnik. Brooklyn: Ugly Duckling Presse.

Sappho (1992). *Poems and Fragments*, trans. J. Balmer. Newcastle upon Tyne: Bloodaxe Books.

Scott, C. (2000). *Translating Baudelaire*. Exeter: University of Exeter Press.

Scott, C. (2012). *Literary Translation and the Rediscovery of Reading*. Cambridge: Cambridge University Press.

Steiner, G., ed. (1970). *Poem into Poem: World Poetry in Modern Verse Translation*. Harmondsworth: Penguin.

Steiner, G. (1992 [1975]). *After Babel: Aspects of Language and Translation*. 2nd ed. Oxford: Oxford University Press.

Vayenas, N. (2010). Eight positions on the translation of poetry. In *The Perfect Order: Selected Poems 1974–2010*. London: Anvil Press Poetry, pp. 130–2.

Waldrop, R. (1989). Joy of the Demiurge. In J. Biguenet and R. Schulte, eds., *The Craft of Translation*. Chicago: University of Chicago Press, pp. 41–8.

Wilson, E. (2018). Translator's note. In Homer, *The Odyssey*, trans. E. Wilson. New York: W.W. Norton, pp. 83–91.

Yao, S. G. (2002). *Translation and the Languages of Modernism: Gender, Politics, Language*. London: Palgrave Macmillan.

Zukofsky, C., and Zukofsky, L., trans. (1969). *Catullus*. London: Cape Golliard Press in association with Grossman Publishers.

# 25

# Translating the Texts of Songs and Other Vocal Music

Peter Low

## 25.1 Introduction

Song texts form part of a distinctive art form, a hybrid one that brings together two of humankind's most brilliant inventions: words and music. This means that they differ from other verbal art forms – not in themselves, since they often resemble poems (see Chapter 24), but in their use. Translators need to recognize their nature as words for singing because otherwise the translations they produce will not be fit for purpose. This applies even if the texts began life as printed poems (e.g., sonnets by major poets). A written poem, when set to music, becomes oral in character, and tends to acquire richer connotations through the song's musical dimension.

A great deal of vocal music has been translated or adapted. Often, an attractive tune has crossed a linguistic frontier and has then inspired someone to import the text as well. Members of the receiving culture are often unaware that a song in their language has actually come from another (for example, 'Autumn Leaves' began life in French, while 'Aux Champs-Élysées' was adapted from English). This process is so widespread that translations exist for thousands of songs and hymns, and hundreds of operas and musicals. We can possibly count a million translations and adaptations – even after we exclude the cases where an existing melody is given not a translation but a set of new, unrelated words.

Song translating, in its best manifestations, is an impressive craft, indeed a genuine art. Yet until the twenty-first century, relatively little was written about it, much less than about poetry translating. There were many song-translators, but few said much about their objectives and strategies, and relatively little scholarly attention was given to their efforts. In the twenty-first century, however, we can list at least five substantial publications in English:

- Dinda Gorlée, ed. (2005) *Song and Significance.*
- Ş. Susam-Sarajeva, ed. (2008) *Translation and Music.* Special issue of *The Translator*, 14(2).
- Helen Minors, ed. (2013) *Music, Text and Translation.*
- Ronnie Apter and Mark Herman (2016) *Translating for Singing.*
- Peter Low (2017) *Translating Song.*

Vocal music is, of course, a very broad field. It has a place in hundreds of cultures, both in public rituals (weddings, funerals, choral festivals) and in private gatherings. The simple word 'song', which for some people calls to mind a three-minute item on the theme of love performed by a soloist at a pop concert, actually denotes a wide diversity of works. It might, for example, be a long narrative ballad, a sacred hymn, a complex aria, a satirical jazz-song or a repetitive chant for dancing. Song is not just a precious way of expressing emotion; it is also a way of telling stories, developing fictional characters, commenting on events, entertaining crowds or making fun of individuals. There are songs intended for the church, the salon, the cabaret, the village fair, the recording studio, the opera house, the rock festival and the nursery. Songs can be secular, sacred, sentimental or satirical. There are glad songs and sad songs, dancing songs, marching songs, harvest songs, drinking songs, lullabies … And vocal music also includes works for more than one voice, from duets and cantatas to massed choirs. Yet all have something in common: the components of words and music – plus subsequent performance.

Clearly, the verbal elements of vocal music cannot cross linguistic borders as readily as the musical elements. People who hear a song in a language they don't know cannot fully understand its verbal elements, although these may actually matter a great deal. This is predictable and regrettable; but it is not irremediable since the skill of translators can to come into play.

Some of the problems of song translation derive from the nature of the texts. These are expressive texts, often creative, sentimental or playful. Many make use of metaphor, rhythm, rhyme, allusion, slang, dialect and raw emotional utterance. These are features encountered also in poetry translation (see Chapter 24). In some cases the texts existed as published poems before they became songs; for example, the musical *Cats*, composed by Andrew Lloyd Webber, which premiered in 1981, uses verses from the poetry collection *Old Possum's Book of Practical Cats* (1939) by the American-English poet T. S. Eliot. In other cases the lyrics were written by poets for the express purpose of musical setting (e.g., the songs in Shakespeare's plays). A third case is where a text for singing is devised to fit an existing instrumental tune.

Other problems, however, relate to the different performance situations in which a translation might be wanted. In some cases, notably in the classical music tradition, a song will be performed in a language unfamiliar to most of the audience, and therefore a translation is needed not for singing but for speaking, reading or studying. In other cases the translation is itself meant to be sung, in the language of the audience, in which case the translator must satisfy numerous requirements, as will be explained presently. It follows that there are different types of song translating, according to the function which the translation is intended to fill. Here we will use the word *skopos* favoured by scholars such as Katharina Reiss and Hans J. Vermeer, for whom the term designates the 'goal or purpose, defined by the commission and if necessary adjusted by the translator' (Vermeer, 1989/2000, p. 230). In focusing thus on function and purpose, this 'Skopos theory' highlights the needs of the end-user of the translation. (A fuller account is given in Chapter 1.)

## 25.2 A Variety of Possible Skopoi

There are still some translators and teachers, not to mention translation machines, for whom there exists 'the translation' or 'the best translation' of any given sentence. They are mistaken – the truth is that all translating is ad hoc (interpreters certainly know this when they are talking to children or hospital patients). The translating of songs proves a good field to apply the approach of the *skopos* theorists. One of their important contentions is that a translation devised with one purpose in mind is unlikely to be ideal for another purpose. When assessing a translation, according to *skopos* theory, 'the standard will not be intertextual coherence but adequacy or appropriateness with regard to the *skopos*' (Nord, 1997, p. 33).

Consider these four sentences, which are all versions of the start of the poem 'Heidenröslein' by Johann Wolfgang von Goethe, published in 1799:

(1) 'Saw a boy a (little) rose to stand, (little) rose on the heath.'
(2) 'A boy saw a wild rose growing, a rose on the heath.'
(3) 'A boy saw a rose growing on the heath.'
(4) 'Once a boy espied a rose growing in the heather.'

The source text (ST) reads: 'Sah ein Knab' ein Röslein stehn,/ Röslein auf der Heide.'

Each of the four versions is very good for at least one particular purpose. Version (1) may seem incoherent, yet it functions well as a 'study translation' for singers who want to know the sense and function of each German word – and who will compare it with Version (2), which is actually printed alongside it in a well-known compendium (Phillips, 1979). Version (2) is also well suited to the needs of people who listen to the song in the source language – they may read this translation either in a printed programme or on a compact disc (CD) insert. The more concise Version (3) would be appropriate for surtitles or subtitles. Given the technical constraints of this *skopos*, the result would probably be a two-line caption, thus:

> A boy saw a rose
> growing on the heath

As for Version (4), it is something different: a 'singable translation' devised for performance with Franz Schubert's well-known music of 1815, whose rhythms it matches perfectly. Although the verb 'espy' is uncommon, it works well enough when sung. And although the last word 'heather' is semantically inaccurate, we must concede (given this *skopos*) that it is a good option, since 'heath' and 'moor' are monosyllabic ('moorland' would be virtually unsingable – it ends in two consonants, whereas the last German syllable is short and open).

Section 25.3 will explore what best practice might be for all but one of the most likely purposes. Section 25.4 will focus on 'singable translations' intended for performance in the target language (TL), be it in the concert hall or the karaoke bar.

Now a little disclaimer: this chapter does not examine 'replacement texts' – those cases where a song-tune has crossed a language border and acquired a completely new set of words. Such texts, since they have taken nothing verbal from the source, are not translations or even adaptations: they are 'non-translations'. And because the verbal dimension is lost (the tune alone is still present), the resulting musico-verbal creation ought not to be called 'the same song'. This practice of writing new words for old tunes is an interesting cultural phenomenon – for example secular words written for sacred tunes or vice versa – but it has no place in a handbook that focuses on translation.

This chapter will also ignore the case of translations made on paper for the purpose of being set to music at a future date – though the remarks in Section 25.4.3.1 concerning 'singability' are relevant to that task. Further, the role of singers will be neglected: performers are very important indeed, but their contribution comes largely after the translating has happened.

### 25.3  Translations to Accompany the Performance of Songs in the Source Language

When a song will be performed in a language unfamiliar to the audience, some kind of translating needs to occur because otherwise the verbal elements of the song will be lost. The listeners may not resent this, but they would not know whether the loss matters or not.

| Skopos | Kind of translation |
| --- | --- |
| 1. Study | Word-for-word/ Gloss |
| 2a. Printed programme | Communicative |
| 2b. CD insert | Semantic |
| 3. Surtitles & subtitles | Communicative/ Gist |
| 4. Spoken intro | Gist |

Figure 25.1 Types of translation for non-singable purposes

This section proposes different kinds of translation, according to what the translation is for. Is it for a singer to study? Is it for an audience to read quickly? Is it to be printed on a CD insert? Is it to be displayed on screens as surtitles or subtitles? Or is it an oral text to be spoken before the performance? With songs there is certainly no one 'all-purpose translation'.

Figure 25.1 shows the kinds of translation appropriate for different non-singable purposes.

### 25.3.1   Study Translations

Study translations are of minority interest only. The users requiring the deepest understanding of the words are performers, choir directors and teachers of singing. Usually they are working in the classical music tradition, where one often sings in a foreign language. But this method could be useful also for foreign performers of, say, American jazz classics – indeed, whenever the song is a complex song in a source language that the singer does not know well. Study translations are designed to help the singer really understand how the text functions in detail, not just its general meaning. They are meant to be read more than once.

In order to be fit for purpose, study translations should be word-for-word versions, or nearly so. They consciously break the normal rules of good translating by excluding some of the tools that competent translators use constantly – tools such as transposing parts of speech, changing word order, and paraphrase.

In addition, such translations can ignore the usual requirement to be economical, to use a similar number of words as the ST. On the contrary, a word-for-word study translation can be suitably complemented by explanations, perhaps in footnotes, of subtleties, obscurities, double meanings, subtextual subtleties and cultural allusions. It may also elucidate linguistic matters such as pronouns or the absence thereof. Translators, after all, are language consultants and cultural go-betweens, and so providing such information is totally appropriate.

### 25.3.2 Programme Translations and CD Inserts

A different *skopos* applies to a translation printed in a recital programme and intended for an audience to read in the concert hall.

A good programme translation needs to be digestible in a relatively limited time. As John Glenn Paton puts it: 'The audience at a recital wants idiomatic English, understandable at a glance' (Paton, 2013, n. p.). Translators should therefore reduce the processing effort required by the reader. This means choosing natural language that is reasonably clear and idiomatic, as the ST usually is. The result is unlikely, however, to do full justice to the depth and subtlety of a poetic song-lyric.

Sometimes, unfortunately, concert programmes have printed translations which were actually intended for singing in the TL. Those translations tend to feature rhyme and archaic words and distorted word order, and are unlikely to convey the meaning with optimal clarity and accuracy.

Since the invention of the World Wide Web (www) by Timothy John Berners-Lee in 1989 and the release to the general public of the first web browser in 1991 (https://en.wikipedia.org/wiki/World_Wide_Web), performers have increasingly been able to choose suitable programme translations from the Internet, for example from a fine database called the LiederNet Archive, www.lieder.net/. The founder of that resource, in 1995, Emily Ezust, says that most of its translations are 'unostentatious (grammatical) prose broken up into lines, or what I like to think of as mostly-literal-but-not-glaringly-so' (Ezust, 2013, n.p.). Such versions are not stand-alone poetry-translations; they are adjunct texts intended to help the musicians to convey the musico-verbal work. A similar and larger website for more popular music is www.lyricstranslate.com.

One of the questions faced by translators who make adjunct texts is this: How reader-friendly should the translation be? This is a matter of style, involving issues like the avoidance of rare words and the domestication of cultural details such as food and drink. The present author finds value in the distinction Peter Newmark draws between 'communicative' translations (written with the reader in mind) and 'semantic' translations (written at the level of the author, as is usually best for poetry). For concert programmes, Newmark (1998, p. 21) favours the reader-friendly option: 'sober, close, "plain prose", parallel, line by line translations'.

Conversely, the 'semantic' option may be better in the case of CD inserts – the little paper booklets sold with many compact discs, some of which print the words of the songs and translations into one or more languages. The slightly different situation of the reader here – not under obvious time pressure – may allow the translator to be more subtle, more literary and less reductive.

### 25.3.3 Subtitles and Surtitles

The present chapter neglects the subject of subtitling, not because it is rarely used with music (on the contrary, many DVDs (digital versatile discs) and TV broadcasts use it) but because this *Handbook* covers it in Chapter 22. It also neglects 'fansubbing', which is subtitling done by fans, often of long videos, a practice that has become common for songs and music theatre. Although the guidelines in the rest of this section are very relevant to fansubbers, these people often choose to work more freely as they are non-professional and may be engaging in playful adaptation rather than true translating.

Surtitling, however, is not the same *skopos* as subtitling. Here the situation is a live performance. There are large screens, usually placed above the stage, which display captions in the language of the audience during the performance. They deliver the translation in fragments – which might be called 'sight-bites'. The electronic display is usually in pale letters on a dark background. Surtitles are commonly used in opera and music theatre, and sometimes in song recitals.

Many audience members use the surtitles provided, either reading every word, or more typically glancing up regularly (like drivers checking the rear-view mirror) in order to keep track of the verbal content. Although spectators who do not speak the language of the performance may often guess what the people on stage are singing about, only the surtitles can tell them what the actors are actually saying. Audiences value this. They notice, however, when surtitling is badly done: they are likely to complain about cases of bad spacing, incorrect spelling, poor hyphenation, and ill-chosen breaks between lines. (They criticize poor timing too, even though that depends not on the translator but on the prompter who operates the computerized display in real time.) Also, because the translation is presented simultaneously with the ST, audience members who know both languages are likely to notice translation errors.

Translators devising surtitles for music theatre should have four priorities:

(1) to help the audience follow the plot;
(2) to enhance understanding of the characters' predicaments;
(3) to blend with the music and the particular production; and
(4) to remain unobtrusive.

Given the visual material that the audience is looking at – set, costumes, gestures, etc. – the need to be unobtrusive is great. People need time to take in the visual components, which may include spectacular effects on a wide stage. Nobody goes to a musical in order to read words!

Surtitles for a musical production should be devised before the first performance, and edited several times. A translator may need to attend some rehearsals in order to be familiar with the concept of the production in question, and to avoid incongruities (such as the phrase 'this man here' when the singer is pointing to someone on the far side of the stage).

Many of the detailed guidelines that apply to subtitling apply to surtitles also. There are space constraints: the technology will impose a limit of, say, thirty-five characters per line. Line breaks must be chosen well. Ideally, each caption should be a self-contained sentence – but where this is impossible, the sentence should be broken judiciously with suspension points. A little loss of content is often acceptable in surtitles and subtitles – the trick is to omit or simplify unimportant details without changing significant ones.

There are also time constraints. This means that complicated vocabulary or syntax should be simplified. Ambiguity should be reduced. Words that are delivered rapidly need to be translated very economically. Punctuation should be minimized. Fortunately, surtitling for music is easier than subtitling for film because floods of words are rare. You may leave captions on screen for four seconds (with one-line captions) and six seconds or more (for two-liners). In trios, as when three opera performers are singing different words, you can offer little or nothing. And you should omit many of the repetitions common in vocal music.

### 25.3.4   Spoken Introductions

It sometimes happens that a performer introduces a foreign song with a spoken translation. This may be the full recitation of a high-quality poem or song-lyric, or merely a brief indication of its verbal content. Such a translation needs to communicate quickly and directly (re-reading is not possible). Good examples tend to be informal, brief and clear. A common context for this is a popular concert; and the spoken words may well be improvised by the performer.

If a translator's services are sought, some considerations should be: to limit the total length, to make the information digestible; to avoid ambiguities (e.g., homophones); to reduce obscurities and complex syntax; and, above all, to communicate. One may also exploit the possible emphases of spoken delivery. Dramatic pauses, and the use of underlining, though usually avoided with printed words, can be good for texts that will be spoken.

## 25.4   Translations to Sing to Existing Tunes

### 25.4.1   Matters of Debate

Sometimes a translator takes a song which is already known and devises a translation that can be sung to the existing music. There is an ongoing debate about the value of such 'singable translations'.

One argument is theoretical. There are purists (perhaps lovers of German Lieder) who say that the resulting song 'doesn't sound the same, and is not as good'. And indeed it is not the same – many of the sounds are different – but how similar does it need to be? Songwriters usually choose words for their meanings, not chiefly for their sounds. As for whether such translations are less good, that is true generally, but not universally.

A second argument is pragmatic: the critic points to the poor quality of many existing 'singable translations' and declares them unusable. This claim carries some weight. In the case of translated hymns, even their continued acceptance for church use cannot excuse their frequent clumsiness. In the case of opera translations, complaints have long been made. Around 1850, a young composer named Richard Wagner criticized German translations of opera on many counts: their ill-fitting accents, their distorted word order, their false vowels and their 'absurdest end-rhymes' (Wagner, 1893, p. 360). In English one finds many translations that merit similar rejection. Not a few are scarred by forced rhymes and marred by archaic language (even words like 'prithee'). The poor quality of many 'singable translations' is one of the reasons why classical artists usually sing the STs. Wagner himself wanted to have his operas translated to a high standard.

But those two arguments are not totally convincing. Even numerous poor-quality examples do not prove that high quality is impossible to achieve, merely that the making of good examples requires good strategy and skill. And, in any case, singable translations are not made for the sake of people who do not need them – who know and savour the detailed wordings in the source language – they are made for foreign audiences who will be exposed to the total song. For example, the many thousands who applauded the English version of the musical *Les Misérables*, with lyrics by Herbert Kretzmer and music by Claude-Michel Schönberg, which ran in London from October 1985 to July 2019, could not have understood the French musical version with lyrics by Alain Boubil, which premiered in Paris in 1980. The musical versions are based on the historical novel *Les Misérables* by Victor Hugo, published in French in 1862.

Besides, how important is understanding the words? There is no short answer to this, since vocal music is extremely varied. Even if we judge that, on average, the words matter less than the music, that still leaves thousands of songs where the words have at least equal importance. In these cases, a foreign audience that is offered no insight into the words cannot appreciate the songs properly and may justly claim to be sold short.

The case against singable translations is strongest in songs where the original words are of poor quality (national anthems, nursery rhymes?) or songs where almost all the emphasis is on the music (frenzied dances, coloratura arias?). Conversely, the case in favour is strongest where the lyrics were composed by singer-songwriters who really care about those words and whose own performances demonstrate this by being audible and clear. Songwriters usually want the audience to understand and not just hear. So do most performers. As the singer and college teacher Arthur Graham puts it, 'the singer needs words that may be sung with sincerity' (Graham, 1989, p. 35). It is generally true in vocal music that both words and music were meant to reach the listeners' ears and brains simultaneously.

The following kinds of song are more likely to be worth translating:

- narrative songs
- comic songs
- dramatic songs.

To these we can add dialogue songs (those using or implying two or more characters). We can say that all these songs are not musico-centric but logocentric (focused on the words). This makes them more rewarding to translate – but not easier!

### 25.4.2   Multiple Constraints

The makers of singable translations face particular challenges. On top of the normal considerations of meaning and naturalness (which apply to translating generally), attention must be given to rhythm, ease of articulation, and often rhyme. This is because of the pre-existing music – its predetermined pitches, note-lengths, rhythms, stresses and phrasings. In a singable translation, the original melody, which fitted the original words, will be reused, virtually unchanged, but will be carrying different words – words in the TL but derived from the ST. In many cases the music had been composed with the ST as its starting-point, in which case the translator works in the opposite direction, proceeding from the music in search of TL words. There are also problems related to the requirements of vocal performance (some words are hard to sing). This unusual mixture of dissimilar considerations has led people to talk of 'multiple trade-offs' and even of a 'juggling act'.

### 25.4.3   Five Criteria

The present author prefers to characterize the task as a 'pentathlon'. This metaphor likens the five criteria which the translator must face to the five dissimilar events in which athletes must compete to maximize their points. They are #A singability, #B sense, #C naturalness, #D rhythm and #E rhyme. Here they are explained in order:

### 25.4.3.1   Singability

This criterion is *physical and phonetic*, and for translators it affects the choice of vowels and consonants. Any translation that scores poorly here is a failure and will not be performed, whatever its other virtues may be.

The words need to be ones which singers can produce effectively. Singability is judged by the suitability of the translation for singing, in term of the challenges of articulation, breathing, dynamics and resonance, with reference to the mouth, throat, lungs and vocal folds. This is best assessed by singers who usually sing in the TL. I heartily endorse Apter and Herman's (2016, p. 23) remark that '[w]hen performers ask for reasonable adjustments or point out bad phonetic choices, translators should accommodate them'.

Some pointers for translators are:

(1) Try to have open syllables, those that do not end with a consonant.
(2) Favour words containing pure vowels.
(3) Avoid placing hard-to-sing words on high notes. Closed vowels are harder to sing on high pitches, and open vowels can sometimes be harder to sing on low notes.
(4) Avoid consonant clusters and other kinds of tongue-twister.
(5) Be sparing with plosive consonants because they stop the air-flow.
(6) Avoid placing short vowels on long notes.

That sixth point calls for explanation. In English and German, one of the most problematic vowels is the [i] as in 'bin'. If it is placed on a long note, singers will tend to lengthen it to an [i:] and distort the meaning.

### 25.4.3.2  Sense

This term denotes the semantic matters that dominate discussions of non-fiction translating: *meaning, content* and *intent*. We see successful transfer of sense whenever the ST meaning survives intact, and mishandling of sense whenever the translation acquires a different verbal meaning. This matter is best assessed by truly bilingual people.

In the case of singable translations, however, sense is only one of several criteria. Pedantic insistence on sense is actually undesirable because it underplays the need for naturalness, and reduces flexibility generally. For singable translations, sense may be acceptably transferred through choices which are imprecise, such as near-synonyms, subordinates, super-ordinates, etc. One might even opt for an adjacent item in the same category. This does not mean we can award 10/10 for a line that translates apples as pears. But it does mean that the penalty for such imperfection may well be outweighed by a better score on another criterion (one might choose 'pear' for its rhyme, or to save one syllable).

When translators score very poorly on this criterion of sense – whether by incompetence or strategic choice – the translation should more accurately be called an adaptation. Harai Golomb puts the strong case for compromise in these words:

> Semantic approximations and loose summaries, that would be hair-raising in music-free contexts and normally rejected as translational

non-starters, can be accommodated, especially if sacrifices of this type earn the text such valued qualities as rhythmical elegance, witty and effective word-music alignment, and immediate communicability.

(Golomb, 2005, p. 133)

Johan Franzon (2005, p. 292) even sees this as a higher kind of fidelity: 'song-translators raise the level of fidelity from the textual-semantic to the contextual-functional'.

An additional consideration is mood. When choosing between two synonyms in the TL, it is desirable to take account of mood as well as meaning, and to recognize that a song's mood is partly a function of the music. A word which is good at conveying the meaning may nevertheless lack the sadness or the happiness that best fits the song.

### 25.4.3.3 Naturalness

This term assumes that the translation will be a text that could have been created spontaneously in the TL – by a songwriter or other wordsmith within the target culture. Ideally, it should give the miraculous impression that it existed first. As one translator put it: 'The target text must sound as if the music had been fitted to it, even though it was actually composed to fit the source text' (Dyer-Bennett, 1965, p. 292). The opposite of naturalness is awkwardness and clumsiness.

Consideration of this criterion coheres with a very common translating principle: Observe the norms of the TL. But this principle is particularly important with songs because singers have to perform them to audiences. Singers like to sing with commitment and soul, and clumsy words prevent that. Naturalness is best assessed by native speakers of the TL. (Note that naturalness is not the same as domestication, which concerns the treatment of foreign cultural details such as people's names, which can often be kept unchanged.)

### 25.4.3.4 Rhythm

It is the rhythm of the music that matters here. This, in vocal music, overrules the rhythm of the words; and so translators must focus on the musical rhythm, with its downbeats, bar-lines, varying note-lengths and syllabic patterns. A good translation will match these musical rhythms, and thus achieve a good rhythmic fit. This is best assessed by people with a strong sense of rhythm.

The challenge is not easy: these are unusual requirements for translators! But song-translations which were not made deliberately to fit the existing music almost never fit. Even when a line of the translation has the same syllable-count as the ST, its strong accents will often fall on inappropriate words, such as articles or short prepositions. Musical setting often increases the difference between stressed and unstressed syllables, and very weak words (such as 'the' or 'a' in English) should never be placed on a downbeat. Confronted with a mismatch, you may at times find a quick solution, like replacing a word with a differently stressed synonym, for example with 'maybe' in place of 'perhaps', or 'lessen' for 'reduce'. At other times you may find that your first draft translation does not fit, and needs more work.

Downbeats matter more than syllable-count. Although it is good to achieve the same syllable-count as the ST, the musical rhythm matters more. In addition, you are seeking a match for the longs and shorts of the music. You must therefore pay attention to the length of vowels – without ignoring the role of consonants. You may also need to take account of rests in the music. For example, a line which on paper looks unbroken may in the song contain a significant rest – and you have to prevent this gap from coming in the middle of a word.

Short phrases need special attention. 'In general', writes Johan Franzon (2008, p. 387), 'the longer the musical lines, the easier it may be for translators to accommodate the syntax of their particular language'. Unfortunately, many songs contain short phrases, often with only two or three syllables. These may be tricky to translate, and they may well be repeated (repetition is of course common in vocal music). But note: there is no rule requiring you to always translate the same source language phrase in the same way.

A problem may arise with prominent words. Although perfect sequential alignment of translation to ST is seldom crucial, there are times when the rhythm and the melody-line highlight particular words of the ST by placing them at the crest of the melody or at the end of a phrase. Such highlighted words should ideally be translated at the same location in the song. 'Musical dynamics or the crest of a phrase will often determine where certain meanings must fall' (Apter and Herman, 2016, p. 207).

### 25.4.3.4.1  Line-endings

Although the lines of song-lyrics often end in stressed syllables, this is far from universal. Even in English, one often finds lines ending in a two-syllable word like 'offer' or 'finish' where the final syllable is weak.

In Spanish and Italian songs, for example, many lines end with an unstressed 'a' or 'o'. Each of these line-endings – sometimes called feminine or trochaic endings – coincides with a similar ending to the musical phrase: the penultimate note has the downbeat, and the final note is soft. This means that the translator needs to find a trochaic word (strong-weak, like 'marry' or 'marrow') preferably ending in a vowel.

Translators working into English need to concentrate to find these rhymes. One of the easier solutions is the '-ing' suffix, but it is boring to overdo this option. Apter and Herman speak of searching for 'syllables such as -es, -le, and -er to match the very light final syllables of words in languages such as German and sung French' (Apter and Herman, 1991, p. 103, also 2016, p. 186).

### 25.4.3.4.2   *In Defence of Tweaking*

Rhythm is certainly an area where tweaks (small adjustments) are often possible. Although it is desirable to retain the original rhythm intact, some flexibility is usually needed. You can tweak the rhythm if, without compromising the melody, you can slur different notes together, or tie instances of the same note.

The best place to add a syllable is on a melisma (where one syllable has two or more notes), and the best place to subtract a syllable is on a repeated note. Apter and Herman (2016, p. 18) give a chart of different tweaks that they call 'splitting notes, combining notes, adding notes, deleting notes, spreading syllables and inserting syllables'.

Adding notes does indeed alter the musical medium, yet alterations of this kind are sometimes insignificant and therefore acceptable. Besides, in strophic songs, where every musical phrase is repeated with different words, variation often exists already in the ST: the composers themselves tweaked their melodies. So, when translators make minor adjustments from verse to verse, they are simply claiming latitudes that are a normal part of songwriting.

### 25.4.3.5   Rhyme

Rhyme is the easiest criterion to assess, and usually the least important. But although this criterion should not have priority over the four discussed already, you need to factor it in from the outset. If you add rhyme only as an afterthought, the results will be awful. It is better to find some rhyming words for your translation (the most crucial ones) early on in the process.

There is actually no consensus, across languages and cultures, decreeing that rhyme is a necessary component of vocal music. Even in Europe, one can point to plenty of unrhymed vocal music – often in Latin. 'It is possible for a translation to dispense with rhyme altogether if care is taken that the sound patterns interweave closely enough that internal sonic tensions override the lack of rhyme at musical phrase endings' (Apter and Herman, 2016, p. 195). Choosing not to rhyme does not mean that one should ignore the vowel-sounds, of course, since they remain a consideration of singability.

A good strategy is to ask: 'Does my translation need to rhyme at all? What is the function of rhyme in the specific song I am considering?' If it has gusto and wit, then an unrhymed translation will probably disappoint (we may bet that some of the ST words were chosen chiefly because they rhymed). Conversely, there may be good grounds for creating a rhymeless translation: if you judge that rhyme is of minor importance in the work, or if the TL does not commonly use rhyme.

In the past, consciously or subconsciously, many song-translators have given rhyme a high priority. This has usually been misguided. In particular, translators into English, French and German tended to place undue weight on the quantity and quality of rhymes.

#### 25.4.3.5.1 *Quantity and Quality?*

There is a common trap here. Some translators say: 'Yes, I will retain rhyme', and promptly set their target at perfect rhymes as numerous as those in the ST, to be placed in the same locations. Often they pay a heavy price in other ways: the rhyme at the end of the line ends up shaping that whole line – the tail wags the dog! Over-emphasis on rhyme compromises sense.

A wiser approach is to seek some margin of flexibility. Here is what I told myself before tackling a rhyming text:

> My rhymes don't have to be as numerous or as perfect as in the ST, and the original rhyme-scheme need not be observed precisely. I will try to get a good score in rhyme, but not at the expense of other considerations. In places I may even restrict my rhyming to the 'clinch rhyme' at the end of each stanza.

A flexible approach can also apply to the location of rhymes, and flexibility certainly helps with rhyme quality. Although the usual requirement for rhyme is that the words should end with the same two phonemes (either vowel-consonant or consonant-vowel), there will be places where imperfect rhymes score better overall. In any case, many original songwriters have themselves settled for near-rhymes. It follows that song-translators, not being entitled to invent meanings at will as songwriters do, have even greater reason to exploit the dozens of near-rhymes available in the TL. Various terms have been used for kinds of near-rhyme, such as weak-rhyme, half-rhyme and slant-rhyme. The term 'off-rhyme' is sometimes used when the same vowel is accompanied by an adjacent consonant (e.g., mine/time, a common near-rhyme in English songs). One online dictionary *www.rhymezone.com* even gives the option of searching for a 'near rhyme'. One can also speak of a general 'rhymingness' when vowel-sounds combine in a pleasing way.

#### 25.4.3.5.2 *Try to Find Your Rhyme-Words in Inverse Order!*

Working backwards is working smart: it reduces the chance of the rhyme seeming forced. Thus, if the ST has a rhyming couplet, translate line two first, and give it a strong ending, before you look for the rhyme that will end line one.

### 25.4.4 Further Considerations

Although all the above five criteria are common, they do not cover all the possible issues.

When a song forms part of a stage musical or opera, it is also important to consider the character's personality and dramatic situation. Every song or aria needs to cohere with the extended stage-work that it belongs to, a need not covered by the five criteria expounded here. The experienced opera-translators Ronnie Apter and Mark Herman insist: 'Most scripts for the stage *are* dramatic and *do* delineate character. Good translations should do the same' (Apter and Herman, 2016, p. 143). Any translator wishing to tackle a whole musical or opera ought to first digest Apter and Herman (2016).

When a song in a film or TV show is being dubbed, it is desirable to fit the translation to the singer's lip movements, at least when the image is a close-up (see further Chapter 22).

## 25.5  Further Discussion

The criteria discussed in this chapter can be used to help assess the quality of singable translations, either to choose between available translations or to identify parts of the translation where improvements should be made. The sporting metaphor of the pentathlon, mentioned in Section 25.4.3, stresses how dissimilar these criteria are, and implies that the objective is a high aggregate score across all these five events. Trade-offs are very likely to be required.

Negotiating the necessary trade-offs calls for greater flexibility than is needed in most other translating. Ordinary translating relies on a standard 'toolbox' of techniques – literal translation, paraphrase, transposition of parts of speech, changes in word-order. But for singable translations, that normal toolbox should be supplemented by a 'box of tricks', such as these: modulation, compensation in place, superordinate and subordinate words, near-synonyms, substitute metaphors, dilution, condensation, repackaging, and what could be called 'utterance-changing': replacing one kind of utterance – be it a statement, exclamation, question or imperative – with another.

## 25.6  Tips and Tricks

Since song translating is not easy, I offer here a number of practical tips based on personal experience:

(1) Begin with the key phrase. This may be either the start, or the line most often repeated, or the crucial phrase of the refrain. If the last line is particularly good, then start your translating there so as to ensure that the lyric ends strongly. Your version of that phrase needs to be convincing – indeed, it may make or break your translation.

(2) Decide whether or not you will use rhymes (and, if so, give early attention to rhyming-words).

(3) Decide your priorities for this particular song. What do you most want to achieve: good rhythm, long vowels, legato phrasing, humour, pathos or . . .? This will help you make good choices – and the features of the text that you judge to have low priority will probably not be well

transferred. This is all the more reason to be very clear about your strategy and objectives.

Singable translations seldom come close to that semantic equivalence which receives high priority in most prose translation. But they can, at best, creatively deliver what some theorists call equivalent effect – and others might call 'the essential spirit of the work'. This objective is not well served by pedantic rules such as 'Never ever alter the rhythm' or 'Retain the identical number of rhymes'. It is better served by making creative use of the methods mentioned in this chapter. Fortunately, the musical dimension of the work will be retained in performance, so that the translation will be transmitted in conjunction with the same non-verbal code – the music – which enhanced the ST.

All good translations are superior to bad ones in respect of (a) showing a deep understanding of the ST, with its original context and purpose; (b) transferring or replicating all its important features, sometimes at the expense of its incidental details; and (c) being fit for the intended purpose in the target culture. A good song-translation is one fit to receive 'the icing on the cake' – the talents that a good performer can bring to it.

## 25.7  Adapting Rather than Translating

Although this chapter has focused on faithful translations of texts, many people choose to deviate from fidelity and make 'free translations' – adaptations rather than strict translations. Some so-called translations of popular music are really freely adapted. The reason for adapting may simply be the difficulty of close translations, but there may also be a desire to domesticate, to appropriate, even to improve on the ST.

Generally, of course, singable translations need to treat the meaning of the ST more freely than normal translations do. Thus, a little adjective may be ignored, a rhyming word may be added, the name of a person or place may be transposed. These changes (omissions, additions and modifications) are made chiefly to adapt the translation to its intended situation in the target culture. But at some point the changes become too great or numerous to be called 'translations'. The present author distinguishes the two with the following definitions:

> *A translation is a target text where all significant details of meaning have been transferred.*
>
>  *An adaptation is a derivative text where significant details of meaning have not been transferred which easily could have been.*

While offering a clear enough distinction, those definitions accept that grey areas exist between the two (not everyone will agree about what is significant or easy). Apter and Herman (2016, p. 58) define translating as 'not changing anything major in the original'. Whereas omitting an adjective is usually trivial, the omission of a thematic element is always significant. Klaus Kaindl's discussion of 'Hymne à l'amour' (words by Edith Piaf and Marguerite Monnot) notes that one version in German 'makes no mention of physical surrender or death' (Minors, 2013, p. 160). Adapting is the right term for this.

A typical adaptation mixes genuine transfer with forms of unforced deviation (omission, addition, modification); it 'draws on an ST but has extensively modified it for a new cultural context' (Munday, 2009, p. 166). Adapting is easier than translating since one has more freedom. This is not to deny that the best adaptations – such as parodies – are excellent, just that their excellence is not owing to translation skills. Adaptation is more common in popular music than in highbrow music, and is more acceptable, too, because the lowbrow tradition assigns less value to fidelity to an original, and even encourages 'covers' of popular songs. It is worth noting, however, that some songwriters are resentful when someone else presents a version of their creative work which they judge to be a travesty or betrayal, or when they hear a serious distortion being presented as a good representation of one of their songs.

## References

Apter, R., and Herman, M. (1991). Opera translation. In M. Larson, ed. *Translation Theory and Practice: Tension and Interdependence*. Amsterdam: John Benjamins, pp. 100–120.

Apter, R., and Herman, M. (2016). *Translating for Singing, the Theory, Art and Craft of Translating Lyrics*. London: Bloomsbury.

Dyer-Bennett, R. (1965). Preface to Schubert, *The Lovely Milleress*. New York: Schirmer.

Ezust, E. (2013). Personal communication.

Franzon, J. (2005). Musical comedy translation: Fidelity and format in the Scandinavian *My Fair Lady*. In D. Gorlée, ed. *Song and Significance: Virtues and Vices of Vocal Translation*. Amsterdam: Rodopi, pp. 263–97.

Franzon, J. (2008). Choices in song translation: Singability in print, subtitles and sung performance. *The Translator*, **14**(2), 373–98.

Golomb, H. (2005). Music-linked translation (MLT) and Mozart's operas. In D. Gorlée, ed., *Song and Significance: Virtues and Vices of Vocal Translation*. Amsterdam: Rodopi, pp. 121–62.

Gorlée, D., ed. (2005). *Song and Significance*. Amsterdam/New York: Rodopi.

Graham, A. (1989). A new look at recital song translation. *Translation Review*, **29**, 31–7.

Low, P. (2017). *Translating Song*. London: Routledge.

Minors, H. J., ed. (2013). *Music, Text and Translation*. London: Bloomsbury.

Munday, J., ed. (2009) *The Routledge Companion to Translation Studies*. London: Routledge.

Newmark, P. (1998). *More Paragraphs on Translation*. Clevedon, UK: Multilingual Matters.

Nord, C. (1997). *Translating as a Purposeful Activity*. Manchester: St Jerome.

Paton, J. G. (2013). Personal communication.

Phillips, L. (1979). *Lieder Line by Line, and Word for Word*. London: Duckworth.

Susam-Sarajeva, Ş., ed. (2008). Special issue: Translation and Music. *The Translator*, **14**(2).

Vermeer, H. J. (1989/2000). Skopos and commission in translational action. Trans. A. Chesterman. In L. Venuti, ed., *The Translation Studies Reader*. London: Routledge, pp. 221–32.

Wagner, R. (1893). *Richard Wagner's Prose Works II*. London: Kegan Paul (original in *Oper und Drama*, 1852).

# Part VI

## Translation in History

# 26

# Translation before the Christian Era

Roberto A. Valdeón

## 26.1 Introduction

In his introduction to translation history, Lieven D'hulst (2010, p. 397) writes that the coupling of translation and history can be done from two perspectives: what translation can mean for the understanding of history, and what history can mean for the multifarious forms of translation. In his approach, D'hulst (2010, p. 398)distinguishes three concepts, namely history, historiography and meta-history, which are rarely integrated because of the difficulties this would pose for the researcher, both in practical terms and as a consequence of the multi-layered nature of historical research. This integration is even more complex for any attempts to study the history of translation during the period comprising the time before our current era, often referred to as Before the Christian Era (BCE) or BC (Before Christ). Indeed, as knowledge of translation BCE is scant, we can only make assumptions about the importance of translation in that period of human history. However, the questions that D'hulst raises may contribute to providing a general picture of what translation meant before our current era: who translated; what has been translated; where did translations become available; what other agents were involved; why did transla-tion occur; how were translations produced; when were they produced; and what were the effects of the translations? This chapter will attempt to answer some of these questions with regards to the role of transla-tion during a period which, given the scarcity of sources and docu-ments, let alone translations, has received only limited attention in the discipline.

One of the difficulties in the study of translation BCE results from the absence of writing in most parts of the world at the time. In fact, according to Lewis (2009), of the approximately seven thousand languages spoken in the world, only a few hundred have a literary tradition. Consequently, if we turn to the entries in handbooks and encyclopaedias on translation and interpreting, authors can assume only that translation must have played a crucial role in both trade and everyday life; multiple linguistic groups are likely to have come into contact with one another, even though there is little or no evidence of this. Bandia (2009, p. 313), for instance, claims that, in Africa, translation must be as old as the spoken word itself, as even today there are hundreds of diverse linguistic communities and, therefore, translation has always been necessary to communicate among them. We also know that in the ninth century BCE, China's Zhou dynasty used interpreters in their meetings with representatives of foreign nations (Hung and Pollard, 2009, p. 369). Elsewhere in Asia, the clay tablets containing Sumerian-Eblatie word lists dating back 4,500 years provide further evidence of the use of translation in ancient times (Delisle and Woodsworth, 2012 p. 3). In that historical period, the number of individuals capable of writing was very small, but scribes, whose identities are unknown, were in charge of keeping records of religious, political and trade issues. Undoubtedly, they were also in charge of recording the transactions between speakers of different languages, and, therefore, the translations used in the process. In fact, a tablet found in contemporary southern Iraq lists a number of professions in hierarchical order, including interpreters (Ruiz Rosendo and Persaud 2016, p. 6).

The conceptualization of translation as a distinct discipline and/or practice also poses additional problems when considering translation at the time. Trivedi (2006, p. 106) notes that in India 'there is no surviving evidence of any text of any kind being translated into an Indian language' until the nineteenth century, while translations from Indian languages into Chinese and Arabic, for instance, were carried out. The multilingual nature of India was, however, reflected in its literature all the same, as it was normal to use two or more languages in one given literary text. This does not mean that translation did not occur. In fact, according to the *Natyasastra*, a Sanskrit treaty of the performing arts attributed to Bharata Muni, one of the roles of a translator was to be able to recreate the same emotions as in the original (Sharma, 2002). This is in line with Gambier's (2018, p. 26) view that translation and creative writing are part of the same process and, in turn, may explain the difficulty of finding an equivalent term in Indian languages for the concept of 'translation'. Even in the case of Western civilizations, such as that of Rome, translation was a problematic concept: the publication of a translated text often followed its oral performance, which meant that the published text may have had little to do with its oral representations (McElduff, 2015, p. 129).

## 26.2    Translation in Ancient Egypt

During the pre-Christian era, in areas such as the Mediterranean and the Middle East, translation was closely connected to political and military expansion, as well as to the spread of various religious faiths. In ancient Egypt, hieroglyphs depicted interpreters, as the establishment of an administration required the hiring of language brokers capable of communicating with foreigners during their military expeditions and trade dealings (Galán 2011), although Hermann (2002/1956) claims that the Egyptians regarded them as barbarians. Thus, interpreters were often used to put words into the mouths of foreigners rather than to translate their words literally (Hermann 2002/1956). Consequently, most interpreters had a low status. Of particular interest is the work of the archaeologist José M. Galán, who has studied, among others, inscriptions dating back to the year 2250 BCE found in the autobiography of an official known as Harkhuf. One inscription, found on Qubbet el-Hawa hill in the Aswan region of southern Egypt, lists Harkhuf's functions, which included the supervision of interpreters. However, it is not clear what this entailed (Galán, 2011, p. 297). Galán also provides us with various examples of inscriptions from different periods recording the use of interpreters, as treaties had to be signed by speakers of different languages. Of particular note is the reproduction of the oaths taken by the various peoples conquered by Egypt, who had to swear their allegiance to the pharaohs. Their words must have been mediated as the conquered did not speak the Egyptian language. Therefore, the scribes or other language brokers must have intervened in the process (Galán, 2011, pp. 301–2). Similarly, traders from Syria, Palestine and Cyprus appear in these inscriptions addressing the pharaohs (Galán, 2011, p. 303).

Another difficulty in accessing historical accounts of ancient Egypt is the Egyptian language (or rather groups of languages). Characterized by its hieroglyphic writing, Egyptian has remained a mystery in many ways. Egyptologists have used a transliteration system to decipher the meaning of texts and for publication purposes (see, for example, Rothe, Miller and Rapp, 2008). Of all the various 'texts' discovered over the past two hundred years, the most influential is the Rosetta Stone, found in 1799 in the Egyptian city of Rashid. It contains a decree issued in Memphis in 196 BCE in three languages, namely ancient Egyptian, Egyptian demotic script and ancient Greek. The Rosetta Stone, currently at the British Museum in London, was crucial to deciphering ancient Egyptian hieroglyphs despite the minor differences among the three versions.

Egyptian hieroglyphic writing might have been created at about the same time as Sumerian, a cuneiform language which may have influenced Egyptian. The influence of Sumerian and other languages can be traced in the adaptation of Egyptian to be used with Semitic systems from around 2000 BCE (Schniedewind and Hunt, 2007, p. 34).

The Egyptian group of languages influenced and was influenced by other languages, such as Greek. In fact, with a long history of almost 3,500 years, the tongue of the pharaohs went through various phases, including Coptic in the final 300 years, before it was replaced by Arabic. The Greeks are considered the first to introduce graphic representations of vowels, derived in turn from the Phoenician alphabet. This system, created around 1000 BC, also influenced Aramaic, Hebrew, Coptic and Arabic (Delisle and Woodsworth, 2012, p. 3). This web of influences meant that, in the final phase of the life of their language, the influence of Greek led Egyptians to introduce vowels following the Greek alphabet, which was used together with characters from traditional hieroglyphic writing. Indeed, the inscriptions found along the Nile demonstrate that this route was frequented by the Greeks and the Romans. For instance, inscriptions at Bir Meniah, in southern Egypt, include portions in Greek and Latin (Rothe, Miller and Rapp, 2008, p. 44), pointing to the encounters among different linguistic communities that undoubtedly needed translators to understand one another.

Despite the mysteries and uncertainties of this civilization, it is clear that ancient Egyptians used papyri (most of which are now lost) and stone inscriptions. Some of these texts point to the difficult interaction among various peoples who inhabited the area. This would ultimately lead to the end of the Nile culture (Kemp, 2006, p. 14).

## 26.3   Translation in the Near and Middle East

In contemporary Syria lay the ancient cities of Ebla (or Tell Mardikh) and Ugarit. In the 1970s the Italian archaeologist Paolo Matthiae discovered almost two thousand tablets in two languages, Sumerian and what is now known as Ebla language, Eblaite or Eblan. As for Ugarit, more than ten thousand tablets inscribed with this language were discovered in the early twentieth century. The tablets, covering a wide variety of topics such as history, economy, literature and religion (Shear, 2004, p. 66), were written in eight different languages and include bilingual and trilingual texts (Pegenaute, 2018, p. 187), although they were composed mainly in Ugaritic, the second oldest Northwest Semitic language with connections to other languages such as Phoenician, Hebrew and Aramaic (Gianto, 2012, p. 29). The tablets date back to around 1300–1190 BCE (Gianto, 2012). As Ugarit was an important cultural centre with scribal schools, some of the tablets included abecedaries or alphabets, notably the bilingual Ugaritic-Akkadian alphabet tablet (Schniedewind and Hunt, 2007, p. 36). More than a hundred of them are believed to have been used to train scribes and translators, as they also included polyglot glossaries (Schniedewind and

Hunt, 2007, p. 34), pointing to the role of language mediation in the area. Ugaritic, which enjoyed some prestige as the official language, was used for letter-writing, record-keeping, documentation as well as for literary purposes (Gzella, 2012, p. 1). Given the variety of linguistic groups that lived in that area over the centuries, translation was clearly crucial for communication purposes and for colonial dominance.

In the same way, the peoples that inhabited the Iranian plateau belonged to various linguistic groups, whose mutual impact is difficult to assess given the scarcity of extant documents. In present-day eastern Iran as well as in the west of Afghanistan, a new religion was taking shape at the same time as Judaism, led by the prophet Zarathustra (who might have lived between 1000 and 500 BCE). The texts that formed the canon of the new religion were transmitted by priests during the first half of the first millennium BCE, and the few extant documents are now gathered in the so-called *Avesta*, which is, in fact, a collection of texts containing the first written version of the religious oral texts of the Zoroastrian religion. These had been passed from generation to generation in Avestan, an Indo-Iranian language which, together with Old Persian, is the oldest Iranian language of which records exist (Martínez and de Vaan, 2014, p. 1). Avestan is also referred to as Gatha-Avestan, as it is the language of the Gathas, or the hymns believed to have been composed by Zarathustra (Beekes, 1988, p. XII).

The Avestan alphabet is considered very comprehensive and to be a variety of Pahlavi (Middle Persian), in turn deriving from Aramaic script (Martínez and de Vaan, 2014, p. 4), the main difference being that it indicates vocalic sounds, which may have been the result of its contact with Greek. It is also worth noting that the alphabet was created at some point between the seventh and ninth centuries of the CE for the transmission of the much older religious texts. However, not all the texts in the *Avesta* are written in the same variety of the language and some are accompanied by versions in Pahlavi or Sanskrit. Interestingly, the manuscripts that contain only Avestan are often referred to as 'pure' as opposed to those with translations, termed 'impure' (Martínez and de Vaan, 2014, p. 2). The texts containing interlinear translation in Pahlavi and Sanskrit are considered the most reliable, though, and the Sanskrit version is believed to have been produced when some of the Zoroastrians moved to India (de Vaan, 2003, p. 18). In fact, it has been argued that the 'pure' texts are copies of those that contained interlinear translations (de Vaan, 2003, p. 19).

As with other religious texts, the connection of the *Avesta* with the present has been made possible via translation. For example, it was translated into German by Friedrich von Spiegel (first published in 1852), and then from the German translation into English in 1864 for the Parsee brethren in India, although a few copies were reserved for English readers. It is worth noting that the translator compared the German version with the original *Zend*, or interpretation of the *Avesta*, to 'guide him a little in his choice of words' (Anonymous, 1864, p. vi), that is, with the original commentaries and glosses, although Bleeck refers to the *Zend* as a language (Anonymous, 1864, p. x). This is of note as it reflects the difficulties that arise when studying ancient texts such as the *Avesta*.

Also in contemporary Iran, we find the Behistun inscriptions at Mount Behistun, near Kermanshah, a city established by Darius I. Cyrus the Great had ruled a large geographical area which included peoples who spoke different languages and dialects. These inscriptions, authored during the reign of Darius the Great (at some point between 522 BCE and 486 BCE) show that although Elamite may have been the principal language of Darius's empire, it was not the only one, as the versions in other languages (Old Persian and Babylonian) were adaptations of the Elamite text (Potts, 1999, p. 317). Potts (1999, p. 311–17) points out that, given the political situation of the time, it is not surprising that more than one language was used. Later, after the conquest of Mesopotamia, Aramaic was also spoken in the empire, often as a lingua franca. It is worth noting that Greek might have been used in certain parts of the empire, given the influence of Greece and the presence of Greek speakers in the area. During the Persian period, which spans from 538 to 333 BCE, Aramaic was finally adopted as the language of the empire and the scribes had to master the language. For instance, during the reign of Darius I, an Egyptian law-code was translated into Aramaic (Bickerman, 1959, p. 9).

From that period date parts of the Hebrew Bible, as Aramaic was increasingly being used by the Jews. The Book of Ezra mentions a concept called *mprs*, meaning 'translate', referring to a translating method used in the Persian chancelleries (Schniedewind, 2013, p. 141). The dominance of Aramaic was such that when the *torah* (or teachings) was read to the people, it had to be translated as Hebrew was no longer understood by the majority (Schniedewind, 2013, p. 141), a situation that would change after the fall of the Persian empire, which gave way to the recovery of Hebrew and the emergence of Greek. During this period, the mutual influence of these languages on each other can be felt in texts with Hebrew vocabulary and Aramaic morphology (Schniedewind, 2013, p. 167).

The history of the Bible is indeed reflective of the movement of peoples and the variety of languages used in Syria-Palestine, where Semitic Akkadian had a predominant status and other, non-Semitic languages (such as Hittite and Hurrian) were spoken and used by the scribes. These non-Semitic languages must have influenced the Semitic languages of the Bible but, given the scarcity of sources, the origin of Semitic languages is difficult to date. What is obvious is that the Bible evolved in a period of great cultural and linguistic diversity (Gzella, 2012, pp. 1–2).

In his history of Hebrew, Schniedewind (2013, p. 28) posits that the spread of alphabetic writing occurred during the rise and fall of the

Egyptian empire, and points to the fact that, in the rabbinic tradition, writing was given to mankind during the creation of the world, an idea that was also known in ancient Egypt and Mesopotamia. The early Israelites were indeed aware of the importance of languages and dialects, for example in Genesis 10, Canaanites, a Semitic-speaking people, were divided according their families and their languages.

One of the most disputed aspects of the Hebrew Bible is the role played by the tablets of stone, 'written by the finger of God' and given to Moses (Schniedewind, 2005, p. 128). These tablets have been the cause of much controversy, in terms of their interpretation and their translation; but, most importantly, they point to the centrality of translation in legitimizing religious and political power. This mythical moment is reminiscent of the birth of a modern religion: in the nineteenth century the angel Moroni allegedly appeared to Joseph Smith, the founder of the Church of Jesus Christ of Latter-day Saints, also known as the Mormon Church. More surprisingly, the inscriptions on the Mormon tablets, which became the basis of a new Christian-based religion, were allegedly written in a language called Ancient Egyptian. The tables and their translation into English exemplified the connection among ancient traditions, modern religions and the importance of fictional or pseudo-translations in the creation of canons, literary or religious (Toury, 1995, pp. 41–2, 2005, pp. 11–14).

## 26.4 Translation in Ancient Greece and Rome

It seems that, in ancient Greece, translation was not considered particularly important, as there are no discussions of the practice in Greek literature. It has been claimed that this may be owing to the fact that the Greeks, like contemporary speakers of English, may have expected other peoples to learn their language, as it functioned as a lingua franca (Connolly and Bacopoulou-Halls, 2009, p. 419). In addition, ancient Greeks opposed what was considered the corruption of their language by foreign tongues. But the influence of the Greeks, far-reaching as they moved towards the East and towards Northern Africa, undoubtedly led to the use of translation. The intervention of the Ten Thousand, an army of Greek soldiers hired by Cyrus the Younger, required interpreters capable of translating from Greek into languages such as Persian, Armenian, Tracian and Macionese, as Xenophon's chronicle records (Santoyo, 2006, p. 14). In the *Anabasis*, written around 370 BCE, Xenophon (1859, pp. 23, 77, 127, 155) mentions the role of interpreters on several occasions. In line with the role of interpreters in the modern age, mediators were sent to approach foreign peoples in advance (Xenophon, 1859, pp. 269, 483). Although most mediators remained anonymous, Xenophon mentions Pigres by name (Xenophon, 1859, p. 77), highlighting his agency, partly as a linguistic mediator, partly as a diplomat. Intercultural communication between Greeks and Persians was also promoted by the existence of the so-called guest friendship (or *xenia*) (Vlassopoulos, 2017, p. 365).

Despite this, when we think of translation in the era before Christ, we tend to associate it with translation in Ancient Greece first, and in Rome later, often in connection with religious and literary texts. In fact, in the same way as modern Bible translation was instrumental in the emergence of translation studies as a scholarly discipline, the translation of religious texts must have been of similar importance for the practice of translation in ancient times. The first translations of the Jewish Bible into Greek (Septuagint), Aramaic (Targum) and Syriac (Peshitta) all date from the third century BCE (Naudé, 2018, p. 391). The translation of the First Testament from Hebrew into Greek has been dated back to the reign of Ptolomy II (circa 283–246 BC), while the Epistle of Aristeas (circa 150 BC) records the approval of the translation by the Hellenistic Jewish community of Alexandria, presumably as the text reproduced the 'sublimity' and 'the sacred associations' of the original rather than the lexis (Weissbort and Eysteinsson, 2006, pp. 11–12). This version, which is called the Septuagint because of the legend that Ptolomy hired seventy scholars to do the work, is believed to have been influenced by Greek schools of philosophy, for example in the references to the four elements and to hedonism (McLaughlin, 2012, pp. 77–8), but it also shows elements of Hebrew and Aramaic origin. In any case, translation was a rudimentary business: translators and scribes would use different equivalents for the same original or resorted to transliterations for want of better options (Bickerman, 1959, p. 17).

Although the accuracy of the Greek translation has been the subject of controversy (Schniedewind, 2005, p. 178), it remains central for today's Christian churches because it represents the unity of the original church (Loba Mkole, 2016, p. 112). In fact, when Greek-speaking Christians accepted it as a sacred text, Hellenized Jews themselves abandoned it as such (Naudé, 2018, p. 391), as they might have regarded it almost as blasphemous. Also of great relevance is the fact that translation is about power and about trust (Lefevere, 1992, p. 3). This is the reason why a text like the Septuagint, which is considered a bad translation as it uses a common rather than a literary style and does not read fluently (Bickerman, 1959), continues to be the 'official' translation used by the Greek Orthodox Church: the translators commissioned to render the originals into Greek are still considered 'trusted translators'. It should also be noted that, although the study of Bible translations no longer occupies a central position in translation studies, Bible translation scholars continue to publish their texts in their periodicals and have often turned to translation studies concepts in their work. For example, Tully (2014) has argued that the study of ancient versions of the Old Testament such as the Greek Septuagint, the Syriac Peshitta and the Aramaic Targum can contribute to contemporary debates, for example the existence of translation universals (see Mauranen and Kujamäki, 2004).

In addition to the crucial role of Greek translations in the dissemination of the teachings of Christianity, Greece also served as a model for Roman architects, sculptors, philosophers and writers. In fact, Roman imperial culture was based on the Greek model, which the Romans had come into contact with after the conquest of Greece in the three centuries BCE. In fact, probably never in the history of humanity has a new state/empire shown such great respect for the culture it had taken. The Roman elite spoke, wrote and translated Greek (McElduff, 2013, p. 1): 'speaking the wrong sort of Greek, not speaking Greek or using it inappropriately marked you as the wrong sort of Roman' (McElduff, 2015, p. 129). Greek literary works served to shape the Roman identity from a small regional power to a world empire in which authors not only translated Greek texts but drew on them for their own creations: in *De republica*, for instance, Cicero translated and integrated parts of Plato's work (McElduff, 2013, p. 5). This practice resulted in a dialogue between Greek originals and Roman authors.

Translation was a part of the Roman education system, central to the disciplines of grammar and rhetoric. However, despite the importance of Greek and Greek literary works, the practice of translation as such played a secondary role in the Roman system: it was used for grammatical commentary and as a form of imitation (Copeland, 1991, p. 10). Some Roman playwrights acknowledged their debt to Greek originals (Garceau 2018), even though they did not discuss the nature and extent of that debt. For instance, in the third century BCE, Gnaeus Naevius, a Roman poet and dramatist, had already translated plays on the Trojan War, whereas Livius Andronicus adapted Greek tragedies and was also a translator of the *Odyssey*, proving that translation was fundamental in the creation of a Roman literary canon well before European writers used translation for the same purpose during the emergence of Europe's nation-states (Gillespie, 2011, p. 2). However, it should be noted that Gnaeus Naevius used translation to create a mythical history of Rome (Merkle, 2018, p. 240), whereas Livius Andronicus combined strategies that preserved the original wording of the *Odyssey* together with many Roman insertions, which produced a blend of imitation and *aemulatio* (Tadeu Gonçalves, 2015, p. 24).

The first classical author to discuss translation practices at some length was Cicero who, in his *De Optimo Genere Oratorum (On the Best Kind of Orators)*, defended the use of free translation. In this essay, Cicero, who introduced two speeches by the Greek orators Demosthenes and Aeschines, made a distinction, possibly for the first time, between literal and free translations (Garceau, 2018; Kitzbichler, 2016, p. 29). Cicero claimed that he had translated the Greek originals not like a translator but like an orator. This may have resulted from the difficulties he encountered in the translation process, which meant that, for instance, he needed four Latin synonyms to convey the term 'arche' (beginning; origin) in just one single passage of Plato (Bickerman, 1959, p. 16). Similarly, in *Ars Poetica* (*The Art of Poetry*), Horace advises against literal translations and provides examples to illustrate what a good translation should look like. Kitzbichler (2016, pp. 29–30), however, points out that both Cicero and Horace have been misquoted or misinterpreted since they did not argue against word-for-word translation but, rather, were suggesting that authors tend to use old material for their own creations. In this sense, it might be argued that Cicero and Horace rejected translation, or the word-for-word rendering of a foreign text, as a mere copy: 'Translation is for both Cicero and Horace a negative foil against which the task of the orator and poet, respectively, gains a sharper profile' (Kitzbichler, 2016, p. 30).

Some authors, on the other hand, have claimed that the status of Greek in Rome should be understood against the backdrop of Rome's feeling of political superiority. McElduff (2015, p. 130) notes that the Romans used Greek interpreters while representing Rome and avoided speaking Greek 'in particularly fraught situations'. It is worth quoting McElduff (2015, pp. 130–1) at some length:

> The Roman general Scipio Africanus the Elder used an interpreter when speaking to the Carthaginian general Hannibal before the battle of Zama in 202 BCE (Polybius 15.6, Livy, From the Founding of Rome 30.30). Although both were fluent in Greek, and Hannibal understood and spoke Latin (although with a strong accent), the presence of an interpreter marked their identities as generals leading armies of two powerful, non-Hellenistic states.

This illustrates the status of the two languages and the relevance of translations to indicate the superiority of one of them. McElduff mentions another notable example: although the senators had to be educated in Greek and Roman oratory (Garceau, 2018, p. 350) and, therefore, could understand Greek, the Romans did not allow the Greeks to use their language in the Senate. Thus, they had to address the senators via interpreters, marking the superiority of one language over another. As Copeland (1991, p. 35) puts it, the Romans acknowledged their debt to Greek culture but appropriated that influence to signal their contemporary superiority.

The importance of Greece was not limited to Europe, Northern Africa and the Middle East. In the last two centuries before our era, the so-called Indo-Greek empire reached Afghanistan and northern India. The Greeks who settled in that area, 'remnants' of Alexander the Great's army (Holt, 2012, p. 1), established a civilization that fused with the local and preserved some of their own culture, as the few extant papyri and rock inscriptions show. For instance, the inscriptions found in 1976 in an altar in Tepe Nimlik, Afghanistan, include a Greek text devoted to a local god by someone with an Iranian name (Holt, 2012, p. 115). More surprisingly, in 1958 it was discovered that emperor Ashoka, who ruled most of the Indian subcontinent before the time of the Indo-Greek empire (mid-third century BCE), had set up a number of rock edicts containing his moral precepts. These edicts, displayed on pillars in public places, used local languages, for example Magadhi Prakrit in the central part of Indian, and Aramaic and Greek in the northwest, showing the cultural and linguistic interplay of the peoples for whom these inscriptions had been ordered (Holt, 2012, p. 121). As regards the former, Lerner (2013, p. 190) posits that the translators of the Prakrit texts had to adapt the concepts for the target readers, as some of them were unknown in Greek. Also of great interest is the fact that Ashoka's conversion to Buddhism led not only to an emphasis on social justice but also to an interest in spreading his new faith. Consequently, it is believed that he sent missionaries fluent in Greek to other Hellenistic kingdoms, although there are no records of these missions (Holt, 2012, p. 122). This underscores the various manners in which translation was used for religious purposes.

## 26.5 Translation in China

In Asia, the continuous flux of peoples led to imperial expansion and to interaction among the peoples of contemporary Korea, Japan, China and others. In China, multi-ethnicity had been a common feature of the tribes that live along the Yellow River (Lung, 2011, p. 5), among which the Huaxia were the most prominent. They were responsible for the Qin and Han dynasties, who considered themselves superior to the other peoples of the Central Plain. As territorial expansion has always led to a need for translators and interpreters, and the Han dynasty (206 BC–AD 220) was in contact with the peoples of the borderlands, translation was required for communication between the Chinese governments and the military outposts in the Inner Central Asian states (Hung, 2005, p. 49). But, although interpreters and translators must have been crucial for the successive Chinese dynasties, few extant documents allow us a glimpse of the importance of language mediators. Lung (2006, p. 228) mentions the case of *Houhanshu*, or History of the Latter Han, which provides an account of the variety of languages spoken in the area, each incomprehensible to non-native speakers. Thus, interpreters were needed to control other tribes and to propagate the culture of Han China (Lung, 2006, p. 236). Interestingly, Lung (2006, p. 237) notes that those interpreters may in fact have been regional officials playing the role of 'cultural ambassadors'.

Translation was also of the utmost importance for the dissemination of religious faiths. In Asia, sutras were characteristic of Buddhism and Hinduism. These oral traditions were used at a time when most of the population was illiterate, so sutras had to be memorized and repeated orally. It was not until the first century BCE that they began to be recorded in written form as well. Sutras were translated into Chinese during the Han dynasty, a period that spans more than 400 years starting in 206 BCE, and must have had a great impact on the practice of translation, as it is widely accepted that there were no theoretical approaches to the problems of translation before the introduction of Buddhism (St André, 2010, p. 73). The production and dissemination of these translations, aimed at rendering religious texts into Chinese, depended on the collaborative nature of projects as well as on the practice of relay translation (St Andre, 2010), which must have characterized the arrival of religious traditions in China via the kingdoms of the Silk Road. Translators were not the only people who participated in the interlinguistic transformation of these texts: other individuals might have helped the translators to understand the meaning of the original texts. Some of them were bilingual while others spoke one language. The process remained similar in the CE, as translation forums included individuals who performed different functions when rendering a text into Chinese (Hung, 2005, p. 49). This is reminiscent of translational practices in other parts of the world. McElduff (2013, p. 9), for instance, stresses that, although Roman translators did not generally mention assistants, translation was 'a shared experience', as they must have needed to consult experts or friends about the precise meaning of words because dictionaries were used only for official translations. In fact, McElduff (2013, p. 9) claims, translation by memory was probably more common than we imagine.

Although the practice of translation in China is to some extent documented, theoretical statements on translation are more difficult to find. However, in *An Anthology on Chinese Discourse on Translation* (2014[2006]), Martha Cheung gathers more than 250 passages, both short excerpts and full texts, all of which mention or discuss translation to some extent. These documents highlight the function of translation as 'cultural representation, and not merely as a process of interlingual communication' (Cheung, 2014[2006], p. 2). Particularly noteworthy is the collection of early views on translation from a Chinese perspective, even though, as mentioned, most of the translational activity, called *fanyi*, was oral at the time. In part one of the anthology, Cheung presents a small number of texts in which the authors discuss the relation between language and ideas. These texts are brief because, as Cheung (2014[2006], p. 21) stresses, 'brevity is a major characteristic of the ways the ancients conducted the activity called writing'. Among the mentions of translation, we can highlight some indirect references by Confucius (Cheung, 2014[2006], pp. 30–1), and to the interpreters that were used in the dealings with other tribes (Cheung, 2014[2006], p. 36). Of particular interest is the following extract by Mengzi (372–289 BCE), where the author muses on the importance of interpretation (Cheung, 2014[2006], p. 37): 'In explaining a poem, one should not allow the words, in their literary patterning, to obscure the lines, and one should not allow the lines to obscure what is compellingly present in the writer's mind. The right way is to read with empathy in order to meet and grasp what is compellingly present in the writer's mind.' In the text, argues Cheung (2014[2006], p. 38), Mengzi stresses that this passage would apply to the later translations of Buddhist sutras; it was quoted by James Legge, one of the most respected translators of Chinese classics in the nineteenth century. Also relevant is the extract attributed to Zhuangzi (369–286 BCE), who wrote that 'the hare trap is for catching hares; once you have got the hare, the trap is forgotten. Words are for catching ideas; once you have got the idea, the words are forgotten' (Cheung, 2014[2006], p. 40).

These sentiments also serve to bring this chapter to its conclusion, as they summarize the difficulties of catching 'words' in translated forms at a time when writing was generally limited to stone inscriptions and papyri, many of which have been lost. However, the discoveries of the past hundred years in areas such as Egypt or the Iranian plateau have demonstrated that the practice of translation was not unknown. Rather, they reflect that the aims of translating into foreign languages were in no way different from the reasons why translation has been used in modern times: conquest, trade, dissemination of religious beliefs and literary appropriation or adaptation were at the heart of it all.

# References

Anonymous. (1864). *Avesta: The Religious Books of the Parsees.* Trans. Henry Bleeck. Herford: Stephen Austin.

Bandia, P. (2009). African tradition. In M. Baker and G. Saldanha, eds., *Routledge Encyclopedia of Translation Studies.* London: Routledge, pp. 313–20.

Beekes, R. (1988). *A Grammar of Gatha-Avestan.* Leiden: Brill.

Bickerman, E. (1959). The Septuagint as a translation. *Proceedings of the American Academy for Jewish Research,* **28**, 1–39.

Cheung, M. P. Y., ed. (2014 [2006]). *An Anthology on Chinese Discourse on Translation. Volume 1: From the Earliest Times to the Buddhist Project.* London: Routledge.

Connolly, D., and Bacopoulou-Halls, A. (2009). Greek tradition. In M. Baker and G. Saldanha, eds., *Routledge Encyclopedia of Translation Studies.* London: Routledge, pp 418–26.

Copeland, R. (1991). *Rhetoric, Hermeneutics and Translation in the Middle Ages: Academic Traditions and Vernacular Texts.* Cambridge: Cambridge University Press.

De Vaan, M. (2003). *The Avestan Vowels.* Amsterdam: Rodopi.

Delisle, J., and Woodsworth, J. (2012). *Translators through History.* Amsterdam: John Benjamins.

D'hulst, L. (2010). Translation history. In Y. Gambier and L. van Doorslaer, eds., *Handbook of Translation Studies*. Amsterdam: John Benjamins, pp. 397–405.

Galán, J. (2011). Intérpretes y traducciones en el Egipto imperial. *SEMATA*, **23**, 295–313.

Gambier, Y. (2018). Concepts of translation. In L. D'hulst and Y. Gambier, eds., *A History of Modern Translation Knowledge: Sources, Concepts, Effect*. Amsterdam: John Benjamins, pp. 19–39.

Garceau, B. (2018). The Fidus interprets and the fact of slavery: Rethinking classical and patristic models of translation. *Translation Studies*, **11**(3), 349–64.

Gianto, A. (2012). Ugaritic. In H. Gzella, ed., *Languages from the World of the Bible*. Berlin: DeGruyter, pp. 27–54.

Gillespie, S. (2011). *English Translation and Classical Reception: Towards a New Literary History*. Oxford: Wiley-Blackwell.

Gzella, H. ed. (2012). *Languages from the World of the Bible*. Berlin: DeGruyter.

Hermann, A. (2002/1956). Interpreting in antiquity. In F. Pöchhacker and M. Schlesinger, eds., *The Interpreting Studies Reader*. London: Routledge, pp. 15–22.

Holt, F. (2012). *Lost World of the Golden King: In Search of Ancient Afghanistan*. Berkeley: University of California Press.

Hung, E. (2005). Cultural borderlines in China's translation history. In E. Hung, ed., *Translation and Cultural Change: Studies in History, Norms and Image-Projection*. Amsterdam: John Benjamins, pp. 43–64.

Hung, E., and Pollard, D. (2009). Chinese tradition. In M. Baker and G. Saldanha, eds., *Routledge Encyclopedia of Translation Studies*. London: Routledge, pp. 369–78.

Kemp, B. (2006). *Ancient Egypt: Anatomy of a Civilization*. London: Routledge.

Kitzbichler, J. (2016). From Jerome to Schleiermacher? Translation methods and the irrationality of languages. In T. Seruya and J. Justo, eds., *Rereading: Translation, Cognition and Culture*. Berlin: Springer, pp. 227–40.

Lefevere, A. (1992). *Translation/History/Culture*. London: Routledge.

Lerner, J. (2013). The Greek inscriptions of Aśoka. In A. Sinitsyn and M. Kholod, eds., *Studies in Honour of Valery P. Nikonorov*. St Petersburg: St Petersburg State University, pp. 188–97.

Lewis, M., ed. (2009). *Ethnologue: Languages of the World*. Dallas, TX: SIL International.

Loba Mkole, J.-C. (2016). Biblical canons in church traditions and translations. *The Bible Translator*, **67**(2), 108–19.

Lung, R. (2006). Translation and historiography: How an interpreter shaped historical records in Latter Han China. *TTR*, **19**(2), 225–52.

Lung, R. (2011). *Interpreters in Early Imperial China*. Amsterdam: John Benjamins.

Martínez, J., and de Vaan, M. (2014). *Introduction to Avestan*. Leiden and Boston: Brill.

Mauranen, A., and Kujamäki, P., eds. (2004). *Translation Universals: Do They Exist?* Amsterdam: John Benjamins.

McElduff, S. (2013). *Roman Theories of Translation: Surpassing the Source.* London: Routledge.

McElduff, S. (2015). Speaking as Greeks, speaking over Greeks: Orality and its problems in Roman translation. *Translation Studies*, **8**(2), 128–40.

McLaughlin, J. (2012). *The Ancient Near East.* Nashville, TN: Abingdon Press.

Merkle, D. (2018). Translation and censorship. In F. Fernández and J. Evans, eds., *The Routledge Handbook of Translation and Politics.* London: Routledge, pp. 238–53.

Naudé, J. (2018). History of translation knowledge of monotheistic religions with written tradition. In L. D'hulst and Y. Gambier, eds., *A History of Modern Translation Knowledge.* Amsterdam: John Benjamins, pp. 390–5.

Pegenaute, L. (2018). Translation and cultural development. In S.-A. Harding and O. Carbonell, eds., *The Routledge Handbook of Translation and Culture.* London: Routledge, pp. 177–206.

Potts, D. (1999). *The Archaeology of Elam: Formation and Transformation of an Ancient Iranian State.* Cambridge: Cambridge University Press.

Rothe, R., Miller, W., and Rapp, G. (2008). *Pharaonic Inscriptions from the Southern Eastern Desert of Egypt.* Winona Lake, IN: Eisenbraus.

Ruiz Rosendo, L., and Persaud, C. (2016). Interpreters and interpreting in conflict zones and scenarios. *Linguistica Antverpiensia, New Series: Themes in Translation Studies*, **15**, 1–35.

Santoyo, J. (2006). Blank spaces in the history of translation. In G. Bastin and P. Bandia, eds., *Charting the Future of Translation.* Ottawa: University of Ottawa Press, pp. 11–44.

Schniedewind, W. (2005). *How the Bible Became a Book: The Textualization of Ancient Israel.* Cambridge: Cambridge University Press.

Schniedewind, W. (2013). *A Social History of Hebrew: Its Origins through the Rabbinic Period.* New Haven, CT: Yale University Press.

Schniedewind, W., and Hunt, J. (2007). *A Primer on Ugaritic: Language, Culture and Literature.* Cambridge: Cambridge University Press.

Sharma, T. (2002). Translating literary texts through Indian poetics: A phenomenological study. *Translation Today*, **1**(1). www.anukriti.net /tt1/article-k/a1.html.

Shear, I. (2004). *Kingship in the Mycean World and Its Reflection in the Oral Tradition.* Philadelphia, PA: INSTAP Academic Press.

St André, J. (2010). Lessons from Chinese history: Translation as a collaborative and multi-stage process. *TTR*, **23**(1), 71–94.

Tadeu Gonçalves, R. (2015). *Performative Plautus: Sophistics, Metatheater and Translation.* Newcastle: Cambridge Scholars Publishing.

Toury, G. (1995). *Descriptive Translation Studies and Beyond.* Amsterdam: John Benjamins.

Toury, G. (2005). Enhancing cultural changes by means of fictitious translations. In E. Hung, ed., *Translation and Cultural Change*. Amsterdam: John Benjamins, pp. 3–18.

Trivedi, H. (2006). In our time, in our own terms: Translation in India. In T. Hermans, ed., *Translating Others*. Manchester: St Jerome, pp. 102–19.

Tully, E. (2014). Translation universals and polygenesis: Implications for textual criticism. *The Bible Translator*, **65**(3), 292–307.

Vlassopoulos, K. (2017). Xenophon on Persia. In M. Flower, ed., *Cambridge Companion to Xenophon*. Cambridge: Cambridge University Press, pp. 360–75.

Weissbort, D., and Eysteinsson, A. (2006). *Translation Theory and Practice: A Critical Reader*. Oxford: Oxford University Press.

Xenophon. (1859). *The Anabasis of Xenophon*. Trans. Thomas Clark. Philadelphia, PA: Charles DeSilver.

# 27

# Translation in the First Millennium

Denise Merkle

## 27.1  Introduction

The first millennium spans the years 1 to 1000. However, historical periodicity does not always line up neatly with conventional Western chronology, calculated from the traditional date of the birth of Christ (AD), now referred to as the Common Era (CE). The section on the Old World in Chapter 28 starts with the Late Middle Ages. By contrast, this chapter covers the period from the beginning of the CE to the advent of the Renaissance, tracing translation activity back to the civilizations that gave rise to cultural and intellectual renewal in Europe. The Eastern Roman and Byzantine, (Holy) Roman, Umayyad and Abbasid as well as Chinese empires, in addition to the Indian subcontinent, have documented translation and interpreting activity during the millennium when expansionist empires and kingdoms rose and fell, and Silk Road trade flourished. Classical Greek, Latin, Persian, Sanskrit and Arabic texts were revered and much translated, as were the texts of two religions founded during the period, Christianity and Islam. The Chinese invented the fabrication of paper early in the second century, which reduced the cost of producing translations. After the Islamic conquest of Samarkand (modern Uzbekistan) in 712, paper made its way throughout the Arabo-Islamic empire and finally to the European continent via Spain in the twelfth century (Salama-Carr, 2012, p. 96). During the so-called dark ages in Europe, intellectual activity was vibrant in the Mediterranean region, northern Africa, Arabia, Persia, the Indian subcontinent and China.

## 27.2  Africa

Translation on the African continent during the first millennium was often a by-product of proselytizing and empire building. Foreign ideas, often religious, were introduced to indigenous peoples notably by

Christians and Muslims. According to Paul Bandia (2009, p. 2), Western representations (e.g., Vansina, 1985; Bascom, 1964; and Finnegan, 1970 cited in Bandia, 2001) contributed to proscribing 'African culture to the realm of orality'. Oral history was handed down by a long line of talented 'professional linguists', who assumed the role of official spokesperson for ethnic groups and royalty. Many worked in the courts of ancient Mali as well as Zimbabwean and Ghanaian kingdoms. These interpreters acted as mediators between the ruling classes and the people in hierarchically organized nations. While they were respected by those who required their services, they were mistrusted by the common people (Bandia, 2009, p. 4). Other forms of translation, involving drum language (Cloarec-Heiss, 1999; Bandia, 2009, p. 4), for example, have also retained the interest of researchers. However, Africa has a long history of written translation going back to the beginning of the first millennium, if not earlier.

Bandia (2009, p. 5) notes that the African pictorial languages of the Akan, Ashanti, Adrinka and Baoulé peoples (Ghana), the Bamileke and Bamun peoples (Cameroon) and the Baluba and Bakuba peoples (Congo) have been translated into Arabic and Roman scripts, for example. However, Africa's tradition of written translation also involves logographic, alphasyllabaric and alphabetic writing systems (Yimam, 1992), such as those developed by the literate cultures of the Nile Valley: Demotic, Coptic, Nubian, Ethiopian and Kush. The British Museum houses, for example, a page from an Old Nubian translation of the Investiture of the Archangel Michael (ninth–tenth century), found at Qasr Ibrim. Old Nubian used a variant of the Coptic alphabet, with three additional letters, two of which were from Meroitic. There is evidence that people south of the first cataract of the Nile had spoken a language different from Ancient Egyptian since the Old Kingdom, also known as the Age of the Pyramids. One more recent indication is the presence of translators who were acting as a link between the Egyptian rulers, who spoke Demotic from year zero to the fifth century and Coptic until the fourteenth century, and the Nubian population (Khalil and Miller, 1996, p. 71).

The Nubian kingdom of Kush, south of Egypt, thrived for centuries at Meroë. The Meroitic period lasted from about 300 BCE until the fourth century CE. Kush had its own dynastic leaders, adaptations of Egyptian religion and alphasyllabic language, Meroitic. Whether the Egyptian rulers were Assyrians, Persians, Greeks or Romans, the Kushites maintained close trading relations with them. The Kingdom of Kush began its final decline during the reign of the Roman Emperor Augustus; however, it was Axumite Kingdom nomads who captured Meroë in the fourth century. During the Meroitic period, literacy was widespread (Millet, 1974, cited by Khalil and Miller, 1996, p. 67) and the ruling families were bilinguals in Meroitic and Egyptian or Demotic, so translation activity can be assumed. Approximately four hundred years elapsed between the last Meroitic documents from the fourth century and the earliest Nubian documents (seventh–eighth centuries), a period of cultural illiteracy (Khalil and Miller, 1996, p. 68).

According to Gawdat Gabra (1996, pp. 59–61), in Egypt, much religious literature was translated into Coptic primarily from Greek, for example St Matthew's Gospel and the Old Testament, but also from Syriac and Aramaic. Since the majority of Egyptians could not read Greek, different versions of the Bible were translated into Coptic and Coptic dialects from the first half of the third century. Many Apocrypha made their way into Egypt primarily during the first centuries of Christianity, and were translated from Greek into Coptic. Works by the Apostles and the Fathers of the Church were primarily translated from Greek, but some from Syriac. Most of the Coptic texts housed at the Nag' Hamâdi library, an important source of information on Gnosticism, were translated from Greek at the end of the fourth century. These texts, essential to our understanding of the history of religions and philosophy, also provide information on the history of the book and on the Coptic language and dialects. Manichæism texts, including letters from Mani, were translated after his death in 276 either from Aramaic or from Greek into the Sub-Akhmimic dialect of Coptic. The last works in Coptic were written by the patriarch Mark III (799–819). By contrast, St Pachomius's works were written in Coptic and some of them were translated into Greek. Between the ninth and the eleventh centuries, Coptic works were translated into Arabic.

Sophia Björnesjö (1996, pp. 94–7, 99) discusses a bilingual Greek-Arabic papyrus from 643 CE, a receipt from the military commander Abdallah b. Gâbir acknowledging receipt of sixty-five sheep to feed his troops. The Greek is not a literal translation of the Arabic, and the names of the two scribes are identified. A three-year correspondence (708–11) between the governor of Umayyad Egypt, Qurra b. Sarik, and the pagarch, Basilios of Upper Egypt, was written in Greek and Arabic, and some letters were bilingual. Basilios may have known an Arabophone able to translate into Arabic. Egypt remained predominantly Christian and Coptic speaking until the tenth century. It was necessary to translate contracts, tax registers, sales receipts and so forth into Coptic as Arabic gained a foothold in the ninth and tenth centuries. Written and oral Coptic was the language of monasteries before being gradually replaced by Arabic. The tenth century marked the beginning of the period when it became necessary to explain liturgy in Arabic and when the first translations of Coptic Christian texts into Arabic appear, as well as Christian texts written in Arabic. A Christian text, probably from the ninth century, deplores the cultural changes that Christians will undergo under Arabic rule, especially the loss of their language to Arabic.

The Kingdom of Aksum, or Axum, was a trading empire centred in Eritrea and northern Ethiopia, which existed from approximately 100 to 940. It became a major trading empire after the fourth century, growing wealthy from trade among Africa, India and Arabia across the Red Sea and the Indian Ocean. Its common language, alphasyllabic Ge'ez, a Semitic language sometimes called Ethiopic, is the ancestor of the modern Tigrinya and Tigré languages. One of the oldest inscriptions of the language, from the early fourth century, is found on the Hawulti obelisk in Matara, Eritrea (Mekonnen, 2020). Axum was an important intermediary between Imperial Rome and India, and Christianity probably spread to Axum through trade routes.

Christianity became the established church of the Ethiopian Axumite Kingdom in the fourth century, when Frumentius, originally from the Eastern Roman Empire, brought Christianity to the Kingdom; he was eventually granted the title of bishop of Ethiopia by the Catholic/Orthodox Church. However, the Coptic Church missionaries who Christianized Axum between the fourth and sixth centuries came from Egypt. The Coptic missionaries were Monophysites (also called Miaphysites) and considered heretics within the Roman and Byzantine empires. The Bible was translated into Ge'ez between the fifth and the seventh centuries (Gaur, 2015). According to E. A. Wallis Budge (1928), the oldest surviving Ge'ez manuscript is believed to be the fifth- or sixth-century illuminated Garima Gospels in two volumes. Qerlos, a collection of Christological writings, including the treatise of bishop St Cyril of Alexandria, dates back to this period. In the latter part of the fifth century, the Aksumite Collection provided a fundamental set of instructions and laws for the new Ethiopian Church. The collection includes a translation of the Apostolic Tradition, lost in the original Greek, and a translation of the monastic Rules of Pachomius. The ambitious translation enterprise undertaken in the early years of the Ethiopian church resulted in the Ge'ez Bible containing eighty-one Books from the Old and New Testaments (Mekonnen, 2020). A number of these are canonical books of the Old Testament. Notably, the complete text of the Book of Enoch has survived in no other language (Mekonnen, 2020).

## 27.3   Arab-Speaking World and Persia

Many peoples inhabiting the Arab-speaking world were bilingual, writing in Syriac or Aramaic, since Arabic did not develop a writing system until the rise of Islam in the seventh century. By contrast, Nestorian Christians, expelled from Byzantium by the First Council of Ephesus (431), settled in southwestern Persia, where they translated Greek, Indian, Chinese and perhaps Sogdian medical texts into Syriac, the official language of the Nestorian Church. However, little translation into Arabic during the same period has been documented, other than a trilingual text (Greek, Syriac and Arabic) dating back to 513, which was found near Aleppo (Baker, 2001, p. 317). The Prophet (c.570–8 June 632), commonly known as Muhammad, sent messages to various non-Arab political rulers, so translation or interpretation would have been required (Baker, 2001, p. 318). By 698, Iraq, Iran and Syria were religiously and politically Islam, and Egypt and North Africa increasingly so. The Umayyad Caliph Abd Al-Malik ibn Marawan (685–705) is credited with establishing Arabic as the lingua franca of a vast empire comprising many ethnic and linguistic groups by declaring it the sole administrative language.

Translation is closely associated with the growth of Arabic as a written literary language, which 'began with the need to fix the form of the Qur'ān' (Baker, 2001, p. 317) that 'includes many words borrowed from Greek, Persian, Syriac and Hebrew' (Baker, 2001, p. 318). The first organized, large-scale translation activity in history, centred in Baghdad, started during the reign of the Umayyads (661–750) and culminated under the ethnically diverse Abbasids (750–1258) with the Golden Era of translation during the reign of Al-Ma'mūn, who adopted Persian practices, including translating foreign works (Salama-Carr, 2012, p. 106). This Arabo-Islamic tradition had its roots in Judeo-Christian schools of translation, for example 'the theological Nestorian Syriac School of Nizip/Nisibis (4th and 5th centuries) [and] the Jacobite Syriac School of Kinnisrin' (Gambier, 2018, p. 29). Greek and Syriac were tightly linked because the Eastern Church used both languages. During the seventh century, Caliph Omar limited translation to pragmatic texts. During the late Umayyad period (first half of the eighth century), the first texts from Persian, Greek and Coptic on alchemy, medicine and astrology, as well as administrative texts, were translated, in addition to Byzantine and Persian songs. The free-thinking Arabo-Persian Ibn Al-Muqaffa' translated from Persian into Arabic famous Hindu fables, for example *Kalila wa dimna* (Baccouche, 2000, p. 396). Towards the end of the Umayyad period, 'Greek gnomologia' texts were translated (Baker, 2001, p. 319).

Under the Abbasids, 'ethnic Arabs excelled [in] theology, jurisprudence and linguistics', whereas Persians, Syrians and Jews excelled in translation and writing in almost all other areas (Baker, 2001, p. 319). Translation policies were adopted with the support of 'aZams (Persian Jews), some of whom had converted to Islam and among whom Caliphs recruited doctors and secretaries (Baccouche, 2000, p. 396). At the beginning of the Abbasid period, Harran (Hellenopolis) housed an important school of translation led by Thabit ibn Kurra. Sabeans translated Greek mathematical and astronomy works, but also Hindu, Babylonian and Chaldean texts (Baccouche, 2000, p. 399). During the period, it was believed that the Qur'ān encouraged translation in order to seek knowledge. Three features distinguished this Golden Era of translation: (1) the 'range of source languages' ('Sanskrit, Persian, Syriac, Greek, Aramaic', etc.); (2) the 'range of topics and subjects' ('mathematics, astronomy, philosophy, logic, medicine, chemistry, politics, etc.') – Arabs were less interested in literary texts because the myths tended to conflict with Islamic religious values and '[they] already had a strong literary tradition'; and (3) the fact that, supported by government, translation was 'institutionalized' in 'transla-lation chambers ... set up to initiate and regulate the flow of translations' (Baker, 2001, p. 318). Al-Mansūr (754–75) established the first translation chamber reserved for great intellectuals, which was expanded by Al-Rashid (786–809) and Al-Ma'mūn (813–33) (Touati, 2014).

The Greek-Arabic translation movement was initiated in 754 by Abbasid Caliph Al-Mansūr in Baghdad, where depositories of the wisdom of the Ancients became as famous as the Alexandria library, likely destroyed at some point between the fifth and the seventh centuries. Knowledge was considered one of the greatest riches that an empire could acquire and translation was mobilized to increase it. Emphasis was placed on great Greek scientific and philosophical classics, many of which were direct translations, as well as Persian and Hindu texts. Syriac and Persian were intermediate languages during the Umayyad period. Under Caliph Al-Ma'mūn, around 830, the House of Wisdom (Bayt Al-Hikma) became even more famous, in large part thanks to the learned men it attracted, as well as the quantity and quality of translations produced. Translators were recruited by the Caliph and paid richly, and they enjoyed great prestige. Collaborative translation between translators and non-translators aimed to enrich the empire and was itself enriched by it.

Two important translators of the period were Yuhanna Ibn Al-Batrīq and Hunayn Ibn Ishāq. Ibn Al-Batrīq was a Syrian scholar who pioneered the translation of ancient Greek texts (e.g., those of Galen, Hippocrates and Ptolemy) into Arabic, by proposing an Arabic equivalent for the meaning of each Greek word without, however, taking syntax and metaphors into account, in addition to borrowing ancient Greek words when no equiva-lent could be found (Baccouche, 2000, p. 397). Hunayn Ibn Ishāq revised the former's translations under Al-Ma'mūn (Baker, 2001, p. 321). He com-piled the encyclopedic *Kitab sirr al-asrar* (the book of the science of govern-ment) translated into Latin as *Secretum Secretorum* (Secret of Secrets) in the mid-twelfth century. The influential book, whose origin is uncertain, treated a wide range of topics, from statecraft to magic.

The ninth-century Syrian Nestorian Hunayn Ibn Ishāq, trained in med-icine, translated 'some 100 manuscripts into Syriac and 39 into Arabic, including the works of Aristotle, Plato and Ptolemy' (Baker, 2001, p. 320). Ibn Ishāq's method of translating Greek originals, which was dominant during the period, translated meaning accurately, while creating an idio-matic target text that could 'be understood by the non-expert in the field of medical science or by him who does not know anything of the ways of philosophy' (Salama-Carr, cited by Baker, 2001, p. 321). Supported by his expertise in medicine and logic, Ibn Ishāq's method guaranteed a fluid and accurate translation. By contrast, his translations of mathematical texts required revision since he was not an expert in the field (Baccouche, 2000, p. 397). 'Al-Ma'mūn recruited the most talented men for the House of Wisdom[,] such as al-Khwarizmi, al-Kindi and al-Hajjaj[,] the first translator

of Euclid's *Elements* into Arabic ..... There they worked with Hunayn ...'
(O'Connor and Robertson, 1999). However,

> [m]ost of the difficulty occurred in searching for the [Greek philosophical
> and scientific] manuscripts which were to be translated. In order to find
> manuscripts of the works of Aristotle and others, Al-Ma'mūn sent a team
> of his most learned men to Byzantium. It is thought that Hunayn, being
> more skilled in the Greek language than any of the other scholars in
> Baghdad, was on this expedition. (O'Connor and Robertson, 1999, para. 5)

His son Ishāq Ibn Hunayn is remembered for his Arabic translation of
Euclid's *Elements*.

During the Golden Era, commentaries on the best methods of translation,
as well as on the limits and reliability of the translation of certain text types,
were written (Baker, 2001, p. 321). This Era 'was followed by a rich period
[during the tenth and eleventh centuries] of original writing in many fields,
including astronomy, alchemy, geography, linguistics, theory and philosophy', the 'most outstanding contributions [coming] from Arabic-speaking
subjects of the Empire', notably Persians (Baker, 2001, p. 321).

## 27.4 India

The primary sources of information for this section are Krishnamurthy
(2001, pp. 469–71) and Salama-Carr (2012, p. 102).

India had been trading with Mediterranean peoples, including Egyptians
and Byzantines, since BCE. Indian thought influenced the writings of the
Greek first- and second-century physicians Dioscorides and Galen, while in
150 a first-century Alexandrian astrological text was translated into Sanskrit
by Yavanesvara in central India. The Indian classical period lasted from
c.100 to 1000. From the third to the fifth centuries, Chinese and Buddhist
scholars translated Indian works on Buddhism, Hinduism, astronomy,
mathematics, pharmacology and logic; some 8,000 titles are listed in catalogues compiled during the Song and Tang dynasties. Caliph Al-Mansūr
translators produced the first translations of astronomy, medicine and
mathematics texts from Sanskrit into Arabic, notably the mathematician-
astronomer Aryabhata's late-fifth-century treatise that presented his number system. Sanskrit medical treatises were also translated into Pali, and
later into Bengali and Nepali, as well as Korean, Khotanese, Tibetan,
Mongolian and Chinese; references to Indian treatises can be found in the
works of the Perso-Arabian physician and philosopher Al-Râzî (c.860–925).
The Nalanda University scholars Arya Deva, Silabhadra and Dharmapala
travelled to Tibet, where their works were translated into Tibetan. The
ninth- or tenth-century *Mahavyutpatti*, a Sanskrit-Tibetan-Chinese dictionary
of Buddhist technical terms, confirms co-operation among Indian, Tibetan
and Chinese scholars.

In the first century, Kushana King Kanishka accelerated the spread of Buddhism in Central Asia and China. Indian Buddhist scholars travelled to China and were responsible for the first translations into Chinese. Northeast India's Nalanda University trained translators from the fourth century. Kumarajiva went to China in 401 and translated the *Life of Nagarjuna*, a major Buddhist leader, into Chinese. Jingupta translated thirty-seven Sanskrit works into Chinese, while Paramartha went to China in the fifth century and translated the *Life of Vasabandu*, an authority on yoga. Two centuries later, the Chinese Buddhist translators Xuan Zang (c.600–64) and Yijing (635–713) went to India to study at Nalanda. The former translated more than thirty Buddhist volumes, while the latter took several hundred books back to China.

The earliest surviving Sanskrit poem from the period is a Chinese translation produced by an Indian scholar. It is believed that the prestigious classical Sanskrit versions of two Hindu epics, *Mahabharata* and *The Ramayana*, were translated from Prakrit, as were vernacular Puranas (ancient stories), to enhance their status. Vernacular Prakrit was a Middle Indo-Aryan language, used contemporaneously with classical Sanskrit (Woolner, 1917). Sanskrit plays started to allow those who were not kings or brahmins to speak in Prakrit. A gloss was provided in Sanskrit for the Prakrit speeches. Animal fables were first translated from Sanskrit into Middle Persian Pahlavi in the sixth century at the order of a Persian emperor. A Syriac translation followed in c.570 and an Arabic translation in the eighth century. The fables continued to be translated into other languages into the second millennium.

In Southern India, where Dravidian languages are spoken, early inscriptions and Jain texts were originally written in Sanskrit and Prakrit, after which they were written in Tamil. Sanskrit works, such as those of the fourth- or fifth-century dramatist and poet Kalidasa, were adapted into Telugu for popular audiences. The first written Kannada texts were adaptations of Sanskrit originals. Yadava kings supported the development of Marathi to render Sanskrit texts, such as the *Bhagavad Gita*, and religious poems inspired by Bhakti texts.

## 27.5  China

The primary source of information for this section is Hung and Pollard (2001, pp. 366–71).

Translation in the fields of diplomacy and commerce is an integral part of China's long history, in part because of the country's many regional languages. The term *yiguan* or *yishi* (literally 'translation official' responsible for government translation work) dates back to the Han Dynasty (206 BCE to 220 CE), during which translators and interpreters accompanied merchants throughout Asia and the Indian subcontinent (Hung and

Pollard, 2001, p. 366). During the Tang Dynasty (618–906), foreigners living in China worked as government interpreters and accompanied Chinese officials on diplomatic missions.

From the mid-first to the fifth centuries, Buddhist scriptures were the primary objects of translation. In the second century, a vast translation movement that lasted for nine centuries, often with government support, started with the spread of Buddhism, which already had a long history in India where it had originated. Some sutras may have been translated as early as 70 CE. Sogdians from Samarkand, who had honed their linguistic skills at the crossroads of the Silk Road, were among the translators of Buddhist scriptures in China. The second-century Parthian prince An Shigao (aka Parthamasiris) is the earliest known translator of sutras into Chinese, and he also introduced elements of Indian astronomy to China. First-phase translations were literal, reproducing source language syntax closely and with liberal recourse to transliteration. For example, in the third century, Zhi Qian produced generally incomprehensible translations of about thirty volumes of Buddhist scriptures. According to Hung and Pollard (2001, p. 367), three-step translation forums were created to inter-pret, record and check translations, while producing detailed annotations under the guidance of a revered foreign Buddhist monk with no knowl-edge of Chinese but who was named the Chief Translator (*yizhu*), while a Chinese (*duyu* or *chuanyu*) interpreted the monk's theological explana-tions. The Chinese translation was compiled by the Recorder (*bishou*).

In the fifth century, the Buddhist monk Dao An oversaw the translation of sutras and invited the Buddhist monk Kumarajiva, who like many other Indian translators during this phase had learned Chinese. Consequently, Kumarajiva did not have to rely on an interpreter, which inaugurated the second phase. A highly revered translator-monk, his forums could attract more than 3,000 participants. Kumarajiva emphasized the transfer of meaning, supported free translation and suggested that translators sign their translations (Zhong, 2003). His translations enabled Buddhism to take root as a serious rival to Taoism. From Kumarajiva's arrival until the seventh century, the quantity of translations of Sanskrit sutras increased and their accuracy improved. The pendulum swung in the opposite direc-tion during this phase of freer translation (*yiyi*), where syntax adhered to target norms and translations achieved a literary quality.

During the third phase (c.589–1100), the famous Tang dynasty monk Xuan Zang (c.600–64) recommended reproducing the style of the original text accurately, that is, without embellishment. He also set down rules for transliteration that were adopted by many translators who succeeded him (Zhong, 2003). In 629, Xuan Zang left for India in search of sacred texts, returning in 645 with gold statues of Buddha, other artefacts and more than 600 manuscripts. The emperor built the 'Great Wild Goose Pagoda' for him in modern Xi'an, where he spent the rest of his life working with a small group of expert collaborators on the Buddhist manuscripts brought back from India. The translations helped to make Buddhism popular throughout China. He also translated some Tao texts, in addition to classical Chinese literature, into Sanskrit. He believed that translation 'must be both truthful and intelligible to the populace' (Zhong, 2003). Dao An had insisted on word-for-word translation, whereas Kumarajiva had favoured freer translation to achieve an elegant and intelligible target text. Xuan Zang's approach fell between the two extremes. He was the first Chinese translator to make use of amplification and omission, among other novel techniques (Zhong, 2003). The quality of translation improved because translations were now produced by Chinese monks who had studied Sanskrit in India. During the Song dynasties (960–1279), schools for the translation of Buddhist scriptures were established, but, with the declining interest in Buddhism in India, the quality and quantity of Chinese translations were no longer comparable with those of the Tang dynasty.

China also had a huge impact on all aspects of Japanese life, including its writing system. In the third and fourth centuries, Korean scribes introduced the Chinese script, which would be used in Japan until 1854. Rather than translate Chinese texts, the Japanese devised an annotation system called *kambun kundoku*, which enabled them to read the Chinese texts without translation. Special marks placed beside Chinese characters converted the foreign texts into understandable Japanese (Kondo and Wakabayashi, 2001, p. 485).

## 27.6   Ancient Rome and the Roman Empires

The primary source of information for this section is Ballard et al. (2019, pp. 45–103).

It is believed that Jesus of Nazareth spoke and taught in Aramaic, and encouraged the use of different languages to convert people to his teachings. The multilingual communication of the day required first oral and then written translation. Hebrew was the sacred language; Greek, the language of the cultivated elite; Latin, the language of the Roman conqueror; and Aramaic, the vehicular language; for example, the apostle Matthew wrote first in Aramaic for Palestinian Christians, before his text was translated into Greek. By the end of the second century, the Christians had started to preach in Latin, which required translations of Christian scripture into Latin, the earliest of which were based on the Septuagint. Aquila Ponticus, also known as Aquila of Sinope, produced a very literal Greek translation of the Hebrew version of the Old Testament for Jews no longer able to read Hebrew, under the authority of a famous rabbi (Simon, 2012, p. 158), at the beginning of the second century. At the end of the second century, two translations were produced: the first by the Jewish proselyte Theodotion whose poor knowledge of Hebrew resulted in an awkward translation, the other by

Symmachus of Samaria whose translation was more intelligible than Aquila's. The three translations replaced the Septuagint in synagogues where Greek rather than Arameen was spoken. Origen's (c.230–40) *Hexapla* is a six-column Bible, including the Old Testament in Hebrew characters, the Greek transcription, and Greek translations by Aquila of Sinope, Symmachus and Theodotion, as well as the Septuagint. Fragments of this work and Latin translations of his commentaries in Greek remain.

Saint Jerome (Eusebius Hieronymus), the patron saint of translators, was born into an affluent family at Stridon (Dalmatia) c.347, and died at Bethlehem in 419 or 420. Christianity had acquired legal status under Emperor Constantine the Great, and became the state religion in 380. Emperor Theodosius made Nicene Christianity the official religion of the Roman Empire. Jerome's native language was Illyrian; he learned Latin when he moved to Rome for his education. Jerome liked rhetoric, and read Cicero and Quintilian, who believed that producing a translation that respected the target language's unique character contributed to improving mastery of one's mother tongue. At around sixteen years old, he befriended Pammachius and was baptized in 366. He embarked on his 374 voyage to the Orient as well as his translation career, taking his personal library with him.

At Antioche, he abandoned pagan literature until it was authorized by Church fathers fifteen years later. In the Chalcis desert, he learned Hebrew and did penance until 378, when he returned to Antioche and was ordained a priest. From 379 to 382, he lived in Constantinople, the capital of the Roman Empire, where he studied theology and started to translate Greek texts into Latin, including the second part of *The Chronicon* by Eusebius of Caesarea, which became a model for translation during the Middle Ages. From 382 to 385, Jerome lived in Rome working as Pope Damas's secretary. The pope tasked him with revising the existing translations of the Old Testament in order to produce a single homogenous Latin text from the *Vetus Latina*, which refers to all of the Latin translations of biblical texts written in Greek in Europe and Africa during the second half of the second century until the mid-third century. He rather decided to produce a new translation of the New Testament, and to (re-)translate parts of the Septuagint he considered poorly translated, which resulted in the Vulgate. Re-translation of canonical Greek texts was considered scandalous, so he had to justify himself in a letter to Marcella in 384. In conflict with authority and unpopular in Rome, Jerome returned to the Middle East in 385 to live in a convent. From 386 to 393, he built monasteries, and he translated.

In 394, Saint Augustin criticized Jerome's work, fearing the dangers of competing interpretations. In his Letter to Pammachius, *De Optimo Genere Interpretandi* (on the best translation method), written in 395–6, Saint Jerome justified his translation of the Bible, writing: 'If I render word for word, the result sounds absurd; if I make any necessary changes in order or wording, I appear to have abandoned the function of a translator' (in Kelly, 1975, p. 72). The letter is foundational for translation studies in that Jerome's justifications are based on the observation of his translation practice, and his method is scientific because his assertions are supported with examples. His well-documented translation work included textual and terminology research, syntheses, annotations and commentaries, thereby contributing to preserving classical texts for posterity.

At the end of the third century, some poetic works were still translated from Greek into Latin, though Greek gradually lost importance in the Western Roman Empire because Romans no longer read the Greek originals. From the second century, Latin translations of Greek philosophical works began to appear. A partial fourth-century translation of Plato's *Timée* produced by Chalcidius accompanied by a long commentary became important for knowledge on Plato in the Middle Ages. First-century Titus Flavius Josephus wanted to make the Jewish religion known in the seven book *The Wars of the Jews* presented as a translation from Aramaic. The first Latin fourth-century translation, which names the translator Iosippus, reduced it to five books. During the fourth and early sixth centuries, two important translators were Caius Marius Victorinus Afer, whose translations of Aristotle and Porphyry of Tyr have been lost, and Anicius Manlius Severinus Boethius. The latter was inspired by Afer's translation of Porphyry's *Isagoge*, and aimed to make the works of Plato and Aristotle accessible in Latin by translating them. Boethius thereby became the main intermediary between classical antiquity and the following centuries. In the sixth century, Cassiodorus, founder of the Vivarium monastery, had monks copy Latin manuscripts. He understood that it was vital for a civilization to conserve and produce translations, thereby continuing the work of Boethius.

Other non-religious works translated in this period include *Physiologus*, an anonymous didactic Christian text written or compiled in Greek, in Alexandria, from the early centuries of the millennium. It consists of written descriptions, sometimes illustrated, of animals, fantastic creatures, stones and plants, followed by an anecdote describing their moral and symbolic qualities. It was translated into Armenian in the fifth century, into Latin between the mid-fourth century and the early sixth century, into Ethiopic and Syriac, after which it was translated into many European and Middle-Eastern languages. A number of illuminated manuscript copies, such as the ninth-century *Bern Physiologus*, survive. A predecessor of bestiaries, it influenced ideas on the symbolic meaning of animals in Europe for more than a thousand years. Medieval poetical literature and medieval ecclesiastical art are replete with symbolism, for example the phoenix rising from its ashes, that can be traced to *Physiologus* (Littmann, 1939).

Romans also translated Greek scientific, especially medical, texts, as early as the first century, when Celsus developed a Latin medical terminology. In the second century, Caelius Aurelianus and, in the fifth or sixth century, Muscio produced Latin adaptations of, for example, a book on gynaecology. Afer translated works by Euclid, Archimedes, Ptolemy and Pythagoras, all of which have been lost. However, his free translation into Latin, titled *Institutio arithmetica*, of the second century Nicomachus of Gerasa's Greek language *Arithmetike eisagoge* (*Introduction to Arithmetic*) became an essential reference from the Middle Ages to the Renaissance, and he came to be considered the author. Starting in the sixth century, anonymous translations of Hippocratus, Galien, Rufus of Ephesus, Alexander of Tralles, Dioscorides and Oribasius appeared.

Theory developed during the first two centuries of the millennium. For Quintilian (c.30–100), like Cicero, translating meant turning Greek into Latin. To do justice to the excellent Greek models, one had to choose the most appropriate Latin terms while respecting target language syntax, style and tone because the languages were fundamentally different. He believed that translation exercises to and from the source language were the best training for orators to improve their self-expression. Pliny the Younger (62–114) shared Quintilian's beliefs, adding that translators read the original more attentively than simple readers did, thereby attributing intellectual legitimacy to translation. Early in the first century, Seneca (4 BCE–65 CE) explained to a philosophy student that it was unnecessary to borrow foreign terms when it was possible to use a target term that expressed the idea more clearly. Aulu-Gelle (125–c.180) defended the translator's, in particular Virgil's, decision to adapt the source text for linguistic, stylistic and moral reasons, explaining that Virgil skilfully deleted certain passages and terms while keeping, even adding, others in his translations of Homer, Hesiod, Callimachus and so on, thereby creating 'interlinguistic intertextuality' (Ballard et al., 2019, p. 74).

The year 476 marked the deposition of the last Western Roman Emperor, Romulus Augustus, the collapse of the Western Roman Empire and the creation of the Kingdom of Italy. The Eastern imperial court survived until 1453. Eastern Empire Churches translated the Septuagint into Coptic (from the second century), Ethiopean (from the fourth to the seventh centuries), Syriac and Armenian. Before undertaking the task of translation, early translators (Ulfila, Mashtots, Cyril and Methodius) were sometimes called upon to create alphabets.

## 27.7 Goths, Armenians and Slavs

Ulfila, also known as Wulfila or Ulphilas, was likely born in modern-day Romania (c.311). After receiving a Christian education, he promoted the Arian doctrine. Arianism was a Christian offshoot that believed that Christ was not divine, only exceptional. In Moesia, he conceived the idea of translating the Bible into the oral language of the Goths, a Germanic people, but he first had to invent an alphabet. Ulfila transcribed the sounds of the spoken Gothic language into letters borrowed from Greek, to which he added Latin and Runic letters. His translation work lasted forty years while he was bishop. He translated the books of the Old Testament from the Septuagint Greek version, and those of the New Testament from the original Greek (Wulfila, 2020), following Greek syntax, but creating neologisms when required. While syntactically literal, his translation included moral censorship aimed at tempering Gothic bellicosity; for example, he did not translate the Books of Kings because they narrated military exploits (Delisle, 2012, p. 5).

Arianism was condemned as heretical by the Concile of Nicaea in 325, but was tolerated until the Roman Emperor Theodosius I excommunicated its followers in 380. Ulfila died in 382 or 383 in Constantinople. His translation reinforced the religious zeal of recent converts, disseminated Arianism among the Goths and contributed to preserving their ethnic identity. While Ulfila's theological legacy was ultimately lost with the demise of Arianism, his invention of the Gothic alphabet and translation of the Bible into the previously unwritten Gothic language are lasting contributions. A few fragments of his translation of the Bible still exist, for example in the Silver Codex (a purple parchment with silver and gold letters) now at Upsala, dating from the fifth century, and in a Milanese codex (Wulfila, 2020). Germanic languages, including English, can trace back words to Ulfila's neologisms (Delisle, 2012, p. 5).

Mesrop Mashtots (361–440) was a dominant figure in Armenia, especially during the fourth century when the country officially adopted Christianity. He was a priest and missionary who spoke Armenian, Greek, Persian and Syriac. Thanks to the benediction and support of the patriarch of the Armenian Church Sahak Partev, he took on the task of creating an Armenian alphabet of thirty-six letters, which were 'Greek supplemented by non-Greek, or Semitic, characters', from 392 to 406, with two letters added in the twelfth century to create the classical Armenian alphabet (Delisle, 2012, p. 7). With Partev, he started translating the scriptures from Greek and Syriac into Armenian (Delisle, 2012, p. 6). Mashtots and his disciples then went to Edessa and Constantinople to locate original texts and translate scripture, while his disciples learnt Greek and Syriac, after which the team returned to Armenia. Partev and Meshtots used the new material to revise their first draft of the Bible translation. Furthermore, Meshtots and his team also translated Aristotle, Plato, Xenon and Eusebius. Widespread literacy and evangelization in Armenia were achieved by creating a very avant-garde 'network of public schools' (Delisle, 2012, p. 7), all of which was intended 'to build a powerful political and cultural identity [and] strengthen the nation's resistance to assimilation by the Byzantines and Persians' (Delisle, 2012, p. 7).

In 862, the Christian ruler of the Slavic state of Great Moravia, Prince Rastislav, asked the Byzantine Emperor Michael III to send missionaries to educate his people and preach the Christian faith in Slavic. The prince wished not only to have sacred texts translated into the language of his people but also to free them from Frankish domination through religious emancipation. Macedonian Slavs Cyril and his brother Methodius spoke Greek and the Slavic dialect. During a diplomatic mission among the Khazars, Cyril learnt Hebrew, Arabic and Khazar (a Turkic language) and discovered Ulfila's Gothic Psalter and Gospels. He needed to create an alphabet; however, to avoid being accused of heresy for translating into a vernacular language, Cyril asked 'God himself [to reveal] the Slavic letters to [him]' (Delisle, 2012, p. 10). The result was the Glagolitic alphabet, which could be adopted by all the dialects of the language group. While in Constantinople, the brothers and some disciples translated the Holy Books, Psalms and liturgical texts into Old Slavonic.

In 863, the brothers travelled to Moravia with the alphabet and translations for Rastislav. Cyril eventually celebrated Church of Rome liturgy fully in Slavonic, which was initially criticized by the pope. However, Pope Adrian II officially recognized the Slavonic liturgy in 868. Cyril died in 869 in Rome, and Methodius continued translating among the Slavs until he died a few years later. The brothers are considered saints in the Roman Catholic and Orthodox Churches. Their disciples created the Cyrillic alphabet, a simplified version of the Glagolitic alphabet (Delisle, 2012, p. 12).

## 27.8  Toledo

In the late seventh century, Toledo became a key centre of literacy and writing in the Iberian peninsula. From 718, Islamic invaders ruled Spain, the only Western European nation to have been controlled by Muslims. Under the tenth-century, Cordoba-based Umayyad caliphate, Spain was the richest part of Europe and Muslim cities were much more advanced in science, medicine and the arts than their counterparts in Christian Europe. On 25 May 1085, Alfonso VI of Castile captured Toledo which became a major cultural and intellectual centre of Christian Europe, acting as a bridge between Arabo-Muslim and Christian traditions. The Christian conquerors, who had until then considered education and science heretical, were struck by the beauty and culture of the multicultural and multilingual Arab city, populated by Mozarabs (Christians who lived under Islamic rule), Conversos (Jews who had converted to Christianity) and Jews (Pym, 2001, p. 552). They discovered the vast literature on medical, among other, subjects that had been translated into Arabic during the Golden Era of Islam by the House of Wisdom. They did not pillage the Arab libraries, and English, French and other international scholars travelled there to translate into Latin. The eleventh-century scholars of Toledo often spoke Arabic and relied on Arabic sources in their work. When they came into contact with Western Christendom, where Latin was the only written language, it became necessary to translate. In the first part of the twelfth century, Archbishop Raymond of Toledo set up a centre in the cathedral library where classical texts were translated. In addition, commentaries and elaborations were written by Arabic scholars, who had access to many works, including classical Greek texts, which European scholars had heard about but never read. These included works by Galen on medicine, Ptolemy on geography, Aristotle on philosophy and so on, in addition to the transfer of anatomic terminology from Ancient Greek and the Islamic Golden Era to medieval Latin Christendom. Scholars, together with Jewish and Christian translators from the area who had previously lived under Muslim rule, produced relay translations in the centre. A Jew or Mozarab produced an oral Romance version of the Arabic text, which a Christian clerk translated into Latin (Pym, 2001, p. 553). Gerard of Cremona (c.1114–87) was the most productive of the translators, completing more than eighty-seven works on statecraft, ethics, physiognomy, astrology, geometry, alchemy, magic and medicine. He translated Avicenna's *Canon of Medicine*, the key work of the Islamic Golden Era of medicine, and '... the leading authors of anatomical Latin words in the Middle Ages ... founded their books on Gerard's translations. The anatomical terms of the *Canon* retain *auctoritas* up to the Renaissance. Thus, terms coined by Gerard such as *diaphragm*, *orbit*, *pupil* or *sagittal* remain relevant in the current official anatomical terminology' (Arráez-Aybar, Bueno-López and Raio, 2015, p. 21).

From 1250, under the sponsorship of Alfonso X, books on Arabic astronomy, among other scientific subjects, were translated directly into Castilian by primarily Jewish scholars, assisted by Christian clerks. A group of Italians also rendered several of the Castilian translations into Latin and French, thus disseminating classical knowledge throughout Christian Europe (Pym, 2001, p. 553).

According to Anthony Pym (2001, p. 553), the source texts were treated as 'sacred' and literally translated just like such texts had been since Boethius. 'The resulting opacity was ... offset by ... marginal notes, glosses and extended commentaries. Omissions and transformations were also used to Christianize certain texts.'

A parallel can be drawn between the translation movement of Toledo and the ninth- and tenth-century translation movement of Baghdad, where Arabic scholars had translated classical Greek texts into Arabic. In Toledo, these texts were translated from Arabic into Latin. The great library of Toledo attracted scholars from across the continent who returned home with copies of books and translations from the library to enrich knowledge in their cities. Newly founded European universities also contributed to the broader circulation of classical texts, thereby establishing the foundation of scientific think-ing. The universities of Bologna, Paris and Oxford used the new trans-lations as their first textbooks. For example, Nicolaus Copernicus read Latin translations of the works of Greek and Arabic astronomers in Bologna. The translation scholars of Baghdad and Toledo contributed significantly to the rebirth of classical antiquity during the Renaissance.

# References

Arráez-Aybar, L.-A., Bueno-López, J.-L., and Raio, N. (2015). Toledo School of Translators and their influence on anatomical terminology. *Annals of Anatomy – Anatomischer Anzeiger*, **198**, 21–33. www.sciencedirect.com /science/article/abs/pii/S0940960215000047.

Baccouche, T. (2000). La traduction dans la tradition arabe. *Meta*, **45**(3), 395–99. https://doi.org/10.7202/001936ar.

Baker, M. (2001) Arabic tradition. In M. Baker and G. Saldanha, eds., *The Routledge Encyclopedia of Translation Studies*. London/New York: Routledge, pp. 316–25.

Ballard, M., D'hulst, L., Mariaule, M., and Wecksteen-Quinio, C., eds. (2019). *Antiquité et traduction: De l'Égypte ancienne à Jérôme*. Villeneuve d'Ascq: Presses Universitaires de Septentrion.

Bandia, P. (2001). African tradition. In M. Baker and G. Saldanha, eds., *The Routledge Encyclopedia of Translation Studies*. London/New York: Routledge, pp. 295–305.

Bandia, P. (2009). Translation matters. In J. Inggs and L. Meintjes, eds., *Translation Studies in Africa*. London/New York: Bloomsbury, Continuum Studies in Translation, pp. 1–20.

Bascom, W. R. (1964) Folklore research in Africa. *Journal of American Folklore*, **77**(303), 12–31.

Björnesjö, S. (1996). L'arabisation de l'Égypte: le témoignage papyrologi-que. *Égypte/Monde arabe*, 27–8, 93–106. https://doi.org/10.4000/ema .1923.

Cloarec-Heiss, F. (1999). From natural language to drum language: An economical encoding procedure in Banda-Linda (Central African Republic). In C. Fuchs and S. Robert, eds., *Language Diversity and Cognitive Representations*. Amsterdam/Philadelphia: John Benjamins, pp. 145–58.

Delisle, J. (2012). Translators and the invention of alphabets. In J. Delisle and J. Woodsworth, eds., *Translators through History*. Amsterdam/ Philadelphia: John Benjamins, pp. 3–20.

Finnegan, R. (1970). *Oral Literature in Africa*. Oxford: Clarendon Press.

Gabra, G. (1996). Langue et littérature coptes (trans. Samia Rizq). *Égypte/ Monde arabe*, 27–8, 57–66. https://doi.org/10.4000/ema.1030.

Gambier, Y. (2018). Concepts of translation. In L. D'hulst and Y. Gambier, eds., *A History of Modern Translation Knowledge*. Amsterdam/Philadelphia: John Benjamins, pp. 19–38.

Gaur, A. (2015). Ge'ez Language. In *Encyclopedia Britannica*. www .britannica.com/topic/Geez-language.

Hung, E., and Pollard, D. (2001). Chinese tradition. In M. Baker and G. Saldanha, eds., *The Routledge Encyclopedia of Translation Studies*. London/New York: Routledge, pp. 365–76.

Kelly, J. N. D. (1975). *Jerome: His Life, Writings and Controversies*. London: Duckworth.

Khalil, M., and Miller, C. (1996). Old Nubian and language uses in Nubia. *Égypte/Monde arabe*, 27–8, 67–76. https://doi.org/10.4000/ema.1032.

Kondo, M., and Wakabayashi, J. (2001). Japanese tradition. In M. Baker and G. Saldanha, eds., *The Routledge Encyclopedia of Translation Studies*. London/New York: Routledge, pp. 485–94.

Krishnamurthy, R. (2001). Indian tradition. In M. Baker and G. Saldanha, eds., *The Routledge Encyclopedia of Translation Studies*. London/New York: Routledge, pp. 464–74.

Littmann, E. (1939). Ethiopic language. In J. Orr, ed., *International Standard Bible Encyclopedia Online*. Originally published by Wm. B. Eerdmans Publishing Co. www.internationalstandardbible.com/E/ethiopic-language.html.

Mekonnen, Z. (2020). Ge'ez: The Untapped Ethiopian Treasure. *Addis Zeybe*. https://addiszeybe.com/featured/geez-the-untapped-ethiopian-treasure.

O'Connor, J. J., and Robertson, E. F. (1999). Hunayn ibn Ishaq (808–873) Biography. *MacTutor History of Mathematics*. St Andrews University. https:// mathshistory.st-andrews.ac.uk/Biographies/Hunayn/.

Pym, A. (2001). Spanish tradition. In M. Baker and G. Saldanha, eds., *The Routledge Encyclopedia of Translation Studies*. London/New York: Routledge, pp. 552–6.

Salama-Carr, M. (2012). The dissemination of knowledge. In J. Delisle and J. Woodsworth, eds., *Translators through History*. Amsterdam/Philadelphia: John Benjamins, pp. 95–124.

Simon, S. (2012). Translators and the spread of religions. In J. Delisle and J. Woodsworth, eds., *Translators through History*. Amsterdam/Philadelphia: John Benjamins, pp. 153–86.

Touati, H. (2014). Bayt al-hikma: la Maison de la sagesse des Abbassides. In H. Touati, ed., *Encyclopédie de l'humanisme méditerranéen*. www .encyclopedie-humanisme.com/?Bayt-al-hikma.

Vansina, J. (1985). *Oral Tradition as History*. Madison: University of Wisconsin Press.

Wallis Budge, E. A. (1928). *A History of Ethiopia: Nubia and Abyssinia*. London: Methuen.

Woolner, A. C. (1917). *Introduction to Prakrit*. Lahore: University of the Punjab. https://archive.org/details/introductiontopr00woolrich.

Wulfila (2020, 11 October). *New World Encyclopedia.* www.newworldencyclo
  pedia.org/p/index.php?title=Wulfila&oldid=1043710.

Yimam, B. (1992). (Ethiopian) Writing system (trans. Samuel Kinde and
  Minga Negash). Wyiyit – Dialogue. *Journal of Addis Ababa University (AAU)*, I,
  1, 3rd series. www.ethiopians.com/bayeyima.html.

Zhong, W. (2003). An overview of translation in China: Practice and theory.
  *Translation Journal*, **7**(2). https://translationjournal.net/journal/24china
  .htm.

# 28

# Translation in the Second Millennium

Denise Merkle

## 28.1 Introduction

The second millennium of the Common Era (CE) spanned the years 1001 to 1999. It encompassed the High (1000–1300) and Late Middle Ages (1300–1500) of the Old World, succeeded by the Early Modern period or the Renaissance, which ended with the beginning of the Industrial Revolution in the late eighteenth century. The period was characterized by the development of vernacular languages in Europe, the invention of the printing press, the Age of Exploration, wars of religion and the Age of Enlightenment or Reason. The Enlightenment launched the Modern era, marked by industrialization, the rise of nation-states and the rapid development of science, technology and public education. The twentieth century saw two world wars, the subsequent formation of the United Nations (UN), increasing globalization, and the expansion of and growing dependence on technology.

The division of history suggested above was developed for, and applies best to, the Old World, particularly Europe. However, by the eighteenth century, as a corollary of extensive world trade and colonization, the histories of civilizations had become increasingly interconnected in a process known today as globalization (Bird and Kopp, 2019).

This chapter presents an overview history of translation and interpreting activity through the second millennium in Africa, the Americas (the 'New World'), Asia (China, India, Japan, Turkey) and the Old World. The last overview concentrates on the time since the thirteenth century, given that between the eleventh and the thirteenth centuries, dominant languages of translation were Arabic and Latin, covered in Chapter 27 of this volume. The chapter concludes with a section on the twentieth century that links the professionalization of translation, terminology and interpretation with the development of transnational organizations (e.g., UNESCO, the United Nations Educational, Scientific and Cultural

Organization) and supranational unions (e.g., the European Union) in the aftermath of World War II, along with continued globalization and technological progress.

## 28.2  Africa

The primary source of information for this section is Bandia (2009).

Translation has played a key role in pre-colonial, colonial and post-colonial Africa. The Arabs had been trading on the continent for centuries, which clearly necessitated interpreting at the very least. In pre-colonial Africa, oral literature and history were transmitted by word of mouth by linguists, called *griots* in French Africa, often acting as spokesmen for kings and chiefs. The *griots* both reworded their patron's message to convey it to the common people and translated between languages. Other forms of translation involved drum language (Cloarec-Heiss, 1999) and pictograms, as used in pre-colonial Egypt (Diop, 1979).

The colonial era ran from the fifteenth century to the mid-twentieth century. Bandia (2009) divides the era into the period that experienced the arrival of Europeans and the slave trade, and the period starting in the nineteenth century, referred to as the pre-independence era, marked by the partitioning of Africa.

The arrival of the Portuguese in 1445 created the need for translation and interpretation between African linguistic communities, between African languages and Arabic, and between African and European languages. Portuguese missionaries were the first to teach African linguistic communities to write using Roman script. However, they quickly learnt that they could evangelize more effectively in local oral languages. Educated slaves, such as Juan Latino (1516–94), who became a professor of Latin at the University of Granada in 1530 after initially serving a Spanish general, transposed African praise poems into Latin. In a context of competition for religious dominance, the Qur'ān and other Islamic texts were translated into such African languages as Yoruba and Hausa, and, in the nineteenth century, large-scale translation of the Bible into African languages began. Evangelizing in local languages led to the creation of the 1880 Group that launched a bilingual Portuguese/Kimbundu journal, which published some of the earliest works translated from European into African languages, as well as to the training of one of Africa's first translator-terminologists, Joaquin Dias Cordeiro da Matta (1857–94), who produced a Kimbundu–Portuguese dictionary.

In the 1890s, full-scale colonization resulted in Africa being divided up. In the British colonies, the use of vernacular literature was encouraged by Protestant missionaries, resulting in the creation of a bilingual literary tradition that evolved into an English-language tradition in the twentieth century. French purist attitudes to their language and culture discouraged literary creativity in the French colonies, while the *griots* lost their historical prestige. French-speaking Africans worked to correct the literary imbalance in the twentieth century by translating oral literature into French, which inspired English-speaking Africans to do likewise. The Ugandan poet Okot p'Bitek (1931–82) wrote first in Acholi and then translated into English, and the Kenyan writer and academic Ngugi Wa Thiong'o (b. 1938) first writes in Kikuyu and then translates into English. By contrast, the Tanzanian activist and politician Julius Nyerer (1922–99) translated Shakespeare into Swahili. While there has been considerable translation between European and African languages, and between European languages in Africa, there has been relatively little translation between African languages.

## 28.3   The Americas

Norse explorers made contact with the Indigenous peoples in Newfoundland, Labrador and along the New Brunswick Coast, and since trade occurred, interpretation activity can be assumed. However, the first explorers to record their encounters with Indigenous peoples throughout the Americas were the Spanish, Portuguese, French and British. Interpreters were trained to facilitate communication in a context of exploration, colonization and evangelization; missionaries are credited with creating alphabets and other writing systems for oral languages in order to translate the Bible into various Indigenous languages.

### 28.3.1   Latin America

The primary sources of information for this section are Bastin (2001, pp. 505–10), Echeverri and Bastin (2019) and Castro (2019).

The first generation of Latin American interpreters were mainly natives who had been captured and taught Spanish. For example, Christopher Columbus (1451–1506) took ten Native Americans to Spain to learn the language and familiarize themselves with the culture, and on his return to America was accompanied by two interpreters. In 1499, other Spanish explorers took captives to serve as *lenguas* (interpreters). However, some Spaniards lived with Indigenous tribes, also acting as interpreters.

The Spanish conquistador Hernán Cortés de Monroy (1485–1547) used three interpreters at a time to interpret, for example, from Spanish into Maya, from Maya into Nahuatl and from Nahuatl back into Spanish. Especially noteworthy was the Nahua woman La Malinche (d. 1529), interpreter of one of the main language families of Mexico and Central America. She was given to Cortés in 1519 and aided him in his conquest of the Aztecs. Interpreting between Quechua and Spanish was not as structured in Peru, but it played a role in the ambush and execution of the Inca chief Atahualpa (b. circa 1502), in 1532, and the downfall of the Inca civilization. Between 1529 and 1630, fifteen decrees relating to interpreters were signed by Carlos V, Philip II and Philip III. Professional interpreter status was achieved in 1563, and interpreters had to take an oath to be neutral, clear and accurate.

Despite religious censorship, books circulated relatively freely in Latin America, which contributed to Spanish becoming the lingua franca. Printing presses were installed in Mexico (1535) and in Peru's capital, Lima (1583). Unfortunately, books were frequently lost or destroyed, resulting in the disappearance of dictionaries and grammars of Native American languages and translations into them. However, a few translations survived, including the bilingual *Historia de las Cosas de Neuva España*, written in Nahuatl under the direction of Fra Bernardino de Sahagún (1500–90) and translated by him into Spanish.

After independence from Spain, Argentina, Chile, Cuba and Venezuela created distinct national identities through translation activity in the nineteenth and early twentieth centuries, which involved rejecting things Spanish and looking to foreign models, such as Rousseau, Diderot and Abbot Raynal. To respect the source culture, translation of literary and philosophical texts related to emancipation was literal. Translation was also linked to the founding of newspapers, literary journals, publishing houses and universities, French being the most common source language, followed later by English. The arrival of immigrants to Argentina promoted intercultural exchanges and produced such influential translators as Jorge Luis Borges (1899–1986), while Chile produced Pablo Neruda (1904–73). Cuba distinguished itself by notable female translators, such as Gertrudis Gomez De Avelaneda (1814–73).

### 28.3.2 Brazil

The primary sources of information for this section are Gonçalves Barbosa and Wyler (2001, pp. 326–30) and Silva-Reis and Milton (2019).

In Brazil, *línguas* (interpreters) were deportees, adventurers and shipwrecked Portuguese, for example João Ramalho (1493–1580), who lived with Indigenous peoples and learnt their languages. The Jesuits, who arrived in 1549 to convert the Indigenous peoples to Christianity, learnt the lingua franca *Abanheenga*, which had been developed for inter-tribal communication, wrote grammars for and simplified it, renaming their version *Nheengatu*. Until 1759, when the Jesuits were expelled from Portugal and Brazil and *Nheengatu* was banned, education was bilingual, and Portuguese–*Nheengatu* interpreters were needed in courts of law. By 1800 the black population who had been brought to Brazil as slaves added languages of the Bantu group to the linguistic mix and developed a Yoruba-based lingua franca.

In 1815 the exiled Portuguese royal family consolidated the position of Portuguese as the major language of Brazil and elevated the country to the category of kingdom. In 1823, when Brazil became independent, Portuguese was adopted as the official language and, in 1938, President Getúlio Vargas (1882–1954) imposed Portuguese as the language of education. Translators were first recognized officially in 1808 as staff members of the *Impressão Régia* (Royal Printing Shop), founded the same year. They were replaced by multilingual copywriters seventy-three years later. During its 14-year monopoly, the printer published 1,100 works, notably in the social and natural sciences and the professions, to respond to the country's technical needs. Many translations appeared after independence, but most were reprints of translations from the French published in Portugal. Because of the high cost of paper and taxes on books produced locally, publishers restricted their activities to textbooks and law books, local authors publishing in London or Paris. By 1920, Brazil was producing its own paper and, by the 1930s, a Brazilian publishing and literary translation industry was flourishing in response to the growing gap between Brazilian and European Portuguese.

### 28.3.3  North America

#### 28.3.3.1  United States

The primary source of information for this section is Venuti (2001, pp. 306–10).

The French and Spanish in Louisiana and Florida, respectively, interacted with Native Americans, the country's first interpreters in the sixteenth century, while British settlers learnt Aboriginal languages in the seventeenth century. Puritans in Massachusetts, for example, profited from the knowledge of English-speaking members of Algonquin tribes. Throughout the eighteenth century and well into the nineteenth, translation and interpretation continued to be used to expropriate Native Americans' land and convert them to Christianity, while extending the western frontier of the United States to block further Spanish and French expansion.

Translation also played a role in Puritan independence from the Anglican Church through the literal translation of Hebrew psalms, as well as in the American Revolution through the translation of Enlightenment writings by Voltaire (1694–1778) and Rousseau (1712–78), on which Benjamin Franklin (1706–90) and Thomas Jefferson (1743–1826) drew in the Declaration of Independence (1775–6). After the American Revolution, foreign works were translated to construct an autonomous identity that could compete with Britain's and Europe's, and, by the 1850s, a distinctly American variety of English was recognizable. Unofficial translation of immigrant languages between 1851 and 1920 contributed to the political and economic domination of newcomers, while helping to form a clear American identity that respected democratic principles.

Translation and interpreting have increasingly served American political and economic interests since World War II. The State Department's Foreign Service employs a language section to review translations of diplomatic documents and provide interpreting services for international conferences, and translation has also performed explicitly ideological functions. For example, during the Cold War, the US Information Agency issued propagandistic materials over the Voice of America in more than thirty languages. American businesses turned increasingly to translation in the second half of the twentieth century to develop foreign markets, creating a vibrant commercial and technical translation industry. The American publishing industry, by contrast, sold far more translation rights than it acquired, a reflection of international interest in American cultural values and an apparently monolingual domestic culture.

### 28.3.3.2 Canada

The primary source of information for this section is Delisle (2001, pp. 356–9).

The first interpreters in Canada were also Indigenous. In 1534, Jacques Cartier (1491–1557) took two young Iroquois men to France to learn French, and in 1535, they acted as interpreters in negotiations with natives at Stadacona (Québec City). By contrast, Samuel de Champlain (1567–1635) used as *truchements* (interpreters) young, often illiterate, Frenchmen, who agreed to live with Indigenous peoples belonging to Algonquin or Huron-Iroquois family groups, to learn their languages and cultures. Until the Seven Years' War, most translation and interpretation work was done by missionaries, who produced dictionaries and grammars of Indian languages; however, the courts and the military also required part-time interpreters for Indian languages, along with English and Dutch to ensure productive commercial interactions.

After the defeat of the French by the British (1759–63), translation was increasingly limited to French and English. Given the dominant French-speaking population, official documents had to be translated into French, and a dual legal system (French civil law and British common law) was adopted. However, interpreting with Indigenous peoples had not stopped. In fact, in 1804, the North West Company employed almost sixty interpreters, the vast majority French-speaking, who played an active role in the exploration and colonization of the western and northern territories that would be annexed to Canada.

Legal and parliamentary translation was given official status by the British North America Act of 1867, which required that both English and French be used in parliament and in Québec; in 1870 this provision was extended to Manitoba, when it joined the Canadian confederation. The arrival of immigrants, primarily from Europe, from the 1880s until post–World War II necessitated translation to and from their languages, most of it unofficial.

In 1934, the translation offices of federal government departments, employing close to 100 translators, were absorbed into the federal Translation Bureau, Québec and New Brunswick creating provincial translation bureaus in the 1980s. Canadian businesses have also depended on translation, and translation firms have existed in Canada since the early twentieth century.

## 28.4  Asia

### 28.4.1  China

The primary source of information for this section is Hung and Pollard (2001, pp. 366–71).

China has a long history of translation activity. Schools of translation of Buddhist scriptures were established during the Song Dynasty (960–1279), though by 1644, translating sutras had lost importance. Under Mongol Yuan rule in the thirteenth century, Arabs began to settle in China. After learning Chinese, members of the erudite elite translated scientific works from Arabic or European languages. An Arabic dictionary of elementary medicine was translated towards the end of the Yuan dynasty in thirty-six volumes and published during the Ming Dynasty (1368–1644) as *Hui Hui Yao Fang*. The next two centuries were not marked by significant translations.

Towards the end of the sixteenth century, Christian missionaries arrived in China. Between 1582 and 1773, more than seventy European missionaries, often assisted by Chinese collaborators, undertook the translation of various works. The Italian Jesuit priest Matteo Ricci (1552–1610) was assisted by, for example, Xu Guangqi (1562–1633), a distinguished scientist and prime minister during the last years of the Ming Dynasty, when he translated Euclid's *Elements* in 1607. In 1612, a six-volume translation by the astronomer Father Sabatino De Ursis (1575–1620) and Xu Guangqi was the first Chinese work on hydrology and reservoirs. Although translations carried out during the Ming Dynasty were mainly on science and technology, there were also translations of philosophy and literature. The mathematician, astronomer and geographer Li Zhizao (1565–1630), assisted by missionaries, translated some of Aristotle's works into Chinese. In 1625, the first translation of *Aesop's Fables* was introduced to Chinese readers in a translation by the Jesuit missionary to China Nicholas Trigault (1577–1628) (Zhong, 2003).

Translation into Chinese all but stopped with the expulsion of foreign missionaries in 1723. It resumed following the British invasion (1840–2) and the subsequent arrival of American and European missionaries. Missionaries dominated scientific and technical translation initially, but

Chinese translators gradually took over the transmission of Western knowledge. According to Weihe Zhong (2003), at the beginning of the nineteenth century, the Yangwu group of highly placed foreign affairs officials initiated the translation of technical documents dealing with subjects like shipbuilding and weapons manufacture, and established some translator training institutions. Many translations of mathematics and chemistry texts were published by the Jiangnan Ordnance Factory, where the sinologist John Fryer (1839–1928) was an official translator.

By 1912, many medical books were available in Chinese, Ding Dubao (1874–1952), a physician and translator, having been responsible for more than fifty medical translations. After the Sino-Japanese War of 1894–5, Yan Fu (1854–1921) was the most influential translator of European political and social science works, and a translation theorist. He supervised several translation institutes operating under government authority; however, it was particularly his 1898 translation of Thomas Henry Huxley's *Evolution and Ethics* (1893) that established his reputation throughout the country. Yan Fu wrote in classical Chinese, and rearranged chapters and paragraphs so that they would be consistent with the Chinese classical style of presentation and organization of ideas. He also contributed to translation theory in China by developing the triple translation criteria of 'Faithfulness, Fluency and Elegance' in the preface of his noteworthy Huxley translation (Zhong, 2003).

### 28.4.2  India

The primary source of information for this section is Krishnamurthy (2001, pp. 469–71).

India's medieval period (circa 1000–1750) was not marked by significant translation activity into Indian languages. Texts produced during the period were not considered translations from Sanskrit but, rather, independent creations acclaimed as original works by those Indians who read them or heard them recited. While Sanskrit classics had been widely translated into the colonizing languages of Arabic and Persian over a thousand years, European languages, notably English, were added only at the end of the eighteenth century. Yet, few foreign texts were translated into Sanskrit (Trivedi, 2018).

In the south, the twelfth-century philosopher Basava (1105–67) was an exponent of the Virashaivas or Lingayats cult. One publication of his teachings is Palkurika Soma's *Basava* (1195), written in Telegu and adapted into Kannada by Sumatibhima in the fourteenth century. The memoirs of Babur (1483–1530), who conquered Delhi in 1526, were translated from Turkish into Persian and later into English. Dara Shukoh (1615–59) had about fifty of the *Upanishads* translated from Sanskrit into Persian by 1657. The French Indiologist Anquetil-Duperron (1731–1805) subsequently translated them into Latin and published them in Paris in 1802. The mathematician and astronomer Sawai Jai Singh of Jaipur (1688–1743) had some classical Greek texts on mathematics (including Euclid) translated into Sanskrit, as well as more recent European works on trigonometry and logarithms, and Arabic texts on astronomy.

In the early sixteenth century, Western science was introduced to India by travellers and merchants, and later Jesuit missionaries. The astronomer Jagannatha Samrat (1652–1744) translated Ptolemy's *Almagest* and Euclid's *Elements* from Arabic into Sanskrit under the titles of *Samrat-Siddhanta* and *Rekhaganita*. In 1730, Nayanasukhopadhyaha translated the geometry treatise *Ukarakhya Grantha* into Sanskrit from a collective Arabic version that had been translated from a Greek original. The establishment of the Native Medical Institution in 1825, along with courses in medicine at the Sanskrit College and Calcutta Madrasa in 1826, required the translation of numerous European textbooks into Sanskrit, Bengali and other local languages. Between 1868 and 1910, at least ten scientific journals and forty-seven technical publications appeared in Bengali.

In 1843, a society for vernacular translation was founded in Delhi under the auspices of Yesudas Ramachandra (1821–80), who translated Tate's *Elements of Mechanism* into Urdu (*Risala Usual Kalon ke bare main*, 1863). According to Syed Ahmad Khan (1817–98), who founded a similar society in 1864, 'Those who are bent on improving India should remember that the best way to do this is through the translation of all the arts and sciences into their own languages' (quoted by Mohammad, 1972, pp. 231–2). Quoting from page 156 of Maya Pandit's 'Translation culture in nineteenth century Maharashtra: An exercise in colonial cultural politics' (Pandit, 2017), Trivedi (2018, para. 8) concludes that 'while translation in precolonial India was "a natural process of organic growth" and a "symbiotic" process, it became under colonial rule a "secondary, subservient act"—just as we became secondary and subservient subjects'.

After initially showing interest in Sanskrit texts in the late eighteenth century, British colonizers soon increased translation from European into Indian languages. The Baptist William Carey (1761–1834) started translating the Gospels into Indian vernaculars, using the first private press in India. In 1813, the British opened India to Western missionaries, and, in 1835, English replaced Persian as the administrative and legal language. The printing press inspired Indians to publish, for example, a bilingual English-Bengali magazine and Hindu texts in Sanskrit. The Independence movement also encouraged translation activity between local languages and English. Rabindranath Tagore (1861–1941) won the Nobel Prize for Literature in 1913, mainly for his own English translation of a collection of poems, *Gitanjali*, that he had first written in Bengali.

### 28.4.3 Japan

The primary source of information for this section is Kondo and Wakabayashi (2001, pp. 485–90).

Military shoguns (commanders) controlled Japan from 1186 to 1867, during which time Japan translated and interpreted to gather information and import ideas. Between 554 CE and 1854 when Japan opened its doors to the West, China exerted great influence on Japan's intellectual, religious and cultural life, and there were two primary languages used for reading and writing in Japan: Chinese, for scholarly works, and Japanese, for literature. Translation from Chinese into Japanese was not required thanks to the development of an annotation system called *kambun kundoku* (interpretive reading of Chinese). However, interplay between the two languages resulted in Japanized Chinese and Sinicized Japanese. In 1611, Tokugawa Ieyasu encouraged Chinese merchants to trade in Nagasaki, which required interpreters of Tang Chinese and resulted in an influx of Chinese books. During this period, the first translations from classical and colloquial Ming Dynasty (1368–1644) Chinese were made.

The arrival of Portuguese and Dutch merchants in the sixteenth and seventeenth centuries, respectively, brought a second wave of foreign languages to Japan. However, the Portuguese presence was short-lived in reaction to its destabilizing preoccupation with evangelization, with missionaries and Christianity banned in 1639. The Dutch, who had arrived in 1609 and made no efforts to convert the Japanese to Christianity, were allowed to remain in Hirado, with the Chinese in Nagasaki and the Koreans in Tsushima.

In 1641, the Dutch trading post was ordered to move to the island Dejima in the port of Nagasaki. The government position of *Oranda tsūji*, Dutch interpreter, was created. By the late eighteenth century, *tsūji* started their linguistic training at age ten. Approximately fifty *tsūji* worked at any given time until the end of their monopoly in the mid-1800s. The translation into Classical Chinese of medical texts was focal, followed by translations of natural and military science, and, lastly, the humanities. *Tsūji* with a scholarly bent taught Dutch and introduced Western knowledge and culture. In *Wage reigon*, Motoki Yoshinaga (1735–94) explained his method of translation, likely the first essay on translation methodology in Japan, while Shizuki Tadao (1760–1806), regarded as the father of physics in Japan, wrote nine books on Dutch, parts of which touch on translation issues.

In 1808, Baba Sajūrō (1787–1822) was ordered by the shogun to settle in Edo where he translated Dutch grammars and taught Dutch to Japanese scholars. From 1811, at the national translation bureau set up to translate barbarian books, he also directed the translation of the Dutch version of a French encyclopaedia, the largest national translation project in the history of Japan. In 1806, the *tsūji* helped Hendrik Doeff (1764–1837), head of the Dejima settlement, compile the Dutch–Japanese *Doeff Haruma* dictionary (1833), the largest dictionary produced during the Edo period.

In 1808, an encounter with a British ship prompted the shogun to order the *tsūji* to learn English. Next came Russian. Since many Russian documents were written in French, authorities ordered the *tsūji* to learn French from Doeff. In 1854, Japan signed the Kanagawa Treaty with the United States. Relay translation and interpretation was required during formal negotiations until English-speaking translators and interpreters learnt Japanese.

The Meiji period (1868–1912) restored the emperor to power and allowed Japanese people to learn foreign languages and travel abroad. English, French, Russian and German books were rapidly translated. The 1877–86 period saw very free translations of political novels that inspired the first Japanese political novels and the fusion of Japanese, Chinese and Western styles to form a new style. After 1885, translations became more literal, translators reproducing idiomatic expressions and personal pronouns, not traditionally used in Japanese.

### 28.4.4  Turkey

The primary source of information for this section is Paker (2001, pp. 571–8).

The multi-ethnic, multilingual Ottoman Empire (1299–1922) at its peak (1481–1566) extended into Central Europe, Crimea, the Middle East and North Africa. The republic of Turkey was created in 1923 and retained some of the linguistico-ethnic plurality of the empire. Turkey's official language is Turkish, with Kurdish the most widely spoken minority language.

In the thirteenth-century Seljuk state that preceded the Ottoman empire, official interpreter-translators, called *tercüman* (dragoman), appointed by royal decree, were held in high esteem. Assisted by translators' clerks, they acted as intermediaries and interpreters for foreigners and wrote correspondence addressed to foreign states. Two dragomans and two clerks were documented during the period. In particular, the translation from Persian and Arabic of religious and sacred writings, except for the Qur'ān written in Arabic, played a vital role in the development of the Turkish language. The earliest interlinear manuscript translation of the Qur'ān into Anatolian Turkish dates back to the fourteenth century.

The fourteenth and fifteenth centuries were marked by Arab–Persian acculturation, with scientific texts written almost exclusively in Arabic, the language of higher learning in madrasas, although some medical texts and encyclopaedic works were translated into or written in Turkish. Persian poetry was translated into Turkish and appropriated with the aim of elevating Turkish to a literary language. Nevertheless, by the end of the sixteenth century, Ottoman poetry had become Persianized. During the fifteenth century, the intellectually curious Sultan Mehmed II (1432–81) had

Byzantine and Persian manuscripts translated into Arabic, rather than Turkish, though Plutarch's *Lives*, for example, was translated from Greek into Turkish.

Professional translation and interpreting were institutionalized in the sixteenth century to deal with diplomatic and commercial activities. By the eighteenth century, dragomans were responsible for foreign affairs, administration of provinces, interpreting for foreign instructors in military institutions, the position of the Naval Dragoman, who also supervised the collection of taxes from non-Muslim subjects, and the diplomatic corps.

The reign of Ahmed III (1673–1736) in the eighteenth century saw an interest in the translation of non-literary works from Western Europe. Twenty-five translators were appointed in 1717 to translate scientific, medical and military texts from European and Oriental languages. A Turkish printing press was set up in 1727, long after Jewish (1493–4), Armenian (1567) and Greek (1627) presses had been established in Istanbul.

In 1839, a series of social, political and institutional reforms called *Tanzimat* opened the doors to Europeanization, through primarily French writings, and limited the role of Naval Dragoman to interpreting. The government Translation Chamber had been established in 1833 and the century was marked by a high volume of translation not only from European sources but also from Persian and Arabic. The Academy of Sciences, founded in 1851, was designed to provide teaching materials for a prospective university, but it was closed in 1862. Three years later, a Translation Committee was formed to continue publishing translations of historical and geographical works. More controversial was the translation into Turkish of potentially heretical European Enlightenment thinking. The first literary translators introduced Western poetry, philosophy and the novel to Turkey, inspiring Ibrahim Şinasi (1826–71) to write the first Turkish domestic comedy in 1860, and to found one of the first private Turkish newspapers, *Tasvir-I Efkâr* (1862), in which he serialized translations written in simple Turkish prose. The years 1873–83 were highly productive for the writers and translators of the *Tanzimat*.

Censorship in the reign of Abdülhamid II (1842–1918) limited translation to popular French fiction. The 1907 Constitutional Revolution, which removed Abdülhamid II from power, prompted renewed interest in the translation of canonical historical, philosophical and social science works, as well as foreign, particularly English, German and Russian, literature.

## 28.5 Old World

Translation during the Late Middle Ages is often associated with the Toledo School, which translated major philosophical, religious, scientific and medical works from Arabic, Greek and Hebrew into Latin during the twelfth and thirteenth centuries. In England, the Franciscan scholar

Roger Bacon (1214–92) affirmed the necessity of thorough mastery of both the source and the target languages as well as disciplinary knowledge to produce a good translation (Hackett, 2015). The poet Geoffrey Chaucer (1343–1400) founded a literary tradition based on translations and adaptations of Latin and French works, while in France, translators from Latin such as the poet Jean de Meung (c.1240–c.1305), the author Pierre Bersuire (1290–1362), the theologian Raoul de Presles (1316–82) and the philosopher Nicole Oresme (c.1325–82) worked towards elevating the literary status of French. Assisted by his followers, the English theologian John Wycliffe (1330–84) translated the Vulgate into English (1382). The Gutenberg moveable type press, invented in the late 1440s and early 1450s, caused a far-reaching socio-cultural revolution in Europe, which paved the way for the European Renaissance through the widespread dissemination of printed material.

The Byzantine scholar George Gemistus Plethon (1355–1452) reintroduced Plato's thought during the 1438–39 Council of Florence, during which he met Cosimo de' Medici (1389–1464) who founded the Platonic Academy. Under the leadership of the Italian scholar and translator Marsilio Ficino (1433–99), the Platonic Academy undertook the translation into Latin of all of Plato's works along with other, Neoplatonic works, which reached a wide audience in Western Europe thanks to Gutenberg's press. Ficino's work and Erasmus's Latin edition of the New Testament led to readers demanding more literal translations on which to base their philosophical and religious beliefs. In Britain, in 1469, Thomas Malory (1415–71) produced *Le Morte Darthur* (*The Death of Arthur*), a free compilation of English stories and translations of thirteenth-century French romances about the legendary Camelot, the Knights of the Round Table and their quest for the Holy Grail. The only known print copy was produced by Britain's first printer William Caxton (c.1422–c.1491), in 1485, the year that marks the end of the Middle Ages in Britain and the beginning of the Early Modern period (British Library, n.d.).

While Gutenberg's press enhanced the work of the Catholic Church, it also aided the Protestant Reformation by disseminating Protestant tracts and exchanges between Martin Luther (1483–1546) and the Catholic Church. Advancements in printing and the growth of the middle class during the sixteenth century further developed translation, as demand for new reading materials increased. From its beginnings in the early sixteenth century, the Reformation led to the Bible being printed in vernacular languages, contributing to the use and development of national languages and cultures throughout Europe and the Nordic countries.

Whereas Luther survived the Inquisition, two famous translators were convicted of heresy: William Tyndale (c.1494–c.1536) and Étienne Dolet (1509–46). In 1525, the *Tyndale New Testament* was printed in Worms, only to be burned in England in 1526. While in hiding in Belgium, Tyndale managed to translate half of the Old Testament from Hebrew, before being executed for heresy in 1536 (Simon, 2012, p. 167). One of his assistants completed the translation of the Old Testament. Thanks to the printing press, the 'Tyndale Bible' became the first mass-produced English translation. Dolet, by contrast, translated classical Greek texts and theorized the practice of translation (Horguelin, 1981). He was condemned in 1544 by the Inquisitors of the Sorbonne's Theological Faculty for being a relapsed atheist. His so-called blasphemous error was to have created a faux sense by adding three words that denied the immortality of the soul to one of his translations (Horguelin, 1996, p. 9).

The 'Belles infidèles', or free translation movement, galvanized the construction of national literatures in seventeenth-century Great Britain and Europe. Alexander Pope (1688–1744), a poet and translator, claimed to have reduced Homer's 'wild paradise' to 'order' in his English translation of the *Iliad* (Russo and Stewart, 2019, p. 107). Though rampant in Europe, the movement was first attributed, circa 1654, to Nicolas Perrot d'Ablancourt (1606–64), who produced elegant but free translations on the assumption that he had the right to improve on the style of authors. During the second half of the seventeenth century, the English poet and translator John Dryden (1631–1700) proposed a tripartite division of translation in his Preface to Ovid's *Epistles* (1680): 'metaphrase', or literal translation; 'paraphrase', or idiomatic translation; and 'imitation', which creates an original text. He rejected both the un-idiomatic and obscure 'metaphrase' and the overly free 'imitation' in favour of the compromise 'paraphrase' (Hopkins, 2014).

In the eighteenth century, Denis Diderot (1713–84) began his encyclopaedia project with the translation into French of *A Medicinal Dictionary* (1743–5) by the physician and translator Robert James (1703–76) and the *Cyclopaedia* (1728) by Ephraim Chambers (1680–1740). Pierre Le Tourneur (1737–88) produced the first complete translation of Shakespeare into French (1776–82). According to Johann Gottfried Herder (1744–1803), a German philosopher, theologian and poet, a translator should translate towards (and not from) his own language. In the *Fragments* (1767–8), he developed an innovative hermeneutic theory of translation in reaction to Dryden. For his part, the Scots historian and lawyer Alexander Fraser Tytler (1747–1813) published the *Essay on the Principles of Translation* (1791), in which he emphasized that reading was more helpful than the use of dictionaries, as had the Polish poet and grammarian Onufry Andrzej Kopczyński (1736–1817) in 1783.

Madame de Staël (1766–1817) published the essay 'De l'esprit des traductions' (1816), which would have a profound influence on translation in Europe. Like de Staël, August Wilhelm von Schlegel (1767–1845) tasked translators with making humankind's intellectual heritage universally accessible, in addition to producing seventeen highly respected translations of Shakespeare. In his seminal lecture 'On the Different Methods of Translating' (1813), the German theologian and philosopher Friedrich

Schleiermacher (1768–1834) distinguished between pragmatic and literary texts, or those without and those with clear cultural content, which led to the distinction between translation methods that moved the writer towards the reader and those that moved the reader towards the author. Schleiermacher favoured the latter approach for the translation of non-pragmatic texts. During the nineteenth century, the development of archaeology and the discovery of ancient tombs and writings encouraged Western scholars to produce erudite literal translations of ancient texts from Arabic, Greek, Persian and Sanskrit, but also between, for example, Shakespearean English and French and between Medieval French and nineteenth-century French.

## 28.6  Twentieth Century

Simultaneous interpreting equipment, invented by the American Edward Filene, appeared in the 1920s. In 1926, IBM patented the Hushaphone Filene-Finley system (also called the International Translator System), and the decade was marked by simultaneous interpreting trials (Blackman, n.d.). The simultaneous interpretation profession was an outcome of the multilingual Nuremberg Trials in 1945–6, in which English, French, Russian and German were the official languages. President Eisenhower's interpreter, Léon Dostert (1904–71), devised the system used at the trials, which he also demonstrated, in 1946, at a UN meeting. The more efficient results convinced UN bodies to switch from consecutive to simultaneous interpretation (Russo, 2010; Setton, 2010). The Canadian parliament introduced simultaneous interpreting in 1959 and the Canadian senate did so in 1961. The 1960s inaugurated research on simultaneous interpretation theory and practice that had a clear impact on the global development of the profession.

Anti-discrimination legislation in the United States along with increasing international migration led to the need for and professionalization of community or public service interpreting during the later decades of the twentieth century. Interpreters working in the courts, police stations, medical contexts, social services, schools or at asylum hearings are generally fluent in the source and target languages (including sign language), understand the public services being used, and have extensive cultural knowledge and cultural sensitivity (Hertog, 2010). Milestones in community interpreting are the US Court Interpreters' Act of 1978, which set standards of interpreting in federal courts (Hertog, 2010), and section 14 of the 1982 Canadian Charter of Rights and Freedoms (Canadian Heritage, n.d.), which provides the right to an interpreter to anyone who does not speak the language in use in a court or is deaf. To encourage the professionalization of community interpreting on a global scale, the Critical Link network was founded in 1992 by Brian Harris of the University of Ottawa.

The first Critical Link International conference on the theme of interpreting in legal, health and social services settings was held in Canada in 1995, followed by the second in 1998 (Critical Link International, n.d.).

The second half of the twentieth century also witnessed the proliferation of translation technology. Extensive research in artificial intelligence was taking place around the world, in the hope that fast, high-quality machine translation (MT) would one day be available. In the 1950s, MT became an object of research in the United States, followed by similar research in the Soviet Union. When investments in MT research did not produce the expected results, funding was reduced a decade later. Interest grew in statistical models for MT and evolved from rule-based to corpus-based MT in the 1990s. By the end of the twentieth century, no autonomous translation system was able to produce high-quality translation of an unrestricted text; however, computer-assisted translation (CAT), from terminology banks to word processing and translation memories, had gained in popularity (see Bowker and Fisher, 2010; Forcada, 2010).

According to the Infoterm website (2015), increasing terminology standardization necessitated the formulation of principles and methods for terminology work during the first half of the twentieth century, and the establishment of the technical (terminology) committee ISA/TC 37 of the International Federation of National Standards Associations (ISA) in 1936. In 1951, ISO/TC 37 (established formally in 1946 by the International Organization for Standardization, ISO) was renamed 'Terminology (principles and co-ordination)' and became operational in 1952. Since 1985, ISO/TC 37 has developed into one of ISO's most important technical committees. Meanwhile, electronic terminology banks were being developed. One of the first was Termium, developed by linguists at the Université de Montréal starting in 1970 and acquired by the Federal Translation Bureau in 1976. As the number of terminology records grew, the Canadian government received a proposal, in 1985, to launch a CD-ROM in order to make the database more accessible to users. By 1990, TERMIUM on CD-ROM was commercially available through subscription, with updates released every three to four months. The Québec government, Siemens, the UN and the European Union (EU), to name but a few, would all develop their own terminology data banks by the end of the century.

Post–World War II translation and interpreting have undergone many other revolutionary advancements from localization and the professionalization of translation and interpretation to the proliferation of translator and interpreter training programmes. Intimately tied to professional training was the creation of professional associations to regulate the professions, many of which became members of the International Federation of Translators, FIT (Fédération internationale des traducteurs).

FIT was created in 1953 under the auspices of UNESCO by the national associations of translators and interpreters in Denmark, France, Italy, Norway, the Federal Republic of Germany and Turkey. In 1956, an international recommendation to promote translation and the professional status of translators in Asia was adopted, a year after *Babel, International Journal of Translation*, was founded with the assistance of UNESCO. Canada's *Journal des Traducteurs*, also founded in 1955, would become known as *Meta* in 1965. While FIT had encouraged international co-operation on terminology since the mid-1950s, in 1958 it adopted a 'recommendation to encourage working together in the area of training translators and terminology research' (FIT, 2019). Translator training, translator status and translator rights, including those of literary translators, in Europe, Asia, the Americas, Africa and Arab-speaking countries, were recurring themes until the end of the century.

The second half of the century was also marked by the creation of a new academic discipline. In 1958, the Second Congress of Slavists in Moscow proposed a separate interdisciplinary science for the study of translation phenomena that was neither linguistics nor literary studies. The same year, within comparative literature, the debate around the place of translation broke out between Haskell Block (1932–2003), against translation, and René Étiemble (1909–2002), among others, in favour of translation (Godbout, 2009). During the 1950s and 1960s, systematic linguistic-oriented studies of translation began to appear, notably the *Stylistique comparée du français et de l'anglais* (1958), a contrastive comparison of French and English, by the French-Canadian linguists Jean-Paul Vinay (1910–99) and Jean Darbelnet (1904–90) (Vinay and Darbelnet, [1958] 1990). In 1964, Eugene Nida (1914–2011) published *Toward a Science of Translating*, a manual for Bible translation that introduced ethnographic approaches to the study of translation (Nida, 1964). In the 1960s and early 1970s, the Czech scholar Jiří Levý (1926–67) and the Slovak scholars Anton Popovič (1933–84) and František Miko (1920–2010) worked on the stylistics of literary translation. The name of the new discipline, 'translation studies', was coined by James S. Holmes (1924–86) in his seminal paper 'The name and nature of translation studies' (Holmes, 1972), in which he called for the consolidation of a separate discipline and proposed a classification of the field. Holmes's proposed map of translation studies would later be presented by Gideon Toury (1942–2016) in *Descriptive Translation Studies and Beyond* (Toury, 1995).

Translation studies gained recognition as an autonomous discipline during the second half of the twentieth century, alongside the growth in translation schools and courses at university level. In 1995, a study of 60 countries revealed that there were 250 post-secondary institutions offering courses in translation or interpreting (Caminade and Pym, 1995). Scholarly interest has been accompanied by a growth in conferences on translation, translation journals and translation-related publications. The visibility acquired by translation has also led to the development of national and international associations of translation studies. The Canadian Association for Translation Studies (Association Canadienne de traductologie) founded in 1987 is the oldest translation studies association in the world, and its official journal is TTR – *Traduction, terminologie, rédaction* (translation, terminology, writing).

# References

Bandia, P. (2009). Translation matters. In J. Inggs and L Meintjes, eds., *Translation Studies in Africa*. London/New York: Bloomsbury, pp. 1–20.

Bastin, G. L. (2001). Latin American tradition, trans. M. Gregson. In M. Baker and G. Saldanha, eds., *The Routledge Encyclopedia of Translation Studies*. London/New York: Routledge, pp. 505–12.

Bird, B., and Kopp, C. (2019). Macroeconomics: Globalization. *Investopedia*. Available at www.investopedia.com/terms/g/globalization.asp.

Blackman, T. (n.d.). The history of simultaneous interpreting equipment. *Bromberg & Associates*. Available at https://brombergtranslations.com /simultaneous-interpreting-equipment-history/.

Bowker, L., and Fisher, D. (2010). Computer-aided translation. In Y. Gambier and L. van Doorslaer, eds., *The Handbook of Translation Studies*, vol. 1. Amsterdam/Philadelphia: John Benjamins, pp. 60–5.

British Library (n.d.). *Le Morte Darthur*. Available at www.bl.uk/collection-items/thomas-ma.lorys-le-morte-darthur.

Caminade, M., and Pym, A. (1995). Special issue: 'Les formations en traduction et interprétation. Essai de recensement mondial'. *Traduire*. Paris: Société Française des Traducteurs.

Canadian Heritage (n.d.). *Canadian Charter of Rights and Freedoms*. Available at www.mcgill.ca/dise/files/dise/cdn_rights.pdf.

Castro, N. (2019). Translation in Central America and Mexico. In Y. Gambier and U. Stecconi, eds., *A World Atlas of Translation*. Amsterdam/Philadelphia: John Benjamins, pp. 419–42.

Cloarec-Heiss, F. (1999). From natural language to drum language: An economical encoding procedure in Banda-Linda (Central African Republic). In C. Fuchs and S. Robert, eds., *Language Diversity and Cognitive Representations*. Amsterdam/Philadelphia: John Benjamins, pp. 145–58.

Critical Link International (n.d.). *Critical Link International*. Available at https://criticallink.org.

Delisle, J. (2001). Canadian tradition, trans. S. C. Lott. In M. Baker and G. Saldanha, eds., *The Routledge Encyclopedia of Translation Studies*. London/New York: Routledge, pp. 356–64.

Diop, C. A. (1979). *Nations nègres et culture*. Paris: Présence Africaine.

Echeverri, Á., and Bastin, G. L. (2019). Hispanic South America. In Y. Gambier and U. Stecconi, eds., *A World Atlas of Translation*. Amsterdam/Philadelphia: John Benjamins, pp. 375–94.

Fédération internationale des traducteurs (FIT). (2019). FIT timeline. *Fédération internationale des traducteurs*. Available at www.fit-ift.org/fit-timeline/.

Forcada, M. L. (2010). Machine translation today. In Y. Gambier and L. van Doorslaer, eds., *The Handbook of Translation Studies*, vol. 1. Amsterdam/Philadelphia: John Benjamins, pp. 215–23.

Godbout, P. (2009). D. G. Jones, poète, comparatiste et traducteur. *TTR*, **22** (2), 23–36.

Gonçalves Barbosa, H., and Wyler, L. (2001). Brazilian tradition. In M. Baker and G. Saldanha, eds., *The Routledge Encyclopedia of Translation Studies*. London/New York: Routledge, pp. 326–33.

Hackett, J. (2015). Roger Bacon. In E. N. Zalta, ed., *The Stanford Encyclopedia of Philosophy*. Available at https://plato.stanford.edu/archives/spr2015/entries/roger-bacon/.

Hertog, E. (2010). Community interpreting. In Y. Gambier and L. van Doorslaer, eds., *The Handbook of Translation Studies*, vol. 1. Amsterdam/Philadelphia:John Benjamins, pp. 49–54.

Holmes, J. ([1972] 1988). The name and nature of translation studies. In J. Holmes, ed., *Translated! Papers on Literary Translation and Translation Studies*. Amsterdam: Rodopi, pp. 67–80.

Hopkins, D. (2014). Dryden as translator. In *Oxford Handbooks Online*. Available at www.oxfordhandbooks.com/view/10.1093/oxfordhb/9780199935338.001.0001/oxfordhb-9780199935338-e-10.

Horguelin, P. A. (1981). *Anthologie de la manière de traduire. Domaine français*. Montréal: Linguatech.

Horguelin, P. A. (1996). *Traducteurs français des xvi$^e$ et xvii$^e$ siècles*. Montréal: Linguatech.

Hung, E., and Pollard, D. (2001). Chinese tradition. In M. Baker and G. Saldanha, eds., *The Routledge Encyclopedia of Translation Studies*. London/New York: Routledge, pp. 365–76.

Infoterm (2015). History of ISO/TC 37. *Infoterm*. Available at www.infoterm.info/standardization/history_standardization_terminological_principles_and_methods.php.

Kondo, M., and Wakabayashi, J. (2001). Japanese tradition. In M. Baker and G. Saldanha, eds., *The Routledge Encyclopedia of Translation Studies*. London/New York: Routledge, pp. 485–94.

Krishnamurthy, R. (2001). Indian tradition. In M. Baker and G. Saldanha, eds., *The Routledge Encyclopedia of Translation Studies*. London/New York: Routledge, pp. 464–74.

Mohammad, S., ed. (1972). *Writings and Speeches of Sir Syed Ahmad Khan*. Bombay: Nachiketa Publications Ltd.

Nida, E. (1964). *Toward a Science of Translating*. Leiden: Brill.

Paker, S. (2001). Turkish tradition. In M. Baker and G. Saldanha, eds., *The Routledge Encyclopedia of Translation Studies*. London/New York: Routledge, pp. 571–82.

Pandit, M. (2017). History of translation culture in nineteenth century Maharashtra: An exercise in colonial cultural politics. In T. Khan, ed.,

*History of Translation in India.* Mysuru: National Translation Mission CIIL, pp. 135–60.

Russo, M. (2010). Simultaneous interpreting. In Y. Gambier and L. van Doorslaer, eds., *The Handbook of Translation Studies*, vol. 1. Amsterdam/ Philadelphia: John Benjamins, pp. 333–6.

Russo, J., and Stewart, C. (2019). *Introductory English Language.* Waltham Abbey, UK: Edtech Press.

Setton, R. (2010). Conference interpreting. In Y. Gambier and L. van Doorslaer, eds., *The Handbook of Translation Studies*, vol. 1. Amsterdam/ Philadelphia: John Benjamins, pp. 66–74.

Silva-Reis, D., and Milton, J. (2019). The history of translation in Brazil through the centuries: In search of a tradition. In Y. Gambier and U. Stecconi, eds., *A World Atlas of Translation.* Amsterdam/Philadelphia: John Benjamins, pp. 395–418.

Simon, S. (2012). Translators and the spread of religions. In J. Delisle and J. Woodsworth, eds., *Translators through History.* Amsterdam/Philadelphia: John Benjamins, pp. 153–86.

Toury, G. (1995). *Descriptive Translation Studies and Beyond.* Amsterdam/ Philadelphia: John Benjamins.

Trivedi, H. (2018). Translation in India: A curious history. *The Book Review,* a monthly review of important books. Available at https://thebookrevie windia.org/.

Venuti, L. (2001). American tradition. In M. Baker and G. Saldanha, eds., *The Routledge Encyclopedia of Translation Studies.* London/New York: Routledge, pp. 305–16.

Vinay, J.-P., and Darbelnet, J. ([1958] 1990). *Stylistique comparée du français et de l'anglais.* Montréal: Beauchemin.

Zhong, W. (2003). An overview of translation in China: Practice and theory. *Translation Journal,* **7**(2). Available at https://translationjournal.net/jour nal/24china.htm.

# 29

# Translation in the Third Millennium

Moritz Schaeffer

## 29.1 Introduction

The impact of technology on translation is likely to play a significant role in how translators and consumers of translations will experience translation itself in the current millennium. It is highly likely that we will come to understand the brain much better and that technology will become much more integrated with humans. Together, these transformations can be expected to have a revolutionary influence on how translation is conceptualized, practised and used. It is not far-fetched to think of brains as databases being harvested, used and maintained. The role of translators is therefore likely to increase rather than diminish, although it will be very different from how it is currently understood. The copyright status of assembled words was already entering a grey area around the 2020s, and the ease with which and the extent to which information can be duplicated will turn the very concept of the original on its head should it become possible to mirror, duplicate or replicate an entire brain. It seems reasonable to suppose that global connectivity will acquire a new meaning once brains are connected the way we are currently connected via machines external to our bodies. Translation will need to be central in the endeavour to build an interface among individuals, not only among those speaking different languages but also among those speaking the same language – Jakobson (1959, p. 134) put it this way: 'No linguistic specimen may be interpreted by the science of language without a translation of its signs into other signs of the same system or into signs of another system.'

Of course, to predict with any degree of certainty how an academic discipline or a profession may develop over a decade is fraught with dangers of all kinds and requires many caveats if these predictions are to be taken seriously. To predict what will happen over the course of a millennium in that same discipline is reckless – if these predictions are to carry the same weight as, for example, economic or financial forecasts. This chapter does not want to burden itself with the responsibility of these kinds of forecasts – instead, the aim is to use the current state of affairs and assume that future developments will follow a linear path, disregarding, thus, events which may impact translation as an object of study and as practised in entirely unexpected ways. The current chapter therefore takes a snapshot at a given point in time – the time of writing – and attempts to tell a coherent story which will more likely than not be turned upside down and sideways by what is to come.

## 29.2  The State of Affairs in the 2020s

The use of machine translation has been growing exponentially – in 2016, Google Translate reported that it had 500 million daily users who between them translated more than 100 billion words a day (www.blog.google /products/translate/ten-years-of-google-translate/). The global market for machine translation was valued at 433 million US dollars in 2016. Nimdzi.com estimates a valuation of about 1 billion US dollars by 2022. In 2019, the same forecaster valued the sales of the translation technology market at 780 million US dollars a year. The demand for automated translation is unlikely to recede and is likely to further transform how translation is practised and consumed. In other words, machine translation has been part and parcel of how humans communicate across linguistic boundaries since the beginning of the third millennium, and the integration between human- and machine-generated language is likely to become increasingly intimate. However, before we venture into predictions about future developments, it is worth having a look at the recent past.

The origins of the development of machine translation can be traced back to a model of communication put forward by Shannon and Weaver in 1949. In their *Mathematical Theory of Communication*, they conceive of communication as involving an information source, a transmitter which encodes the information, a channel through which the encoded information is transmitted, a receiver which decodes the transmitted information, and a destination – 'the person (or thing) for whom the message is intended' (Shannon and Weaver, 1949, p. 2). One tacit assumption that is implicit in much machine learning, and in the model proposed by Shannon and Weaver, is that the phenomena that are learnt from the data are stationary ergodic processes. In other words, the assumption is that the language (combination) considered is a deterministic dynamical system. Further, it is assumed that the patterns determining the dynamics of this language (combination) do not contain any random aspects and are thus predictable – as long as enough data is considered. Machine translation systems learn from large corpora (millions or even billions of words) of source texts and their translations. On the basis of the patterns that are extracted from these corpora, the machine translation system makes predictions about text that it may not have seen before. The system assumes that the new data is a recombination of data that it has already seen. One prerequisite for this learning to work is therefore that the learnt patterns exhaust the possible patterns given the language (combination) in question. However, natural languages are not stationary or ergodic – they change over time – so the model as envisaged by Shannon and Weaver operates under the assumption that the intended message is distorted by a number of factors pertaining to the source and the receiving person (or thing) in addition to noise that infiltrates the transmission. In sum, communication in these circumstances is modelled with a certain degree of uncertainty; formally, this measure is called entropy. Schaeffer and colleagues (Carl and Schaeffer, 2017; Schaeffer et al., 2016; Schaeffer and Carl, 2014) proposed measures of translation difficulty which are formally calculated as entropy and capture the uncertainty associated with a translation – in terms of the lexical target items or the word order a translator chooses. Given a source, the translator may often have a choice regarding lexical target items and the order in which these are output. While Schaeffer and colleagues make no claim regarding why a particular translator may choose a particular word order, they show that the degree of uncertainty has an effect on behaviour during translation: the higher the entropy of a source item, the more cognitively effortful is the translation of this source item, given that more uncertainty (or noise) is associated with that source item and translators need longer to, for example, produce a translation.

Shannon and Weaver's model has not only been applied to machine translation; it has also been used to understand communication between humans, given that verbal communication – even within the same linguistic system – involves essentially the same uncertainties regarding the source, the channel of transmission and the interpretation or decoding of the intended message. Malmkjær (2011) aptly points out how difficult it is to model translation without recourse to a theory of meaning or communication. She shows how tacit assumptions inherent in influential translation theories have been challenged by philosophers of language. These axiomatic assumptions are that translators have 'unmediated access to the aspects of context that the target and source texts both relate to' and that there is a universally shared language-independent meaning (Malmkjær, 2011, p. 115). She concludes that a considerable amount of uncertainty is involved in both monolingual communication and translation, given that 'meaning is formed on each occasion of linguistic interaction and is therefore unique and not replicable' (Malmkjær, 2011, p. 122). To the extent that either unmediated access to the aspects of context that the target and source texts both relate to or universally shared language-independent meaning or both can be formalized, automatization of the translation process is trivial. In other words, to rid the translation process of the associated uncertainties pertaining to source, channel and recipient makes it trivial. However, to do so is by no means an easy feat if what is required is a one size fits all (language combinations and texts) solution.

Jakobson (1959) ponders on the question of to what extent and in which circumstances translation is either possible or impossible. The first half of Jakobson's essay argues that translation is not only always possible but rather always necessary: 'the cognitive level of language not only admits but directly requires recoding interpretation, i.e., translation' (Jakobson, 1959, p. 236). In other words, this definition of translation encompasses every act of cognition which involves linguistic representations: the act of linguistic interaction with the world involves the translation of linguistic signs into cognitive representations in addition to the associated noise as conceptualized and quantified by Shannon and Weaver (1949).

## 29.3  Noisy Translation

In 1968, Delgado et al. reported studies involving psychiatric patients who had been fitted with what the authors call a 'stimoceiver' – a device which both records an electroencephalography (EEG) signal and delivers small electric shocks intracranially, that is, inside the brain – controlled via radio. Delgado and colleagues could induce or control aggressive behaviour in humans at the press of a button remotely and observe the immediate and local effect on electrophysical activity in the brain. While this crude inter-action consisting of electric shocks can hardly be called communication, the 1968 study by Delgado and colleagues was the first in a series of studies which investigate the interaction between brains via machines and between brains and machines. Prior studies had done so with animals (e.g., Delgado, 1966). Advances in the decoding of the brain have led researchers to talk about brain-machine interfaces (Lebedev and Nicolelis, 2006) which are systems that decode neuronal activity into a language which is understood by some other device, such as a prosthetic limb or a cursor on a screen. Deadwyler et al. (2013) report on a study involving rats. The animals had to perform a task which was taxing in terms of working memory. The rats receive a reward via a lever, then proceed to a photocell on the opposite side of the cage, poke it with their nose, after which two levers appear where there was only one before. The reward is now delivered via the new lever and not the one the rats received the reward from previously. The animal is thus presented with a sample stimulus and, after a short delay, the sample stimulus is shown again along with a novel alternative. The animal is there-fore rewarded for selecting the novel stimulus. In addition, the delay between the first reward and the second reward via the novel stimulus is varied (1–30 seconds): the time between the first reward and the second reward via the novel lever is controlled by the photocell which lights up only after a certain time in response to a nose poke indicating that the novel lever has appeared. This delayed-non-match-to-sample task involves memorizing a complex sequence of actions.

Deadwyler et al. (2013) recorded the activity in cell ensembles of the hippocampus involved in the formation of memory. Two types of cell ensemble are involved in this, and one ensemble (hippocampal area CA3) projects to the second (hippocampal area CA1). The authors recorded the activity in the CA3 ensembles, used it as input in the form of machine learning (generalized Volterra model (GVM)) in order to predict the activation of the CA1 cell ensemble. In other words, they trained rats to perform the task described above, recorded the neuronal activity of the CA3 and CA1 ensembles and used the activation of the former in order to predict the activation of the latter, which made it possible to learn which kind of activation is associated with a successful completion of the task (finding the reward in the novel lever after a certain delay). The training data (the neural activation in the two cell ensembles) came from more than 2,000 animals who performed the task many times. In other words, this machine learning problem and its solution does not differ in essence from machine translation: while the input in Deadwyler et al.'s (2013) experiment was neuronal activation in CA3 cells and the output was neuronal activation in CA1 cells of the hippocampus, the input to a machine translation system is text in one language and the output is text in a different language. However, the basic assumption is the same: large amounts of training data make it possible to learn the patterns inherent in this data which cover – to a certain extent – possible patterns of new data. Deadwyler et al. (2013) proceeded to run the same task described here with two differently trained sets of rats: those that had learnt to wait for the photocell to switch on after eight, twelve or sixteen seconds before the novel lever would appear, and rats which had never experienced this delay. These delay-naïve rats were very good at performing the task without a delay, but completed the task correctly only about half of the times if a delay was introduced. However, Deadwyler et al. (2013) stimulated the CA1 cell ensemble with the information from the rats which had learnt the delayed version of the task – that is, they transplanted a formed memory from one rat to another resulting in a gain of about twenty percentage points of the success rate. In other words, the basis for this transfer of memories from one animal to another is a model (described in more detail in Song et al., 2009) which decodes neuronal activation by associating it with a particular behavioural pattern; recreating this pattern in an otherwise naïve animal is then relatively trivial or technical. However, while the naïve rats performed significantly and to a large extent better with the transplanted memory than without it, they performed worse than the rats which had been trained. In other words, brain-to-brain communication in these animals involved some kind of loss and was noisy to a certain extent.

In a similar experiment, Pais-Vieira et al. (2013) employed a slightly simpler model, but had rats perform as a dyad: two rats were in identical cages with two levers, one on each side. For one rat (the 'encoder' rat), an LED over the lever which would produce the reward would light up. The other ('decoder') rat had an identical cage with two levers and two LEDs, but both were always on. Neuronal activity from the motor cortex was recorded in the encoder rat. In this case, only ten trials were used to construct a template of typical activity for the correct behavioural response. While the encoder rat performed the task, the difference between the encoder rat's neuronal activity and the template derived previously was calculated, transformed, and the decoder rat received intra-cortical micro-stimulation proportional to the difference between the encoder's actual neuronal activity for the particular response and the template. If the decoder rat chose the correct lever, not only did it receive a reward itself but so did the encoder rat. In other words, the encoder rat, which chose the correct lever on the basis of the LEDs, received a reward if the decoder rat chose the correct lever on the basis of the spatial information extracted from the encoder rat via the brain-to-brain connection only. Their only connection was a direct link between their brains, and they co-operated: the decoder rat significantly increased the percentage of correct trials above chance as a result of the neuronal activity transferred from the encoder rat. In addition, the encoder rat learnt from the other rat's mistakes: the encoder rat's response latency reduced from about twenty seconds to about fifteen seconds after the decoder rat had made a mistake. This co-operation based on brain-to-brain communication was also possible when the animals were separated by thousands of kilometres and the neuronal information was transmitted via the Internet. Pais-Vieira et al. (2013, p. 5) highlight that the neuronal information 'recorded from ... the encoder rat's [brain] during a single trial w[as] sufficient for decoder rats to repeatedly perform [the] tasks, significantly above chance levels, in real-time'. Pais-Vieira et al. (2013, p. 7) further argue that the brain-to-brain interface tested in this study constitutes 'a discrete noisy channel' as defined by Shannon and Weaver (1949). They suggest that, instead of connecting just two brains, it would be possible to connect several brains in this manner, thus increasing substantially the computing power of such a 'grid of multiple reciprocally interconnected brains' (Pais-Vieira et al., 2013, p. 7), resulting in an organic computer. Pais-Vieira et al. (2013) and Deadwyler et al. (2013) experimented with animal models; however, grids of multiple reciprocally interconnected human brains are, of course, theoretically possible and research in this direction exists: for example, Jiang et al. (2019) tested to what extent three participants' interconnected brains were able to solve a task collectively. The authors used brain recording: EEG and brain stimulation (transcranial magnetic stimulation (TMS)) – both of which are non-invasive methods and were used for obvious ethical reasons. In the study by Jiang et al. (2019), the task was to play a version of the Tetris game where blocks have to be rotated in order to fill gaps on a screen. Two participants transmitted their decision whether to rotate a particular block or not by controlling a horizontally moving cursor via steady-state visually evoked potentials. The brain responds to light sources at particular frequencies with electrical activity proportional to the frequency of the light source. These potentials can be isolated in the record obtained from recordings on the scalp. In other words, these evoked potentials respond to visual stimulation at specific frequencies. Participants looked at different LEDs (flashing at different frequencies) depending on whether they decided that rotating a particular block was conducive or not. Their brains therefore generated electrical activity at a frequency that corresponded to the frequency of the particular LED they were looking at and this information was recorded and transmitted to a third person who did not see the blocks by translating the evoked potential of the participants who saw the blocks into very short (one millisecond) pulses of TMS which resulted in perceived flashes of light called phosphenes (similar to what those who suffer from a particular form of migraine experience). The intensity of the pulses was varied depending on whether the sender participant was looking at an LED signifying a 'yes' or 'no' response to the question of whether a block should be rotated or not. The receiver participant then either perceived a phosphene or did not. The reliability of the two senders was manipulated so that the receiver had to decide which sender to trust more. Results showed that the triad performed consistently above chance.

A company called Neuralink (Musk and Neuralink, 2019) develops implants which connect the brain directly with a computer. Much of the research is geared towards making the devices larger and more durable – and to allow for wireless connection rather than having to establish a connection between brain and computer via some form of cable which would, of course, increase the risk of infection and other complications. Musk and Neuralink (2019, p. 10) argue that what they develop 'serves two main purposes: it is a research platform for use in rodents and serves as a prototype for future human clinical implants'. In other words, it is Neuralink's explicit aim to produce implants which make it possible to connect a human brain to a computer in order to allow direct communication between machine and human, presumably in order to augment their capabilities. Musk and Neuralink suggest that their implants may serve clinical purposes, but this kind of research has also been funded by companies with a far less obviously clinical background. For instance, Facebook funded research (Moses et al., 2019) that used the kinds of implants developed by Neuralink in order to translate neuronal activity in auditory and sensorimotor cortical brain regions into spoken language. Three participants who were going to undergo surgery for epilepsy were fitted with implants which could record neuronal activity intracranially for the purposes of identifying the parts of the brain where seizures were located. This made it possible for the researchers to record data inside the brains of otherwise normal humans. Participants listened to a set of pre-recorded questions and could choose from a set of predetermined answers. The machine learning task in this case was to predict which question participants heard on the basis of the neuronal activity recorded in the auditory brain regions and to predict which answer they had uttered on the basis of the neuronal data gathered in sensorimotor cortical brain regions. While this is a limited set of linguistic items (four groups of partly identical questions and twenty-four possible answers in total) and while the information that was being translated is on the surface of language (phonetic transcriptions), the success rate in predicting what participants were hearing or saying was higher in some participants than others, but for all participants it was significantly above chance.

The study by Moses et al. (2019) decoded and translated phonetic and sensorimotor information intracranially, but there are also attempts to decode semantic information based on data gathered from human participants in a non-invasive manner: Huth et al. (2016) map groups of related concepts on particular areas in the brain and can predict, on the basis of functional MRI data, what kind of concept is active where in the brain at which point in time.

## 29.4  Noiseless Translation

While all of the studies attempting to decode aspects of how the brain encodes information are successful to some degree, their decoding involves some levels of uncertainty: communication between rat brains in Pais-Vieira et al.'s (2013) study is noisy, as is the channel between Deadwyler et al.'s (2013) rats or Facebook's (Moses et al., 2019) epileptic human patients. The study by Huth et al. (2016) manages to predict *the kind of* concept a human is processing at a specific moment in time at some particular location in their brain on the basis of changes in oxygen-levels in the blood passing through the brain. The fact that more or less direct communication with the brains of (human) animals involves some kind of noise or uncertainty does not mean that it might not be possible to establish a direct channel of communication without any loss at some point in the current millennium. For some time, the technologies used to study the brain have been seen as potential threats to 'mental privacy' by, for example, Mecacci and Haselager (2019), who discuss the potential consequences of a situation in which it is not possible for a subject to conceal their internal mental states because some technology is capable of decoding these. Mecacci and Haselager (2019, p. 445) formulate a set of benchmarks and tools which allow policymakers to evaluate 'current (as of 2018) and near future (approximately 5–10 years later, based on currently ongoing research) brain reading technology'. In other words, these authors expect existing technologies to become a potential threat to humans who might not be aware of or consent to some other person or institution having access to content of their mind which they do not divulge freely. The time frame that this chapter deals with goes considerably beyond the next decade or so. It might therefore not be too bold to claim that the brain will be completely decoded within the current millennium.

The studies referred to here all used a small number of participants, but it is not uncommon to have much larger data sets: the Cam-CAN data repository (Taylor et al., 2017) is based on data from approximately 700 participants and contains brain imaging and cognitive-behavioural data. A number of brain banks around the world collect actual brains post-mortem not only of patients with neuro-degenerative diseases but also, increasingly, of healthy controls. The Neuropathology Data Set, for example, available from the National Alzheimer's Coordinating Center (www .alz.washington.edu/index.html), currently contains brain tissue from approximately 17,000 humans. Fast-forwarding maybe just a couple of hundred years, it is not unreasonable to expect that rather than images of brains, actual brains inside living human bodies will become databases. It might be expected that forms not unlike current consent forms for data privacy and anonymization will then be available and willingly signed by participants.

In sum, this chapter is an incomplete snapshot of the current state of affairs which – if it develops in a linear fashion – may result in a situation in which brains can be decoded completely and noiselessly. Whether this will actually occur and, if it does, whether it will be achieved by implanting interfacing devices intracranially or whether remote methods will be used is essentially irrelevant. Central in the endeavour is the degree to which the translation of a brain is accurate, faithful, or adequate and noiseless. Once a high degree of accuracy in the translation of a brain is achieved and once this translation is possible in both directions, that is, once it is possible to connect two human brains in a manner similar to the way in which Pais-Vieira et al. (2013) have connected two or even more (Pais-Vieira et al., 2015) rat brains, then a whole new set of questions will arise. A millennium allows for many developments and the current rate of discovery is likely to continue at the same pace or to increase exponentially; it is therefore likely to be only a question of time before human brains can and will be connected directly. While Orwellian scenarios are certainly not new and may now be more relevant than at the turn of the century, they might obscure the potential for translation to play a central role in radically altering global economies of knowledge: assuming that it is possible (a) to decode a human brain without loss and (b) to encode information directly without loss and (c) if it becomes possible to connect not only a small number of individuals in this way but humanity as such, 'the individuum' will cease to be a meaningful description of an embodied brain. An incommensurable number of opposites will cease to be: the subjective will not have an opposite objective perspective, neither will they be complementary – if humanity is connected, language and communication will be closed, ergodic systems (Shannon and Weaver, 1949, pp. 8–9) and there will be no transmission of information, given that there will be no *other* to any particular human with whom to exchange information that is not already known to all humans. Politics, governance, manipulation and its other will resolve into a common will, decision or behaviour of the connected humankind.

Of course, extrapolating current technologies and developments to future realities allows for less peaceful visions: Kosinski, Stillwell and Graepel (2013) showed how to access, on the basis of publicly available data, some aspects of what Mecacci and Haselager (2019, p. 447) refer to as 'mental states': '[mental states] ... encompass every aspect of an individual's psychology, including, but not limited to, personality traits and dispositions (e.g. sexual preferences, personal tastes and habits ...), qualitative states (e.g. perceptions, emotions, feelings ...), propositional states (e.g. knowledge, beliefs), intentions and goals, plans, memories etc.'. The potential for misuse of this technology has been amply discussed and it is equally likely that the possibility of translating a human brain – with or without its (bearer's) consent – will lead to a more extreme form of the current potential to influence large swaths of populations. In sum, irrespective of how and whether humans will communicate in a thousand years' time, it is extremely likely that the translation of the brain will lead to collapsing global boundaries and hitherto well-defined entities resulting in a radical reorientation affecting global realities.

# References

Carl, M., and Schaeffer, M. J. (2017). Why translation is difficult : A corpus-based study of non-literality in post-editing and from-scratch translation. *Hermes – Journal of Language and Communication in Business*, **56**, 43–57.

Deadwyler, S. A., Berger, T. W., Sweatt, A. J., Song, D., Chan, R. H. M., Opris, I., Gerhardt, G. A., Marmarelis, V. Z., and Hampson, R. E. (2013). Donor/recipient enhancement of memory in rat hippocampus. *Frontiers in Systems Neuroscience*, **7**. https://doi.org/10.3389/fnsys.2013.00120.

Delgado, J. M. R. (1966). Aggressive behavior evoked by radio stimulation in monkey colonies. *American Zoologist*, **6**, 669–81. https://doi.org/10.1093/icb/6.4.669.

Delgado, J. M. R., Mark, V., Sweet, W., Ervin, F., Weiss, G., Bach-y-Rita, G., and Hagiwara, R. (1968). Intracerebral radio stimulation and recording in completely free patients. *Journal of Nervous and Mental Disease*, **147**, 329–40. https://doi.org/10.1097/00005053-196810000-00001.

Huth, A. G., de Heer, W. A., Griffiths, T. L., Theunissen, F. E., and Gallant, J. L. (2016). Natural speech reveals the semantic maps that tile human cerebral cortex. *Nature*, **532**, 453–8. https://doi.org/10.1038/nature17637.

Jakobson, R. (1959). On linguistic aspects of translation. In R. Brower, ed., *On Translation*. Cambridge, MA: Harvard University Press, pp. 232–9.

Jiang, L., Stocco, A., Losey, D. M., Abernethy, J. A., Prat, C. S., and Rao, R. P. N. (2019). BrainNet: A multi-person brain-to-brain interface for direct collaboration between brains. *Scientific Reports*, **9**, 6115. https://doi.org/10.1038/s41598-019-41895-7.

Kosinski, M., Stillwell, D., and Graepel, T. (2013). Private traits and attributes are predictable from digital records of human behavior. *Proceedings of the National Academy of Sciences*, **110**, 5802–5. https://doi.org/10.1073/pnas.1218772110.

Lebedev, M. A., and Nicolelis, M. A. L. (2006). Brain–machine interfaces: Past, present and future. *Trends in Neurosciences*, **29**, 536–46. https://doi.org/10.1016/j.tins.2006.07.004.

Malmkjær, K. (2011). Meaning and translation. In K. Malmkjær and K. Windle, eds., *The Oxford Handbook of Translation Studies*. Oxford: Oxford University Press, pp. 108–22. https://doi.org/10.1093/oxfordhb/9780199239306.013.0009.

Mecacci, G., and Haselager, P. (2019). Identifying criteria for the evaluation of the implications of brain reading for mental privacy. *Science and Engineering Ethics*, **25**, 443–61. https://doi.org/10.1007/s11948-017-0003-3.

Moses, D. A., Leonard, M. K., Makin, J. G., and Chang, E. F. (2019). Real-time decoding of question-and-answer speech dialogue using human cortical activity. *Nature Communications*, **10**, 3096. https://doi.org/10.1038/s41467-019-10994-4.

Musk, E., and Neuralink. (2019). An integrated brain-machine interface platform with thousands of channels (preprint). *Neuroscience*. https://doi.org/10.1101/703801.

Pais-Vieira, M., Chiuffa, G., Lebedev, M., Yadav, A., and Nicolelis, M. A. L. (2015). Building an organic computing device with multiple interconnected brains. *Scientific Reports*, **5**, 11869. https://doi.org/10.1038/srep11869.

Pais-Vieira, M., Lebedev, M., Kunicki, C., Wang, J., and Nicolelis, M. A. L. (2013). A brain-to-brain interface for real-time sharing of sensorimotor information. *Scientific Reports*, **3**, 1319. https://doi.org/10.1038/srep01319.

Schaeffer, M. J., and Carl, M. (2014). Measuring the cognitive effort of literal translation processes. In U. Germann, M. Carl, P. Koehn, G. Sanchis-Trilles, F. Casacuberta, R. Hill and S. O'Brien, eds., *Proceedings of the Workshop on Humans and Computer-Assisted Translation (HaCaT)*. Stroudsburg, PA: Association for Computational Linguistics, pp. 29–37.

Schaeffer, M. J., Dragsted, B., Hvelplund, K. T., Winther Balling, L., and Carl, M. (2016). Word translation entropy: Evidence of early target language activation during reading for translation. In M. Carl, S. Bangalore and M. Schaeffer, eds., *New Directions in Empirical Translation Process*

*Research: Exploring the CRITT TPR-DB.* Cham: Springer, pp. 183–210. https://
doi.org/10.1007/978-3-319-20358-4.

Shannon, C. E., and Weaver, W. (1949). *The Mathematical Theory of
Communication.* Urbana: University of Illinois Press.

Song, D., Chan, R. H. M., Marmarelis, V. Z., Hampson, R. E., Deadwyler, S. A.,
and Berger, T. W. (2009). Nonlinear modeling of neural population
dynamics for hippocampal prostheses. *Neural Networks,* **22,** 1340–51.
https://doi.org/10.1016/j.neunet.2009.05.004.

Taylor, J. R., Williams, N., Cusack, R., Auer, T., Shafto, M. A., Dixon, M.,
Tyler, L. K., Cam-CAN and Henson, R. N. (2017). The Cambridge Centre
for Ageing and Neuroscience (Cam-CAN) data repository: Structural and
functional MRI, MEG, and cognitive data from a cross-sectional adult
lifespan sample. *NeuroImage,* **144,** 262–9. https://doi.org/10.1016/j
.neuroimage.2015.09.018.

# Index

Printed in the United States
by Baker & Taylor Publisher Services